Durland

Standard Plate Number Catalog

MINT PLATE BLOCK EVALUATIONS FOR SPECIFIC NUMBERS

Compiled and edited by

GEORGE V.H. GODIN

This catalog is a carefully prepared analysis forming an authoritative guide to the retail value of specific plate numbers and positions.

It should be noted that prices on rare numbers, and all issues prior to 1935 are for reasonably well centered plate blocks, generally described as fine to very fine. Blocks in very fine to superb condition frequently sell for prices higher than those listed, and conversely poorly centered blocks sell for substantial discounts.

BUREAU ISSUES ASSOCIATION, Inc.
P.O. Box 1047 • Belleville, IL 62223

Library of Congress Catalogue No. 55-22466
ISBN O-930412-19-2

Printed in the United States of America
by Frank Newman Printing Company
St. Louis, MO 63116

PLEASE CAREFULLY READ THE DEFINITIONS ON PAGE 5, THE IMPRINT TYPE INFORMATION ON PAGES 6 & 7 AND THE INFORMATION CONCERNING TYPES OF THE 2¢ 1894 ISSUE ON PAGE 8.

INDEX

INDEX Continued

APPENDICES

Much of our plate number information stems from studies made by members of the Bureau Issues Association and published in their magazine. Serious plate number collectors should join this organization. For further information write to:

George V.H. Godin, Executive Secretary, P.O. Box 1047, Belleville, IL 62223-1047

PLEASE READ THIS PAGE CAREFULLY

POSITION ABBREVIATIONS

Flat Press: T = Top; **TL** = Top Left; **TR** = Top Right (with **F** unless noted); **L** = Left side; **R** = Right side; **B** = Bottom. See rotary press for other flat plate abbreviations, e.g. for #1053.

Rotary Press: UL = Upper Left; **UR** = Upper Right; **LL** = Lower Left; **LR** = Lower Right.

See Appendix C for newer type presses.

The listing of the early plate numbers does NOT guarantee that plate number blocks exist. The data used is based on the research by Mr. C.B. Durland and is supplemented by the plate number surveys conducted by the Bureau Issues Association. Many of the reports are based on plate number only and were not accompanied by a Scott Catalog Number. As a result there will be some numbers listed under various Scott Catalog Numbers, which could exist but have NOT been reported. These are listed with a †. We have dropped some previously listed numbers in the 1923-1929 regular issued based on direct inquiry with collectors who collect the various perforation varieties. The surveys did NOT require the respondent to report whether his copy was a plate block, a plate single, or mint or used.

We are using a series of symbols throughout the catalog to qualify either the plate number or the position. The symbols and their meanings are:

- * = a scarce plate number. (Not used when plate has been priced)
- † = an unreported plate number or unreported position.
- ‡ = the position does NOT exist, or exists and cannot be readily identified.
- **o** = the same plate number issued both tagged and untagged.
- **P** = this number has only been reported as a Bureau Precancel.
- **N** = read footnote.
- **Z** = read footnote.

The prices in this edition are based on plate blocks in *VERY FINE* condition. All commemoratives and regular rotary press issues use a format which lists the price followed by an appropriate numbers of blank □ for the positions. Flat plate commemoratives show a price for the top positions followed by boxes and then another price followed by boxes for the remaining positions. If the position has not been reported a † appears in the place of the □. If the position does not exist, a ‡ appears in the place of the □. If the price of a position is different, this is noted by a subscript number (example $\square_3$ means 3 times the listed price) for that position. Multiply the listed price by the number shown in the subscript to obtain the price for the position.

The prices in this book are based for the greater part on a reasonable return for the cost, including labor, involved in the sale of one specific plate block to one customer. Where we have used auction prices as a basis, the price is in italics and does not include the buyers 10% if applicable.

We wish to point out very explicitly that a low quantity of impressions of any plate does not mean that the number is scarce. The criterion is the number of copies that were saved and are available to collectors.

On any issue where there is a limited amount of information available that does not permit proper evaluation of the price, we have left the price column blank. This does not mean that the price is necessarily higher or lower than the other plates in the issue. It does mean that there is a difference of opinion concerning the price.

The listings of the plate numbers on rotary press coil stamps and booklet panes prior to 1981 are those that have been sent to the pressroom. They are listed with the intent that they be used as a checklist by those people who own partial plate numbers. Not all of the numbers have been reported to exist.

Up to about 1981, we list the actual plate number digits appearing in the selvedge of the plate block. After the changeover to the new system of using a single or double digit to represent each plate used in the printing, we tabulate the single or multiple digit representative number. Following the table are the various combinations of representative numbers followed by a price and then the boxes for the positions. Where a hyphen appears between these numbers, the portion to the left is usually gravure or offset and the portion to the right is intaglio.

After 1985 the five digit series of plate number became part of the six digit miscellaneous series used to identify all BEP printing.

Please read page 215 for additional information on the new plate numbering system.

We wish to acknowledge with our sincere thanks the cooperation and assistance given by:

P.R. Beutel, W. Wallace Cleland, Kenneth E. Diehl, Joseph M. Napp, Jacques C. Schiff Jr., William O. Schuman, Frank J. Waggener, and Charles H. Yeager.

IMPRINTS

Following the precedent established by the BANK NOTE COMPANIES in exhibiting their imprint on the margins of the sheets of Postage Stamps, the BUREAU OF ENGRAVING & PRINTING adopted the practice when awarded the contract in 1894. BUREAU IMPRINTS appeared, beginning with Plate #1 (approved June 19, 1894) until December, 1911 when it was discontinued for reasons of economy.

In the "PLATE NUMBER CHECK LIST" compiled and issued by the BUREAU ISSUES ASSOCIATION reference is made to the several types of Imprint and Plate Number Combinations herein illustrated.

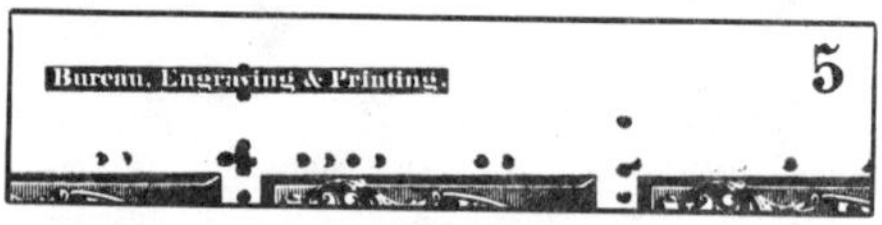

IMPRINT I

IMPRINT - Colored rectangle with weak frame line. Colorless shaded letters -Measurement - 26.6 mm. x 2 mm.

PLATE NUMBER - Shaded numerals - 3.2 mm. high.

——————INITIAL PLATE — #1.

IMPRINT II

IMPRINT - Outer frame line strong. Ends ornamented with rosettes and arrowheads - Meas. 37 mm. x 3.2 mm.

PLATE NUMBER - Shaded numerals as Imprint I - 3.2 mm.

Plate 74 was the first Imprint II plate assigned but 76 was the first one certified and used to print stamps.

——————INITIAL PLATE — #76.

IMPRINT III

IMPRINT - Colorless, shaded capitals. Outer frame line. Ornate ends. Measurement - 56.75 mm. x 2 mm.

PLATE NUMBER - Shaded numerals -3.2 mm.

Used on SPECIAL DELIVERY, NEWSPAPER & PERIODICAL stamp plates.

——————INITIAL PLATE — #77.

IMPRINT IV

IMPRINT - Same as Imprint II.

PLATE NUMBER - Heavily shaded numerals 2.7 mm. in height.

——————INITIAL PLATE — #155.

IMPRINT V

IMPRINT - Same as Type II.

PLATE NUMBER - Thin line numerals 2.7 mm. high.

Used generally, with modifications, on all subsequent plates.

——————INITIAL PLATE — #255.

IMPRINT VI

IMPRINT - Same as Imprint III.

PLATE NUMBER - Same as Imprint IV.

Used - SPECIAL DELIVERY, NEWSPAPER & PERIODICAL stamp plates.

——————INITIAL PLATE — #257.

IMPRINTS

IMPRINT VII

IMPRINT - Same as Imprint III.
PLATE NUMBER - Numerals same as Imprint V.
Used only on SPECIAL DELIVERY stamp plates.

———————**INITIAL PLATE — #381.**

IMPRINT VIII

IMPRINT - Shaded colorless capitals in colored rectangle. Thin Frame. Fork & Arrow-head ornaments at ends. 35.75 x 1.3 mm.
PLATE NUMBER - Numerals same as Imprint V.
Used - TRANS-MISSISSIPPI issue, only.

———————**INITIAL PLATE — #590.**

IMPRINT IX

IMPRINT - omitted.
PLATE NUMBER - Numerals same as Imprint V.
First Use - "STAMP BOOKLET" plates.

———————**INITIAL PLATE — #988.**

IMPRINT X

IMPRINT & PLATE NUMBER similar to Imprint V with OPEN STAR 2.7 mm. high between.
Used on plates having varying gutter widths between the vertical rows of stamp subjects.

———————**INITIAL PLATE — #4968.**

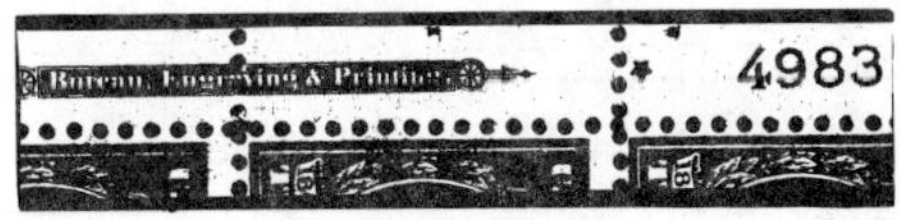

IMPRINT XI

IMPRINT & PLATE NUMBER - similar to Imprint X. Small solid STAR 1.3 mm. high substituted for open star.
Used similarly to Imprint X on plates of the LINCOLN COMMEMORATIVE and one 1¢ ordinary - #4980.

———————**INITIAL PLATE — #4976.**

IMPRINT XII

IMPRINT & PLATE NUMBER - similar to Imprint V with capital "A" added between the imprint and number. "A" is 3.2 mm.
Used for plates having uniform vertical spacing between rows of subjects, but wider than in those with Imprint V.

———————**INITIAL PLATE — #5557.**

IMPRINT XIII

IMPRINT - omitted
Used on plates having the same characteristics as Imprint XII.

———————**INITIAL PLATE — #5805.**

IMPRINT XIV

PLATE NUMBER - together with the DENOMINATION in large capital letters 4.6 mm. high.
The VALUE was conspicuously displayed in the sheet margins that an error may not so easily occur due to all denominations being in the same color.
Used on PARCEL POST stamp plates -series, 1912.

———————**INITIAL PLATE — #6161.**

2¢ TYPES 1894-1898 ISSUES

TYPE I

The horizontal lines of the ground work run across the double triangles and are of the same thickness.

Plate numbers used are between 1 and 125 plus 144.

TYPE II

The horizontal lines of the groundwork run across the double triangles but are thinner within the triangles.

Plate numbers used are 126, 131, 132, 133, 169 and part of 170.

TYPE III

The horizontal lines of the groundwork do not run across the double lines of the triangles. The lines inside the inner triangle are thin like type II.

Plate numbers used are 141, 142, 143, 145, 146, 148-158, 160, part of 170, and between 171 and 503.

TYPE IV

Refer to "The Bureau Specialist" for details of differences. See pages 283-293 October 1955 and pages 100, 118-119 April 1957.

Plate numbers used are between 505 and 1493.

1894 REGULAR ISSUE

Unwatermarked Perf. 12

FLAT PRESS

When the Bureau of Engraving and Printing took over the printing of United States postage stamps from private contractors in 1894 there was considerable interest in the collecting of the new plate numbers.

These were usually collected in strips of three stamps showing the plate number and the imprint so imprint blocks of six are very difficult to find on many plates.

1894 REGULAR ISSUE
Continued

As the seemingly endless plate numbers climbed higher and higher few collectors kept up their interest and so many of the later plates are considerably more difficult to find.

No printing records are available so there is no way of being certain but we have marked with an asterisk those plates which we have found to be difficult to find.

#246 1¢ FRANKLIN (Ultramarine)
12 Plates

Basic Price	T, L, R, B
Imprint Strip of 3	$90
Imprint Block of 6	$325

Imprint I

2	6	15	17	18
21	24	27	29	31
33	35			

#247 1¢ FRANKLIN (Blue)
16 Plates

Basic Price	T, L, R, B
Imprint Strip of 3	$225
Imprint Block of 6	$650

Imprint I

*18	*21	24	*27	29
*31	33	35		

Imprint II

98	99	101	102	*119
*120	*121	122		

#248 2¢ WASHINGTON (Pink)
20 Plates

Basic Price	T, L, R, B	Type I
Imprint Strip of 3		$75
Imprint Block of 6		$225

Imprint I

1	3	4	5	7
8	9	10	11	12
13	16	19	20	22
23	25	26	30	32

#249 2¢ WASHINGTON (Carmine Lake)
39 Plates

Basic Price	T, L, R, B	Type I
Imprint Strip of 3		$500
Imprint Block of 6		$1,500

Imprint I

1	3	4	5	7
8	9	10	11	12
13	16	19	20	22
23	25	26	30	32

#249 2¢ WASHINGTON Cont.

Imprint II

78	79	80	82	88
*89	96	97	110	111
112	113	114	115	116
*117	124	125	144	

#250 2¢ WASHINGTON (Carmine)
39 Plates

Basic Price	T, L, R, B	Type I
Imprint Strip of 3		$90
Imprint Block of 6		$325

Imprint I

1	3	4	5	*7
8	9	*10	11	12
13	16	19	20	22
23	25	26	30	32

Imprint II

78	79	80	82	88
*89	96	97	110	111
112	113	114	115	116
*117	124	125	144	

#251 2¢ WASHINGTON (Carmine)
4 Plates

Basic Price	T, L, R, B	Type II
Imprint Strip of 3		$675
Imprint Block of 6		$2,500

Imprint II

126	131	132	133

#252 2¢ WASHINGTON (Carmine)
16 Plates

Basic Price	T, L, R, B	Type III
Imprint Strip of 3		$350
Imprint Block of 6		$1,200

Imprint II

141	142	143	145	146
148	149	150	151	152
153	154			

Imprint IV

155	156	157	158

#253 3¢ JACKSON 8 Plates

Basic Price	T, L, R, B
Imprint Strip of 3	$325
Imprint Block of 6	$1,000

Imprint I

44	46	47	48

The following have no side plate numbers.

Basic Price	T, B
Imprint Strip of 3	$325
Imprint Block of 6	$1,000

Imprint II

91	95	103	107

1894 REGULAR ISSUE

Continued

#254 4¢ LINCOLN (Dark Brown)
8 Plates

Basic Price **T, L, R, B**
Imprint Strip of 3 .... $375
Imprint Block of 6 .... $1,250

Imprint I

45 50 51 59

The following have no side plate numbers.

Basic Price **T, B**
Imprint Strip of 3 .... $375
Imprint Block of 6 .... $1,250

Imprint II

92 94 *104 106

#255 5¢ GRANT (Chocolate)
12 Plates

Basic Price **T, L, R, B**
Imprint Strip of 3 .... $275
Imprint Block of 6 .... $875

Imprint I

*49 53 54 *56

The following have no side plate numbers.

Basic Price **T, B**
Imprint strip of 3 .... $275
Imprint Block of 6 .... $875

Imprint II

128 129 130 134

Imprint IV

161 162 163 164

#256 6¢ GARFIELD (Dull Brown)
1 Plate

Price **T, B only**
Imprint Strip of 3 .... $550
Imprint Block of 6 .... $1,750

Imprint I

28

#257 8¢ SHERMAN 1 Plate

Price **T, B only**
Imprint Strip of 3 .... $425
Imprint Block of 6 .... $1,250

Imprint I

58

#258 10¢ WEBSTER (Green)
4 Plates

Basic Price **T, L, R, B**
Imprint Strip of 3 .... $775
Imprint Block of 6 .... $2,750

Imprint I

55 62 63 64

#259 15¢ CLAY (Dark Blue)
1 Plate

Price **T, B only**
Imprint Strip of 3 .... $1,200
Imprint Block of 6 .... $4,250

Imprint I

52

#260 50¢ JEFFERSON 1 Plate

Price **T, B only**
Imprint Strip of 3 .... $1,700
Imprint Block of 6 .... $7,000

Imprint I

75

#261 $1 PERRY 1 Plate

On plate number 76, a two hundred subject plate, the top and bottom plate blocks from the right pane will contain two stamps of type I and four of type II. The strip of three will have one copy of type I and two of type II.

Price **BL Only** **Type I**
Imprint Strip of 3 .... $4,250
Imprint Block of 6 .... $16,500

Imprint II

76

#261A $1 PERRY 1 Plate

Basic Price **BR only** **Type I and Type II**
Imprint Strip of 3 .... $6,500
Imprint Block of 6 .... $27,500

Imprint II

76

#262 $2 MADISON 1 Plate

Price **B only**
Imprint Strip of 3 .... $10,500
Imprint Block of 6 .... $40,000

Imprint II

84

#263 $5 MARSHALL 1 Plate

Price **B only**
Imprint Strip of 3 .... $17,000
Imprint Block of 6 .... $87,500

Imprint II

85

No top positions of the $1, $2, or $5 have been reported.

1895-98 REGULAR ISSUE

Double Line Wmk. Perf. 12
FLAT PRESS

#264 1¢ FRANKLIN (Blue)
77 Plates

Basic Price T, L, R, B
Imprint Strip of 3 . . . . $25
Imprint Block of 6 . . . . $185

Imprint I

*24	*29	*33	*35	

Imprint II

98	99	101	102	119
120	121	122		

Imprint IV

165	166	167	168	177
178	179	180	234	237
240	245	276	277	278
280	294	295	296	297
298	299	300	301	304
308	310	313	314	

Imprint V

333	334	335	336	344
345	346	347	348	350
352	355	360	362	365
366	367	369	370	371
439	440	441	442	443
444	445	446	452	453
454	455	493	494	495
496				

#265 2¢ WASHINGTON (Carmine)
17 Plates

Basic Price T, L, R, B **Type I**
Imprint Strip of 3 . . . . $100
Imprint Block of 6 . . . . $375

Imprint II

78	79	80	82	88
96	97	111	112	113
114	115	*116	117	124
125	144			

#266 2¢ WASHINGTON (Carmine)
6 Plates

Basic Price T, L, R, B **Type II**
Imprint Strip of 3 . . . . $115
Imprint Block of 6 . . . . $425

Imprint II

126	131	132	133

Imprint IV

169	170N

#267 2¢ WASHINGTON (Carmine)
207 Plates

Basic Price T, L, R, B **Type III**
Imprint Strip of 3 . . . . $ 20
Imprint Block of 6 . . . . $135

#267 2¢ WASHINGTON (Carmine)
Continued

Imprint II

141	142	143	145	146
148	149	150	151	152
153	154			

Imprint IV

155	156	157	158	160
170N	171	172	173	174
175	176	181	182	183
185	186	187	188	191
198	199	201	202	203
204	205	206	207	209
210	211	212	213	214
215	216	217	218	219
220	221	222	223	224
225	226	227	228	229
230	231	232	233	235
236	238	239	241	242
243	244	274	275	279
281	282	283	290	291
292	293	307	311	312
315	316	317	318	319
320	321	322	323	324
325	326	327		

N The first three rows of the left of plate 170 are triangle II so the block and strip from the left side positions will be type II's. All other positions, will show triangle III stamps only.

Imprint V

328	329	330	331	332
337	338	339	340	341
342	343	349	354	356
358	361	363	364	368
372	374	376	379	382
383	384	385	387	388
393	394	395	396	397
398	399	400	401	402
403	404	405	406	411
412	413	414	415	416
417	418	419	420	421
422	423	424	425	426
427	*428	429	430	431
432	433	434	435	436
437	438	464	465	466
467	468	469	470	471
472	473	474	475	476
477	478	479	480	481
482	483	484	485	486
487	488	489	490	491
497	498	499	500	501
502	503			

1895-98 REGULAR ISSUE

#268 3¢ JACKSON 12 plates

Basic Price **T, B only**
Imprint Strip of 3 . . . . $135
Imprint Block of 6 . . . . $650

Imprint II
91 95 103 107

Imprint V
447 448 449 450 1213
1214 1215 1216

#269 4¢ LINCOLN (Dark Brown)
16 Plates

Basic Price **T, B only**
Imprint Strip of 3 . . . . $135
Imprint Block of 6 . . . . $650

Imprint II
92 94 104 106

Imprint IV
194 195 196 197

Imprint V
456 457 458 459 460
461 462 463

#270 5¢ GRANT (Chocolate)
24 Plates

Basic Price **T, B only**
Imprint Strip of 3 . . . . $125
Imprint Block of 6 . . . . $650

Imprint II
128 129 130 134

Imprint IV
161 162 163 164 189
190 192 193 250 251
252 253

Imprint V
351 353 *357 359 389
390 391 392

#271 6¢ GARFIELD (Dull Brown)
6 Plates

Basic Price **T, B only**
Imprint Strip of 3 . . . . $325
Imprint Block of 6 . . . . $1,250

Imprint I
28

Imprint IV
184 248

Imprint V
373 386 451

#272 8¢ SHERMAN 11 Plates

Basic Price **T, B only**
Imprint Strip of 3 . . . . $135
Imprint Block of 6 . . . . $700

#272 8¢ SHERMAN Cont.

Imprint I
58

Imprint IV
249

Imprint V
555 928 *929 *930 931
1094 1095 1096 1097

#273 10¢ WEBSTER (Green)
8 Plates

Basic Price **T, L, R, B**
Imprint Strip of 3 . . . . $250
Imprint Block of 6 . . . . $1,300

Imprint I
55 62 63 64

Imprint IV
302 303 305 306

#274 15¢ CLAY (Dark Blue)
2 Plates

Basic Price **T, B only**
Imprint Strip of 3 . . . . $800
Imprint Block of 6 . . . . $3,500

Imprint I
52

Imprint IV
264

#275 50¢ JEFFERSON 1 Plate

Price **T, B only**
Imprint Strip of 3 . . . . $1,150
Imprint Block of 6 . . . . $6,750

Imprint I
75

#276 $1 PERRY 1 Plate

On plate number 76, a two hundred subject plate, the top and bottom plate blocks from the right pane will contain two stamps of type I and four of type II. The strip of three will have one copy of type I and two of type II.

1895-98 REGULAR ISSUE

#276 $1 PERRY Cont.

Price	TL, BL	Type I
Imprint Strip of 3		$3,000
Imprint Block of 6		$11,500

Imprint II

76

#276A $1 PERRY **1 Plate**

Price	TR, BR	Type I and Type II
Imprint Strip of 3		5,250
Imprint Block of 6		$23,500

Imprint II

76

#277 $2 MADISON **1 Plate**

Price	T, B only	
Imprint Strip of 3		$4,250
Imprint Block of 6		$21,000

Imprint II

84

#278 $5 MARSHALL **1 Plate**

Price	T,B, only	
Imprint Strip of 3		$9,000
Imprint Block of 6		$60,000

Imprint II

85

(For plate 288 see Appendix EE)

1898 REGULAR ISSUE

Double Line Wmk. Perf. 12

FLAT PRESS

#279 1¢ FRANKLIN (Green)

273 Plates

Basic Price	T, L, R, B
Imprint Strip of 3	$40
Imprint Block of 6	$185

Imprint V

439	440	*441	446	452
493	494	495	496	526
527	528	529	534	535
536	537	538	539	540
541	542	543	544	545
546	547	548	549	564
565	566	567	572	573
574	575	766	767	768
769	770	771	772	773
794	795	796	797	810
811	812	813	818	819
820	821	822	823	824
825	826	827	828	829
830	831	832	833	846
847	848	849	862	863
864	865	936	937	938
939	940	941	942	943
944	945	946	947	952
953	954	*955	956	957
*958	*959	*960	961	*962
*963	*964	*965	*966	*967
*968	*969	*970	*971	*972
*973	*974	*975	*976	*977
978	*979	984	985	*986
987	992	993	994	995
*1000	1001	1002	1003	1004
1005	1006	1007	1012	1013
1014	1015	1016	1017	1018
1019	1020	1021	1022	*1023
1028	1029	1030	1031	1042
1043	1044	1045	1050	1051
1052	1053	1058	1059	1060
1061	1062	1063	1064	1065
1130	1131	1132	1133	1146
*1147	*1148	*1149	1157	1158
1159	1160	1161	1162	1163
*1164	1183	1184	1185	*1186
1188	1189	*1190	1191	1204
1205	1206	1207	1209	1210
1211	1212	1287	1288	1289
1290	1303	*1304	1305	1306
1315	1316	1317	1318	1328
1329	1330	1331	1340	1341
1342	*1343	1376	*1377	1378
*1379	1392	*1393	1394	*1395
1396	1397	1398	*1399	*1400
*1401	1402	*1403	1404	1405
1406	1407	1408	*1409	*1410
1411Z	1420	*1421	1422	*1423
*1424	1425	*1426	*1427	1453

1898 REGULAR ISSUE

#279 1¢ FRANKLIN (Green) Cont.

*1454	*1455	*1456	*1457	1458
1459	*1460	*1469	*1470	1471
*1472	1485	1486	1487	*1488
*1501	*1502	*1503	*1504	1505
1506	1507	1508		

z On plate **1411** the plate number on the left top position precedes the imprint.

#279B 2¢ WASHINGTON (Red)
309 Plates

Basic Price	T, L, R, B	Type IV
Imprint Strip of 3		$35
Imprint Block of 6		$175

Imprint V

505	506	507	508	509
510	511	512	513	514
515	516	517	522	523
524	525	550	551	552
553	556	557	558	559
560	561	562	563	568
569	570	571	593	594
595	596	745	746	747
748	753	754	755	756
758	759	760	761	762
763	764	765	774	775
776	777	778	779	780
781	782	783	784	785
786	787	788	789	798
799	800	801	802N	803
804	805	806	807	808
809	814	815	816	817
838	839	840	841	842
843	844	845	850	851
852	853	854	855	856
857	858	859	860	861
866	867	869	870	875
876	877	878	885	886
887	888	895	896	897
898	904	905	906	907
909	910	911	912	913
914	915	916	917	918
919	920	921	926	927
1024	1025	1026	1027	1032
1033	1034	1035	1038	1039
1040	1041	1046	1047	1048

N The top imprint and plate numbers on plate 802 are spread out so that a strip of four or a block of eight stamps are required.

All other positions are normal.

#279B 2¢ WASHINGTON (Red) Cont.

1049	1054	1055	1056	1057
1066	1067	1068	1069	1070
1071	1072	1073	1074	*1075
1076	1077	1080	1081	1082
1083	1088	1089	1090	1091
1104	1105	1106	1107	1108
1109	1110	1111	1152	1153
1154	1155	1251	1252	1265
1266	1267	1268	1269	1270
1275	1276	1277	1278	1279
1280	1281	1282	1283	1284
1285	1286	1291	1292	1293
1294	1295	1296	1297	1298
1299	1300	1301	1302	1307
1308	1309	1310	1311	1312
1313	1314	*1319	*1320	*1321
*1322	1344	1345	1346	1347
1348	1349	1350	1351	1352
1353	1354	1355	1356	1357
1358	1359	1360	1361	1362
1363	1364	1365	1366	1367
1372	1373	1374	1375	1380
1381	1382	1383	1384	1385
1386	1387	1412	1413	1414
1415	1416	1417	1418	1419
1428	1429	1430	1431	*1433
1434	1435	1436	*1437	1438
1439	1440	1441	1442	1443
1444	*1449	*1450	*1451	1452
1461	1462	1463	1464	*1465
*1466	*1467	*1468	*1493	

#280 4¢ LINCOLN (Rose Brown)
20 Plates

Basic Price	T, B only
Imprint Strip of 3	$125
Imprint Block of 6	$700

Imprint V

460	461	462	463	530
531	532	*533	790	791
792	793	1100	1101	1102
*1103	*1332	*1333	*1334	*1335

#281 5¢ GRANT (Dark Blue)
32 Plates

Basic Price	T, B only
Imprint Strip of 3	$155
Imprint Block of 6	$800

Imprint V

389	390	391	392	407

1898 REGULAR ISSUE

#281 5¢ GRANT (Dark Blue) **Cont.**

408	409	410	834	835
836	837	948	949	950
951	*980	*981	*982	*983
1084	1085	*1086	1087	1199
1200	1201	1202	1217	1218
1219	1220			

#282 6¢ GARFIELD (Lake)

5 Plates

Basic Price **T, B only**

Imprint Strip of 3..................$210

Imprint Block of 6 ....$1,200

Imprint V

554 922 923 924 925

#282C 10¢ WEBSTER (Brown)

9 Plates

Basic Price **T, L, R, B** **Type I**

Imprint Strip of 3..................$650

Imprint Block of 6 ....$3,250

Imprint IV

302 303 305 306

Imprint V

518 *519 *520 521 932**N**

#283 10¢ WEBSTER (Brown)

12 Plates

Basic Price **T, B, R, B** **Type II**

Imprint Strip of 3..................$400

Imprint Block of 6 ....$1,800

Imprint V

*932**N**	*933	*934	*935	996
997	998	999		

The following have no side plate numbers.

Basic Price **T, B only** **Type II**

Imprint Strip of 3..................$750

Imprint Block of 6 ....$3,250

*1336 *1337 *1338 *1339

N On plate 932 all stamps are Type 1 except 7 entries of Type II. Since one of these is position 86 of the lower left pane, the bottom plate block contains one Type II example.

#284 15¢ CLAY (Olive Green)

1 plate

Price **T, B only**

Imprint Strip of 3..................$475

Imprint Block of 6 ....$2,500

Imprint IV

264

BOOKLET PANES

Double Line Wmk. Perf. 12

BOOKLET PANES OF 6

FLAT PRESS

#279Be 2¢ WASHINGTON (Red)

20 Plates

Top plate number only

Basic Price T $750

Imprint IX

360 Subjects

*988	*989	990	991	*1008
*1009	*1010	*1011		

180 Subjects

1324	1325	1326	1327	*1368
*1369	*1370	*1371	1489	1490
1491	1492			

1898 COMMEMORATIVES

Double Line Wmk. Perf. 12
FLAT PRESS **Positions T, B**
Imprint VIII

#285 1¢ TRANS-MISSISSIPPI
Basic Prices: **14 Plates**
Imprint Pair $70
Imprint Block of 4 .... $200

	T	B		T	B		T	B
590	☐	☐	591	☐	☐	592	☐	☐
598	☐	☐	600	☐	☐	601	☐	☐
*605	☐	☐	607	☐	☐	612	☐	☐
635	☐	☐	*709	☐	☐	710	☐	☐
711	☐	☐	712	☐	☐			

#286 2¢ TRANS-MISSISSIPPI
Basic Prices: **121 Plates**
Imprint Pair $65
Imprint Block of 4 .... $185

597	☐	☐	608	☐	☐	610	☐	☐
611	☐	☐	615	☐	☐	*616	☐	☐
619	☐	☐	621	☐	☐	622	☐	☐
623	☐	☐	624	☐	☐	625	☐	☐
626	☐	☐	*627	☐	☐	628	☐	☐
629	☐	☐	630	☐	☐	631	☐	☐
632	☐	☐	633	☐	☐	638	☐	☐
639	☐	☐	640	☐	☐	641	☐	☐
642	☐	☐	644	☐	☐	645	☐	☐
646	☐	☐	647	☐	☐	648	☐	☐
649	☐	☐	650	☐	☐	651	☐	☐
*652	☐	☐	653	☐	☐	654	☐	☐
655	☐	☐	656	☐	☐	657	☐	☐
658	☐	☐	659	☐	☐	*660	☐	☐
661	☐	☐	*662	☐	☐	663	☐	☐
*664	☐	☐	665	☐	☐	666	☐	☐
*667	☐	☐	668	☐	☐	669	☐	☐
670	☐	☐	*671	☐	☐	672	☐	☐
*673	☐	☐	*674	☐	☐	*675	☐	☐
676	☐	☐	677	☐	☐	678	☐	☐
679	☐	☐	680	☐	☐	*681	☐	☐
683	☐	☐	684	☐	☐	*685	☐	☐
686	☐	☐	687	☐	☐	688	☐	☐
689	☐	☐	690	☐	☐	*691	☐	☐
692	☐	☐	693	☐	☐	*694	☐	☐
695	☐	☐	696	☐	☐	697	☐	☐
698	☐	☐	699	☐	☐	700	☐	☐
701	☐	☐	*702	☐	☐	703	☐	☐
704	☐	☐	705	☐	☐	706	☐	☐
707	☐	☐	708	☐	☐	713	☐	☐
714	☐	☐	715	☐	☐	716	☐	☐
717	☐	☐	718	☐	☐	719	☐	☐
720	☐	☐	721	☐	☐	722	☐	☐
724	☐	☐	725	☐	☐	726	☐	☐
727	☐	☐	728	☐	☐	729	☐	☐
732	☐	☐	733	☐	☐	734	☐	☐
735	☐	☐	737	☐	☐	738	☐	☐
739	☐	☐	740	☐	☐	741	☐	☐
742	☐	☐	743	☐	☐	744	☐	☐
749	☐	☐	*750	☐	☐	751	☐	☐
752	☐	☐						

#287 4¢ TRANS-MISSISSIPPI
Basic Prices: **3 Plates**
Imprint Pair $350
Imprint Block of 4 .... $1,100

599 ☐ ☐ 634 ☐ ☐ *636 ☐ ☐

#288 5¢ TRANS-MISSISSIPPI
Basic Prices: **3 Plates**
Imprint Pair $300
Imprint Block of 4 .... $1,000

602 ☐ ☐ 614 ☐ ☐ 618 ☐ ☐

#289 8¢ TRANS-MISSISSIPPI
Basic Prices: **2 Plates**
Imprint Pair $400
Imprint Block of 4 .... $1,750

609 ☐ ☐ 643 ☐ ☐

#290 10¢ TRANS-MISSISSIPPI
Basic Prices: **3 Plates**
Imprint Pair $450
Imprint Block of 4 .... $2,250

604 ☐ ☐ 617 ☐ ☐ 620 ☐ ☐

#291 50¢ TRANS-MISSISSIPPI
Basic Price **1 Plate**
Imprint Pair $1,750
Imprint Block of 4 .... $14,500

603 ☐ ☐

#292 $1 TRANS-MISSISSIPPI
Basic Price **1 Plate**
Imprint Pair $4,500
Imprint Block of 4 .... $45,000

606 ☐ ☐

#293 $2 TRANS-MISSISSIPPI
Basic Price **1 Plate**
Imprint Pair $6,500
Imprint Block of 4 .... $90,000

613 ☐ ☐

1901 COMMEMORATIVES

These plates are collected in top and bottom strips of three and blocks of six with the frame plate number only or in bottom strips of five or blocks of ten showing both frame and vignette plate numbers. This combination comes from the bottom left position of the sheet. Some of the 1¢ and 2¢ combinations are very scarce.

FLAT PRESS

Double Line Wmk. Perf. 12

#294 1¢ PAN-AMERICAN

Basic Prices:

Imprint Strip of 3, **T or B** $85
Imprint Block of 6, **T or B** $300
Imprint Strip of 5, **B** $175
Imprint Block of 10, **B** $600

8 Frame Plates *Imprint V*

	T	B		T	B		T	B
1112	☐	☐	1116	☐	☐	1123	☐	☐
1139	☐	☐	1172	☐	☐	1175	☐	☐
1179	☐	☐	*1181	☐	☐			

20 Vignette Plates *Imprint IX*

	B		B		B		B
1113	☐	1117	☐	1125	☐	1136	☐
1156	☐	1168	☐	1170	☐	1177	☐
1180	☐	1194	☐	*1196	☐	*1225	☐
*1226	☐	*1227	☐	*1228	☐	*1233	☐
*1234	☐	*1235	☐	*1236	☐	*1248	☐

#295 2¢ PAN-AMERICAN

Basic Prices:

Imprint Strip of 3, **T or B** $70
Imprint Block of 6, **T or B** $300
Imprint Strip of 5, **B** $185
Imprint Block of 10, **B** $675

12 Frame Plates *Imprint V*

1078	☐	☐	1092	☐	☐	1098	☐	☐
1114	☐	☐	1119	☐	☐	1122	☐	☐
1126	☐	☐	1129	☐	☐	*1165	☐	☐
1167	☐	☐	*1169	☐	☐	1176	☐	☐

36 Vignette Plates *Imprint IX*

1079	☐	1093	☐	1115	☐	1118	☐
1124	☐	1127	☐	1128	☐	1134	☐
1135	☐	1137	☐	1138	☐	1166	☐
1171	☐	1173	☐	1174	☐	1178	☐
1182	☐	1187	☐	1192	☐	1193	☐
*1195	☐	*1197	☐	1198	☐	1208	☐
1221	☐	1222	☐	1223	☐	1224	☐
1229	☐	*1230	☐	*1231	☐	*1232	☐
*1238	☐	1239	☐	*1240	☐	*1241	☐

#296 4¢ PAN-AMERICAN

Imprint Strip of 3, **T or B** $600
Imprint Block of 6, **T or B** $3,500
Imprint Strip of 5, **B** $800
Imprint Block of 10, **B** $5,500

1 Frame Plate *Imprint V*

1145 ☐ ☐

1 Vignette Plate *Imprint IX*

1142 ☐

#297 5¢ PAN-AMERICAN

Imprint Strip of 3, **T or B** $650
Imprint Block of 6, **T or B** $3,750
Imprint Strip of 5, **B** $800
Imprint Block of 10, **B** $6,000

1 Frame Plate *Imprint V*

1140 ☐ ☐

1 Vignette Plate *Imprint IX*

1141 ☐

#298 8¢ PAN-AMERICAN

Imprint Strip of 3, **T or B** $800
Imprint Block of 6, **T or B** $7,000
Imprint Strip of 5, **B** $1,200
Imprint Block of 10, **B** $10,000

1 Frame Plate *Imprint V*

1150 ☐ ☐

1 Vignette Plate *Imprint IX*

1143 ☐

#299 10¢ PAN-AMERICAN

Imprint Strip of 3, **T or B** $1,200
Imprint Block of 6, **T or B** $8,000
Imprint Strip of 5, **B** $1,800
Imprint Block of 10, **B** $11,500

1 Frame Plate *Imprint V*

1151 ☐ ☐

1 Vignette Plate *Imprint IX*

1144 ☐

1902-03 REGULAR ISSUE

Double Line Wmk. Perf. 12
FLAT PRESS
Imprint V

#300 1¢ FRANKLIN 823 Plates

Basic Price T, L, R, B

Imprint Strip of 3 .... $40

Imprint Block of 6 .... $185

1541	1542	1543	1544	1545
1546	1547	1548	1549	1550
1551	1552	1578	1579	1580
1581	1608	1609	1610	1611
1625	1626	1627	1628	1634
1635	*1636	1637	1638	1639
1640	1641	1651	1652	1653
1654	1655	1656	1657	1658
1659	1660	1661	1662	1680
1681	1682	1683	1700	1701
1702	1703	1720	1721	1722
1723	1725	1726	1727	1728
1733	1734	1735	1736	1737
1738	1739	1740	1793	1794
1795	1796	1801	1802	1803
1804	1821	1822	1823	1824
1865	1866	1867	1868	1869
1870	*1871	1872	1873	1874
*1875	*1876	1881	*1882	1883
1884	*1897	1898	1899	1900
1945	*1946	*1947	1948	1953
*1954	1955	1956	1957	1958
*1959	*1960	1973	1974	1975
1976	1977	1978	1979	1980
1981	1982	1983	1984	1985
1986	1987	1988	2029	2030
2031	2032	*2037	2038	2039
2048	*2053	2054	2055	2056
2061	2062	2063	2064	2077
2078	2079	2080	2085	2086
2087	2088	2089	2090	2091
2092	2141	2142	2143	2144
2173	2174	2175	2176	2181
2186	2187	2188	2193	2194
2195	2196	2257	2258	2259
2260	2273	2274	2275	2276
2281	2282	2283	2284	2285
2286	2287	2288	2310	2311
2312	2313	2391	2392	2393
2394	2407	2408	2409	2410
2415	2416	2417	2418	2451
2452	2453	2454	2468	2469
2470	2471	2484	2485	2486
2487	2492	2493	2494	2495
2500	2501	2502	2503	2552
2553	2554	2555	2560	2561
2562	2563	2580	2581	2582
2583	2584	2585	2586	2587
2645	2646	2647	2648	2675
2676	2677	2678	2693	2694
2695	2696	2697	2698	2699
2700	2733	2734	2735	2736
2737	2738	2739	2740	2745
2746	2747	2748	2749	*2750

#300 1¢ FRANKLIN Continued

2751	2752	2753	2754	2755
2756	2757	2758	2759	2760
2761	2762	2763	2764	*2789
2790	2791	2792	2797	2798
2799	2800	2801	2818	2819
2820	2821	2822	2823	*2824
2825	2907	2908	2909	2910
2911	2912	2913	2914	2915
2916	2917	2918	2919	2920
2921	2922	2927	2928	2929
2930	2935	2936	2937	2938
2939	2940	2941	2942	2943
2944	2945	2946	2947	2948
2949	2950	2991	2992	2993
*2994	2995	2996	2997	2998
2999	3000	3001	3002	3015
3016	3017	3018	3024	3026
3029	3034	3035	3037	3038
3039	3040	3041	3043	3082
3095	3096	3103	*3104	3119
3120	3121	3122	3123	3124
3125	3126	3127	3128	3129
3130	3131	3132	3133	3134
3178	3182	3186	3189	3194
3201	3203	3207	3214	3217
3220	3223	3224	3225	3226
3227	3228	3229	3230	3231
3232	3233	3234	3239	3243
3244	3245	3246	3247	3252
3261	3266	3283	3284	3285
3286	3287	3290	3293	3320
3364	3365	3366	3367	3370
3371	3373	3374	3377	3378
3379	3380	3381	3382	3383
3384	3385	3386	3391	3392
3393	3394	3396	3400	3401
3402	3404	3407	3476	3477
3482	3483	3485	3489	*3492
*3494	3495	3499	3500	3506
3509	3515	3518	3529	3530
3535	3558	3567	3588	*3590
3596	3598	*3599	3692	3696
3704	3710	3714	3719	3725
3726	3731	*3738	3741	3742
3746	3747	3748	3749	3750
3751	3752	3757	3760	3761
3764	3768	3769	3771	3772
3776	3777	3778	3781	3782
*3783	3785	*3786	*3788	*3789
*3790	†3791	*3793	*3794	*3795
3797	3798	3800	3803	3805

1902-03 REGULAR ISSUE

#300 1¢ FRANKLIN Continued

*3809 3813 3815 3818 3874
3875 3880 3881 3882 3885
3887 3889 *3890 3891 3893
3894 *3898 3900 3901 3905
*3907 *3909 3910 3914 3917

3919 3921 3922 3926 3930
3933 3936 3937 3938 3942
3943 3944 3947 3949 3950
3951 3952 3953 3957 3958
3959 3960 3961 3965 3966
3967 3968 3971 3972 3973
3974 3976 3977 3978 3979
3980 3982 3983 3984 3986
3987 3988 3990 3991 *3992
3993 3994 3995 3996 4130

4131 4134 4135 4136 4137
4138 4139 4142 *4143 4144
4147 4148 4149 4150 4151
4154 4155 4156 *4157 4160
4161 4162 4163 4164 4165
4168 4169 4170 4171 4172
4176 4177 4178 4179 4181
4183 *4191 4192 4193 4198
4199 4201 4216 4221 *4228
*4229 4232 4233 *4234 4236

4237 4240 4241 4246 4252
4253 4257 4258 4259 4265
4266 4270 4273 4274 4278
4281 4282 4287 *4288 *4290
*4293 *4294 4295 4296 4297
*4301 4302 *4303 *4304 4305
4309 4310 4311 4314 4319
4324 *4325 *4328 *4334 4340
4341 4347 4348 4349 4354
4355 4356 4362 4366 4370

4371 4376 4386 4387 4392
4397 4403 4412 4413 4421
4422 4427 4428 4432 4436
4440 4450 4453 4455 4458
4462 4466 4467 4472 4473
4474 4478 4479 4480 4484
4485 4486 4491 4492 4493
*4494 4498 4499 4504 4505
4506 4511 4517 4529 4533
4539 4547 4554 4559 4562

4565 *4566 *4567 4571 *4573
4574 4578 4582 4585 4586
4591 4592 4597 4600 4601
4603 4605 4606 4608 4609
4610 4618 4619 4620 4621
4622 4623 4626 4629 4630
4633 4637 4640 4641 4645
4656 4673 4674 4675 4679
4680 4681 4682 4688 *4691
*4694 4698 4699 4700 *4702

4705 4706 4710 4712 4713
4717 4719 4722 4723 4724
4727 4729 4733 4734 4737
4738 4742 4744 4748 4752
4753 *4757 4758

#301 2¢ WASHINGTON (FLAG)

Basic Price T, L, R, B 145 Plates

Imprint Strip of 3 . . . .$45
Imprint Block of 6 . . . .$200

1513 1514 1515 1516 1517
1518 1519 1520 1521 1522
1523 1524 1525 1526 1527
1528 1529 1530 1531 1532
1533 1534 1535 1536 1553
1554 1555 1556 1557 1559
1560 1561 1562 1563 1564
1565 1566 1567 1568 1569
1570 1571 1572 1573 *1574
*1575 1576 1577 1603 1604

1605 1606 1612 1613 1614
1615 1616 1617 1618 1619
1621 1622 1623 1624 1643
1644 1645 1646 1647 1648
1649 1650 1668 1669 1670
1671 1672 1673 1674 1675
1676 1677 1678 1679 1684
1685 1686 1687 1692 1693
1694 1695 1696 1697 1698
1699 1704 1705 1706 1707

1708 1709 1710 1711 1712
1713 1714 1715 1716 1717
1718 1719 1724 1729 1730
1731 1732 1741 1742 1743
1744 *1745 1746 1747 *1748
1749 *1750 *1751 1752 1753
*1754 *1755 1756 1757 *1758
1759 1760 1761 1762 *1763
1764 *1765 *1766 *1767 *1768

#302 3¢ JACKSON 16 Plates

Basic Price T, L, R, B

Imprint Strip of 3 . . . .$250
Imprint Block of 6 . . . .$1,000

1586 1587 1588 1589 2516
2517 2518 2519 2806 2807
2808 2809 3511 3523 3527
3536

1902-03 REGULAR ISSUE

#303 4¢ GRANT 24 Plates

Basic Price T, L, R, B

Imprint Strip of 3 . . . . $250
Imprint Block of 6 . . . . $1,000

1477 1478 1479 1480 1797
1798 1799 1800 2298 2299
2300 2301 4214 4255 4264
4271 4501 4512 4520 4527
4747 4754 4759 4761

#304 5¢ LINCOLN 34 Plates

Basic Price T, L, R, B

Imprint Strip of 3 . . . . $250
Imprint Block of 6 . . . . $1,100

1537 1538 1539 1540 1663
1885 1886 1887 1888 2225
2226 2227 2297 2951 2952
2953 2954 3147 3153 3157
3158 3159 3484 3488 3493
3498 4073 4074 4075 4076
4190 4194 4203 4209

#305 6¢ GARFIELD 8 Plates

Basic Price T, L, R, B

Imprint Strip of 3 . . . . $300
Imprint Block of 6 . . . . $1,250

1598 1599 1600 1601 *4658
4660 *4664 4666

#306 8¢ MARTHA WASHINGTON

Basic Price T, L, R, B **12 Plates**

Imprint Strip of 3. . . . . $165
Imprint Block of 6 . . . . $850

1497 1498 1499 1500 2802
2803 2804 2805 3557 3565
3570 3576

#307 10¢ WEBSTER 12 Plates

Basic Price T, L, R, B

Imprint Strip of 3 . . . . $325
Imprint Block of 6 . . . . $1,500

1590 1591 1592 1593 2289
2290 2291 2292 2826 2827
2828 2829

#308 13¢ HARRISON 8 Plates

Basic Price T, L, R, B

Imprint Strip of 3. . . . . $150
Imprint Block of 6 . . . . $650

1473 1474 1475 1476 3827
3831 3835 3840

#309 15¢ CLAY 6 Plates

Basic Price T, B

Imprint Strip of 3 . . . . $750
Imprint Block of 6 . . . . $4,000

1607 2330

Basic Price T, L, R, B

Imprint Strip of 3 . . . . $750
Imprint Block of 6 . . . . $4,000

3202 3206 3208 3209

1902-03 REGULAR ISSUE

#310 50¢ JEFFERSON 1 Plate

Price T, B

Imprint Strip of 3 . . . . $2,500
Imprint Block of 6 . . . . $9,000

1602

#311 $1 FARRAGUT 1 Plate

Price T, B

Imprint Strip of 3 . . . . $ 4,000
Imprint Block of 6 . . . . $17,500

1629

#312 $2 MADISON 1 Plate

Price T, B

Imprint Strip of 3 . . . . $ 6,500
Imprint Block of 6 . . . . $25,000

1630

#313 $5 MARSHALL 1 Plate

Price T, B

Imprint Strip of 3 . . . . $12,000
Imprint Block of 6 . . . . $65,000

1620

BOOKLET PANES

Double Line Wmk. Perf. 12

BOOKLET PANES OF 6

FLAT PRESS

Imprint IX

#300b 1¢ FRANKLIN 20 Plates

Top plate number only
Basic Price T $1,000

3339	3340	3341	*3342	3468
3469	3471	3472	†3474	†3475
†3479	*3480	3503	3508	3510
3514	†4544	*4550	*4553	*4557

BOOKLET PANES

#301c 2¢ WASHINGTON (FLAG)

Top plate number only **20 Plates**
Basic Price T $1,000

1582	1583	*1584	*1585	*1594
*1595	*1596	1597	1664	*1665
1666	*1667	*1688	*1689	*1690
1691	*1769	1770	*1771	*1772

IMPERFORATE

FLAT PRESS Double Line Wmk.
Blocks of 6

Imprint V

#314 1¢ FRANKLIN 38 Plates

Basic Price T, L, R, B
Imprint Block of 6 . . . . $275

3119	3120	3121	3122	3227
3228	3230	3231	3364	3365
3366	3367	3373	3374	*4147
4149	4296	*4324	*4354	4370
4371	4376	4386	4474	4493
4498	4499	4505	4559	4562
*4605	4608	4681	4682	4688
*4712	4713	*4734		

#314A 4¢ GRANT 1 Plate

4255

Imperforate stamp was issued but all known examples have Schermack perforations type III.

#315 5¢ LINCOLN 6 Plates

Basic Price T, L, R, B
Imprint Block of 6 . . . . $6,000

2951	2952	2953	2954	4073
4075				

1902-03 REGULAR ISSUE

Doubleline Wmk. Perf. 12 ***Imprint V***

#319 2¢ WASHINGTON (SHIELD) (DIE I) 1450 Plates

Basic Price T, L, R, B

Imprint Strip of 3 . . . . $25
Imprint Block of 6 . . . . $100

1805	1806	1807	1808	1809
1810	1811	1812	1813	1814
1815	1816	1817	1818	1819
1820	1825	1826	1827	1828
1829	1830	1831	1832	1833
1834	1835	1836	1837	1838
1839	1840	1841	1842	1843
1844	1849	1850	*1851	1852
1853	1854	1855	1856	1857
1858	*1860	1861	1862	1863
1864	1877	1878	1879	1880
1893	1894	1895	1896	1901
1902	1903	1904	1905	1906
1907	1908	*1909	1910	1911
1913	1914	1915	1916	1917
1918	1919	1920	1921	1922
1923	1924	1925	1926	*1927
*1928	1929	*1930	1931	1932
1933	1934	1935	1936	1937
1938	1940	1941	1942	1943
1944	1961	1962	1963	1964
1965	1966	1967	*1968	1969
1970	1971	1972	1989	1990
1991	1992	1993	1994	1995
1996	1997	1998	1999	2000
2001	2002	2003	2004	2005
*2006	2007	2008	2013	2014
2015	2016	2017	2018	2019
2020	2021	2022	2023	2024
2025	2026	2027	2028	2033
2034	2035	2036	2040	2041
2042	2043	2044	2045	2046
2047	2049	2051	2052	2057
2058	2059	2060	2065	2066
2067	2068	2073	2074	2075
2076	2133	2134	2135	2136
2169	2170	2171	2172	2189
2191	2192	2201	2202	2203
2204	2205	2206	2207	2208
2209	2210	2211	2212	2213
2214	2215	2216	2217	2218
2219	2220	2221	2222	2223
2224	2229	2230	2231	2232
2237	2238	2239	2240	2241
2242	2243	2244	2245	2246
2247	2248	2249	2250	2251
2252	2253	2254	2255	2256
2261	2262	2263	*2264	2265
2266	2267	2268	2269	2270
2271	2272	2277	2278	2279
2280	2293	2294	2295	2296
2306	*2307	2308	2309	2314
2315	2316	2317	2318	2319
2320	2321	2322	2323	2324
2325	2326	2327	2328	2329
2331	2332	2333	2334	2335
2336	2337	2338	2339	2340
2341	2342	2343	2344	2345
2346	2347	2348	2349	2350
2351	2352	2353	2354	2355
2356	2357	2358	2359	2360
2361	2362	2363	2364	2365
2366	2367	2368	2369	2370
2379	2380	2381	2382	2383
2384	2385	2386	2387	2388
2389	2390	2395	2396	2397
2398	2399	2400	2401	2402
2403	2404	2405	2406	2419
2420	2421	2422	2423	2424
2425	2426	2427	2428	2429
2430	2431	2432	2433	2434
2435	2436	2437	2438	2439
2440	2441	2442	2443	2444
2445	2446	2447	2448	2449
2450	2455	2456	2457	2458
2459	2460	2461	2462	2463
2464	2465	2466	2472	2473
2474	2475	2476	2477	2478
2479	2480	2481	2482	2483
2488	2489	2490	2491	2508
2509	2510	2511	2512	2513
2514	2515	2520	2521	2522
2523	2524	2525	2526	2527
2528	2529	2530	2531	2532
2533	2534	2535	2536	2537
2538	2539	2540	2541	2542
2543	2544	2545	2546	2547
2556	2557	2558	2559	2564
2565	2566	2567	2568	2569
2570	2571	2572	2573	2574
2575	2576	2577	2578	2579
2588	2589	2590	2591	2592
2593	2594	2595	2596	2597
2598	2599	2608	2609	2610
2611	2612	2613	2614	2615
2616	2617	2618	2619	2620
2621	2622	2623	2624	2625
2626	2627	2628	2629	2630
2631	2632	2633	2634	2635
2636	2637	2638	2639	2640
2641	2642	2643	2644	2649
2650	2651	2652	2653	2654
2655	2656	2657	2658	2659
2660	2661	2662	2663	2664
2665	2666	2667	2668	2669
2670	2671	2672	2673	2674
2679	2680	2681	2682	2683
2684	2685	2686	2687	2688
2689	2690	2691	2692	2701
2702	2703	2704	2705	2706
2707	2708	2709	2710	2711
2712	2717	2718	2719	2720
2721	2722	2723	2724	2725
2726	2727	2728	2729	2730
2731	2732	2741	2742	2743
2744	2765	2766	2767	2768
2773	2774	2775	2776	2777
2778	2779	2785	2786	2787

1902-03 REGULAR ISSUE

#319 2¢ WASHINGTON (SHIELD) (DIE I) Continued

2788 2793 2794 *2795 2796
2810 2811 2812 2813 2814

2815 2816 2817 2830 2831
2832 2833 2834 2835 2836
2837 2838 2839 2840 2841
2842 2843 2844 2845 2846
2847 2848 2849 2850 2851
2852 2853 2854 2855 2856
2857 2858 2859 2860 2861
2862 2863 2864 2865 2866
2867 2868 2869 2870 2871
2872 2873 2874 2875 2876

2877 2878 2883 2884 2885
2886 2887 2888 2889 2890
2891 2892 2893 2894 2895
2896 2897 2898 2899 2900
2901 2902 2903 2904 2905
2906 2959 2960 2961 2962
2963 2964 2965 2966 2967
2968 2969 2970 2971 2972
2973 2974 2975 2976 2977
2978 2979 *2980 2981 2982

2983 2984 2985 2986 2987
2988 2989 2990 3003 3004
3005 3006 3007 3008 3009
3010 3036 3042 3044 3045
3046 3047 3048 3049 3050
3051 3052 3053 3054 3055
3056 3057 3058 3059 3060
3061 3062 3063 3064 3065
3066 3067 3068 3069 3070
3071 3072 3073 3074 3075

3076 3077 3078 3079 3080
3081 3083 3084 3085 3086
3087 3088 3089 3090 3091
3092 3093 3094 3097 3098
3099 3100 3101 3102 3105
3106 3107 3108 3109 3110
3111 3112 3113 3114 3115
3116 3117 3118 3135 3136
3137 3138 3139 3140 3141
3142 3143 *3144 3145 3146

3148 3149 3150 3151 3152
3154 3155 3156 3160 3161
3162 3163 3164 3166 3167
3168 3169 3170 3171 3172
3173 3174 3175 3176 3179
3180 3183 3184 3185 3187
3188 3190 3191 3193 *3200
3204 3205 3210 3211 3212
*3213 3218 3222 3248 3249
3250 3251 3253 3254 3255

3256 3257 3258 3259 3260
3262 3623 3264 *3265 3267
3268 3269 3270 3271 3272
3273 3274 3275 3276 3277
3278 3279 3280 3281 3282
3288 3289 3291 3292 3294
3295 3296 3297 3298 3301
3304 3305 3306 3309 3310
3313 3314 3315 3316 3317

3318 3319 3321 3322 3323

3324 3325 3326 3327 3328
3329 3330 3331 3332 3333
3334 3335 3336 3337 3338
3343 3344 3345 3346 3347
3348 3349 3350 3351 3352
3353 3356 3357 3358 3361
3362 3363 3368 3369 3372
*3375 3376 3389 *3390 3395
3399 3403 3408 3411 3412
3415 3416 3417 3418 3419

3420 3423 3424 3425 3426
3427 3428 3429 3430 3431
3432 3433 3434 3435 3438
3439 3440 3441 3442 *3445
3446 3447 3448 3451 3452
3453 3454 3455 3456 3457
3458 3461 3462 3463 *3465
3466 3467 3470 3473 3478
3481 3486 3487 *3490 3491
3496 3497 3501 3502 3507

3516 3519 3528 3533 3534
3537 3539 3547 3548 3551
3552 3555 *3559 3562 3563
3564 3566 *3568 3569 3571
3572 *3573 *3574 *3575 3581
3582 3584 3586 3587 3589
3600 3605 3606 3607 3608
3609 3611 3612 3614 3615
3616 3617 3620 3621 3622
3623 3624 3625 3626 3627

3628 3629 3630 *3631 3632
3633 3634 3635 3640 3641
3642 3643 3644 3549 3650
3651 3652 3653 3654 3659
3660 3663 3665 3668 3674
3675 3676 3679 *3680 3681
3682 3683 3684 3685 3686
3687 3688 3689 3690 *3691
3693 3694 3695 3697 3698
*3699 3700 *3701 3702 3703

3705 *3706 *3707 *3708 *3709
3711 3712 3713 3715 *3716
3717 3718 3721 3722 3723
3724 3727 *3728 3729 *3730
*3732 3735 *3736 3737 3743
3744 3745 3758 3759 3765
*3767 3773 3774 3779 3784
*3792 3796 3801 *3806 *3808
*3811 3812 3816 3820 *3821
3823 3824 3825 3826 3828

3829 3830 3832 3833 3834
3836 3837 3838 3839 3841
3842 3843 3844 3845 3846
3847 3848 *3849 *3850 3851
3852 3853 3854 3855 3856
3857 *3858 3859 3860 *3861
3862 3863 3864 3865 3866
3867 3868 *3869 3870 3871

1902-03 REGULAR ISSUE

#319 2¢ WASHINGTON (SHIELD) (DIE I) Continued

3872	3873	3876	3877	3878
3879	3883	*3884	3886	3888
3892	3895	3896	3897	3899
3902	3903	3904	3906	3908
3911	3912	3913	3915	3916
3918	3920	3925	3929	3931
3932	3934	3935	3939	3940
3941	3945	3946	3948	3954
3955	3956	3962	3963	3964
3969	3970	3975	3981	3985
*3989	3998	4000	4005	4006
4009	4010	4011	4012	4013
4014	4015	4016	4017	4018
4019	4020	4021	4022	4023
4024	4025	4026	4027	4028
4029	4030	4031	4032	*4033
4034	*4035	4036	4037	4038
4039	4040	4041	*4042	4043
4044	4045	4046	4047	*4048
4049	4050	*4051	4053	*4054
*4055	4056	*4058	4059	4060
4063	4064	4065	4066	4067
*4068	4069	4070	4071	4072
4077	4078	4079	4080	4081
*4082	4083	4084	4085	4086
*4087	4088	4089	4090	4091
4092	4093	4094	*4095	4096
4097	4098	4099	4100	4101
4102	4103	4104	4105	4110
4111	4112	4113	4116	4117
4119	4122	*4123	4124	*4125
*4126	*4127	*4128	4129	4132
4133	4140	4141	4145	4146
4152	4153	4158	4159	4166
4167	4173	4174	4175	*4180
4182	*4184	4185	4186	*4187
4188	*4189	4195	4196	4197
4200	4202	*4204	*4205	4206
4207	4208	4210	4211	4212
4213	*4215	4217	4218	4219
*4220	*4222	*4224	4225	4226
4227	4238	4243	4244	4245
4249	4250	4251	4254	4256
4260	4261	4262	4263	4267
4268	4269	4272	4276	4277
4280	4284	4285	4286	4291
4292	4298	4299	4300	*4306
4307	4308	4312	*4313	4315
*4316	4317	4318	4320	4321
4322	4323	4326	4327	4329
4330	4331	4332	4333	4335
4336	4337	4338	*4342	4345

#319f 2¢ WASHINGTON (SHIELD) (DIE II) 225 Plates

Basic Price T, L, R, B

Imprint Strip of 3 . . . .$ 27.50
Imprint Block of 6 . . . .$175

4339	4343	4344	4346	4350
4351	4352	4353	4359	4360
4361	4365	4369	4372	4373
4377	4378	*4380	4381	4383
4384	4385	4388	4389	4390
4391	4393	4394	4395	4396
4398	4399	4400	4401	4402
4404	4405	4406	4407	4408
4409	4410	4411	4414	4415
4416	4417	4419	4420	4424
4425	4426	4429	4431	4433
4434	4437	4438	4447	4448
4449	4452	4454	4456	4459
4460	4461	4463	4465	4468
4469	4470	4471	4475	4476
4477	4481	4482	4483	4487
4488	4489	4490	4495	4496
4497	4500	4502	4503	4507
4508	4509	4510	4513	4514
4515	4516	4518	4519	4521
4522	4523	4524	4525	4526
4528	4530	4531	4532	4534
4535	4536	4537	4538	4540
4541	4542	4543	4545	4546
4548	4549	4552	4555	4556
4560	4561	4569	4575	4581
4587	4588	4595	4596	4599
4604	4611	4612	4615	4616
4617	4624	4625	4627	4628
4631	4632	4634	4635	4636
4638	4639	4642	4643	4644
4646	4647	4648	4649	4650
4651	*4652	4653	4654	4655
4657	4659	4661	4662	4663
4665	4667	4668	4669	4670
4671	4672	4676	4677	4678
4683	4684	4685	4686	4687
4689	4690	4692	4693	4695
4696	4697	4701	4703	4704
4707	4708	4709	4711	4714
4715	4716	4718	4720	4721
4725	4726	4728	4730	4731
4732	4735	4736	4739	4740
4741	4743	4745	*4746	*4750
4756	4764	4769	4772	4776

1902-03 REGULAR ISSUE

BOOKLET PANES

Imprint IX

Double Line Wmk. Perf. 12

BOOKLET PANES OF 6

FLAT PRESS

#319g 2¢ WASHINGTON (SHIELD) (DIE I) 232 Plates

Top plate number only

Basic Price T $200

*1845 †1846 †1847 †1848 *1889
1890 1891 1892 *1949 *1950
1951 *1952 *2009 *2010 *2011
*2012 *2109 2110 2111 2112
*2121 *2122 *2123 *2124 *2233
†2234 2235 2236 *2302 2303
*2304 2305 *2371 *2372 *2373
*2374 2375 *2376 2377 2378
*2411 *2412 *2413 *2414 2467
*2496 *2497 *2498 *2499 *2504

2505 *2506 2507 2548 2549
2550 2551 2600 *2601 *2602
*2603 *2604 †2605 *2606 *2607
2713 2714 2715 2716 2769
2770 2771 2772 2781 2782
*2783 *2784 *2879 2880 2881
2882 *2923 *2924 2925 *2926
*2931 *2932 2933 *2934 *2955
2956 2957 *2958 *3011 *3012
*3013 *3014 *3019 3020 3021

*3022 3023 *3025 *3027 *3028
3030 3031 *3032 *3033 *3196
3197 3198 3199 †3215 †3216
*3219 *3221 †3235 †3236 †3237
*3238 †3240 *3241 *3242 3299
3300 3302 *3303 *3307 *3308
*3311 *3312 3354 *3355 3359
*3360 3387 3388 *3397 *3398
†3405 †3406 3409 *3410 †3413
†3414 †3421 †3422 *3436 *3437

†3443 *3444 *3449 †3450 *3459
*3460 †3464 *3521 3525 3526
†3531 *3532 3549 *3550 3553

#319g 2¢ WASHINGTON (SHIELD) (DIE I) Continued

*3636 †3637 †3638 †3639 *3645
*3646 *3647 *3648 *3661 3662
*3664 †3666 †3667 *3669 †3670
3673 *3733 *3734 *3739 3740
*3753 3754 *3755 †3756 3762
3763 3766 3810 3814 3817
3819 3822 *3923 3924 3928

3997 3999 4001 *4002 †4003
†4004 †4007 †4008 *4052 †4057
*4061 †4062 4106 †4107 4108
†4109 *4114 4115 *4118 *4120
†4223 *4230 *4231 *4235 *4239
*4242 †4247 *4248 †4275 *4279
*4283 *4289

#319h 2¢ WASHINGTON (SHIELD) (DIE II) 40 Plates

Top plate number only

Basic Price T $300

†4357 4358 4363 *4364 4367
4368 *4374 *4375 *4379 4382
4418 4423 4430 *4435 *4439
4441 4442 4443 *4444 4445
4446 4451 4457 4464 4551
4558 4564 *4570 *4577 †4580
4584 4590 4594 *4598 4602
*4607 4749 4751 4755 4760

IMPERFORATE

FLAT PRESS Double Line Wmk.

Blocks of 6

Imprint V

#320 2¢ WASHINGTON (SHIELD) (DIE I) 37 Plates

Basic Price T, L, R, B

Imprint Block of 6 . . . . $300

*3136 3160 3161 3162 3164
3222 3248 3249 3250 3251
*3295 *3298 *3301 3305 3399
3451 3452 3453 3454 *3706
*3709 4146 4152 4153 *4204
*4218 4219 4227 4243 4245
4250 4262 4268 4269 *4277
4315 4323

#320a 2¢ WASHINGTON (SHIELD) (DIE II) 6 Plates

Basic Price T, L, R, B

Imprint Block of 6 . . . .$1,000

*4617 4651 4671 4701 4704
4718

1904 COMMEMORATIVES

Double Line Wmk. Perf. 12
FLAT PRESS **Positions T, B**
Imprint V

#323 1¢ LOUISIANA PURCHASE

Basic Prices: **24 Plates**
Imprint Pair $70
Imprint Block of 4 . . . . $200

	T	B		T	B		T	B
2113	☐	☐	2114	☐	☐	2115	☐	☐
2116	☐	☐	2117	☐	☐	2118	☐	☐
2119	☐	☐	2120	☐	☐	2129	☐	☐
2130	☐	☐	2131	☐	☐	2132	☐	☐
2137	☐	☐	2138	☐	☐	2139	☐	☐
2140	☐	☐	*2149	☐	☐	2150	☐	☐
2151	☐	☐	2152	☐	☐	2161	☐	☐
2162	☐	☐	2163	☐	☐	2164	☐	☐

#324 2¢ LOUISIANA PURCHASE

Basic Prices: **40 Plates**
Imprint Pair $65
Imprint Block of 4 . . . . $200

2069	☐	☐	2070	☐	☐	2071	☐	☐
2072	☐	☐	2081	☐	☐	2082	☐	☐
2083	☐	☐	2084	☐	☐	2093	☐	☐
2094	☐	☐	2095	☐	☐	2096	☐	☐
2125	☐	☐	2126	☐	☐	2127	☐	☐
2128	☐	☐	2145	☐	☐	2146	☐	☐
2147	☐	☐	2148	☐	☐	2153	☐	☐
2154	☐	☐	2155	☐	☐	2156	☐	☐
2157	☐	☐	2158	☐	☐	2159	☐	☐
2160	☐	☐	*2165	☐	☐	2166	☐	☐
2167	☐	☐	2168	☐	☐	*2177	☐	☐
2178	☐	☐	2179	☐	☐	2180	☐	☐
*2182	☐	☐	2183	☐	☐	2184	☐	☐
*2185	☐	☐						

#325 3¢ LOUISIANA PURCHASE

Basic Prices **4 Plates**
Imprint Pair $225
Imprint Block of 4 . . . . $650

2101	☐	☐	2102	☐	☐	2103	☐	☐
2104	☐	☐						

#326 5¢ LOUISIANA PURCHASE

Basic Prices: **4 Plates**
Imprint Pair $275
Imprint Block of 4 . . . . $800

	T	B		T	B		T	B
2097	☐	☐	2098	☐	☐	2099	☐	☐
2100	☐	☐						

#327 10¢ LOUISIANA PURCHASE

Basic Prices: **4 Plates**
Imprint Pair $550
Imprint Block of 4 . . . . $2,000

2105	☐	☐	2106	☐	☐	2107	☐	☐
2108	☐	☐						

1907 COMMEMORATIVES

Double Line Wmk. Perf. 12
FLAT PRESS **Positions T, B**
Imprint V

#328 1¢ JAMESTOWN 9 Plates

Basic Prices:
Imprint Strip of 3 . . . . $80
Imprint Block of 6 . . . . $300

	T	B		T	B		T	B
3538	☐	☐	3540	☐	☐	3541	☐	☐
3542	☐	☐	3543	☐	☐	3544	☐	☐
3545	☐	☐	3546	☐	☐	*3799	☐	☐

#329 2¢ JAMESTOWN 32 Plates

Basic Prices:
Imprint Strip of 3 . . . . $100
Imprint Block of 6 . . . . $375

3504	☐	☐	3505	☐	☐	3512	☐	☐
3513	☐	☐	3517	☐	☐	3520	☐	☐
3522	☐	☐	3524	☐	☐	3577	☐	☐
3578	☐	☐	3579	☐	☐	3580	☐	☐
3592	☐	☐	3593	☐	☐	*3594	☐	☐
*3595	☐	☐	3601	☐	☐	3602	☐	☐
3603	☐	☐	3604	☐	☐	3610	☐	☐
3613	☐	☐	3618	☐	☐	3619	☐	☐
*3655	☐	☐	*3656	☐	☐	3657	☐	☐
*3658	☐	☐	3671	☐	☐	*3672	☐	☐
3677	☐	☐	3678	☐	☐			

#330 5¢ JAMESTOWN 4 Plates

Basic Prices:
Imprint Strip of 3 . . . . $500
Imprint Block of 6 . . . . $3,000

3554	☐	☐	3556	☐	☐	3560	☐	☐
3561	☐	☐						

1908-09 REGULAR ISSUE

Double Line Wmk. Perf. 12
FLAT PRESS

#331 1¢ FRANKLIN 158 Plates

Imprint V

Basic Price	T	$100
Basic Price	L, R, B	$95

4874	4875	4880	*4881	4882
4885	*4886	*4888	4889	4890
4891	4892	4894	*4895	*4897
*4898	4899	*4900	4901	*4902
4903	*4904	*4906	*4907	4908
4909	4910	4911	*4912	4913
*4914	4915	*4960	*4962	*4966
*4967	4971	4972	4974	4975

Imprint XI

Basic Price	T	$850
Basic Price	L, R, B	$800

*4980

Imprint X

Basic Price	T	$90
Basic Price	L, R, B	$85

4985	*4986	4989	4991	4993
4994	4995	4997	4998	4999
5000	5001	5002	5003	5004
*5005	*5006	*5007	*5008	*5009
5010	5011	5012	5013	*5014
*5023	*5024	*5076	*5077	5078
5079	*5080	5081	*5082	5083
5084	*5085	*5086	*5087	5089
5091	5093	5097	5098	5100
5101	5103	5111	5118	5124
5137	5152	5153	5159	5162
5166	5169	5179	5180	5186
5187	5192	5193	5198	5206
5216	5223	5227	5232	5234
5242	5255	5259	5279	5287
5294	5301	5313	5320	5322
5330	5333	5336	5340	5345
5352	5359	5360	5373	5378
5380	5382	5383	5385	5386
5387	5401	5402	5403	5404
5413	5414	5416	5418	5420
5429	5432	5435	5438	5441
5444	5474	5476	5488	5489
5490	5491			

#332 2¢ WASHINGTON 266 Plates

Imprint V

Basic Price	T	$80
Basic Price	L, R, B	$75

4807	4809	4810	4811	4812
4813	*4814	4815	4816	4817
4818	4819	4820	4821	4822
*4823	4824	4825	*4827	4828
4829	4830	4831	4833	4834
4835	4837	*4838	4839	4840
4841	*4842	4843	*4844	4845
4846	*4847	4848	4849	4850
4851	4852	4853	4854	*4855
4856	4857	4858	4859	*4860
4861	4862	4863	4864	4865
4866	4868	4871	4872	4873

#332 2¢ WASHINGTON Continued

4876	4878	4879	4883	4884
4887	4893	4896	4905	

Imprint XI

Basic Price	T	$850
Basic Price	L, R, B	$800

*4988

Imprint X

Basic Price	T	$85
Basic Price	L, R, B	$80

*4968	4969	*4987	*4990	*4992
4996	5015	5016	5017	5018
5019	5020	5021	5022	5025
5026	*5027	*5028	5031	5032
5033	5036	*5039	5044	5045
5046	5049	5050	5051	5052
5053	5054	5055	*5056	5057
*5058	*5059	5060	5061	5062
5063	5064	5065	*5066	5067
5068	5069	*5070	5071	5072
*5073	*5074	5075	5092	5094
5102	5105	5107	5109	5110
5114	5115	5116	5117	5119
5120	5122	5123	5125	5127
5128	5129	5133	5134	5135
5140	5141	5147	5148	5149
5150	5151	5155	5156	5157
5160	5161	5163	5164	5165
5167	5168	5174	5175	5176
5177	5178	5181	5182	5183
5184	5185	5188	5189	5190
5191	5194	5195	5196	5197
5256	5258	5260	5265	5269
5270	5271	5272	5273	5274
5275	5276	5277	5278	5280
5281	5282	5283	5284	5285
5286	5288	5289	5290	5291
5292	5293	5295	5296	5297
5298	5299	5300	5302	5303
5304	5305	5306	5307	5308
5309	5310	5311	5312	5314
5315	5316	5317	5318	5319
5321	5323	5324	5325	5326
5327	5328	5329	5331	5332
5334	5335	5337	5338	5339
5342	5343	5346	5347	5348
5349	5351	5361	5362	5363
5364	5365	5366	5367	5368
5369	5371	5374	5375	5377
5381				

1908-09 REGULAR ISSUE

#333 3¢ WASHINGTON TYPE I

Imprint V — 8 Plates

Basic Price	T	$325
Basic Price	L, R, B	$300

4918 4925 4926 4927

Imprint X

Basic Price	T	$350
Basic Price	L, R, B	$325

5121 5126 5131 5136

#334 4¢ WASHINGTON 20 Plates

Imprint V

Basic Price	T	$400
Basic Price	L, R, B	$375

4932 4933 4934 4935

Imprint X

Basic Price	T	$400
Basic Price	L, R, B	$375

5132 5138 5146 *5158 5199
5212 5217 5226 5405 5406
5407 *5408 5415 5417 5422
*5426

#335 5¢ WASHINGTON 12 Plates

Imprint V

Basic Price	T	$550
Basic Price	L, R, B	$525

4928 4929 4930 4931 4958
4959 4961 4973

Imprint X

Basic Price	T	$575
Basic Price	L, R, B	$500

5341 5376 5379 5396

#336 6¢ WASHINGTON 4 Plates

Imprint V

Basic Price	T	$850
Basic Price	L, R, B	$800

4936 4937 4938 4939

#337 8¢ WASHINGTON 4 Plates

Imprint V

Basic Price	T	$550
Basic Price	L, R, B	$500

4919 4922 4923 4924

#338 10¢ WASHINGTON 4 Plates

Imprint V

Basic Price	T	$850
Basic Price	L, R, B	$800

4940 4941 4943 4944

#339 13¢ WASHINGTON 4 Plates

Imprint V

Basic Price	T	$500
Basic Price	L, R, B	$450

4942 4945 4946 4948

#340 15¢ WASHINGTON 4 Plates

Imprint V

Basic Price	T	$650
Basic Price	L, R, B	$600

4949 4951 4952 4954

#341 50¢ WASHINGTON 1 Plate

Imprint V

Price	T	$7,000
Price	B	$6,500

4956

#342 $1 WASHINGTON 1 Plate

Imprint V

Price	T	$10,000
Price	B	$9,500

4957

1908-09 REGULAR ISSUE

BOOKLET PANES

Double Line Wmk. Perf. 12

BOOKLET PANES OF 6

FLAT PRESS

#331a 1¢ FRANKLIN 16 Plates

Imprint IX

Basic Price T $190

180 Subject Plates

*4867 *4869 *4870 *4877 5029
5030 5034 5035 5037 5038
5040 5041

360 Subject Plates

5263 5264 5267 5268

#332a 2¢ WASHINGTON 44 Plates

Imprint IX

Basic Price T $160

180 Subject Plates

*4803 *4804 *4805 *4806 *4808
*4826 *4832 *4836 4947 4950
4953 4955 4963 4964 4965
4970 *5042 *5043 *5047 5048
*5088 *5090 5095 *5096 5099
5104 *5106 5108 5112 *5113
*5139 *5154

360 Subject Plates

5130 5261 5262 5266 5445
5446 5448 5450 5451 5456
5458 5459

IMPERFORATE

FLAT PRESS Double Line Wmk.

Blocks of 6

#343 1¢ FRANKLIN 87 Plates

Imprint V

Basic Price T $90
Price L, R, B $85

4874 4875 4880 *4881 4882
4889 4890 4892 4894 *4895
4899 *4900 *4902 4903 4908
*4962 4971 4972 4974 4975

Imprint XI

Price T $600
Price L, R, B $550

*4980

Imprint X

Basic Price T $95
Basic Price L, R, B $90

4985 4989 4991 4993 *4994
4997 *5001 5002 *5003 5004
*5005 *5006 *5009 5011 *5014
*5023 *5024 5084 *5085 5089
5091 5093 5097 5103 5152
5159 5162 5166 *5169 5179
5180 5186 5193 5198 5206

#343 1¢ FRANKLIN Continued

5227 5232 5234 5242 5259
5279 5287 5294 5301 5313
5320 5322 5330 5333 5336
5345 5352 5359 5360 5373
5378 5380 5387 5413 5414
5416 5435 5488 *5490 5491
5495

#344 2¢ WASHINGTON 116 Plates

Imprint V

Basic Price T $150
Basic Price L, R, B $140

4812 4813 *4814 4815 4816
4817 4818 4820 4821 4824
4829 4830 4831 4833 4848
4849 4856 4858 4859 4862
4864 4865 4866 4868 4872
4873 4876 4878 4879 4883
4884 4887 4893 4896 4905

Imprint X

Basic Price T $140
Basic Price L, R, B $130

*4987 *4992 4996 *5015 5017
5020 5021 5031 5032 5033
5036 *5059 5068 5075 5092
5114 5117 5119 5122 5123
5129 5133 5134 5135 5141
5150 5151 5155 5156 5157
5167 5168 5178 5181 5183
5188 5189 5256 5258 5260
5273 5280 *5283 5284 5285
5286 5292 5293 5295 5296
5297 5298 5299 5300 *5303
5305 5306 *5307 5308 5309
5310 5311 5312 5314 5321
5323 5326 5327 5344 5347
5349 5361 5363 5365 5366
5367 5368 5371 5375 5377
5381

#345 3¢ WASHINGTON TYPE I

Imprint V 4 Plates

Basic Price T $300
Basic Price L, R, B $275

4918 4925 4926 4927

1908-09 REGULAR ISSUE

IMPERFORATE

Double Line Wmk.

#346 4¢ WASHINGTON 14 Plates

Imprint V

Price	T	$450
Price	L, R, B	$400

4932 4933 4934 4935

Imprint X

Basic Price	T	$500
Basic Price	L, R, B	$450

5199 5212 5217 5226 5405
5406 5407 5408 5415 5417

#347 5¢ WASHINGTON 8 Plates

Imprint V

Basic Price	T	$750
Basic Price	L, R, B	$700

4928 4929 4930 4931 4958
4959 4961 4973

IMPERFORATE COIL STAMPS

Double Line Wmk. FLAT PRESS

Starting with the 1908 issue, we will list the plate numbers that have been authenticated for the imperforate coil stamps including those used by the vending and affixing machines. The latter will be identified by showing initials for company and type in parentheses under sub-heading of Private Perf.

#343E 1¢ FRANKLIN

Imprint X

5352 5387 5413 5414 5416

#343S 1¢ FRANKLIN

none reported

#344E 2¢ WASHINGTON

Imprint X

5120 5122 5260 5273 5274
5283 5293 5295 5296 5297
5298 5299 5302 5303 5305
5306

Imprint V
Private Perf.

4876 (S III) 4905 (USAV)

#344S 2¢ WASHINGTON

Imprint V

4873

Imprint X

*5258 5260 *5273 5296 5299

IMPERFORATE COIL STAMPS Continued

#345S 3¢ WASHINGTON

Imprint V

Private Perf.

4925 (USAV II) 4927 (USAV III)

#346E 4¢ WASHINGTON

Imprint X

*5122 5199 5217

Imprint V

Private Perf.

4932 (USAV I) 4934 (B11)

#347E 5¢ WASHINGTON

Imprint V

4958 4959 4961 4973

Private Perf

4931 (B II)

Other plate numbers may exist on these Imperforate Coils with fake perforations to represent the more expensive Perforated Coil Stamps.

COIL STAMPS

Perf. 12 Horizontally
FLAT PRESS Double Line Wmk.

#348 1¢ FRANKLIN

Imprint V

4903 4974

Imprint X

5186 5198 5255 5352 5387
5403 5404 5418 5420 5429
5432 5474 5487 5489 5496
5497 5498

#349 2¢ WASHINGTON

Imprint X

5115 5116 5119 5120 5122
5177 5260 5273 5295 5296
5298 5299 5302 5305 5306
5307 5315 5316 5319 5321

#350 4¢ WASHINGTON

Imprint X

5212 5415 5417 5422 5426

#351 5¢ WASHINGTON

Imprint V

4924 4928 4929 4930

1908-09 REGULAR ISSUE

COIL STAMPS

Perf. 12 Vertically
FLAT PRESS Double Line Wmk.

#352 1¢ FRANKLIN

Imprint V

4972 4975

Imprint X

5169 5179 5180 5255 5382

#353 2¢ WASHINGTON

Imprint V

4858

Imprint X

5160 5177 5180 5183 5184
5194 5256 5272 5273 5332
5334 5348 5367 5369

#354 4¢ WASHINGTON

Imprint V

4932 4935

#355 5¢ WASHINGTON

Imprint V

4929 4958 4959 4961 4973

#356 10¢ WASHINGTON

Imprint V

4944

CLAY PAPER

The following plate number singles all have Philatelic Foundation certificates as qenuine CLAY paper stamps. Report courtesy of R.H. White

Double Line Wmk. Perf. 12

#359 3¢ WASHINGTON TYPE I

4927

#361 5¢ WASHINGTON

4929 4931

#365 13¢ WASHINGTON

4942

#366 15¢ WASHINGTON

4949

BLUISH PAPER

Double Line Wmk. Perf. 12

#357 1¢ FRANKLIN (BLUISH)

	Imprint V	**7 plates**
Basic Price	T	$1,200
Basic Price	L, R, B	$1,100

4889 4890 4892 4894 4899

	Imprint X	
Basic Price	T	$3,500
Basic Price	L, R, B	$3,250

4994 4997

BLUISH PAPER

#358 2¢ WASHINGTON (BLUISH)

	Imprint V	**8 Plates**
Basic Price	T	$1,200
Basic Price	L, R, B	$1,100

4837 *4860 4861 4863

	Imprint X	
Basic Price	T	$1,700
Basic Price	L, R, B	$1,600

4996 5015 5016 *5017

#359 3¢ WASHINGTON TYPE I (BLUISH) **4 Plates**

	Imprint V	
Basic Price	T	$15,000
Basic Price	L, R, B	$14,000

4918 4925 4926 4927

#360 4¢ WASHINGTON (BLUISH)

	Imprint V	**1 Plate**
Basic Price	T	—
Basic Price	L, R, B	—

4934

#361 5¢ WASHINGTON (BLUISH)

	Imprint V	**1 Plate**
Basic Price	T	$30,000
Basic Price	L, R, B	—

4931

#362 6¢ WASHINGTON (BLUISH)

	Imprint V	**4 Plates**
Basic Price	T	$10,000
Basic Price	L, R, B	$9,500

4936 4937 4938 4939

#363 8¢ WASHINGTON (BLUISH)

	Imprint V	**1 Plate**
Basic Price	T	—
Basic Price	L, R, B	—

4922

#364 10¢ WASHINGTON (BLUISH)

	Imprint V	**3 Plates**
Basic Price	T	—
Basic Price	L, R, B	$11,000

4940 4943 4944

#365 13¢ WASHINGTON (BLUISH)

	Imprint V	**3 Plates**
Basic Price	T	$17,500
Basic Price	L, R, B	—

4942 4945 4948

#366 15¢ WASHINGTON (BLUISH)

	Imprint V	**4 Plates**
Basic Price	T	$10,000
Basic Price	L, R, B	$9,500

4949 4951 4952 4954

1909 COMMEMORATIVES

Double Line Wmk. Perf 12

FLAT PRESS **Imprint Block of 6**

#367 2¢ LINCOLN 8 Plates

Imprint XI

	T			L	R	B
4976	$175	☐	$165	☐	☐	☐
4977	$175	☐	$165	☐	☐	☐
4978	$175	☐	$165	☐	☐	☐
4979	$175	☐	$165	☐	☐	☐
4981	$175	☐	$165	☐	☐	☐
4982	$175	☐	$165	☐	☐	☐
4983	$175	☐	$165	☐	☐	☐
4984	$175	☐	$165	☐	☐	☐

#368 2¢ LINCOLN IMPERFORATE

Imprint XI **8 Plates**

4976	$300	☐	$275	☐	☐	☐
4977	$300	☐	$275	☐	☐	☐
4978	$300	☐	$275	☐	☐	☐
4979	$300	☐	$275	☐	☐	☐
4981	$300	☐	$275	☐	☐	☐
4982	$300	☐	$275	☐	☐	☐
4983	$300	☐	$275	☐	☐	☐
4984	$300	☐	$275	☐	☐	☐

#369 2¢ LINCOLN BLUISH PAPER

Imprint XI **4 Plates**

4976	$4,500	☐	$4,000	☐	☐	☐
4977	$4,500	☐	$4,000	☐	☐	☐
4978	$4,500	☐	$4,000	☐	☐	☐
4979	$4,500	☐	$4,000	☐	☐	☐

#370 2¢ ALASKA-YUKON 20 Plates

Imprint V

5142	$325	☐	$300	☐	☐	☐
5143	$325	☐	$300	☐	☐	☐
5144	$325	☐	$300	☐	☐	☐
5145	$325	☐	$300	☐	☐	☐
5170	$325	☐	$300	☐	☐	☐
5171	$325	☐	$300	☐	☐	☐
5172	$325	☐	$300	☐	☐	☐
5173	$325	☐	$300	☐	☐	☐
5208	$325	☐	$300	☐	☐	☐
5209	$325	☐	$300	☐	☐	☐
5210	$325	☐	$300	☐	☐	☐
5211	$325	☐	$300	☐	☐	☐
*5235	—	☐	—	☐	☐	☐
5236	$325	☐	$300	☐	☐	☐
5237	$325	☐	$300	☐	☐	☐
*5241	—	☐	—	☐	☐	☐

1909 COMMEMORATIVES

#370 2¢ ALASKA-YUKON Cont.

5249	$325	☐	$300	☐	☐	☐
5250	$325	☐	$300	☐	☐	☐
5251	$325	☐	$300	☐	☐	☐
5257	$325	☐	$300	☐	☐	☐

#371 2¢ ALASKA-YUKON IMERF.

Imprint V **9 Plates**

*5209	—	☐	—	☐	☐	☐
*5235	—	☐	—	☐	☐	☐
5236	$350	☐	$300	☐	☐	☐
5237	$350	☐	$300	☐	☐	☐
*5241	—	☐	—	☐	☐	☐
5249	$350	☐	$300	☐	☐	☐
5250	$350	☐	$300	☐	☐	☐
5251	$350	☐	$300	☐	☐	☐
5257	$350	☐	$300	☐	☐	☐

#372 2¢ HUDSON-FULTON

Imprint V **8 Plates**

5388	$350	☐	$325	☐	☐	☐
5389	$350	☐	$325	☐	☐	☐
5390	$350	☐	$325	☐	☐	☐
5391	$350	☐	$325	☐	☐	☐
5392	$350	☐	$325	☐	☐	☐
5393	$350	☐	$325	☐	☐	☐
5394	$350	☐	$325	☐	☐	☐
5395	$350	☐	$325	☐	☐	☐

#373 2¢ HUDSON-FULTON IMPERF

Imprint V **8 Plates**

5388	$400	☐	$350	☐	☐	☐
5389	$400	☐	$350	☐	☐	☐
5390	$400	☐	$350	☐	☐	☐
5391	$400	☐	$350	☐	☐	☐
5392	$400	☐	$350	☐	☐	☐
5393	$400	☐	$350	☐	☐	☐
5394	$400	☐	$350	☐	☐	☐
5395	$400	☐	$350	☐	☐	☐

1910-11 REGULAR ISSUE

Single Line Wmk. Perf. 12

#374 1¢ FRANKLIN 114 Plates

Imprint X

Basic Price T $85

Basic Price L, R, B $80

5159	5232	5255	5301	*5313
5322	5345	5352	5359	5360
5382	5383	*5384	5385	*5387
5401	5402	5403	5404	5413
5414	5416			

1910-11 REGULAR ISSUE

#374 1¢ FRANKLIN Continued

5418	5420	5429	5432	5435
5438	5441	5444	5473	5474
5475	5476	5477	5478	5479
5480	5481	5482	5483	5484
5485	5486	5487	5488	5489
5490	5491	5493	5494	5495
5496	5497	5498	5499	5591
5592	5595	5596	5598	5599
5600	5601	5602	5603	5604
5605	5607	5620	5622	5631
5632	5633	5634	5637	5639
5640	5643	5644	5647	5651
5672	5673	*5794	*5799	

Imprint XII

Basic Price T $100
Basic Price L, R, B $95

5566	5567	5572	5573	5656
5657	5658	5659	5663	5664
*5665	5666	5677	5678	5679
5682	5699	*5705	5706	5707
5708	5709	*5710	*5712	*5713
5714	5715	5716		

(see Appendix B)

#375 2¢ WASHINGTON 146 Plates

Imprint X

Basic Price T $80
Basic Price L, R, B $75

5092	5274	5276	5280	5281
5282	5283	5284	5293	5296
5297	5298	5299	5300	5303
5305	5306	5307	5308	5309
5310	5311	5312	5314	5317
5318	5319	5321	5323	5324
5325	*5326	5327	5328	5329
5331	5332	5334	5335	5337
5338	5339	5342	5343	*5344
5347	5348	5349	5351	
5353	5358	5362	*5366	5369
5370	5375	5508	5509	5512
5515	5516	5517	5518	5528
5542	5543	5544	5545	5546
5547	5548	5549	5550	5551
5552	5553	5554	5555	5556
5578	5581	5585	5589	5590
5606	5608	5609	5610	5611
5612	5616	5617	5618	5619
5621	5623	5624	5625	5626
5627				
5628	5629	5630	5635	5636
5642	5645	5648	5650	*5652
5654	5655	5671	*5795	*5796

Imprint XII

Basic Price T $90
Basic Price L, R, B $85

5557	5558	5559	5560	5561
5562	5563	5564	5565	5660
5661	*5662	5667	5668	5669
5670	5674	5683	5684	*5685
5686	5687	5688	5689	5690
5693	5694	5711	5717	*5797
*5798				

#376 3¢ WASHINGTON TYPE I 12 Plates

Imprint X

Basic Price T $200
Basic Price L, R, B $175

5121	5126	5131	5136	5421
5424	5428	5433		

Imprint IX

Basic Price T $200
Basic Price L, R, B $170

6044	6048	6050	6052

#377 4¢ WASHINGTON 12 Plates

Imprint X

Basic Price T $250
Basic Price L, R, B $225

5568	5569	5570	5571	5574
5575	5576	5577		

Imprint IX

Basic Price T $275
Basic Price L, R, B $250

6002	6004	6010	6025

#378 5¢ WASHINGTON 24 Plates

Imprint V

Basic Price T $300
Basic Price L, R, B $275

4958	4959	4961	4973

Imprint X

Basic Price T $300
Basic Price L, R, B $275

5341	5376	5379	5396	5638
5641	5649	*5653		

Imprint XIII

Basic Price T $300
Basic Price L, R, B $275

5894	5898	5902	5906

Imprint IX

Basic Price T $300
Basic Price L, R, B $275

6348	6349	6352	6353	6733
6734	6736	6739		

#379 6¢ WASHINGTON 12 Plates

Imprint V

Basic Price T $550
Basic Price L, R, B $500

4936	4937	4938	4939

Imprint X

Basic Price T $500
Basic Price L, R, B $450

5203	5215	5222	5231	5419
5423	5425	5430		

1910-11 REGULAR ISSUE

#380 8¢ WASHINGTON 8 Plates

Imprint V

Basic Price T $1,250
Basic Price L, R, B $1,150

1010 1022 1023 1021

Imprint X

Basic Price T $2,000
Basic Price L, R, B $1,800

*5204 5214 *5233 5238

#381 10¢ WASHINGTON 8 Plates

Imprint V

Basic Price T $1,300
Basic Price L, R, B $1,200

4940 4941 4943 4944

Imprint X

Basic Price T $1,200
Basic Price L, R, B $1,100

5200 5213 5220 5239

#382 15¢ WASHINGTON 4 Plates

Imprint V

Basic Price T $2,500
Basic Price L, R, B $2,250

4949 4951 4952 4954

BOOKLET PANES

Single Line Wmk. Perf. 12

BOOKLET PANES OF 6

FLAT PRESS ***Top plate number only***

#374a 1¢ FRANKLIN 12 Plates

Imprint IX

Basic Price T $175

5263 5264 5267 5268 5447
5449 5452 5454 †5455 †5457
*5460 *5463

#375a 2¢ WASHINGTON 19 Plates

Imprint IX

Basic Price T $150

5130 5261 5262 5266 5445
5446 5448 5450 5451 5456
5458 5459 5461 5462 5464
5466 5467 †5469 *5472

IMPERFORATE

FLAT PRESS Single Line Wmk.

Blocks of 6

#383 1¢ FRANKLIN 84 Plates

Imprint X

Basic Price T $65
Basic Price L, R, B $60

*5232 5322 5359 5360 5378
5380 5383 5384 5385 5401
5402 5403 5404 5418 5420
5429 5432 5438 5473 5475
5477 5478 5479 5480 5481
5482 5483 5484 5485 5486

IMPERFORATE

#383 1¢ FRANKLIN Continued

5488 5489 5490 5491 5494
5495 5496 5497 5498 5592
5596 5598 5599 5600 5601
5000 5004 5005 5007 5020
5622 5631 5632 5633 5634
5637 5639 5640 5643 5644
5647 5651 5672 5673 *5677
*5794 *5799

Imprint XII

Basic Price T $125
Basic Price L, R, B $115

5566 5567 *5572 5573 5656
5657 5658 5659 5664 5665
*5679 5709 5712 5713 5714
5715 5716

(see Appendix B)

#384 2¢ WASHINGTON 95 Plates

Imprint X

Basic Price T $200
Basic Price L, R, B $190

5092 5134 5151 5280 5282
5283 5284 5296 5297 5298
5299 5300 5303 5307 *5308
*5309 *5311 5312 5314 5318
*5321 *5323 5325 *5327 5328
5329 5332 5337 5342 5348
5353 5358 *5362 5370 5375
5509 5512 5516 5517 5518
5528 5542 5549 5551 *5552
5553 *5554 5585 5589 5590
5608 5609 5611 *5612 *5616
5618 5619 *5623 5624 5627
*5628 *5635 5636 5642 5645
5648 5654 5655

Imprint XII

Basic Price T $225
Basic Price L, R, B $215

5557 5558 5559 5560 5561
5562 5563 5564 5565 5660
5661 5662 5667 *5668 5669
5685 5686 5687 5688 *5689
5690 5693 5694 5711 5717
5797 *5798

IMPERFORATE COIL STAMPS

FLAT PRESS Single Line Wmk.

Starting with the 1908 issue, we will list the plate numbers that have been authenticated for the imperforate coil stamps including those used by the vending and affixing machines. The latter will be identified by showing initials for company and type in parentheses under sub-heading of Private Perf.

#383E 1¢ FRANKLIN

Imprint X

5322 5360 5378 5383 5401
5402 5403 5404 5418 5420
5432 5438 5473 5475 5480
5481 5599 5673

1910-13 REGULAR ISSUE

IMPERFORATE COIL STAMPS

FLAT PRESS Single Line Wmk.

#383E 1¢ FRANKLIN Continued

Imprint XII

5572 5573 5656 5657 5658
5659

#383S 1¢ FRANKLIN

Imprint XII

5573 5657 5658 5659 5661

Imprint X

Private Perf.
5634 (USAV II)

#384E 2¢ WASHINGTON

Imprint X

5283 5307 5308 5309 5311
5312 *5616 *5635

Imprint XII

5557 5558 5559 5560 5561
5562 5564 5660 5661 5662
5667 5668 5669 5689

#384S 2¢ WASHINGTON

Imprint XII

5557 5558 5561 5661

Private Perf.
5686 (S III b)

Other plate numbers may exist on these Imperforate Coils with fake perforations to represent the more expensive Perforated Coil Stamps.

COIL STAMPS

Perf. 12 Horizontally
FLAT PRESS Single Line Wmk.

#385 1¢ FRANKLIN

Imprint X

5159 5179 5255 5322 5352
5359 5387 5403 5414 5416
5418 5420 5429 5432 *5438
5441 5474 5475 *5476 5479
5489 5496 5497 5498

Imprint XII

All copies examined to date have been authentic #383E with added fake perforations.

#386 2¢ WASHINGTON

Imprint X

5116 5307 *5309 *5331 5558
5560 5667

Imprint XII

All copies examined to date have been authentic #384E with added fake perforations.

COIL STAMPS

Perf. 12 Vertically
FLAT PRESS Single Line Wmk.

#387 1¢ FRANKLIN

none reported

#388 2¢ WASHINGTON

Imprint X

5334 5351 5558

Imprint XII

All copies examined to date have been authentic #384S with added fake perfora tions.

#389 3¢ WASHINGTON

Imprint X

5126

COIL STAMPS

Perf. 8½ Horizontally
FLAT PRESS Single Line Wmk.

#390 1¢ FRANKLIN

Imprint X

All examples are probably fake perforated versions of #383E

Imprint XII

5566 5567 5572 5573 5656
5657 5658 5659 5666 5677
5678 5679 5699 5705 5709
5714 5715 5716

#391 2¢ WASHINGTON

Imprint X

All examples are probably fake perforated versions of #384E.

Imprint XII

5307 5309 5319 5557 5558
5559 5560 5561 5562 5563
5564 *5565 5661 *5667 *5668
5674 5686 5687 5688 5690

COIL STAMPS

Perf. 8½ Vertically
FLAT PRESS Single Line Wmk.

#392 1¢ FRANKLIN

Imprint X

All examples are probably fake perforated versions of #383S

Imprint XII

5566 5567 5572 5573 5656
5657 5658 5659 *5669 5682
5699 5705 5706 5709 *5715
5716

1910-13 REGULAR ISSUE

COIL STAMPS

Perf. 8½ Vertically
FLAT PRESS Single Line Wmk.

#393 2¢ WASHINGTON

Imprint X

All examples are probably fake perforated versions of #384S.

Imprint XII

5557 5558 5559 5560 5561
5562 5563 5667 5668 5670
5674 5688 5795 5798

#394 3¢ WASHINGTON

Imprint X

5121 5126 5131 5136 5421
5424 5428 5433

#395 4¢ WASHINGTON

Imprint X

5574 5575 5576 5577

Imprint IX

6002

#396 5¢ WASHINGTON

Imprint XIII

5894 5898 5902 5906

1912-15 COMMEMORATIVES

Single Line Wmk. Perf. 12
FLAT PRESS **Block of 6**

Imprint IX

#397 1¢ PANAMA-PACIFIC 12 Plates

		T		L	R	B
6127	$200	☐	$175	☐	☐	☐
6128	$200	☐	$175	☐	☐	☐
6131	$200	☐	$175	☐	☐	☐
6132	$200	☐	$175	☐	☐	☐
6144	$200	☐	$175	☐	☐	☐
6146	$200	☐	$175	☐	☐	☐
6147	$200	☐	$175	☐	☐	☐
6148	$200	☐	$175	☐	☐	☐
6548	$200	☐	$175	☐	☐	☐
6549	$200	☐	$175	☐	☐	☐
6550	$200	☐	$175	☐	☐	☐
6551	$200	☐	$175	☐	☐	☐

1912-15 COMMEMORATIVES

#398 2¢ PANAMA-PACIFIC

23 Plates		T		L	R	B
6306	$325	☐	$300	☐	☐	☐
6307	$325	☐	$300	☐	☐	☐
6308	$325	☐	$300	☐	☐	☐
6309	$325	☐	$300	☐	☐	☐
6310	$325	☐	$300	☐	☐	☐
6311	$325	☐	$300	☐	☐	☐
6312	$325	☐	$300	☐	☐	☐
6313	$325	☐	$300	☐	☐	☐
6314	$325	☐	$300	☐	☐	☐
6315	$325	☐	$300	☐	☐	☐
6316	$325	☐	$300	☐	☐	☐
6317	$325	☐	$300	☐	☐	☐
6320	$325	☐	$300	☐	☐	☐
6321	$325	☐	$300	☐	☐	☐
6322	$325	☐	$300	☐	☐	☐
6323	$325	☐	$300	☐	☐	☐
6432	$325	☐	$300	☐	☐	☐
6442	$325	☐	$300	☐	☐	☐
6447	$325	☐	$300	☐	☐	☐
6647	$325	☐	$300	☐	☐	☐
6648	$325	☐	$300	☐	☐	☐
6649	$325	☐	$300	☐	☐	☐
6650	$325	☐	$300	☐	☐	☐

#399 5¢ PANAMA-PACIFIC 4 Plates

6129	$2,500	☐	$2,250	☐	☐	☐
6133	$2,500	☐	$2,250	☐	☐	☐
6134	$2,500	☐	$2,250	☐	☐	☐
6138	$2,500	☐	$2,250	☐	☐	☐

1912-15 COMMEMORATIVES

Single Line Wmk. Perf. 12

Imprint IX

#400 10¢ PANAMA-PACIFIC

4 Plates	T			L	R	B
6130	$3,500	☐	$3,250	☐	☐	☐
6135	$3,500	☐	$3,250	☐	☐	☐
6139	$3,500	☐	$3,250	☐	☐	☐
6143	$3,500	☐	$3,250	☐	☐	☐

#400A 10¢ PANAMA-PACIFIC

4 Plates						
6130	$10,000	☐	$9,000	☐	☐	☐
6135	$10,000	☐	$9,000	☐	☐	☐
6139	$10,000	☐	$9,000	☐	☐	☐
6143	$10,000	☐	$9,000	☐	☐	☐

Single Line Wmk. Perf. 10

FLAT PRESS **Block of 6**

Imprint IX

#401 1¢ PANAMA-PACIFIC 8 Plates

6548	$375	☐	$350	☐	☐	☐
6549	$375	☐	$350	☐	☐	☐
6550	$375	☐	$350	☐	☐	☐
6551	$375	☐	$350	☐	☐	☐
6875	$375	☐	$350	☐	☐	☐
6880	$375	☐	$350	☐	☐	☐
6891	$375	☐	$350	☐	☐	☐
6944	$375	☐	$350	☐	☐	☐

#402 2¢ PANAMA-PACIFIC

11 Plates						
*6322	—	☐	—	☐	☐	☐
*6432	—	☐	—	☐	☐	☐
6447	$2,000	☐	$1,750	☐	☐	☐
6647	$2,000	☐	$1,750	☐	☐	☐
6648	$2,000	☐	$1,750	☐	☐	☐
6649	$2,000	☐	$1,750	☐	☐	☐
6650	$2,000	☐	$1,750	☐	☐	☐
7034	$2,000	☐	$1,750	☐	☐	☐
7035	$2,000	☐	$1,750	☐	☐	☐
7038	$2,000	☐	$1,750	☐	☐	☐
7039	$2,000	☐	$1,750	☐	☐	☐

1912-15 COMMEMORATIVES

#403 5¢ PANAMA-PACIFIC

4 Plates	T			L	R	B
6129	$5,000	☐	$4,750	☐	☐	☐
6133	$5,000	☐	$4,750	☐	☐	☐
6134	$5,000	☐	$4,750	☐	☐	☐
6138	$5,000	☐	$4,750	☐	☐	☐

#404 10¢ PANAMA-PACIFIC

4 Plates						
6130	$18,000	☐	$17,000	☐	☐	☐
6135	$18,000	☐	$17,000	☐	☐	☐
6139	$18,000	☐	$17,000	☐	☐	☐
6143	$18,000	☐	$17,000	☐	☐	☐

1912-14 REGULAR ISSUE

Single Line Wmk. Perf 12

FLAT PRESS **Block of 6**

#405 1¢ WASHINGTON 289 Plates

Imprint XII

Basic Price T $120

Basic Price L, R, B $115

5727	5728	5730	5731	5732
5733	5734	5735	5736	*5737
5738	*5739	5781	5787	5801

Imprint XIII

Basic Price T $130

Basic Price L, R, B $125

5806	5807	5822	5828	5831
5833	5834	5837	5840	5843
5849	5853	5855	5858	5859
5862	5864	5867	5870	5873
5874	5878	5880	5881	5882
5884	5885	5886	5887	5891
5892	5893	5895	5897	5900
5901	5903	5905	5910	*5913
5915	5916	5918		

Imprint IX

Basic Price T $100

Basic Price L, R, B $95

5921	5924	5930	6005	6006
6007	6008	6009	6011	6012

1912-14 REGULAR ISSUE

#405 1¢ WASHINGTON Continued

Imprint IX

6013 6014 6015 6016 6017
6018 6019 6020 6026 6027
6028 6029 6030 6031 6032
6033 6034 6035 6036 6037
6038 6039 6040 6041 6042
6045 6114 6115 6117 6118
6120 6121 6122 *6150 6154
6272 6273 6282 6283 6301
6305 6327 6328 6342 6344
6354 6373 6437 *6443 *6450
6455 *6465 *6468 *6472 6473
*6474 6475 6476 6477 6478
6479 *6480 6481 6482 6483
6484 6485 6486 6487 6488
6521 6528 6532 6533 6534
6535 6539 6540 6541 6542
6543 6544 6545 6546 6547
6574 6575 6576 6577 6578
6588 6600 6601 6606 6607
6608 6609 6610 6611 6612
6613 6614 6615 6616 6617
*6618 *6619 *6621 *6623 *6624
6628 6631 6632 *6634 6636
6676 *6678 *6680 6681 *6682
*6683 6688 *6691 6713 6718
6719 6720 6721 *6722 6723
6724 *6725 6726 6727 6775
6776 6777 6778 6781 6782
6783 6785 6787 6788 6789
6792 6793 6798 6804 6805
6808 6810 6811 6812 6814
6816 6820 6821 6823 6824
6826 6829 6831 6832 6834
6835 6836 6837 6841 6844
6845 6849 6851 6854 6858
6861 6937 6940 6941 6942
6945 6946 6947 6948 6949
6953 6954 6955 6958 6959
6961 6962 6967 6968 6970
6974 6975 6981 6982 6983
6987 6989 6990 6996 7001
7003 7008 7010 7012 7017
7023 7027 7030 7032 7103
7106 7142 7144 7149 7151
7153

#406 2¢ WASHINGTON 566 Plates

Imprint XII

Basic Price T $130
Basic Price L, R, B $120

5740 5743 5754 5759 5763
5769 5777 5779 5785 *5788
5789 5790 *5791 5792 5800
5802 5803

Imprint XIII

Basic Price T $120
Basic Price L, R, B $110

5805 5808 5809 5810 5811
5812 5813 5814 5815 5816

#406 2¢ WASHINGTON Continued

Imprint XIII

5817 5818 5819 5820 5821
5823 5824 5825 5826 5827
5830 5832 5835 5836 5838
5839 5841 5842 5845 5851
5856 5861 5865 5866 5868
5869 5872 5876 5877 5883
5888 5889 5890 5896 5899
5904 5907 5908 5909 5911
5912 5914 5917

Imprint IX

Basic Price T $110
Basic Price L, R, B $100

5919 5920 5922 5923 5925
5926 5927 5928 *5929 5931
5932 5933 5934 5935 5936
5940 5944 5945 5946 *5948
*5949 *5950 5951 5952 5953
5954 5955 5956 5959 5960
5961 5962 5963 5964 5965
5966 *5967 5968 5969 5970
5971 5972 5973 5974 5975
5976 5977 5978 5979 5980
5981 5982 5983 5984 5985
5986 5987 5988 5989 5991
5992 5993 5994 5995 5996
5997 5998 5999 6000 6001
6003 6024 6051 6054 6055
6058 6059 6062 6063 6064
6065 6066 6067 6068 6069
6070 6071 6072 6073 6074
6075 6077 6078 6080 6081
6082 6083 6084 6085 6087
6088 6089 6090 6091 6092
6093 6094 6095 6096 6097
6098 6099 6100 6101 6102
6103 6104 6105 6106 6107
6108 6109 6110 6111 6151
6153 6155 6157 6158 6159
6190 6223 6267 6268 6269
6270 6271 6278 6281 6284
6285 6286 6289 6290 6291
6292 6293 6294 *6295 6297
6298 6300 6302 6303 6304
6318 6319 6324 6325 6326
6329 6343 6358 6362 6368
6372 6387 *6398 6403 6406
6413 6414 6415 6419 6422
6429 6430 6436 6438 6440
6444 6445 6446 6451 6452
6453 6454 6456 6457 6459
6460 6461 6462 6464 6466
6467 6469 6471 6489 6490
6491 6492 6493 6494 6495
6496 6497 6498 6499 6500
6501 6502 6503 6504 6505
6506 6507 6508 6509 6510
6511 6512 6513 6514 6515
6516 6517 6518 6519 6520
6522 6523 6524 6525 6526

1912-14 REGULAR ISSUE

#406 2¢ WASHINGTON Continued

Imprint IX

6527	6529	6530	6531	6536
6537	6538	6620	6622	6625
6626	6627	6629	6630	6633
6635	6637	6638	6639	6640
6641	6642	6643	6644	6645
6646	6651	6652	6653	6654
6655	6656	6657	6658	6659
6660	6661	6662	6663	6664
6665	6666	6667	6668	6669
*6670	6671	6672	6673	*6674
6675	6677	*6679	6684	6685
6686	6687	6689	6690	*6692
6693	6694	6698	6699	*6700
6715	*6716	6717	6731	6737
6738	6740	6741	6743	6744
*6746	*6747	6748	6750	6753
6754	6756	6757	6758	6759
6760	6761	6762	*6764	6765
6766	*6767	6768	*6769	6770
6771	6772	6773	6774	6779
6780	6784	6786	6790	6791
*6794	6795	*6796	6797	6799
6800	6802	6806	6807	6815
6817	6818	6827	6828	6830
6838	6839	6840	6842	6843
6846	6847	6848	6850	6852
6853	6855	6859	6860	6862
6866	6867	6870	6871	6873
6874	6876	6877	*6881	6883
6886	6887	6888	6889	6890
6893	6894	6895	6896	6897
6898	6912	6939	6943	6950
6951	*6952	6956	6960	6963
6969	6971	6972	6976	6977
6978	6979	6980	6984	6985
6986	6988	6991	6992	6993
6994	6995	6997	6998	6999
7000	7002	7004	7005	7006
7007	7009	7011	7013	7014
7015	7019	7020	7024	7025
7026	7028	7029	7031	7041
7043	7044	7045	7046	7047
7048	7050	7051	7052	7053
7054	7055	7056	7058	7059
7060	7061	7062	7063	7064
7065	7066	7067	7068	7069
7070	7071	7072	7074	7075
7076	7077	7078	7079	7080
7081	7082	7083	7084	7085
7086	7087	7088	*7094	7099
7100	7115	7117	7120	7125
7128	*7150	7158	*7177	7178

Electrolytic Plate

Price	T	$275
Price	R, L, B	$250

6023

#407 7¢ WASHINGTON 4 Plates

Imprint IX

Basic Price	T	$1,350
Basic Price	L, R, B	$1,250

6903	6904	6916	6919

BOOKLET PANES

Single Line Wmk. Perf. 12

BOOKLET PANES OF 6

FLAT PRESS ***Top plate number only***

#405b 1¢ WASHINGTON 16 Plates

Imprint IX

Basic Price	T	$90

5741	5744	5748	5750	5753
5757	5762	5768	5776	6076
6079	6086	6355	6363	6364
6369				

#406a 2¢ WASHINGTON 33 Plates

Imprint IX

Basic Price	T	$90

5756	5761	*5767	5772	*5778
*5783	5786	5793	5844	5937
5938	5939	5941	5942	5943
5947	6047	6053	*6057	*6061
*6112	*6113	*6116	*6119	6554
6559	6560	6561	*6562	*6563
*6564	*6565	*6696		

IMPERFORATE

FLAT PRESS Single Line Wmk.

Blocks of 6

#408 1¢ WASHINGTON 207 Plates

Imprint XII

Basic Price	T	$60
Basic Price	L, R	$55
Basic Price	R	$750

5727	5728	5730	5732	5733
5735	5737	5739	5781	5787

Imprint XIII

Basic Price	T	$35.00
Basic Price	L, R, B	$32.50

5806	5807	5828	5831	5833
5834	5837	5840	5843	5849
5858	5859	5862	5864	5867

1912-14 REGULAR ISSUE

#408 1¢ WASHINGTON Continued

Imprint XIII Continued

5873 5874 5878 5880 5881
5882 *5885 5886 5887 5891
5892 5895 5897 5900 5901
5903 5905 5915 5918

Imprint IX

Basic Price	T	$25.00
Basic Price	L, R, B	$22.50

6006 6007 6008 6009 6011
6012 6013 6014 *6016 6018
6020 6038 6041 6114 6150
6154 6282 6283 6301 *6327
*6472 6474 6475 6476 6477
6478 6485 6486 6487 6488
6528 6532 6533 6534 6542
6543 6544 6545 6546 6547
6606 6607 6608 6609 6610
6611 6612 6613 6614 6615

6616 6617 6619 6628 *6631
6632 6681 6713 6720 6721
6722 6723 6724 6725 6775
6776 6777 6778 6782 *6787
6789 6793 6798 6804 *6805
6811 6812 6814 *6816 6820
6821 *6823 6829 6831 *6832
6841 *6845 *6851 *6854 6861
6940 6941 6942 6945 6955
6958 6970 6974 6975 6982

*6983 6987 7017 7023 7027
7030 7032 7106 7107 7108
7110 7113 7114 7116 7118
7119 7148 7149 7153 7281
7283 7284 7285 7288 7289
7290 7291 7292 7293 7294
7299 7300 7301 7302 7312
7320 7326 7329 7363 7364
7375 *7382 7464 7485 *7493
7500 7514 7515 7516 7517

7518 7519 7520 7525 7533
7534 *7535 7546 *7547 *7549
7671 7674

#409 2¢ WASHINGTON 348 Plates

Imprint XII

Basic Price	T	$70
Basic Price	L, R, B	$65

5754 5785 5789 5792 5802

Imprint XIII

Basic Price	T	$70
Basic Price	L, R, B	$65

5811 5814 5815 5818 5819
*5824 5827 5830 5832 5835
5836 5838 5839 5841 5842
5845 5851 5856 5861 5866
5868 5869 5872 5876 5877
5888 5889 5890 5896 5899
5904 5907 5908 5911 *5912
5917 *5963

#409 2¢ WASHINGTON Continued

Imprint IX

Basic Price	T	$50
Basic Price	L, R, B	$45

5919 5920 5923 *5925 *5928
5929 5932 5940 5960 5962
*5963 5964 5965 5966 5969
*5972 5975 5976 5978 *5979
5980 5981 5982 5983 5985
5986 5987 5988 5991 5992
5993 5994 5995 5996 5998
*6000 6001 6003 *6024 6051
6054 6055 6058 6059 6063
6064 6065 6067 6070 6071

6072 6073 6077 6082 6089
*6090 6091 6093 6094 6095
6096 6097 6098 6099 6111
6151 6157 6159 6190 *6269
6286 *6289 6294 *6297 6300
6302 6303 6319 6329 6343
6358 *6362 6436 6445 6446
6451 6452 6453 6454 6456
6461 6464 *6466 *6467 *6469
6489 6490 6491 6492 6493

6494 6495 6496 6497 6498
6499 6501 *6502 6503 *6505
*6506 6507 6508 6509 6510
6511 *6513 6522 *6524 6536
6537 6620 *6622 6629 6630
6633 6639 6641 6643 6645
6646 6651 6654 6670 6671
6672 6673 6757 6758 6761
6765 6770 6771 6772 6773
6774 6780 6784 6794 6796

6799 6815 6817 6818 6827
6839 6842 6867 6873 6877
6886 6943 6950 6951 6952
6956 6963 6969 6971 6978
6979 6980 *6984 6988 6991
6992 *7005 *7006 7043 7044
*7045 7046 7048 7052 7054
7058 7059 7060 7067 *7068
7075 7076 7077 7078 7080
*7081 7082 7088 *7091 7115

7117 7120 7124 *7158 7178
7184 7185 7186 7187 7197
*7206 *7222 7223 7224 7225
7226 7227 *7245 7259 7261
7265 7311 7313 7314 7315
*7318 *7319 7322 7328 7336
7337 7340 7342 7347 7349
7350 7352 7356 7368 7373
7376 7377 7386 7388 7389
7390 7391 7392 7393 7394

7395 7396 *7399 7400 7401
7402 *7403 7404 7416 7420
7421 7424 7451 7454 7455
7459 7472 *7473 *7476 *7477
7478 7481 7486 7487 *7494
7495 7501 7568 7569 7571

1912-14 REGULAR ISSUE

#409 2¢ WASHINGTON Continued

Imprint IX

7572 7573 7574 7575 7576
7578 7579 7580 7582 7583
7589 7590 7591 7593 7594
7609 7610 7611 7612 *7639
7701 *7703 *7708 *7714 7724
7732 7735 *7737

IMPERFORATE COIL STAMPS

FLAT PRESS Single Line Wmk.

Starting with the 1908 issue, we will list the plate numbers that have been authenticated for the imperforate coil stamps including those used by the vending and affixing machines. The latter will be identified by showing initials for company and type in parentheses under sub-heading of Private Perf.

#408E 1¢ WASHINGTON

Imprint XII

5787 5801

Imprint XIII

5837 5843 5862 5881 5882

Imprint IX

6475 6477 6478 6479 6485
6486 6487 6528 6535

Private Perf.

Imprint XIII — 5867 (SIII)

Imprint IX — 6547 (M IV)

#408S 1¢ WASHINGTON

Imprint XIII

5837 5840 6465 5843

Imprint IX

6154 6282 6283 6465 6528
6546

Private Perf.

Imprint XIII — 5878 (USAV II)

Imprint IX — 6283 (S III)

#409E 2¢ WASHINGTON

Imprint XIII

5836 5839 5841 5845 5856
5866

Imprint IX

5920 6024 6055 6063 6286
6300 6444 6445 6446 6451
6452 6453 6460 6461 6462
6466 6467 6469 6489 *6492
6494 6496 6497 6498 6501

Private Perf.

Imprint XII — 5802 (S III)

Imprint IX — 5995 (B I), 5998 (USAV I)

#409S 2¢ WASHINGTON

Imprint IX

5919 5920 5923 6505 6515

Imprint XIII

5819 (USAV II) 5830 (USAV II)
5830 (USAV III) *5872 (MOM IV)

Other plate numbers may exist on these Imperforate Coils with fake perforations to represent the more expensive Perforated Coil Stamps.

COIL STAMPS

Perf. 8½ Horizontally
FLAT PRESS Single Line Wmk.

#410 1¢ WASHINGTON

Imprint XII

5727

Imprint XIII

5853 5880 5887 5891 5892
5893 5897 5904 5905

Imprint IX

6005 6006 6008 6014 6117
6305 6327 6328 6437 6344
6455 6472 6473 6474 6475
6476 6477 6478 6479 6480
6485 6486 6487 6488 6535
6539 6540 6541 6581 *6582
6974

#411 2¢ WASHINGTON

Imprint XII

5740 5754

Imprint XIII

5820 5821 5907 *5914

Imprint IX

5925 5927 5933 5955 5972
5978 5981 6051 6054 6055
6058 6059 6063 6070 6071
6075 6083 6302 6326 6329
6403 6436 6501

COIL STAMPS

Perf. 8½ Vertically
FLAT PRESS Single Line Wmk.

#412 1¢ WASHINGTON

Imprint XIII

5807 5828 5831 5840 5859
5862 5864 5867 5870

COIL STAMPS

#412 1¢ WASHINGTON Cont.

Imprint IX

6014	6015	6034	6035	6037
*6040	6114	6117	*6154	6282
6301	6327	6437	6477	6480
6521	6535	6545	*6546	6547
*6613	6615	6616	6617	*6719
*6775	6811	6812	6814	6820
6831	6832	6837	6841	6844
*6851	6858	6937		

#413 2¢ WASHINGTON

Imprint XII

All examples are probably fake perforated versions of #409S

Imprint XIII

5827	5830	5838	5839	5872
5907				

Imprint IX

5920	5955	5960	5988	5989
5991	5995	5996	6065	6069
6070	6072	6075	6090	6094
6158	6267	6270	6278	6294
6326	6372	6444	6454	6457
6493	6498	6513	6530	6531
6522	6536	6629	6630	6637
6640	6642	6646	6664	6666
6677	6753	6786	6799	6800
6802	6806	6807	6840	6871
6874	6883	6943	6951	6960
6971	6972	6976	6995	7487

1912-14 REGULAR ISSUE

Single Line Wmk. Perf. 12
FLAT PRESS **Block of 6**

#414 8¢ FRANKLIN 4 Plates

Imprint XII

Basic Price	T	$500
Basic Price	L, R, B	$450

5718 5719 5721 5722

#415 9¢ FRANKLIN 4 Plates

Imprint IX

Basic Price	T	$800
Basic Price	L, R, B	750

6901 6905 6907 6915

#416 10¢ FRANKLIN 8 Plates

Imprint XII

Basic Price	T	$600
Basic Price	L, R, B	$550

5745 5751 5764 5770 5773
5784

1912-14 REGULAR ISSUE

#416 10¢ FRANKLIN Continued

Imprint XIII

Basic Price	T	$650
Basic Price	L, R, B	$600

5847 5852

#417 12¢ FRANKLIN 4 Plates

Imprint IX

Basic Price	T	$550
Basic Price	L, R, B	$500

6900 6902 6910 6913

#418 15¢ FRANKLIN 12 Plates

Imprint XII

Basic Price	T	$850
Basic Price	L, R, B	$800

5747 5755 5760 5766 5771
5775 5780

Imprint XIII

Basic Price	T	$900
Basic Price	L, R, B	$850

5850

Imprint IX

Basic Price	T	$850
Basic Price	L, R, B	$800

6809 6819 6825 6833

#419 20¢ FRANKLIN 4 Plates

Imprint IX

Basic Price	T	$2,250
Basic Price	L, R, B	$2,150

6908 6909 6920 6926

#420 30¢ FRANKLIN 4 Plates

Imprint IX

Basic Price	T	$2,000
Basic Price	L, R, B	$1,900

6899 6911 6914 6917

#421 50¢ FRANKLIN 4 Plates

Imprint IX

Basic Price	T	$10,000
Basic Price	L, R, B	$9,500

7040 7042 7049 7057

1912 REGULAR ISSUE

Double Line Wmk. Perf. 12

#422 50¢ FRANKLIN 1 Plate

Imprint XII

Price	T	$6,000
Price	B	$5,500

5749

1912 REGULAR ISSUE

#423 $1 FRANKLIN 1 Plate

Imprint XII

Basic Price	T	$11,000
Basic Price	B	$10,000

5782

1914-15 REGULAR ISSUE

Single Line Wmk. Perf. 10
FLAT PRESS **Block of 6**

#424 1¢ WASHINGTON 181 Plates

Imprint IX

Basic Price	T	$50
Basic Price	L, R, B	$45

6845	6942	6946	6947	6948
6949	6953	6955	6958	6959
6961	6962	6967	6968	6970
6974	6975	6981	6982	6983
6987	6989	6990	6996	7001
7003	7008	7010	7012	7017
7023	7027	7030	7032	7103
7106	7107	7108	7110	7113
7114	7116	7118	7119	7142
7144	7145	7146	7148	7149
7151	7153	7156	7157	7159
7161	7164	7165	7167	7169
7173	7281	7282	7283	7284
7285	7288	7289	7290	7291
7292	7293	7294	7295	7296
7297	7298	7299	7300	7301
7302	7303	7304	7305	7306
7307	7308	7309	7310	7312
7320	7326	7329	7332	7338
7351	7359	7361	7363	7364
7365	7370	7371	7374	7375
7380	7381	7382	7384	7464
7485	7493	7500	7514	7515
7516	7517	7518	7519	7520
7525	7526	7527	7528	7529
7530	7531	7532	7533	7534
7535	7536	7537	7538	7539
7540	7541	7542	7543	7544
7545	7546	7547	7549	7570
7577	7585	7592	7596	7602
7644	7645	7646	7647	7649
7650	7651	7652	7654	7655

1914-15 REGULAR ISSUE

#424 1¢ WASHINGTON Continued

Imprint IX

7656	7657	7658	7659	7660
7663	7664	7665	7666	7667
7668	7669	7670	7671	7674
7725	7736			

#424b 1¢ WASHINGTON

7142

COIL PLATES Blocks of 10

Side plate numbers only

Basic Price	UR, LL	$175

6581 6582 6585 6589

These were flat plates prepared for endwise coils. When rotary press plates replaced them the excess stock was perforated and sold as sheet stamps.

The words 'COIL STAMPS' do not appear with the UL and LR plate numbers. These positions would be collected in blocks of six.

#425 2¢ WASHINGTON Block of 6

Imprint IX **338 Plates**

Basic Price	T	$37.50
Basic Price	L, R, B	$35.00

6806	6815	6852	6971	6972
6993	6994	6995	6997	6998
6999	7000	7002	7013	7014
7015	7019	7024	7026	7028
7029	7044	7045	7046	7047
7048	7050	7051	7052	7053
7055	7058	7059	7060	7061
7062	7063	7064	7065	7066
7067	7068	7069	7070	7071
7072	7074	7075	7076	7077
7078	7079	7080	7081	7082
7083	7084	7085	7086	7087
7088	7090	7091	7092	7094
7097	7099	7100	7101	7102
7104	7105	7109	7111	7112
7115	7117	7120	7124	7125
7128	7150	7152	7154	7155
7158	7162	7168	7177	7178
7184	7185	7186	7187	7188
7189	7190	7191	7192	7193

1914-15 REGULAR ISSUE

#425 2¢ WASHINGTON Continued

Imprint IX

7194	7195	7196	7197	7198
7199	7200	7201	7202	7203
7206	7207	7208	7209	7210
7211	7212	7214	7216	7217
7218	7219	7220	7221	7222
7223	7224	7225	7226	7227
7228	7229	7232	7233	7234
7244	7245	7246	7248	7251
7252	7255	7257	7259	7261
7264	7265	7311	7313	7314
7315	7316	7317	7318	7319
7321	7322	7323	7324	7327
7328	7330	7333	7334	7335
7336	7337	7339	7340	7341
7342	7343	7344	7345	7346
7347	7349	7350	7352	7353
7354	7355	7356	7357	7360
7366	7367	7368	7373	7376
7377	7378	7383	7386	7387
7388	7389	7390	7391	7392
7393	7394	7395	7396	7397
7398	7399	7400	7401	7402
7403	7404	7405	*7406	7407
7416	7420	7421	7424	7447
7448	7450	7451	7454	7455
7456	7459	7460	7461	7465
7466	7471	7472	7473	7475
7476	7477	7478	7479	7481
7486	7487	7488	7491	7492
7494	7495	7501	7568	7569
7571	7572	7573	7574	7575
7576	7578	7579	7580	7581
7582	7583	7584	7586	7587
7588	7589	7590	7591	7593
7594	7595	7597	7601	7603
7604	7605	7607	7608	7609
7610	7611	7612	7613	7614
7615	7618	7620	7638	7639
7640	7641	7681	7682	7683
7684	7685	7692	7693	7694
7695	7696	7697	7698	7699
7700	7701	7702	7703	7704
7705	7706	7707	7708	7709
7710	7711	7712	7713	7714
7715	7716	7717	7721	7722
7724	7728	7729	7730	7732
7735	7737	7760	7762	7774
7776	7777	7778		

COIL PLATES
Blocks of 10

Side plate numbers only

Basic Price UR, LL $175

6568	6570	6571	6572	†6573

These were flat plates prepared for endwise coils. When rotary press plates replaced them the excess stock was perforated and sold as sheet stamps.

The words 'COIL STAMPS' do not appear with the UL and LR plate numbers. These positions would be collected in blocks of six.

Single Line Wmk. Perf. 10

#426 3¢ WASHINGTON TYPE I
Blocks of 6 16 Plates

Imprint IX

Basic Price T $150
Basic Price L, R, B $140

6044	6048	6050	6052	6749
6751	6755	6763	6863	6868
6878	6882	7253	7254	7258
7267				

#427 4¢ WASHINGTON 12 Plates

Imprint IX

Basic Price T $425
Basic Price L, R, B $400

6002	6004	6010	6025	6728
6729	6730	6732	7263	7269
7273	7276			

#428 5¢ WASHINGTON 20 Plates

Imprint IX

Basic Price T $325
Basic Price L, R, B $300

6733	6734	6736	6739	7016
7018	7021	7022	7235	7236
7237	7238	7239	7240	7241
7242	7622	7623	7632	7633

#429 6¢ WASHINGTON 12 Plates

Imprint X

Basic Price T $325
Basic Price L, R, B $300

5203	5215	5222	5231	5419
5423	5425	5430		

Imprint IX

Basic Price T $325
Basic Price L, R, B $300

7136	7137	7138	7139

1914-15 REGULAR ISSUE

#430 7¢ WASHINGTON 12 Plates

Imprint IX

Basic Price	T	$1,100
Basic Price	L, R, B	$1,000

6903 6904 6916 6919 6923
6929 6932 6936 7718 7719
7720 7723

#431 8¢ FRANKLIN 8 Plates

Imprint XII

Basic Price	T	$400
Basic Price	L, R, B	$375

5718 5719 5721 5722 5724
5725 5804

Imprint XIII

Price	T	$450
Price	L, R, B	$425

5846

#432 9¢ FRANKLIN 4 Plates

Imprint IX

Basic Price	T	$650
Basic Price	L, R, B	$600

6901 6905 6907 6915

#433 10¢ FRANKLIN 12 Plates

Imprint XII

Basic Price	T	$600
Basic Price	L, R, B	$550

5770 5773

Imprint XIII

Basic Price	T	$600
Basic Price	L, R, B	$550

5847 5852

Imprint IX

Basic Price	T	$550
Basic Price	L, R, B	$500

6735 6742 6745 6752 7204
7205 7213 7215

#434 11¢ FRANKLIN 4 Plates

Imprint IX

Basic Price	T	$225
Basic Price	L, R, B	$200

7498 7499 7504 7505

#435 12¢ FRANKLIN 4 Plates

Imprint IX

Basic Price	T	$275
Basic Price	L, R, B	$250

6900 6902 6910 6913

#437 15¢ FRANKLIN 8 Plates

Imprint XII

Basic Price	T	$950
Basic Price	L, R, B	$900

*5771 *5775 *5780

Imprint XII

Price	T	$950
Price	L, R, B	$900

5850

Imprint IX

Basic Price	T	$900
Basic Price	L, R, B	$850

6809 6819 6825 6833

1914-15 REGULAR ISSUE

#438 20¢ FRANKLIN 4 Plates

Imprint IX

Basic Price	T	$3,000
Basic Price	L, R, B	$2,800

6908 6909 6920 6926

#439 30¢ FRANKLIN 4 Plates

Imprint IX

Basic Price	T	$4,500
Basic Price	L, R, B	$4,000

6899 6911 6914 6917

#440 50¢ FRANKLIN 4 Plates

Imprint IX

Basic Price	T	$10,000
Basic Price	L, R, B	$9,500

7040 7042 7049 7057

COIL STAMPS

Perf. 10 Horizontally
FLAT PRESS Single Line Wmk.

#441 1¢ WASHINGTON

No paste up numbers exist since sheets with side plate numbers only were used for this issue and thus the plate numbers were trimmed in the stripping process.

#442 2¢ WASHINGTON 13 Plates

Imprint XIII

5883

Imprint IX

5965	6055	6438	6446	6451
6452	6453	6457	6492	6496
6498	6501			

COIL STAMPS

Perf. 10 Vertically
FLAT PRESS Single Line Wmk.

#443 1¢ WASHINGTON 36 Plates

Imprint IX

6480	6821	6824	6826	6831
6834	6835	6845	6849	6854
6861	6937	6946	6947	6948
6949	6954	6958	6959	6961
6967	*6970	*6975	6989	6990
6996	7001	7003	7010	7023
*7026	7030	7032	7106	*7103
7291				

#444 2¢ WASHINGTON 64 Plates

Imprint XIII

5917

Imprint IX

5919	5920	5923	6513	6786
6800	6847	6852	6859	6889

COIL STAMPS

#444 2¢ WASHINGTON Continued

Imprint IX

*6876	6895	6896	6897	6898
6912	*6939	6956	6976	6984
6985	6986	*6994	6995	6998
7000	7019	7024	7026	7028
7029	7047	7048	7051	7053
7059	7060	*7061	7062	7063
7079	7080	7081	7082	7083
7084	7085	7086	7087	7090
7091	7092	7124	7125	7128
7150	7178	*7194	7200	7202
7207	7224			

#445 3¢ WASHINGTON 4 Plates

Imprint IX

6044 6048 6050 6052

#446 4¢ WASHINGTON 8 Plates

Imprint IX

6002	6004	6010	6025	6728
6729	*6730	6732		

#447 5¢ WASHINGTON 4 Plates

Imprint IX

6733 6734 6736 6739

ROTARY COILS

Endwise Coils

Single Line Wmk. Perf. 10
HORIZONTAL

#448 1¢ WASHINGTON

7433 7434

#449 2¢ WASHINGTON TY. I

6279 6280

#450 2¢ WASHINGTON TY. III

7561 7562

The listed plates were used to print the stamps. No examples have been reported to date. Please send clear xerox with your report to the editor.

Sidewise Coils Perf. 10

Single Line Wmk.

★7170	7171	7182	7183	7552
7553	★7558	★7559	7565	7566
7567	7619	7626	7627	7690
7691				

#453 2¢ WASHINGTON TY. I

6856	6857	7174	7175	7230
7231	7270	7271	7408	7409
7417	7418	7422	7423	

#454 2¢ WASHINGTON TY. II

7425 7426 7427 7428 7429
★7430 ★7437 ★7438 7443 7444
★7457 7458 7462 7463 7467
7468 7469 7470 7482 7483
7489 7490 ★7496 7497 7502
7503

#455 2¢ WASHINGTON TY. III

7510 7511 7512 7513 7421
7522 7523 7524 7617 7621
★7624 ★7625 7630 ★7631 7636
7637 7661 7662 7672 7673
7677 7678 7679 7680 7686
★7687 7688 7689 7782

#456 3¢ WASHINGTON TY. I

7441 7442

#457 4¢ WASHINGTON

7440 7452

#458 5¢ WASHINGTON

7435 7436

Sidewise Coils

Single Line Wmk. Imperforate

#459 2¢ WASHINGTON TY. I

6856 6857

The listed plates were used to print the stamps. ★ preceding number indicates a report. Please send clear xerox with your report to the editor of any examples you may have which are not listed.

BOOKLET PANES

Single Line Wmk. Perf. 10
BOOKLET PANES OF 6
FLAT PRESS

#424d 1¢ WASHINGTON 31 Plates

Top Plate Number only

Basic Price	T	$7.50

6355 6363 6364 6369 6695
6697 6707 6710 6864 6865
6869 6872 6879 6884 6885
6892 *7160 *7163 *7166 *7172
7176 7179 7180 7181 7268
7275 7277 7278 7474 7480
7484

#425e 2¢ WASHINGTON 48 Plates

Top Plate Number only

Basic Price	T	$20

*6562 *6563 *6564 *6565 6696
6701 6702 6708 6709 6711
6712 6714 6801 6803 6813
6822 6964 6965 6966 6973
7089 7093 7095 7096 7098
*7123 7127 7131 7133 7135
7140 7143 7147 7243 7247
7249 7250 7256 7260 7325
7548 7550 *7551 7554 7555
7556 7557 *7560

1915 ISSUE

Double Line Wmk. Perf. 10
FLAT PRESS **Block of 6**

#460 $1 FRANKLIN 1 Plate

Imprint XII

Price	T	$12,500
Price	B	$12,000

5782

Single Line Wmk. Perf. 11
FLAT PRESS **Block of 6**

#461 2¢ WASHINGTON 4 Plates

Imprint IX

Basic Price	T	$1,000
Basic Price	L, R, B	$ 950

7259 7261 7264 7265

1916-17 REGULAR ISSUE

Unwatermarked Perf. 10
FLAT PRESS **Block of 6**

#462 1¢ WASHINGTON 84 Plates

Imprint IX

Basic Price	T	$150
Basic Price	L, R, B	$140

6953 *7532 *7533 *7535 7647
7649 7650 7651 7652 7654
7655 7656 *7658 7659 *7660
*7663 7664 7665 7666 7667
7668 7669 7670 7671 7674
7725 7726 7727 7731 7733
7736 7741 7743 7749 7750
7753 7754 7755 7756 7757
7758 7759 7761 7764 7765
7831 7832 7838 7850 7862
7863 7864 7865 7874 7875
7876 7877 7878 7879 7883
7884 7886 7888 7889 7890
7891 7892 7893 7894 7895
7896 7897 7898 7899 7900
*7901 7902 7903 7904 7905
7906 7907 7908 7938

1916-17 REGULAR ISSUE

Unwatermarked. Perf. 10
FLAT PRESS **Block of 6**

#463 2¢ WASHINGTON 158 Plates

Imprint IX

Basic Price	T	$125
Basic Price	L, R, B	$115

7225	7322	*7398	*7401	7405
7406	7407	7410	7456	7475
7495	7501	7569	7581	*7583
7589	7590	7594	7638	7639
7640	7641	7682	7698	7699
*7701	*7703	7705	7706	7707
7708	7709	7710	7711	7712
*7713	*7714	*7715	7716	*7717
*7721	7722	7724	7728	7729
7730	7732	7735	7737	7760
7762	7768	7769	7770	7771
7772	7773	7774	7775	7776
7777	7778	7779	7780	7781
7783	7784	7792	7793	7794
7795	7796	7797	7798	7799
7800	7801	7802	7805	7806
7807	7808	7809	7810	7811
7812	7815	7816	7817	7818
7819	7820	7821	7823	7824
7825	7833	7839	7840	7842
7843	7844	7845	7846	7847
7848	7849	7851	7854	7855
7856	7857	7858	7859	7866
7867	7868	7869	7870	7871
7872	7873	7921	7922	7923
7930	7931	7932	7935	7936
7941	7942N	7944	7945	7946
7947	7948	7949	7951	7952
7955	7982	7983	7985	7986
7987	7988	7989	7995	7996
8000	8001	8002	8004	8005
8006	8009	8010		

N Plate 7942 is not scarce but it is the sheet on which the 5¢ errors are found and, for that reason, the plates bring a substantial premium. *The errors do not appear in any of the plate blocks.* See #467

#464 3¢ WASHINGTON TYPE I 8 Plates

Imprint IX

Basic Price	T	$1,300
Basic Price	L, R, B	$1,200

7253	7254	7258	7262	7266
7267	7272	7274		

#465 4¢ WASHINGTON 7 Plates

Imprint IX

Basic Price	T	$950
Basic Price	L, R, B	$900

7331	7348	7362	7372	7598
7599	7606			

1916-17 REGULAR ISSUE

#466 5¢ WASHINGTON 8 Plates

Imprint IX

Basic Price	T	$1,000
Basic Price	L, R, B	$950

7622	7623	7632	7633	7787
7788	7789	7790		

#467 5¢ ERROR PLATE

Price	T	$50
Price	L, R, B	$45

7942N

N The 2¢ stamp plate 7942 is not scarce but it is the sheet on which the 5¢ errors are found.

The errors are located at stamps #74 and #84 of the upper left pane and stamp #18 in the lower right pane of plate 7942. *The errors, therefore, do not appear in any of the plate blocks.*

#468 6¢ WASHINGTON 4 Plates

Imprint IX

Basic Price	T	$1,200
Basic Price	L, R, B	$1,100

7136 7137 7138 7139

#469 7¢ WASHINGTON 8 Plates

Imprint IX

Basic Price	T	$1,500
Basic Price	L, R, B	$1,400

7718	7719	7720	7723	7919
7920	7924	7925		

#470 8¢ FRANKLIN 4 Plates

Imprint XII

Basic Price	T	$625
Basic Price	L, R, B	$600

5724 5725 5804

Imprint XIII

Price	T	$650
Price	L, R, B	$625

5846

#471 9¢ FRANKLIN 4 Plates

Imprint IX

Basic Price	T	$700
Basic Price	L, R, B	$650

6901 6905 6907 6915

#472 10¢ FRANKLIN 7 Plates

Imprint IX

Basic Price	T	$1,600
Basic Price	L, R, B	$1,500

7204	7213	7215	7358	7369
7379	7385			

1916-17 REGULAR ISSUE

#473 11¢ FRANKLIN 4 Plates

Imprint IX

Basic Price T $350
Basic Price L, R, B $325

7498 7499 7504 7505

#474 12¢ FRANKLIN 4 Plates

Imprint IX

Basic Price T $600
Basic Price L, R, B $550

6900 6902 6910 6913

#475 15¢ FRANKLIN 6 Plates

Imprint XII

Price T —
Price L, R, B —

*5771 *5780

Imprint IX

Basic Price T $2,750
Basic Price L, R, B $2,500

6809 6819 6825 6833

#476 20¢ FRANKLIN 4 Plates

Imprint IX

Basic Price T $3,500
Basic Price L, R, B $3,250

6908 6909 6920 6926

#476 A 30¢ FRANKLIN 2 Plates

Imprint IX

Price T —
Price L, R, B —

*6914 *6917

#477 50¢ FRANKLIN 4 Plates

Imprint IX

Basic Price T $22,500
Basic Price L, R, B $20,000

7040 7042 7049 7057

#478 $1 FRANKLIN 1 Plate

Imprint XII

Price T $13,000
Price B $12,500

5782

#479 $2 MADISON 1 Plate

Imprint IX

Basic Price T $6,500
Basic Price L, R, B $6,250

8015

#480 $5 MARSHALL 1 Plate

Imprint IX

Basic Price T $5,250
Basic Price L, R, B $5,000

8016

BOOKLET PANES

Unwatermarked. Perf. 10

BOOKLET PANES OF 6

FLAT PRESS

#462a 1¢ WASHINGTON 12 Plates

Top plate number only

Basic Price T $17.50

7179	7275	7277	7278	7449
7474	7480	7484	7785	7786
7791	7880			

#463a 2¢ WASHINGTON 12 Plates

Top plate number only

Basic Price T $100

7555	7556	7557	7560	7881
7882	7885	7887	7968	7969
7970	7971			

IMPERFORATE

FLAT PRESS Unwatermarked

Blocks of 6

#481 1¢ WASHINGTON 153 Plates

Imprint IX

Basic Price T $15
Basic Price L, R, B $14

7535	7669	7671	7674	7725
7736	7741	7743	7749	7750
7753	7754	7755	*7756	7757
7850	7862	7863	7865	7875
7877	7878	7879	*7889	*7890
7894	7898	7899	7900	7901
7902	7905	7907	7908	8038
8039	8040	8042	8045	8046

1916-17 REGULAR ISSUE

#481 1¢ WASHINGTON Continued

Imprint IX

8068	8115	8116	8117	8168
8259	8372	8373	8374	8377
8378	8387	8388	8389	8390
8397	8398	*8431	8457	8915
*8931	9477	*9478	9479	9480
9481	10073	10075	10076	10083
10084	10085	10091	10092	10110
10112	10113	10195	10197	10232
10248	10258	10260	10264	10265
10278	10279	10280	10281	10282
10284	10285	10290	10292	10293
10298	*10299	10344	10351	10365
*10369	*10599	*10600	*10659	10682
*10757	*10783	10799	*10800	11728
11806	*11807	12493	*12494	*12501
12505	12548	12611	12616	12617
12924	*13199	*13267	13301	13303
13304	13306	13308	13316	13317
13319	*13320	13332	13337	13338
13339	13340	13349	13350	*13356
13359	13361	13363	*13366	13368
13370	13371	13378	13379	13380
13381				

Electrolytic Plates

Basic Price	T	$250
Basic Price	L, R, B	$225

13376 13377

#482 2¢ WASHINGTON TYPE I

Imprint IX **154 Plates**

Basic Price	T	$27.50
Basic Price	L, R, B	$25.00

7322	7393	*7583	7639	7699
7701	7714	7729	7730	7760
7762	7771	7780	7781	7783
7784	7792	7800	7801	7802
7805	7806	7807	7808	7809
7816	7817	7818	7819	7820
7821	7824	*7867	*7930	7935
*7936	7942N	7944	7945	7946
7947	7985	7986	7987	7995
*8009	*8010	8011	8012	8014
8018	8022	8023	8024	8025
8026	8067	8069	8070	8501
*8522	8535	8536	8537	*8539
*8541	8548	8550	8870	8871
8886	*9119	*9163	*9166	9168
9169	9172	9173	9191	9192
*9221	*9224	9231	9238	9239
9411	9420	*9421	*9425	*9434
9443	9445	9448	9455	9456
10240	10267	10272	10304	10305
10313	10314	10354	*10378	10379
10392	10393	10398	10419	10424
10425	10426	10427	10428	10429
*10554	*10560	*10569	10577	*10578
10579	10585	10593	10594	*12960

IMPERFORATE (Cont.)

#482 2¢ WASHINGTON Continued

Imprint IX

12963	*12964	12977	12978	12979
12980	12981	12993	*12996	13207
13208	13209	13227	*13454	*13495
*13524	*13550	13669	13670	13671
13672	13683	13728	13729	*13869
13884	13885	13886	13887	

N The 2¢ stamp plate 7942 is the plate on which the 5¢ errors are found. See #485.

#482A 2¢ WASHINGTON TYPE Ia

10208 10209

All of the stamps on these two plates are type Ia except for two entries on the lower left pane of plate 10208.

Imperforate type Ia was issued but all known examples have Schermack perforations type III.

#483 3¢ WASHINGTON TYPE I

Imprint IX **36 Plates**

Basic Price	T	$200
Basic Price	L, R, B	$190

7272	8091	*8092	8120	8121
8123	8126	8128	8129	8130
8131	8132	8134	8135	8137
8138	8139	8140	8141	8142
8143	8144	8146	8161	8192
*8193	8195	8196	8197	8204
*8206	8209	8230	8232	*8235
*8236				

#484 3¢ WASHINGTON TYPE II

Imprint IX **26 Plates**

Basic Price	T	$150
Basic Price	L, R, B	$140

8308	8310	8316	8317	8319
*8320	8325	8330	8338	8351
8352	8354	8355	8356	8357
8358	8362	8364	8365	8366
8371	8386	8456	8462	8473
8476				

1916-17 REGULAR ISSUE
IMPERFORATE (Cont.)

#485 5¢ ERROR PLATE

Price	T	$175
Price	L, R, B	$150

7942N

N **The 2¢ plate 7942 is the plate on which the 5¢ errors are found.**

The errors are located at stamps #74 and #84 of the upper left pane and stamp #18 in the lower right pane of plate 7942. *The errors, therefore, do not appear in any of the plate blocks.*

ROTARY COILS
Endwise Coils
Unwatermarked. Perf. 10

HORIZONTAL

#486 1¢ WASHINGTON

7433 7434 7563 7564 8079
8080 10081 10082 10408 10409
10410 10411 13928 13929

#487 2¢ WASHINGTON TY. II

7431 7432

#488 2¢ WASHINGTON TY. III

7628 7629 8077 8078 10767
10768 13629 13630 13631 13632

#489 3¢ WASHINGTON TY. I

7634 7635 8111 8112

Sidewise Coils
Unwatermarked. Perf. 10

VERTICAL

#490 1¢ WASHINGTON

7506 7507 7508 7690 7691
7744 7745 7763 7766 7767
7957 7958 7963 7964 7978
7979 8081 8082 8336 8337
8339 8340 9099 9111 9112
9113 9114 9141 9142 9151
9152 9450 9451 9452 9453
9463 9464 9467 9468 10087
10088 10089 10090 10103 10104
10184 10185 10202 10203 10345
10346 10347 10348 10349 10350
10361 10640 10641 10643 10686
10687 10688 10689 10690 10691
10692 10693 10694 10695 11740
11741 11742 11743 11764 11765
11766 11767 13312 13313 13314
13315 13445 13446 13447 13448
13491 13492 13575 13576 13611
13612 13615 13616 13810 13811
13812 13813 13820 13821 13826

ROTARY COILS (Cont.)

#490 1¢ WASHINGTON

13827 13856 13857 13872 13873
13896 13897 13906 13907 13910
13911 13930 13931 13942 13943
13968 13969 13976 14104

#491 2¢ WASHINGTON TY. II

7445 7446 7462 7463

#492 2¢ WASHINGTON TY. III

7661 7662 7672 7673 7686
7738 7739 7746 7747 7751
7752 7782 7803 7804 7813
7814 7826 7829 7830 7835
7836 7852 7853 7909 7910
7915 7916 7939 7940 7953
7961 7962 7965 7967 7976
8049 8050 8051 8052 8056
8057 8061 8062 8071 8072
8073 8074 8075 8076 8169
8170 8171 8172 8326 8327
8328 8329 8928 8939 8940
9103 9104 9105 9106 9153
9154 9233 9234 9235 9236
9237 9457 9458 9465 9466
9469 9470 10097 10098 10115
10116 10175 10176 10177 10178
10183 10295 10296 10297 10306
10307 10308 10315 10316 10317
10318 10384 10386 10387 10388
10389 10444 10445 10446 10447
10448 10449 10450 10451 10452
10453 10466 10467 10468 10469
10470 10471 10478 10479 10480
10485 10486 10487 10488 10489
10491 10492 19648 10649 10650
10651 10652 10670 10671 10680
10681 10723 10724 10725 10726
10727 10728 10729 10730 10731
10732 10733 10738 10739 10740
10741 10750 11718 11719 11724
11725 11726 11727 11730 11731
11732 11733 11734 11735 11736
11737 11769 11770 11771 11772
11797 11798 11799 11800 11808
11809 11810 11811 12464 12465
12466 12469 12470 12471 12472
12473 12474 12475 12476 12483
12484 12485 12486 12513 12514
12515 12516 12517 12518 12519
12520 12529 12530 12531 12532
12601 12602 12603 12604 12918
12919 12920 12921 12922 12927
12928 12929 12970 12971 12972
12973 13002 13004 13005 13239
13240 13253 13254 13286 13287
13288 13289 13290 13291 13292
13293 13294 13295 13386 13387
13388 13397 13398 13399 13400
13401 13402 13413 13414 13417

ROTARY COILS (Cont.)

#492 2¢ WASHINGTON TY. III

13418	13425	13426	13417	13428
13505	13506	13507	13508	13509
13510	13511	13512	13514	13536
13537	13538	13539	13583	13584
13585	13586	13595	13596	13597
13598	13599	13600	13601	13602
13603	13604	13605	13606	13607
13608	13637	13638	13641	13642
13647	13648	13651	13652	13657
13678	13677	13678	13692	13693
13694	13695	13718	13719	13720
13721	13740	13741	*13742	13743
13764	13765	13766	13767	13776
13777	13778	*13779	13786	*13787
*13788	13789	13800	13801	*13802
13803	13804	13805	13807	13809
13814	13815	13830	13831	13840
13841	*13842	*13843	13874	13875
13894	13895	13938	*13939	*13958
*13959	13960	13961	13970	13971
13984	13985	14030	*14031	*14032
14033	*14038	*14039	*14040	14041
14050	14051	14052	*14053	14054
14055	*14056	14057		

#493 3¢ WASHINGTON TY. I

7441	7442	8107	8108	8109
8110	8124	8125	8151	8152
8153	8154	8155	8201	8202
8203	8216	8218	8219	8226
8227	8228	8229	8233	8234
8237	8238	8239	8240	8244
8245	8247	8248	8250	8251

#494 3¢ WASHINGTON TY. II

8269	8275	8276	8281	8282
8402	8408	8409	8428	8429
8442	8454	8455	8458	8459
8464	8467	8468	8469	8470
8471	8472	8474	8475	8482
8483	8923	8924	8949	8950
8951	9107	9108	9109	9110
9133	9134	9135	9136	9143
9144	9145	9146	9181	9182

#495 4¢ WASHINGTON

7440	7452	7675	7676

#496 5¢ WASHINGTON

7435	7436	13633	13634

#497 10¢ FRANKLIN

13625	13626

1917-19 REGULAR ISSUE

All Imprint IX except as noted.

Unwatermarked. Perf. 11
FLAT PRESS **Block of 6**

#498 1¢ WASHINGTON 655 Plates

Basic Price	T	$15
Basic Price	L, R, B	$14

7532	7533	7535	7647	7651
7655	7656	7658	7659	7668
7669	7670	7671	7674	7726
7727	7733	7741	7743	7750
7754	7755	*7756	7757	*7758
7759	7761	7764	7765	7831
7832	7889	7890	7891	7892
7895	7896	7897	*7898	*7899
*7900	7901	7902	7903	7904
7906	*7907	7911	7912	7913
*7914	7933	7937	7938	7943
7950	7956	7959	7999	8003
8007	8008	8013	8034	8035
8036	8037	8038	8039	8040
8042	8043	8044	8045	8046
8047	8048	8054	8060	8068
8115	8116	8117	8164	8165
8166	8167	8168	8173	8174
8175	8176	8257	8258	*8259
8260	8261	8335	8341	*8342
*8343	8344	8345	*8346	*8347
8348	8349	8350	8360	8361
8368	8369	8372	8373	8374
8377	8378	8387	8388	8389
8390	8391	8392	8393	8394
8395	8396	8397	8398	8399
8400	8401	8404	8405	8406
8407	8422	8423	8424	8425
8426	8427	8430	8431	8432
8433	8434	8439	8440	8443
8444	8445	8446	8447	8450
8453	8457	8461	8465	8510
8511	8512	8513	8526	8527
8528	8529	8884	8885	8907
8908	8909	8910	8911	8912
8913	8914	8915	8916	8917
8918	8919	8920	8921	8922

1917-19 REGULAR ISSUE

#498 1¢ WASHINGTON Continued

8925	8926	8927	8929	8930
8931	8932	8933	8934	8935
8937	8941	8942	8944	9477
9478	9479	9480	9481	10073
10074	10075	10076	10083	10084
10085	10086	10091	10092	10099
10100	10101	10102	10105	10106
10107	10108	10109	10110	10111
10112	10113	10114	10117	10118
10119	10120	10121	10122	10123
10124	10125	10126	10127	10128
10129	10130	10131	10132	10133
10134	10153	10154	10155	10156
*10157	10158	10159	10160	10161
*10162	10163	10164	10165	10166
10167	10168	10173	10174	10186
10187	10188	10189	10194	10195
10196	10197	10230	10231	10232
10233	10242	10243	*10244	*10245
10246	10247	*10248	*10249	10258
*10259	10260	10261	10262	*10263
10264	10265	10278	10279	10280
10281	10282	10283	10284	10285
10290	10291	10292	10293	10298
10299	10343	10344	10351	10352
10357	10358	10359	10360	10362
10363	10364	10365	10366	10367
10368	10369	10370	10371	10374
10375	10376	10377	10380	10381
10382	10383	10390	10391	10394
10395	10396	10397	10414	10415
10417	10420	10421	10422	10423
10440	10441	10454	10455	10472
10473	10529	10530	10539	10540
10557	10558	10565	10566	10567
10568	10571	10572	10573	10574
10575	10576	10580	10583	10584
10586	10587	10588	10591	10592
10595	10596	10599	10600	10601
10602	10603	10604	10613	10614
10615	10616	10625	10626	10644
10645	10646	10647	10654	10656
10657	10658	10659	10660	10661
10662	10663	10664	10665	10676
10677	10678	10679	10682	10683
10684	10685	10696	10697	10698
10699	10701	10702	10703	10708
10709	10710	10711	10712	10713
10742	10743	10744	10745	10746
10747	10748	10749	10751	10752
10753	10754	10755	10756	10757
10758	10759	10760	10761	10762
10769	10770	10771	10772	10773
10774	10779	10780	10781	10782
10783	10784	10789	10790	10799
10800	10801	10802	10803	10804
10805	10806	10807	10808	10809
10810	10811	10812	10814	10815
10816	*11720	11721	11722	11723
11728	11729	11786	11787	11788

#498 1¢ WASHINGTON Continued

11789	11790	11791	11792	11802
11803	11804	11805	11806	11807
11812	11813	12491	12492	12493
12494	12497	12498	12499	12500
12501	12502	12503	12504	12505
12506	12507	12508	12521	12522
12523	12524	12525	12527	12528
12533	12534	12535	12536	12537
12538	12539	12540	12541	12542
12543	12544	12545	12546	12547
12548	12609	12610	12611	12612
12613	12614	12615	12616	12617
12923	12924	12925	12926	13198
13199	13200	13201	13214	13216
13217	13219	13220	13221	13222
13223	13224	13225	13226	13231
13232	13233	13234	13249	13250
13251	13252	13256	13257	13258
13259	13265	13266	13267	13300
13301	13302	13303	13304	13305
13306	*13307	13308	13309	13310
13311	13316	13317	13318	13319
13320	13321	13322	13323	13324
*13325	*13326	*13327	*13328	13329
13330	13331	13332	13333	13334
13335	13336	13337	13338	13339
13340	13341	13342	13343	13344
13345	13346	13347	13348	13349
13350	13351	*13356	13357	13358
13359	13360	13361	*13362	13363
13364	13365	13366	13367	13368
13369	13370	13371	*13378	13379
13380	13381	*13544	*13545	13546
13547				

Electrolytic Plates

Basic Price	T	$200
Basic Price	L, R, B	$190

*13376 *13377 *13389 †13390

#499 2¢ WASHINGTON 830 Plates

Basic Price	T	$17.50
Basic Price	L, R, B	$15.00

5990	*7322	7393	*7398	7456
7501	7569	7581	7589	7590
7640	7641	7682	7698	7699
7701	7703	7705	7707	*7708
7709	7710	7711	7713	7714
7716	7724	7728	7730	7732
7737	*7773	7792	7795	7797
7801	7802	*7808	7809	7816
7817	7818	7819	7823	7839
7840	7841	7842	7843	7845
7847	*7848	7854	7855	7856
7857	7858	7859	7866	7867
7868	7869	7870	7871	*7873
7921	7922	7923	7930	7931
*7932	7934	7935	7936	7941
*7942N	7944	7945	7946	7947

1917-19 REGULAR ISSUE

#499 2¢ WASHINGTON Continued

7948 7949 7951 7952 7955
7982 7983 7985 7986 7987
7988 7989 7995 7996 8000
8001 8002 8004 8005 8006

8009 8010 8011 8012 8014
8017 8018 8019 8020 8021
8022 8023 8024 8025 8026
8027 8028 8029 8030 8031
8032 8033 8041 8053 8055
8058 8059 8063 8064 8065
8066 8067 8069 8070 8083
8084 8085 8086 8087 8088
8089 8090 8180 8181 8182
8498 8499 8500 8501 8502

8503 8504 8505 8514 8515
8516 8517 8518 8519 8520
8521 8522 8523 8524 8525
8531 8532 8533 8534 8535
8536 8537 8538 8539 8540
8541 8542 8546 8547 8548
8549 8550 8551 8552 8553
8870 8871 8872 8874 8875
8876 8877 8886 8887 8952
8953 8954 9098 9100 9101

9102 9119 9120 9121 9122
9123 9124 9125 9126 9127
9128 9131 9132 9139 9140
9156 9157 9158 9159 9160
9161 9162 9163 9165 9166
9167 9168 9169 9170 9171
9172 9173 9174 9175 9176
9183 9184 9185 9186 9187
9188 9189 9190 9191 9192
9197 9198 9199 9200 9201

9202 9203 9204 9205 9206
9207 9208 9209 9210 9211
9212 9213 9214 9215 9216
9217 9218 9219 9220 9221
9222 9223 9224 9225 9226
9227 9228 9229 9230 9231
9232 9238 9239 9240 9241
9410 9411 9420 9421 9422
9423 9424 9425 9434 9435
9436 9437 9438 9439 9440

9441 9442 9443 9444 9445
9446 9447 9448 9449 9454
9455 9456 9459 9460 9461
9462 10190 10191 10192 10193
10198 10199 10200 10201 10204
10205 10206 10207 *10208Z 10210
10211 10212 10213 10214 10215
10216 10217 10226 10227 10228
10229 10234 10235 10236 10237
10238 10239 10240 10241 10266

10267 10268 10269 10270 10271
10272 10273 10286 10287 10288
10289 10304 10305 10313 10314
10319 10320 10321 10322 10323
10324 10333 10334 10339 10340
10341 10342 *10353 10354 10355
10356 10372 10373 10378 10379

#499 2¢ WASHINGTON Continued

10392 10393 10398 10399 10412
10413 10418 10419 10424 10425
10426 10427 10428 10429 10434

10435 10442 10443 10456 10457
10462 10463 10464 10465 10481
10482 10483 10484 10493 10495
10496 10497 10498 10499 10500
10505 10506 10507 10508 10515
10516 10517 10518 10519 10520
10521 10522 10523 10524 10531
10532 10533 10534 10535 10536
10537 *10538 *10545 *10546 10547
10548 *10549 *10550 10551 *10552

*10553 10554 10555 10556 10559
10560 10561 10562 10563 10564
10569 10570 10577 10578 10579
10581 10582 10585 10589 10590
10593 10594 10597 10598 12938
12939 12940 12941 12942 12943
12944 12945 12946 12947 12948
12949 12950 12951 12952 12953
12954 12955 12956 12957 12958
12959 12960 12961 12962 12963

12964 12965 12966 12967 12968
12969 12974 12975 12976 12977
12978 12979 12980 12981 12982
12983 12984 12985 12986 12987
12988 12989 12990 12991 12993
12994 12995 12996 12997 12998
12999 13000 13001 13006 13007
13008 13009 13014 13015 13016
13017 13194 13195 13196 13197
13202 13203 13204 13205 13206

13207 13208 13209 13227 13228
13229 13230 13235 13236 13237
13238 13241 13242 13243 13244
13245 13246 13247 13248 13260
13261 13262 13263 13296 13297
13298 13299 13433 13434 13435
13436 13437 13438 13439 13440
13441 13442 13451 13452 13453
13454 13455 13456 13457 13458
13475 13476 13477 13478 13479

13480 13481 13482 13483 13484
13485 13486 13487 13488 13489
13490 13493 13494 13495 13496
13518 13519 13520 13521 13524
13525 13526 13527 13532 13533
13534 13535 13540 13541 13542
13543 13548 13549 13550 13551
13560 13561 13562 13563 13564
13565 13566 13567 13587 13588
13589 13590 13591 13592 13593

13594 13659 13660 13661 13662
13663 13664 13665 13666 13667
13668 13669 13670 13671 13672
13673 13674 13679 13680 13681
13682 13683 13684 13685 13686
13687 13689 13690 13691 13698
13699 13700 13701 13702 13703
13704 13705 13706 13707 13708

1917-19 REGULAR ISSUE

#499 2¢ WASHINGTON Continued

13709 13710 13711 13712 13713
13714 13715 13716 13717 13724
13725 13726 13727 13728 13729
13730 13731 13732 13733 13734
13735 13736 13737 13738 13739
13746 13747 13748 13749 13758
13759 13760 13761 13768 13769
13770 13771 13772 13773 13774
13775 13780 13781 13782 13783
13792 13793 13794 13795 13848
13849 13850 13851 13864 13865
13866 13867 13868 13869 13870
13871 13878 13879 13880 13881
13882 13883 13884 13885 13886
13887 13888 13889 13898 13899
13900 13901 13902 13903 13904
13905 13912 13913 13914 13915
13924 13925 13926 13927 13932
13933 13934 13935 13944 13945
13946 13947 13954 13955 13956
13957 13972 13973 13974 13975
13978 13979 13980 13981 13986
13987 13988 13989 13992 13993
13994 13995 13996 13997 13998
13999 14002 14003 14004 14005
14008 14009 14010 *14011 14014
14015 14016 14017 14019 14020
14021 14022 14023 14024 14025

N Plate 7942 is not scarce but it is the sheet on which the 5¢ errors are found and, for that reason, the plates bring a substantial premium. *The errors do not appear in any of the plate blocks.* See #505

Z See #500 TYPE Ia

#500 2¢ WASHINGTON TYPE Ia

Basic Price **T** $2,400
Basic Price **L, R, B** $2,300

10208 10209

All of the stamps on these two plates are type Ia except for two entries on the lower left pane 10208. A bottom plate block of this pane shows the combination of type I and type Ia. These are quite scarce.

This Block is valued at $6,750

#501 3¢ WASHINGTON TYPE I

90 Plates
Basic Price **T** $175
Basic Price **L, R, B** $165

7253 7254 7258 7262 7266
7267 7272 7274 8091 8092
8093 8094 8099 8100 8101
8102 8103 8104 8105 8106
8118 8119 8120 8121 8122
8123 8126 8127 8128 8129
8130 8131 8132 8133 8134

#501 3¢ WASHINGTON Continued

8135 8136 8137 8138 8139
8140 8141 8142 8143 8144
8145 8146 8147 8148 *8149
8156 *8157 8158 8159 8160
8161 8163 8192 8193 8195
8196 8197 8198 8199 8204
8206 8207 8208 8209 8210
8215 8221 8222 8223 8224
8225 8230 8232 8235 8236
8241 8242 8243 8246 8249
8252 8253 8254 8255 8256

#502 3¢ WASHINGTON TYPE II

85 Plates
Basic Price **T** $220
Basic Price **L, R, B** $210

8262 8263 8264 8265 8266
8267 8268 8271 8273 8274
8277 8278 *8279 *8280 *8283
8284 *8285 *8286 *8287 *8288
*8289 *8290 8291 8292 *8293
*8294 8295 8296 *8297 *8298
*8299 *8300 8305 8306 8307
8308 8309 *8310 8311 8312
8313 8314 *8315 *8316 *8317
*8318 *8319 8320 *8321 8322
8323 8324 8325 8330 8338
8351 8352 8353 8354 8355
8356 8357 8358 8359 8362
8363 8364 8365 8366 8367
8371 8386 8456 8462 8473
8476 *8481 †8866 †8867 *8868
*8869 †8903 *8904 *8905 *8906

#503 4¢ WASHINGTON 33 Plates

Basic Price **T** $185
Basic Price **L, R, B** $175

7331 7598 7599 7600 7606
7972 7973 7974 7975 8494
8495 8496 8497 8880 8881
8888 8889 10474 10475 10476
10477 12549 12550 12551 12552
13556 13557 13558 13559 13569
13570 13571 13572

1917-19 REGULAR ISSUE

#504 5¢ WASHINGTON 88 Plates

Basic Price T $150
Basic Price L, R, B $140

7622 7623 7632 7633 7787
7788 7789 7790 7993 7994
7997 7998 8200 8205 8220
8231 8484 8485 8486 8487
8882 8883 8901 8902 9115
9116 9117 9118 10139 10140
10141 10142 10222 10223 10224
10225 10309 10310 10311 10312
10458 10459 10460 10461 10541
10542 10543 10544 10666 10667
10668 10669 10704 10705 10706
10707 11748 11749 11750 11751
12479 12480 12481 12482 12509
12510 12511 12512 12553 12554
12555 12556 13272 13273 13274
13275 13463 13464 13465 13466
13497 13498 13499 13500 *13822
13823 *13824 *13825

#505 5¢ ERROR PLATE

Price T $20
Price L, R, B $17.50

7942N

N The 2¢ stamp plate 7942 is not scarce but it is the sheet on which the 5¢ errors are found.

The errors are located at stamps #74 and #84 of the upper left pane and stamp #18 in the lower right pane of plate 7942. *The errors, therefore, do not appear in any of the plate blocks.*

#506 6¢ WASHINGTON 24 Plates

Basic Price T $220
Basic Price L, R, B $210

7136 7137 7138 7139 7822
7828 7834 7837 10093 10094
10095 10096 10763 10764 10765
10766 12557 12558 12559 12560
13372 13373 13374 13375

#507 7¢ WASHINGTON 54 Plates

Basic Price T $375
Basic Price L, R, B $350

7718 7719 7919 7920 7924
7925 8488 8489 8490 8491
8897 8898 8899 8943 *10169
*10170 *10171 *10172 10300 10301
10302 10303 *10511 10512 *10513
10514 10636 10637 10638 10639
10795 10796 10797 10798 11752
11753 11754 11755 12561 12562
12563 12564 13276 13277 13278
13279 13750 13751 13752 13753
13950 13951 13952 13953

#508 8¢ FRANKLIN 24 Plates

Imprint XII

Basic Price T $250
Basic Price L, R, B $225

5724 5725 5804

Imprint XIII

Price T $275
Price L, R, B $250

5846

Imprint IX

Basic Price T $225
Basic Price L, R, B $200

7734 7740 7742 7748 10785
10786 10787 10788 12565 12566
12567 12568 13382 13383 13384
13385 13852 13853 13854 13855

#509 9¢ FRANKLIN 17 Plates

Basic Price T $200
Basic Price L, R, B $175

6901 6905 6907 6915 6918
6922 6925 6930 11773 11774
11775 11776 12569 12570 12571
12572 *13754

#510 10¢ FRANKLIN 65 Plates

Imprint XIII

Price T $250
Price L, R, B $225

5847

Imprint IX

Basic Price T $325
Basic Price L, R, B $300

7204 7205 7213 7215 7358
7369 7379 7385 8301 8302
8303 8304 8435 8436 8437
8438 10143 10144 10145 10146
10254 10255 10256 10257 10525
10526 *10527 10528 10605 10606
10607 10608 10627 10628 10629
10630 *10734 10735 10736 10737

1917-19 REGULAR ISSUE

#510 10¢ FRANKLIN Continued

11744 11745 11746 11747 12573
12574 12575 12576 12605 12606
12607 12608 13403 13404 13405
13406 13501 13502 13503 13504
13796 13797 13798 13799

#511 11¢ FRANKLIN 12 Plates

Basic Price	T	$140
Basic Price	L, R, B	$130

7498 7499 7504 7505 12577
12578 12579 12580 *13467 *13468
*13469 *13470

#512 12¢ FRANKLIN 16 Plates

Basic Price	T	$140
Basic Price	L, R, B	$130

6900 6902 6910 6913 6931
6934 7036 7037 10621 10622
10623 10624 12581 12582 12583
12584

#513 13¢ FRANKLIN 8 Plates

Basic Price	T	$150
Basic Price	L, R, B	$140

9147 9148 9149 9150 12585
12586 12587 12588

#514 15¢ FRANKLIN 36 Plates

Basic Price	T	$700
Basic Price	L, R, B	$650

6809 6819 6825 6833 7926
7927 7928 7929 8878 8879
8890 8891 10179 10180 10181
10182 10501 *10502 10503 10504
10617 10618 10619 10620 12589
12590 12591 12592 13280 13281
13282 13283 *13860 *13861 *13862
*13863

1917-19 REGULAR ISSUE

#515 20¢ FRANKLIN 32 Plates

Basic Price	T	$775
Basic Price	L, R, B	$725

6908 6909 6920 6926 6933
6935 6938 7033 10135 10136
10137 10138 10325 10326 10327
10328 11793 11795 11796 11801
12593 12594 12595 12596 13471
13472 13473 13474 13836 13837
13838 13839

#516 30¢ FRANKLIN 8 Plates

Basic Price	T	$650
Basic Price	L, R, B	$600

6899 6911 6914 6917 6921
6924 6927 6928

#517 50¢ FRANKLIN 8 Plates

Basic Price	T	$1,750
Basic Price	L, R, B	$1,650

7040 7042 7049 7057 13653
13654 13655 13656

#518 $1 FRANKLIN 1 Plate

Imprint XII

Price	T	$1,250
Price	B	$1,150

5782

1917 ISSUE

Double Line Wmk. Perf. 11
FLAT PRESS **Block of 6**

#519 2¢ WASHINGTON 8 Plates

Imprint V

Basic Price	T	$2,500
Basic Price	L, R, B	$2,400

4818 4848 4856 4864 4865
4866 4868 4905

Some early imperforate sheets of Scott's #344 were returned to the Bureau and perforated with the 11 gauge.

1918 ISSUE

Unwatermarked Perf. 11
FLAT PRESS **Block of 8**

#523 $2 FRANKLIN

Top plate numbers only

Price	T	$20,000
Frame Plate	8177	
Vignette Plate	8179	

#524 $5 FRANKLIN

Top plate numbers only

Price	T	$6,500
Frame Plate	8178	
Vignette Plate	8179	

BOOKLET PANES

Unwatermarked Perf. 11
BOOKLET PANES OF 6

#498e 1¢ WASHINGTON 73 Plates

Top plate number only

Basic Price T $3

6885	7179	7275	7277	7278
7449	7474	7480	7484	7785
7786	7791	7880	*7980	7981
7990	7991	8183	8184	8185
8186	8187	8188	8189	8194
8945	8946	8947	8948	9177

1918 ISSUE

#498e 1¢ WASHINGTON Cont.

Top plate number only

9178	9179	9180	10077	10078
10079	10080	*10250	10251	*10252
10253	10430	10431	10432	10433
*10714	10715	10716	10717	11756
11757	11758	11759	11761	11762
11763	11768	13268	13269	13270
13271	13421	13422	13423	13424
13429	13430	13431	13432	13459
13460	13461	13462		

#499e 2¢ WASHINGTON 100 Plates

Top plate number only

Basic Price T $4

7881	7882	7885	7887	7968
7969	7970	7971	8191	8893
8894	8895	9471	9472	9473
9474	10147	10148	10149	10150
10218	10219	10220	10221	10329
10330	10331	10332	*10400	*10401
*10402	10403	10404	10405	*10406
10407	10609	10610	10611	10612
10672	10673	10674	*10675	10718
10719	10720	10721	*10775	*10776
*10777	10778	10791	10792	10793
10794	*11777	11778	11779	11780
11781	11782	11783	11784	*12487
12488	*12489	*12490	12930	12931
12932	12933	12934	12935	12936
*12937	13010	13011	13012	13013
13210	13211	13212	13213	13528
13529	13530	13531	13617	13618
13619	13620	*13621	13622	13623
13624	13964	13965	13966	13967

#501b 3¢ WASHINGTON TYPE I

Top plate number only **4 plates**

Basic Price T $100

8095	8096	8097	8098

#502b 3¢ WASHINGTON TYPE II

Top plate number only **12 Plates**

Basic Price T $65

8331	8332	8333	8334	8448
8449	8452	8460	9129	9130
9137	9138			

1918-1920 OFFSET PRINTING

Unwatermarked Perf. 11
Positions T, L, R, B Blocks of 6

Early in 1918 the Bureau of Engraving and Printing began producing the lower values of the current issue of postage stamps by the offset printing method. The stamps were much inferior to the engraved work and as soon as the volume of work in the Bureau would permit the engraving of postage stamp plates was resumed.

1918-1920 OFFSET PRINTING

Collectors, in general, were not greatly interested in these stamps and the printing method is such that the stamps abound in major and minor defects and varieties. Both of these factors make the issue a very rewarding field for study today.

Many varieties appear on the plate blocks of this issue and two of the most popular are the CRNTS and 'OAM' varieties. These are priced under the type Va plates, Scott #528.

#525 1¢ OFFSET 259 Plates

Basic Price	T	$30.00
Basic Price	L, R, B	$27.50

*9095 *9096 *9242 9245 9247
9248 9249 9250 9257 9258
9259 9260 9261 9266 9267
9283 9284 9285 9290 9291
9306 9307 9308 9318 9320
9321 9322 9328 9399 9402
9403 *9486 9487 9488 9489
9496 *9497 *9498 9499 9508
9509 9510 9511 9515 9516
9517 9518 9519 9521 9522

9523 9524 9525 9526 9527
9539 9540 *9541 9555 9556
9557 9558 *9640 9641 9643
9661 9662 9672 9673 9674
9675 9676 *9677 *9678 9679
*9680 *9681 *9682 *9685 9692
9693 *9694 *9698 *9699 9700
9703 9710 *9711 *9712 9713
9714 9715 *9716 9717 †9718
†9720 9721 9723 9724 9725

9753 9754 9755 9756 *9763
9764 9765 9766 9767 9768
9772 9773 *9774 *9779 9780
9781 *9782 *9787 *9788 9789
9790 †9791 9792 *9802 *9803
9804 *9805 *9806 *9807 9809
9810 9811 9812 9817 9818
9819 *9820 9821 *9822 9824
9825 9828 9829 *9830 9837
*9838 9839 †9840 *9841 *9842

*9843 *9844 *9859 9860 9861
9870 *9871 9874 9876 *9878
*9879 9893 *9894 9895 *9896
9897 *9906 *9907 9909 9916
9917 9918 9920 9949 *9950
9951 *9952 *9953 *9954 *9965
*9966 9967 *9968 9969 9970
*9971 *9972 *9973 *9974 9975
*9976 9977 *9978 †9979 9980
*9981 9982 *9983 *9984 9985

*9986 9987 *9988 *9989 *9990
*9991 †9992 9993 *9995 *9996
*9997 *9998 9999 10000 10001
10002 10003 *10005 10006 10007
10008 10009 10010 10011 *10012
10013 10014 10015

#525 1¢ OFFSET Continued

10016 *10017 *10020 *10021 10022
*10023 10024 10025 10026 10027
10028 10029 10030 †10031 10032
10033 *10034 10035 10036 10037

*10038 10041 10042 10043 10044
†10045 *10049 *10050 10052 *10053
*10054

#526 2¢ OFFSET Type IV 95 Plates

Basic Price	T	$250
Basic Price	L, R, B	$225

*10818 *10819 10820 10821 10822
10823 10824 10825 10826 10827
10828 10829 *10830 10831 10832
*10833 10834 *10835 10836 10837
*10839 10840 *10841 10842 *10843
10844 *10845 *10852 10853 10854
10855 10856 10857 *10858 *10859
10860 *10861 10862 *10863 10864
*10866 *10871 *10872 *10873 *10874
*10876 *10878 *10879 10880 10881

*10882 *10883 10884 10885 *10886
10887 10888 *10890 *10892 *10893
*10894 10895 10896 10897 10898
*10899 *10900 10901 *10902 10904
10905 *10906 10907 10908 10909
10910 10912 10913 10914 10915
10916 *10917 10918 *10919 *10921
*10922 *10923 10927 10928 10929
10931 10932 *10933 10934 *10935

#527 2¢ OFFSET Type V 302 Plates

Basic Price	T	$150
Basic Price	L, R, B	$140

†10924 *10936 10948 *10949 10950
*10951 *10953 10954 *10955 10956
10957 *10958 10959 *10960 10961
*10962 *10965 *10968 10969 *10970
10971 *10972 *10973 *10974 *10975
*10976 10977 †10978 †10981 *10982
*10983 *10984 10986 *10987 *10988
*10989 10990 10991 *10992 10993
*10994 *10995 *10996 *10997 *10998
*10999 11000 *11001 *11002 *11003

11004 *11005 11006 *11007 *11008
11009 *11010 *11011 *11012 *11013
*11014 *11015 *11016 *11017 11018
11019 *11020 11021 11022 11023
*11024 11025 *11026 11027 11028
*11029 *11031 11032 *11033 11034
*11035 11036 *11037 *11038 *11039
11040 11041 *11042 11043 *11044
11045 11046 *11047 *11048 11050
†11051 11052 *11053 *11054 *11057

*11058 *11059 *11060 *11061 *11062
11063 *11064 *11065 11066 11067
11069 11070 11071 *11072 *11073
*11074 11075 *11076 11077 *11078
*11079 11080 11081 *11082 11083
11084 11085 11086 *11087 11088

1918-1920 OFFSET PRINTING

#527 2¢ OFFSET Type V Continued

11090	11091	*11092	*11093	*11094
11095	*11097	*11098	11099	*11100
*11101	*11102	*11103	*11104	*11105
11106	*11107	11109	*11110	*11111
*11112	*11114	11115	*11116	11120
11121	11122	11124	11125	11126
11127	11128	11129	*11130	11131
11132	11133	11134	11135	11136
*11137	11139	11140	*11142	11143
*11144	†11145	11146	*11147	*11149
11150	11151	11152	*11153	11154
11155	11156	11157	11159	11160
11161	11162	*11164	11165	11166
11168	11169	11170	*11171	11172
11173	11174	11175	11176	*11177
*11178	11179	11180	11181	11182
11183	*11184	11185	11186	11187
*11188	*11189	*11190	11191	11193
*11196	11197	*11198	11199	*11200
11202	11203	11204	11205	11206
11209	*11210	11211	11212	*11213
*11214	11215	*11216	11218	11219
*11220	†11221	*11222	*11223	*11224
11226	*11227	11229	11230	11231
*11232	11233	11234	11235	11236
11237	11238	11241	*11242	11243
*11245	11246	*11247	11248	11249
11250	11251	11252	*11253	11254
11256	*11257	11260	*11261	11262
11263	†11264	*11265	*11272	11273
*11274	*11275	*11276	11277	*11278
11279	*11281	*11282	11283	11284
11386	11878	11879	11883	11892
11893	11894	11895	11896	11934
11936	11937			

#528 2¢ OFFSET Type Va 548 Plates

Basic Price	T	$65
Basic Price	L, R, B	$60

The plate printers initials O A M are found on the plate number blocks of at least 19 plates.

These blocks are valued at..........$90

A defective "E" in CENTS that causes the word to look almost as though it was spelled CRNTS occurs on the stamp directly below the top plate number on many plates.

These blocks are valued at..........$80

*11266	11267	11285	*11286	11287
*11288	*11289	11290	*11291	11292
*11293	11294	*11295	*11299	11300
11301	*11302	*11303	11304	11305
11306	11307	*11308	11309	†11310
11311	11312	11313	11315	11316
11317	*11318	*11319	*11320	*11321
*11323	11324	*11325	11326	*11327
*11328	11329	11330	11331	*11332
11333	11335	*11336	*11337	*11338

#528 2¢ OFFSET Type Va Cont.

11339	11340	11341	11342	11343
11344	*11345	*11346	11347	11348
11349	*11350	*11351	*11353	11354
*11355	11356	*11358	11359	11360
11361	*11362	11363	*11364	11365
*11366	11367	11368	11369	*11370
11371	11373	*11374	*11375	*11376
11378	11379	11380	11381	11382
11383	11384	11385	11388	*11389
11390	11391	11392	11393	11395
11397	11398	11399	*11400	11402
11403	11404	*11405	11406	*11407
11408	11409	11410	11411	11412
11413	11414	11415	11416	11417
11418	11419	*11420	11421	11422
11423	*11424	11425	11426	*11427
11428	11429	11430	11431	11433
11434	11435	11436	11439	11440
11441	*11443	11444	*11445	11446
11447	*11448	*11449	*11450	*11451
*11452	*11453	11455	*11456	11457
*11458	*11459	*11460	11461	*11462
11463	11464	*11466	*11467	11468
11469	*11470	11472	*11473	*11474
11475	*11476	*11477	11478	*11479
†11480	11481	*11482	11483	*11485
*11487	11488	11489	11490	*11491
11492	*11493	*11494	11495	11497
*11498	*11499	†11500	*11501	11503
*11504	11505	11506	11507	*11508
*11509	*11510	11511	11512	*11513
11514	11515	11516	11517	11518
11519	11520	*11521	11522	*11523
11524	*11525	11526	*11527	11528
11529	11530	11531	11532	11533
11535	11536	*11537	11538	*11539
11540	*11541	*11542	*11543	11544
11545	11546	11547	11548	*11549
11550	11551	11552	*11553	*11555
*11556	*11558	11559	*11560	11561
†11563	11564	*11565	11566	11567
*11570	11571	*11572	11573	11574
11575	*11576	11577	11578	*11579
*11580	11581	11582	*11583	11591
11592	*11593	11594	11595	*11596
11597	11823	*11824	*11825	11826
11827	11828	*11829	*11831	11832
11835	11836	*11837	11838	11839
11840	†11841	11842	*11843	11845
11846	11847	11848	11849	11850
*11851	11852	11853	11854	11855
11856	*11857	*11858	11859	11860
*11861	11862	11863	11864	11865
11866	11867	11868	11869	*11870
11871	11872	11873	11874	11875
11876	11887	11888	*11889	11890
11891	11897	11898	11899	11900
11901	11902	11903	11904	11905
11906	11908	11909	11910	11911
11912	11913	11914	11915	11916
*11917	11918	11920	*11921	†11922

1918-20 OFFSET PRINTING

#528 2¢ OFFSET Type Va Cont.

11924	11925	11926	11927	11928
*11929	*11930	11931	*11932	11933
11938	*11939	11944	11945	11946
11947	11948	11949	11950	11952
11957	11958	11959	11962	11964
11965	11967	11968	11969	*11970
11971	*11972	11973	*11974	11975
*11976	*11977	*11979	*11980	11981
11982	11983	11984	*11985	11986
11987	11988	*11989	11990	11991
11992	11993	*11994	11996	11997
11998	*12000	*12001	*12002	12003
12004	12005	12007	12011	12012
12013	12014	12015	*12017	12018
12019	12020	12021	*12022	12023
12024	12025	12026	12027	12028
12029	*12030	12031	12032	12033
12034	12035	12036	12037	12038
12039	12040	12041	12042	12043
12044	12047	12048	12049	12050
12051	12052	*12053	*12054	12056
12057	12058	12059	12060	12061
12062	12063	12064	12066	12067
12068	12069	12070	12071	12072
12073	12074	12075	*12076	*12077
*12078	12079	12081	12082	*12084
*12085	12086	*12089	12090	12091
12092	12093	*12094	*12095	12096
12097	12099	12100	12101	*12102
12103	12104	12105	12106	12107
12108	12109	12110	12111	12112
*12114	12115	*12117	12118	12119
12120	12121	*12122	12123	12124
*12125	12126	†12127	*12128	*12129
12130	12132	*12133	12134	12135
12136	12137	12138	12140	12141
12142	12143	12144	12145	†12148
†12149	12155	*12838	12850	*12851
*12852	*12854	12855		

#528A 2¢ OFFSET Type VI 103 Plates

Basic Price	T	$350
Basic Price	L, R, B	$325

The plate printers initials O A M are found on the plate number block of 11590 top. Valued at...................$500

†11562	*11585	*11586	*11587	11588
11590	11599	11600	11601	11603
11604	11605	11606	11607	11608
11609	11611	11612	*11613	11615
11616	*11617	*11618	*11620	11624
*11629	11630	*11631	11632	*11633
*11634	*11635	*11636	11637	11638
11639	11641	11642	11643	*11646
11647	11648	11649	11650	11651
11652	*11653	11654	11655	11656
11657	11658	*11659	11660	*11661
11662	11663	11664	*11665	11666
11667	11668	*11669	11670	11671
11673	11674	11675	11676	11677

#528A 2¢ OFFSET Type VI Cont.

11678	11679	11680	11681	11682
11683	11684	*11685	11686	11688
†11690	11691	11692	11693	11694
11695	11696	11697	11698	11699
11700	11703	11706	†11707	11708
11709	11710	11712	11713	11717
11818	11819	*11820		

#528B 2¢ OFFSET Type VII 604 Plates

Basic Price	T	$160
Basic Price	L, R, B	$150

12151	12152	12153	12157	*12158
12159	12160	†12161	12162	12164
12165	12166	12167	12168	12169
12170	12171	12172	12173	12174
12175	12176	12177	12178	*12179
12180	12182	12183	12184	12185
12186	12187	†12188	*12189	12190
12191	*12192	12193	12194	12195
12197	12198	12199	12200	12201
12202	12203	12205	*12207	12208
12209	12210	12212	12213	12215
12217	12219	12220	12221	12222
12223	12224	12225	12226	12227
12228	*12229	12230	12239	†12240
12241	12242	12243	12244	12245
12246	12247	12248	*12249	12250
*12251	12252	12253	12254	12255
12256	12257	*12258	12259	12260
*12262	12263	12264	12265	12266
12267	12268	12269	12270	12271
12272	12274	12275	12276	12277
12278	12279	12280	12281	12282
12283	12284	12285	12286	12287
12288	12289	12290	12291	12292
12293	*12294	12295	12296	12297
12298	*12299	12301	12302	12303
12304	12305	12306	12307	*12308
12309	*12310	*12311	12312	12313
12314	12315	12316	12318	*12319
12320	12321	12324	*12325	12326
12327	12328	12329	12330	12331
12332	12333	12334	12335	12336
12338	*12339	12340	*12341	12342
12343	†12344	*12345	12346	12347
†12348	*12349	12350	12351	12352
12353	12354	*12355	12356	12357
*12358	12359	*12360	†12361	12362
12363	*12364	*12365	*12367	12368
12370	*12371	12372	*12373	12374
*12375	12376	*12377	12378	*12379
12380				
12381	*12391	12393	12394	12396
†12397	*12398	12399	*12402	12403
12404	†12405	12406	12407	12408
12409	12410	12411	12412	12413
12415	*12416	12417	*12618	12619
*12620	*12621	12623	*12624	*12625
†12626	12627	*12629	*12630	*12631
*12633	*12634	12635	12636	12637
12638	12640	*12641	*12642	12643

1918-1920 OFFSET PRINTING

#528B 2¢ OFFSET Type VII Cont.

12644	12645	†12646	*12647	*12648
12649	12650	12651	12652	12653
12654	12655	†12656	12657	12658
12659	12660	12661	12662	12663
*12664	*12665	*12666	12667	12668
12669	12670	12671	12672	12673
12674	12675	12677	*12678	12679
12680	12682	12683	*12684	12685
12686	12687	*12688	*12689	12690
12691	12692	12693	12694	*12695
12696	12697	12698	12699	†12700
12701	12702	12703	*12704	*12705
12706	12707	12709	12710	12711
*12712	*12713	*12714	12715	12716
12717	12718	12719	*12720	*12721
*12722	12723	*12724	*12725	*12726
12727	12728	12729	*12730	†12731
*12732	12733	12734	*12735	12736
†12738	12739	12740	12741	12742
*12743	12744	*12745	12746	12747
12748	12749	*12750	12751	12752
*12754	12756	12758	*12762	12764
*12765	12767	12768	*12769	†12770
*12771	12772	*12773	12774	*12776
*12777	*12778	*12779	12780	12781
*12782	12785	*12786	*12789	*12790
*12791	12792	†12794	†12795	†12796
12797	12798	12799	12800	12801
12803	†12804	*12805	12806	12807
*12808	12809	12810	12811	12812
*12813	12814	12815	12816	*12817
12818	12819	12821	12822	12823
12824	12825	12826	12827	12828
12829	12830	*12831	12832	12833
12834	12835	*12840	*12841	*12843
*12844	12845	12846	12847	†12848
*12858	*12859	12860	12861	*12862
12863	*12864	12868	*12869	12870
*12871	12872	*12873	12874	12875
12876	12877	12879	12880	*12881
12882	12883	12884	12885	12886
12887	*12888	12889	12890	12891
12892	12893	12894	12895	12896
*12897	12898	12899	12900	*12903
12904	12905	*12907	*12908	*12909
12910	12911	*12912	12913	*12914
*12915	12916	12917	13018	13019
13020	*13021	13022	13023	*13024
13025	*13026	*13027	13028	*13029
13030	*13031	*13032	13033	*13034
*13035	*13037	*13038	*13039	*13040
*13041	13042	*13043	*13044	*13045
*13046	*13047	*13048	*13049	13050
*13051	13052	13053	*13054	*13055
*13056	*13057	13058	*13059	13060
13061	13062	*13063	*13064	13066
*13067	13069	13070	13071	13072
13073	13075	13076	13077	13078
*13079	13080	*13081	*13082	13083
13084	*13085	13086	*13087	*13088

#528B 2¢ OFFSET Type VII Cont.

13089	13090	13091	13092	13093
13095	13096	13097	13098	13099
13100	13101	13102	13103	13106
13107	13108	*13109	13110	13111
13112	*13113	*13114	13115	*13116
*13117	*13118	13119	*13120	*13121
13122	*13123	13124	13125	13126
13127	13128	13129	13130	13131
13132	13133	*13134	13136	13137
13139	13141	13142	*13143	*13145
*13157	13158	*13159	13160	13161
†13162	*13163	*13164		

#529 3¢ OFFSET Type III 127 Plates

Basic Price	T	$65
Basic Price	L, R, B	$60

*8370	8375	8379	*8380	8381
8382	8383	8384	8385	8411
8412	8413	*8414	8415	8417
8418	8420	8421	8554	8556
8557	8558	*8559	8560	8561
*8562	8563	*8564	*8565	8567
8568	8569	8572	8573	*8574
8578	8579	8580	8581	8582
*8583	8584	8585	*8586	8587
8588	*8589	*8590	*8591	8592
*8593	8596	8597	8598	*8599
8600	8601	8602	8604	8605
8606	*8607	8608	8609	8610
*8611	8612	*8613	8614	8615
8616	†8617	*8618	*8619	*8620
*8621	*8622	8625	8626	8627
8628	8629	8630	8631	8632
8633	8634	8635	8636	8637
8639	8640	8641	8642	8643
8644	8645	8646	*8647	8648
8649	8650	8651	8652	8653
8654	8655	8656	8657	8658
*8659	*8660	*8661	8662	8663
8664	8665	8666	8667	8668
8669	*8670	*8671	8672	8674
*8700	†8717			

#530 3¢ OFFSET Type IV 566 Plates

Basic Price	T	$12.50
Basic Price	L, R, B	$12.00

†8720	*8721	*8722	*8723	8724
†8725	8726	8728	*8730	8731
8732	8733	8734	8735	8736
8737	8738	8739	8740	8741
8742	8743	8744	8745	8746
8747	8748	8749	*8750	8751
8752	8754	8755	8756	8757
8759	8760	8761	8762	*8763
8764	8765	8766	8769	8772
8773	8774	8775	8776	*8777
8778	8779	8780	8781	8782
8784	8785	8786	8787	8788
8789	8790	8791	8792	8793
8794	8795	8796	8797	8798

1918-1920 OFFSET PRINTING

#530 3¢ OFFSET Type IV Cont.

8804 8805 8808 8809 8810
8811 8812 8813 †8814 8815
8816 8817 8818 8819 8820
8821 8824 8825 *8828 8829
8830 8831 8832 8833 8834
8835 8836 8837 8838 8839
8840 8841 8842 8844 8845
8846 8848 8852 8853 *8854
8855 *8856 *8857 8859 8860
8861 8862 *8863 8955 *8956

*8958 8959 8961 8962 8963
8965 8966 8967 8968 †8969
8970 8971 8972 8973 *8974
*8975 8976 8977 8978 8979
8980 8981 8982 8983 8985
*8986 8987 8988 *8989 8990
8991 8992 8995 8996 8997
8998 8999 9000 9001 9002
9003 9004 9005 9006 9007
9008 9009 9010 9011 9012

*9013 9014 *9015 9016 9017
9018 9019 9020 9021 9023
9024 *9026 9027 9028 9029
*9030 *9033 *9034 9035 9036
*9037 9038 *9039 *9042 *9044
*9045 9046 *9047 *9048 9050
*9051 9052 9055 9056 9057
9058 9059 9061 9062 9063
9064 *9065 9066 9069 *9071
9072 9073 9074 9075 9077

9078 9079 9080 *9081 9082
9083 9084 9085 9086 9087
9088 9089 9090 9091 9092
9093 9094 9251 9252 9253
9254 9255 9256 9263 9265
9268 9270 9274 9275 *9278
9279 9280 9281 9286 9287
9288 9289 9292 9293 9294
9295 9296 *9297 9298 9300
9301 9302 9303 9304 9305

9309 9310 9311 9312 9313
9314 9323 9324 9325 9326
9327 9330 9331 9332 9333
9334 *9335 9336 9337 9338
9339 *9340 9341 *9342 9343
9344 9346 9347 9348 9349
9350 9351 9352 9353 9354
9355 9356 9357 9358 9359
9360 9361 9362 9363 *9365
9366 *9367 9368 9369 9371

9372 9373 9374 9375 9376
9377 9378 9379 9380 *9381
9382 9383 9384 9385 9386
9388 9389 *9390 9391 *9392
9393 9394 *9395 9396 9398
9405 9406 *9407 9408 9482
9483 9484 *9485 9490 9491
9492 9493 9494 9495 9500
9501 9502 9503 9504 9505
9506 9507 9512 9513 9514
9529 9530 9531 9532 9533

#530 3¢ OFFSET Type IV Cont.

9534 9535 9536 9537 9538
9543 9544 9545 *9546 9547
*9548 9549 9550 9553 9554
9559 9561 9562 *9566 9572
9573 9574 9575 9576 9577
9578 9579 9580 9581 9583

9585 9586 9587 9588 9589
9590 9591 9592 9593 9594
9595 9596 9597 *9598 9599
9600 *9601 9602 9603 9604
*9605 *9606 *9607 9608 *9609
*9611 9612 9613 9614 9615
*9616 9617 9618 9619 9620
9621 *9622 *9623 9624 9625
9626 9627 9628 9629 9630
9631 9632 *9633 9634 9635

9636 *9637 9638 9639 9646
*9647 9648 9649 *9650 9651
9652 *9653 9654 9655 *9656
9657 9658 9659 *9660 9666
*9667 9668 9669 9670 *9671
9686 *9687 *9688 *9689 *9690
9691 9695 9696 9697 9704
9705 9706 9707 *9708 *9709
*9726 *9727 9728 9729 9730
9731 9732 9733 9784 *9785

9786 9799 *9800 9801 *9813
9814 9815 9816 9832 9845
9846 9847 9848 9849 *9850
9851 9852 9853 9854 9855
9856 9857 9858 9863 9864
9865 9866 9867 9868 9882
9883 9884 9885 9886 9887
9888 9889 9898 *9899 9900
*9901 9903 *9904 9905 9910
*9911 *9912 *9913 9922 9923

9924 9925 9926 *9927 9930
*9933

#531 1¢ OFFSET IMPERFORATE

22 Plates

Basic Price	T	$110
Basic Price	L, R, B	$100

9402 9509 9521 9523 9527
9540 9558 9789 *9808 9817
9818 9819 9828 *9830 †9840
*9906 *9920 9951 *9952 *9954
*9965 *9967

#532 2¢ OFFSET Type IV IMPERF.

7 Plates

Basic Price	T	$350
Basic Price	L, R, B	$300

10864 10881 *10892 10896 10915
10918 *10919

#533 2¢ OFFSET Type V IMPERF.

4 Plates

Basic Price	T	$2,000
Basic Price	L, R, B	$1,900

11260 11893 11895 11896

1918-1920 OFFSET PRINTING

#534 2¢ OFFSET Type Va IMPERF

33 Plates

Basic Price	T	$125
Basic Price	L, R, B	$115

11356	11373	11380	11384	11390
11403N	11410	11412	11414	11415
11422	11425	11428	11431	11433
11434N	11439	*11443	*11493	11853
11854	*11860	11862	11864	11865
11866	11887	*12002	12007	*12025
12028	12109	12119		

N O A M blocks are valued at .... $250.

#534A 2¢ OFFSET Type VI IMPERF

12 Plates

Basic Price	T	$425
Basic Price	L, R, B	$400

*11629	11641	11654	11667	11668
*11669	11673	11688	11696	*11699
11703	11710			

#534B 2¢ OFFSET Type VII IMPERF

8 Plates

Basic Price	T	$12,000
Basic Price	L, R, B	$11,000

12252	12274	12275	12280	12288
12305	*12778	12809		

#535 3¢ OFFSET Type IV IMPERF

29 Plates

Basic Price	T	$85
Basic Price	L, R, B	$75

8781	8787	8979	9004	9019
9023	9024	*9048	9050	*9055
9252	9255	9256	9323	9324
9331	9332	9333	9334	9384
9385	9386	9391	9393	9394
9408	*9637	9926	*9930	

#536 1¢ OFFSET Perf. 12½ 7 Plates

Basic Price	T	$200
Basic Price	L, R, B	$190

9985	9993	10001	10025	10032
10033	10052			

1919 COMMEMORATIVE

Unwatermarked Perf. 11
FLAT PRESS Block of 6

#537 3¢ VICTORY 16 Plates

		TL	TR	L	R	B
9412	$150	☐	☐	☐	☐	☐
9413	$150	☐	☐	☐	☐	☐
9414	$150	☐	☐	☐	☐	☐
9415	$150	☐	☐	☐	☐	☐
9416	$150	☐	☐	☐	☐	☐
9417	$150	☐	☐	☐	☐	☐
9418	$150	☐	☐	☐	☐	☐
9419	$150	☐	☐	☐	☐	☐
9426	$150	☐	☐	☐	☐	☐

1919 COMMEMORATIVES

#537 3¢ VICTORY Continued

		TL	TR	L	R	B
9427	$150	☐	☐	☐	☐	☐
9428	$150	☐	☐	☐	☐	☐
9429	$150	☐	☐	☐	☐	☐
9430	$150	☐	☐	☐	☐	☐
9431	$150	☐	☐	☐	☐	☐
9432	$150	☐	☐	☐	☐	☐
9433	$150	☐	☐	☐	☐	☐

1919 REGULAR ISSUE COIL WASTE

Please refer to Appendix D for description of marginal markings

Unwatermarked Perf. 11x10
ROTARY PRESS **Block of 4**

#538 1¢ WASHINGTON 86 Plates

Arrangement #10

Basic Price	T	$125

8336	8339	8340	9099	*9111
9112	9113	*9114	9141	9142
*9151	9152	*9450	*9451	9452
9453	*9463	9464	9467	9468
*10087	10090	10103	10104	10184
10185	10202	*10203	10347	10348
10350	*10361	*10640	*10641	*10643
*10686	10687	*10688	*10689	10690
10691	10692	10693	10694	10695
*11740	*11741	11742	11743	11764
*11765				
11766	*11767	13312	13313	13314
13315				

Arrangement #8

Basic Price	T	$125

13445	13446	13447	13448	13575
13576	13611	13612		

Arrangement #11

Basic Price	T	$125

*13810	*13811	*13812	13813	*13820
*13826	13827	*13856	13857	13872
13873	13896	13897	*13910	*13911
*13930	13942	*13943	13968	13976
14104				

1919 REGULAR ISSUE

COIL WASTE

#538a 1¢ WASHINGTON 2 Plates

N IMPERFORATE HORIZONTALLY

Arrangement #8

Basic Price T $700

13611 13612

#539 2¢ WASHINGTON 2 Plates

Arrangement #3 ***Blocks of 4***

Price T $12,500

*7462 *7463

#540 2¢ WASHINGTON 267 Plates

Arrangement #11

Basic Price T $125

*8171 *8172 8327 *8328 8329
8928 8939 8940 9103 9104
9105 9106 9153 9154 *9233
*9234 9235 9236 9237 *9458
*9465 9466 *9469 9470 *10097
*10098 *10115 *10116 *10175 *10176
*10177 *10178 *10183 *10295 *10296
*10297 *10306 *10307 *10308 *10315
*10316 10317 *10318 10384 *10386
*10387 10388 *10389 10444 10445
*10446 *10447 10448 10449 10450
10451 10452 10453 *10466 *10467
*10468 *10469 *10470 10471 10478
10479 10480 10485 10486 *10489
*10491 *10492 *10648 *10649 *10650
10651 10652 10670 10671 10680
10681 *10723 *10724 *10725 *10726
*10727 *10728 *10729 10730 10731
*10732 *10733 10738 10739 10740
10741 *11726 *11727 *11730 11731
11732 *11733 *11734 11735 11736
*11737 11769 *11770 *11771 *11772
*11798 *11799 *11800 *11808 *11809
*11810 *11811 *12464 *12465 *12466
12469 *12470 12471 12472 *12473
*12474 12475 12476 12483 12484
12485 12486 *12513 12514 12515
*12516 12517 *12518 12519 12520
*12529 12530 12531 12532 12601
12602 12603 12604 12918 12919

COIL WASTE

#540 2¢ WASHINGTON Continued

*12920 12921 12922 *12927 *12928
12929 *12970 *12971 *12972 *12973
13002 13004 13005 13239 13240
13253 13254 13286 *13287 *13288
*13289 *13290 13291 13292 *13293
*13294 13295 13386 13387 13388
13536 13537 13538 *13539

Arrangement #10 ***S 30 inverted***

Price T $650

10471

Arrangement #8

Basic Price T $125

13397 13398 13399 13400 *13414
*13418 *13511 *13512 *13514 *13583
*13584 13585 13586 13595 13596
13597 13598 13599 13600 13601
13602 13603 13604 *13647 *13648
13651 13652 *13657 *13658 13677
13678 13692 13693 13694 13695
*13718 13719 13720 *13721 13740
*13764

Arrangement #11

Basic Price T $125

13741 13742 13743 *13765 *13766
13767 *13777 *13778 *13779 13786
*13788 *13789 13802 *13803 *13807
*13809 *13814 13815 *13831 13840
*13938 13939 13958 *13959 13984
13985 14030 14031 *14032 *14033
14038 14039 *14040 14041 *14050
*14051 14052 14053 14054 14055
14056 14057

#540a 2¢ WASHINGTON

N IMPERFORATE HORIZONTALLY

Arrangement #8

Basic Price T $700

13740

Arrangement #11

Basic Price T $700

13741

N Do not confuse these with blocks imperforate only between top margin and stamps.

COIL WASTE (Cont.)

#541 3¢ WASHINGTON 20 Plates

Arrangement #8

Basic Price T $425

8454 8482 8483 8923 8924
8949 8950 8951 9107 9108
9109 9110 9133 9134 9135
9136 *9143 *9144 9145 9146

1920 REGULAR ISSUE

ROTARY PRESS PERF 10 x 11

Block of 6

#542 1¢ WASHINGTON 12 Plates

Side plate numbers only

Basic Price L, R $150

10151 10152 10436 10437 10439
10509 10510 10635 11738 11739
12467 12468

ROTARY PRESS PERF 10

#543 1¢ WASHINGTON 64 Plates

Block of 6

Side plate numbers only

Basic Price L, R $40

12467 12468 12495 12496 12597
12598 12599 12600 13284 13285
13352 13353 13354 13355 13419
13420 13522 13523 13573 13574
13609 13610 13613 13614 13649
13650 13675 13676

Block of 4

With corner plate numbers

Basic Price UL, UR, LL, LR $20

13744 13745 13762 13763 13784
13785 13790 13791 13858 13859
13876 13877 13890 13891 13892
13893 13908 13909 13937 13940
13941 13948 13949 13962 13963
13982 13983 13990 13991 14000
14001 14006 14007 14012 14013
14293

ROTARY PRESS PERF. 11

#544 1¢ WASHINGTON

No plate number ever reported.

1920 REGULAR ISSUE
COIL WASTE

(See Appendix D)

ROTARY PRESS PERF. 11

Top plate only **Block of 4**

#545 1¢ WASHINGTON 38 Plates

Arrangement #10

Basic Price T $1000

10090 *10640 *10686 10687 11764
*11765 11766 *11767 13314 13315

1920 REGULAR ISSUE
COIL WASTE

#545 1¢ WASHINGTON Continued

Arrangement #8

Basic Price T $1,000

13445 13446 *13447 *13448 13491
13492 13575 13576 13611 13612
*13615 13616

Arrangement #11

Basic Price T $1,000

*13812 13813 *13826 13827 13856
13857 13872 13873 13896 13897
13906 13907 13910 13931 13969
13976

#546 2¢ WASHINGTON 80 Plates

Arrangement #10

Basic Price T $750

10651 *10670 10671 *10750 *11726
*11727 *11730 11731 11732 *11734
*12465 *12466 12470 *12473 *12474
12483 12484 12485 12486 *12513
12514 12515 *12516 12517 *12518
12519 *12529 12918 12919 *12920
12922 12929 *13292 *13293 *13386
*13387 *13388

Arrangement #8

Basic Price T $750

*13397 *13398 *13508 *13511 *13512
13583 13584 13595 13596 *13647
*13648 13651 13652 *13657 *13658
13677 13678 13692 13693 13694
*13718 13719

Arrangement #11

Basic Price T $750

*13807 13814 13815 *13840 *13841
*13842 13843 13874 13875 *13894
*13895 *13938 13939 13958 13959
*13960 *13970 *13971 14031 *14040
14041

FLAT PRESS PERF 11

Position T only.

#547 $2 FRANKLIN

Price Block of 8 $7,500

Frame Plate 8177
Vignette Plate 8179

1920 COMMEMORATIVES

FLAT PRESS PERF 11
Plate Block of 6

#548 1¢ PILGRIM 12 Plates

		TL	TR	L	R	B
12418	$50	☐	☐	☐	☐	☐
12419	$50	☐	☐	☐	☐	☐
12420	$50	☐	☐	☐	☐	☐
12421	$50	☐	☐ N	☐	☐	☐
12428	$50	☐	☐ N	☐	☐	☐
12429	$50	☐	☐	☐	☐	☐
12431	$50	☐	☐	☐	☐	☐
12436	$50	☐	☐	☐	☐	☐
12437	$50	☐	☐	☐	☐	☐
12438	$50	☐	☐	☐	☐	☐
12439	$50	☐	☐	☐	☐	☐
12448	$50	☐	☐	☐	☐	☐

N The letter F is on the left bottom position and is inverted in relation to the plate number. The right bottom has only the plate number. The TR position has no letter F.

#549 2¢ PILGRIM 20 Plates

		TL	TR	L	R	B
12422	$75	☐	☐	☐	☐	☐
12423	$75	☐	☐	☐	☐	☐
12424	$75	☐	☐	☐	☐	☐
12425	$75	☐	☐	☐	☐	☐
12432	$75	☐	☐	☐	☐	☐
12433	$75	☐	☐	☐	☐	☐
12434	$75	☐	☐	☐	☐	☐
12435	$75	☐	☐	☐	☐	☐
12440	$75	☐	☐	☐	☐	☐

#549 2¢ PILGRIM Continued

		TL	TR	L	R	B
12441	$90	☐	☐	☐	☐	☐
12442	$90	☐	☐	☐	☐	☐
12443	$90	☐	☐	☐	☐	☐
12444	$90	☐	☐	☐	☐	☐
12445	$90	☐	☐	☐	☐	☐
12446	$90	☐	☐	☐	☐	☐
12447	$90	☐	☐	☐	☐	☐
12452	$90	☐	☐	☐	☐	☐
12453	$90	☐	☐	☐	☐	☐
12454	$90	☐	☐	☐	☐	☐
12455	$90	☐	☐	☐	☐	☐

#550 5¢ PILGRIM 2 Plates

12426	$700	☐	☐	☐	☐	☐
12427	$700	☐	☐	☐	☐	☐

1922-25 REGULAR ISSUE

FLAT PRESS PERF. 11
Plate Blocks of 6

#551 ½¢ NATHAN HALE 49 Plates

Basic Price **TL, TR, L, R, B** $6.50

17017	17018	17019	17020	17029
17030	17031	17032	17033	17034
17035	17036	17037	17038	17039
17040	17041	17042	17043	17044

1922-25 REGULAR ISSUE

#551 ½¢ NATHAN HALE Cont.

17045	17046	17047	17048	17049
17050	17051	17052	17054	17055
17056	17057	17058	17071	17072
17073	17074	17075	17076	17077
17078	17079	17080	17081	17082
17083	17084	17085	17086	

#552 1¢ FRANKLIN 255 Plates

Basic Price TL, TR, L, R, B $25

14157	14158	14159	14160	14191
14192	14193	14194	14215	14216
14217	14218	14243	14244	14245
14246	14254	14255	14256	14257
14281	14283	14284	*14975	*14976
14977	*14978	*15021	15022	15023
15024	*15043	15044	15045	15046
15047	15048	15049	15050	15069
15070	15071	15072	15073	15074
15075	15076	*15093	15094	15095
15096	15105	15106	15107	15108
15133	*15134	15135	15136	15143
15144	15145	15146	*15159	15160
15161	15162	15185	15186	15187
15188	15215	15216	15217	15218
15267	15268	15269	15270	15285
15286	15287	15288	15292	15293
*15294	15295	15296	*15297	15298
15299	*15300	*15301	*15302	15303
15310	*15311	*15312	15313	15314
*15315	15316	15317	15318	15319
15320	15321	15328	15329	15330
15331	15332	15333	15334	15335
15342	*15343	15344	15345	15358
15359	15360	15361	15366	15367
15368	15369	15372	15373	15374
*15375	15380	15381	15382	15383
15384	*15385	15386	15387	15398
15399	15400	15401	15408	15409
15410	15411	15420	15421	15422
15423	15429	15430	15431	15432
15437	15438	15439	15440	15453
15454	15455	15456	15489	15490
15491	15492	15584	15585	15586
15587	15953	15954	15955	15956
15979	15980	15981	15982	15983
15984	15985	15986	15987	15988
15989	15990	15991	*15992	*15993
15994	15995	15996	15997	15998
15999	16000	16001	16002	16003
16004	16005	16006	16007	16008
16009	16010	16017	16018	16019
16020	16023	16024	16025	16026
16027	16028	16029	16030	16031
16032	16033	16034	16035	16036
16037	16038	16041	16042	16043
16044	16049	16050	16051	16052
16055	16056	16057	16058	16061
16062	16556	16557	16558	16559
16560	16561	†16562	16563	16564
16565	16568	16569	16570	*16571

#553 1½¢ HARDING (PROFILE)

66 Plates

Basic Price TL, TR, L, R, B $40

16829	16830	16831	16832	16837
16838	16839	16840	16841	16842
16843	16844	16845	16846	16847
16848	16861	16862	16863	16864
16865	16866	16867	16868	16869
16870	16871	16872	16873	16874
16875	16876	16877	16878	16879
16880	16910	16911	16912	16913
16914	16915	16916	16917	16930
16931	*16932	16933	16934	16935
16936	*16937	16938	16939	16940
16941	*16968	16970	16971	16972
16973	16974	16975	16982	*16983
*16984				

#554 2¢ WASHINGTON 1363 Plates

Basic Price TL, TR, L, R, B $25

14074	14075	14076	14077	14082
14083	14084	14085	14086	14087
14088	14089	14090	14091	14092
14093	14100	14101	14102	14103
14105	14106	14107	14108	14113
14114	14115	14116	14119	14120
14121	14122	14127	14128	14129
14130	14139	14140	14141	14142
14143	14144	14145	14146	14151
14152	14153	14154	14161	14162
14163	14164	14165	14166	14167
14168	14177	14178	14179	14180
14185	14186	14187	14188	14195
14196	14197	14198	14211	14212
14213	14214	14225	14226	14227
14228	14258	14259	14260	14261
*14277	14278	14279	14280	14300
14301	14302	14303	14307	14308
14309	14310	14313	14314	14315
14316	14317	14318	14319	14320
14322	14323	14324	14325	14332
14333	14334	14335	14336	14337
14338	14339	14344	14345	14346
14347	14350	14351	14352	14353
14354	14355	14356	14357	14360
14361	14362	14363	14364	14365
14366	14367	14374	14375	14376
14377	14378	14379	14380	14381
14386	14387	14388	14389	14390
14391	14392	14393	14396	14397
14398	14399	14400	14401	14402
14403	14408	14409	14410	14411
14412	14413	14414	14415	14422
14423	14424	14425	14426	14427
14428	14429	14430	14431	14432
14433	14440	14441	14442	14443
14444	14445	14446	14447	14448
14449	14450	14451	14452	14453
14454	14455	14458	14459	14460
14461	14466	14467	14468	14469
14470	14471	14472	14473	14474

1922-25 REGULAR ISSUE

#554 2¢ WASHINGTON Continued

14475 14496 14497 14498 14500
14501 14502 14503 14504 14505
14506 14507 14508 14509 14510
14511 14518 14519 14520 14521
14522 14523 14524 14525 14529
14530 14531 14532 14533 14534
14535 14536 14539 14540 14541
14542 14543 14544 14545 14546
14555 *14556 14557 14558 14575

14576 14577 14578 14620 14621
14622 14623 14626 14627 14628
14629 14636 14637 14638 14639
14644 14645 14646 14647 14656
14657 14658 14668 14669 14670
14671 14672 14673 14674 14675
14676 14677 14678 14679 14684
14685 14686 14687 14688 14689
14690 14691 14692 14693 14694
14695 14696 14697 14698 14699

14700 14701 14702 14703 14708
14709 14710 14711 14712 14713
14714 14715 14716 14717 14718
14719 14722 14723 14724 14725
14726 14727 14729 14738 14739
14740 14741 14742 14743 14744
14745 14746 14747 14748 14749
14750 14751 14752 *14753 *14758
14759 14760 14761 14762 14763
14764 14765 14768 14769 14770

14771 14772 14773 14774 14775
14778 14779 14780 14781 14782
14783 14784 14785 14786 14787
14788 14789 14790 14791 14792
14793 14800 14801 14802 14803
14804 14805 14806 14807 14820
14821 14822 14823 14832 14833
14834 14835 14836 14837 14838
14839 14922 14923 14924 14925
15247 15248 15249 15250 15281

15282 15283 15284 15306 15307
15308 15309 *15324 15325 15326
15327 15336 15337 15338 15339
15354 15355 15356 15357 15362
15363 15364 15365 15376 15377
15378 15379 15388 15389 15390
15391 15394 15395 15396 *15397
15402 15403 15404 15405 15424
15425 15426 15427 †15433 15434
15435 15436 15445 15446 15447

15448 15457 *15458 15459 15460
15465 15466 15467 15468 15469
15470 15471 15472 15481 15482
15483 15484 15493 15494 15495
15496 15501 15502 15503 15504
15514 15515 15516 15517 15592
15593 15594 15595 15596 15597
15598 15599 15602 15603 15604
15605 15606 15607 15608 15609
15612 15613 15614 15615 15622

15623 15624 15625 15626 15627

#554 2¢ WASHINGTON Continued

15628 15629 15630 15631 15632
15633 15634 15635 15636 15637
15640 15641 15642 15643 15644
15645 15646 15647 15648 15649
15650 15651 15656 15657 15658
15659 15660 15661 15662 15663
15668 15669 15670 15671 15672
15673 15674 15675 15680 15681
15682 15683 15684 15685 15686

15687 15688 15689 15690 15691
15696 15697 15698 15699 15700
15701 *15702 15703 15708 15709
15710 15711 15712 15713 15714
15715 15716 15717 15718 15719
15726 15727 15728 15729 15736
15737 15738 15739 15748 15749
15750 15751 15770 15771 15772
15773 15812 15813 15814 15815
15816 15817 15818 15819 15834

15835 15836 15837 15842 15843
15844 15845 15850 15851 15852
15853 15864 15865 15866 15867
15872 15873 15874 15875 15878
15879 15880 15881 15882 15883
15884 15885 15896 15897 15898
15899 15904 15905 15906 15907
15912 15913 15914 15915 15932
15933 15934 15935 15969 15970
15971 15972 16095 16096 16097

16098 16099 16100 16101 16102
16103 16104 16105 16106 16111
16112 16113 16114 16115 16116
16117 16118 16123 16124 16125
16126 *16127 16128 16129 16130
16131 16132 16133 16134 16140
16141 16142 16143 16148 16149
16150 16151 *16152 16153 *16154
16155 16157 *16158 16159 16160
16165 16166 16167 16168 16179

16180 16181 16182 16183 16184
16185 16186 16187 16188 16189
16190 16197 16198 16199 16200
16205 16206 16207 16208 16221
16222 16223 16224 16225 16226
16227 16228 16231 16232 16233
16234 16235 16236 16237 16238
16239 16240 16241 16242 16253
16254 16255 16256 16258 16259
16260 16261 16266 16267 16268

16269 16272 16273 16274 16275
16280 16281 16282 16283 16292
16293 16294 16295 16296 16297
16298 16299 16314 16315 16316
16317 16322 16323 16324 16325
16343 16344 16345 16346 16347
16348 16349 16350 16351 16352
16353 16354 16371 16372 16373
16374 16383 16384 16385 16386
16407 16408 16409 16410 16417

16418 16419 16420 16427 16428

1922-25 REGULAR ISSUE

#554 2¢ WASHINGTON Continued

16429	16430	16431	16432	16433
16434	16439	16440	16441	16442
16487	16488	16489	16490	16491
16492	16493	16494	16497	16498
16499	16500	16501	16502	16503
16504	16505	16506	16507	16508
16518	16519	16520	16521	16526
16527	16528	16529	16530	16531
16532	16533	16534	16535	16536
16537	16538	16539	16540	16541
16546	16547	16548	16549	16550
16551	16552	16553	16580	16581
16582	16583	16630	16631	16632
16633	16634	16635	16636	16637
16638	16639	16640	16641	16642
16643	16644	16645	16650	16651
16652	16653	16656	16657	16658
16659	16697	16698	16699	16700
16713	16714	16715	16716	16717
16718	16719	16720	16721	16722
16723	16724	*16737	*16738	16739
16740	16741	16742	16743	16744
16745	16746	16747	16748	16753
16754	16755	16756	16757	16758
16759	*16760	16761	16762	16763
16764	16785	16786	16787	16788
*16789	16790	16791	16792	17107
17108	17109	17110	17111	17112
17113	17114	17115	17116	17117
17118	17119	17120	17121	17122
17123	17124	17125	17126	17147
17148	17149	17150	17151	17152
17153	17154	17163	17164	17165
17166	17179	17180	17181	17182
17187	17188	17189	17190	17195
17196	17197	17198	17207	*17209
17210	17215	17216	17217	17218
17219	17220	17221	17222	17243
17244	17245	17246	17255	17256
17257	17258	17263	17264	17265
17266	17267	17268	17269	17270
17286	17287	17288	17289	17292
17293	17294	17295	17296	17297
17298	17299	17300	17301	17302
17303	17308	17309	17310	17311
17312	17313	17314	17315	17317
17318	17319	17320	17325	17326
17327	17328	17329	17330	17331
17332	17333	17334	17335	17336
17337	*17338	17339	17340	17341
17342	17343	17344	17345	17346
17347	17348	17349	17350	17351
17352	17357	*17358	17359	17360
17361	17362	17363	17364	17367
17368	17369	17370	17371	17372
17373	17374	17375	*17376	17377
17378	17380	17381	17382	17383
17384	17385	17386	17387	17388
*17389	*17390	*17391	*17392	17393
*17394	*17395	17396	*17397	*17398

#554 2¢ WASHINGTON Continued

*17399	17402	*17403	*17404	*17405
17489	17490	17491	17492	17534
17535	17536	17537	*17538	17539
*17540	17541	*17550	17551	17552
17553	17554	17555	17556	17557
17576	17577	17578	17579	17580
17581	*17582	17583	17592	17593
*17594	17595	*17596	*17597	17598
*17599	17602	17603	*17604	*17605
*17606	17607	17608	17609	17629
17630	17631	17632	17645	17646
*17647	17648	17654	17655	17656
17657	17658	*17659	17660	17661
17666	17667	17668	17669	17670
17671	17672	17673	17676	*17677
17678	17679	17687	17688	17689
17690	17695	17696	17697	17698
17699	17700	17701	17702	17705
17706	17707	17708	17709	17710
17711	17712	17717	17718	17719
17720	17721	17722	17723	17724
17726	17727	17728	17730	17731
17732	17733	17734	17735	17736
17737	17740	17741	17742	17743
17744	17745	17746	17747	17748
17749	17750	17751	17752	17753
*17754	17755	*17756	*17757	17758
*17759	17764	17765	17766	17767
17768	*17769	17770	*17771	17778
17779	17780	17781	17782	*17783
17784	17785	17788	17789	17790
17791	17794	17795	17796	17797
17802	17803	17804	17805	17808
17809	17810	17811	17812	17813
17814	17815	17818	17819	17820
17821	17828	17829	17830	17831
17834	17835	17836	17837	17838
17839	17840	17841	17842	17843
17844	17845	17848	17849	17850
17851	17860	17861	17862	17863
17864	17865	17866	17867	17868
17869	17870	17871	17874	17875
17876	17877	17890	17891	17892
17893	17894	17895	17896	17897
18167	18168	18169	18170	18175
18176	18177	18178	18197	18198
18199	18200	18203	18204	18205
18206	18207	18208	18209	*18210
18211	18212	18213	18214	18215
18216	18217	18218	18219	*18220
*18221	18222	18223	18224	18225
18226	18227	18228		

Star Plates

In 1925 flat plate stamps were issued with a slightly wider vertical spacing between the designs. Most of these plates were marked with a star beside the top or right side plate number of the upper right pane.

1922-25 REGULAR ISSUE

#554 2¢ WASHINGTON Continued

Star Plates

Small five pointed star at left of top plate number of upper right pane.

Price TR $250

16758

Six pointed star at left of top plate number of upper right pane.

Basic Price TR $375

16741 16761 16787 17107 17109
17117 17124 17179 17187 17188
17190

Six pointed star below side plate number of upper right pane.

Price RS $1,000

17196

Large five pointed star at left of top plate number of upper right pane.

Basic Price TR $300

16763 16764 16785 16786 16790
16791 16792 17108 17110 17112
17113 17114 17115 17116 17119
17120 17121 17122 17123 17125
17126 17147 17148 17149 17150
17151 17152 17153 17154 17163
17164 17165 17166 17180 17181
17182 17195 17198

Large five pointed star below side plate number of upper right pane.

Basic Price RS $50

16788 17189 17197 17207 *17209
17210 17215 17216 17217 17218
17219 17220 17221 17222 17243
17244 17245 17246 17255 17256
17257 17258 17263 17264 17265
17266 17267 17268 17269 17270
17286 17287 17288 17289 17292
17293 17294 17295 17296 17297
17298 17299 17300 17301 17302
17303 17308 17309 17310 17311

17312 17313 17314 17315 17317
17318 17319 17320 17325 17326
17327 17328 17329 17330 17331
17332 17333 17334 17335 17336

#554 2¢ WASHINGTON Continued

Star Plates

17337 *17338 17339 17340 17341
17342 17343 17344 17345 17346
17347 17348 17349 17350 17351
17352 17357 *17358 17359 17360
17361 17362 17363 17364 17367
17368 17369 17370 17371 17372

17373 17374 17375 *17376 17377
17378 17380 17381 17382 17383
17384 17385 17386 17387 17388
*17389 *17390 *17391 *17392 17393
*17394 *17395 17396 *17397 *17398
*17399 17402 *17403 *17404 *17405
17489 17490 17491 17492 17534
17535 17536 17537 *17538 17539
*17540 17541 *17550 17551 17552
17553 17554 17555 17556 17557

17576 17577 17578 17579 17580
17581 *17582 17583 17592 17593
*17594 17595 *17596 *17597 17598
*17599 17602 17603 *17604 *17605
*17606 17607 17608 17609 17629
17630 17631 17632 17645 17646
*17647 17648 17654 17655 17656
17657 17658 *17659 17660 17661
17666 17667 17668 17669 17670
17671 17672 17673 17676 *17677

17678 17679 17687 17688 17689
17690 17695 17696 17697 17698
17699 17700 17701 17702 17705
17706 17707 17708 17709 17710
17711 17712 17717 17718 17719
17720 17721 17722 17723 17724
17726 17727 17728 17730 17731
17732 17733 17734 17735 17736
17737 17740 17741 17742 17743
17744 17745 17746 17747 17748

17749 17750 17751 17752 17753
*17754 17755 *17756 *17757 17758
*17759 17764 17765 17766 17767
17768 *17769 17770 *17771 17778
17779 17780 17781 17782 *17783
17784 17785 17788 17789 17790
17791 17794 17795 17796 17797
17802 17803 17804 17805 17808
17809 17810 17811 17812 17813
17814 17815 17818 17819 17820

17821 17828 17829 17830 17831
17834 17835 17836 17837 17838
17839 17840 17841 17842 17843
17844 17845 17848 17849 17850
17851 17860 17861 17862 17863
17864 17865 17866 17867 17868
17869 17870 17871 17874 17875
17876 17877 17890 17891 17892
17893 17894 17895 17896 17897
18167 18168 18169 18170 18175

18176 18177 18178 18197 18198
18199 18200 18203 18204 18205
18206 18207 18208 18209 *18210

1922-25 REGULAR ISSUE

#554 2¢ WASHINGTON Continued

Star Plates

18211	18212	18213	18214	18215
18216	18217	18218	18219	*18220
*18221	18222	18223	18224	18225
18226	18227	18228		

#555 3¢ LINCOLN 44 Plates

Basic Price TL, TR, L, R, B $200

14296	14297	14298	14299	14734
14735	14736	14737	15171	15172
15173	15174	15550	15551	15552
15553	15725	16399	16400	16401
16402	16473	16474	16475	16476
16666	16667	16668	16669	16709
16710	16711	16712	16769	16770
*17921	17922	17923	17924	17925
18120	18121	*18122	18123	

#556 4¢ MARTHA WASHINGTON

36 Plates

Basic Price TL, TR, L, R, B $225

14094	14095	14096	14097	14796
14797	14798	14799	15085	15086
15087	15088	15219	15220	15221
15222	15251	15252	15253	15254
15526	15527	15528	15529	16211
16212	16213	16214	16335	16336
16337	16338	16367	16368	*16369
16370				

#557 5¢ THEODORE ROOSEVELT

75 Plates

Basic Price TL, TR, L, R, B $250

14066	14067	14068	14069	14078
14079	14080	14081	14285	14286
14287	14288	*14549	14550	*14551
14552	14565	14566	14567	14568
14602	14603	14604	14605	14848
14849	14850	14851	14880	*14881
14882	14883	14916	14917	14918
14919	14930	14931	14932	14933

#557 5¢ THEODORE ROOSEVELT Continued

15147	15148	15149	15150	15203
15204	15205	15206	15227	15228
15229	15230	15544	15545	15546
15547	15568	15569	15570	15571
15952	16330	16331	16332	16333
16363	16364	16365	16366	16391
*16392	16393	16394	*18035	*18060

#557a 5¢ THEODORE ROOSEVELT

IMPERFORATE

Only one sheet known. Now broken and bottom plate block realized $6,500 at auction in April 1983.

15568

#558 6¢ GARFIELD 22 Plates

Basic Price TL, TR, L, R, B $450

14169	14170	14171	14172	14962
14963	14694	14973	15892	15893
15894	15895	16045	16046	16047
16048	16243	16334	16469	16470
16471	16472			

#559 7¢ McKINLEY 61 Plates

Basic Price TL, TR, L, R, B $95

14584	14585	*14586	14587	*14812
*14813	14814	14815	14950	*14951
14952	14953	15181	15182	15183
15184	15211	15212	15213	15214
15271	15272	15273	15274	*15794
16135	16136	16137	16138	16139
*16156	16247	*16248	*16249	*16250
*16251	16252	16453	16454	16455
16456	16662	16663	16664	16665
17452	17453	17454	17455	17621
*17622	17623	17624	18116	18117
18118	18119	18163	*18164	*18165
*18166				

#560 8¢ GRANT 54 Plates

Basic Price TL, TR, L, R, B $700

14569	14570	14571	14572	15223
*15224	15225	15226	15263	15264
15265	15266	15477	15478	15479
15480	*15946	15947	15948	15949
*16011	16012	16013	16014	16169
16170	16171	16172	16175	16176
16177	*16178	16215	16216	16217
16218	16449	16450	16451	16452
16701	16702	16703	16704	16765
16768	16795	*16796	17467	17916
17917	17918	17919	17920	

Star Plate

Price —

*16796 Two TL plate singles reported

1922-25 REGULAR ISSUE

#561 9¢ JEFFERSON 16 Plates

Basic Price TL, TR, L, R, B $200

14239	14240	14241	14242	15235
15236	15237	15238	15259	15260
15261	15262	17521	*17522	*17523
*17524				

#562 10¢ MONROE 103 Plates

Basic Price TL, TR, L, R, B $325

14229	14230	14231	14232	14233
14234	14235	14236	14492	14493
14494	14495	14580	*14581	14582
14583	14606	14607	14608	14609
14610	14611	14612	14613	14808
14809	14810	*14811	14816	14817
14818	14819	14844	14845	14846
*14847	15199	*15125	*15126	15127
15128	15200	15201	15202	15275
15276	15277	15278	*15346	15347
15348	15349	15509	*15510	*15511
*15512	*15513	15554	15555	15556
15557	15734	15735	15924	15925
15926	15927	15940	15941	15942
15943	16069	16070	16071	*16072
16075	16076	16077	16078	16355
16356	16357	16358	16359	16360
16361	16362	16375	16376	16377
16378	16379	16380	16381	16382
16387	16388	16389	16390	*17468
*17469	*18033	*18034		

#562a 10¢ MONROE

IMPERFORATE

Price

14818 Only Lower Left Reported.

#563 11¢ HAYES 28 Plates

Basic Price TL, TR, L, R, B $35

14058	14059	14060	14061	15798
15799	15800	15801	16445	16446
16447	16448	17414	17415	17416
17417	17456	17457	17458	17459

#563 11¢ HAYES Continued

17617	17618	17619	17620	19135
19136	19137	19138		

#564 12¢ CLEVELAND 35 Plates

Basic Price TL, TR, L, R, B $90

14404	14405	14406	14407	15350
15351	15352	15692	15693	15694
15695	16257	16404	16405	16406
16515	17418	17419	17420	17421
17470	17471	17472	18031	18032
18398	18399	18424	18921	18922
18923	19161	19162	19163	19442

Star Plates

Large five pointed star below side plate number of upper right pane.

Basic Price RS $165

17418	17419	17420	18398

Six pointed star below side plate number of upper right pane.

Price RS $350

17421

#565 14¢ AMERICAN INDIAN

20 Plates

Basic Price TL, TR, L, R, B $70

14512	14513	14514	14515	14526
15795	15796	15797	16625	17464
17465	17466	19417	19418	19419
19420	19438	19439	19440	19441

#566 15¢ STATUE OF LIBERTY

41 Plates

Basic Price TL, TR, L, R, B $300

14070	14071	14072	14073	14910
14911	14912	14913	17422	17423
17424	17425	17430	17431	17432
17433	17460	17461	17462	17463
17525	17526	17527	17528	*17529
17931	17932	17933	17934	18928

1922-25 REGULAR ISSUE

#566 15¢ STATUE OF LIBERTY Cont.

18929 18930 19139 19140 19141
19142 19462 *19463

The following have no side plate numbers.

*20180 *20181 *20182

Star Plates

Large five pointed star below side plate number of upper right pane.

Basic Price RS $475

17422 17423 17424 17425 17430
17431 17432 17433

#567 20¢ GOLDEN GATE 76 Plates

Basic Price TL, TR, L, R, B $300

14559 14560 14561 14562 14966
14967 14968 14969 15536 15537
15538 15539 15572 15573 15574
15575 16646 16647 16648 *16649
17227 17228 17229 17230 17426
17427 17428 17429 17530 17531
17532 17533 17682 17683 17684
17685 17686 18377 18668 18669
18670 18671 18672 18673 18674
18675 18688 18689 18690 18691
18925 18926 18927 19131 19132
19133 19134 19468 19646 19647
19648 19649 19872 20033 20034
20037 20038

The following have no side plate numbers.

*17725 20195 20196 20197 20198
*20271 *20272 *20273 *20274

Star Plates

Large five pointed star below side plate number of upper right pane.

Basic Price RS $700

17227 17228 17229 17230 17426
17427 17428 17429 18668 18669
18670 18671 18672 18673 18674
18675 18688 18689 18690 18691

#568 25¢ NIAGARA FALLS 12 Plates

Basic Price TL, TR, L, R, B $250

14062 14063 14064 14065 16626
16627 16628 16629 17442 17443
17444 17445

#569 30¢ BISON 24 Plates

Basic Price TL, TR, L, R, B $450

14436 14437 14438 14439 16065
16066 16067 16068 16465 16466
16467 16468 17446 17447 17448
17449 17558 17559 17560 17561

The following have no side plate numbers

20191 20192 *20193 *20194

#570 50¢ AMPHITHEATRE 16 Plates

Basic Price TL, TR, L, R, B $800

14042 14043 14044 14045 15151
15152 15153 15154 17479 17480
17481 17482 19143 19144 19145
19146

#571 $1 LINCOLN MEMORIAL 5 Plates

Basic Price TL, TR, B $500

14268 18642 18680 18681 18682

#572 $2 U.S. CAPITOL 1 Plate

Price TL, TR, B $1,250

14306

#573 $5 AMERICA 1 Combination

Price T Block of 8 $3,250

Frame Plate 14327
Vignette Plate 14326

1922-25 REGULAR ISSUE

BOOKLET PANES

FLAT PRESS PERF. 11

BOOKLET PANES OF 6

#552a 1¢ FRANKLIN 20 Plates

Top plate number only

Basic Price T $8.50

14221	14222	14223	14224	14250
14251	14252	14253	14269	14270
14271	14272	15961	15962	15963
15964	15965	15966	15967	15968

#554c 2¢ WASHINGTON 194 Plates

Top plate number only

Basic Price T $11

14181	14182	14183	14184	14199
14200	14201	14202	14207	14208
*14209	14210	14418	14419	14420
14421	14462	14463	14464	14465
14476	14477	14478	14479	14480
14481	14482	14483	14484	14485
14486	14487	14488	14489	14490
14491	14934	14935	14937	14974
14983	14984	14985	14986	15255
15256	15257	15258	15289	15414
15415	15416	15417	15505	15506
15507	15508	15522	*15523	15524
15525	15558	*15559	*15560	*15561
15576	15577	15578	15579	*15724
*15730	*15731	*15732	15733	15790
15791	15792	*15793	*15804	*15805
15806	15807	16085	*16086	16087
16088	16146	16147	16193	16194
16195	16196	16288	16290	16291
16306	16307	16308	16309	16318
16319	16320	16321	16326	16327
16328	16329	16592	16593	16594
16595	16600	16601	16602	16603
16613	16614	16615	*16616	16617
16618	16619	*16620	*16621	*16622
16623	16624	16705	*16706	16707
16708	16773	*16774	16775	16776
17475	17476	17477	17478	17483
17484	17485	17486	*17494	17495
17496	*17497	17880	17881	17882
*17883	17886	17887	*17888	17889
*17910	17911	*17912	17913	17927
17928	17929	17930	*17941	*17942
*17943	*17944	17951	17952	*17953
*17954	*17955	17956	17957	*17958
18259	*18260	*18261	18262	*18297
18298	18299	18300	18373	18374
*18383	*18384	18385	*18386	18400
*18401	*18408	*18409	*18521	

IMPERFORATE

FLAT PRESS **Blocks of 6**

#575 1¢ FRANKLIN 47 Plates

Basic Price **TL, TR, L, R, B** $100

14157	14158	14159	14160	14217
14244	14245	15045	15069	15106
15136	15146	15268	15269	15328
15331	15344	15366	15372	15385
15398	15399	15400	15401	15408
*15410	15422	15432	15440	15456
15489	15490	15954	15991	16043
16049	16050	16061	16062	16556
16557	16558	16559	16560	16561
16568	16569			

#576 1½¢ HARDING (PROFILE)

40 Plates

Basic Price **TL, TR, L, R, B** $35

16829	16830	16831	16832	16837
16838	16839	*16840	*16841	16842
16843	16845	16846	*16847	16848
16861	16862	16863	16864	16865
16866	16867	16868	16869	16870
16872	16873	16911	16917	*16932
*16933	16936	16938	16939	16940
16971	16972	16973	16974	16982

#577 2¢ WASHINGTON 117 Plates

Basic Price **TL, TR, L, R, B** $30

14091	14093	14177	14178	14179
14180	14195	14196	14197	14198
14323	14325	14332	14334	14449
14455	14536	14555	14577	*14691
14759	14760	14761	14763	14764
14771	14781	14788	14820	14821
14822	14823	15640	*15642	15686
15690	15699	15739	15835	15836
15843	15881	15970	15971	16096
16097	16098	16099	*16101	16104
16105	16130	16151	16190	16208
16235	16520	16580	16645	16651
16714	16722	16724	16739	16743
16755	17122	17222	*17357	17490
17492	17608	17671	*17677	17679
17696	*17701	17706	17708	17709
17710	17721	17724	17727	17728
17731	17740	17741	17742	17743
17745	17746	17747	17748	17874
17875	17876	17877	17891	18197
18198	18199	18200	18206	18207
18208	18217	18219	*18220	*18221
18222	18223	18224	18225	18226
18227	18228			

1922-25 REGULAR ISSUE

#577 2¢ WASHINGTON Continued

STAR PLATES

Large five pointed star below side plate number of upper right pane.

Basic Price RS $75

17222	17490	17492	17608	17671
*17677	17679	17696	17706	17708
17709	17710	17721	17724	17727
17728	17731	17740	17741	17742
17743	17745	17746	17747	17748
17874	17875	17876	17877	17891
18197	18198	18199	18200	18206
18207	18208	18217	18219	*18220
*18221	18222	18223	18224	18225
18226	18227	18228		

1923-26 REGULAR ISSUE

COIL WASTE

ROTARY PRESS PERF. 11 x 10

Blocks of 4

#578 1¢ FRANKLIN 24 Plates

Arrangement #11 ***(See Appendix D)***

Basic Price T $200

14563	14564	14573	14574	14588
14589	14590	14591	14600	14601
14618	14619	14633	14661	15290
15291	15304	15323	15370	15428
15721	15723	15743	15810	

#579 2¢ WASHINGTON 181 Plates

Arrangement #11 ***(See Appendix D)***

Basic Price T $100

14098	14099	14109	14110	14111
14112	14117	14118	14123	14124
14125	14126	14131	14132	14133
14134	14135	14136	14138	14147
14148	14149	14150	14173	14174
14175	14176	14203	14204	14219
14220	14237	14238	14247	14248
14249	14266	14267	14289	14290
14291	14292	14304	14305	14311
14312	14340	14341	14342	14343

COIL WASTE (Cont.)

#579 2¢ WASHINGTON Continued

14358	14359	14368	14369	14372
14373	14384	14385	14416	14417
14434	14435	14456	14457	14517
14537	14538	14547	14548	14553
14554	14664	14665	14666	14667
14680	14681	14682	14683	14704
14705	14706	14707	14730	14731
14732	14733	14754	14755	14756
14757	14766	14767	14776	14777
14794	14795	14864	14865	14914
14915	14920	14921	14926	14927
14928	14929	14944	14945	14958
14959	14970	14971	14979	14980
15003	15004	15015	15016	15033
15034	15051	15052	15142	15392
15393	15419	15441	15449	15451
15461	15462	15463	15464	15473
15474	15475	15476	15485	15486
15487	15488	15497	15498	15499
15500	15531	15532	15533	15540
15542	15564	15566	15567	15580
15582	15583	15588	15589	15600
15601	15616	15619	15639	15664
15667	15840	15841	15847	15848
15849	15868	15869	15888	15889
15890	15891	15910	15919	15920
15921				

1923-26 REGULAR ISSUE

ROTARY PRESS PERF. 10

Blocks of 4

#581 1¢ FRANKLIN 56 Plates

Basic Price **UL, UR, LL, LR** $125

14205	14206	14348	14349	14370
14371	*14382	*14383	14394	14395
*14527	14528	14624	14625	*14630
*14631	14642	*14643	14651	*14652
*14653	14662	14663	*14960	14961
*14981	14982	15548	15549	15652
*15653	*15655	*15944	*15945	15950
*15951	*15957	*15958	*15959	*15960
15977	*15978	16173	16174	*16191
16192	*16201	*16209	*16210	*16751
*16752	16811	16812	18730	18731
18732				

#582 1½¢ HARDING (PROFILE)

37 Plates

Basic Price **UL, UR, LL, LR** $42.50

16825	*16826	*16849	16850	16851
16852	16885	16886	16887	*16888
16905	*16906	*16948	*16949	*16950
16951	17008	*17022	*17023	*17024
*17487	*17488	*18235	18357	18358
18359	18360	18412	18413	*18482
*18483	18488	18489	*18693	*18699
18701	18702			

1923-26 REGULAR ISSUE

ROTARY PRESS PERF. 10

#583 2¢ WASHINGTON 283 Plates

Basic Price		UL, UR, LL, LR		$30
*15412	15413	*15518	15519	15534
15535	*15562	*15563	15610	15611
*15620	15621	15764	15765	15802
15803	15820	15821	15822	15823
15900	15901	15902	*15903	*16262
*16263	16270	16271	16286	16287
*16304	*16305	*16413	*16414	*16415
*16416	*16463	16464	*16749	*16750
17273	17274	†17284	*17285	17305
17321	*17322	*17365	17366	17400
17401	17473	17474	17498	*17499
17500	*17501	*17507	17508	*17856
*17857	17914	17915	17935	17936
17949	17950	17959	17960	17965
17966	17969	17970	17971	17972
17977	17978	17979	17980	17993
17994	18005	18006	18007	18008
18009	18010	18011	18012	18042
18043	18044	18045	18056	18057
18061	18062	18063	18064	18065
18066	18092	18093	18094	18095
†18124	†18125	18139	18140	18161
18162	18231	18232	18233	18234
18240	18241	18242	18243	18251
18252	*18273	*18274	18283	18284
18289	18290	18295	18296	*18301
18302	*18317	*18318	18329	*18330
18337	18338	18343	18344	*18351
*18352	18355	*18356	*18363	*18364
18368	18369	18517	*18518	18519
18520	*18525	*18526	18527	18528
18529	18530	18531	*18534	18535
18537	18548	*18549	18584	*18585
18586	18587	18588	18589	18590
18591	18592	18593	18602	18603
18604	18605	18610	18611	18616
18617	18620	18621	18628	18629
18630	18631	18632	18633	18654
18655	18656	18657	18658	*18659
18660	18661	18763	18764	18779
18780	18781	18782	18783	18784
18787	18788	18795	18796	18797
18798	18801	18802	18809	*18810
18811	18812	18813	18814	18815
*18816	18826	18827	18828	18829
18834	18835	18836	18837	*18852
18853	*18856	18857	18858	18859
18862	18863	18864	18865	18868
18869	18870	18871	18872	18873
18874	18875	18876	18877	*18878
*18879	*18880	*18881	18882	18883
18884	18885	18886	18887	18888
18889	18895	*18896	18901	18902
18931	18932	18933	18934	18935
18936	18937	18939	18940	18941
18943	*18944	18945	18946	*18947
*18948	*18951	*18952		

#584 3¢ LINCOLN 22 Plates

Basic Price		UL, UR, LL, LR		$275
*17155	*17156	17161	*17162	*17511
*17512	*17568	*17569	17616	17653
17898	17899	*17900	*17901	18114
18115	18379	18380	18439	18440
18445	18446			

#585 4¢ MARTHA WASHINGTON 13 Plates

Basic Price		UL, UR, LL, LR		$200
16079	16080	16660	16661	17436
17437	17739	17760	17761	17989
17990	*18083	18365		

#586 5¢ THEODORE ROOSEVELT 36 Plates

Basic Price		UL, UR, LL, LR		$175
*16089	16090	16495	16566	*16567
16608	16654	16670	16671	17493
17519	17520	17586	17587	*17651
*17652	17762	17763	17772	17773
18157	18158	18159	18160	18394
18395	18418	18419	18441	18442
18459	18460	*18789	*18790	*18850
*18854				

#587 6¢ GARFIELD 10 Plates

Basic Price		UL, UR, LL, LR		$75
16083	16084	*17584	*17585	17588
17589	17967	17968	18036	18421

#588 7¢ McKINLEY 8 Plates

Basic Price		UL, UR, LL, LR		$115
17786	*17787	17798	17799	18179
18180	18195	18196		

#589 8¢ GRANT 8 Plates

Basic Price		UL, UR, LL, LR		$300
17816	17817	*17832	*17833	18189
18190	18775	18777		

#590 9¢ JEFFERSON 4 Plates

Basic Price		UL, UR, LL, LR		$65
17854	17855	18193	18194	

#591 10¢ MONROE 28 Plates

Basic Price		UL, UR, LL, LR		$675
16107	16108	*17440	17441	17590
17591	17614	17615	17649	*17650
17693	17694	18135	18136	*18137
18138	18387	18388	18414	18415
*18532	18533	18538	18539	18614
18615	18622	18623		

1923-26 REGULAR ISSUE

BOOKLET PANES

ROTARY PRESS PERF. 10
BOOKLET PANES OF 6

#583a 2¢ WASHINGTON 15 Plates

Basic Price UL, LL $100

*17450	*17451	*18550	*18551	*18662
*18663	†18695	†18696	*18697	*18698
*18705	*18706	*18707	*18708	*18710

COIL WASTE

ROTARY PRESS PERF. 11
Blocks of 4

#594 1¢ FRANKLIN

No plate number reported to date.

COIL WASTE

ROTARY PRESS PERF. 11
Blocks of 4

#595 2¢ WASHINGTON 95 Plates

Arrangement #11 ***(See Appendix D)***
Basic Price T $300

14098	14099	14109	14110	14111
14112	14117	14118	14123	14124
14125	14126	14131	14132	14133
14134	14135	14136	14138	14147
14148	14149	14150	14173	14174
14175	14176	14203	14204	14219
14220	14237	14238	14247	14248
14249	14266	14267	14289	14290
14291	14292	14304	14305	14311
14340	14341	14343	14358	14359
14368	14369	14372	14373	14384
14416	14417	14434	14435	14456
14457	14517	14538	14547	14548
14553	14554	14664	14665	14666
14667	14680	14681	14682	14683
14704	14705	14706	14707	14730
14731	14733	14754	14756	14766
14767	14776	14794	14795	14864
14914	14915	14920	14921	14926

1923-29 REGULAR ISSUE

SIDE COIL PLATES

ROTARY PRESS
PERF. 10 VERTICALLY

#597 1¢ FRANKLIN 104 Plates

Top plate number only

14563	14564	14573	14574	14588
14589	14590	14591	14600	14601
14618	14619	14633	14640	†14641
14648	14649	14654	†14655	†14660
14661	15290	15291	15304	†15322
15323	†15340	15341	15370	†15371
15428	15676	15677	15678	15679
15704	15705	†15706	†15707	15720
15721	15722	15723	15741	15742
15743	15774	15775	15776	15777
†15808	15809	15810	15811	†15973
†15975	†15976	†16015	†16022	†16039
16053	†16054	†16063	16064	16074
16081	16082	†16109	†16110	16777
†16779	16780	16827	†19356	19581
19582	19583	19584		

With top and bottom plate numbers

19756	19757	19758	19759	19860
19861	19862	19863	19864	19865
19868	19869	19870	19871	20043
20044	20045	20046	20051	20052
20073	20074	20093	20094	20102
20103				

#598 1½¢ HARDING (PROFILE)

Top plate number only **62 Plates**

16828	16853	†16854	16855	16856
16881	16882	†16883	16884	16907
16908	16909	16942	16943	16944
†16945	16946	16947	16976	16977
16994	†16995	16996	16997	†16998
16999	17025	17026	17067	17068
†17069	18478	18479	18492	†18513
†18514	18515	18516	18643	18644
18645	18713	18714	18715	†18759
18760	†18761	18762	†18817	18818
18821	18822	18823	18824	19320
19321	19322	19323	19324	19325
19326	19327			

#599 2¢ WASHINGTON (DIE 1)

Top plate number only **686 Plates**

14098	14099	14109	14110	14111
14112	14117	14118	14123	14124
14125	14126	14131	14132	14133
14134	14135	14136	14138	14147
14148	14149	14150	14173	14174
14175	14176	14203	14204	14219
14220	14237	14238	14247	14248
14249	14266	14267	14289	14290
14291	14292	14304	14305	14311
14312	14340	14341	14342	14343
14358	14359	14368	14369	14372

1923-26 REGULAR ISSUE SIDE COIL PLATES

ROTARY PRESS PERF. 10 VERTICALLY

#599 2¢ WASHINGTON (DIE 1) Continued

Top plate number only

14373 14384 14385 14416 14417
14434 14435 14456 14457 14517
14537 14538 14547 14548 14553
14554 14664 14665 14666 14667
14680 14681 14682 14683 14704
14705 14706 14707 14730 14731
14732 14733 14754 14755 14756
14757 14766 14767 14776 14777
14794 14795 14864 14865 14914

14915 14920 14921 14926 14927
14928 14929 14944 14945 14958
14959 14970 14971 14979 †14980
15003 15004 15015 15016 15033
15034 15051 15052 †15141 15142
15392 15393 †15406 †15407 †15418
15419 15441 †15442 †15443 †15444
15449 †15450 15451 15461 15462
15463 15464 15473 15474 15475
15476 15485 15486 15487 15488

15497 15498 15499 15500 15521
15530 15531 15532 15533 15540
†15541 15542 †15543 15564 †15565
15566 15567 15580 †15581 15582
15583 15588 15589 †15590 15591
15600 15601 15616 †15617 †15618
15619 †15638 15639 15664 †15665
†15666 15667 †15824 †15825 15826
15827 †15838 †15839 15840 15841
†15846 15847 15848 15849 15868

15869 †15870 15871 15888 15889
15890 15891 †15908 †15909 15910
†15911 †15916 15917 †15918 15919
15920 15921 15922 15923 †15928
†15929 †15930 †15931 †15936 †15937
†15938 †15939 †16161 †16162 16163
†16164 †16203 †16204 †16219 †16220
16230 †16264 †16265 †16284 †16285
16300 16301 16302 16303 16395
†16396 †16397 16398 16411 16412

16421 †16422 †16423 †16424 †16435
†16436 †16437 16438 †16457 †16458
†16459 †16460 †16461 †16462 †16479
†16480 †16481 †16482 †16483 16484
†16485 †16486 †16509 †16510 †16511
†16512 †16513 16514 †16516 †16517
†16522 †16523 †16524 †16525 †16542
†16543 †16544 †16545 †16676 16677
16682 †16683 †16684 †16685 †16695
†16696 16725 †16726 16727 †16728

†16729 †16730 †16731 16732 16733
†16734 16735 †16736 †16809 †16810
16821 †16822 16823 †17271 †17272
†17275 †17276 †17277 †17278 †17279
†17280 †17281 †17282 †17283 †17290
†17291 †17306 †17307 †17316 †17323
†17324 †17502 †17503 †17504 †17505
†17510 †17517 †17518 †17562 †17563

#599 2¢ WASHINGTON (DIE 1) Continued

Top plate number only

†17563 †17574 †17575 †17600 †17601
17633 17634 †17635 †17636 †17662

†17663 †17664 †17665 †17674 †17675
†17691 17692 †17703 †17713 17714
†17715 17716 †17774 †17775 †17776
†17777 17792 †17800 †17801 †17806
†17807 17822 †17823 †17824 †17825
†17826 †17827 †17846 †17847 17852
17853 17858 †17859 17872 †17873
†17878 †17879 †17902 17903 †17904

†17905 †17973 †17974 17975 †17976
†17981 †17982 †17985 17986 17987
17988 †17991 17992 17995 †17996
17997 17998 †17999 18000 18001
18002 18004 18013 †18014 †18015
†18016 18017 †18018 18019 18020
†18040 †18041 †18046 18047 †18048
†18049 †18050 †18051 †18052 †18053
†18055 †18067 18068 †18069 18070
†18071 18072 †18073 †18074 †18075

18076 †18077 †18078 18088 18089
†18090 18091 †18100 †18101 †18102
†18103 18104 18105 †18128 †18129
18141 18142 †18147 †18148 18171
18172 †18173 †18174 18244 18245
18253 †18254 †18271 18272 18291
†18292 †18293 18294 †18303 18304
18305 †18306 †18315 18316 †18324
†18339 18340 18341 18342 †18353
†18354 †18366 18367 18392 †18393

18402 18403 18404 †18405 18416
18417 18426 †18427 †18447 †18448
19049 19050 19051 †19052 19090
19091 19092 19093 19102 19103
†19177 †19178 †19179 †19180 †19219
19220 19223 †19224 19229 19230
19231 19306 19307 19308 19309
19310 19311 19312 19313 †19367
19368 19369 19370 †19386 19387
19388 19389 19394 19395 19396

19397 †19450 19451 19460 19461
†19471 19472 19473 19474 19483
19484 †19485 19486 †19491 †19492
19499 19512 †19513 19514 19515
†19516 19517 †19524 †19533 19534
†19535 †19536 19539 19540

With top and bottom plate numbers

19752 19753 19754 19755 19765
19766 19767 19768 19769 19770
19771 19772 19773 19774 19814
19815 19816 †19817 19818 19819
19820 19821 19822 19823 19833
19836 19837 19842 19843 19885
19886 19887 19888 19889 19890
19891 19892 19893 19894 19899

1923-26 REGULAR ISSUE

ROTARY PRESS
PERF. 10 VERTICALLY

#599 2¢ WASHINGTON (DIE 1) Cont.

19900 19901 19902 19909 19910
19913 19914 19917 19918 19923
19924 19939 19940 19960 19961
19970 19971 19974 19975 19982
19983 19984 19985 19992 19993
19996 19997 20002 20003 20006
20007 20017 20018 20021 20022
20023 20024 20118 20119 20120
20121 20122 20123 20166 20167
20176 20177 20183 20184 20199
20200 20207 20208 20223 20224
20301 20302 20315 20316 20329
20330 20339 20349 20350 20353
20354 20363 20777 20778 20779
20780 20785 20786 20787 20788
20797 20798 20799

#599A 2¢ WASHINGTON (DIE II)

Top plate number only **9 Plates**

†19682 †19683 †19684 19685 19686

With top and bottom plate numbers

19748 19749 19750 †19751

Joint line pairs or strips showing plate number 19748 or plate number 19515 may be the combination type I and type II pieces.

#600 3¢ LINCOLN 20 Plates

Top plate number only

14720 †14721 †16425 16426 †17434
†17435 17906 †17907 17908 †17909
18799 18800 18807 18808 18838
18839 18840 18841

With top and bottom plate numbers.

20376 20377

#601 4¢ MARTHA WASHINGTON

Top plate number only **8 Plates**

14189 14190 14294 14321 17937
17938 17939 17940

#602 5¢ THEODORE ROOSEVELT

Top plate number only **10 Plates**

15279 †15280 16443 16444 16477
16478 17945 17946 17947 17948

6¢ GARFIELD

See #723 page 104

#603 10¢ MONROE 9 Plates

Top plate number only

†16339 †16340 16341 16342 17610
17961 17962 †17963 17964

END COIL PLATES

ROTARY PRESS
PERF. 10 HORIZONTALLY

#604 1¢ FRANKLIN 8 Plates

Position L only.

15179 15180 15239 15240

Position L, R

20355 20356 20357 20358

#605 1½¢ HARDING (PROFILE)

Position R only. **2 Plates**

†17027 †17028

#606 2¢ WASHINGTON (DIE I)

Position L only. **18 Plates**

†14155 †14156 15193 15194 15243
†15244 18755 18756 18757 18758
19287 19289

Position R only. **6 Plates**

15245 15246 17570 †17571 17572
†17573

1923 COMMEMORATIVES

FLAT PRESS PERF. 11

#610 2¢ HARDING 166 Plates

		TL	TR	L	R	B
14852	$30	☐	☐	☐	☐	☐
14853	$30	☐	☐	☐	☐	☐
14854	$30	☐	☐	☐	☐	☐
14855	$30	☐	☐	☐	☐	☐
14856	$30	☐	☐	☐	☐	☐
14857	$30	☐	☐	☐	☐	☐
14858	$30	☐	☐	☐	☐	☐
14859	$30	☐	☐	☐	☐	☐
14860	$30	☐	☐	☐	☐	☐
14861	$30	☐	☐	☐	☐	☐
14862	$30	☐	☐	☐	☐	☐
14863	$30	☐	☐	☐	☐	☐
14868	$30	☐	☐	☐	☐	☐
14869	$30	☐	☐	☐	☐	☐
14870	$30	☐	☐	☐	☐	☐
14871	$30	☐	☐	☐	☐	☐
14872	$30	☐	☐	☐	☐	☐
14873	$30	☐	☐	☐	☐	☐
14874	$30	☐	☐	☐	☐	☐
14875	$30	☐	☐	☐	☐	☐
14876	$30	☐	☐	☐	☐	☐
14877	$30	☐	☐	☐	☐	☐
14878	$30	☐	☐	☐	☐	☐
14879	$30	☐	☐	☐	☐	☐
14884	$30	☐	☐	☐	☐	☐
14885	$30	☐	☐	☐	☐	☐
14886	$30	☐	☐	☐	☐	☐
14887	$30	☐	☐	☐	☐	☐
14888	$30	☐	☐	☐	☐	☐
14889	$30	☐	☐	☐	☐	☐

1923 COMMEMORATIVES

#610 2¢ HARDING Continued

Plate	Price	TL	TR	L	R	B
14890	$30	☐	☐	☐	☐	☐
14891	$30	☐	☐	☐	☐	☐
14892	$30	☐	☐	☐	☐	☐
14893	$30	☐	☐	☐	☐	☐
14894	$30	☐	☐	☐	☐	☐
14895	$30	☐	☐	☐	☐	☐
14896	$30	☐	☐	☐	☐	☐
14897	$30	☐	☐	☐	☐	☐
14898	$30	☐	☐	☐	☐	☐
14899	$30	☐	☐	☐	☐	☐
14902	$30	☐	☐	☐	☐	☐
14903	$30	☐	☐	☐	☐	☐
14904	$30	☐	☐	☐	☐	☐
14905	$30	☐	☐	☐	☐	☐
14906	$30	☐	☐	☐	☐	☐
14907	$30	☐	☐	☐	☐	☐
14908	$30	☐	☐	☐	☐	☐
14909	$30	☐	☐	☐	☐	☐
14940	$30	☐	☐	☐	☐	☐
14941	$30	☐	☐	☐	☐	☐
14942	$30	☐	☐	☐	☐	☐
14943	$30	☐	☐	☐	☐	☐
14946	$30	☐	☐	☐	☐	☐
14947	$30	☐	☐	☐	☐	☐
14948	$30	☐	☐	☐	☐	☐
14949	$30	☐	☐	☐	☐	☐
14954	$30	☐	☐	☐	☐	☐
14955	$30	☐	☐	☐	☐	☐
14956	$30	☐	☐	☐	☐	☐
14972	$30	☐	☐	☐	☐	☐
14987	$30	☐	☐	☐	☐	☐
14988	$30	☐	☐	☐	☐	☐
14989	$30	☐	☐	☐	☐	☐
14990	$30	☐	☐	☐	☐	☐
14991	$30	☐	☐	☐	☐	☐
14992	$30	☐	☐	☐	☐	☐
14993	$30	☐	☐	☐	☐	☐
14994	$30	☐	☐	☐	☐	☐
14997	$30	☐	☐	☐	☐	☐
14998	$30	☐	☐	☐	☐	☐
14999	$40	☐	☐	☐	☐	☐
15000	$50	☐	☐	☐	☐	☐
15005	$30	☐	☐	☐	☐	☐
15006	$40	☐	☐	☐	☐	☐
15007	$35	☐	☐	☐	☐	☐
15008	$30	☐	☐	☐	☐	☐
15009	$30	☐	☐	☐	☐	☐
15010	$50	☐	☐	☐	☐	☐
15011	$60	☐	☐	☐	☐	☐
15012	$30	☐	☐	☐	☐	☐
15017	$60	☐	☐	☐	☐	☐
15018	$30	☐	☐	☐	☐	☐
15019	$30	☐	☐	☐	☐	☐
15020	$40	☐	☐	☐	☐	☐
15025	$30	☐	☐	☐	☐	☐
15026	$30	☐	☐	☐	☐	☐
15027	$30	☐	☐	☐	☐	☐
15028	$30	☐	☐	☐	☐	☐
15029	$50	☐	☐	☐	☐	☐
15030	$35	☐	☐	☐	☐	☐

#610 2¢ HARDING Continued

Plate	Price	TL	TR	L	R	B
15031	$40	☐	☐	☐	☐	☐
15032	$30	☐	☐	☐	☐	☐
15035	$30	☐	☐	☐	☐	☐
15036	$30	☐	☐	☐	☐	☐
15037	$30	☐	☐	☐	☐	☐
15038	$30	☐	☐	☐	☐	☐
15039	$30	☐	☐	☐	☐	☐
15040	$30	☐	☐	☐	☐	☐
15041	$60	☐	☐	☐	☐	☐
15042	$30	☐	☐	☐	☐	☐
15053	$30	☐	☐	☐	☐	☐
15054	$40	☐	☐	☐	☐	☐
15055	$30	☐	☐	☐	☐	☐
15056	$30	☐	☐	☐	☐	☐
15057	$30	☐	☐	☐	☐	☐
15058	$30	☐	☐	☐	☐	☐
15059	$35	☐	☐	☐	☐	☐
15060	$40	☐	☐	☐	☐	☐
15061	$30	☐	☐	☐	☐	☐
15062	$30	☐	☐	☐	☐	☐
15063	$30	☐	☐	☐	☐	☐
15064	$35	☐	☐	☐	☐	☐
15065	$30	☐	☐	☐	☐	☐
15066	$30	☐	☐	☐	☐	☐
15067	$30	☐	☐	☐	☐	☐
15068	$40	☐	☐	☐	☐	☐
15077	$30	☐	☐	☐	☐	☐
15078	$30	☐	☐	☐	☐	☐
15079	$30	☐	☐	☐	☐	☐
15080	$30	☐	☐	☐	☐	☐
15081	$30	☐	☐	☐	☐	☐
15082	$30	☐	☐	☐	☐	☐
15083	$30	☐	☐	☐	☐	☐
15084	$30	☐	☐	☐	☐	☐
15089	$30	☐	☐	☐	☐	☐
15090	$30	☐	☐	☐	☐	☐
15091	$30	☐	☐	☐	☐	☐
15092	$30	☐	☐	☐	☐	☐
15097	$30	☐	☐	☐	☐	☐
15098	$30	☐	☐	☐	☐	☐
15099	$30	☐	☐	☐	☐	☐
15100	$30	☐	☐	☐	☐	☐
15109	$30	☐	☐	☐	☐	☐
15110	$30	☐	☐	☐	☐	☐
15111	$30	☐	☐	☐	☐	☐
15112	$30	☐	☐	☐	☐	☐
15113	$30	☐	☐	☐	☐	☐
15114	$30	☐	☐	☐	☐	☐
15115	$40	☐	☐	☐	☐	☐
15116	$30	☐	☐	☐	☐	☐
15117	$30	☐	☐	☐	☐	☐
15118	$30	☐	☐	☐	☐	☐
15119	$30	☐	☐	☐	☐	☐
15120	$30	☐	☐	☐	☐	☐
15121	$30	☐	☐	☐	☐	☐
15122	$30	☐	☐	☐	☐	☐
15129	$30	☐	☐	☐	☐	☐
15130	$30	☐	☐	☐	☐	☐
15131	$30	☐	☐	☐	☐	☐
15132	$30	☐	☐	☐	☐	☐

1923 COMMEMORATIVES

#610 2¢ HARDING Continued

		TL	TR	L	R	B
15137	$30	☐	☐	☐	☐	☐
15138	$30	☐	☐	☐	☐	☐
15139	$30	☐	☐	☐	☐	☐
15155	$30	☐	☐	☐	☐	☐
15156	$30	☐	☐	☐	☐	☐
15157	$30	☐	☐	☐	☐	☐
15158	$30	☐	☐	☐	☐	☐
15163	$30	☐	☐	☐	☐	☐
15164	$30	☐	☐	☐	☐	☐
15165	$50	☐	☐	☐	☐	☐
15167	$40	☐	☐	☐	☐	☐
15177	$30	☐	☐	☐	☐	☐
15178	$50	☐	☐	☐	☐	☐
15191	$40	☐	☐	☐	☐	☐
15192	$60	☐	☐	☐	☐	☐
15195	$100	☐	☐	☐	☐	☐

Plate 15195 is considered the scarcest number. In our experience, it is rare.

IMPERFORATE ERROR

Tentative valuation $5,000

Plate 14870 **Position TL, L**

This plate was never used for the #611 Imperforate printings. A single Upper Left pane of the imperforate error was discovered in an otherwise normal package of **perforated** sheets **before** the stamp was **issued** in **imperforate** form. Therefore the pane was a #610 unperforated error. Through the later release of the regularly issued imperforates, the plain copies in the error pane lost their identity.

#611 2¢ HARDING 6 Plates

FLAT PRESS IMPERFORATE

		TL	TR	L	R	B
15019	$50	☐	☐	☐	☐	☐
15025	$50	☐	☐	☐	☐	☐
15027	$50	☐	☐	☐	☐	☐
15028	$50	☐	☐	☐	☐	☐
15054	$2,200	☐	☐	☐	☐	☐
15059	$1,350	†	†	☐	☐	☐

(See 14870 under #610)

#612 2¢ HARDING 8 Plates

ROTARY PRESS PERF 10

This is a poorly centered issue. The basic price is for reasonably fine condition.

		UL	UR	LL	LR
14866	$350	☐	☐	☐	☐
14867	$350	☐	☐	☐	☐
14900	$350	☐	☐	☐	☐
14901	$350	☐	☐	☐	☐
14938	$350	☐	☐	☐	☐
14939	$350	☐	☐	☐	☐
14995	$350	☐	☐	☐	☐
14996	$350	☐	☐	☐	☐

1924 COMMEMORATIVES

FLAT PRESS PERF. 11

#614 1¢ HUGUENOT-WALLOON

12 Plates

		TL	TR	L	R	B
15756	$50	☐	☐	☐	☐	☐
15757	$50	☐	☐	☐	☐	☐
15758	$50	☐	☐	☐	☐	☐
15759	$50	☐	☐	☐	☐	☐
15778	$50	☐	☐	☐	☐	☐
15779	$50	☐	☐	☐	☐	☐
15780	$50	☐	☐	☐	☐	☐
15781	$50	☐	☐	☐	☐	☐
15782	$50	☐	☐	☐	☐	☐
15783	$50	☐	☐	☐	☐	☐
15784	$50	☐	☐	☐	☐	☐
15785	$50	☐	☐	☐	☐	☐

1924 COMMEMORATIVES

#615 2¢ HUGUENOT-WALLOON

16 Plates

Plate	Price	TL	TR	L	R	B
15744	$85	☐	☐	☐	☐	☐
15745	$85	☐	☐	☐	☐	☐
15746	$85	☐	☐	☐	☐	☐
15747	$85	☐	☐	☐	☐	☐
15760	$85	☐	☐	☐	☐	☐
15761	$85	☐	☐	☐	☐	☐
15762	$85	☐	☐	☐	☐	☐
15763	$85	☐	☐	☐	☐	☐
15766	$85	☐	☐	☐	☐	☐
15767	$85	☐	☐	☐	☐	☐
15768	$85	☐	☐	☐	☐	☐
15769	$85	☐	☐	☐	☐	☐
15786	$85	☐	☐	☐	☐	☐
15787	$85	☐	☐	☐	☐	☐
15788	$85	☐	☐	☐	☐	☐
15789	$85	☐	☐	☐	☐	☐

#616 5¢ HUGUENOT-WALLOON

4 Plates

Plate	Price	TL	TR	L	R	B
15752	$450	☐	☐	☐	☐	☐
15753	$450	☐	☐	☐	☐	☐
15754	$450	☐	☐	☐	☐	☐
15755	$450	☐	☐	☐	☐	☐

TR plate blocks of 15754 contain three examples of the "broken-circle" variety and are considered worth about 20% more than normal blocks.

1925 COMMEMORATIVES

#617 1¢ LEXINGTON-CONCORD

4 Plates

Plate	Price	TL	TR	L	R	B
16797	$50	☐	☐	☐	☐	☐
16798	$50	☐	☐	☐	☐	☐
16799	$50	☐	☐	☐	☐	☐
16800	$50	☐	☐	☐	☐	☐

#618 2¢ LEXINGTON-CONCORD

8 Plates

Plate	Price	TL	TR	L	R	B
16801	$95	☐	☐	☐	☐	☐
16803	$95	☐	☐	☐	☐	☐
16804	$95	☐	☐	☐	☐	☐
16813	$95	☐	☐	☐	☐	☐
16814	$95	☐	☐	☐	☐	☐
16815	$95	☐	☐	☐	☐	☐
16816	$95	☐	☐	☐	☐	☐
17004	$95	☐	☐	☐	☐	☐

#619 5¢ LEXINGTON-CONCORD

4 Plates

Plate	Price	TL	TR	L	R	B
16805	$400	☐	☐	☐	☐	☐
16806	$400	☐	☐	☐	☐	☐
16807	$400	☐	☐	☐	☐	☐
16808	$400	☐	☐	☐	☐	☐

1925 COMMEMORATIVES

BICOLORED

#620 2¢ NORSE-AMERICAN

Blocks of 8, with Arrow and Plate-Number combination. *Top only* —

Basic Price $200

4 Frame Plates \ 8 Vignette Plates	16687	16688	16689	16960	17353	17355	17356	17379
16694					*		*	
16924								
16958						*		
16959								

All 32 Number combinations exist

#621 5¢ NORSE-AMERICAN

Blocks of 8, with Arrow and Plate-Number combination. *Top only* —

Basic Price $750

4 Frame Plates \ 4 Vignette Plates	16927	16928	16929	16957
16925				
16926				
16961				
16963				*

All 16 Number combinations exist

1925-26 REGULAR ISSUE

FLAT PRESS PERF 11

#622 13¢ HARRISON 15 Plates

Basic Price TL, TR, L, R, B $210

18106	18107	18108	18109N	18110
18111	18112	18113N	18924	19104
19105	19119	19120	19121	19122

N 18109 and 18113 are "Star" plates. On these plates there is a large 5-pointed star below the plate number on right plate blocks from upper-right panes. The star was not entered in any other position. Value *$1,700.*

#623 17¢ WILSON 8 Plates

Basic Price TL, TR, L, R, B $250

18021	18022	18023	18024	18025
18026	18027	18028		

1926 COMMEMORATIVES

#627 2¢ SESQUICENTENNIAL EXPO (LIBERTY BELL) 60 Plates

		TL	TR	L	R	B
18540	$50	☐	☐	☐	☐	☐
18541	$50	☐	☐	☐	☐	☐
18542	$50	☐	☐	☐	☐	☐
18543	$50	☐	☐	☐	☐	☐
18544	$50	☐	☐	☐	☐	☐
18545	$50	☐	☐	☐	☐	☐
18546	$50	☐	☐	☐	☐	☐
18547	$50	☐	☐	☐	☐	☐
18552	$50	☐	☐	☐	☐	☐
18553	$50	☐	☐	☐	☐	☐
18554	$50	☐	☐	☐	☐	☐
18555	$50	☐	☐	☐	☐	☐
18556	$50	☐	☐	☐	☐	☐
18557	$50	☐	☐	☐	☐	☐
18558	$50	☐	☐	☐	☐	☐
18559	$50	☐	☐	☐	☐	☐
18560	$50	☐	☐	☐	☐	☐
18561	$50	☐	☐	☐	☐	☐
18562	$50	☐	☐	☐	☐	☐
18563	$50	☐	☐	☐	☐	☐
18564	$50	☐	☐	☐	☐	☐
18565	$50	☐	☐	☐	☐	☐
18566	$50	☐	☐	☐	☐	☐
18567	$50	☐	☐	☐	☐	☐
18568	$50	☐	☐	☐	☐	☐
18569	$50	☐	☐	☐	☐	☐
18570	$50	☐	☐	☐	☐	☐
18571	$50	☐	☐	☐	☐	☐
18572	$50	☐	☐	☐	☐	☐
18573	$50	☐	☐	☐	☐	☐
18574	$50	☐	☐	☐	☐	☐
18575	$50	☐	☐	☐	☐	☐
18576	$50	☐	☐	☐	☐	☐
18577	$50	☐	☐	☐	☐	☐
18578	$50	☐	☐	☐	☐	☐
18579	$50	☐	☐	☐	☐	☐
18580	$50	☐	☐	☐	☐	☐
18581	$50	☐	☐	☐	☐	☐
18582	$50	☐	☐	☐	☐	☐
18583	$50	☐	☐	☐	☐	☐
18634	$50	☐	☐	☐	☐	☐
18635	$50	☐	☐	☐	☐	☐
18636	$50	☐	☐	☐	☐	☐
18637	$50	☐	☐	☐	☐	☐
18638	$50	☐	☐	☐	☐	☐
18639	$50	☐	☐	☐	☐	☐
18640	$50	☐	☐	☐	☐	☐
18641	$50	☐	☐	☐	☐	☐
18646	$50	☐	☐	☐	☐	☐
18647	$50	☐	☐	☐	☐	☐
18648	$50	☐	☐	☐	☐	☐
18649	$50	☐	☐	☐	☐	☐
18650	$50	☐	☐	☐	☐	☐
18651	$50	☐	☐	☐	☐	☐
18652	$50	☐	☐	☐	☐	☐
18653	$50	☐	☐	☐	☐	☐
18664	$50	☐	☐	☐	☐	☐
18665	$50	☐	☐	☐	☐	☐
18666	$50	☐	☐	☐	☐	☐
18667	$50	☐	☐	☐	☐	☐

1926 COMMEMORATIVES

#628 5¢ ERICSSON MEMORIAL

12 Plates

		TL	TR	L	R	B
18595	$110	☐	☐	☐	☐	☐
18597	$110	☐	☐	☐	☐	☐
18598	$110	☐	☐	☐	☐	☐
18599	$110	☐	☐	☐	☐	☐
18600	$110	☐	☐	☐	☐	☐
18601	$110	☐	☐	☐	☐	☐
18606	$110	☐	☐	☐	☐	☐
18607	$110	☐	☐	☐	☐	☐
18608	$110	☐	☐	☐	☐	☐
18609	$110	☐	☐	☐	☐	☐
18612	$110	☐	☐	☐	☐	☐
18613	$110	☐	☐	☐	☐	☐

#629 2¢ WHITE PLAINS 5 Plates

		TL	TR	L	R	B
18765	$60	☐	☐	☐	☐	☐
18766	$60	☐	☐	☐	☐	☐
18767	$60	☐	☐	☐	☐	☐
18768	$60	☐	☐	☐	☐	☐
18769	$60	☐	☐	☐	☐	☐

#630 2¢ WHITE PLAINS SOUVENIR SHEET

Each pane has the plate number at top, left, right and bottom. The positions listed below are for panes of 25.

		UL	UR	LL	LR
18770	$500	☐	☐	☐	☐
18771	$500	☐	☐	☐	☐
18773	$500	☐	☐	☐	☐
18774	$500	☐	☐	☐	☐

1926-29 REGULAR ISSUE

Condition and centering are very important factors in the valuation of the scarce plate numbers of this issue. These were produced during the Depression years and this may account for the small supply of well centered plate number blocks that are available. *Plate number singles are more plentiful and some of the better plates are available in quantity as plate singles.*

ROTARY PRESS IMPERFORATE

#631 1½¢ HARDING (PROFILE)

2 Plates

		UL	UR	LL	LR
18360	$70	☐	☐	☐	☐
18413	$70	☐	☐	☐	☐

ROTARY PRESS PERF. 11 x 10½

#653 ½¢ NATHAN HALE 12 Plates

		UL	UR	LL	LR
19650	$1.25	☐	☐	☐	☐
19651	$1.25	☐	☐	☐	☐
19652	$1.25	☐	☐	☐	☐
19653	$1.25	☐	☐	☐	☐

1926-29 REGULAR ISSUE

#653 ½¢ NATHAN HALE Continued

		UL	UR	LL	LR
20370	$1.25	☐	☐	☐	☐
20371	$1.25	☐	☐	☐	☐
20408	$1.25	☐	☐	☐	☐
20409	$1.25	☐	☐	☐	☐
20922	$1.25	☐	☐	☐	☐
20923	$1.25	☐	☐	☐	☐
20924	$1.25	☐	☐	☐	☐
20925	$1.25	☐	☐	☐	☐

#632 1¢ FRANKLIN 133 Plates

		UL	UR	LL	LR
15549	$2.50	☐	☐	☐	☐
16811	$6.00	☐	☐	☐	☐
16812	$2.50	☐	☐	☐	☐
18730	$2.50	☐	☐	☐	☐
18731	$3.00	☐	☐$_{2}$	☐	☐
18732	$2.50	☐	☐	☐	☐
18955	$2.50	☐	☐	☐	☐
18956	$2.50	☐	☐	☐	☐
18957	$2.50	☐	☐	☐	☐
18958	$2.50	☐	☐	☐	☐
19215	$3.00	☐	☐$_{2}$	☐	☐$_{2}$
19216	$2.50	☐	☐	☐	☐
19217	$3.00	☐	☐$_{2}$	☐	☐
19218	$6.00	☐	☐	☐	☐
19264	$30.00	☐	☐	☐	☐
19265	$2.50	☐	☐	☐	☐
19266	$3.00	☐$_{2}$	☐	☐$_{2}$	☐$_{2}$
19267	$3.00	☐$_{2}$	☐	☐$_{2}$	☐
19300	$7.00	☐	☐	☐	☐
19301	$12.00	☐	☐	☐	☐
19302	$12.00	☐	☐	☐	☐
19303	$6.00	☐	☐	☐	☐
19336	$2.50	☐	☐	☐	☐
19337	$3.00	☐$_{2}$	☐	☐	☐$_{2}$
19338	$2.50	☐	☐	☐	☐
19339	$2.50	☐	☐	☐	☐
19537	$3.00	☐$_{2}$	☐$_{2}$	☐	☐$_{2}$
19538	$2.50	☐	☐	☐	☐
19593	$4.00	☐$_{2}$	☐	☐	☐$_{2}$
19594	$2.50	☐	☐	☐	☐
19595	$2.50	☐	☐	☐	☐
19596	$2.50	☐	☐	☐	☐
19601	$2.50	☐	☐	☐	☐
19602	$2.50	☐	☐	☐	☐
19603	$2.50	☐	☐	☐	☐

#632 1¢ FRANKLIN Continued

		UL	UR	LL	LR
19604	$50.00	☐	☐	☐	☐
19852	$2.50	☐	☐	☐	☐
19853	$2.50	☐	☐	☐	☐
19854	$2.50	☐	☐	☐	☐
19855	$2.50	☐	☐	☐	☐
19873	$2.50	☐	☐	☐	☐
19874	$2.50	☐	☐	☐	☐
19875	$2.50	☐	☐	☐	☐
19876	$2.50	☐	☐	☐	☐
20027	$3.00	☐	☐	☐$_{2}$	☐$_{2}$
20028	$3.00	☐	☐	☐$_{2}$	☐$_{2}$
20029	$2.50	☐	☐	☐	☐
20030	$2.50	☐	☐	☐	☐
20031	$2.50	☐	☐	☐	☐
20032	$2.50	☐	☐	☐	☐
20039	$2.50	☐	☐	☐	☐
20040	$3.00	☐$_{2}$	☐$_{2}$	☐	☐
20047	$2.50	☐	☐	☐	☐
20048	$6.00	☐	☐$_{2}$	☐$_{2}$	☐
20049	$2.50	☐	☐	☐	☐
20050	$2.50	☐	☐	☐	☐
20075	$2.50	☐	☐	☐	☐
20076	$2.50	☐	☐	☐	☐
20081	$2.50	☐	☐	☐	☐
20082	$2.50	☐	☐	☐	☐
20083	$2.50	☐	☐	☐	☐
20084	$2.50	☐	☐	☐	☐
20098	$2.50	☐	☐	☐	☐
20099	$2.50	☐	☐	☐	☐
20104	$2.50	☐	☐	☐	☐
20105	$3.00	☐	☐	☐$_{2}$	☐$_{2}$
20114	$2.50	☐	☐	☐	☐
20115	$2.50	☐	☐	☐	☐
20126	$25.00	☐	☐	☐	☐
20127	$35.00	☐	☐	☐	☐
20138	$2.50	☐	☐	☐	☐
20139	$2.50	☐	☐	☐	☐
20144	$2.50	☐	☐	☐	☐
20145	$3.00	☐$_{3}$	☐$_{2}$	☐	☐
20148	$2.50	☐	☐	☐	☐
20149	$2.50	☐	☐	☐	☐

		UL	UR	LL	LR
20152	$50.00	☐	☐	☐$_{2}$	☐
20153	$50.00	☐	☐	☐$_{2}$	☐
20156	$6.00	☐	☐	☐$_{2}$	☐
20157	$4.00	☐$_{2}$	☐	☐$_{3}$	☐$_{3}$
21220	$12.50	☐$_{2}$	☐	☐$_{2}$	☐$_{3}$
21221	$2.50	☐	☐	☐	☐
21226	$3.00	☐	☐$_{2}$	☐	☐

1926-29 REGULAR ISSUE

#632 1¢ FRANKLIN Continued

		UL	UR	LL	LR
21227	$2.50	□	□	□	□
21228	$2.50	□	□	□	□
21229	$2.50	□	□	□	□
21230	$2.50	□	□	□	□
21232	$2.50	□	□	□	□
21233	$2.50	□	□	□	□
21270	$2.50	□	□	□	□
21271	$2.50	□	□	□	□
21272	$2.50	□	□	□	□
21273	$2.50	□	□	□	□
21286	$2.50	□	□	□	□
21287	$2.50	□	□	□	□
21288	$2.50	□	□	□	□
21289	$2.50	□	□	□	□
21292	$2.50	□	□	□	□
21293	$2.50	□	□	□	□
21294	$2.50	□	□	□	□
21295	$2.50	□	□	□	□
21296	$2.50	□	□	□	□
21297	$2.50	□	□	□	□
21304	$2.50	□	□	□	□
21305	$2.50	□	□	□	□
21306	$2.50	□	□	□	□
21307	$2.50	□	□	□	□
21343	$2.50	□	□	□	□
21344	$2.50	□	□	□	□
21345	$2.50	□	□	□	□
21346	$2.50	□	□	□	□
21371	$2.50	□	□	□	□
21372	$2.50	□	□	□	□
21379	$2.50	□	□	□	□
21380	$2.50	□	□	□	□
21387	$2.50	□	□	□	□
21388	$2.50	□	□	□	□
21412	$2.50	□	□	□	□
21413	$2.50	□	□	□	□
21414	$2.50	□	□	□	□
21415	$2.50	□	□	□	□
21433	$2.50	□	□	□	□
21434	$2.50	□	□	□	□
21435	$2.50	□	□	□	□
21436	$2.50	□	□	□	□
21568	$2.50	□	□	□	□
21569	$2.50	□	□	□	□
21572	$2.50	□	□	□	□
21573	$2.50	□	□	□	□
21594	$12.00	□	□	□	□
21595	$12.00	□	□	□$_{3}$	□$_{3}$
21620	$2.50	□	□	□	□
21621	$2.50	□	□	□	□

#633 1½¢ HARDING (PROFILE)
42 Plates

		UL	UR	LL	LR
18358	$90	□	□	□	□
18359	$90	□	□	□	□
18360	$90	□	□	□	□
18412	$90	□	□	□	□
18413	$225	†	□	□	†
18488	$90	□	□	□	□

#633 1½¢ HARDING (PROFILE) Continued

		UL	UR	LL	LR
18489	$90	□	□	□	□
18693	—	†	†	†	†
18694	$225	□	□	□	□
18699	—	†	†	†	†
18700	$225	□	□	□	□
18701	$90	□	□	□	□
18702	$90	□	□	□	□
18703	$90	□	□	□	□
18704	$90	□	□	□	□
18722	$90	□	□	□	□
18723	$90	□	□	□	□
18728	$90	□	□	□	□
18729	$90	□	□	□	□
18737	$90	□	□	□	□
18738	$90	□	□	□	□
18825	$90	□	□	□	□
19047	$90	□	□	□	□
19048	$90	□	□	□	□
19057	$90	□	□	□	□
19058	$90	□	□	□	□
19072	$90	□	□	□	□
19073	$90	□	□	□	□
19125	$90	□	□	□	□
19126	$90	□	□	□	□
19181	$90	□	□	□	□
19182	$90	□	□	□	□
19191	$90	□	□	□	□
19192	$90	□	□	□	□
19201	$90	□	□	□	□
19202	$90	□	□	□	□
19213	$90	□	□	□	□
19214	$90	□	□	□	□
19290	$90	□	□	□	□
19291	$90	□	□	□	□
19292	$90	□	□	□	□
19293	$90	□	□	□	□

#634 2¢ WASHINGTON
483 Plates

		UL	UR	LL	LR
18043	$7.50	□	□	□	□
18061	$10.00	□	□	□	□
18095	$10.00	□	□	□	□
18139	$10.00	□	□	□	□
18231	$10.00	□	□	□	□
18234	$20.00	□	□	□	□
18243	$20.00	□	□	□	□
18284	$50.00	†	□	□	†
18368	$10.00	□	□	□	□
18369	$1.25	□$_{4}$	□$_{4}$	□$_{4}$	□$_{3}$
18517	$10.00	□	□	□	□
18520	$2.00	□$_{2}$	□$_{3}$	□	□
18529	$3.50	□	□	□	□
18584	—	†	†	†	†
18586	$7.50	□	□	□	□
18588	$15.00	□	□	□	□
18589	$1.25	□$_{6}$	□$_{4}$	□$_{8}$	□$_{8}$

1926-29 REGULAR ISSUE

#634 2¢ WASHINGTON Continued

Plate	Price	UL	UR	LL	LR
18605	$7.50	☐4	☐4	☐4	☐
18610	$7.50	☐	☐	☐	☐
18611	$50.00	†	†	☐	†
18616	$1.25	☐4	☐5	☐4	☐2
18617	$50.00	†	†	†	☐
18620	$1.25	☐8	☐4	☐8	☐
18621	$50.00	†	☐	†	†
18628	$1.25	☐3	☐6	☐6	☐
18629		†	†	†	†
18630		†	†	†	†
18633		†	†	†	†
18655	$10.00	☐	☐	☐	☐
18657	$35.00	☐	☐	☐	☐
18658	$50.00	†	†	☐	†
18659	$50.00	†	†	☐	†
18660	$7.50	☐	☐	☐	☐
18661	$7.50	☐	☐	☐	☐
18763	$5.00	☐	☐	☐	☐
18764	$35.00	☐	☐	☐	☐
18779	$4.00	☐	☐	☐	☐
18780	$4.00	☐	☐	☐	☐
18781	$10.00	☐	☐	☐	☐
18782	$7.50	☐	☐	☐	☐
18783	$10.00	☐	☐	☐	☐
18784	$2.00	☐2	☐	☐2	☐
18787	$30.00	☐	☐	☐	☐
18788	$15.00	☐	☐	☐	☐
18795	$3.75	☐	☐2	☐2	☐2
18796	$3.75	☐	☐	☐	☐
18797	$15.00	☐	☐	☐	☐
18798	$7.50	☐	☐2	☐2	☐2
18801	$50.00	†	☐	†	†
18802	$50.00	†	†	☐	†
18809	$3.75	☐	☐	☐	☐
18810	$35.00	☐	☐	☐	☐
18811	$3.75	☐2	☐	☐	☐
18812	$3.75	☐2	☐2	☐	☐
18813	$2.50	☐3	☐3	☐	☐3
18814	$3.75	☐	☐2	☐2	☐
18815	$3.75	☐	☐	☐	☐2
18816	$35.00	☐	☐	☐	☐
18826	$1.25	☐6	☐2	☐3	☐2
18827	$1.25	☐3	☐2	☐3	☐2
18828	$3.75	☐2	☐2	☐	☐
18829	$3.75	☐2	☐2	☐	☐
18834	$1.25	☐8	☐8	☐3	☐6
18835	$7.50	☐	☐	☐	☐

#634 2¢ WASHINGTON Continued

Plate	Price	UL	UR	LL	LR
18836	$1.50	☐	☐2	☐5	☐5
18837	$1.25	☐2	☐6	☐8	☐3
18852	$1.25	☐2	☐3	☐3	☐3
18853	$1.25	☐6	☐	☐3	☐2
18856	$5.00	☐2	☐2	☐	☐2
18857	$5.00	☐	☐2	☐2	☐2
18858	$1.25	☐	☐3	☐	☐3
18859	$1.25	☐	☐3	☐2	☐3
18862	$25.00	☐	☐	☐	☐
18863	$25.00	☐	☐	☐	☐
18864	$5.00	☐	☐	☐	☐
18865	$1.25	☐3	☐3	☐2	☐2
18868	$3.75	☐	☐2	☐	☐2
18869	$3.75	☐	☐2	☐	☐
18870	$12.50	☐	☐	☐	☐
18871	$1.25	☐2	☐2	☐2	☐3
18872	$2.50	☐4	☐4	☐4	☐3
18873	$1.25	☐8	☐3	☐3	☐2
18874	$1.25	☐3	☐3	☐2	☐3
18875	$5.00	☐2	☐2	☐	☐
18876	$5.00	☐2	☐2	☐	☐
18877	$10.00	☐	☐	☐	☐
18878	$7.50	☐2	☐2	☐	☐2
18879	$12.50	☐	☐	☐	☐
18880	$15.00	☐	☐	☐	☐
18881	$15.00	☐	☐	☐	☐
18882	$35.00	☐	☐	☐	☐
18883	$50.00	☐	☐	☐	☐
18884	$12.50	☐	☐	☐	☐
18885	$2.50	☐4	☐	☐4	☐4
18886	$12.50	☐	☐	☐	☐
18887	$15.00	☐	☐	☐	☐
18888	$3.75	☐	☐	☐	☐
18889	$20.00	☐	☐	☐	☐
18895	$10.00	☐	☐	☐	☐
18896	$5.00	☐2	☐2	☐	☐
18901	$7.50	☐2	☐2	☐	☐2
18902	$25.00	☐	☐	☐	☐
18931	$1.25	☐2	☐2	☐2	☐3
18932	$1.25	☐2	☐2	☐2	☐3
18933	$1.25	☐3	☐2	☐3	☐2
18934	$1.25	☐3	☐3	☐3	☐2
18935	$2.50	☐	☐	☐	☐
18936	$1.25	☐3	☐3	☐2	☐2
18937	$1.25	☐2	☐3	☐2	☐
18938	$3.75	☐	☐	☐	☐
18939	$1.25	☐3	☐3	☐3	☐2
18940	$1.25	☐2	☐3	☐3	☐2
18941	$2.50	☐	☐	☐	☐
18942	$2.50	☐	☐	☐	☐
18943	$1.25	☐3	☐2	☐2	☐2
18944	$1.25	☐3	☐2	☐2	☐2
18945	$2.50	☐	☐	☐	☐
18946	$2.50	☐	☐	☐	☐
18947	$2.50	☐	☐	☐	☐
18948	$1.25	☐2	☐3	☐2	☐2
18949	$2.50	☐3	☐	☐	☐
18950	$2.50	☐	☐	☐	☐
18951	$1.00	☐3	☐4	☐4	☐3
18952	$1.00	☐3	☐4	☐3	☐3

1926-29 REGULAR ISSUE

#634 2¢ WASHINGTON Continued

Plate	Price	UL	UR	LL	LR
18953	$1.25	☐$_2$	☐$_6$	☐$_3$	☐$_2$
18954	$1.25	☐$_2$	☐$_3$	☐$_2$	☐$_2$
18959	$1.75	☐$_2$	☐	☐	☐$_4$
18962	$1.25	☐$_2$	☐$_2$	☐$_2$	☐$_3$
18963	$1.25	☐$_2$	☐	☐	☐$_3$
18964	$1.25	☐	☐$_2$	☐	☐$_3$
18965	$25.00	☐	☐	☐	☐
18966	$25.00	☐	☐	☐	☐
18967	$3.75	☐$_2$	☐	☐	☐$_2$
18968	$1.25	☐$_3$	☐$_4$	☐$_3$	☐$_6$
18969	$1.25	☐$_2$	☐$_3$	☐$_3$	☐$_3$
18970	$1.25	☐$_2$	☐$_3$	☐$_6$	☐$_2$
18971	$7.50	☐	☐	☐	☐
18972	$7.50	☐	☐	☐	☐
18973	$25.00	☐	☐	☐	☐
18974	$25.00	☐	☐	☐	☐
18975	$1.25	☐$_3$	☐$_6$	☐$_2$	☐$_2$
18976	$3.75	☐$_2$	☐$_2$	☐	☐
18977	$1.25	☐$_2$	☐$_3$	☐$_3$	☐$_3$
18978	$3.75	☐	☐	☐	☐
18979	$12.50	☐$_2$	☐	☐$_2$	☐$_2$
18980	$10.00	☐	☐	☐	☐
18981	$10.00	☐	☐	☐	☐
18982	$10.00	☐	☐	☐	☐
18983	$1.25	☐$_2$	☐$_3$	☐	☐$_3$
18984	$1.25	☐	☐	☐	☐
18985	$3.75	☐	☐$_2$	☐	☐
18986	$3.75	☐	☐	☐	☐$_2$
18987	$1.25	☐	☐$_2$	☐$_3$	☐$_3$
18988	$1.25	☐	☐$_2$	☐$_3$	☐$_3$
18989	$1.25	☐$_2$	☐	☐	☐
18990	$1.25	☐$_3$	☐	☐$_3$	☐$_2$
18991	$1.75	☐	☐$_2$	☐$_2$	☐$_2$
18992	$1.25	☐$_2$	☐$_3$	☐$_2$	☐$_3$
18993	$1.25	☐$_2$	☐$_3$	☐$_3$	☐
18994	$1.25	☐$_2$	☐$_3$	☐$_3$	☐$_3$
18995	$1.25	☐$_3$	☐$_3$	☐$_3$	☐$_2$
18996	$1.25	☐$_3$	☐$_2$	☐$_3$	☐$_2$
19009	$1.25	☐$_2$	☐$_3$	☐$_2$	☐$_6$
19010	$1.25	☐$_2$	☐$_3$	☐$_2$	☐$_3$
19011	$3.75	☐$_2$	☐$_2$	☐$_2$	☐
19017	$3.75	☐$_2$	☐$_2$	☐$_2$	☐
19018	$1.25	☐$_2$	☐$_3$	☐$_2$	☐$_2$
19019	$1.25	☐$_2$	☐$_3$	☐$_3$	☐$_2$
19020	$1.25	☐	☐$_3$	☐$_2$	☐
19021	$1.25	☐	☐$_3$	☐$_2$	☐

#634 2¢ WASHINGTON Continued

Plate	Price	UL	UR	LL	LR
19022	$1.25	☐	☐$_2$	☐$_2$	☐$_2$
19023	$1.25	☐	☐	☐$_2$	☐
19024	$1.25	☐$_2$	☐$_2$	☐	☐
19025	$1.25	☐	☐	☐	☐$_2$
19026	$1.25	☐	☐$_3$	☐$_2$	☐$_2$
19027	$1.25	☐	☐$_3$	☐$_3$	☐$_3$
19028	$10.00	☐	☐	☐	☐
19029	$15.00	☐	☐	☐	☐
19030	$1.25	☐$_2$	☐$_2$	☐	☐
19031	$1.25	☐$_2$	☐$_3$	☐	☐
19032	$1.25	☐$_2$	☐$_3$	☐$_3$	☐$_3$
19033	$3.75	☐	☐	☐	☐
19034	$1.25	☐$_2$	☐	☐	☐
19043	$1.25	☐	☐	☐	☐$_2$
19044	$1.25	☐	☐$_3$	☐$_2$	☐
19045	$1.25	☐	☐$_3$	☐	☐
19046	$1.25	☐$_2$	☐$_3$	☐	☐
19053	$1.25	☐$_3$	☐$_2$	☐	☐$_2$
19054	$1.25	☐$_3$	☐$_2$	☐$_3$	☐$_3$
19055	$7.50	☐	☐	☐	☐
19056	$1.25	☐$_2$	☐$_3$	☐$_3$	☐$_3$
19059	$1.25	☐$_3$	☐$_2$	☐$_3$	☐$_2$
19060	$1.25	☐	☐$_2$	☐$_3$	☐$_3$
19070	$1.25	☐$_2$	☐$_2$	☐$_3$	☐
19071	$1.25	☐	☐$_3$	☐$_2$	☐
19074	$3.75	☐	☐	☐	☐
19075	$1.25	☐$_3$	☐$_3$	☐$_2$	☐$_3$
19080	$1.25	☐$_2$	☐$_3$	☐$_3$	☐$_3$
19081	$1.25	☐$_2$	☐	☐$_2$	☐$_2$
19086	$1.25	☐	☐$_2$	☐$_2$	☐$_3$
19087	$1.25	☐	☐$_3$	☐	☐$_2$
19094	$1.25	☐$_2$	☐	☐$_2$	☐$_2$
19095	$2.00	☐	☐	☐	☐
19107	$1.75	☐	☐	☐	☐
19108	$1.50	☐	☐	☐	☐
19109	$1.50	☐	☐	☐	☐
19110	$1.25	☐$_2$	☐	☐	☐
19115	$1.25	☐$_2$	☐$_3$	☐$_2$	☐$_2$
19116	$1.25	☐$_2$	☐$_3$	☐$_2$	☐$_2$
19117	$2.50	☐	☐$_3$	☐	☐
19118	$1.25	☐$_3$	☐$_2$	☐$_2$	☐$_2$
19123	$1.25	☐$_3$	☐	☐$_2$	☐$_2$
19124	$1.25	☐$_4$	☐$_4$	☐$_3$	☐$_4$
19149	$1.25	☐$_2$	☐	☐	☐$_2$
19150	$1.25	☐$_2$	☐$_3$	☐$_3$	☐$_3$
19151	$3.75	☐	☐	☐	☐
19152	$1.25	☐$_3$	☐$_3$	☐$_3$	☐$_2$
19153	$1.25	☐$_3$	☐$_3$	☐$_3$	☐$_2$
19154	$5.00	☐$_2$	☐	☐$_2$	☐$_2$
19157	$10.00	☐	☐	☐	☐
19158	$10.00	☐	☐	☐	☐
19159	$1.25	☐$_2$	☐$_3$	☐$_2$	☐$_2$
19160	$2.50	☐$_3$	☐$_2$	☐$_3$	☐$_3$
19165	$7.50	☐	☐	☐	☐
19166	$25.00	☐	☐	☐	☐
19167	$1.25	☐$_2$	☐$_3$	☐	☐$_3$
19168	$12.50	☐	☐	☐	☐
19171	$7.50	☐	☐	☐	☐
19172	$3.00	☐	☐	☐	☐

1926-29 REGULAR ISSUE

#634 2¢ WASHINGTON Continued

		UL	UR	LL	LR
19173	$1.25	□2	□2	□3	□3
19174	$2.00	□	□	□	□
19175	$1.50	□2	□	□	□2
19176	$1.25	□3	□2	□3	□3
19185	$1.25	□	□	□	□
19186	$12.00	□	□	□	□
19187	$15.00	□	□	□	□
19188	$20.00	□	□	□	□
19189	$5.00	□5	□4	□4	□4
19190	$3.75	□	□	□	□
19195	$3.75	□2	□	□	□3
19196	$1.25	□	□2	□	□
19197	$25.00	□	□	□	□
19198	$10.00	□	□	□	□
19203	$10.00	□	□	□	□
19204	$1.25	□2	□	□	□2
19205	$1.25	□2	□2	□2	□
19206	$1.25	□6	□2	□3	□6
19209	$1.25	□6	□2	□3	□6
19210	$1.25	□3	□3	□2	□3
19211	$1.25	□	□	□	□
19212	$1.25	□2	□	□	□2
19221	$2.50	□8	□3	□8	□8
19222	$10.00	□	□	□	□
19227	$7.50	□	□	□	□
19228	$15.00	□	□	□	□
*19232	—	□	□	□	□
19233	$35.00	□	□	□	□
*19240	—	†	□	□	□
19241	$15.00	□	□	□	□
19242	$2.50	□	□	□	□
19243	$3.00	□	□	□	□
19244	$1.25	□3	□6	□6	□2
19245	$1.25	□3	□3	□2	□3
19250	$5.00	□	□	□	□
19251	$3.75	□	□	□	□
19252	$3.75	□	□	□	□2
19253	$25.00	□	□	□	□

		UL	UR	LL	LR
19258	$1.50	□	□2	□2	□
19259	$5.00	□	□	□	□
19268	$35.00	□	□	□	□
19269	$10.00	□	□	□	□
19270	$7.50	□	□	□	□
19271	$15.00	□	□	□	□
19272	$1.00	□5	□5	□2	□2
19273	$2.00	□	□	□	□
19284	$3.75	□	□	□	□

#634 2¢ WASHINGTON Continued

		UL	UR	LL	LR
19285	$3.75	□	□	□	□
19304	$2.50	□2	□2	□3	□3
19305	$2.00	□	□	□	□
19318	$1.50	□	□	□	□
19319	$1.25	□	□	□	□
19328	$2.00	□	□	□	□
19329	$2.50	□2	□2	□2	□
19330	$2.50	□	□	□	□
19331	$5.00	□5	□5	□3	□5
19332	$1.50	□	□	□	□
19333	$2.00	□	□	□	□
19334	$1.25	□3	□2	□3	□3
19335	$15.00	□	□	□	□
19340	$2.00	□	□	□	□
19341	$2.00	□	□	□	□
19342	$5.00	□3	□2	□3	□3
19343	$25.00	□	□	□	□
19344	$15.00	□	□	□	□
19345	$5.00	□2	□2	□3	□3
19346	$2.50	□	□	□	□
19347	$1.25	□	□	□	□
19348	$25.00	□	□	□	□
19349	$20.00	□	□	□	□
19378	$10.00	□	□	□	□
19379	$2.00	□	□	□	□
19380	$2.00	□	□	□	□
19381	$1.50	□	□	□	□
19382	$1.75	□	□	□	□
19383	$5.00	□3	□3	□	□
19384	$1.50	□	□	□	□
19385	$2.00	□	□	□	□
19398	$3.75	□	□2	□	□
19399	$1.25	□	□	□	□
19400	$1.25	□	□	□	□
19401	$1.25	□	□	□	□
19402	$1.25	□	□	□	□
19403	$2.50	□	□4	□4	□
19415	$5.00	□4	□3	□4	□4
19416	$3.75	□	□2	□2	□2
19421	$1.25	□	□	□	□
19422	$1.25	□3	□2	□2	□3
*19424	—	□	□	□	□
19428	$7.50	□	□	□	□
19429	$5.00	□4	□4	□4	□3
19430	$2.50	□	□	□2	□
19431	$2.50	□	□	□4	□2
19432	$2.00	□	□	□	□
19433	$1.25	□3	□3	□3	□2
19434	$60.00	□	□	□	□
19435	$1.25	□3	□3	□3	□2
19436	$1.25	□	□	□	□2
19437	$1.25	□	□	□	□
19446	$2.50	□	□	□	□
19447	$2.50	□3	□3	□	□
19448	$1.25	□	□	□	□
19449	$20.00	□	□	□	□
19453	$2.25	□	□	□	□
19454	$2.00	□	□	□	□
19455	$1.25	□3	□3	□3	□2

1926-29 REGULAR ISSUE

#634 2¢ WASHINGTON Continued

		UL	UR	LL	LR
19456	$1.25	☐	☐	☐	☐
19457	$1.25	☐	☐	☐	☐
19458	$2.50	☐	☐	☐	☐
19459	$2.00	☐	☐	☐	☐
19475	$1.25	☐	☐	☐	☐
19476	$15.00	☐	☐	☐	☐
19477	$20.00	☐	☐	☐	☐
19478	$2.00	☐	☐	☐	☐
19479	$17.50	☐2	☐2	☐2	☐
19480	$17.50	☐	☐	☐	☐
19481	$5.00	☐	☐	☐	☐
19482	$1.25	☐	☐	☐	☐
19518	$1.25	☐	☐	☐	☐
19519	$1.25	☐2	☐3	☐3	☐3
19792	$2.00	☐	☐	☐	☐
*19793	—	☐	☐	☐	☐
19810	$10.00	☐	☐	☐	☐
19811	$7.50	☐	☐	☐	☐
19812	$20.00	☐	☐	☐	☐
19813	$2.50	☐6	☐2	☐4	☐3
19856	$2.00	☐	☐	☐	☐
19857	$1.25	☐	☐	☐	☐
19858	$1.25	☐	☐	☐	☐
19859	$1.25	☐	☐	☐	☐
19866	$2.00	☐	☐	☐	☐
19867	$1.25	☐	☐	☐	☐
19895	$2.00	☐	☐	☐	☐
19896	$1.25	☐	☐	☐	☐
19897	$1.25	☐	☐	☐	☐
19898	$1.25	☐	☐	☐	☐
19903	$1.25	☐	☐	☐	☐
19904	$1.25	☐	☐	☐	☐
19905	$10.00	☐	☐	☐	☐
19906	$1.25	☐	☐	☐	☐
19907	$1.25	☐	☐	☐	☐
19908	$1.25	☐	☐	☐	☐
19911	$1.25	☐	☐	☐	☐
19912	$1.25	☐	☐	☐	☐
19915	$1.25	☐	☐	☐	☐
19916	$1.25	☐	☐	☐	☐
19919	$1.25	☐	☐	☐	☐
19920	$1.25	☐	☐	☐	☐
19925	$1.25	☐	☐	☐	☐
19926	$1.25	☐	☐	☐	☐
19927	$1.25	☐	☐	☐	☐
19928	$1.25	☐	☐	☐	☐
19929	$1.25	☐	☐	☐	☐
19930	$1.00	☐3	☐5	☐5	☐5
19931	$1.25	☐	☐	☐	☐
19932	$1.25	☐	☐	☐	☐
19937	$1.25	☐	☐	☐	☐
19938	$1.25	☐	☐	☐	☐
19949	$1.25	☐	☐	☐	☐
19950	$1.25	☐	☐	☐	☐
19951	$1.25	☐	☐	☐	☐
19952	$1.25	☐	☐	☐	☐
19955	$1.25	☐	☐	☐	☐
19956	$1.25	☐	☐	☐	☐
19958	$1.25	☐	☐	☐	☐
19959	$1.25	☐	☐	☐	☐
19964	$1.25	☐3	☐3	☐	☐2

#634 2¢ WASHINGTON Continued

		UL	UR	LL	LR
19965	$1.25	☐	☐	☐	☐
19966	$1.25	☐	☐	☐	☐
19967	$1.25	☐	☐	☐	☐
19968	$1.25	☐	☐	☐	☐
19969	$1.25	☐	☐	☐	☐
19976	$2.00	☐	☐	☐	☐
19977	$2.50	☐	☐	☐	☐
19978	$1.25	☐	☐	☐	☐
19979	$1.25	☐	☐	☐	☐
19980	$1.25	☐	☐	☐	☐
19981	$1.25	☐	☐	☐	☐
19986	$1.25	☐	☐	☐	☐
19987	$1.25	☐	☐	☐	☐
19988	$1.25	☐	☐	☐	☐
19989	$1.25	☐	☐	☐	☐
19994	$1.25	☐	☐	☐	☐
19995	$1.25	☐	☐	☐	☐
19998	$1.25	☐	☐	☐	☐
19999	$1.25	☐4	☐2	☐2	☐
20000	$1.25	☐	☐	☐	☐
20001	$1.25	☐	☐	☐	☐
20011	$1.25	☐	☐	☐	☐
20012	$1.25	☐	☐	☐	☐
20013	$1.25	☐	☐	☐	☐
20014	$1.25	☐	☐	☐	☐
20015	$35.00	☐	☐	☐	☐
20016	$1.25	☐	☐	☐	☐
20019	$1.25	☐2	☐4	☐	☐2
20020	$1.25	☐	☐	☐	☐
20025	$2.50	☐2	☐	☐2	☐2
20026	$2.50	☐3	☐	☐3	☐3
20146	$2.00	☐	☐	☐	☐
20147	$2.00	☐	☐	☐	☐
20150	$1.50	☐	☐	☐	☐
20151	$1.25	☐	☐	☐	☐
20154	$1.50	☐	☐	☐	☐
20155	$1.50	☐	☐	☐	☐
20178	$1.25	☐	☐	☐	☐
20179	$3.00	☐	☐	☐	☐
20185	$1.25	☐	☐	☐	☐
20186	$2.00	☐	☐	☐	☐
20201	$1.25	☐	☐	☐	☐
*20202	—	☐	☐	☐	☐
20205	$1.25	☐3	☐4	☐3	☐3
20206	$1.25	☐3	☐4	☐4	☐6
20221	$1.25	☐	☐	☐2	☐2
20222	$1.25	☐	☐	☐2	☐2
20233	$1.25	☐	☐	☐	☐
20234	$1.25	☐	☐	☐	☐
20243	$1.25	☐	☐	☐	☐
20244	$1.25	☐	☐	☐2	☐
20255	$1.25	☐	☐	☐	☐
20256	$1.25	☐	☐	☐	☐
20285	$30.00	☐	☐	☐	☐
20286	$1.25	☐	☐	☐	☐
20295	$20.00	☐	☐	☐	☐
20296	$7.50	☐	☐	☐	☐
20297	$7.50	☐2	☐2	☐2	☐
20298	$7.50	☐	☐	☐	☐
20303	$2.50	☐3	☐4	☐3	☐3

1926-29 REGULAR ISSUE

#634 2¢ WASHINGTON Continued

		UL	UR	LL	LR
20304	$1.25	☐	☐	☐	☐
20321	$1.25	☐	☐	☐	☐
20322	$1.25	☐	☐	☐	☐
20331	$2.00	☐$_2$	☐	☐	☐$_2$
20332	$1.25	☐	☐	☐	☐
20341	$1.25	☐	☐	☐	☐
20342	$1.25	☐	☐	☐	☐
20347	$1.25	☐	☐	☐	☐
20348	$8.75	☐$_2$	☐$_2$	☐$_2$	☐
20351	$1.25	☐	☐	☐	☐
20352	$1.25	☐	☐	☐	☐
20382	$5.00	☐	☐	☐	☐
20383	$1.25	☐	☐	☐	☐
20529	$1.25	☐	☐	☐	☐
20530	$1.25	☐	☐	☐	☐
20531	$1.25	☐	☐	☐	☐
20532	$12.00	☐	☐	☐	☐
20541	$1.25	☐	☐	☐	☐
20542	$1.25	☐	☐	☐	☐
21147	$1.25	☐	☐	☐	☐
21148	$1.25	☐	☐	☐	☐
21377	$1.25	☐	☐	☐	☐
21378	$1.25	☐	☐	☐	☐
21383	$15.00	☐	☐	☐	☐
21384	$15.00	☐	☐	☐	☐
21555	$1.25	☐	☐	☐	☐
21556	$1.25	☐	☐	☐	☐

EXPERIMENTAL-EYE PLATES

The first two of these plates made their appearance early in February 1935; the others went to press between March 1935 and January 1938. By June 1940 all had been cancelled.

This issue has special importance since it is Eye Printing No. 1, the forerunner of all Electric-Eye issues. Because of the unusual position for a rotary-press number (3-up or 3-down from the corner of the sheet), collectors were at loss to know what size pieces to take.

Today, position collectors want to show the corner sheet margins. In order to do this, a block of 6 is the minimum requirement. This size has a chopped-off appearance and is not popular, but a vertical corner block of 10 is well balanced and desirable in every respect.

#634 Experimental Eye Plates

Corner Vertical Blocks of 10

28 Plates		UL	UR	LL	LR
21149	$4.75	☐	☐	☐	☐
21150	$4.75	☐	☐	☐	☐
21367	$9.50	☐	☐	☐	☐
21368	$9.50	☐	☐	☐	☐
21399	$4.75	☐	☐	☐	☐
21402	$4.75	☐	☐	☐	☐
21411	$4.75	☐	☐	☐	☐

#634 Experimental-Eye Plates Cont.

		UL	UR	LL	LR
21416	$4.75	☐	☐	☐	☐
21417	$4.75	☐	☐	☐	☐
21418	$4.75	☐	☐	☐	☐
21419	$4.75	☐	☐	☐	☐
21420	$4.75	☐	☐	☐	☐
21421	$4.75	☐	☐	☐	☐
21422	$4.75	☐	☐	☐	☐
21423	$4.75	☐	☐	☐	☐
21424	$4.75	☐	☐	☐	☐
21437	$4.75	☐	☐	☐	☐
21438	$4.75	☐	☐	☐	☐
21441	$4.75	☐	☐	☐	☐
21442	$4.75	☐	☐	☐	☐

		UL	UR	LL	LR
21447	$7.00	☐	☐	☐	☐
21448	$7.00	☐	☐	☐	☐
21676	$15.00	☐	☐	☐	☐
21677	$15.00	☐	☐	☐	☐
21678	$15.00	☐	☐	☐	☐
21679	$15.00	☐	☐	☐	☐
21688	$15.00	☐	☐	☐	☐
21689	$15.00	☐	☐	☐	☐

#634A WASHINGTON DIE II 6 Plates

Plate blocks of this scarce die are usually off center. Prices vary greatly according to condition.

Plate Blocks of 4.

		UL	UR	LL	LR
19644	$2,250	☐	☐	☐	☐

1926-29 REGULAR ISSUE

#634A 2¢ WASHINGTON DIE II Cont.

		UL	UR	LL	LR
19645	$2,500	☐	☐	☐	☐
19744	$2,250	☐	☐	☐	☐
19745	$2,250	☐	☐	☐	☐
19746	$2,250	☐	☐	☐	☐
19747	$2,250	☐	☐	☐	☐

#635 3¢ LINCOLN 30 Plates

		UL	UR	LL	LR
18114	$30	☐	☐	☐	☐
18115	$45	☐	☐	☐	☐
18126	$8	☐	☐	☐	☐
18127	$8	☐	☐	☐	☐
18379	$3	☐ 3	☐ 5	☐ 5	☐ 3
18380	$15	☐	☐	☐	☐
18439	$15	☐	☐	☐	☐
18440	$15	☐	☐	☐	☐
18445	$9	☐ 2	☐	☐	☐ 2
18446	$8	☐	☐	☐	☐
18457	$15	☐	☐	☐	☐
18458	$15	☐	☐	☐	☐
18791	$5	☐ 3	☐ 6	☐ 6	☐ 7
18792	$15	☐	☐ 2	☐	☐
18803	$8	☐	☐	☐	☐
18804	$35	☐	☐	☐	☐
18830	$8	☐	☐	☐	☐
18831	$9	☐	☐ 2	☐	☐
18832	$8	☐	☐	☐	☐
18833	$9	☐ 2	☐ 2	☐	☐
19096	$3	☐ 4	☐ 4	☐ 5	☐ 3
19097	$3	☐ 3	☐ 5	☐ 3	☐ 3
19098	$3	☐ 3	☐ 7	☐ 3	☐ 5
19099	$3	☐ 3	☐ 5	☐ 5	☐ 3
19111	$8	☐	☐	☐	☐
19112	$8	☐	☐	☐	☐
20432	$8	☐	☐	☐	☐
20433	$8	☐	☐	☐	☐

#635a (1932) 3¢ LINCOLN REISSUE

21185	$3.50	☐	☐	☐	☐
21186	$3.50	☐	☐	☐	☐

#636 4¢ MARTHA WASHINGTON

8 Plates		UL	UR	LL	LR
17761	$100	☐	☐	☐	☐
17989	$100	☐	☐	☐	☐
17990	$100	☐	☐	☐	☐
18038	$100	☐	☐	☐	☐
18039	$100	☐	☐	☐	☐
18082	$100	☐	☐	☐	☐
18083	$100	☐	☐	☐	☐
18365	$100	☐	☐	☐	☐

#637 5¢ THEODORE ROOSEVELT

21 plates

18394	$22.50	☐	☐	☐	☐
18441	$22.50	☐	☐	☐	☐
18459	$55.00	☐	☐	☐	☐
18460	$40.00	☐	☐	☐	☐
18785	$22.50	☐	☐	☐	☐
18850	$55.00	☐	☐	☐	☐
18851	$45.00	☐	☐	☐	☐
18854	$55.00	☐	☐	☐	☐
18855	$22.50	☐	☐	☐	☐
18907	$45.00	☐	☐	☐	☐
18908	$22.50	☐	☐	☐	☐
18909	$22.50	☐	☐	☐	☐
18910	$22.50	☐	☐	☐	☐
18911	$22.50	☐	☐	☐	☐
18912	$22.50	☐	☐	☐	☐
18913	$22.50	☐	☐	☐	☐
18914	$22.50	☐	☐	☐	☐
19088	$22.50	☐	☐	☐	☐
19089	$22.50	☐	☐	☐	☐
19100	$22.50	☐	☐	☐	☐
19101	$22.50	☐	☐	☐	☐

#638 6¢ GARFIELD 12 Plates

18029	$22.50	☐	☐	☐	☐
18030	$22.50	☐	☐	☐	☐
18036	$22.50	☐	☐	☐	☐
18037	$22.50	☐	☐	☐	☐
18396	$22.50	☐	☐	☐	☐
18397	$22.50	☐	☐	☐	☐
18420	$22.50	☐	☐	☐	☐
18421	$22.50	☐	☐	☐	☐
18860	$22.50	☐	☐	☐	☐
18861	$22.50	☐	☐	☐	☐

1926-29 REGULAR ISSUE

#638 6¢ GARFIELD Continued

		UL	UR	LL	LR
18866	$22.50	☐	☐	☐	☐
18867	$22.50	☐	☐	☐	☐

#639 7¢ McKINLEY 10 Plates

		UL	UR	LL	LR
18195	$22.50	☐	☐	☐	☐$_{2}$
18196	$22.50	☐	☐	☐	☐$_{2}$
18735	$22.50	☐	☐	☐	☐
18736	$22.50	☐	☐	☐	☐
18739	$22.50	☐	☐	☐	☐
18740	$22.50	☐	☐	☐	☐
19236	$22.50	☐	☐	☐	☐
19237	$22.50	☐	☐	☐	☐
19238	$22.50	☐	☐	☐	☐
19239	$22.50	☐	☐	☐	☐

#640 8¢ GRANT 26 Plates

		UL	UR	LL	LR
18189		†	†	†	†
*18190	—	☐	☐	☐	☐
18191	$22.50	☐	☐	☐	☐
18192	$22.50	☐	☐	☐	☐
18733	$22.50	☐	☐	☐	☐
18734	$32.50	☐	☐	☐	☐
18753	$37.50	☐	☐	☐	☐
18754	$37.50	☐	☐	☐	☐
18775	$32.50	☐	☐	☐	☐
18776	$27.50	☐$_{2}$	☐$_{2}$	☐$_{2}$	☐$_{3}$
18777	$32.50	☐	☐	☐	☐
18778	$55.00	☐	☐	☐	☐
19246	$27.50	☐	☐	☐$_{2}$	☐
19247	$27.50	☐$_{2}$	☐$_{2}$	☐	☐
19262	$22.50	☐	☐	☐	☐
19263	$22.50	☐	☐	☐	☐
19372	$32.50	☐	☐	☐	☐
19373	$32.50	☐	☐	☐	☐
19374	$22.50	☐	☐	☐	☐
19375	$22.50	☐	☐	☐	☐
19376	$22.50	☐	☐	☐	☐
19377	$22.50	☐	☐	☐	☐
20128	$22.50	☐	☐	☐	☐
20129	$22.50	☐	☐	☐	☐
20364	$10.00	☐$_{7}$	☐$_{8}$	☐$_{8}$	☐$_{9}$
20365	$10.00	☐$_{6}$	☐$_{7}$	☐$_{6}$	☐$_{7}$

#641 9¢ JEFFERSON 16 Plates

		UL	UR	LL	LR
17884	$16.25	☐$_{2}$	☐$_{2}$	☐$_{3}$	☐$_{3}$
17885	$16.25	☐$_{2}$	☐$_{3}$	☐$_{3}$	☐$_{3}$
18193	$27.50	☐	☐	☐$_{2}$	☐
18194	$16.25	☐$_{2}$	☐$_{2}$	☐$_{3}$	☐$_{3}$
18201	$16.25	☐$_{2}$	☐$_{2}$	☐$_{3}$	☐$_{3}$
18202	$22.50	☐	☐	☐	☐
18741	$16.25	☐$_{3}$	☐$_{3}$	☐$_{2}$	☐$_{2}$
18742	$16.25	☐$_{3}$	☐$_{3}$	☐$_{2}$	☐$_{2}$
18743	$55.00	☐	☐	☐	☐
18744	$60.00	☐	☐	☐	☐
19350	$22.50	☐	☐	☐	☐
19351	$32.50	☐	☐	☐	☐
19352	$22.50	☐	☐	☐	☐
19353	$22.50	☐	☐	☐	☐
19354	$22.50	☐	☐	☐	☐
19355	$22.50	☐	☐	☐	☐

#642 10¢ MONROE 26 Plates

		UL	UR	LL	LR
*18532P	—	☐	☐	☐	☐
*18533	—	†	†	†	☐
*18538P	—	†	☐	†	†
*18539	—	†	☐	†	†
18614	$35	☐	☐	☐	☐
18615	$35	☐	☐	☐	☐
18622	$35	☐	☐	☐	☐
18623	$35	☐	☐	☐	☐
18626	$35	☐	☐	☐	☐
18627	$35	☐	☐	☐	☐
18846	$35	☐	☐	☐	☐
18847	$35	☐	☐	☐	☐
18848	$35	☐	☐	☐	☐
18849	$60	☐	☐	☐	☐
19234	$35	☐	☐	☐	☐
19235	$15	☐$_{4}$	☐$_{3}$	☐$_{3}$	☐$_{3}$
19254	$35	☐	☐	☐	☐
19255	$35	☐	☐	☐	☐
19256	$35	☐	☐	☐	☐
19257	$35	☐	☐	☐	☐
19489	$35	☐	☐	☐	☐
19490	$35	☐	☐	☐	☐
19504	$35	☐	☐	☐	☐
19505	$35	☐	☐	☐	☐
19506	$35	☐	☐	☐	☐
19507	$35	☐	☐	☐	☐

1926-29 REGULAR ISSUE

BOOKLET PANES

ROTARY PRESS PERF. 11 x 10½

BOOKLET PANES OF 6

Positions UL, LL

#632a 1¢ FRANKLIN 14 Plates

18915	18916	18917	18918	19529
19530	19531	19532	19561	19562
19563	19564	19921	19922	

#634d 2¢ WASHINGTON (DIE I)

78 Plates

*18662	*18663	*18697	18698	18705
*18706	*18707	*18708	*18709	*18710
†18711	*18712	*18716	*18717	18718
*18719	18720	*18721	18842	18843
18844	*18845	*19183	*19184	19193
19194	19199	*19200	19274	19275
*19276	*19277	19278	19279	19314
19315	*19316	*19317	19357	19358
*19359	*19360	19361	*19362	*19404
*19405	*19406	*19407	19408	19409
19760	*19761	*19762	*19763	19834
19835	19844	19845	19846	19847
19848	19849	19850	19851	19962
19963	*19972	19973	19990	19991
20041	20042	20096	20097	20100
20101	20106	20107		

1927 COMMEMORATIVES

FLAT PRESS PERF. 11

#643 2¢ VERMONT SESQUICENTENNIAL

8 Plates

Plate	Price	TL	TR	L	R	B
19035	$50	☐	☐	☐	☐	☐
19036	$50	☐	☐	☐	☐	☐
19037	$50	☐	☐	☐	☐	☐
19038	$50	☐	☐	☐	☐	☐
19039	$50	☐	☐	☐	☐	☐
19040	$50	☐	☐	☐	☐	☐
19041	$50	☐	☐	☐	☐	☐
19042	$50	☐	☐	☐	☐	☐

#644 2¢ BURGOYNE 10 Plates

Plate	Price	TL	TR	L	R	B
19061	$42.50	☐	☐	☐	☐	☐
19062	$42.50	☐	☐	☐	☐	☐
19063	$42.50	☐	☐	☐	☐	☐
19064	$42.50	☐	☐	☐	☐	☐
19065	$42.50	☐	☐	☐	☐	☐
19066	$42.50	☐	☐	☐	☐	☐
19067	$42.50	☐	☐	☐	☐	☐
19068	$42.50	☐	☐	☐	☐	☐
19069	$42.50	☐	☐	☐	☐	☐
19106	$42.50	☐	☐	☐	☐	☐

1927 COMMEMORATIVES

#645 2¢ VALLEY FORGE 8 Plates

Plate	Price	TL	TR	L	R	B
19493	$45	☐	☐	☐	☐	☐
19494	$45	☐	☐	☐	☐	☐
19495	$45	☐	☐	☐	☐	☐
19496	$45	☐	☐	☐	☐	☐
19497	$45	☐	☐	☐	☐	☐
19500	$45	☐	☐	☐	☐	☐
19501	$45	☐	☐	☐	☐	☐
19502	$45	☐	☐	☐	☐	☐

1928 COMMEMORATIVES

ROTARY PRESS PERF. 11 x 10½

#646 2¢ MOLLY PITCHER OVERPRINT

2 Plates

Plate	Price	UL	UR	LL	LR
19070	$45	☐	☐	☐	☐
19071	$45	☐	☐	☐	☐

#647 2¢ HAWAII OVERPRINT 4 Plates

Plate	Price	UL	UR	LL	LR
18983	$150	☐	☐	☐	☐
18984	$150	☐	☐	☐	☐
19054	$150	☐	☐	☐	☐
19055	$150	☐	☐	☐	☐

#648 5¢ HAWAII OVERPRINT 2 Plates

Plate	Price	UL	UR	LL	LR
18907	$325	☐	☐	☐	☐
18908	$325	☐	☐	☐	☐

FLAT PRESS PERF. 11

#649 2¢ AERONAUTICS 16 Plates

Plate	Price	TL	TR	L	R	B
19654	$20	☐	☐	☐	☐	☐
19655	$20	☐	☐	☐	☐	☐
19656	$20	☐	☐	☐	☐	☐
19657	$20	☐	☐	☐	☐	☐
19662	$20	☐	☐	☐	☐	☐
19663	$20	☐	☐	☐	☐	☐
19664	$20	☐	☐	☐	☐	☐
19665	$20	☐	☐	☐	☐	☐
19678	$20	☐	☐	☐	☐	☐
19679	$20	☐	☐	☐	☐	☐
19680	$20	☐	☐	☐	☐	☐
19681	$20	☐	☐	☐	☐	☐
19708	$20	☐	☐	☐	☐	☐
19709	$20	☐	☐	☐	☐	☐
19710	$20	☐	☐	☐	☐	☐
19711	$20	☐	☐	☐	☐	☐

#650 5¢ AERONAUTICS 4 Plates

Plate	Price	TL	TR	L	R	B
19658	$85	☐	☐	☐	☐	☐
19659	$85	☐	☐	☐	☐	☐
19660	$85	☐	☐	☐	☐	☐
19661	$85	☐	☐	☐	☐	☐

12 FRAME PLATES

12 VIGNETTE PLATES

	19720		19721		19722		19723		19724		19725		19726		19727		19740		19741		19742		19743	
	L	R	L	R	L	R	L	R	L	R	L	R	L	R	L	R	L	R	L	R	L	R	L	R
19728																								
19729																								
19730																								
19731																								
19732																								
19733																								
19734																								
19735																								
19736																								
19737																								
19738																								
19739																								

1929 COMMEMORATIVES

FLAT PRESS PERF. 11

#651 2¢ CLARK (BICOLORED)

Only Two Positions, TL, TR

TL Blocks of six:
Red plate, Black plate, Red Top

TR Blocks of six:
Black TOP, Black F plate, Red F plate

Basic Price $16

Every red (Frame) plate exists in combination with every black (Vignette) plate. Thus, a complete collection of left and right pane combinations has 288 blocks. Although there are no rare combinations, completion is difficult and mixed centering is to be expected.

REGULAR ISSUE

#653 ½¢ NATHAN HALE

See page 68

1929 COMMEMORATIVES

FLAT PRESS PERF. 11

#654 2¢ EDISON 4 Plates

		TL	TR	L	R	B
19775	$40	☐	☐	☐	☐	☐
19776	$40	☐	☐	☐	☐	☐
19777	$40	☐	☐	☐	☐	☐
19778	$40	☐	☐	☐	☐	☐

ROTARY PRESS PERF. 11 x 10½

#655 2¢ EDISON 8 Plates

		UL	UR	LL	LR
19779	$60	☐	☐	☐	☐
19780	$60	☐	☐	☐	☐
19796	$60	☐	☐	☐	☐
19797	$60	☐	☐	☐	☐
19806	$80	☐	☐	☐	☐
19807	$90	☐	☐	☐	☐
19808	$90	☐	☐	☐	☐
19809	$80	☐	☐	☐	☐

ROTARY PRESS
PERF. 10 VERTICALLY

#656 2¢ EDISON SIDE COILS

8 Plates

19781 19782 19794 19795 19802
19803 19804 19805

FLAT PRESS PERF. 11

#657 2¢ SULLIVAN 4 Plates

		TL	TR	L	R	B
19783	$37.50	☐	☐	☐	☐	☐
19784	$37.50	☐	☐	☐	☐	☐
19785	$37.50	☐	☐	☐	☐	☐
19786	$37.50	☐	☐	☐	☐	☐

1929 KANSAS, NEBRASKA STATE OVERPRINTS

Completion of these issues in matched sets is rarely accomplished. The 2¢ Kansas plates are the biggest obstacle, for at least half of the numbers are troublesome when one is searching for missing positions. There is no general agreement as to which are the scarcest plates, and the positions show up so infrequently that there is no established market value. To a lesser degree the 2¢ Nebraska plates present the same problem.

1¢ Kansas 18957 and 19302 are often referred to as much harder than the other two 1¢ Kansas plates, but their scarcity does not approach that of the difficult 2¢ numbers. 3¢ Kansas 18804 is definitely scarce. Among the higher denominations we have found the 9¢ and 10¢ Nebraska plates about the hardest to locate in fine condition, but centering is a problem on most of the State Overprints, and we do not know of one complete collection that is fine throughout.

KANSAS

ROTARY PRESS PERF. 11 x 10½

#658 1¢ KANSAS 4 Plates

		UL	UR	LL	LR
18957	$50	☐	☐	☐	☐
19302	$50	☐	☐	☐	☐
19338	$35	☐	☐	☐	☐
19339	$35	☐	☐	☐	☐

#659 1½¢ KANSAS 2 Plates

19181	$45	☐	☐	☐	☐
19191	$45	☐	☐	☐	☐

#660 2¢ KANSAS 12 Plates

19174	$42.50	☐	☐	☐	☐
19175	$42.50	☐	☐	☐	☐
19273	$85.00	☐	☐	☐	☐
19379	$42.50	☐	☐	☐	☐
19383	$42.50	☐	☐	☐	☐
19384	$42.50	☐	☐	☐	☐
19385	$42.50	☐	☐	☐	☐
19398	$42.50	☐	☐	☐	☐
19430	$75.00	☐	☐	☐	☐
19431	$75.00	☐	☐	☐	☐
19436	$75.00	☐	☐	☐	☐
19447	$75.00	☐	☐	☐	☐

#661 3¢ KANSAS 3 Plates

18126	$175	☐	☐	☐	☐
18803	$175	☐	☐	☐	☐
18804	$225	☐	☐	☐	☐

#662 4¢ KANSAS 2 Plates

18038	$175	☐	☐	☐	☐
18082	$175	☐	☐	☐	☐

1929 KANSAS OVERPRINTS

#663 5¢ KANSAS 2 Plates

		UL	UR	LL	LR
18907	$185	☐	☐	☐	☐
18908	$185	☐	☐	☐	☐

#664 6¢ KANSAS 2 Plates

18030	$450	☐	☐	☐	☐
18037	$450	☐	☐	☐	☐

#665 7¢ KANSAS 2 Plates

18736	$400	☐	☐	☐	☐
18740	$400	☐	☐	☐	☐

#666 8¢ KANSAS 2 Plates

18191	$800	☐	☐	☐	☐
18192	$800	☐	☐	☐	☐

#667 9¢ KANSAS 2 Plates

18742	$200	☐	☐	☐	☐
18744	$200	☐	☐	☐	☐

#668 10¢ KANSAS 2 Plates

19234	$375	☐	☐	☐	☐
19235	$375	☐	☐	☐	☐

NEBRASKA

ROTARY PRESS PERF. 11 x 10½

#669 1¢ NEBRASKA 2 Plates

19338	$35	☐	☐	☐	☐
19339	$35	☐	☐	☐	☐

#670 1½¢ NEBRASKA 2 Plates

19182	$37.50	☐	☐	☐	☐
19192	$37.50	☐	☐	☐	☐

#671 2¢ NEBRASKA 9 Plates

18989	$32.50	☐	☐	☐	☐
18990	$32.50	☐	☐	☐	☐
19059	$32.50	☐	☐	☐	☐
19204	$32.50	☐	☐	☐	☐
19205	$32.50	☐	☐	☐	☐
19233	$32.50	☐	☐	☐	☐
19378	$32.50	☐	☐	☐	☐
19430	$32.50	☐	☐	☐	☐
19431	$32.50	☐	☐	☐	☐

1929 NEBRASKA OVERPRINTS

#672 3¢ NEBRASKA 2 Plates

		UL	UR	LL	LR
18803	$175	☐	☐	☐	☐
18804	$175	☐	☐	☐	☐

#673 4¢ NEBRASKA 2 Plates

		UL	UR	LL	LR
18038	$200	☐	☐	☐	☐
18082	$200	☐	☐	☐	☐

#674 5¢ NEBRASKA 2 Plates

		UL	UR	LL	LR
18907	$250	☐	☐	☐	☐
18908	$250	☐	☐	☐	☐

#675 6¢ NEBRASKA 2 Plates

		UL	UR	LL	LR
18030	$550	☐	☐	☐	☐
18037	$550	☐	☐	☐	☐

#676 7¢ NEBRASKA 2 Plates

		UL	UR	LL	LR
18736	$250	☐	☐	☐	☐
18740	$250	☐	☐	☐	☐

#677 8¢ NEBRASKA 2 Plates

		UL	UR	LL	LR
18191	$350	☐	☐	☐	☐
18192	$350	☐	☐	☐	☐

#678 9¢ NEBRASKA 2 Plates

		UL	UR	LL	LR
18742	$400	☐	☐	☐	☐
18744	$400	☐	☐	☐	☐

#679 10¢ NEBRASKA 2 Plates

		UL	UR	LL	LR
19234	$950	☐	☐	☐	☐
19235	$950	☐	☐	☐	☐

1929 COMMEMORATIVES

FLAT PRESS PERF. 11

#680 2¢ FALLEN TIMBERS 8 Plates

		TL	TR	L	R	B
19824	$60	☐	☐	☐	☐	☐
19825	$40	☐	☐	☐	☐	☐
19826	$60	☐	☐	☐	☐	☐
19827	$40	☐	☐	☐	☐	☐
19828	$60	☐	☐	☐	☐	☐
19829	$40	☐	☐	☐	☐	☐
19830	$40	☐	☐	☐	☐	☐
19831	$60	☐	☐	☐	☐	☐

1929 COMMEMORATIVES

#681 2¢ OHIO RIVER CANALIZATION

5 Plates		TL	TR	L	R	B
19838	$32.50	☐	☐	☐	☐	☐
19839	$32.50	☐	☐	☐	☐	☐
19840	$32.50	☐	☐	☐	☐	☐
19841	$32.50	☐	☐	☐	☐	☐
20005	$32.50	☐	☐	☐	☐	☐

1930 COMMEMORATIVES

#682 2¢ MASS. BAY COLONY

8 Plates		TL	TR	L	R	B
20053	$40	☐	☐	‡	‡	☐
20054	$40	☐	☐	‡	‡	☐
20055	$40	☐	☐	‡	‡	☐
20056	$40	☐	☐	‡	‡	☐
20057	$40	☐	☐	‡	‡	☐
20058	$40	☐	☐	‡	‡	☐
20059	$40	☐	☐	‡	‡	☐
20060	$40	☐	☐	‡	‡	☐

#683 2¢ CAROLINA-CHARLESTON

4 Plates		TL	TR	L	R	B
20061	$65	☐	☐	‡	‡	☐
20062	$65	☐	☐	‡	‡	☐
20063	$65	☐	☐	‡	‡	☐
20064	$65	☐	☐	‡	‡	☐

#688 2¢ BRADDOCK 4 Plates

		TL	TR	L	R	B
20168	$52.50	☐	☐	‡	‡	☐
20169	$52.50	☐	☐	‡	‡	☐
20170	$52.50	☐	☐	‡	‡	☐
20171	$52.50	☐	☐	‡	‡	☐

#689 2¢ VON STEUBEN 8 Plates

		TL	TR	L	R	B
20267	$32.50	☐	☐	‡	‡	☐
20268	$32.50	☐	☐	‡	‡	☐
20269	$32.50	☐	☐	‡	‡	☐
20270	$32.50	☐	☐	‡	‡	☐
20281	$32.50	☐	☐	‡	‡	☐
20282	$32.50	☐	☐	‡	‡	☐
20283	$32.50	☐	☐	‡	‡	☐
20284	$32.50	☐	☐	‡	‡	☐

1931 COMMEMORATIVES

FLAT PRESS PERF. 11

#690 2¢ PULASKI 12 Plates

		TL	TR	L	R	B
20416	$20	☐	☐	‡	‡	☐
20417	$20	☐	☐	‡	‡	☐
20418	$20	☐	☐	‡	‡	☐
20419	$20	☐	☐	‡	‡	☐
20420	$20	☐	☐	‡	‡	☐
20421	$20	☐	☐	‡	‡	☐
20422	$20	☐	☐	‡	‡	☐
20423	$20	☐	☐	‡	‡	☐
20424	$20	☐	☐	‡	‡	☐
20425	$20	☐	☐	‡	‡	☐
20426	$20	☐	☐	‡	‡	☐
20427	$20	☐	☐	‡	‡	☐

1930 REGULAR ISSUE

ROTARY PRESS PERF. 11 x 10½

#684 1½¢ HARDING (FULL FACE)

52 Plates

Plate	Price	UL	UR	LL	LR
20259	$3	☐	☐	☐	☐
20260	$3	☐	☐	☐	☐
20265	$3	☐	☐	☐	☐
20266	$8	☐	☐	☐	☐
20390	$3	☐	☐	☐	☐
20391	$3	☐	☐	☐	☐
20394	$3	☐	☐	☐	☐
20395	$3	☐	☐	☐	☐
20398	$3	☐	☐	☐	☐
20399	$3	☐	☐	☐	☐
20412	$3	☐	☐	☐	☐
20413	$3	☐	☐	☐	☐
20414	$3	☐	☐	☐	☐
20415	$3	☐	☐	☐	☐
20430	$3	☐	☐	☐	☐
20431	$3	☐	☐	☐	☐
21080	$3	☐	☐	☐	☐
21081	$3	☐	☐	☐	☐
21082	$3	☐	☐	☐	☐
21083	$3	☐	☐	☐	☐
21088	$3	☐	☐	☐	☐
21089	$3	☐	☐	☐	☐
21090	$9	☐	☐	☐	☐
21091	$3	☐	☐	☐	☐
21092	$3	☐	☐	☐	☐
21093	$3	☐	☐	☐	☐
21094	$70	☐	☐	☐	☐
21095	$3	☐	☐	☐	☐
21381	$3	☐	☐	☐	☐
21382	$3	☐	☐	☐	☐

Plate	Price	UL	UR	LL	LR
21389	$3	☐	☐	☐	☐
21390	$3	☐	☐	☐	☐
21503	$6	☐	☐	☐	☐
21504	$6	☐	☐	☐	☐
21549	$3	☐	☐	☐	☐
21550	$3	☐	☐	☐	☐
21551	$3	☐	☐	☐	☐
21552	$3	☐	☐	☐	☐
21570	$10	☐	☐	☐	☐
21571	$3	☐	☐	☐	☐
21584	$3	☐	☐	☐	☐
21585	$7	☐	☐	☐	☐
21586	$3	☐	☐	☐	☐
21587	$3	☐	☐	☐	☐

1930 REGULAR ISSUE

#684 1½¢ HARDING (FULL FACE) Continued

Plate	Price	UL	UR	LL	LR
21744	$3	☐	☐	☐	☐
21745	$3	☐	☐	☐	☐
21749	$3	☐	☐	☐	☐
21750	$3	☐	☐	☐	☐
21752	$8	☐	☐	☐	☐
21753	$8	☐	☐	☐	☐
21758	$9	☐	☐	☐	☐
21759	$9	☐	☐	☐	☐

#685 4¢ TAFT 10 Plates

Plate	Price	UL	UR	LL	LR
20136	$8.50	☐	☐	☐	☐
20137	$8.50	☐	☐	☐	☐
20140	$8.50	☐	☐	☐	☐
20141	$8.50	☐	☐	☐	☐
20172	$8.50	☐	☐	☐	☐
20173	$8.50	☐	☐	☐	☐
20174	$8.50	☐	☐	☐	☐
20175	$12.50	☐	☐	☐	☐
20203	$12.50	☐	☐	☐	☐
20204	$12.50	☐	☐	☐	☐

1930 REGULAR ISSUE
SIDE COIL PLATES

ROTARY PRESS

PERF. 10 VERTICALLY

Positions T, B

#686 1½¢ HARDING COIL (FULL FACE) 20 Plates

20261	20262	20263	20264	20388
20389	20392	20393	20396	20397
20402	20403	20410	20411	21112
21113	21487	21488	21511	21512

#687 4¢ TAFT COIL 4 Plates

20134	20135	20142	20143

1931 REGULAR ISSUE

ROTARY PRESS PERF. 11 x 10½

#692 11¢ HAYES 5 Plates

Plate	Price	UL	UR	LL	LR
20533	$17.50	☐	☐	☐	☐
20534	$17.50	☐	☐	☐	☐
20617	$17.50	☐	☐	☐	☐
20618	$17.50	☐	☐	☐	☐
21078	$17.50	☐	☐	☐	☐

1930 REGULAR ISSUES Cont.

#693 12¢ CLEVELAND 6 Plates

		UL	UR	LL	LR
20543	$35.00	☐	☐	☐	☐
20614	$35.00	☐	☐	☐	☐
20708	$35.00	☐	☐	☐	☐
20709	$35.00	☐	☐	☐	☐
21179 N	$500.00	☐	†	†	†
21180 N	$500.00	☐	†	†	†

N Rare in **mint** condition. All positions exist precancelled and are less difficult.

#694 13¢ HARRISON 5 Plates

20545	$20	☐	☐	☐	☐
20546	$20	☐	☐	☐	☐
20712	$20	☐	☐	☐	☐
20713	$20	☐	☐	☐	☐
21079	$20	☐	☐	☐	☐

#695 14¢ AMERICAN INDIAN
2 Plates

20549	$25	☐	☐	☐	☐
20550	$25	☐	☐	☐	☐

#696 15¢ STATUE OF LIBERTY

6 Plates

20547	$50	☐	☐	☐	☐
20548	$50	☐	☐	☐	☐
20722	$50	☐	☐	☐	☐
20723	$50	☐	☐	☐	☐
21181	N $100	☐	☐	☐	☐
21182	N $100	☐	☐	☐	☐

N Very scarce in **mint** condition. All positions also exist precancelled and are less difficult in that form.

1931 REGULAR ISSUE

ROTARY PRESS PERF. 10½ x 11

#697 17¢ WILSON 2 Plates

		UL	UR	LL	LR
20535	$30	☐	☐	☐	☐
20536	$30	☐	☐	☐	☐

1931 REGULAR ISSUE

ROTARY PRESS PERF. 10½ x 11

#698 20¢ GOLDEN GATE 4 Plates

		UL	UR	LL	LR
20537	$55	☐	☐	☐	☐
20538	$55	☐	☐	☐	☐
20688	$55	☐	☐	☐	☐
20689	$55	☐	☐	☐	☐

#699 25¢ NIAGARA FALLS 4 Plates

20539	$60	☐	☐	☐	☐
20540	$60	☐	☐	☐	☐
20729	$60	☐	☐	☐	☐
20730	$60	☐	☐	☐	☐

#700 30¢ BISON 4 Plates

20551	$100	☐	☐	☐	☐
20552	$100	☐	☐	☐	☐
20743	$100	☐	☐	☐	☐
20744	$100	☐	☐	☐	☐

#701 50¢ AMPHITHEATRE 2 Plates

20553	$300	☐	☐	☐	☐
20554	$300	☐	☐	☐	☐

Much of our plate number information stems from studies made by members of the Bureau Issues Association and published in their magazine. Serious plate number collectors should join this organization. For further information write to:

George V.H. Godin, Executive Secretary
P.O. Box 1047, Belleville IL 62223-1047

1931 COMMEMORATIVES

FLAT PRESS PERF. 11

#702 2¢ RED CROSS BICOLORED

Plate Combination Block of 4

TL - BLACK NO. - RED NO.

TR - RED NO. - F BLACK NO.

BL - BLACK NO. - RED NO.

BR - RED NO. - BLACK NO.

Basic Price $2.50

The last 4 frame plates had short runs and are comparatively scarce. We place a tentative valuation of $5.00 on combinations blocks containing 20514, 20515, 20516 — and $9.00 on 20525 which had the fewest impressions.

20 VIGNETTE PLATES

24 FRAME PLATES

24 FRAME PLATES		20445		20446		20447		20448		20449		20489		20490		20491		20492		20493		20494		20495		20496		20497		20498		20499		20500		20501		20502		20503	
		L	R	L	R	L	R	L	R	L	R	L	R	L	R	L	R	L	R	L	R	L	R	L	R	L	R	L	R	L	R	L	R	L	R	L	R	L	R	L	R
20434	T																																								
	B																																								
20435	T																																								
	B																																								
20436	T																																								
	B																																								
20437	T																																								
	B																																								
20438	T																																								
	B																																								
20439	T																																								
	B																																								
20440	T																																								
	B																																								
20441	T																																								
	B																																								
20450	T																																								
	B																																								
20451	T																																								
	B																																								
20452	T																																								
	B																																								
20453	T																																								
	B																																								
20454	T																																								
	B																																								
20455	T																																								
	B																																								
20456	T																																								
	B																																								
20457	T																																								
	B																																								
20466	T																																								
	B																																								
20467	T																																								
	B																																								
20468	T																																								
	B																																								
20469	T																																								
	B																																								
20514	T																																								
	B																																								
20515	T																																								
	B																																								
20516	T																																								
	B																																								
20525	T																																								
	B																																								

1931 COMMEMORATIVES

#703 2¢ YORKTOWN BICOLORED

Plate Combination Block of 4

FIRST LAYOUT WITHOUT ARROW

Printed from 100-subject plates divided into left and right panes.

16 Frame Plates

22 Vignette Plates		20461 L	20461 R	20462 L	20462 R	20463 L	20463 R	20464 L	20464 R	20465 L	20465 R	20478 L	20478 R	20479 L	20479 R	20480 L	20480 R	20481 L	20481 R	20482 L	20482 R	20483 L	20483 R	20484 L	20484 R	20485 L	20485 R	20486 L	20486 R	20487 L	20487 R	20488 L	20488 R
20470	T																																
	B																																
20472	T																																
	B																																
20473	T																																
	B																																
20474	T																																
	B																																
20475	T																																
	B																																
20476	T																																
	B																																
20477	T																																
	B																																
20504	T																																
	B																																
20505	T																																
	B																																
20506	T																																
	B																																
20507	T																																
	B																																
20508	T																																
	B																																
20509	T																																
	B																																
20510	T																																
	B																																
20511	T																																
	B																																
20512	T																																
	B																																
20597	T																																
	B																																
*20598	T																																
	B																																
*20599	T																																
	B																																
*20600	T																																
	B																																
*20601	T																																
	B																																
*20602	T																																
	B																																

*The last 5 plates are scarcer than the others. 20602 is the most difficult.

1931 COMMEMORATIVES

#703 2¢ YORKTOWN BICOLORED

FIRST LAYOUT WITHOUT ARROW

In the first layout every red (frame) plate exists in combination with every black (vignette) plate. There are 352 **number** combinations

Plate Combination Block of 4

Basic Price **TL, TR, BL, BR** $4

SECOND LAYOUT WITH ARROW

Basic Combination Block of 6

Basic Price **TL, TR, B** $5.50

SECOND LAYOUT WITH ARROW

The vignette plates made for the second layout contained only 50 subjects, so there are no left and right vignette panes. Every vignette number exists in combination with every frame plate. There are 128 **number** combinations. Most of the vignette plates were used with only one side of the frame plates; that is, left or right panes only. Therefore, on these there are just 2 positions, top and bottom. A few of the vignette numbers were used with both left and right frame plates. These bottom positions can be identified in blocks of 10 (2 x 5) only.

8 Frame Plates / 16 Vignette Plates

16 Vignette Plates		20646		20647		20648		20649		20668		20669		20670		20671	
		L	R	L	R	L	R	L	R	L	R	L	R	L	R	L	R
20650	T	s	c	s	c	s	c	s	c		c		c		c		c
	B	s	c	s	c	s	c	s	c		c		c		c		c
20651	T	c	s	c	s	c	s	c	s	c		c		c		c	
	B	c	s	c	s	c	s	c	s	c		c		c		c	
20652	T		c	s	c	s	c	s	c		c		c		c		c
	B		c	s	c	s	c	s	c		c		c		c		c
20653	T	s	c	s	c	s	c	s	c		c		c		c		c
	B	s	c	s	c	s	c	s	c		c		c		c		c
20656	T	c	s	c	s	c	s	c	s	c		c		c		c	
	B	c	s	c	s	c	s	c	s	c		c		c		c	
20657	T	c		c		c		c		c	s	c		c		c	
	B	c		c		c		c		c	s	c		c		c	
20658	T	c		c		c		c		c	s	c		c		c	
	B	c		c		c		c		c	s	c		c		c	
20659	T	s	c	s	c	s	c	s	c		c		c		c		c
	B	s	c	s	c	s	c	s	c		c		c		c		c
20660	T	c		c		c		c		c		c		c	s	c	
	B	c		c		c		c		c		c		c	s	c	
20661	T		c		c		c		c		c		c		c		c
	B		c		c		c		c		c		c		c		c
20662	T		c		c		c		c	s	c		c		c		c
	B		c		c		c		c	s	c		c		c		c
20663	T	c		c		c		c		c		c		c		c	
	B	c		c		c		c		c		c		c		c	
20664	T		c		c		c		c		c		c		c		c
	B		c		c		c		c		c		c		c		c
20665	T	c		c		c		c		c		c		c		c	
	B	c		c		c		c		c		c		c		c	
20666	T	c		c		c		c		c		c		c		c	
	B	c		c		c		c		c		c		c		c	
20667	T		c		c		c		c		c		c		c		c
	B		c		c		c		c		c		c		c		c

c - - common   s - - scarce

Identifying plate block positions

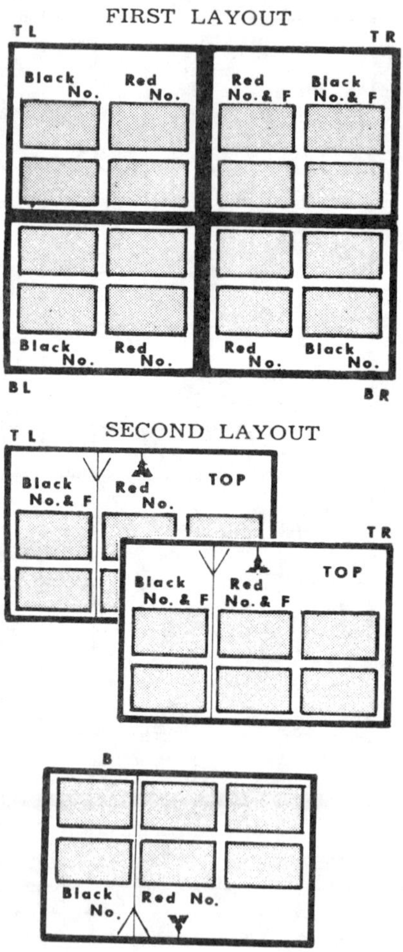

1932 WASHINGTON BICENTENNIAL ISSUE

ROTARY PRESS PERF 11 x 10½

#704 ½¢ BICENTENNIAL 6 Plates

Plate	Price	UL	UR	LL	LR
20559	$5	☐	☐	☐	☐
20560	$5	☐	☐	☐	☐
20605	$5	☐	☐	☐	☐
20629	$5	☐	☐	☐	☐
20698	$8	☐	☐	☐	☐
20699	$8	☐	☐	☐	☐

#705 1¢ BICENTENNIAL 28 Plates

Plate	Price	UL	UR	LL	LR
20561	$5	☐	☐	☐	☐
20562	$5	☐	☐	☐	☐
20573	$5	☐	☐	☐	☐
20574	$5	☐	☐	☐	☐
20654	$5	☐	☐	☐	☐
20655	$5	☐	☐	☐	☐
20690	$5	☐	☐	☐	☐
20691	$5	☐	☐	☐	☐
20692	$5	☐	☐	☐	☐
20693	$5	☐	☐	☐	☐
20714	$5	☐	☐	☐	☐
20715	$5	☐	☐	☐	☐
20739	$5	☐	☐	☐	☐
20740	$5	☐	☐	☐	☐
20741	$5	☐	☐	☐	☐
20742	$5	☐	☐	☐	☐
20747	$5	☐	☐	☐	☐
20766	$5	☐	☐	☐	☐
20775	$5	☐	☐	☐	☐
20776	$5	☐	☐	☐	☐
20831	$15	☐	☐	☐	☐
20832	$15	☐	☐	☐	☐
20835	$5	☐	☐	☐	☐
20836	$5	☐	☐	☐	☐
20839	$15	☐	☐	☐	☐
20840	$9	☐	☐	☐	☐
20843	$5	☐	☐	☐	☐
20844	$5	☐	☐	☐	☐

#706 1½¢ BICENTENNIAL 8 Plates

Plate	Price	UL	UR	LL	LR
20632	$22.50	☐	☐	☐	☐
20633	$22.50	☐	☐	☐	☐
20634	$22.50	☐	☐	☐	☐
20635	$22.50	☐	☐	☐	☐
20678	$22.50	☐	☐	☐	☐
20679	$22.50	☐	☐	☐	☐
20680	$22.50	☐	☐	☐	☐
20681	$22.50	☐	☐	☐	☐

#707 2¢ BICENTENNIAL 60 Plates

Plate	Price	UL	UR	LL	LR
20555	$2	☐	☐	☐	☐
20556	$2	☐	☐	☐	☐
20577	$2	☐	☐	☐	☐
20578	$2	☐	☐	☐	☐
20583	$2	☐	☐	☐	☐
20584	$2	☐	☐	☐	☐
20630	$2	☐	☐	☐	☐

#707 2¢ BICENTENNIAL Cont.

Plate	Price	UL	UR	LL	LR
20631	$2	☐	☐	☐	☐
20644	$2	☐	☐	☐	☐
20645	$2	☐	☐	☐	☐
20684	$2	☐	☐	☐	☐
20685	$2	☐	☐	☐	☐
20696	$2	☐	☐	☐	☐
20697	$2	☐	☐	☐	☐
20706	$2	☐	☐	☐	☐
20707	$2	☐	☐	☐	☐
20716	$2	☐	☐	☐	☐
20717	$2	☐	☐	☐	☐
20726	$2	☐	☐	☐	☐
20727	$2	☐	☐	☐	☐
20733	$5	☐	☐	☐	☐
20734	$2	☐	☐	☐	☐
20749	$2	☐	☐	☐	☐
20750	$2	☐	☐	☐	☐
20751	$2	☐	☐	☐	☐
20752	$15	☐	☐	☐	☐
20753	$2	☐	☐	☐	☐
20754	$2	☐	☐	☐	☐
20755	$2	☐	☐	☐	☐
20756	$2	☐	☐	☐	☐
20759	$2	☐	☐	☐	☐
20760	$2	☐	☐	☐	☐
20761	$2	☐	☐	☐	☐
20762	$2	☐	☐	☐	☐
20763	$2	☐	☐	☐	☐
20764	$2	☐	☐	☐	☐
20767	$2	☐	☐	☐	☐
20768	$2	☐	☐	☐	☐
20771	$2	☐	☐	☐	☐
20772	$2	☐	☐	☐	☐
20773	$2	☐	☐	☐	☐
20774	$2	☐	☐	☐	☐
20781	$2	☐	☐	☐	☐
20782	$2	☐	☐	☐	☐
20783	$2	☐	☐	☐	☐
20784	$2	☐	☐	☐	☐
20789	$2	☐	☐	☐	☐
20790	$2	☐	☐	☐	☐
20791	$2	☐	☐	☐	☐
20792	$2	☐	☐	☐	☐
20793	$2	☐	☐	☐	☐
20794	$2	☐	☐	☐	☐
20795	$2	☐	☐	☐	☐
20796	$2	☐	☐	☐	☐
20801	$2	☐	☐	☐	☐
20802	$20	☐	☐	☐	☐
20803	$20	☐	☐	☐	☐
20804	$2	☐	☐	☐	☐
20805	$2	☐	☐	☐	☐
20806	$10	☐	☐	☐	☐

1932 WASHINGTON BICENTENNIAL ISSUE

ROTARY PRESS PERF. 11 x 10½

#708 3¢ BICENTENNIAL 12 Plates

		UL	UR	LL	LR
20557	$17.50	☐	☐	☐	☐
20558	$17.50	☐	☐	☐	☐
20694	$17.50	☐	☐	☐	☐
20695	$17.50	☐	☐	☐	☐
20847	$60.00	☐	☐	☐	☐
20848	$60.00	☐	☐	☐	☐
21014	$17.50	☐	☐	☐	☐
21015	$17.50	☐	☐	☐	☐
21042	$17.50	☐	☐	☐	☐
21043	$17.50	☐	☐	☐	☐
21044	$37.50	☐	☐	☐	☐
21045	$37.50	☐	☐	☐	☐

#709 4¢ BICENTENNIAL 4 Plates

20567	$7	☐	☐	☐	☐
20568	$7	☐	☐	☐	☐
20593	$7	☐	☐	☐	☐
20594	$7	☐	☐	☐	☐

#710 5¢ BICENTENNIAL 4 Plates

20636	$23	☐	☐	☐	☐
20637	$23	☐	☐	☐	☐
20638	$23	☐	☐	☐	☐
20639	$23	☐	☐	☐	☐

#711 6¢ BICENTENNIAL 2 Plates

20569	$75	☐	☐	☐	☐
20570	$75	☐	☐	☐	☐

#712 7¢ BICENTENNIAL 4 Plates

20563	$7	☐	☐	☐	☐
20564	$7	☐	☐	☐	☐
20731	$7	☐	☐	☐	☐
20732	$7	☐	☐	☐	☐

#713 8¢ BICENTENNIAL 2 Plates

20565	$85	☐	☐	☐	☐
20566	$85	☐	☐	☐	☐

1932 WASHINGTON BICENTENNIAL ISSUE

ROTARY PRESS PERF. 11 x 10½

#714 9¢ BICENTENNIAL 2 Plates

		UL	UR	LL	LR
20640	$50	☐	☐	☐	☐
20641	$50	☐	☐	☐	☐

#715 10¢ BICENTENNIAL 4 Plates

20642	$150	☐	☐	☐	☐
20643	$150	☐	☐	☐	☐
20686	$150	☐	☐	☐	☐
20687	$150	☐	☐	☐	☐

1932 COMMEMORATIVES

FLAT PRESS PERF. 11

#716 2¢ OLYMPIC LAKE PLACID
12 Plates

		TL	TR	L	R	B
20815	$18	☐	☐	‡	‡	☐
20816	$18	☐	☐	‡	‡	☐
20817	$18	☐	☐	‡	‡	☐
20818	$18	☐	☐	‡	‡	☐
20819	$18	☐	☐	‡	‡	☐
20820	$18	☐	☐	‡	‡	☐
20821	$18	☐	☐	‡	‡	☐
20822	$18	☐	☐	‡	‡	☐
20823	$18	☐	☐	‡	‡	☐
20824	$18	☐	☐	‡	‡	☐
20825	$18	☐	☐	‡	‡	☐
20826	$18	☐	☐	‡	‡	☐

ROTARY PRESS PERF. 11 x 10½

#717 2¢ ARBOR DAY 6 Plates

		UL	UR	LL	LR
20872	$10	☐	☐	☐	☐
20873	$10	☐	☐	☐	☐
20874	$10	☐	☐	☐	☐
20875	$10	☐	☐	☐	☐
20876	$10	☐	☐	☐	☐
20877	$10	☐	☐	☐	☐

#718 3¢ OLYMPIC RUNNER
6 Plates

20864	$20	☐	☐	☐	☐
20865	$20	☐	☐	☐	☐
20906	$20	☐	☐	☐	☐
20907	$20	☐	☐	☐	☐
20908	$20	☐	☐	☐	☐
20909	$20	☐	☐	☐	☐

#719 5¢ DISCUS THROWER
4 Plates

20868	$35	☐	☐	☐	☐
20869	$35	☐	☐	☐	☐
20870	$35	☐	☐	☐	☐
20871	$35	☐	☐	☐	☐

1932 REGULAR ISSUE

ROTARY PRESS

#720 3¢ "STUART" WASHINGTON

This stamp is very popular with collectors who enjoy tackling a long run of plate numbers. There are 206 plates for a total of 824 pieces if one is to go for all 4 positions. Although the stamp is common and the majority of the plates are not classed as difficult, it is quite an achievement to complete even the easier numbers in all positions. Beyond that the struggle begins, for the scarce to rare plates offer a stout challenge.

The issue is not noted for very fine centering. Although it is possible to obtain many of the blocks in fine or better condition, anyone starting a "Stuart" collection with the idea of being super-fussy should be warned at the beginning that there is no such thing as an important showing of the plates except in mixed condition. Even the best possible "Stuart" collection will contain a percentage of less-than-fine specimens. Nevertheless, the condition on the whole should be reasonably attractive to warrant our evaluations.

206 Plates		UL	UR	LL	LR
20878	$1.75	☐	☐	☐	☐
20879	$1.75	☐	☐	☐	☐
20880	$6.00	☐$_3$	☐$_3$	☐$_2$	☐$_3$
20881	$5.00	☐$_5$	☐$_3$	☐$_4$	☐$_6$
20884	$1.75	☐	☐	☐	☐
20885	$1.75	☐	☐	☐	☐
20886	$1.75	☐	☐	☐	☐
20887	$1.75	☐	☐	☐	☐
20888	$6.00	☐	☐$_2$	☐	☐
20889	$6.00	☐	☐$_5$	☐$_2$	☐$_2$
20890	$4.00	☐	☐	☐	☐
20891	$1.75	☐	☐	☐	☐
20892	$1.75	☐	☐	☐	☐
20893	$1.75	☐	☐	☐	☐
20894	$1.75	☐	☐	☐	☐
20895	$1.75	☐	☐	☐	☐
20910	$1.75	☐	☐	☐	☐
20911	$1.75	☐	☐	☐	☐
20912	$20.00	☐	☐	☐	☐
20913	$1.75	☐	☐	☐	☐
20914	$5.00	☐$_4$	☐$_9$	☐$_1$	☐$_4$
20915	$1.75	☐	☐	☐	☐

#720 3¢ "STUART" WASHINGTON

Continued		UL	UR	LL	LR
20920	$1.75	☐	☐	☐	☐
20921	$1.75	☐	☐	☐	☐
20932	$1.75	☐	☐	☐	☐
20933	$1.75	☐	☐	☐	☐
20934	$1.75	☐	☐	☐	☐
20935	$1.75	☐	☐	☐	☐
20950	$1.75	☐	☐	☐	☐
20951	$4.00	☐	☐	☐	☐
20952	$1.75	☐	☐	☐	☐
20953	$1.75	☐	☐	☐	☐
20954	$1.75	☐	☐	☐	☐
20955	$1.75	☐	☐	☐	☐
20956	$2.50	☐$_2$	☐$_2$	☐	☐$_2$
20957	$1.75	☐	☐	☐	☐
20958	$1.75	☐	☐	☐	☐
20959	$1.75	☐	☐	☐	☐
20960	$1.75	☐	☐	☐	☐
20961	$12.50	☐$_3$	☐$_8$	☐$_3$	☐$_3$
20962	$2.00	☐$_4$	☐$_7$	☐$_6$	☐$_6$
20963	$1.75	☐	☐	☐	☐
20964	$1.75	☐	☐	☐	☐
20965	$1.75	☐	☐	☐	☐
20966	$1.75	☐	☐	☐	☐
20967	$1.75	☐	☐	☐	☐
20970	$1.75	☐	☐	☐	☐
20971	$1.75	☐	☐	☐	☐
20972	$1.75	☐	☐	☐	☐
20973	$1.75	☐	☐	☐	☐
20974	$1.75	☐	☐	☐	☐
20975	$1.75	☐	☐	☐	☐
20980	$12.00	☐	☐	☐	☐$_2$
20981	$30.00	☐	☐	☐	☐
20982	$1.75	☐	☐	☐	☐
20983	$1.75	☐	☐	☐	☐
20984	$25.00	☐$_5$	☐$_4$	☐$_3$	☐$_4$
20985	$1.75	☐	☐	☐	☐
20986	$1.75	☐	☐	☐	☐
20987	$1.75	☐	☐	☐	☐
20988	$1.75	☐	☐	☐	☐
20989	$1.75	☐	☐	☐	☐
20990	$1.75	☐	☐	☐	☐
20991	$1.75	☐	☐	☐	☐
20992	$1.75	☐	☐	☐	☐
20993	$1.75	☐	☐	☐	☐
20996	$1.75	☐	☐	☐	☐
20997	$1.75	☐	☐	☐	☐
20998	$1.75	☐	☐	☐	☐
20999	$1.75	☐	☐	☐	☐
21000	$1.75	☐	☐	☐	☐
21001	$1.75	☐	☐	☐	☐
21004	$1.75	☐	☐	☐	☐
21005	$1.75	☐	☐	☐	☐
21006	$1.75	☐	☐	☐	☐
21007	$1.75	☐	☐	☐	☐
21008	$1.75	☐	☐	☐	☐
21009	$1.75	☐	☐	☐	☐
21018	$4.00	☐	☐	☐	☐
21019	$4.00	☐	☐	☐	☐

1932 REGULAR ISSUE

ROTARY PRESS

#720 3¢ "STUART" WASHINGTON Continued

Plate	Price	UL	UR	LL	LR
21022	$4.00	☐	☐	☐	☐
21023	$1.75	☐	☐	☐	☐
21024	$1.75	☐	☐	☐	☐
21025	$1.75	☐	☐	☐	☐
21114	$1.75	☐	☐	☐	☐
21115	$1.75	☐	☐	☐	☐
21116	$1.75	☐	☐	☐	☐
21117	$2.50	☐	☐	☐	☐2
21224	$1.75	☐	☐	☐	☐
21225	$2.50	☐	☐	☐2	☐
21266	$1.75	☐	☐	☐	☐
21267	$2.50	☐	☐	☐2	☐
21268	$1.75	☐	☐	☐	☐
21269	$1.75	☐	☐	☐	☐
21282	$1.75	☐	☐	☐	☐
21283	$1.75	☐	☐	☐	☐
21284	$1.75	☐	☐	☐	☐
21285	$1.75	☐	☐	☐	☐
21290	$1.75	☐	☐	☐	☐
21291	$1.75	☐	☐	☐	☐
21298	$1.75	☐	☐	☐	☐
21299	$1.75	☐	☐	☐	☐
21300	$1.75	☐	☐	☐	☐
21301	$1.75	☐	☐	☐	☐
21308	$1.75	☐	☐	☐	☐
21309	$1.75	☐	☐	☐	☐
21310	$1.75	☐	☐	☐	☐
21311	$1.75	☐	☐	☐	☐
21347	$1.75	☐	☐	☐	☐
21348	$1.75	☐	☐	☐	☐
21349	$1.75	☐	☐	☐	☐
21350	$1.75	☐	☐	☐	☐
21351	$1.75	☐	☐	☐	☐
21352	$2.50	☐	☐3	☐	☐
21353	$1.75	☐	☐	☐	☐
21354	$1.75	☐	☐	☐	☐
21355	$1.75	☐	☐	☐	☐
21356	$1.75	☐	☐	☐	☐
21357	$1.75	☐	☐	☐	☐
21358	$3.00	☐	☐2	☐	☐2
21359	$1.75	☐	☐	☐	☐
21360	$1.75	☐	☐	☐	☐
21361	$1.75	☐	☐	☐	☐
21362	$1.75	☐	☐	☐	☐
21363	$1.75	☐	☐	☐	☐
21364	$1.75	☐	☐	☐	☐
21365	$1.75	☐	☐	☐	☐
21366	$1.75	☐	☐	☐	☐
21369	$1.75	☐	☐	☐	☐
21370	$1.75	☐	☐	☐	☐
21373	$1.75	☐	☐	☐	☐
21374	$1.75	☐	☐	☐	☐
21375	$1.75	☐	☐	☐	☐
21376	$1.75	☐	☐	☐	☐
21385	$1.75	☐	☐	☐	☐
21386	$1.75	☐	☐	☐	☐
21397	$1.75	☐	☐	☐	☐
21398	$1.75	☐	☐	☐	☐
21400	$1.75	☐	☐	☐	☐

Plate	Price	UL	UR	LL	LR
21401	$1.75	☐	☐	☐	☐
21403	$1.75	☐	☐	☐	☐
21404	$1.75	☐	☐	☐	☐
21425	$1.75	☐	☐	☐	☐
21426	$1.75	☐	☐	☐	☐
21427	$1.75	☐	☐	☐	☐
21428	$1.75	☐	☐	☐	☐
21429	$1.75	☐	☐	☐	☐
21430	$1.75	☐	☐	☐	☐
21431	$1.75	☐	☐	☐	☐
21432	$1.75	☐	☐	☐	☐
21439	$1.75	☐	☐	☐	☐
21440	$1.75	☐	☐	☐	☐
21449	$1.75	☐	☐	☐	☐
21450	$1.75	☐	☐	☐	☐
21451	$1.75	☐	☐	☐	☐
21452	$1.75	☐	☐	☐	☐
21453	$1.75	☐	☐	☐	☐
21454	$1.75	☐	☐	☐	☐
21521	$1.75	☐	☐	☐	☐
21522	$1.75	☐	☐	☐	☐
21523	$1.75	☐	☐	☐	☐
21524	$1.75	☐	☐	☐	☐
21525	$1.75	☐	☐	☐	☐
21526	$1.75	☐	☐	☐	☐
21529	$1.75	☐	☐	☐	☐
21530	$1.75	☐	☐	☐	☐
21545	$1.75	☐	☐	☐	☐
21546	$1.75	☐	☐	☐	☐
21547	$1.75	☐	☐	☐	☐
21548	$1.75	☐	☐	☐	☐
21574	$1.75	☐	☐	☐	☐
21575	$1.75	☐	☐	☐	☐
21580	$1.75	☐	☐	☐	☐
21581	$1.75	☐	☐	☐	☐
21582	$1.75	☐	☐	☐	☐
21583	$1.75	☐	☐	☐	☐
21616	$1.75	☐	☐	☐	☐
21617	$1.75	☐	☐	☐	☐
21618	$1.75	☐	☐	☐	☐
21619	$1.75	☐	☐	☐	☐
21649	$1.75	☐	☐	☐	☐
21650	$1.75	☐	☐	☐	☐
21659	$1.75	☐	☐	☐	☐
21660	$1.75	☐	☐	☐	☐
21661	$1.75	☐	☐	☐	☐
21662	$1.75	☐	☐	☐	☐
21667	$1.75	☐	☐	☐	☐
21668	$1.75	☐	☐	☐	☐
21669	$2.50	☐	☐2	☐2	☐2
21670	$5.00	☐	☐	☐	☐
21672	$1.75	☐	☐	☐	☐
21673	$5.00	☐	☐	☐	☐8
21718	$2.50	☐	☐2	☐	☐
21748	$2.50	☐	☐2	☐	☐
21754	$1.75	☐	☐	☐	☐
21755	$1.75	☐	☐	☐	☐
21762	$1.75	☐	☐	☐	☐
21763	$1.75	☐	☐	☐	☐

1932 REGULAR ISSUE

ROTARY PRESS

#720 3¢ "STUART" WASHINGTON

Continued		UL	UR	LL	LR
21764	$1.75	□	□	□	□
21765	$1.75	□	□	□	□
21766	$3.00	□$_3$	□$_3$	□$_2$	□$_2$
21767	$3.00	□$_3$	□$_2$	□$_2$	□$_3$
21768	$2.50	□$_2$	□	□$_2$	□
21769	$2.50	□$_2$	□	□	□
21772	$6.00	□	□$_4$	□$_2$	□
21773	$6.00	□	□$_4$	□$_2$	□

COILS and BOOKLET PANES

When rotary-press coils and booklet panes are perfectly cut, the plate numbers are removed, but off-center and/or widely cut specimens show part of the plate, the percentage visible depending, of course, on the width of the margin containing the number. It follows that the bigger the percentage, the greater the desirability. It is possible to obtain 100% complete numbers on several booklet-pane plates, but, although seen infrequently, their scarcity does not compare with that of 100% coil numbers. Any complete coil-plate number is **rare.**

It is possible to **reconstruct** numerous coil-plate numbers by joining partial plates.

The full numbers seen on booklet panes are invariably upper- or lower-left positions. The cutting is never as wide on upper and lower rights, and booklet-pane specialists are usually satisfied when right-pane plate-number percentages are large enough to be identified.

1932 REGULAR ISSUE

#720b 3¢ "STUART" 16 Plates

BOOKLET PANES OF 6

ROTARY PRESS

20900 20901 20902 20903 20904
20905 21010 21011 21012 21013
21489 21490 21515 21516 21519
21520

ROTARY PRESS PERF. 10 VERTICALLY

#721 3¢ "STUART" SIDE COILS

Positions T or B **88 Plates**

20916 20917 20918 20919 20936
20937 20938 20939 20940 20941
20942 20943 20944 20945 20946
20947 20948 20949 20976 20977
20978 20979 20994 20995 21002
21003 21016 21017 21020 21021

1932 REGULAR ISSUE

#721 3¢ "STUART" SIDE COILS

Continued

21026 21027 21050 21051 21052
21053 21060 21061 21062 21063
21076 21077 21084 21085 21086
21087 21222 21223 21477 21478
21479 21480 21481 21482 21483
21484 21513 21514 21541 21542
21543 21544 21553 21554

Plates through 21554 were entered approximately 1/16 inch from the stamp design. Those that follow were wide spaced, about 1/8 inch from the design. Because of the wide spacing, very few of the numbers are known to exist.

21592 †21593 †21596 †21597 †21639
†21640 †21641 †21642 †21643 †21644
†21646 †21647 21648 21675 †21702
†21703 †21704 21790 †21791 †21792
21799 †21800 †21803 †21804

ROTARY PRESS

PERF. 10 HORIZONTALLY

#722 3¢ "STUART" END COILS

Positions L, R **2 Plates**

20930 20931

ROTARY PRESS

PERF. 10 VERTICALLY

#723 6¢ GARFIELD SIDE COILS

Positions T or B **2 plates**

20968 20969

1932 COMMEMORATIVES

FLAT PRESS PERF. 11

Blocks of 6

#724 3¢ PENN 12 Plates

		TL	TR	L	R	B
21064	$15	□	□	‡	‡	□
21065	$15	□	□	‡	‡	□
21066	$15	□	□	‡	‡	□
21067	$15	□	□	‡	‡	□
21068	$15	□	□	‡	‡	□
21069	$15	□	□	‡	‡	□
21070	$15	□	□	‡	‡	□
21071	$15	□	□	‡	‡	□
21072	$15	□	□	‡	‡	□
21073	$15	□	□	‡	‡	□
21074	$15	□	□	‡	‡	□
21075	$15	□	□	‡	‡	□

#725 3¢ WEBSTER

12 Plates		TL	TR	L	R	B
21034	$27.50	□	□	‡	‡	□
21035	$27.50	□	□	‡	‡	□
21036	$27.50	□	□	‡	‡	□
21037	$27.50	□	□	‡	‡	□

1932 COMMEMMORATIVES

FLAT PRESS PERF. 11 **Blocks of 6**

#725 3¢ WEBSTER Continued

		TL	TR	L	R	B
21038	$27.50	☐	☐	‡	‡	☐
21039	$27.50	☐	☐	‡	‡	☐
21040	$27.50	☐	☐	‡	‡	☐
21041	$27.50	☐	☐	‡	‡	☐
21046	$27.50	☐	☐	‡	‡	☐
21047	$27.50	☐	☐	‡	‡	☐
21048	$27.50	☐	☐	‡	‡	☐
21049	$27.50	☐	☐	‡	‡	☐

1933 COMMEMORATIVES

FLAT PRESS PERF. 11 **Blocks of 6**

#726 3¢ OGLETHORPE

There are no F numbers on Oglethorpe plates. Instead, the initials C.S., indicating chromed steel, appear in the top margin over the stamp second to the left of the plate-number copy. The inscription is entered on right panes only. Since Blocks of 6 stamps may be from either pane, we list them as T (Top).

Top blocks of 10 showing the C. S., or its absence, sell for about double the basic price.

16 Plates		T	CS	L	R	B
21096	$17.50	☐	☐	‡	‡	☐
21097	$17.50	☐	☐	‡	‡	☐
21098	$17.50	☐	☐	‡	‡	☐
21099	$17.50	☐	☐	‡	‡	☐
21100	$17.50	☐	☐	‡	‡	☐
21101	$17.50	☐	☐	‡	‡	☐
21102	$17.50	☐	☐	‡	‡	☐
21103	$17.50	☐	☐	‡	‡	☐
21104	$17.50	☐	☐	‡	‡	☐
21105	$17.50	☐	☐	‡	‡	☐
21106	$17.50	☐	☐	‡	‡	☐
21107	$17.50	☐	☐	‡	‡	☐
21108	$17.50	☐	☐	‡	‡	☐
21109	$17.50	☐	☐	‡	‡	☐
21110	$17.50	☐	☐	‡	‡	☐
21111	$17.50	☐	☐	‡	‡	☐

1933 COMMEMMORATIVES

ROTARY PRESS **Blocks of 4**

#727 3¢ NEWBURGH

6 Plates		UL	UR	LL	LR
21118	$6.50	☐	☐	☐	☐
21119	$6.50	☐	☐	☐	☐
21120	$6.50	☐	☐	☐	☐
21121	$6.50	☐	☐	☐	☐
21123	$6.50	☐	☐	☐	☐
21124	$6.50	☐	☐	☐	☐

#728 1¢ CENTURY OF PROGRESS

10 Plates

		UL	UR	LL	LR
21131	$3	☐	☐	☐	☐
21132	$3	☐	☐	☐	☐
21133	$3	☐	☐	☐	☐
21134	$3	☐	☐	☐	☐
21135	$3	☐	☐	☐	☐
21136	$3	☐	☐	☐	☐
21139	$6	☐	☐	☐	☐
21140	$6	☐	☐	☐	☐
21141	$20	☐	☐	☐	☐
21142	$20	☐	☐	☐	☐

#7293¢ CENTURY OF PROGRESS

8 Plates

		UL	UR	LL	LR
21125	$4.50	☐	☐	☐	☐
21126	$4.50	☐	☐	☐	☐
21127	$4.50	☐	☐	☐	☐
21128	$4.50	☐	☐	☐	☐
21129	$4.50	☐	☐	☐	☐
21130	$4.50	☐	☐	☐	☐
21137	$4.50	☐	☐	☐	☐
21138	$4.50	☐	☐	☐	☐

1933 COMMEMMORATIVES

1933 CENTURY OF PROGRESS SOUVENIR SHEETS

IMPERFORATE PANES OF 25

Issued Without Gum FLAT PRESS

#730 1¢ SHEET 2 Plates

21145	$35	☐
21159	$35	☐

#731 3¢ SHEET 2 Plates

21146	$30	☐
21160	$30	☐

#732 3¢ N.R.A. ROTARY PRESS

14 Plates		UL	UR	LL	LR
21151	$2.25	☐	☐	☐	☐
21152	$2.25	☐	☐	☐	☐
21153	$2.25	☐	☐	☐	☐
21154	$2.25	☐	☐	☐	☐
21155	$2.25	☐	☐	☐	☐
21156	$2.25	☐	☐	☐	☐
21157	$2.25	☐	☐	☐	☐
21158	$2.25	☐	☐	☐	☐

1933 COMMEMORATIVES Continued

#732 3¢ N. R. A. Continued

		UL	UR	LL	LR
21161	$2.25	□	□	□	□
21162	$2.25	□	□	□	□
21163	$2.25	□	□	□	□
21164	$2.25	□	□	□	□
21165	$5.00	□	□	□	□
21166	$5.00	□	□	□	□

FLAT PRESS PERF. 11

#733 3¢ BYRD 4 Plates

		TL	TR	L	R	B
21167	$25	□	‡	‡	‡	□
21168	$25	□	‡	‡	‡	□
21169	$25	□	‡	‡	‡	□
21170	$25	□	‡	‡	‡	□

#734 5¢ KOSCIUSZKO 4 Plates

		TL	TR	L	R	B
21173	$50	□	‡	‡	‡	□
21174	$50	□	‡	‡	‡	□
21175	$50	□	‡	‡	‡	□
21176	$50	□	‡	‡	‡	□

1934 COMMEMORATIVES

#735 BYRD SOUVENIR SHEET IMPERFORATE PANE OF 6

Issued Without Gum

21184	$20	□

#736 3¢ MARYLAND

FLAT PRESS PERF. 11

8 Plates

		TL	TR	L	R	B
21188	$14	□	□	‡	‡	□
21189	$14	□	□	‡	‡	□
21190	$14	□	□	‡	‡	□
21191	$14	□	□	‡	‡	□
21196	$14	□	□	‡	‡	□
21197	$14	□	□	‡	‡	□
21198	$14	□	□	‡	‡	□
21199	$14	□	□	‡	‡	□

#737 3¢ MOTHER'S DAY

ROTARY PRESS PERF. 11 x 10½

10 plates

		UL	UR	LL	LR
21210	$2	□	□	□	□
21211	$2	□	□	□	□
21212	$2	□	□	□	□
21213	$2	□	□	□	□
21214	$2	□	□	□	□
21215	$2	□	□	□	□
21216	$2	□	□	□	□
21217	$2	□	□	□	□
21218	$2	□	□	□	□
21219	$2	□	□	□	□

1934 COMMEMORATIVES

FLAT PRESS PERF. 11

#738 3¢ MOTHER'S DAY

4 Plates

		TL	TR	L	R	B
21202	$6	□	□	‡	‡	□
21203	$6	□	□	‡	‡	□
21204	$6	□	‡	‡	‡	□
21205	$6	□	□	‡	‡	□

#739 3¢ WISCONSIN

8 Plates

		TL	TR	L	R	B
21238	$5.00	□	□	‡	‡	□
21239	$5.00	□	□	‡	‡	□
21240	$5.00	□	□	‡	‡	□
21241	$5.00	□	□	‡	‡	□
21242	$5.00	□	□	‡	‡	□
21243	$5.00	□	□	‡	‡	□
21244	$5.00	□	□	‡	‡	□
21245	$5.00	□	□	‡	‡	□

1934 NATIONAL PARKS

FLAT PRESS PERFORATED

#740 1¢ YOSEMITE PERF. 11

8 Plates

		TL	TR	L	R	B
21246	$1.75	□	□	‡	‡	□
21247	$1.75	□	□	‡	‡	□
21248	$1.75	□	□	‡	‡	□
21249	$1.75	□	□	‡	‡	□
21250	$1.75	□	□	‡	‡	□
21251	$1.75	□	□	‡	‡	□
21252	$1.75	□	□	‡	‡	□
21253	$1.75	□	□	‡	‡	□

#741 2¢ GRAND CANYON PERF. 11

8 Plates

		TL	TR	L	R	B
21254	$2	□	□	‡	‡	□
21255	$2	□	□	‡	‡	□
21256	$2	□	□	‡	‡	□
21257	$2	□	□	‡	‡	□
21258	$2	□	□	‡	‡	□
21259	$2	□	□	‡	‡	□
21260	$2	□	□	‡	‡	□
21261	$2	□	□	‡	‡	□

#742 3¢ MT. RAINIER PERF. 11

9 Plates

		TL	TR	L	R	B
21262	$2.75	□	□	‡	‡	□
21263	$2.75	□	□	‡	‡	□
21264	$2.75	□	□	‡	‡	□
21265	$2.75	□	□	‡	‡	□
21274	$2.75	□	□	‡	‡	□
21275	$2.75	□	□	‡	‡	□
21276	$2.75	□	□	‡	‡	□
21277	$2.75	□	□	‡	‡	□
21332	$2.75	□	□	‡	‡	□

#743 4¢ MESA VERDE PERF. 11

4 Plates

		TL	TR	L	R	B
21328	$12	□	□	‡	‡	□
21329	$12	□	□	‡	‡	□
21330	$12	□	□	‡	‡	□
21331	$12	□	□	‡	‡	□

1934 NATIONAL PARKS
Continued

#744 5¢ OLD FAITHFUL PERF. 11

4 Plates		TL	TR	L	R	B
21278	$15	☐	☐	‡	‡	☐
21279	$15	☐	☐	‡	‡	☐
21280	$15	☐	☐	‡	‡	☐
21281	$15	☐	☐	‡	‡	☐

#745 6¢ CRATER LAKE PERF. 11

4 Plates		TL	TR	L	R	B
21320	$27.50	☐	☐	‡	‡	☐
21321	$27.50	☐	☐	‡	‡	☐
21322	$27.50	☐	☐	‡	‡	☐
21323	$27.50	☐	☐	‡	‡	☐

#746 7¢ ACADIA PERF. 11

4 Plates		TL	TR	L	R	B
21333	$15	☐	☐	‡	‡	☐
21334	$15	☐	☐	‡	‡	☐
21335	$15	☐	☐	‡	‡	☐
21336	$15	☐	☐	‡	‡	☐

#747 8¢ ZION PARK PERF. 11

4 Plates		TL	TR	L	R	B
21324	$30	☐	☐	‡	‡	☐
21325	$30	☐	☐	‡	‡	☐
21326	$30	☐	☐	‡	‡	☐
21327	$30	☐	☐	‡	‡	☐

#748 9¢ GLACIER PARK PERF. 11

4 Plates		TL	TR	L	R	B
21316	$27.50	☐	☐	‡	‡	☐
21317	$27.50	☐	☐	‡	‡	☐
21318	$27.50	☐	☐	‡	‡	☐
21319	$27.50	☐	☐	‡	‡	☐

#749 10¢ GREAT SMOKY MOUNTAINS PERF. 11

4 Plates		TL	TR	L	R	B
21337	$50	☐	☐	‡	‡	☐
21339	$50	☐	☐	‡	‡	☐
21340	$50	☐	☐	‡	‡	☐
21342	$50	☐	☐	‡	‡	☐

IMPERFORATE SOUVENIR SHEETS
Issued With Gum

#750 3¢ MT. RAINIER PANE OF 6

21303	$37.50	☐

#751 1¢ YOSEMITE PANE OF 6

21341	$15	☐

1935 "FARLEY" REPRINTS SPECIAL PRINTINGS
Issued Without Gum

#752 3¢ NEWBURGH

ROTARY PRESS PERFORATED

2 Plates		UL	UR	LL	LR
21118	$15	☐	☐	☐	☐
21119	$15	☐	☐	☐	☐

FLAT PRESS PERFORATED

#753 3¢ BYRD 4 Plates

4 Plates		TL	TR	L	R	B
21167	$20	☐	‡	‡	‡	☐
21168	$20	☐	‡	‡	‡	☐
21169	$20	☐	‡	‡	‡	☐
21170	$20	☐	‡	‡	‡	☐

#754 3¢ MOTHER'S DAY IMPERF.

4 Plates		TL	TR	L	R	B
21202	$17.50	☐	☐	‡	‡	☐
21203	$17.50	☐	☐	‡	‡	☐
21204	$17.50	☐	‡	‡	‡	☐
21205	$17.50	☐	☐	‡	‡	☐

#755 3¢ WISCONSIN IMPERFORATE

4 Plates		TL	TR	L	R	B
21238	$17.50	☐	☐	‡	‡	☐
21239	$17.50	☐	☐	‡	‡	☐
21240	$17.50	☐	☐	‡	‡	☐
21241	$17.50	☐	☐	‡	‡	☐

#756 1¢ PARK IMPERFORATE

4 Plates		TL	TR	L	R	B
21246	$6	☐	☐	‡	‡	☐
21247	$6	☐	☐	‡	‡	☐
21248	$6	☐	☐	‡	‡	☐
21249	$6	☐	☐	‡	‡	☐

#757 2¢ PARK IMPERFORATE

4 Plates		TL	TR	L	R	B
21254	$7	☐	☐	‡	‡	☐
21255	$7	☐	☐	‡	‡	☐
21256	$7	☐	☐	‡	‡	☐
21257	$7	☐	☐	‡	‡	☐

#758 3¢ PARK IMPERFORATE

4 Plates		TL	TR	L	R	B
21262	$17.50	☐	☐	‡	‡	☐
21263	$17.50	☐	☐	‡	‡	☐
21264	$17.50	☐	☐	‡	‡	☐
21265	$17.50	☐	☐	‡	‡	☐

#759 4¢ PARK IMPERFORATE

4 Plates		TL	TR	L	R	B
21328	$22.50	☐	☐	‡	‡	☐
21329	$22.50	☐	☐	‡	‡	☐
21330	$22.50	☐	☐	‡	‡	☐
21331	$22.50	☐	☐	‡	‡	☐

1935 "FARLEY" REPRINTS SPECIAL PRINTINGS
Continued

#760 5¢ PARK IMPERFORATE

4 plates		TL	TR	L	R	B
21278	$30	☐	☐	‡	‡	☐
21279	$30	☐	☐	‡	‡	☐
21280	$30	☐	☐	‡	‡	☐
21281	$30	☐	☐	‡	‡	☐

#761 6¢ PARK IMPERFORATE

4 Plates

21320	$45	☐	☐	‡	‡	☐
21321	$45	☐	☐	‡	‡	☐
21322	$45	☐	☐	‡	‡	☐
21323	$45	☐	☐	‡	‡	☐

#762 7¢ PARK IMPERFORATE

4 Plates

21333	$40	☐	☐	‡	‡	☐
21334	$40	☐	☐	‡	‡	☐
21335	$40	☐	☐	‡	‡	☐
21336	$40	☐	☐	‡	‡	☐

#763 8¢ PARK IMPERFORATE

4 Plates

21324	$50	☐	☐	‡	‡	☐
21325	$50	☐	☐	‡	‡	☐
21326	$50	☐	☐	‡	‡	☐
21327	$50	☐	☐	‡	‡	☐

#764 9¢ PARK IMPERFORATE

4 Plates

21316	$50	☐	☐	‡	‡	☐
21317	$50	☐	☐	‡	‡	☐
21318	$50	☐	☐	‡	‡	☐
21319	$50	☐	☐	‡	‡	☐

#765 10¢ PARK IMPERFORATE

4 Plates

21337	$55	☐	☐	‡	‡	☐
21339	$55	☐	☐	‡	‡	☐
21340	$55	☐	☐	‡	‡	☐
21342	$55	☐	☐	‡	‡	☐

IMPERFORATE SOUVENIR SHEETS

Blocks of 50 containing 2 complete panes of 25 stamps.

#766 1¢ CENTURY OF PROGRESS

21145	$100	☐
21159	$100	☐

#767 3¢ CENTURY OF PROGRESS

21146	$90	☐
21160	$90	☐

1935 "FARLEY" REPRINTS SPECIAL PRINTINGS
Continued

IMPERFORATE SOUVENIR SHEETS

Blocks of 12 containing 2 complete panes of 6 stamps.

#768 3¢ BYRD

21184	$70	☐

#769 1¢ YOSEMITE

21341	$25	☐

#770 3¢ MT. RAINIER

21303	$70	☐

#771 16¢ SPECIAL DELIVERY AIR MAIL IMPERFORATE

4 Plates		TL	TR	L	R	B
21312	$80	☐	☐	‡	‡	☐
21313	$80	☐	☐	‡	‡	☐
21314	$80	☐	☐	‡	‡	☐
21315	$80	☐	☐	‡	‡	☐

1935 COMMEMORATIVES
ROTARY PRESS

#772 3¢ CONNECTICUT 6 Plates

		UL	UR	LL	LR
21391	$2	☐	☐	☐	☐
21392	$2	☐	☐	☐	☐
21393	$2	☐	☐	☐	☐
21394	$2	☐	☐	☐	☐
21395	$2	☐	☐	☐	☐
21396	$2	☐	☐	☐	☐

1935 COMMEMORATIVES

#773 3¢ SAN DIEGO 6 Plates

21405	$1.75	☐	☐	☐	☐
21406	$1.75	☐	☐	☐	☐
21407	$1.75	☐	☐	☐	☐
21408	$1.75	☐	☐	☐	☐
21409	$1.75	☐	☐	☐	☐
21410	$1.75	☐	☐	☐	☐

#774 3¢ BOULDER DAM
FLAT PRESS

12 Plates		TL	TR	L	R	B
21455	$2.25	☐	☐	‡	‡	☐
21456	$2.25	☐	☐	‡	‡	☐
21457	$2.25	☐	☐	‡	‡	☐
21458	$2.25	☐	☐	‡	‡	☐
21459	$2.25	☐	☐	‡	‡	☐
21460	$2.25	☐	☐	‡	‡	☐
21461	$2.25	☐	☐	‡	‡	☐
21462	$2.25	☐	☐	‡	‡	☐
21463	$2.25	☐	☐	‡	‡	☐
21464	$2.25	☐	☐	‡	‡	☐
21465	$2.25	☐	☐	‡	‡	☐
21466	$2.25	☐	☐	‡	‡	☐

1935 COMMEMORATIVES

#775 3¢ MICHIGAN

ROTARY PRESS

4 Plates		UL	UR	LL	LR
21467	$1.75	☐	☐	☐	☐
21469	$1.75	☐	☐	☐	☐
21470	$1.75	☐	☐	☐	☐
21471	$1.75	☐	☐	☐	☐

1936-37 COMMEMORATIVES

ROTARY PRESS

#776 3¢ TEXAS 4 Plates

Plate	Price	UL	UR	LL	LR
21537	$1.75	☐	☐	☐	☐
21538	$1.75	☐	☐	☐	☐
21539	$1.75	☐	☐	☐	☐
21540	$1.75	☐	☐	☐	☐

#777 3¢ RHODE ISLAND 4 Plates

Plate	Price	UL	UR	LL	LR
21559	$1.75	☐	☐	☐	☐
21560	$1.75	☐	☐	☐	☐
21561	$1.75	☐	☐	☐	☐
21562	$1.75	☐	☐	☐	☐

1936 EXHIBITION SHEET

FLAT PRESS IMPERFORATE

#778 TIPEX PANE OF 4 2 Plates

Plate	Price	
21557	$3.00	☐
21558	$3.00	☐

#782 3¢ ARKANSAS 4 Plates

ROTARY PRESS

Plate	Price	UL	UR	LL	LR
21564	$1.50	☐	☐	☐	☐
21565	$1.50	☐	☐	☐	☐
21566	$1.50	☐	☐	☐	☐
21567	$1.50	☐	☐	☐	☐

#783 3¢ OREGON 4 Plates

Plate	Price	UL	UR	LL	LR
21576	$1.25	☐	☐	☐	☐
21577	$1.25	☐	☐	☐	☐
21578	$1.25	☐	☐	☐	☐
21579	$1.25	☐	☐	☐	☐

#784 3¢ SUSAN ANTHONY 4 Plates

Plate	Price	UL	UR	LL	LR
21588	$1.00	☐	☐	☐	☐
21589	$1.00	☐	☐	☐	☐
21590	$1.00	☐	☐	☐	☐
21591	$1.00	☐	☐	☐	☐

1936-37 COMMEMORATIVES

ARMY and NAVY ISSUES

ROTARY PRESS

#785 1¢ ARMY 4 Plates

Plate	Price	UL	UR	LL	LR
21600	$1.00	☐	☐	☐	☐
21601	$1.00	☐	☐	☐	☐
21602	$1.00	☐	☐	☐	☐
21603	$1.00	☐	☐	☐	☐

1936-37 COMMEMORATIVES

ARMY and NAVY ISSUES

ROTARY PRESS

#786 2¢ ARMY 4 Plates

Plate	Price	UL	UR	LL	LR
21608	$1.00	☐	☐	☐	☐
21609	$1.00	☐	☐	☐	☐
21610	$1.00	☐	☐	☐	☐
21611	$1.00	☐	☐	☐	☐

#787 3¢ ARMY 4 Plates

Plate	Price	UL	UR	LL	LR
21634	$1.50	☐	☐	☐	☐
21636	$1.50	☐	☐	☐	☐
21637	$1.50	☐	☐	☐	☐
21638	$1.50	☐	☐	☐	☐

#788 4¢ ARMY 4 Plates

Plate	Price	UL	UR	LL	LR
21651	$12.50	☐	☐	☐	☐
21652	$12.50	☐	☐	☐	☐
21653	$12.50	☐	☐	☐	☐
21654	$12.50	☐	☐	☐	☐

#789 5¢ ARMY 4 Plates

Plate	Price	UL	UR	LL	LR
21680	$13.50	☐	☐	☐	☐
21681	$13.50	☐	☐	☐	☐
21682	$13.50	☐	☐	☐	☐
21683	$13.50	☐	☐	☐	☐

#790 1¢ NAVY 4 Plates

Plate	Price	UL	UR	LL	LR
21604	$1.00	☐	☐	☐	☐
21605	$1.00	☐	☐	☐	☐
21606	$1.00	☐	☐	☐	☐
21607	$1.00	☐	☐	☐	☐

#791 2¢ NAVY 4 Plates

Plate	Price	UL	UR	LL	LR
21612	$1.00	☐	☐	☐	☐
21613	$1.00	☐	☐	☐	☐
21614	$1.00	☐	☐	☐	☐
21615	$1.00	☐	☐	☐	☐

#792 3¢ NAVY 4 Plates

Plate	Price	UL	UR	LL	LR
21630	$1.50	☐	☐	☐	☐
21631	$1.50	☐	☐	☐	☐
21632	$1.50	☐	☐	☐	☐
21633	$1.50	☐	☐	☐	☐

#793 4¢ NAVY 4 Plates

Plate	Price	UL	UR	LL	LR
21655	$12.50	☐	☐	☐	☐
21656	$12.50	☐	☐	☐	☐
21657	$12.50	☐	☐	☐	☐
21658	$12.50	☐	☐	☐	☐

#794 5¢ NAVY 4 Plates

Plate	Price	UL	UR	LL	LR
21684	$13.50	☐	☐	☐	☐
21685	$13.50	☐	☐	☐	☐
21686	$13.50	☐	☐	☐	☐
21687	$13.50	☐	☐	☐	☐

1936-37 COMMEMORATIVES

ROTARY PRESS

#795 3¢ ORDINANCE 4 Plates

Plate	Price	UL	UR	LL	LR
21691	$1.25	☐	☐	☐	☐
21692	$1.25	☐	☐	☐	☐
21693	$1.25	☐	☐	☐	☐
21694	$1.25	☐	☐	☐	☐

1936-37 COMMEMORATIVES Continued

#796 5¢ VIRGINIA DARE 4 Plates

FLAT PRESS		TL	TR	L	R	B
21697	$9.00	☐	‡	‡	‡	☐
21698	$9.00	☐	‡	‡	‡	☐
21699	$9.00	☐	‡	‡	‡	☐
21700	$9.00	☐	‡	‡	‡	☐

1937 EXPOSITION SHEET

FLAT PRESS IMPERFORATE

#797 10¢ S.P.A. 2 Plates

21695	$1.00	☐
21696	$1.00	☐

#798 3¢ CONSTITUTION 4 Plates

ROTARY PRESS		UL	UR	LL	LR
21705	$1.50	☐	☐	☐	☐
21706	$1.50	☐	☐	☐	☐
21707	$1.50	☐	☐	☐	☐
21708	$1.50	☐	☐	☐	☐

#799 3¢ HAWAII 4 Plates

		UL	UR	LL	LR
21710	$1.75	☐	☐	☐	☐
21711	$1.75	☐	☐	☐	☐
21712	$1.75	☐	☐	☐	☐
21713	$1.75	☐	☐	☐	☐

#800 3¢ ALASKA 4 Plates

		UL	UR	LL	LR
21714	$1.75	☐	☐	☐	☐
21715	$1.75	☐	☐	☐	☐
21716	$1.75	☐	☐	☐	☐
21717	$1.75	☐	☐	☐	☐

#801 3¢ PUERTO RICO 4 Plates

		UL	UR	LL	LR
21721	$1.75	☐	☐	☐	☐
21722	$1.75	☐	☐	☐	☐
21723	$1.75	☐	☐	☐	☐
21724	$1.75	☐	☐	☐	☐

#802 3¢ VIRGIN ISLANDS 4 Plates

		UL	UR	LL	LR
21730	$1.75	☐	☐	☐	☐
21731	$1.75	☐	☐	☐	☐
21732	$1.75	☐	☐	☐	☐
21733	$1.75	☐	☐	☐	☐

1938 PRESIDENTIAL SERIES

CONDITION IMPORTANT: There are no plates in the Presidential Series which cannot be found in very fine condition, and our evaluations are based on "Generally Very Fine." While centering requirements for the very scarce to rare plates may be considered somewhat less exacting, most of them, including the scarcest positions, exist in attractive condition, and our evaluations are based accordingly.

The plates of the Presidential Series have great popular appeal, for the issue marks an important milestone in philatelic history — the conversion from "ordinary" to electronic perforation control. All denominations from the ½¢ to 50¢ show the change from "Pre-Eye" to "Eye" plates, and the 2¢ and 3¢ give us examples of the Experimental-Eye printings with plate numbers 3-up or 3-down from the corner stamps of the sheets.

ROTARY PRESS PERF. 11 x 10½

#803 ½¢ FRANKLIN 6 Plates
Pre-Eye

		UL	UR	LL	LR
21885	$1	☐	☐	☐	☐
21887	$1	☐	☐	☐	☐
21888	$1	☐	☐	☐	☐
21889	$1	☐	☐	☐	☐
21899	$1	☐	☐	☐	☐
21900	$1	☐	☐	☐	☐

#803 ½¢ FRANKLIN 10 Plates

Eye Plates		UL	UR	LL	LR
22406	$.40	☐	☐	☐	☐
22407	$.40	☐	☐	☐	☐
22470	$.40	☐	☐	☐	☐
22471	$.40	☐	☐	☐	☐
22898	$.40	☐	☐	☐	☐
22899	$.40	☐	☐	☐	☐
23408	$.40	☐	☐	☐	☐
23409	$.40	☐	☐	☐	☐
23445P	$2.00	☐	☐	☐	☐
23446P	$2.00	☐	☐	☐	☐

P These plate numbers have been reported only on precancelled stamps

#804 1¢ WASHINGTON 55 Plates
Pre-Eye

		UL	UR	LL	LR
21823	$.25	☐	☐	☐	☐
21824	$.25	☐	☐	☐	☐
21825	$.25	☐	☐	☐	☐
21826	$.75	☐	☐	☐ 3	☐
21828	$.25	☐	☐	☐	☐
21829	$.25	☐	☐	☐	☐
21830	$.30	☐ 2	☐ 2	☐ 3	☐ 3
21831	$.25	☐	☐	☐	☐
21832	$.25	☐	☐	☐	☐
21833	$.25	☐	☐	☐	☐

1938 PRESIDENTIAL SERIES

#804 1¢ WASHINGTON Continued
Pre-Eye Plates

Plate	Price	UL	UR	LL	LR
21834	$100.00	☐7	☐7	☐8	☐8
21859	$2.50	☐	☐	☐	☐
21860	$.60	☐	☐	☐	☐
21861	$2.00	☐	☐	☐	☐
21862	$.25	☐	☐	☐	☐
21863	$.25	☐	☐	☐	☐
21864	$50.00	☐7	☐8	☐7	☐8
21865	$2.75	☐	☐	☐	☐
21866	$1.00	☐	☐	☐	☐
21867	$6.00	☐	☐	☐	☐

Plate	Price	UL	UR	LL	LR
21868	$50.00	☐1	☐1	☐9	☐8
21869	$2.75	☐	☐	☐	☐
21870	$5.00	☐	☐	☐	☐
22150	$7.50	☐	☐	☐	☐
22151	$4.00	☐	☐	☐	☐
22152	$1.25	☐	☐	☐	☐
22153	$1.75	☐	☐	☐	☐
22240	$1.00	☐	☐	☐	☐
22241	$1.00	☐	☐	☐	☐
22242	$.50	☐2	☐3	☐2	☐2
22243	$.75	☐	☐	☐	☐
22244	$2.75	☐	☐	☐	☐
22245	$2.00	☐	☐	☐	☐
22246	$1.25	☐	☐	☐	☐
22247	$1.25	☐	☐	☐	☐
22253	$.75	☐	☐	☐	☐
22254	$.75	☐	☐	☐	☐

#804 1¢ WASHINGTON
Pre-Eye Plates — Continued

Plate	Price	UL	UR	LL	LR
22255	$5.00	☐5	☐5	☐2	☐3
22256	$1.75	☐	☐	☐	☐
22261	$1.00	☐5	☐4	☐3	☐4
22262	$1.00	☐5	☐4	☐3	☐4
22263	$2.00	☐	☐	☐	☐
22264	$2.00	☐	☐	☐	☐
22265	$4.00	☐4	☐2	☐3	☐7
22266	$4.00	☐5	☐2	☐3	☐7
22267	$15.00	☐	☐	☐	☐
22268	$3.00	☐4	☐4	☐4	☐5
22275	$5.00	☐3	☐5	☐3	☐2
22276	$5.00	☐3	☐5	☐3	☐2
22277	$10.00	☐	☐	☐	☐2
22278	$10.00	☐	☐	☐	☐2
22279	$10.00	☐	☐3	☐2	☐
22280	$16.00	☐	☐	☐	☐
22281	$4.00	☐6	☐8	☐7	☐6
22282	$4.00	☐6	☐7	☐7	☐6

#804 1¢ WASHINGTON 72 Plates
Eye Plates

Plate	Price	UL	UR	LL	LR
22337	$.25	☐	☐	☐	☐
22338	$.25	☐	☐	☐	☐
22359	$.25	☐	☐	☐	☐
22360	$.25	☐	☐	☐	☐
22408	$.25	☐	☐	☐	☐
22409	$.25	☐	☐	☐	☐
22410	$.25	☐	☐	☐	☐
22411	$.25	☐	☐	☐	☐
22430	$.25	☐	☐	☐	☐
22431	$.25	☐	☐	☐	☐
22904	$.25	☐	☐	☐	☐
22905	$.25	☐	☐	☐	☐
22906	$.25	☐	☐	☐	☐
22907	$.25	☐	☐	☐	☐
23101	$.25	☐	☐	☐	☐
23107	$.25	☐	☐	☐	☐
23108	$.25	☐	☐	☐	☐
23139	$.25	☐	☐	☐	☐
23228	$.25	☐	☐	☐	☐
23229	$.25	☐	☐	☐	☐

1938 PRESIDENTIAL SERIES

#804 1¢ WASHINGTON Continued

Eye Plates		UL	UR	LL	LR
23303	$.25	☐	☐	☐	☐
23304	$.25	☐	☐	☐	☐
23330	$.25	☐	☐	☐	☐
23331	$.25	☐	☐	☐	☐
23332	$.25	☐	☐	☐	☐
23333	$.25	☐	☐	☐	☐
23406	$.25	☐	☐	☐	☐
23407	$.25	☐	☐	☐	☐
23414	$.25	☐	☐	☐	☐
23415	$.25	☐	☐	☐	☐
23433	$.25	☐	☐	☐	☐
23434	$.25	☐	☐	☐	☐
23436	$.25	☐	☐	☐	☐
23437	$.25	☐	☐	☐	☐
23451	$.25	☐	☐	☐	☐
23452	$.25	☐	☐	☐	☐
23455	$.25	☐	☐	☐	☐
23456	$.25	☐	☐	☐	☐
23529	$.25	☐	☐	☐	☐
23530	$.25	☐	☐	☐	☐
23650	$.25	☐	☐	☐	☐
23651	$.25	☐	☐	☐	☐
23679	$.25	☐	☐	☐	☐
23680	$.25	☐	☐	☐	☐
23746	$.25	☐	☐	☐	☐
23747	$.25	☐	☐	☐	☐
23748	$.25	☐	☐	☐	☐
23749	$.25	☐	☐	☐	☐
23754	$.25	☐	☐	☐	☐
23755	$.25	☐	☐	☐	☐
23782	$.25	☐	☐	☐	☐
23783	$.25	☐	☐	☐	☐
23837	$.25	☐	☐	☐	☐
23838	$.25	☐	☐	☐	☐
24003	$.25	☐	☐	☐	☐
24004	$.25	☐	☐	☐	☐
24007	$.25	☐	☐	☐	☐
24008	$.25	☐	☐	☐	☐
24009	$.25	☐	☐	☐	☐
24010	$.25	☐	☐	☐	☐
24015	$.25	☐	☐	☐	☐
24016	$.25	☐	☐	☐	☐
24023	$.25	☐	☐	☐	☐
24024	$.25	☐	☐	☐	☐
24131	$.25	☐	☐	☐	☐
24132	$.25	☐	☐	☐	☐
24276	$.25	☐	☐	☐	☐
24277	$.25	☐	☐	☐	☐
24282	$.25	☐	☐	☐	☐
24288	$.25	☐	☐	☐	☐
24289	$1.25	☐	☐	☐	☐
24290	$1.25	☐	☐	☐	☐

#805 1½¢ MARTHA WASHINGTON

Pre-Eye — **31 Plates**

Plate	Price	UL	UR	LL	LR
21873	$1.00	☐	☐	☐	☐

#805 1½¢ MARTHA WASHINGTON Continued

Plate	Price	UL	UR	LL	LR
21874	$.25	☐	☐	☐	☐
21876	$1.75	☐	☐	☐	☐
21877	$1.75	☐	☐	☐	☐
21878	$.25	☐	☐	☐	☐
21879	$.25	☐	☐	☐	☐
21880	$50.00	☐ 3	☐ 2	☐	☐
21881	$.25	☐	☐	☐	☐
21882	$.25	☐	☐	☐	☐
21883	$.25	☐	☐	☐	☐
21884	$1.25	☐	☐	☐	☐
21934	$.90	☐	☐	☐	☐
21935	$.90	☐	☐	☐	☐

Plate	Price	UL	UR	LL	LR
21936	$.75	☐	☐	☐	☐
21937	$.75	☐	☐	☐	☐
22077	$2.00	☐	☐	☐	☐
22078	$2.00	☐	☐	☐	☐
22079	$.75	☐	☐	☐	☐
22080	$1.00	☐	☐	☐	☐ 2
22154	$10.00	☐ 1	☐ 8	☐ 1	☐ 9
22155	$.75	☐	☐	☐	☐
22172	$2.50	☐	☐	☐	☐
22173	$.75	☐	☐	☐	☐
22174	$.75	☐	☐	☐	☐
22175	$.75	☐	☐	☐	☐
22315	$1.00	☐	☐	☐	☐
22316	$1.00	☐	☐	☐	☐
22317	$2.00	☐	☐	☐	☐
22318	$2.00	☐	☐	☐	☐
22339	$7.00	☐	☐	☐	☐
22340	$7.00	☐	☐	☐	☐

#805 1½¢ MARTHA WASHINGTON

Eye Plates — **66 Plates**

Plate	Price	UL	UR	LL	LR
22412	$.25	☐	☐	☐	☐
22413	$.25	☐	☐	☐	☐
22414	$.25	☐	☐	☐	☐
22415	$.25	☐	☐	☐	☐
22432	$.25	☐	☐	☐	☐
22433	$.25	☐	☐	☐	☐

1938 PRESIDENTIAL SERIES

#805 1½¢ MARTHA WASHINGTON
Eye Plates Continued

Plate	Price	UL	UR	LL	LR
22464	$.25	☐	☐	☐	☐
22465	$.75	☐$_5$	☐$_2$	☐$_3$	☐$_5$
22466	$.25	☐	☐	☐	☐
22467	$.50	☐$_7$	☐$_3$	☐$_3$	☐$_3$
22472	$.25	☐	☐	☐	☐
22473	$.25	☐	☐	☐	☐
22645	$.25	☐	☐	☐	☐
22646	$.25	☐	☐	☐	☐
22876	$.25	☐	☐	☐	☐
22877	$.25	☐	☐	☐	☐
22880 N	$2.00	☐	☐	☐	☐
22881	$.25	☐	☐	☐	☐
22916	$.25	☐	☐	☐	☐
22917	$.25	☐	☐	☐	☐
22918	$.25	☐	☐	☐	☐
22919	$.25	☐	☐	☐	☐
23083	$.25	☐	☐	☐	☐
23084	$.25	☐	☐	☐	☐
23085	$.25	☐	☐	☐	☐
23086	$.25	☐	☐	☐	☐
23087	$.25	☐	☐	☐	☐
23088	$.25	☐	☐	☐	☐
23089	$.25	☐	☐	☐	☐
23090	$.25	☐	☐	☐	☐
23203	$.25	☐	☐	☐	☐
23204	$.25	☐	☐	☐	☐
23205	$.25	☐	☐	☐	☐
23206	$.25	☐	☐	☐	☐
23209	$.25	☐	☐	☐	☐
23210	$.25	☐	☐	☐	☐
23289	$.25	☐	☐	☐	☐
23290	$.25	☐	☐	☐	☐
23371	$.25	☐	☐	☐	☐
23372	$.25	☐	☐	☐	☐
23373	$.25	☐	☐	☐	☐
23374	$.25	☐	☐	☐	☐
23379	$.25	☐	☐	☐	☐
23380	$.25	☐	☐	☐	☐
23453	$.25	☐	☐	☐	☐
23454	$.25	☐	☐	☐	☐
23697	$.60	☐	☐$_3$	☐$_3$	☐
23698	$.60	☐	☐$_3$	☐$_3$	☐
23730	$.50	☐	☐	☐	☐
23731	$.50	☐	☐	☐	☐
23734	$.75	☐	☐	☐	☐
23735	$.75	☐	☐	☐	☐
23742	$.50	☐	☐	☐	☐
23743	$.50	☐	☐	☐	☐
23756	$.50	☐	☐	☐	☐
23757	$.50	☐	☐	☐	☐

N This plate, although not scarce, is of special interest because the second 8 is inverted.

#805 1½¢ MARTHA WASHINGTON
Eye Plates Continued

Plate	Price	UL	UR	LL	LR
23764	$.50	☐	☐	☐	☐
23765	$.50	☐	☐	☐	☐
23766	$.50	☐	☐	☐	☐
23767	$.50	☐	☐	☐	☐
23778	$.50	☐	☐	☐	☐
23779	$.50	☐	☐	☐	☐
23823	$.75	☐	☐	☐	☐
23824	$.75	☐	☐	☐	☐
23870	$1.75	☐	☐	☐	☐
23871	$1.75	☐	☐	☐	☐

#806 2¢ JOHN ADAMS 12 Plates
Pre-Eye

Plate	Price	UL	UR	LL	LR
21891	$.40	☐	☐	☐	☐
21892	$.40	☐	☐	☐	☐
21893	$.40	☐	☐	☐	☐
21894	$.40	☐	☐	☐	☐
22283	$.90	☐	☐	☐	☐
22284	$.90	☐	☐	☐	☐
22285	$.75	☐	☐	☐	☐
22286	$.75	☐	☐	☐	☐
22297	$7.00	☐	☐	☐	☐
22298	$1.75	☐	☐	☐	☐
22299	$.50	☐	☐	☐	☐
22300	$.50	☐	☐	☐	☐

#806 2¢ JOHN ADAMS
EXPERIMENTAL-EYE PLATES
Corner Vertical Blocks of 10 6 Plates

Plate	Price	UL	UR	LL	LR
21895	$20.00	☐	☐	☐	☐
21896	$4.00	☐	☐	☐	☐
21897	$20.00	☐	☐	☐	☐
21898	$4.00	☐	☐	☐	☐
22000	$6.00	☐	☐	☐	☐
22001	$6.00	☐	☐	☐	☐

#806 2¢ JOHN ADAMS
Eye Plates Blocks of 4 92 Plates

Plate	Price	UL	UR	LL	LR
21999	$.35	☐	☐	☐	☐
22002	$.35	☐	☐	☐	☐
22051	$1.25	☐	☐	☐	☐
22052	$1.25	☐	☐	☐	☐
22053	$1.50	☐	☐	☐	☐
22054	$1.50	☐	☐	☐	☐
22156	$1.00	☐	☐	☐	☐
22157	$1.00	☐	☐	☐	☐
22158	$1.00	☐	☐	☐	☐
22159	$4.00	☐	☐	☐	☐
22319	$1.00	☐	☐	☐	☐
22320	$.35	☐	☐	☐	☐
22420	$1.00	☐$_5$	☐$_3$	☐$_3$	☐$_5$
22421	$.35	☐	☐	☐	☐
22424	$.35	☐	☐	☐	☐
22425	$.35	☐	☐	☐	☐
22444	$.35	☐	☐	☐	☐
22445	$.35	☐	☐	☐	☐

1938 PRESIDENTIAL SERIES

#806 2¢ JOHN ADAMS Continued

Eye Plates		UL	UR	LL	LR
22453	$.35	☐	☐	☐	☐
22454	$.35	☐	☐	☐	☐
22468	$.35	☐	☐	☐	☐
22469	$.35	☐	☐	☐	☐
22647	$.35	☐	☐	☐	☐
22648	$.35	☐	☐	☐	☐
22649	$.35	☐	☐	☐	☐
22650	$.35	☐	☐	☐	☐
23796	$.35	☐	☐	☐	☐
23797	$.35	☐	☐	☐	☐
23981	$.35	☐	☐	☐	☐
23982	$.35	☐	☐	☐	☐
23983	$.35	☐	☐	☐	☐
23984	$.35	☐	☐	☐	☐
23987	$.35	☐	☐	☐	☐
23988	$.35	☐	☐	☐	☐
23989	$.35	☐	☐	☐	☐
23990	$.35	☐	☐	☐	☐
23991	$.35	☐	☐	☐	☐
23992	$.35	☐	☐	☐	☐
23993	$.35	☐	☐	☐	☐
23994	$.35	☐	☐	☐	☐
23995	$.35	☐	☐	☐	☐
23996	$.35	☐	☐	☐	☐
23997	$.35	☐	☐	☐	☐
23998	$.35	☐	☐	☐	☐
23999	$.35	☐	☐	☐	☐
24000	$.35	☐	☐	☐	☐
24112	$1.00	☐	☐	☐	☐
24113	$.35	☐	☐	☐	☐
24127	$.35	☐	☐	☐	☐
24128	$.35	☐	☐	☐	☐
24300	$.35	☐	☐	☐	☐
24301	$.35	☐	☐	☐	☐
24304	$.35	☐	☐	☐	☐
24305	$.35	☐	☐	☐	☐
24306	$.35	☐	☐	☐	☐
24307	$.35	☐	☐	☐	☐
24316	$.35	☐	☐	☐	☐
24319	$.35	☐	☐	☐	☐
24324	$.35	☐	☐	☐	☐
24325	$.35	☐	☐	☐	☐
24330	$.35	☐	☐	☐	☐
24331	$.35	☐	☐	☐	☐
24346	$.35	☐	☐	☐	☐
24347	$1.00	☐	☐	☐	☐
24372	$.35	☐	☐	☐	☐
24373	$.35	☐	☐	☐	☐
24378	$.35	☐	☐	☐	☐
24379	$.35	☐	☐	☐	☐
24382	$.35	☐	☐	☐	☐
24383	$.35	☐	☐	☐	☐
24483	$1.00	☐	☐	☐	☐
24484	$.35	☐	☐	☐	☐
24540	$.35	☐	☐	☐	☐

#806 2¢ JOHN ADAMS Continued

Eye Plates		UL	UR	LL	LR
24541	$.35	☐	☐	☐	☐
24566	$.35	☐	☐	☐	☐
24567	$.35	☐	☐	☐	☐
24601	$.35	☐	☐	☐	☐
24602	$.35	☐	☐	☐	☐
24711	$.35	☐	☐	☐	☐
24712	$.35	☐	☐	☐	☐
24713	$.35	☐	☐	☐	☐
24714	$.35	☐	☐	☐	☐
24721	$.35	☐	☐	☐	☐
24722	$.35	☐	☐	☐	☐
24723	$.35	☐	☐	☐	☐
24724	$.35	☐	☐	☐	☐
24741	$.35	☐	☐	☐	☐
24742	$3.00	☐	☐	☐	☐
24811	$.35	☐	☐	☐	☐
24812	$.35	☐	☐	☐	☐
24910	$.35	☐	☐	☐	☐
24911	$.35	☐	☐	☐	☐

#807 3¢ JEFFERSON 48 Plates

Pre-Eye					
21925	$.50	☐	☐	☐	☐
21926	$2.50	☐	☐	☐	☐
21927	$1.00	☐	☐	☐	☐
21928	$.50	☐	☐	☐	☐
21929	$1.00	☐	☐	☐	☐
21930	$.50	☐	☐	☐	☐
21931	$.50	☐	☐	☐	☐
21932	$.50	☐	☐	☐	☐
21938	$.50	☐	☐	☐	☐
21939	$.50	☐	☐	☐	☐
21940	$.50	☐	☐	☐	☐
21941	$.50	☐	☐	☐	☐
21942	$.50	☐	☐	☐	☐
21943	$1.00	☐	☐	☐	☐
21944	$1.00	☐	☐	☐	☐
21945	$.50	☐	☐	☐	☐
22055	$1.00	☐	☐	☐	☐
22056	$1.00	☐	☐	☐	☐

1938 PRESIDENTIAL SERIES

#807 3¢ JEFFERSON
Pre-Eye Plates Continued

Plate	Price	UL	UR	LL	LR
22057	$2.00	☐$_{2}$	☐$_{3}$	☐$_{3}$	☐$_{2}$
22058	$1.00	☐	☐	☐	☐
22059	$1.00	☐	☐	☐	☐
22060	$1.50	☐$_{2}$	☐$_{2}$	☐	☐
22061	$1.25	☐	☐	☐	☐
22062	$1.00	☐	☐	☐	☐
22063	$1.00	☐	☐	☐	☐
22064	$2.00	☐	☐	☐	☐
22065	$2.00	☐	☐	☐	☐
22066	$1.00	☐	☐	☐	☐
22067	$1.75	☐	☐	☐	☐
22068	$1.00	☐	☐	☐	☐
22069	$2.00	☐	☐	☐	☐
22070	$1.00	☐	☐	☐	☐
22104	$1.75	☐	☐	☐	☐
22105	$1.25	☐	☐	☐	☐
22106	$3.50	☐	☐	☐	☐
22107	$1.25	☐	☐	☐	☐
22131	$2.50	☐	☐	☐	☐
22132	$9.00	☐	☐	☐	☐
22133	$2.50	☐	☐	☐	☐
22134	$5.00	☐$_{3}$	☐$_{3}$	☐$_{4}$	☐$_{4}$
22137	$2.50	☐	☐	☐	☐
22138	$2.50	☐	☐	☐	☐$_{2}$
22139	$12.00	☐	☐	☐	☐
22140	$15.00	☐	☐	☐	☐
22141	$15.00	☐$_{4}$	☐$_{5}$	☐$_{2}$	☐$_{3}$
22142	$15.00	☐$_{3}$	☐$_{5}$	☐$_{2}$	☐$_{3}$
22160	$17.50	☐	☐	☐	☐
22161	$15.00	☐	☐	☐	☐

#807 3¢ JEFFERSON 6 Plates
EXPERIMENTAL-EYE PLATES
Corner Vertical Blocks of 10

Plate	Price	UL	UR	LL	LR
22301	$15.00	☐	☐	☐	☐
22302	$15.00	☐	☐	☐	☐
22355	$15.00	☐	☐	☐	☐
22356	$15.00	☐	☐	☐	☐
22357	$15.00	☐	☐	☐	☐
22358	$15.00	☐	☐	☐	☐

#807 3¢ JEFFERSON
Eye Plates Blocks of 4 302 Plates

Plate	Price	UL	UR	LL	LR
22361	$1.00	☐	☐	☐	☐
22362	$1.75	☐	☐	☐	☐
22363	$.35	☐	☐	☐	☐
22364	$.35	☐	☐	☐	☐
22422	$.35	☐	☐	☐	☐
22423	$.35	☐	☐	☐	☐
22426	$.35	☐	☐	☐	☐
22427	$2.00	☐	☐	☐	☐
22446	$1.00	☐	☐	☐	☐
22447	$2.00	☐	☐	☐$_{2}$	☐
22455	$1.25	☐	☐	☐	☐
22456	$4.00	☐	☐	☐	☐

#807 3¢ JEFFERSON
Eye Plates Continued

Plate	Price	UL	UR	LL	LR
22462	$1.00	☐	☐	☐	☐
22463	$1.00	☐	☐	☐	☐
22651	$1.25	☐	☐	☐	☐
22652	$.35	☐	☐	☐	☐
22653	$.35	☐	☐	☐	☐
22654	$.35	☐	☐	☐	☐
22655	$.35	☐	☐	☐	☐
22656	$.35	☐	☐	☐	☐
22920	$.35	☐	☐	☐	☐
22921	$.35	☐	☐	☐	☐
22928	$.35	☐	☐	☐	☐
22929	$.35	☐	☐	☐	☐
22936	$.35	☐	☐	☐	☐
22937	$.35	☐	☐	☐	☐
23056	$.35	☐	☐	☐	☐
23057	$.35	☐	☐	☐	☐
23066	$.35	☐	☐	☐	☐
23067	$.35	☐	☐	☐	☐
23091	$.35	☐	☐	☐	☐
23092	$.35	☐	☐	☐	☐
23095	$1.25	☐	☐	☐	☐
23096	$.35	☐	☐	☐	☐
23193	$.35	☐	☐	☐	☐
23194	$.35	☐	☐	☐	☐
23199	$2.50	☐$_{3}$	☐$_{3}$	☐$_{4}$	☐$_{5}$
23200	$2.50	☐$_{3}$	☐$_{3}$	☐$_{7}$	☐$_{6}$
23201	$.35	☐	☐	☐	☐
23202	$.35	☐	☐	☐	☐
23250	$.35	☐	☐	☐	☐
23251	$.35	☐	☐	☐	☐
23254	$.35	☐	☐	☐	☐
23255	$.35	☐	☐	☐	☐
23316	$.35	☐	☐	☐	☐
23317	$.35	☐	☐	☐	☐
23318	$.35	☐	☐	☐	☐
23319	$.35	☐	☐	☐	☐
23320	$.35	☐	☐	☐	☐
23321	$.35	☐	☐	☐	☐
23322	$.35	☐	☐	☐	☐
23323	$.35	☐	☐	☐	☐
23359	$.35	☐	☐	☐	☐
23360	$.35	☐	☐	☐	☐
23363	$.35	☐	☐	☐	☐
23364	$.35	☐	☐	☐	☐
23384	$.35	☐	☐	☐	☐
23385	$.35	☐	☐	☐	☐
23386	$.35	☐	☐	☐	☐
23387	$.35	☐	☐	☐	☐
23390	$.35	☐	☐	☐	☐
23391	$.35	☐	☐	☐	☐
23396	$.35	☐	☐	☐	☐
23397	$.35	☐	☐	☐	☐
23401	$.35	☐	☐	☐	☐
23402	$.35	☐	☐	☐	☐
23403	$.35	☐	☐	☐	☐

1938 PRESIDENTIAL SERIES

#807 3¢ JEFFERSON
Eye Plates — Continued

		UL	UR	LL	LR
23404	$.35	☐	☐	☐	☐
23418	$.35	☐	☐	☐	☐
23419	$.35	☐	☐	☐	☐
23424	$.35	☐	☐	☐	☐
23425	$.35	☐	☐	☐	☐
23426	$.35	☐	☐	☐	☐
23427	$.35	☐	☐	☐	☐
23443	$.35	☐	☐	☐	☐
23444	$.35	☐	☐	☐	☐
23457	$.35	☐	☐	☐	☐
23458	$.35	☐	☐	☐	☐
23527	$.35	☐	☐	☐	☐
23528	$.35	☐	☐	☐	☐
23539	$.35	☐	☐	☐	☐
23540	$.35	☐	☐	☐	☐
23541	$.35	☐	☐	☐	☐
23542	$.35	☐	☐	☐	☐
23543	$.35	☐	☐	☐	☐
23544	$.35	☐	☐	☐	☐
23545	$.35	☐	☐	☐	☐
23546	$.35	☐	☐	☐	☐
23547	$.35	☐	☐	☐	☐
23548	$.35	☐	☐	☐	☐
23550	$.35	☐	☐	☐	☐
23551	$.35	☐	☐	☐	☐
23552	$.35	☐	☐	☐	☐
23554	$.35	☐	☐	☐	☐
23555	$.35	☐	☐	☐	☐
23556	$.35	☐	☐	☐	☐
23557	$.35	☐	☐	☐	☐
23565	$.35	☐	☐	☐	☐
23566	$.35	☐	☐	☐	☐
23569	$.35	☐	☐	☐	☐
23570	$6.00	☐ 3	☐ 3	☐ 3	☐ 2
23571	$.35	☐	☐	☐	☐
23572	$.35	☐	☐	☐	☐
23575	$.35	☐	☐	☐	☐
23646	$.35	☐	☐	☐	☐
23647	$7.50	☐	☐	☐	☐ 3
23675	$.35	☐	☐	☐	☐
23676	$.35	☐	☐	☐	☐
23677	$.35	☐	☐	☐	☐
23678 **N**	$.35	☐	☐	☐	☐
23695	$.35	☐	☐	☐	☐
23696	$.35	☐	☐	☐	☐
23699	$.35	☐	☐	☐	☐
23700	$.35	☐	☐	☐	☐
23701	$.35	☐	☐	☐	☐
23702	$.35	☐	☐	☐	☐
23703	$.35	☐	☐	☐	☐
23704	$.35	☐	☐	☐	☐

N Common plate but of interest because of number entry about 1/8" from design — like pre-eye and experimental-eye plates of the series. All other Pres. eye numbers were entered about 1/16" from design.

#807 3¢ JEFFERSON
Eye Plates — Continued

		UL	UR	LL	LR
23705	$.35	☐	☐	☐	☐
23706	$.35	☐	☐	☐	☐
23724	$.35	☐	☐	☐	☐
23725	$.35	☐	☐	☐	☐

		UL	UR	LL	LR
23726	$.35	☐	☐	☐	☐
23727	$.35	☐	☐	☐	☐
23728	$.35	☐	☐	☐	☐
23729	$.35	☐	☐	☐	☐
23732	$.35	☐	☐	☐	☐
23733	$.35	☐	☐	☐	☐
23760	$5.00	☐ 4	☐ 5	☐ 5	☐ 4
23761	$.35	☐	☐	☐	☐
23790	$.35	☐	☐	☐	☐
23791	$.35	☐	☐	☐	☐
23794	$.35	☐	☐	☐	☐
23795	$.35	☐	☐	☐	☐
23827	$.35	☐	☐	☐	☐
23828	$.35	☐	☐	☐	☐
23862	$.35	☐	☐	☐	☐
23863	$.35	☐	☐	☐	☐
23868	$.35	☐	☐	☐	☐
23869	$.35	☐	☐	☐	☐
23886	$.35	☐	☐	☐	☐
23887	$.35	☐	☐	☐	☐
23894	$.35	☐	☐	☐	☐
23895	$.35	☐	☐	☐	☐
23914	$.35	☐	☐	☐	☐
23915	$.35	☐	☐	☐	☐
23951	$.35	☐	☐	☐	☐
23952	$.35	☐	☐	☐	☐
23959	$.35	☐	☐	☐	☐
23960	$.35	☐	☐	☐	☐
23971	$.35	☐	☐	☐	☐
23972	$.35	☐	☐	☐	☐
24001	$.35	☐	☐	☐	☐
24002	$.35	☐	☐	☐	☐
24005	$.35	☐	☐	☐	☐
24006	$.35	☐	☐	☐	☐
24011	$.35	☐	☐	☐	☐
24012	$.35	☐	☐	☐	☐

1938 PRESIDENTIAL SERIES

#807 3¢ JEFFERSON
Eye Plates — Continued

		UL	UR	LL	LR
24013	$.35	☐	☐	☐	☐
24014	$.35	☐	☐	☐	☐
24017	$.35	☐	☐	☐	☐
24018	$.35	☐	☐	☐	☐
24044	$.35	☐	☐	☐	☐
24045	$.35	☐	☐	☐	☐
24054	$.35	☐	☐	☐	☐
24055	$.35	☐	☐	☐	☐
24056	$.35	☐	☐	☐	☐
24057	$.35	☐	☐	☐	☐

		UL	UR	LL	LR
24071	$.35	☐	☐	☐	☐
24072	$.35	☐	☐	☐	☐
24105	$.35	☐	☐	☐	☐
24106	$.35	☐	☐	☐	☐
24109	$.35	☐	☐	☐	☐
24110	$.35	☐	☐	☐	☐
24111	$.35	☐	☐	☐	☐
24114	$.35	☐	☐	☐	☐
24115	$.35	☐	☐	☐	☐
24124	$.35	☐	☐	☐	☐
24125	$.35	☐	☐	☐	☐
24133	$.35	☐	☐	☐	☐
24170	$.35	☐	☐	☐	☐
24171	$5.00	☐ 6	☐ 7	☐ 8	☐ 6
24172	$.35	☐	☐	☐	☐
24173	$.35	☐	☐	☐	☐
24197	$.35	☐	☐	☐	☐
24198	$.35	☐	☐	☐	☐
24201	$.35	☐	☐	☐	☐
24202	$.35	☐	☐	☐	☐
24213	$.35	☐	☐	☐	☐
24214	$.35	☐	☐	☐	☐
24220	$.35	☐	☐	☐	☐
24221	$.35	☐	☐	☐	☐
24241	$.35	☐	☐	☐	☐
24242	$.35	☐	☐	☐	☐
24249	$.35	☐	☐	☐	☐
24250	$.35	☐	☐	☐	☐
24251	$1.25	☐ 6	☐	☐ 2	☐ 8
24252	$1.25	☐ 6	☐	☐ 2	☐ 8

#807 3¢ JEFFERSON
Eye Plates — Continued

		UL	UR	LL	LR
24265	$.35	☐	☐	☐	☐
24266	$.35	☐	☐	☐	☐
24267	$.35	☐	☐	☐	☐
24268	$.35	☐	☐	☐	☐
24294	$.35	☐	☐	☐	☐
24295	$.35	☐	☐	☐	☐
24314	$.35	☐	☐	☐	☐
24315	$.35	☐	☐	☐	☐
24320	$.35	☐	☐	☐	☐
24321	$.35	☐	☐	☐	☐
24322	$.35	☐	☐	☐	☐
24323	$.35	☐	☐	☐	☐
24326	$.35	☐	☐	☐	☐
24327	$.35	☐	☐	☐	☐
24334	$.35	☐	☐	☐	☐
24335	$.35	☐	☐	☐	☐
24336	$.35	☐	☐	☐	☐
24337	$.35	☐	☐	☐	☐
24338	$.35	☐	☐	☐	☐
24339	$.35	☐	☐	☐	☐
24340	$.35	☐	☐	☐	☐
24345	$.35	☐	☐	☐	☐
24350	$.35	☐	☐	☐	☐
24351	$.35	☐	☐	☐	☐
24352	$.35	☐	☐	☐	☐
24353	$1.00	☐	☐	☐	☐ 2
24354	$.35	☐	☐	☐	☐
24355	$.35	☐	☐	☐	☐
24356	$.35	☐	☐	☐	☐
24357	$.35	☐	☐	☐	☐
24358	$.35	☐	☐	☐	☐
24359	$.35	☐	☐	☐	☐
24452	$.35	☐	☐	☐	☐
24453	$.35	☐	☐	☐	☐
24469	$.35	☐	☐	☐	☐
24470	$.35	☐	☐	☐	☐
24485	$.35	☐	☐	☐	☐
24486	$.35	☐	☐	☐	☐
24488	$.35	☐	☐	☐	☐
24489	$.35	☐	☐	☐	☐
24490	$1.00	☐ 2	☐	☐	☐ 2
24542	$.35	☐	☐	☐	☐
24543	$.35	☐	☐	☐	☐
24544	$.35	☐	☐	☐	☐
24545	$.35	☐	☐	☐	☐
24546	$.35	☐	☐	☐	☐
24547	$.35	☐	☐	☐	☐
24568	$.35	☐	☐	☐	☐
24569	$.35	☐	☐	☐	☐
24570	$.35	☐	☐	☐	☐
24586	$.35	☐	☐	☐	☐
24587	$.35	☐	☐	☐	☐
24588	$.35	☐	☐	☐	☐
24590	$.35	☐	☐	☐	☐
24591	$.35	☐	☐	☐	☐

1938 PRESIDENTIAL SERIES

#807 3¢ JEFFERSON
Eye Plates — Continued

		UL	UR	LL	LR
24617	$.35	□	□	□	□
24618	$.35	□	□	□	□
24619	$.35	□	□	□	□
24620	$.35	□	□	□	□
24621	$.35	□	□	□	□
24622	$.35	□	□	□	□
24623	$.35	□	□	□	□
24624	$.35	□	□	□	□
24625	$.35	□	□	□	□
24626	$.35	□	□	□	□
24659	$.35	□	□	□	□
24660	$.35	□	□	□	□
24731	$.35	□	□	□	□
24732	$.35	□	□	□	□
24737	$.35	□	□	□	□
24738	$.35	□	□	□	□
24765	$.35	□	□	□	□
24766	$.35	□	□	□	□
24773	$.35	□	□	□	□
24774	$.35	□	□	□	□
24775	$.35	□	□	□	□
24776	$.35	□	□	□	□
24777	$.35	□	□	□	□
24778	$.35	□	□	□	□
24779	$.35	□	□	□	□
24780	$.35	□	□	□	□
24787	$.35	□	□	□	□
24788	$.35	□	□	□	□
24789	$.35	□	□	□	□
24790	$.35	□	□	□	□
24791	$.35	□	□	□	□
24792	$.35	□	□	□	□
24795	$.35	□	□	□	□
24796	$.35	□	□	□	□
24799	$.35	□	□	□	□
24800	$.35	□	□	□	□
24807	$.35	□	□	□	□
24808	$.35	□	□	□	□
24817	$.35	□	□	□	□
24818	$.35	□	□	□	□
24821	$.35	□	□	□	□
24822	$.35	□	□	□	□
24823	$.35	□	□	□	□
24824	$.35	□	□	□	□
24837	$.35	□	□	□	□
24838	$.35	□	□	□	□
24839	$.35	□	□	□	□
24840	$.35	□	□	□	□
24841	$.35	□	□	□	□

#808 4¢ MADISON
Pre-Eye Plates — 2 Plates

		UL	UR	LL	LR
21960	$5	□	□	□	□
21961	$5	□	□	□	□

#808 4¢ MADISON
Eye-Plates — 12 Plates

		UL	UR	LL	LR
22341	$4.00	□	□	□	□
22342	$4.00	□	□	□	□
22819	$6.00	□	□	□	□
22820	$6.00	□	□	□	□
24501	$4.00	□	□	□	□
24502	$4.00	□	□	□	□
24506	$16.00	□	□	□	□
24507	$16.00	□	□	□	□
24508	$7.00	□	□	□	□
24509	$7.00	□	□	□	□
24510	$7.00	□	□	□	□
24511	$7.00	□	□	□	□

#809 4½¢ WHITE HOUSE
Pre-Eye Plates — 2 Plates

		UL	UR	LL	LR
21972	$1.75	□	□	□	□
21973	$1.75	□	□	□	□

#809 4½¢ WHITE HOUSE
Eye-Plates — 4 Plates

		UL	UR	LL	LR
22343	$1.75	□	□	□	□
22344	$1.75	□	□	□	□
22843 P	$10.00	□	□	□	□
24073 P	$10.00	□	□	□	□

#810 5¢ MONROE
Pre-Eye Plates — 4 Plates

		UL	UR	LL	LR
22003	$1.00	□	□	□	□
22004	$1.00	□	□	□	□
22005	$4.50	□	□	□	□
22006	$4.50	□	□	□	□

#810 5¢ MONROE
Eye-Plates — 12 Plates

		UL	UR	LL	LR
22345	$1.00	□	□	□	□
22346	$1.00	□	□	□	□
22835	$1.00	□	□	□	□
22836	$1.00	□	□	□	□
22837	$1.00	□	□	□	□
22838	$1.00	□	□	□	□
23784	$1.00	□	□	□	□
23785	$1.00	□	□	□	□
24269	$1.00	□	□	□	□
24270	$1.00	□	□	□	□
24562	$4.00	□	□	□	□
24563	$4.00	□	□	□	□

#811 6¢ JOHN QUINCY ADAMS
Pre-Eye plates — 4 Plates

		UL	UR	LL	LR
21964	$3.00	□	□	□	□
21965	$3.00	□	□	□	□
21966	$3.00	□	□	□	□
21967	$3.00	□	□	□	□

P These plates numbers have been reported only on precancelled stamps

1938 PRESIDENTIAL SERIES

#811 6¢ JOHN QUINCY ADAMS
Eye Plates — **14 Plates**

Plate	Price	UL	UR	LL	LR
22347	$1.50	☐	☐	☐	☐
22348	$1.50	☐	☐	☐	☐
22745	$1.50	☐	☐	☐	☐
22800	$1.50	☐	☐	☐	☐
23531	$1.50	☐	☐	☐	☐
23532	$1.50	☐	☐	☐	☐
23880	$1.50	☐	☐	☐	☐
23881	$1.50	☐	☐	☐	☐
24074	$1.50	☐	☐	☐	☐
24075	$1.50	☐	☐	☐	☐
24475	$1.50	☐	☐	☐	☐
24476	$1.50	☐	☐	☐	☐
24847	$1.50	☐	☐	☐	☐
24848	$1.50	☐	☐	☐	☐

#812 7¢ JACKSON
Pre-Eye Plates — **2 Plates**

Plate	Price	UL	UR	LL	LR
22031	$2.50	☐	☐	☐	☐
22033	$2.50	☐	☐	☐	☐

#812 7¢ JACKSON
Eye Plates — **6 Plates**

Plate	Price	UL	UR	LL	LR
22796	$1.50	☐	☐	☐	☐
22797	$1.50	☐	☐	☐	☐
22801	$3.00	☐	☐	☐	☐
22802	$3.00	☐	☐	☐	☐
24845	$1.50	☐	☐	☐	☐
24846	$1.50	☐	☐	☐	☐

#813 8¢ VAN BUREN
Pre-Eye Plates — **4 Plates**

Plate	Price	UL	UR	LL	LR
21968	$2.25	☐	☐	☐	☐
21969	$3.00	☐ 4	☐ 5	☐ 5	☐ 5
21970	$2.25	☐	☐	☐	☐
21971	$3.00	☐ 4	☐ 5	☐ 5	☐ 5

#813 8¢ VAN BUREN
Eye Plates — **12 Plates**

Plate	Price	UL	UR	LL	LR
22349	$4.00	☐	☐	☐	☐
22350	$5.00	☐	☐	☐	☐
22839	$2.25	☐	☐	☐	☐
22840	$2.25	☐	☐	☐	☐
22844	$2.25	☐	☐	☐	☐
23167	$2.25	☐	☐	☐	☐
23780	$2.25	☐	☐	☐	☐
23781	$2.25	☐	☐	☐	☐
24076	$10.00	☐	☐	☐	☐
24107	$10.00	☐	☐	☐	☐
24302	$2.25	☐	☐	☐	☐
24303	$2.25	☐	☐	☐	☐

#814 9¢ WILLIAM HARRISON
Pre-Eye Plates — **2 Plates**

Plate	Price	UL	UR	LL	LR
22035	$3.50	☐	☐	☐	☐
22036	$3.50	☐	☐	☐	☐

#814 9¢ WILLIAM HARRISON
Eye Plates — **8 Plates**

Plate	Price	UL	UR	LL	LR
22798	$2.25	☐	☐	☐	☐
22799	$2.25	☐	☐	☐	☐
22803	$2.25	☐	☐	☐	☐
22804	$2.25	☐	☐	☐	☐
23788	$2.25	☐	☐	☐	☐
23789	$2.25	☐	☐	☐	☐
24310	$2.25	☐	☐	☐	☐
24311	$2.25	☐	☐	☐	☐

#815 10¢ TYLER
Pre-Eye Plates — **4 Plates**

Plate	Price	UL	UR	LL	LR
22039	$3.00	☐	☐	☐	☐
22040	$3.00	☐	☐	☐	☐
22041	$7.50	☐	☐	☐	☐
22042	$6.50	☐	☐	☐	☐

#815 10¢ TYLER
Eye Plates — **14 Plates**

Plate	Price	UL	UR	LL	LR
22351	$1.75	☐	☐	☐	☐
22352	$1.75	☐	☐	☐	☐
22448	$1.75	☐	☐	☐	☐
22449	$1.75	☐	☐	☐	☐
22983	$1.75	☐	☐	☐	☐
22984	$1.75	☐	☐	☐	☐
23634	$1.75	☐	☐	☐	☐
23635	$1.75	☐	☐	☐	☐
23876	$1.75	☐	☐	☐	☐
23877	$1.75	☐	☐	☐	☐
24077	$3.00	☐	☐	☐	☐
24126	$3.00	☐	☐	☐	☐
24471	$1.75	☐	☐	☐	☐
24472	$1.75	☐	☐	☐	☐

#816 11¢ POLK
Pre-Eye Plates — **2 Plates**

Plate	Price	UL	UR	LL	LR
22043	$5.00	☐	☐	☐	☐
22044	$5.00	☐	☐	☐	☐

#816 11¢ POLK
Eye Plates — **3 Plates**

Plate	Price	UL	UR	LL	LR
22045	$3.75	☐	☐	☐	☐
22046	$3.75	☐	☐	☐	☐
22845	$3.75	☐	☐	☐	☐

#817 12¢ TAYLOR
Pre-Eye Plates — **2 Plates**

Plate	Price	UL	UR	LL	LR
22047	$9.00	☐	☐	☐	☐
22049	$9.00	☐	☐	☐	☐

#817 12¢ TAYLOR
Eye Plates — **6 Plates**

Plate	Price	UL	UR	LL	LR
22048	$6.00	☐	☐	☐	☐
22050	$6.00	☐	☐	☐	☐
22846	$12.00	☐	☐	☐	☐
23910	$12.00	☐	☐	☐	☐
24757	$25.00	☐	☐	☐	☐
24758	$25.00	☐	☐	☐	☐

1938 PRESIDENTIAL SERIES

#818 13¢ FILLMORE
Pre-Eye Plates — **2 Plates**

Plate	Price	UL	UR	LL	LR
22073	$12.00	☐	☐	☐	☐
22074	$12.00	☐	☐	☐	☐

#818 13¢ FILLMORE
Eye Plates — **4 Plates**

Plate	Price	UL	UR	LL	LR
22075	$8.50	☐	☐	☐	☐
22076	$8.50	☐	☐	☐	☐
22847	$12.00	☐	☐	☐	☐
23911	$12.00	☐	☐	☐	☐

#819 14¢ PIERCE
Pre-Eye Plates — **2 Plates**

Plate	Price	UL	UR	LL	LR
22087	$3.00	☐$_{3}$	☐$_{3}$	☐$_{5}$	☐$_{3}$
22090	$3.00	☐$_{3}$	☐$_{3}$	☐$_{5}$	☐$_{3}$

#819 14¢ PIERCE
Eye Plates — **4 Plates**

Plate	Price	UL	UR	LL	LR
22088	$5.00	☐	☐	☐	☐
22089	$5.00	☐	☐	☐	☐
22848	$15.00	☐$_{7}$	☐$_{2}$	☐$_{2}$	☐$_{3}$
23928	$15.00	☐$_{7}$	☐$_{2}$	☐$_{3}$	☐$_{3}$

#820 15¢ BUCHANAN
Pre-Eye Plates — **2 Plates**

Plate	Price	UL	UR	LL	LR
22124	$4.25	☐	☐	☐	☐
22125	$4.25	☐	☐	☐	☐

#820 15¢ BUCHANAN
Eye Plates — **17 Plates**

Plate	Price	UL	UR	LL	LR
22126	$2.75	☐	☐	☐	☐
22127	$2.75	☐	☐	☐	☐
22922	$2.75	☐	☐	☐	☐
22923	$2.75	☐	☐	☐	☐
22924	$2.75	☐	☐	☐	☐
23223	$2.75	☐	☐	☐	☐
23707	$2.75	☐	☐	☐	☐
23786	$2.75	☐	☐	☐	☐
23787	$17.50	☐	☐	☐	☐
24312	$2.75	☐	☐	☐	☐
24313	$2.75	☐	☐	☐	☐
24727	$2.75	☐	☐	☐	☐
24728	$2.75	☐	☐	☐	☐
24733	$2.75	☐	☐	☐	☐
24734	$2.75	☐	☐	☐	☐
24735	$6.00	☐	☐	☐	☐
24736	$6.00	☐	☐	☐	☐

#821 16¢ LINCOLN
Pre-Eye Plates — **2 Plates**

Plate	Price	UL	UR	LL	LR
22129	$10.00	☐	☐	☐	☐
22130	$10.00	☐	☐	☐	☐

P These plate numbers have been reported only on precancelled stamps

#821 16¢ LINCOLN
Eye Plates — **4 Plates**

Plate	Price	UL	UR	LL	LR
22815	$7.00	☐	☐	☐	☐
22816	$7.00	☐	☐	☐	☐
23037	$9.50	☐	☐	☐	☐
23929	$9.50	☐	☐	☐	☐

#822 17¢ JOHNSON
Pre-Eye Plates — **2 Plates**

Plate	Price	UL	UR	LL	LR
22108	$9.00	☐	☐	☐	☐
22110	$9.00	☐	☐	☐	☐

#822 17¢ JOHNSON
Eye Plates — **4 Plates**

Plate	Price	UL	UR	LL	LR
22109	$6.00	☐	☐	☐	☐
22111	$6.00	☐	☐	☐	☐
22985	$6.00	☐	☐	☐	☐
23930	$6.00	☐	☐	☐	☐

#823 18¢ GRANT
Pre-Eye Plates — **2 Plates**

Plate	Price	UL	UR	LL	LR
22143	$18.00	☐	☐	☐	☐
22144	$18.00	☐	☐	☐	☐

#823 18¢ GRANT
Eye Plates — **4 Plates**

Plate	Price	UL	UR	LL	LR
22817	$10.00	☐	☐	☐	☐
22818	$10.00	☐	☐	☐	☐
23931	$16.00	☐	☐	☐	☐
24078	$16.00	☐	☐	☐	☐

#824 19¢ HAYES
Pre-Eye Plates — **2 Plates**

Plate	Price	UL	UR	LL	LR
22135	$13.50	☐	☐	☐	☐
22136	$13.50	☐	☐	☐	☐

#824 19¢ HAYES
Eye Plates — **5 Plates**

Plate	Price	UL	UR	LL	LR
22823	$9.00	☐	☐	☐	☐
22824	$9.00	☐	☐	☐	☐
23045 P	$75.00	☐$_{2}$	☐$_{3}$	†	†
23932	$9.00	☐	☐	☐	☐
24079	$13.50	☐	☐	☐	☐

1938 PRESIDENTIAL SERIES

#825 20¢ GARFIELD
Pre-Eye Plates **2 Plates**

		UL	UR	LL	LR
22145	$7.50	□	□	□	□
22146	$7.50	□	□	□	□

#825 20¢ GARFIELD
Eye Plates **11 Plates**

		UL	UR	LL	LR
22176	$500.00	□8	□9	□7	□8
22183	$4.00	□	□	□	□
22184	$4.00	□	□	□	□
22855	$4.00	□	□	□	□
23549	$4.00	□	□	□	□
23558	$4.00	□	□	□	□
23904	$4.00	□	□	□	□
24060	$4.00	□	□	□	□
24061	$4.00	□	□	□	□
24572	$4.00	□	□	□	□
24573	$4.00	□	□	□	□

#826 21¢ ARTHUR
Pre-Eye Plates **2 plates**

		UL	UR	LL	LR
22112	$13.00	□	□	□	□
22113	$13.00	□	□	□	□

#826 21¢ ARTHUR
Eye Plates **4 Plates**

		UL	UR	LL	LR
22114	$10.00	□	□	□	□
22115	$10.00	□	□	□	□
23053 P	$50.00	†	□2	□	†
23933 P	$50.00	†	□3	□	†

#827 22¢ CLEVELAND
Pre-Eye Plates **2 Plates**

		UL	UR	LL	LR
22147	$20.00	□	□	□	□
22148	$20.00	□	□	□	□

#827 22¢ CLEVELAND
Eye Plates **4 Plates**

		UL	UR	LL	LR
22825	$14.00	□	□	□	□
22826	$14.00	□	□	□	□
23934	$20.00	□	□	□	□
24081	$20.00	□	□	□	□

#828 24¢ BENJAMIN HARRISON
Pre-Eye Plates **2 Plates**

		UL	UR	LL	LR
22162	$7.50	□5	□4	□4	□4
22163	$7.50	□5	□4	□4	□4

#828 24¢ BENJAMIN HARRISON
Eye Plates **2 Plates**

		UL	UR	LL	LR
22827	$20.00	□	□	□	□
22828	$20.00	□	□	□	□

P These plate numbers have been reported only on precancelled stamps.

#829 25¢ McKINLEY
Pre-Eye Plates **2 Plates**

		UL	UR	LL	LR
22116	$12.00	□	□	□	□
22117	$12.00	□	□	□	□

#829 25¢ McKINLEY
Eye Plates **10 Plates**

		UL	UR	LL	LR
22118	$4.00	□	□	□	□
22119	$4.00	□	□	□	□
23115	$4.00	□	□	□	□
23878	$4.00	□	□	□	□
23879	$4.00	□	□	□	□
24082	$4.00	□	□	□	□
24699	$4.00	□	□	□	□
24700	$4.00	□	□	□	□
24959	$4.00	□	□	□	□
24960	$4.00	□	□	□	□

#830 30¢ THEODORE ROOSEVELT
Pre-Eye Plates **2 Plates**

		UL	UR	LL	LR
22164	$42.50	□	□	□	□
22165	$42.50	□	□	□	□

#830 30¢ THEODORE ROOSEVELT
Eye Plates **4 Plates**

		UL	UR	LL	LR
22833	$25.00	□	□	□	□
22834	$25.00	□	□	□	□
23116	$25.00	□	□	□	□
23906	$25.00	□	□	□	□

#831 50¢ TAFT
Pre-Eye Plates **2 Plates**

		UL	UR	LL	LR
22207	$60.00	□	□	□	□
22212	$60.00	□	□	□	□

#831 50¢ TAFT
Eye Plates **4 Plates**

		UL	UR	LL	LR
22205	$35.00	□	□	□	□
22206	$35.00	□	□	□	□
22353	$35.00	□	□	□	□
22354	$35.00	□	□	□	□

PRESIDENTIAL $1, $2, $5 BICOLORED

FLAT PRESS PERF. 11

Top position only

All first printings of these denominations were in the 22,000 series, and all were **with** arrow.

Later printings of the 22,000 series are **without** arrow. All number combinations of this series exist both with and without arrow.

There are **no arrows** on any combinations containing vignette or frame plates of the 23,000 or 24,000 series.

1938 PRESIDENTIAL SERIES

#832 $1 WILSON With Arrow

16 Plate Combination Blocks of 4

Vignette-Frame		T
22096-22085	*$40.00*	☐
22096-22086	*$40.00*	☐
22096-22094	*$40.00*	☐
22096-22095	*$40.00*	☐
22097-22085	*$40.00*	☐
22097-22086	*$40.00*	☐
22097-22094	*$40.00*	☐
22097-22095	*$40.00*	☐
22098-22085	*$40.00*	☐
22098-22086	*$40.00*	☐
22098-22094	*$40.00*	☐
22098-22095	*$40.00*	☐
22099-22085	*$40.00*	☐
22099-22086	*$40.00*	☐
22099-22094	*$40.00*	☐
22099-22095	*$40.00*	☐

#832 $1 WILSON Without Arrow

57 Plate Combination Blocks of 4

Vignette-Frame		T
22096-22085	*$45*	☐
22096-22086	*$45*	☐
22096-22094	*$45*	☐
22096-22095	*$45*	☐
22097-22085	*$45*	☐
22097-22086	*$45*	☐
22097-22094	*$45*	☐
22097-22095	*$45*	☐
22098-22085	*$45*	☐
22098-22086	*$45*	☐
22098-22094	*$45*	☐
22098-22095	*$45*	☐
22099-22085	*$45*	☐
22099-22086	*$45*	☐
22099-22094	*$45*	☐
22099-22095	*$45*	☐
24477-22085	*$45*	☐
24477-22086	$110	☐
24477-22094	*$45*	☐
24477-22095	*$45*	☐
24477-24478	*$45*	☐
24477-24497	*$45*	☐
24477-24498	*$45*	☐
24477-24499	*$45*	☐
24477-24500	*$45*	☐
24493-22085	*$45*	☐
24493-22086	$110	☐
24493-22094	$110	☐
24493-22095	$110	☐
24493-24478	*$45*	☐
24493-24497	*$45*	☐

#832 $1 WILSON Without Arrow

Continued

		T
24493-24498	*$45*	☐
24493-24499	*$45*	☐
24493-24500	*$45*	☐
24494-22085	$110	☐
24494-22086	*$45*	☐
24494-22094	$110	☐
24494-22095	*$45*	☐
24494-24478	*$45*	☐
24494-24497	*$45*	☐
24494-24498	*$45*	☐
24494-24499	*$45*	☐
24494-24500	*$45*	☐
24495-22085	$140	☐
24495-22086	$125	☐
24495-22094	*$45*	☐
24495-22095	$110	☐
24495-24478	*$45*	☐
24495-24497	*$45*	☐
24495-24498	*$45*	☐
24495-24499	*$45*	☐
24495-24500	*$45*	☐
24496-24478	*$45*	☐
24496-24497	*$45*	☐
24496-24498	*$45*	☐
24496-24499	*$45*	☐
24496-24500	*$45*	☐

#832b $1 WILSON Without Arrow

16 Plate Combination Blocks of 4

On USIR Watermarked Paper

Vignette-Frame		T
22096-22085	$2,500	☐
22096-22086		†
22096-22094	$2,500	☐
22096-22095	$2,500	☐
22097-22085	$2,500	☐
22097-22086		†
22097-22094	$2,500	☐
22097-22095	$2,500	☐
22098-22085		†
22098-22086	$2,500	☐
22098-22094	$2,500	☐
22098-22095	$2,500	☐
22099-22085	$2,500	☐
22099-22086	*$1,540*	☐
22099-22094	$2,500	☐
22099-22095	$2,500	☐

In 1953 several sheets of the $1 Presidential were discovered printed in error on watermarked paper intended for revenue stamps.

The quantity printed must have been large, for cancelled copies have been reported with postmarks from coast to coast.

1938 PRESIDENTIAL SERIES

The period during which the watermarked stamps were printed and distributed is not known, but it is certain that they were **not** early printings. We surmise that they may have been **printed** between 1950-51 or perhaps earlier.

The watermarked error will be found on **without**-arrow blocks only, and occurs only in the 22000 series combinations.

#832C $1 WILSON Without Arrow

1954 New Printing on Dry Paper.

From 400 Subject Sheets

With top and bottom plate-number entries. Left pane and right pane plate combinations are alike.

25 Plate Combination Blocks of 4

Vignette-Frame		T	B
25017-24836	*$35*	☐	☐
25017-25015	*$35*	☐	☐
25017-25016	*$35*	☐	☐
25017-25026	*$35*	☐	☐
25017-25027	*$35*	☐	☐
25018-24836	*$35*	☐	☐
25018-25015	*$35*	☐	☐
25018-25016	*$35*	☐	☐
25018-25026	*$35*	☐	☐
25018-25027	*$35*	☐	☐
25019-24836	*$35*	☐	☐
25019-25015	*$35*	☐	☐
25019-25016	*$35*	☐	☐
25019-25026	*$35*	☐	☐
25019-25027	*$35*	☐	☐
25020-24836	*$35*	☐	☐
25020-25015	*$35*	☐	☐
25020-25016	*$35*	☐	☐
25020-25026	*$35*	☐	☐
25020-25027	*$35*	☐	☐
25025-24836	$300	☐	☐
25025-25015	*$35*	☐	☐
25025-25016	*$35*	☐	☐
25025-25026	*$35*	☐	☐
25025-25027	*$35*	☐	☐

#833 $2 HARDING With Arrow

4 Plate Combination Blocks of 4

Vignette-Frame		T
22120-22122	*$135*	☐
22120-22123	*$135*	☐
22121-22122	*$135*	☐
22121-22123	*$135*	☐

#833 $2 HARDING Without Arrow

20 Plate Combination Blocks of 4

Vignette-Frame		T
22120-22122	*$175*	☐
22120-22123	*$175*	☐
22120-23477	*$175*	☐
22120-23478	*$175*	☐
22120-24480	*$175*	☐
22121-22122	*$175*	☐
22121-22123	*$175*	☐
22121-23477	*$175*	☐
22121-23478	*$175*	☐
22121-24480	*$175*	☐
23479-22122	*$175*	☐
23479-22123	*$175*	☐
23479-23477	*$175*	☐
23479-23478	*$175*	☐
23479-24480	*$175*	☐
23480-22122	*$175*	☐
23480-22123	*$175*	☐
23480-23477	*$175*	☐
23480-23478	*$175*	☐
23480-24480	*$175*	☐

#834 $5 COOLIDGE With Arrow

4 Plate Combination Blocks of 4

Vignette-Frame		T
22166-22168	*$485*	☐
22166-22169	*$485*	☐
22167-22168	*$485*	☐
22167-22169	*$485*	☐

1938 PRESIDENTIAL SERIES

#834 $5 COOLIDGE Without Arrow

25 Plate Combination Blocks of 4

Vignette-Frame		T
22166-22168	*$465*	☐
22166-22169	*$465*	☐
22166-23475	*$465*	☐
22166-23476	*$465*	☐
22166-24482	$1100	☐
22167-22168	*$465*	☐
22167-22169	*$465*	☐
22167-23475	*$465*	☐
22167-23476	*$465*	☐
22167-24482	*$465*	☐
23481-22168	*$465*	☐
23481-22169	*$465*	☐
23481-23475	*$465*	☐
23481-23476	*$465*	☐
23481-24482	*$465*	☐
23482-22168	*$465*	☐
23482-22169	*$465*	☐
23482-23475	*$465*	☐

BOOKLET PANES

ROTARY PRESS **PANES OF 6**

Most of the Presidential Booklet Pane plates can be found with good percentages (65% or more) of the number showing in the UL and LL positions. Right pane positions are seen infrequently and the percentages are often too small for plate number identification.

#834 $5 COOLIDGE Without Arrow

		T
23482-23476	*$465*	☐
23482-24482	*$465*	☐
24481-22168	$1100	☐
24481-22169	*$465*	☐
24481-23475	*$465*	☐
24481-23476	$1000	☐
24481-24482	*$465*	☐

#834a $5 COOLIDGE Without Arrow

22167-22169	☐

#804b 1¢ WASHINGTON 14 Plates

*22007	*22008	22009	22010	22234
22235	22389	22390	22402	22403
22930	22931	22977	22978	

#806b 2¢ JOHN ADAMS 8 Plates

22011	22012	22392	22404	22405
22461	24298	24299		

#807a 3¢ JEFFERSON 63 Plates

21995	21996	21997	21998	22170
22171	22434	22435	22436	22437
22886	22887	22932	22933	22973
22974	22975	22976	23158	23159
23160	23161	23283	23284	23291
23292	23412	23413	23422	23423
23573	23574	23594	23595	23758
23759	23770	23771	*23847	*23848
24089	24090	24255	24256	24257
24258	24412	24413	24418	24419
24420	24421	24422	24423	24424
24425	24426	24427	24428	24429
24443	24739	24740		

1938 PRESIDENTIAL SERIES

PRESIDENTIAL SIDE COILS

Most of the 1¢ to 3¢ Presidential **side** coils exist with plate number percentages exceeding 50%. The **end** coils and the 4¢, 4½¢, 5¢, 10¢ side coils rarely show as much as 50%.

Almost complete numbers are very scarce and full 100% plates are rare. Reconstructed 100% numbers are usually difficult, and frequently impossible, to complete even on plates that can be found with 50% or more of the number. This is because **one** of the positions, Top or Bottom, may not have been cut wide enough to show more than a small percentage of the number.

Positions T, B **STRIPS OF 5**

#839 1¢ WASHINGTON 52 Plates

170 Subject Plates STRIPS OF 5

21871	21978	†21979	21980	21981
21982	22219	22220	22225	22226
22236	22237	22248	22249	22250
22251	22900	22901	22902	22903
23081	23082	23117	23118	23119
23120	23301	23302	23388	23389
23392	23393	23461	23462	23632
23633	23762	23763	23792	23793
23817	23818	23839	23840	24025
24026	24099	24100	24274	24275
24384	24385			

#840 1½¢ MARTHA WASHINGTON 24 Plates

170 Subject Plates STRIPS OF 5

21983	21984	21985	21986	22221
22222	22227	22228	22238	22239
22311	22312	23207	23208	23567
23568	23578	23579	23768	23769
25164	25165	25166	†25167	

#841 2¢ JOHN ADAMS 36 Plates

170 Subject Plates STRIPS OF 5

21987	21988	21989	21990	22203
22204	22257	22258	22259	22260
22269	22270	22271	22272	22313
22314	22325	22326	22882	22883
22884	22885	22892	22893	22894
22895	22896	22897	23058	23059
23068	23069	24390	24391	24398
24399				

#842 3¢ JEFFERSON 224 Plates

170 Subject Plates STRIPS OF 5

21991	21992	21993	21994	22213
22214	22215	22216	†22223	†22224
22287	22288	22307	22308	22309
22310	22321	22322	22323	22324
22327	22328	22329	22330	22335
22428	22429	22638	22908	22909
22910	22911	22912	22913	22914
22915	23060	23061	23064	23065
23133	23215	23216	23217	23218
23221	23222	23232	23233	23234
23235	23236			
23240	23241	23242	23243	23248
23249	23344	23345	23346	23347
23361	23362	23369	23370	23375
23376	23377	23378	23394	23395
23410	23411	23416	23417	23420
23421	23440	23459	23460	23537
23538	23576	23577	23584	23585
23613	23614	23615	23616	23648
23649	23662	23663	23673	23674
23708	23709	23740	23741	23750
23751	23752	23753	23808	23809
23810	23811	23849	23850	23916
23917	23926	23927	24019	24020
24021	24022	24046	24047	24048
24049	24050	24051	24101	24102
24104	24129	24130	24174	24175
24176	24177	24178	24179	24180
24181	24189	24190	24199	24200
24215	24216	24222	24223	24231
24232	24272	24273	24278	24279
24280	24281	24286	24287	24292
24293	24296	24297	24308	24309
24332	24333	24360	24361	24362
24363	24364	24365	24404	24405
24406	24407	24408	24409	24434
24435	24458	24459	24460	24461
24462	24467	24468	24491	24492
24597	24598	24599	24600	24609
24610	24653	24654	24655	24656
24667	24668	24707	24708	24709
24710	24715	24716	24717	24718
24743	24744	24793	24794	24797
24798	24801	24802	24813	24815
24816	24819	24820	24855	24856
24873	24874			

1938 PRESIDENTIAL SERIES

PRESIDENTIAL SIDE COILS

#843 4¢ MADISON 8 Plates
170 Subject Plates **STRIPS OF 5**

22015 22016 22017 22018 24052
24053 24512 24513

#844 4½¢ WHITE HOUSE 2 Plates
170 Subject Plates **STRIPS OF 5**

22081 22082

#845 5¢ MONROE 6 Plates
170 Subject Plates **STRIPS OF 5**

22019 22020 22021 22022 23722
23723

#846 6¢ JOHN QUINCY ADAMS
6 Plates
170 Subject Plates **STRIPS OF 5**

22023 22024 22025 22026 24857
24858

#847 10¢ TYLER 4 Plates
170 Subject Plates **STRIPS OF 5**

22100 22101 22102 †22103

PRESIDENTIAL END COILS

Positions L, R STRIPS OF 5

#848 1¢ WASHINGTON 2 Plates
150 Subject Plates **STRIPS OF 5**

22179 22180

#849 1½¢ MARTHA WASHINGTON
4 Plates
150 Subject Plates **STRIPS OF 5**

22193 22194 †22208 †22209

#850 2¢ JOHN ADAMS 2 Plates
150 Subject Plates **STRIPS OF 5**

22210 22211

#851 3¢ JEFFERSON 2 Plates
150 Subject Plates **STRIPS OF 5**

22189 22190

1938 COMMEMORATIVES

ROTARY PRESS

#835 3¢ RATIFICATION

4 Plates		UL	UR	LL	LR
21905	$4.00	☐	☐	☐	☐
21906	$4.00	☐	☐	☐	☐
21907	$4.00	☐	☐	☐	☐
21908	$4.00	☐	☐	☐	☐

FLAT PRESS

#836 3¢ DELAWARE

8 Plates		TL	TR	L	R	B
21952	$3.00	☐	☐	‡	‡	☐
21953	$3.00	☐	☐	‡	‡	☐
21954	$3.00	☐	☐	‡	‡	☐
21955	$3.00	☐	☐	‡	‡	☐
21956	$3.00	☐	☐	‡	‡	☐
21957	$3.00	☐	☐	‡	‡	☐
21958	$3.00	☐	☐	‡	‡	☐
21959	$3.00	☐	☐	‡	‡	☐

ROTARY PRESS

#837 3¢ SECOND NORTHWEST

4 Plates		UL	UR	LL	LR
22027	$11.00	☐	☐	☐	☐
22028	$11.00	☐	☐	☐	☐
22029	$11.00	☐	☐	☐	☐
22030	$11.00	☐	☐	☐	☐

#838 3¢ IOWA 2 Plates

22091	$6.00	☐	☐	☐	☐
22092	$6.00	☐	☐	☐	☐

1939 COMMEMORATIVES

#852 3¢ GOLDEN GATE 4 Plates

		UL	UR	LL	LR
22289	$1.50	☐	☐	☐	☐
22290	$1.50	☐	☐	☐	☐
22291	$1.50	☐	☐	☐	☐
22292	$1.50	☐	☐	☐	☐

#853 3¢ NEW YORK 4 Plates

22293	$1.75	☐	☐	☐	☐
22294	$1.75	☐	☐	☐	☐
22295	$1.75	☐	☐	☐	☐
22296	$1.75	☐	☐	☐	☐

FLAT PRESS

#854 3¢ INAUGURATION

9 Plates		TL	TR	L	R	B
22365	$4.50	☐	☐	‡	‡	☐
22366	$3.00	☐	☐	‡	‡	☐
22367	$3.00	☐	☐	‡	‡	☐
22368	$3.00	☐	☐	‡	‡	☐
22369	$3.00	☐	☐	‡	‡	☐
22370	$3.00	☐	☐N	‡	‡	☐
22371	$3.00	☐	☐	‡	‡	☐
22372	$5.75	☐	☐	‡	‡	☐
22373	$3.00	☐	☐	‡	‡	☐

N Has no F but 3 of plate number has 2 dots.

ROTARY PRESS

#855 3¢ BASEBALL

4 Plates		UL	UR	LL	LR
22385	$3.50	☐	☐	☐	☐
22386	$3.50	☐	☐	☐	☐
22387	$3.50	☐	☐	☐	☐
22388	$3.50	☐	☐	☐	☐

FLAT PRESS

#856 3¢ PANAMA CANAL

8 Plates		TL	TR	L	R	B
22394	$4.00	☐	☐	‡	‡	☐
22395	$4.00	☐	☐	‡	‡	☐
22396	$4.00	☐	☐	‡	‡	☐
22397	$4.00	☐	☐	‡	‡	☐
22398	$4.00	☐	☐	‡	‡	☐
22399	$4.00	☐	☐	‡	‡	☐
22400	$4.00	☐	☐	‡	‡	☐
22401	$4.00	☐	☐	‡	‡	☐

ROTARY PRESS

#857 3¢ PRINTING PRESS

4 Plates		UL	UR	LL	LR
22438	$1.25	☐	☐	☐	☐
22439	$1.25	☐	☐	☐	☐
22440	$1.25	☐	☐	☐	☐
22450	$1.25	☐	☐	☐	☐

1939 COMMEMORATIVES

#858 3¢ FOUR STATES 4 Plates

		UL	UR	LL	LR
22457	$1.50	☐	☐	☐	☐
22458	$1.50	☐	☐	☐	☐
22459	$1.50	☐	☐	☐	☐
22460	$1.50	☐	☐	☐	☐

1940 FAMOUS AMERICANS

AUTHORS

#859 1¢ IRVING 2 Plates

22474	$1.15	☐	☐	☐	☐
22475	$1.15	☐	☐	☐	☐

#860 2¢ COOPER 4 Plates

22477	$1.25	☐	☐	☐	☐
22478	$1.25	☐	☐	☐	☐
22479	$1.25	☐	☐	☐	☐
22490	$1.25	☐	☐	☐	☐

#861 3¢ EMERSON 4 Plates

22480	$1.75	☐	☐	☐	☐
22481	$1.75	☐	☐	☐	☐
22482	$1.75	☐	☐	☐	☐
22491	$1.75	☐	☐	☐	☐

#862 5¢ ALCOTT 2 Plates

22483	$11.00	☐	☐	☐	☐
22484	$11.00	☐	☐	☐	☐

#863 10¢ CLEMENS 2 Plates

22486	$50.00	☐	☐	☐	☐
22488	$50.00	☐	☐	☐	☐

POETS

#864 1¢ LONGFELLOW 2 Plates

22502	$1.75	☐	☐	☐	☐
22503	$1.75	☐	☐	☐	☐

#865 2¢ WHITTIER 2 Plates

22505	$1.75	☐	☐	☐	☐
22506	$1.75	☐	☐	☐	☐

#866 3¢ LOWELL 2 Plates

22508	$3.00	☐	☐	☐	☐
22510	$3.00	☐	☐	☐	☐

#867 5¢ WHITMAN 2 Plates

22511	$11.00	☐	☐	☐	☐
22512	$11.00	☐	☐	☐	☐

#868 10¢ RILEY 2 Plates

22514	$40.00	☐	☐	☐	☐
22515	$40.00	☐	☐	☐	☐

EDUCATORS

#869 1 MANN 2 Plates

22521	$2.00	☐	☐	☐	☐
22522	$2.00	☐	☐	☐	☐

1940 FAMOUS AMERICANS
EDUCATORS Continued

#870 2¢ HOPKINS 2 Plates

Plate	Price	UL	UR	LL	LR
22524	$1.50	☐	☐	☐	☐
22525	$1.50	☐	☐	☐	☐

#871 3¢ ELIOT 2 Plates

Plate	Price	UL	UR	LL	LR
22527	$3.00	☐	☐	☐	☐
22528	$3.00	☐	☐	☐	☐

#872 5¢ WILLARD 2 Plates

Plate	Price	UL	UR	LL	LR
22530	$12.50	☐	☐	☐	☐
22532	$12.50	☐	☐	☐	☐

#873 10¢ BOOKER WASHINGTON 2 Plates

Plate	Price	UL	UR	LL	LR
22533	$30.00	☐	☐	☐	☐
22535	$30.00	☐	☐	☐	☐

SCIENTISTS

#874 1¢ AUDUBON 2 Plates

Plate	Price	UL	UR	LL	LR
22546	$1.00	☐	☐	☐	☐
22547	$1.00	☐	☐	☐	☐

#875 2¢ LONG 2 Plates

Plate	Price	UL	UR	LL	LR
22549	$1.00	☐	☐	☐	☐
22550	$1.00	☐	☐	☐	☐

#876 3¢ BURBANK 2 Plates

Plate	Price	UL	UR	LL	LR
22552	$1.25	☐	☐	☐	☐
22553	$1.25	☐	☐	☐	☐

#877 5¢ REED 2 Plates

Plate	Price	UL	UR	LL	LR
22555	$9.00	☐	☐	☐	☐
22556	$9.00	☐	☐	☐	☐

#878 10¢ ADDAMS 2 Plates

Plate	Price	UL	UR	LL	LR
22558	$30.00	☐	☐	☐	☐
22560	$30.00	☐	☐	☐	☐

MUSICIANS

#879 1¢ FOSTER 2 Plates

Plate	Price	UL	UR	LL	LR
22564	$1.25	☐	☐	☐	☐
22565	$1.25	☐	☐	☐	☐

#880 2¢ SOUSA 2 Plates

Plate	Price	UL	UR	LL	LR
22567	$1.25	☐	☐	☐	☐
22568	$1.25	☐	☐	☐	☐

#881 3¢ HERBERT 2 Plates

Plate	Price	UL	UR	LL	LR
22570	$1.50	☐	☐	☐	☐
22571	$1.50	☐	☐	☐	☐

#882 5¢ MacDOWELL 2 Plates

Plate	Price	UL	UR	LL	LR
22574	$12.50	☐	☐	☐	☐
22575	$12.50	☐	☐	☐	☐

1940 FAMOUS AMERICANS
MUSICIANS Continued

#883 10¢ NEVIN 2 Plates

Plate	Price	UL	UR	LL	LR
22576	$45.00	☐	☐	☐	☐
22577	$45.00	☐	☐	☐	☐

ARTISTS

#884 1¢ STUART 2 Plates

Plate	Price	UL	UR	LL	LR
22587	$1.00	☐	☐	☐	☐
22588	$1.00	☐	☐	☐	☐

#885 2¢ WHISTLER 2 Plates

Plate	Price	UL	UR	LL	LR
22602	$1.00	☐	☐	☐	☐
22603	$1.00	☐	☐	☐	☐

#886 3¢ SAINT-GAUDENS 2 Plates

Plate	Price	UL	UR	LL	LR
22593	$1.00	☐	☐	☐	☐
22594	$1.00	☐	☐	☐	☐

#887 5¢ FRENCH 2 Plates

Plate	Price	UL	UR	LL	LR
22596	$11.00	☐	☐	☐	☐
22597	$11.00	☐	☐	☐	☐

#888 10¢ REMINGTON 2 Plates

Plate	Price	UL	UR	LL	LR
22599	$32.50	☐	☐	☐	☐
22600	$32.50	☐	☐	☐	☐

INVENTORS

#889 1¢ WHITNEY 2 Plates

Plate	Price	UL	UR	LL	LR
22619	$2.25	☐	☐	☐	☐
22620	$2.25	☐	☐	☐	☐

#890 2¢ MORSE 2 Plates

Plate	Price	UL	UR	LL	LR
22622	$1.25	☐	☐	☐	☐
22624	$1.25	☐	☐	☐	☐

#891 3¢ McCORMICK 2 Plates

Plate	Price	UL	UR	LL	LR
22625	$2.00	☐	☐	☐	☐
22626	$2.00	☐	☐	☐	☐

#892 5¢ HOWE 2 Plates

Plate	Price	UL	UR	LL	LR
22628	$17.50	☐	☐	☐	☐
22629	$17.50	☐	☐	☐	☐

#893 10¢ BELL 2 Plates

Plate	Price	UL	UR	LL	LR
22631	$85.00	☐	☐	☐	☐
22632	$85.00	☐	☐	☐	☐

1940 COMMEMORATIVES

#894 3¢ PONY EXPRESS 4 Plates

Plate	Price	UL	UR	LL	LR
22579	$4.00	☐	☐	☐	☐
22580	$4.00	☐	☐	☐	☐
22581	$4.00	☐	☐	☐	☐
22582	$4.00	☐	☐	☐	☐

#895 3¢ PAN-AMERICAN UNION 2 plates

Plate	Price	UL	UR	LL	LR
22561	$3.50	☐	☐	☐	☐
22562	$3.50	☐	☐	☐	☐

1940 COMMEMORATIVES

#896 3¢ IDAHO 4 Plates

		UL	UR	LL	LR
22615	$2.50	☐	☐	☐	☐
22616	$2.50	☐	☐	☐	☐
22617	$2.50	☐	☐	☐	☐
22618	$2.50	☐	☐	☐	☐

#897 3¢ WYOMING 4 Plates

22583	$2.00	☐	☐	☐	☐
22584	$2.00	☐	☐	☐	☐
22585	$2.00	☐	☐	☐	☐
22586	$2.00	☐	☐	☐	☐

#898 3¢ CORONADO 4 Plates

22634	$2.00	☐	☐	☐	☐
22635	$2.00	☐	☐	☐	☐
22636	$2.00	☐	☐	☐	☐
22637	$2.00	☐	☐	☐	☐

1940 DEFENSE ISSUE

ROTARY PRESS

#899 1¢ DEFENSE 28 Plates

		UL	UR	LL	LR
22661	$.60	☐	☐	☐	☐
22662	$.60	☐	☐	☐	☐
22663	$.60	☐	☐	☐	☐
22664	$.60	☐	☐	☐	☐
22673	$.60	☐	☐	☐	☐
22674	$.60	☐	☐	☐	☐
22679	$.60	☐	☐	☐	☐
22684	$.60	☐	☐	☐	☐
22685	$.60	☐	☐	☐	☐
22698	$.60	☐	☐	☐	☐
22699	$.60	☐	☐	☐	☐
22709	$.60	☐	☐	☐	☐
22746	$.60	☐	☐	☐	☐
22747	$.60	☐	☐	☐	☐
22768	$.60	☐	☐	☐	☐
22769	$.60	☐	☐	☐	☐
22782	$.60	☐	☐	☐	☐
22783	$.60	☐	☐	☐	☐
22790	$.60	☐	☐	☐	☐
22791	$.60	☐	☐	☐	☐
22849	$2.00	☐	☐	☐	☐
22850	$2.00	☐	☐	☐	☐
22856	$12.00	☐	☐	☐	☐
22857	$12.00	☐	☐	☐	☐
22862	$3.00	☐	☐	☐	☐
22863	$3.00	☐	☐	☐	☐
22868	$4.50	☐	☐	☐	☐
22869	$4.50	☐	☐	☐	☐

#900 2¢ DEFENSE 28 Plates

22665	$.60	☐	☐	☐	☐
22666	$.60	☐	☐	☐	☐
22667	$.60	☐	☐	☐	☐
22668	$.60	☐	☐	☐	☐
22675	$.60	☐	☐	☐	☐
22676	$.60	☐	☐	☐	☐

1940 DEFENSE ISSUE

#900 2¢ DEFENSE Continued

		UL	UR	LL	LR
22686	$.60	☐	☐	☐	☐
22687	$.60	☐	☐	☐	☐
22700	$.60	☐	☐	☐	☐
22701	$.60	☐	☐	☐	☐
22710	$.60	☐	☐	☐	☐
22711	$.60	☐	☐	☐	☐
22748	$.60	☐	☐	☐	☐
22749	$.60	☐	☐	☐	☐
22770	$.60	☐	☐	☐	☐
22771	$.60	☐	☐	☐	☐
22784	$.60	☐	☐	☐	☐
22785	$.60	☐	☐	☐	☐
22792	$1.50	☐	☐	☐	☐
22793	$1.50	☐	☐	☐	☐
22851	$1.50	☐	☐	☐	☐
22852	$1.50	☐	☐	☐	☐
22858	$1.50	☐	☐	☐	☐
22859	$1.50	☐	☐	☐	☐
22864	$1.50	☐	☐	☐	☐
22865	$1.50	☐	☐	☐	☐
22870	$3.00	☐	☐	☐	☐
22871	$3.00	☐	☐	☐	☐

#901 3¢ DEFENSE 44 Plates

22669	$.75	☐	☐	☐	☐
22670	$.75	☐	☐	☐	☐
22671	$.75	☐	☐	☐	☐
22672	$.75	☐	☐	☐	☐
22677	$.75	☐	☐	☐	☐
22678	$.75	☐	☐	☐	☐
22688	$.75	☐	☐	☐	☐
22689	$.75	☐	☐	☐	☐
22690	$.75	☐	☐	☐	☐
22691	$.75	☐	☐	☐	☐
22692	$.75	☐	☐	☐	☐
22693	$.75	☐	☐	☐	☐
22694	$.75	☐	☐	☐	☐
22695	$.75	☐	☐	☐	☐
22696	$.75	☐	☐	☐	☐
22697	$.75	☐	☐	☐	☐
22702	$.75	☐	☐	☐	☐
22703	$.75	☐	☐	☐	☐
22704	$.75	☐	☐	☐	☐
22705	$.75	☐	☐	☐	☐

1940 DEFENSE ISSUE

#901 3¢ DEFENSE Continued

Plate	Price	UL	UR	LL	LR
22712	$.75	☐	☐	☐	☐
22713	$.75	☐	☐	☐	☐
22750	$.75	☐	☐	☐	☐
22751	$.75	☐	☐	☐	☐
22772	$2.50	☐	☐	☐	☐
22773	$2.50	☐	☐	☐	☐
22786	$.75	☐	☐	☐	☐
22787	$.75	☐	☐	☐	☐
22788	$2.50	☐	☐	☐	☐
22789	$2.50	☐	☐	☐	☐
22794	$2.00	☐	☐	☐	☐
22795	$2.00	☐	☐	☐	☐
22853	$3.75	☐	☐	☐	☐
22854	$3.75	☐	☐	☐	☐
22860	$2.00	☐$_{2}$	☐$_{3}$	☐$_{3}$	☐$_{2}$
22861	$5.00	☐	☐	☐	☐
22866	$2.50	☐$_{5}$	☐$_{4}$	☐$_{3}$	☐$_{2}$
22867	$2.50	☐$_{6}$	☐$_{4}$	☐$_{3}$	☐$_{3}$
22872	$17.50	☐$_{2}$	☐$_{2}$	☐$_{3}$	☐$_{2}$
22873	$17.50	☐$_{2}$	☐$_{2}$	☐$_{3}$	☐$_{2}$
22874	$5.00	☐$_{6}$	☐$_{3}$	☐$_{4}$	☐$_{3}$
22875	$6.00	☐$_{6}$	☐$_{2}$	☐$_{3}$	☐$_{3}$
22878	$4.00	☐$_{8}$	☐$_{2}$	☐$_{2}$	☐$_{2}$
22879	$4.00	☐$_{5}$	☐$_{2}$	☐$_{2}$	☐$_{2}$

1940 COMMEMORATIVE

#902 3¢ EMANCIPATION 4 Plates

Plate	Price	UL	UR	LL	LR
22680	$4.50	☐	☐	☐	☐
22681	$4.50	☐	☐	☐	☐
22682	$4.50	☐	☐	☐	☐
22683	$4.50	☐	☐	☐	☐

1941 COMMEMORATIVE

#903 3¢ VERMONT 2 Plates

Plate	Price	UL	UR	LL	LR
22706	$2.00	☐	☐	☐	☐
22707	$2.00	☐	☐	☐	☐

1942 COMMEMORATIVES

#904 3¢ KENTUCKY 2 Plates

Plate	Price	UL	UR	LL	LR
22925	$1.75	☐	☐	☐	☐
22926	$1.75	☐	☐	☐	☐

#905 3¢ WIN THE WAR 86 Plates

Plate	Price	UL	UR	LL	LR
22938	$.50	☐	☐	☐	☐
22939	$.50	☐	☐	☐	☐
22940	$.50	☐	☐	☐	☐
22941	$.50	☐	☐	☐	☐
22942	$.50	☐	☐	☐	☐
22943	$.50	☐	☐	☐	☐
22944	$.50	☐	☐	☐	☐
22945	$.50	☐	☐	☐	☐
22946	$.50	☐	☐	☐	☐
22947	$.50	☐	☐	☐	☐
22948	$.50	☐	☐	☐	☐
22949	$.50	☐	☐	☐	☐

1942 COMMEMORATIVES

#905 3¢ WIN THE WAR Continued

Plate	Price	UL	UR	LL	LR
22950	$.50	☐	☐	☐	☐
22951	$.50	☐	☐	☐	☐
22952	$.50	☐	☐	☐	☐
22953	$.50	☐	☐	☐	☐
22957	$.50	☐	☐	☐	☐
22958	$1.75	☐	☐	☐	☐
22959	$.50	☐	☐	☐	☐
22960	$.50	☐	☐	☐	☐
22961	$.50	☐	☐	☐	☐
22962	$.50	☐	☐	☐	☐
22965	$.50	☐	☐	☐	☐
22966	$.50	☐	☐	☐	☐
22967	$.50	☐	☐	☐	☐
22968	$.50	☐	☐	☐	☐
22969	$.50	☐	☐	☐	☐
22970	$.50	☐	☐	☐	☐
22971	$.50	☐	☐	☐	☐
22972	$.50	☐	☐	☐	☐
23030	$.50	☐	☐	☐	☐
23031	$.50	☐	☐	☐	☐
23032	$.50	☐	☐	☐	☐
23036	$.50	☐	☐	☐	☐
23039	$.50	☐	☐	☐	☐
23040	$.50	☐	☐	☐	☐
23041	$.50	☐	☐	☐	☐
23042	$.50	☐	☐	☐	☐
23046	$.50	☐	☐	☐	☐
23047	$.50	☐	☐	☐	☐
23050	$.50	☐	☐	☐	☐
23051	$.50	☐	☐	☐	☐
23062	$.50	☐	☐	☐	☐
23063	$.50	☐	☐	☐	☐
23073	$.50	☐	☐	☐	☐
23074	$.50	☐	☐	☐	☐
23075	$.50	☐	☐	☐	☐
23076	$.50	☐	☐	☐	☐
23077	$.50	☐	☐	☐	☐
23078	$.50	☐	☐	☐	☐
23079	$.50	☐	☐	☐	☐
23080	$.50	☐	☐	☐	☐
23093	$1.25	☐	☐	☐	☐
23094	$1.25	☐	☐	☐	☐
23097	$2.50	☐	☐	☐	☐
23098	$.50	☐	☐	☐	☐
23099	$.50	☐	☐	☐	☐
23100	$.50	☐	☐	☐	☐
23154	$.50	☐	☐	☐	☐
23155	$.50	☐	☐	☐	☐
23176	$.50	☐	☐	☐	☐
23177	$.50	☐	☐	☐	☐
23178	$.50	☐	☐	☐	☐
23183	$.50	☐	☐	☐	☐
23184	$.50	☐	☐	☐	☐
23185	$.50	☐	☐	☐	☐
23186	$.50	☐	☐	☐	☐
23187	$.50	☐	☐	☐	☐
23188	$.50	☐	☐	☐	☐
23189	$.50	☐	☐	☐	☐

1942 COMMEMORATIVES

#905 3¢ WIN THE WAR Continued

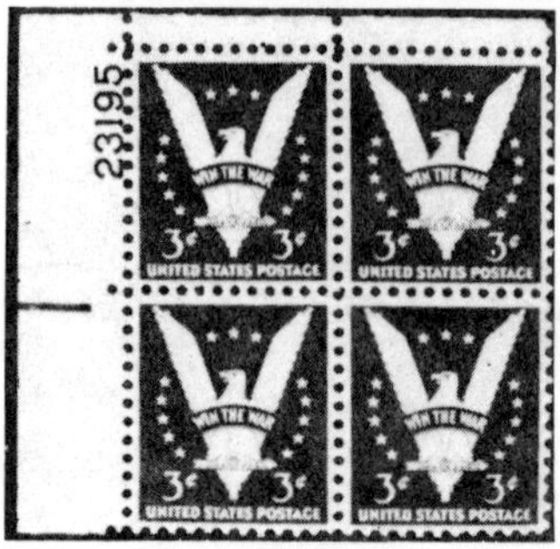

		UL	UR	LL	LR
23191	$1.00	☐	☐	☐$_3$	☐
23192	$1.00	☐	☐	☐$_3$	☐
23195	$75.00	☐$_4$	☐$_2$	☐$_3$	☐$_2$
23196	$75.00	☐$_4$	☐$_2$	☐$_3$	☐$_2$
23198	$1.50	☐$_3$	☐	☐$_2$	☐$_4$
23213	$1.00	☐	☐	☐	☐$_3$
23214	$1.00	☐$_3$	☐	☐$_3$	☐$_3$
23219	$1.50	☐	☐	☐	☐$_2$
23224	$1.50	☐	☐	☐	☐
23225	$1.50	☐	☐	☐	☐
23226	$1.50	☐	☐	☐	☐$_2$
23227	$1.50	☐	☐	☐	☐$_2$
23244	$2.50	☐$_3$	☐$_3$	☐$_2$	☐$_4$
23245	$2.50	☐$_3$	☐$_3$	☐$_2$	☐$_4$
23246	$6.00	☐$_3$	☐	☐$_5$	☐
23247	$6.00	☐$_3$	☐	☐$_3$	☐

#906 5¢ CHINA 2 Plates

22954	$15.00	☐	☐	☐	☐
22955	$15.00	☐	☐	☐	☐

1943 COMMEMORATIVES

#907 1943 2¢ UNITED NATIONS

16 Plates		UL	UR	LL	LR
22986	$.35	☐	☐	☐	☐
22987	$.35	☐	☐	☐	☐
22988	$.35	☐	☐	☐	☐
22989	$.35	☐	☐	☐	☐
22990	$.35	☐	☐	☐	☐
22991	$.35	☐	☐	☐	☐
22992	$.35	☐	☐	☐	☐
22993	$.35	☐	☐	☐	☐
22994	$1.50	☐	☐	☐	☐
22995	$1.50	☐	☐	☐	☐
22996	$1.50	☐	☐	☐	☐
22997	$1.50	☐	☐	☐	☐
22998	$1.50	☐	☐	☐	☐
22999	$1.50	☐	☐	☐	☐
23000	$2.50	☐$_2$	☐	☐	☐$_2$
23001	$2.50	☐$_2$	☐	☐	☐$_2$

1943 COMMEMORATIVES

#908 1943 1¢ FOUR FREEDOMS

14 Plates		UL	UR	LL	LR
23006	$.60	☐	☐	☐	☐
23007	$.60	☐	☐	☐	☐
23008	$.60	☐	☐	☐	☐
23009	$.60	☐	☐	☐	☐
23010	$.60	☐	☐	☐	☐
23011	$.60	☐	☐	☐	☐
23015	$.60	☐	☐	☐	☐
23016	$.60	☐	☐	☐	☐
23017	$.60	☐	☐	☐	☐
23018	$.60	☐	☐	☐	☐
23019	$6.00	☐	☐$_2$	☐$_2$	☐
23020	$5.00	☐	☐$_2$	☐$_2$	☐
23021	$1.25	☐	☐$_2$	☐	☐$_2$
23022	$1.25	☐	☐$_2$	☐	☐$_2$

1943-44 OVERRUN COUNTRIES

FLAG STAMPS **FLAT PRESS**

This issue was printed by the American Banknote Co.

13 Varieties	Name Blocks of 4	
#909 POLAND	$8.00	☐
#910 CZECHOSLOVAKIA	$3.50	☐
#911 NORWAY	$1.50	☐
#912 LUXEMBOURG	$1.50	☐
#913 NETHERLANDS	$1.50	☐
#914 BELGIUM	$1.50	☐
#915 FRANCE	$1.50	☐
#916 GREECE	$15.00	☐
#917 YUGOSLAVIA	$8.50	☐
#918 ALBANIA	$7.50	☐
#919 AUSTRIA	$5.00	☐
#920 DENMARK	$7.50	☐
#921 KOREA	$6.50	☐

1944 COMMEMORATIVES

ROTARY PRESS

#922 3¢ RAILROAD 2 Plates

		UL	UR	LL	LR
23142	$1.75	☐	☐	☐	☐
23143	$1.75	☐	☐	☐	☐

#923 3¢ STEAMSHIP 2 Plates

23145	$1.75	☐	☐	☐	☐
23146	$1.75	☐	☐	☐	☐

#924 3¢ TELEGRAPH 2 Plates

23151	$1.00	☐	☐	☐	☐
23152	$1.00	☐	☐	☐	☐

#925 3¢ CORREGIDOR 2 Plates

23162	$1.25	☐	☐	☐	☐
23163	$1.25	☐	☐	☐	☐

1944 COMMEMORATIVES

ROTARY PRESS

#926 3¢ MOTION PICTURES
2 Plates

Plate	Price	UL	UR	LL	LR
23180	$1.00	☐	☐	☐	☐
23181	$1.00	☐	☐	☐	☐

1945 COMMEMORATIVES

ROTARY PRESS

#927 3¢ FLORIDA 2 Plates

Plate	Price	UL	UR	LL	LR
23237	$.75	☐	☐	☐	☐
23239	$.75	☐	☐	☐	☐

#928 5¢ UNITED NATIONS 4 Plates

Plate	Price	UL	UR	LL	LR
23265	$.50	☐	☐	☐	☐
23266	$.50	☐	☐	☐	☐
23267	$.50	☐	☐	☐	☐
23276	$.50	☐	☐	☐	☐

#929 3¢ IWO JIMA 6 Plates

Plate	Price	UL	UR	LL	LR
23295	$.40	☐	☐	☐	☐
23296	$.40	☐	☐	☐	☐
23297	$.40	☐	☐	☐	☐
23298	$.40	☐	☐	☐	☐
23305	$.40	☐	☐	☐	☐
23306	$.40	☐	☐	☐	☐

#930 1¢ ROOSEVELT 6 Plates

Plate	Price	UL	UR	LL	LR
23307	$.20	☐	☐	☐	☐
23308	$.20	☐	☐	☐	☐
23309	$.20	☐	☐	☐	☐
23310	$.20	☐	☐	☐	☐
23311	$.20	☐	☐	☐	☐
23312	$.20	☐	☐	☐	☐

#931 2¢ ROOSEVELT 2 Plates

Plate	Price	UL	UR	LL	LR
23313	$.30	☐	☐	☐	☐
23314	$.30	☐	☐	☐	☐

#932 3¢ ROOSEVELT 6 Plates

Plate	Price	UL	UR	LL	LR
23285	$.40	☐	☐	☐	☐
23286	$.40	☐	☐	☐	☐
23287	$.40	☐	☐	☐	☐
23288	$.40	☐	☐	☐	☐
23293	$.40	☐	☐	☐	☐
23294	$.40	☐	☐	☐	☐

#933 5¢ ROOSEVELT (1946) 2 Plates

Plate	Price	UL	UR	LL	LR
23381	$.50	☐	☐	☐	☐
23382	$.50	☐	☐	☐	☐

#934 3¢ ARMY 4 Plates

Plate	Price	UL	UR	LL	LR
23324	$.40	☐	☐	☐	☐
23325	$.40	☐	☐	☐	☐
23326	$.40	☐	☐	☐	☐
23327	$.40	☐	☐	☐	☐

1945 COMMEMORATIVES

#935 3¢ NAVY 6 Plates

Plate	Price	UL	UR	LL	LR
23338	$.40	☐	☐	☐	☐
23339	$.40	☐	☐	☐	☐
23340	$.40	☐	☐	☐	☐
23341	$.40	☐	☐	☐	☐
23342	$.40	☐	☐	☐	☐
23343	$.40	☐	☐	☐	☐

#936 3¢ COAST GUARD 4 Plates

Plate	Price	UL	UR	LL	LR
23334	$.40	☐	☐	☐	☐
23335	$.40	☐	☐	☐	☐
23336	$.40	☐	☐	☐	☐
23337	$.40	☐	☐	☐	☐

#937 3¢ AL SMITH 4 Plates

Plate	Price	UL	UR	LL	LR
23353	$.40	☐	☐	☐	☐
23354	$.40	☐	☐	☐	☐
23355	$.40	☐	☐	☐	☐
23358	$.40	☐	☐	☐	☐

#938 3¢ TEXAS 4 Plates

Plate	Price	UL	UR	LL	LR
23365	$.40	☐	☐	☐	☐
23366	$.40	☐	☐	☐	☐
23367	$.40	☐	☐	☐	☐
23368	$.40	☐	☐	☐	☐

1946 COMMEMORATIVES

ROTARY PRESS

#939 3¢ MERCHANT MARINE
4 Plates

Plate	Price	UL	UR	LL	LR
23398	$.40	☐	☐	☐	☐
23399	$.40	☐	☐	☐	☐
23400	$.40	☐	☐	☐	☐
23405	$.40	☐	☐	☐	☐

#940 3¢ DISCHARGE EMBLEM
6 Plates

Plate	Price	UL	UR	LL	LR
23428	$.40	☐	☐	☐	☐
23429	$.40	☐	☐	☐	☐
23430	$.40	☐	☐	☐	☐
23435	$.40	☐	☐	☐	☐
23438	$.40	☐	☐	☐	☐
23439	$.40	☐	☐	☐	☐

#941 3¢ TENNESSEE 4 Plates

Plate	Price	UL	UR	LL	LR
23447	$.40	☐	☐	☐	☐
23448	$.40	☐	☐	☐	☐
23449	$.40	☐	☐	☐	☐
23450	$.40	☐	☐	☐	☐

#942 3¢ IOWA 6 Plates

Plate	Price	UL	UR	LL	LR
23467	$.40	☐	☐	☐	☐
23468	$.40	☐	☐	☐	☐
23469	$.40	☐	☐	☐	☐
23470	$.40	☐	☐	☐	☐
23471	$.40	☐	☐	☐	☐
23472	$.40	☐	☐	☐	☐

1946 COMMEMORATIVES

ROTARY PRESS

#943 3¢ SMITHSONIAN 6 Plates

Plate	Price	UL	UR	LL	LR
23463	$.40	☐	☐	☐	☐
23464	$.40	☐	☐	☐	☐
23465	$.40	☐	☐	☐	☐
23466	$.40	☐	☐	☐	☐
23473	$.40	☐	☐	☐	☐
23474	$.40	☐	☐	☐	☐

#944 3¢ KEARNY EXPEDITION 8 Plates

Plate	Price	UL	UR	LL	LR
23511	$.40	☐	☐	☐	☐
23512	$.40	☐	☐	☐	☐
23513	$.40	☐	☐	☐	☐
23514	$.40	☐	☐	☐	☐
23519	$.40	☐	☐	☐	☐
23520	$.40	☐	☐	☐	☐
23521	$1.00	☐	☐	☐	☐
23522	$1.00	☐	☐	☐	☐

1947 COMMEMORATIVES

ROTARY PRESS

#945 3¢ EDISON 6 Plates

Plate	Price	UL	UR	LL	LR
23559	$.40	☐	☐	☐	☐
23560	$.40	☐	☐	☐	☐
23561	$.40	☐	☐	☐	☐
23562	$.40	☐	☐	☐	☐
23563	$.40	☐	☐	☐	☐
23564	$.40	☐	☐	☐	☐

#946 3¢ PULITZER 6 Plates

Plate	Price	UL	UR	LL	LR
23622	$.40	☐	☐	☐	☐
23623	$.40	☐	☐	☐	☐
23624	$.40	☐	☐	☐	☐
23625	$.40	☐	☐	☐	☐
23626	$.40	☐	☐	☐	☐
23627	$.40	☐	☐	☐	☐

#947 3¢ POSTAGE CENTENARY 4 Plates

Plate	Price	UL	UR	LL	LR
23596	$.40	☐	☐	☐	☐
23597	$.40	☐	☐	☐	☐
23598	$.40	☐	☐	☐	☐
23599	$.40	☐	☐	☐	☐

#948 15¢ CIPEX SHEET (Imperf)

The plate numbers of this souvenir sheet were trimmed off after printing so no plate numbers were regularly issued.

#949 3¢ DOCTOR 8 Plates

Plate	Price	UL	UR	LL	LR
23656	$.40	☐	☐	☐	☐
23657	$.40	☐	☐	☐	☐
23658	$.40	☐	☐	☐	☐
23659	$.40	☐	☐	☐	☐
23660	$.40	☐	☐	☐	☐
23661	$.40	☐	☐	☐	☐
23665	$.40	☐	☐	☐	☐
23666	$.40	☐	☐	☐	☐

1947 COMMEMORATIVES

#950 3¢ UTAH 6 Plates

Plate	Price	UL	UR	LL	LR
23686	$.40	☐	☐	☐	☐
23687	$.40	☐	☐	☐	☐
23688	$.40	☐	☐	☐	☐
23689	$.40	☐	☐	☐	☐
23690	$.40	☐	☐	☐	☐
23691	$.40	☐	☐	☐	☐

#951 3¢ FRIGATE CONSTITUTION 6 Plates

Plate	Price	UL	UR	LL	LR
23710	$.40	☐	☐	☐	☐
23711	$.40	☐	☐	☐	☐
23712	$.40	☐	☐	☐	☐
23713	$.40	☐	☐	☐	☐
23714	$.40	☐	☐	☐	☐
23715	$.40	☐	☐	☐	☐

#952 3¢ EVERGLADES 6 Plates

Plate	Price	UL	UR	LL	LR
23736	$.40	☐	☐	☐	☐
23737	$.40	☐	☐	☐	☐
23738	$.40	☐	☐	☐	☐
23739	$.40	☐	☐	☐	☐
23744	$.40	☐	☐	☐	☐
23745	$.40	☐	☐	☐	☐

1948 COMMEMORATIVES

ROTARY PRESS

#953 3¢ CARVER 4 Plates

Plate	Price	UL	UR	LL	LR
23653	$.40	☐	☐	☐	☐
23654	$.40	☐	☐	☐	☐
23655	$.40	☐	☐	☐	☐
23664	$.40	☐	☐	☐	☐

#954 3¢ CALIFORNIA GOLD 6 Plates

Plate	Price	UL	UR	LL	LR
23772	$.40	☐	☐	☐	☐
23773	$.40	☐	☐	☐	☐
23774	$.40	☐	☐	☐	☐
23775	$.40	☐	☐	☐	☐
23776	$.40	☐	☐	☐	☐
23777	$.40	☐	☐	☐	☐

#955 3¢ MISSISSIPPI 6 Plates

Plate	Price	UL	UR	LL	LR
23802	$.40	☐	☐	☐	☐
23803	$.40	☐	☐	☐	☐
23804	$.40	☐	☐	☐	☐
23805	$.40	☐	☐	☐	☐
23806	$.40	☐	☐	☐	☐
23807	$.40	☐	☐	☐	☐

#956 3¢ FOUR CHAPLAINS 6 plates

Plate	Price	UL	UR	LL	LR
23819	$.40	☐	☐	☐	☐
23820	$.40	☐	☐	☐	☐
23821	$.40	☐	☐	☐	☐
23822	$.40	☐	☐	☐	☐
23825	$.40	☐	☐	☐	☐
23826	$.40	☐	☐	☐	☐

1948 COMMEMORATIVES

#957 3¢ WISCONSIN 4 Plates

		UL	UR	LL	LR
23812	$.40	☐	☐	☐	☐
23813	$.40	☐	☐	☐	☐
23814	$.40	☐	☐	☐	☐
23816	$.40	☐	☐	☐	☐

#958 5¢ SWEDISH PIONEER 4 Plates

		UL	UR	LL	LR
23829	$.60	☐	☐	☐	☐
23830	$.60	☐	☐	☐	☐
23831	$.60	☐	☐	☐	☐
23832	$.60	☐	☐	☐	☐

#959 3¢ PROGRESS OF WOMEN 4 Plates

		UL	UR	LL	LR
23841	$.40	☐	☐	☐	☐
23842	$.40	☐	☐	☐	☐
23843	$.40	☐	☐	☐	☐
23844	$.40	☐	☐	☐	☐

#960 3¢ WILLIAM ALLEN WHITE 4 Plates

		UL	UR	LL	LR
23855	$.50	☐	☐	☐	☐
23856	$.50	☐	☐	☐	☐
23857	$.50	☐	☐	☐	☐
23858	$.50	☐	☐	☐	☐

#961 3¢ CANADA FRIENDSHIP 4 Plates

		UL	UR	LL	LR
23853	$.40	☐	☐	☐	☐
23854	$.40	☐	☐	☐	☐
23859	$.40	☐	☐	☐	☐
23860	$.40	☐	☐	☐	☐

#962 3¢ FRANCIS SCOTT KEY 2 Plates

		UL	UR	LL	LR
23835	$.40	☐	☐	☐	☐
23836	$.40	☐	☐	☐	☐

#963 3¢ SALUTE TO YOUTH 4 Plates

		UL	UR	LL	LR
23864	$.40	☐	☐	☐	☐
23865	$.40	☐	☐	☐	☐
23866	$.40	☐	☐	☐	☐
23867	$.40	☐	☐	☐	☐

#964 3¢ OREGON 4 Plates

		UL	UR	LL	LR
23872	$.50	☐	☐	☐	☐
23873	$.50	☐	☐	☐	☐
23874	$.50	☐	☐	☐	☐
23875	$.50	☐	☐	☐	☐

#965 3¢ HARLAN FISKE STONE 4 Plates

		UL	UR	LL	LR
23890	$1.00	☐	☐	☐	☐
23891	$1.00	☐	☐	☐	☐
23892	$2.25	☐	☐	☐	☐
23893	$2.25	☐	☐	☐	☐

#966 3¢ PALOMAR 4 Plates

		UL	UR	LL	LR
23884	$1.25	☐	☐	☐	☐
23885	$1.25	☐	☐	☐	☐
23888	$2.50	☐	☐	☐	☐
23889	$2.50	☐	☐	☐	☐

#967 3¢ CLARA BARTON 4 Plates

		UL	UR	LL	LR
23896	$.40	☐	☐	☐	☐
23897	$.40	☐	☐	☐	☐
23898	$.40	☐	☐	☐	☐
23899	$.40	☐	☐	☐	☐

#968 3¢ POULTRY INDUSTRY 4 Plates

		UL	UR	LL	LR
23900	$.45	☐	☐	☐	☐
23901	$.45	☐	☐	☐	☐
23902	$.45	☐	☐	☐	☐
23903	$.45	☐	☐	☐	☐

#969 3¢ GOLD STAR 2 Plates

		UL	UR	LL	LR
23833	$.45	☐	☐	☐	☐
23834	$.45	☐	☐	☐	☐

#970 3¢ FORT KEARNY 4 Plates

		UL	UR	LL	LR
23907	$.45	☐	☐	☐	☐
23908	$.45	☐	☐	☐	☐
23912	$.45	☐	☐	☐	☐
23913	$.45	☐	☐	☐	☐

#971 3¢ VOLUNTEER FIREMAN 4 Plates

		UL	UR	LL	LR
23918	$.45	☐	☐	☐	☐
23919	$.45	☐	☐	☐	☐
23924	$.45	☐	☐	☐	☐
23925	$.45	☐	☐	☐	☐

#972 3¢ INDIAN CENTENNIAL 4 Plates

		UL	UR	LL	LR
23920	$.45	☐	☐	☐	☐
23921	$.45	☐	☐	☐	☐
23922	$.45	☐	☐	☐	☐
23923	$.45	☐	☐	☐	☐

#973 3¢ ROUGH RIDERS 4 Plates

		UL	UR	LL	LR
23947	$.45	☐	☐	☐	☐
23948	$.45	☐	☐	☐	☐
23949	$.45	☐	☐	☐	☐
23950	$.45	☐	☐	☐	☐

#974 3¢ JULIETTE LOW 4 Plates

		UL	UR	LL	LR
23953	$.45	☐	☐	☐	☐
23954	$.45	☐	☐	☐	☐
23955	$.45	☐	☐	☐	☐
23956	$.45	☐	☐	☐	☐

#975 3¢ WILL ROGERS 4 Plates

		UL	UR	LL	LR
23943	$.50	☐	☐	☐	☐
29344	$.50	☐	☐	☐	☐
29345	$.50	☐	☐	☐	☐
29346	$.50	☐	☐	☐	☐

1948 COMMEMORATIVES

ROTARY PRESS

#976 3¢ FORT BLISS 4 Plates

Plate	Price	UL	UR	LL	LR
23935	$1.50	☐	☐	☐	☐
23936	$1.50	☐	☐	☐	☐
23937	$1.50	☐	☐	☐	☐
23938	$1.50	☐	☐	☐	☐

#977 3¢ MOINA MICHAEL 4 Plates

Plate	Price	UL	UR	LL	LR
23965	$.45	☐	☐	☐	☐
23966	$.45	☐	☐	☐	☐
23967	$.45	☐	☐	☐	☐
23968	$.45	☐	☐	☐	☐

#978 3¢ GETTYSBURG 4 Plates

Plate	Price	UL	UR	LL	LR
23961	$.45	☐	☐	☐	☐
23962	$.45	☐	☐	☐	☐
23963	$.45	☐	☐	☐	☐
23964	$.45	☐	☐	☐	☐

#979 3¢ TURNERS SOCIETY 4 Plates

Plate	Price	UL	UR	LL	LR
23939	$.45	☐	☐	☐	☐
23940	$.45	☐	☐	☐	☐
23941	$.45	☐	☐	☐	☐
23942	$.45	☐	☐	☐	☐

#980 3¢ JOEL CHANDLER HARRIS 2 Plates

Plate	Price	UL	UR	LL	LR
23882	$.50	☐	☐	☐	☐
23883	$.50	☐	☐	☐	☐

1949 COMMEMORATIVES

ROTARY PRESS

#981 3¢ MINNESOTA 6 Plates

Plate	Price	UL	UR	LL	LR
24029	$.40	☐	☐	☐	☐
24030	$.40	☐	☐	☐	☐
24032	$.40	☐	☐	☐	☐
24033	$.40	☐	☐	☐	☐
24034	$.40	☐	☐	☐	☐
24035	$.40	☐	☐	☐	☐

#982 3¢ WASHINGTON & LEE 6 Plates

Plate	Price	UL	UR	LL	LR
24036	$.40	☐	☐	☐	☐
24037	$.40	☐	☐	☐	☐
24038	$.40	☐	☐	☐	☐
24039	$.40	☐	☐	☐	☐
24040	$.40	☐	☐	☐	☐
24041	$.40	☐	☐	☐	☐

#983 3¢ PUERTO RICO 4 Plates

Plate	Price	UL	UR	LL	LR
24062	$.40	☐	☐	☐	☐
24063	$.40	☐	☐	☐	☐
24064	$.40	☐	☐	☐	☐
24065	$.40	☐	☐	☐	☐

1949 COMMEMORATIVES

#984 3¢ ANNAPOLIS 6 Plates

Plate	Price	UL	UR	LL	LR
24093	$.40	☐	☐	☐	☐
24094	$.40	☐	☐	☐	☐
24095	$.40	☐	☐	☐	☐
24096	$.40	☐	☐	☐	☐
24097	$.40	☐	☐	☐	☐
24098	$.40	☐	☐	☐	☐

#985 3¢ G. A. R. VETERANS 6 Plates

Plate	Price	UL	UR	LL	LR
24135	$.40	☐	☐	☐	☐
24136	$.40	☐	☐	☐	☐
24137	$.40	☐	☐	☐	☐
24138	$.40	☐	☐	☐	☐
24139	$.40	☐	☐	☐	☐
24140	$.40	☐	☐	☐	☐

#986 3¢ EDGAR ALLAN POE 4 Plates

Plate	Price	UL	UR	LL	LR
24143	$.50	☐	☐	☐	☐
24144	$.50	☐	☐	☐	☐
24145	$.50	☐	☐	☐	☐
24146	$.50	☐	☐	☐	☐

1950 COMMEMORATIVES

ROTARY PRESS

#987 3¢ BANKERS ASSOCIATION 6 Plates

Plate	Price	UL	UR	LL	LR
24160	$.40	☐	☐	☐	☐
24161	$.40	☐	☐	☐	☐
24162	$.40	☐	☐	☐	☐
24163	$.40	☐	☐	☐	☐
24164	$.40	☐	☐	☐	☐
24165	$.40	☐	☐	☐	☐

#988 3¢ SAMUEL GOMPERS 4 Plates

Plate	Price	UL	UR	LL	LR
24166	$.40	☐	☐	☐	☐
24167	$.40	☐	☐	☐	☐
24168	$.40	☐	☐	☐	☐
24169	$.40	☐	☐	☐	☐

#989 3¢ STATUE OF FREEDOM 6 Plates

Plate	Price	UL	UR	LL	LR
24183	$.40	☐	☐	☐	☐
24184	$.40	☐	☐	☐	☐
24185	$.40	☐	☐	☐	☐
24186	$.40	☐	☐	☐	☐
24187	$.40	☐	☐	☐	☐
24188	$.40	☐	☐	☐	☐

#990 3¢ EXECUTIVE MANSION 6 Plates

Plate	Price	UL	UR	LL	LR
24209	$.40	☐	☐	☐	☐
24210	$.40	☐	☐	☐	☐
24211	$.40	☐	☐	☐	☐
24212	$.40	☐	☐	☐	☐
24218	$.40	☐	☐	☐	☐
24219	$.40	☐	☐	☐	☐

1950 COMMEMORATIVES

ROTARY PRESS

#991 3¢ SUPREME COURT BLDG.
4 Plates

		UL	UR	LL	LR
24243	$.40	☐	☐	☐	☐
24244	$.40	☐	☐	☐	☐
24245	$.40	☐	☐	☐	☐
24246	$.40	☐	☐	☐	☐

#992 3¢ U. S. CAPITOL 2 Plates

24284	$.40	☐	☐	☐	☐
24285	$.40	☐	☐	☐	☐

#993 3¢ CASEY JONES 6 Plates

24191	$.40	☐	☐	☐	☐
24192	$.40	☐	☐	☐	☐
24193	$.40	☐	☐	☐	☐
24194	$.40	☐	☐	☐	☐
24195	$.40	☐	☐	☐	☐
24196	$.40	☐	☐	☐	☐

#994 3¢ KANSAS CITY 6 Plates

24203	$.40	☐	☐	☐	☐
24204	$.40	☐	☐	☐	☐
24205	$.40	☐	☐	☐	☐
24206	$.40	☐	☐	☐	☐
24208	$.40	☐	☐	☐	☐
24217	$.40	☐	☐	☐	☐

#995 3¢ BOY SCOUTS 6 Plates

24224	$.40	☐	☐	☐	☐
24225	$.40	☐	☐	☐	☐
24227	$.40	☐	☐	☐	☐
24228	$.40	☐	☐	☐	☐
24229	$.40	☐	☐	☐	☐
24230	$.40	☐	☐	☐	☐

#996 3¢ INDIANA TERRITORY
6 Plates

24233	$.40	☐	☐	☐	☐
24234	$.40	☐	☐	☐	☐
24235	$.40	☐	☐	☐	☐
24236	$.40	☐	☐	☐	☐
24237	$.40	☐	☐	☐	☐
24238	$.40	☐	☐	☐	☐

#997 3¢ CALIFORNIA STATEHOOD
4 Plates

24259	$.40	☐	☐	☐	☐
24260	$.40	☐	☐	☐	☐
23261	$.40	☐	☐	☐	☐
24262	$.40	☐	☐	☐	☐

1951 COMMEMORATIVES

ROTARY PRESS

#998 3¢ CONFEDERATE VETERANS
4 Plates

		UL	UR	LL	LR
24366	$.40	☐	☐	☐	☐
24367	$.40	☐	☐	☐	☐
24368	$.40	☐	☐	☐	☐
24369	$.40	☐	☐	☐	☐

1951 COMMEMORATIVES

#999 3¢ NEVADA 6 Plates

		UL	UR	LL	LR
24414	$.40	☐	☐	☐	☐
24415	$.40	☐	☐	☐	☐
24416	$.40	☐	☐	☐	☐
24417	$.40	☐	☐	☐	☐
24430	$.40	☐	☐	☐	☐
24431	$.40	☐	☐	☐	☐

#1000 3¢ LANDING OF CADILLAC
6 Plates

24436	$.40	☐	☐	☐	☐
24437	$.40	☐	☐	☐	☐
24438	$.40	☐	☐	☐	☐
24439	$.40	☐	☐	☐	☐
24440	$.40	☐	☐	☐	☐
24441	$.40	☐	☐	☐	☐

#1001 3¢ COLORADO 6 Plates

24446	$.40	☐	☐	☐	☐
24447	$.40	☐	☐	☐	☐
24448	$.40	☐	☐	☐	☐
24449	$.40	☐	☐	☐	☐
24450	$.40	☐	☐	☐	☐
24451	$.40	☐	☐	☐	☐

#1002 3¢ AMERICAN CHEMICAL SOCIETY 6 Plates

24463	$.40	☐	☐	☐	☐
24464	$.40	☐	☐	☐	☐
24465	$.40	☐	☐	☐	☐
24466	$.40	☐	☐	☐	☐
24473	$.40	☐	☐	☐	☐
24474	$.40	☐	☐	☐	☐

#1003 3¢ BATTLE OF BROOKLYN
6 Plates

24556	$.40	☐	☐	☐	☐
24557	$.40	☐	☐	☐	☐
24558	$.40	☐	☐	☐	☐
24559	$.40	☐	☐	☐	☐
24560	$.40	☐	☐	☐	☐
24561	$.40	☐	☐	☐	☐

1952 COMMEMORATIVES

ROTARY PRESS

#1004 3¢ BETSY ROSS 6 Plates

		UL	UR	LL	LR
24574	$.50	☐	☐	☐	☐
24575	$.50	☐	☐	☐	☐
24576	$.50	☐	☐	☐	☐
24577	$.50	☐	☐	☐	☐
24578	$.50	☐	☐	☐	☐
24579	$.50	☐	☐	☐	☐

#1005 3¢ 4-H CLUB 4 Plates

24580	$.40	☐	☐	☐	☐
24581	$.40	☐	☐	☐	☐
24582	$.40	☐	☐	☐	☐
24583	$.40	☐	☐	☐	☐

1952 COMMEMORATIVES

#1006 3¢ B. & O. RAILROAD

6 Plates		UL	UR	LL	LR
24603	$.50	☐	☐	☐	☐
24604	$.50	☐	☐	☐	☐
24605	$.50	☐	☐	☐	☐
24606	$.50	☐	☐	☐	☐
24607	$.50	☐	☐	☐	☐
24608	$.50	☐	☐	☐	☐

#1007 3¢ A. A. A. ANNIVERSARY

6 Plates

24611	$.40	☐	☐	☐	☐
24612	$.40	☐	☐	☐	☐
24613	$.40	☐	☐	☐	☐
24614	$.40	☐	☐	☐	☐
24615	$.40	☐	☐	☐	☐
24616	$.40	☐	☐	☐	☐

#1008 3¢ NATO 18 Plates

24629	$.40	☐	☐	☐	☐
24630	$.40	☐	☐	☐	☐
24631	$.40	☐	☐	☐	☐
24632	$.40	☐	☐	☐	☐
24633	$.40	☐	☐	☐	☐
24634	$.40	☐	☐	☐	☐
24635	$.40	☐	☐	☐	☐
24636	$.40	☐	☐	☐	☐
24637	$.40	☐	☐	☐	☐
24638	$.40	☐	☐	☐	☐
24639	$.90	☐	☐	☐	☐
24640	$.90	☐	☐	☐	☐
24641	$.90	☐	☐	☐	☐
24642	$.90	☐	☐	☐	☐
24643	$.40	☐	☐	☐	☐
24644	$.40	☐	☐	☐	☐
24645	$.40	☐	☐	☐	☐
24646	$.40	☐	☐	☐	☐

#1009 3¢ GRANDE COULEE DAM

6 Plates

24647	$.40	☐	☐	☐	☐
24648	$.40	☐	☐	☐	☐
24649	$.40	☐	☐	☐	☐
24650	$.40	☐	☐	☐	☐
24651	$.40	☐	☐	☐	☐
24652	$.40	☐	☐	☐	☐

#1010 3¢ LaFAYETTE 6 Plates

24661	$.40	☐	☐	☐	☐
24662	$.40	☐	☐	☐	☐
24663	$.40	☐	☐	☐	☐
24664	$.40	☐	☐	☐	☐
24665	$.40	☐	☐	☐	☐
24666	$.40	☐	☐	☐	☐

#1011 3¢ MT. RUSHMORE 6 Plates

24669	$.40	☐	☐	☐	☐
24670	$.40	☐	☐	☐	☐
24671	$.40	☐	☐	☐	☐
24672	$.40	☐	☐	☐	☐
24673	$.40	☐	☐	☐	☐
24674	$.40	☐	☐	☐	☐

1952 COMMEMORATIVES

#1012 3¢ CIVIL ENGINEERS

6 Plates		UL	UR	LL	LR
24675	$.40	☐	☐	☐	☐
24676	$.40	☐	☐	☐	☐
24677	$.40	☐	☐	☐	☐
24678	$.40	☐	☐	☐	☐
24679	$.40	☐	☐	☐	☐
24680	$.40	☐	☐	☐	☐

#1013 3¢ SERVICE WOMEN

6 Plates

24681	$.40	☐	☐	☐	☐
24682	$.40	☐	☐	☐	☐
24683	$.40	☐	☐	☐	☐
24684	$.40	☐	☐	☐	☐
24685	$.40	☐	☐	☐	☐
24686	$.40	☐	☐	☐	☐

#1014 3¢ GUTENBURG BIBLE

6 Plates

24687	$.40	☐	☐	☐	☐
24688	$.40	☐	☐	☐	☐
24689	$.40	☐	☐	☐	☐
24690	$.40	☐	☐	☐	☐
24691	$.40	☐	☐	☐	☐
24692	$.40	☐	☐	☐	☐

#1015 3¢ NEWS BOYS 6 Plates

24693	$.40	☐	☐	☐	☐
24694	$.40	☐	☐	☐	☐
24695	$.40	☐	☐	☐	☐
24696	$.40	☐	☐	☐	☐
24697	$.40	☐	☐	☐	☐
24698	$.40	☐	☐	☐	☐

#1016 3¢ RED CROSS 6 Plates

24701	$.40	☐	☐	☐	☐
24702	$.40	☐	☐	☐	☐
24719	$.40	☐	☐	☐	☐
24720	$.40	☐	☐	☐	☐
24725	$.40	☐	☐	☐	☐
24726	$.40	☐	☐	☐	☐

1953 COMMEMORATIVES

ROTARY PRESS

#1017 3¢ NATIONAL GUARD

6 Plates		UL	UR	LL	LR
24745	$.40	☐	☐	☐	☐
24746	$.40	☐	☐	☐	☐
24747	$.40	☐	☐	☐	☐
24748	$.40	☐	☐	☐	☐
24749	$.40	☐	☐	☐	☐
24750	$.40	☐	☐	☐	☐

#1018 3¢ OHIO 4 Plates

24751	$.50	☐	☐	☐	☐
24752	$.50	☐	☐	☐	☐
24753	$.50	☐	☐	☐	☐
24754	$.50	☐	☐	☐	☐

1953 COMMEMORATIVES

ROTARY PRESS

#1019 3¢ WASHINGTON TERRITORY

6 Plates

		UL	UR	LL	LR
24759	$.40	☐	☐	☐	☐
24760	$.40	☐	☐	☐	☐
24761	$.40	☐	☐	☐	☐
24762	$.40	☐	☐	☐	☐
24763	$.40	☐	☐	☐	☐
24764	$.40	☐	☐	☐	☐

#1020 3¢ LOUISIANA 6 Plates

24767	$.40	☐	☐	☐	☐
24768	$.40	☐	☐	☐	☐
24769	$.40	☐	☐	☐	☐
24770	$.40	☐	☐	☐	☐
24771	$.40	☐	☐	☐	☐
24772	$.40	☐	☐	☐	☐

#1021 5¢ PERRY 4 Plates

24803	$1.00	☐	☐	☐	☐
24804	$1.00	☐	☐	☐	☐
24805	$1.00	☐	☐	☐	☐
24806	$1.00	☐	☐	☐	☐

#1022 3¢ BAR ASSOCIATION

6 Plates

24829	$.40	☐	☐	☐	☐
24830	$.40	☐	☐	☐	☐
24831	$.40	☐	☐	☐	☐
24832	$.40	☐	☐	☐	☐
24833	$.40	☐	☐	☐	☐
24834	$.40	☐	☐	☐	☐

#1023 3¢ SAGAMORE HILL 6 Plates

24849	$.40	☐	☐	☐	☐
24850	$.40	☐	☐	☐	☐
24851	$.40	☐	☐	☐	☐
24852	$.40	☐	☐	☐	☐
24853	$.40	☐	☐	☐	☐
24854	$.40	☐	☐	☐	☐

#1024 3¢ FUTURE FARMERS

4 Plates

24825	$.40	☐	☐	☐	☐
24826	$.40	☐	☐	☐	☐
24827	$.40	☐	☐	☐	☐
24828	$.40	☐	☐	☐	☐

#1025 3¢ TRUCKING INDUSTRY

6 Plates

24867	$.40	☐	☐	☐	☐
24868	$.40	☐	☐	☐	☐
24869	$.40	☐	☐	☐	☐
24870	$.40	☐	☐	☐	☐
24871	$.40	☐	☐	☐	☐
24872	$.40	☐	☐	☐	☐

1953 COMMEMORATIVES

#1026 3¢ PATTON 6 Plates

		UL	UR	LL	LR
24875	$.55	☐	☐	☐	☐
24876	$.55	☐	☐	☐	☐
24877	$.55	☐	☐	☐	☐
24878	$.55	☐	☐	☐	☐
24879	$.55	☐	☐	☐	☐
24880	$.55	☐	☐	☐	☐

#1027 3¢ NEW YORK CITY

6 Plates

24881	$.40	☐	☐	☐	☐
24882	$.40	☐	☐	☐	☐
24883	$.40	☐	☐	☐	☐
24884	$.40	☐	☐	☐	☐
24885	$.40	☐	☐	☐	☐
24886	$.40	☐	☐	☐	☐

#1028 3¢ GADSDEN PURCHASE

6 Plates

24888	$.40	☐	☐	☐	☐
24889	$.40	☐	☐	☐	☐
24890	$.40	☐	☐	☐	☐
24891	$.40	☐	☐	☐	☐
24892	$.40	☐	☐	☐	☐
24893	$.40	☐	☐	☐	☐

1954 COMMEMORATIVES

#1029 3¢ COLUMBIA UNIVERSITY

4 Plates

		UL	UR	LL	LR
24894	$.40	☐	☐	☐	☐
24895	$.40	☐	☐	☐	☐
24896	$.40	☐	☐	☐	☐
24897	$.40	☐	☐	☐	☐

#1060 3¢ NEBRASKA 4 Plates

24967	$.40	☐	☐	☐	☐
24968	$.40	☐	☐	☐	☐
24969	$.40	☐	☐	☐	☐
24970	$.40	☐	☐	☐	☐

#1061 3¢ KANSAS 4 Plates

24986	$.40	☐	☐	☐	☐
24987	$.40	☐	☐	☐	☐
24988	$.40	☐	☐	☐	☐
24989	$.40	☐	☐	☐	☐

#1062 3¢ EASTMAN 3 Plates

25008	$.40	☐	☐	☐	☐
25009	$.40	☐	☐	☐	☐
25010	$.40	☐	☐	☐	☐

#1063 3¢ LEWIS AND CLARK

Dry Printed **4 Plates**

25021	$.40	☐	☐	☐	☐
25022	$.40	☐	☐	☐	☐
25023	$.40	☐	☐	☐	☐
25024	$.40	☐	☐	☐	☐

1954 REGULAR ISSUE

The advent of this series brought a sharp increase in the collecting of plate number blocks. Collectors took advantage of the opportunity to start at the beginning of a new and interesting group of plates.

The Bureau of Engraving and Printing has done considerable experimenting during this period. Today stamps are printed by a dry process on pre-gummed paper instead of the wet method formerly in use. New equipment has made startling changes in printing methods. The 8¢ bi-colored Liberty is printed from a single plate instead of individual plates for each color.

The monthly publishing of reports on cancelled plates with the number of impressions gave collectors ample advance warning of short runs in time to search the Post Offices. This has prevented many of these plates from being considered rare.

Tremendous accumulations of these plates exist in the hands of some dealers and collectors and, as a result, prices will probably fluctuate until these stocks come onto the market and the existing quantities of the more difficult plate numbers can be estimated more accurately.

ROTARY PRESS PERF. 11 x 10½

#1030 ½¢ FRANKLIN 12 Plates

		UL	UR	LL	LR
Wet Printed					
25263	$.25	☐	☐	☐	☐
25264	$.25	☐	☐	☐	☐
Dry Printed					
25980	$.25	☐	☐	☐	☐
25981	$.25	☐	☐	☐	☐
26002	$.25	☐	☐	☐	☐
26003	$.25	☐	☐	☐	☐
26708	$.90	☐	☐	☐	☐
26709	$.90	☐	☐	☐	☐
26906	$.25	☐	☐	☐	☐
26907	$.25	☐	☐	☐	☐
26911	$.60	☐	☐	☐	☐
26912	$.60	☐	☐	☐	☐

#1031 1¢ WASHINGTON 64 Plates

		UL	UR	LL	LR
Wet Printed					
25030	$.20	☐	☐	☐	☐
25031	$.20	☐	☐	☐	☐
25032	$.20	☐	☐	☐	☐
25033	$.20	☐	☐	☐	☐
25281	$.20	☐	☐	☐	☐
25282	$.20	☐	☐	☐	☐
Dry Printed					
25326	$.20	☐	☐	☐	☐
25327	$.20	☐	☐	☐	☐
25361	$.20	☐	☐	☐	☐

#1031 1¢ WASHINGTON Continued

		UL	UR	LL	LR
25362	$.20	☐	☐	☐	☐
25677	$.20	☐	☐	☐	☐
25678	$.20	☐	☐	☐	☐
25679	$.20	☐	☐	☐	☐
25680	$.20	☐	☐	☐	☐
25681	$.20	☐	☐	☐	☐
25682	$.20	☐	☐	☐	☐
25687	$.20	☐	☐	☐	☐
25688	$.20	☐	☐	☐	☐
25691	$.20	☐	☐	☐	☐
25692	$.20	☐	☐	☐	☐
25695	$.20	☐	☐	☐	☐
25696	$.20	☐	☐	☐	☐
25703	$.60	☐	☐	☐	☐
25704	$.60	☐	☐	☐	☐
25707	$.20	☐	☐	☐	☐
25708	$.20	☐	☐	☐	☐
25714	$.20	☐	☐	☐	☐
25715	$.20	☐	☐	☐	☐
25727	$.60	☐	☐	☐	☐
25728	$.60	☐	☐	☐	☐
25991	$.20	☐	☐	☐	☐
25992	$.20	☐	☐	☐	☐
26063	$.20	☐	☐	☐	☐
26064	$.20	☐	☐	☐	☐
26163	$.20	☐	☐	☐	☐
26164	$.20	☐	☐	☐	☐
26189	$.20	☐	☐	☐	☐
26190	$.20	☐	☐	☐	☐
26408	$.20	☐	☐	☐	☐
26409	$.20	☐	☐	☐	☐
26429	$.20	☐	☐	☐	☐
26430	$.20	☐	☐	☐	☐
26460	$.20	☐	☐	☐	☐
26461	$.20	☐	☐	☐	☐
26606	$.20	☐	☐	☐	☐
26607	$.20	☐	☐	☐	☐
26612	$.20	☐	☐	☐	☐
26613	$.20	☐	☐	☐	☐
26927	$.60	☐	☐	☐	☐
26928	$.60	☐	☐	☐	☐
26929	$.20	☐	☐	☐	☐
26930	$.20	☐	☐	☐	☐
26971	$.20	☐	☐	☐	☐
26972	$.20	☐	☐	☐	☐
26987	$.20	☐	☐	☐	☐
26988	$.20	☐	☐	☐	☐
26994	$.20	☐	☐	☐	☐
26995	$.20	☐	☐	☐	☐
27151	$.20	☐	☐	☐	☐
27152	$.20	☐	☐	☐	☐
27221	$.20	☐	☐	☐	☐
27222	$.20	☐	☐	☐	☐
27228	$.20	☐	☐	☐	☐
27229	$.20	☐	☐	☐	☐

1954 REGULAR ISSUE

#1031A 1¼¢ SANTA FE 6 Plates

Dry Printed

Plate	Price	UL	UR	LL	LR
26619	$.60	□	□	□	□
26620	$.60	□	□	□	□
26641	$.60	□	□	□	□
26642	$.60	□	□	□	□
26724	$.60	□	□	□	□
26725	$.60	□	□	□	□

#1032 1½¢ MOUNT VERNON 5 Plates

Dry Printed

Plate	Price	UL	UR	LL	LR
25365	$4.00	□	□	□	□
25366	$4.00	□	□	□	□
25368	$4.00	□	□	□	□
25369	$4.00	□	□	□	□
25410	$4.00	□	□	□	□

#1033 2¢ JEFFERSON 78 Plates

Dry Printed

Plate	Price	UL	UR	LL	LR
25046	$.25	□	□	□	□
25047	$.25	□	□	□	□
25050	$.25	□	□	□	□
25051	$10.00	□	□	□	□
25056	$.25	□	□	□	□
25057	$.25	□	□	□	□
25061	$.25	□	□	□	□
25062	$.25	□	□	□	□
25079	$.25	□	□	□	□
25080	$.25	□	□	□	□
25129	$.25	□	□	□	□
25130	$.25	□	□	□	□
25131	$.25	□	□	□	□
25132	$.25	□	□	□	□
25137	$.25	□	□	□	□
25138	$.25	□	□	□	□
25143	$.50	□	□	□	□
25144	$.50	□	□	□	□
25149	$.25	□	□	□	□
25150	$.25	□	□	□	□
25189	$.25	□	□	□	□
25190	$.25	□	□	□	□
25203	$.25	□	□	□	□
25204	$.25	□	□	□	□
25213	$.60	□	□	□	□
25214	$.60	□	□	□	□
25215	$.90	□	□	□	□
25216	$.90	□	□	□	□
25241	$.60	□	□	□	□
25242	$.60	□	□	□	□
25277	$.25	□	□	□	□
25278	$.60	□	□	□	□
25283	$.60	□	□	□	□
25284	$.25	□	□	□	□
25290	$.25	□	□	□	□
25291	$.25	□	□	□	□
25457	$.25	□	□	□	□
25458	$.25	□	□	□	□
25459	$.25	□	□	□	□
25460	$.60	□	□	□	□
25461	$.25	□	□	□	□

#1033 2¢ JEFFERSON Continued

Plate	Price	UL	UR	LL	LR
25462	$.25	□	□	□	□
25463	$.25	□	□	□	□
25464	$.60	□	□	□	□
25465	$.25	□	□	□	□
25466	$.25	□	□	□	□
25467	$.25	□	□	□	□
25468	$.25	□	□	□	□
25471	$.60	□	□	□	□
25472	$.60	□	□	□	□
25565	$.25	□	□	□	□
25566	$.90	□	□	□	□
25573	$.25	□	□	□	□
25574	$.25	□	□	□	□
25579	$.25	□	□	□	□
25580	$.25	□	□	□	□
25585	$.25	□	□	□	□
25586	$.25	□	□	□	□
25589	$.25	□	□	□	□
25590	$.25	□	□	□	□
25591	$.50	□	□	□	□
25592	$.50	□	□	□	□
25594	$.25	□	□	□	□
25595	$.25	□	□	□	□
25596	$.25	□	□	□	□
25817	$.25	□	□	□	□
25818	$.25	□	□	□	□
25823	$.25	□	□	□	□
25824	$.25	□	□	□	□
25872	$.25	□	□	□	□
25875	$.25	□	□	□	□
25876	$.25	□	□	□	□
25877	$.25	□	□	□	□
25878	$.25	□	□	□	□
25887	$.25	□	□	□	□
25888	$.25	□	□	□	□
25901	$.25	□	□	□	□
25902	$.25	□	□	□	□

#1034 2½¢ BUNKER HILL 6 Plates

Dry printed

Plate	Price	UL	UR	LL	LR
26308	$.60	□	□	□	□
26309	$.60	□	□	□	□
26310	$.60	□	□	□	□
26322	$.60	□	□	□	□
27090	$50.00	□	□$_6$	†	□$_2$
27091	$50.00	□	†	†	□$_2$

1954 REGULAR ISSUE

#1035 3¢ LIBERTY 64 Plates

Wet Printed

Plate	Price	UL	UR	LL	LR
24943	$.40	☐	☐	☐	☐
24944	$.40	☐	☐	☐	☐
24945	$.40	☐	☐	☐	☐
24946	$.40	☐	☐	☐	☐
24947	$.40	☐	☐	☐	☐
24948	$.40	☐	☐	☐	☐
24949	$.40	☐	☐	☐	☐
24950	$.40	☐	☐	☐	☐
24951	$.40	☐	☐	☐	☐
24952	$.40	☐	☐	☐	☐
24953	$.40	☐	☐	☐	☐
24954	$.40	☐	☐	☐	☐
24955	$.40	☐	☐	☐	☐
24957	$.40	☐	☐	☐	☐
24958	$.40	☐	☐	☐	☐
24961	$.40	☐	☐	☐	☐
24962	$.40	☐	☐	☐	☐
24963	$.40	☐	☐	☐	☐
24964	$.40	☐	☐	☐	☐
24965	$.40	☐	☐	☐	☐
24966	$.40	☐	☐	☐	☐
24979	$.40	☐	☐	☐	☐
24994	$.40	☐	☐	☐	☐
24998	$.40	☐	☐	☐	☐
24999	$.40	☐	☐	☐	☐
25000	$.40	☐	☐	☐	☐
25001	$.40	☐	☐	☐	☐
25004	$.40	☐	☐	☐	☐
25005	$.40	☐	☐	☐	☐
25011	$.40	☐	☐	☐	☐
25012	$.40	☐	☐	☐	☐
25028	$.40	☐	☐	☐	☐
25029	$.40	☐	☐	☐	☐
25073	$.40	☐	☐	☐	☐
25074	$.40	☐	☐	☐	☐
25077	$.40	☐	☐	☐	☐
25078	$.40	☐	☐	☐	☐
25083	$.40	☐	☐	☐	☐
25084	$.40	☐	☐	☐	☐
25085	$.40	☐	☐	☐	☐
25086	$.40	☐	☐	☐	☐
25092	$.40	☐	☐	☐	☐
25093	$.40	☐	☐	☐	☐
25109	$.40	☐	☐	☐	☐
25110	$.40	☐	☐	☐	☐
25111	$.40	☐	☐	☐	☐
25112	$.40	☐	☐	☐	☐
25113	$.40	☐	☐	☐	☐
25114	$.40	☐	☐	☐	☐
25115	$.40	☐	☐	☐	☐
25116	$.40	☐	☐	☐	☐
25187	$.40	☐	☐	☐	☐
25188	$.40	☐	☐	☐	☐
25199	$.40	☐	☐	☐	☐
25200	$.40	☐	☐	☐	☐
25201	$.40	☐	☐	☐	☐

#1035 3¢ LIBERTY Continued

Plate	Price	UL	UR	LL	LR
25202	$.40	☐	☐	☐	☐
25205	$.40	☐	☐	☐	☐
25206	$.40	☐	☐	☐	☐
25211	$.40	☐	☐	☐	☐
25212	$.40	☐	☐	☐	☐
25229	$1.00	☐	☐	☐	☐
25230	$1.00	☐	☐	☐	☐
25233	$.40	☐	☐	☐	☐

#1035 3¢ LIBERTY 224 Plates

Dry Printed — UNTAGGED

Plate	Price	UL	UR	LL	LR
25235	$1.00	☐	☐	☐	☐
25236	$5.00	☐ 1	☐ 1	☐ 5	☐ 8
25239	$1.00	☐	☐	☐	☐
25240	$1.00	☐	☐	☐	☐
25253	$.40	☐	☐	☐	☐
25254	$2.00	☐	☐	☐	☐
25255	$2.00	☐	☐	☐	☐
25256	$.40	☐	☐	☐	☐
25259	$.40	☐	☐	☐	☐
25260	$1.25	☐	☐	☐	☐
25261	$.40	☐	☐	☐	☐
25262	$.40	☐	☐	☐	☐
25265	$.40	☐	☐	☐	☐
25266	$.40	☐	☐	☐	☐
25268	$1.25	☐	☐	☐	☐
25269	$.40	☐	☐	☐	☐
25270	$1.00	☐	☐	☐	☐
25271	$4.00	☐	☐	☐	☐
25272	$.40	☐	☐	☐	☐
25273	$.40	☐	☐	☐	☐
25274	$.40	☐	☐	☐	☐
25275	$.40	☐	☐	☐	☐
25276	$.40	☐	☐	☐	☐
25279	$.40	☐	☐	☐	☐
25280	$.40	☐	☐	☐	☐
25285	$1.50	☐	☐	☐	☐
25286	$1.50	☐	☐	☐	☐
25287	$1.75	☐	☐	☐	☐
25288	$.40	☐	☐	☐	☐
25292	$.40	☐	☐	☐	☐

1954 REGULAR ISSUE

#1035 3¢ LIBERTY Continued

		UL	UR	LL	LR
25293	$1.00	☐	☐	☐	☐
25294	$.40	☐	☐	☐	☐
25295	$1.00	☐	☐	☐	☐
25296	$.40	☐	☐	☐	☐
25297	$.40	☐	☐	☐	☐
25298	$1.00	☐	☐	☐	☐
25306	$.40	☐	☐	☐	☐
25307	$.40	☐	☐	☐	☐
25308	$.40	☐	☐	☐	☐
25311	$.40	☐	☐	☐	☐
25312	$.40	☐	☐	☐	☐
25351	$.40	☐	☐	☐	☐
25352	$.40	☐	☐	☐	☐
25504	$.40	☐	☐	☐	☐
25505	$.40	☐	☐	☐	☐
25506	$1.00	☐	☐	☐	☐
25507	$1.00	☐	☐	☐	☐
25508	$.40	☐	☐	☐	☐
25509	$.40	☐	☐	☐	☐
25510	$3.50	☐	☐	☐	☐
25511	$.40	☐	☐	☐	☐
25512	$.40	☐	☐	☐	☐
25513	$.40	☐	☐	☐	☐
25514	$1.00	☐	☐	☐	☐
25515	$.40	☐	☐	☐	☐
25516	$.40	☐	☐	☐	☐
25517	$2.00	☐	☐	☐	☐
25518	$2.00	☐	☐	☐	☐
25519	$.40	☐	☐	☐	☐
25520	$3.00	☐	☐	☐	☐
25521	$3.00	☐	☐	☐	☐
25522	$.40	☐	☐	☐	☐
25523	$.40	☐	☐	☐	☐
25524	$1.50	☐	☐	☐	☐
25525	$.40	☐	☐	☐	☐
25526	$4.00	☐	☐	☐	☐
25528	$.40	☐	☐	☐	☐
25529	$.40	☐	☐	☐	☐
25530	$.40	☐	☐	☐	☐
25531	$.40	☐	☐	☐	☐
25532	$.40	☐	☐	☐	☐
25537	$.40	☐	☐	☐	☐
25538	$.40	☐	☐	☐	☐
25539	$.40	☐	☐	☐	☐
25540	$7.50	☐	☐	☐	☐
25543	$.40	☐	☐	☐	☐
25544	$.40	☐	☐	☐	☐
25545	$.40	☐	☐	☐	☐
25546	$.40	☐	☐	☐	☐
25547	$.40	☐	☐	☐	☐
25548	$.40	☐	☐	☐	☐
25549	$.40	☐	☐	☐	☐
25550	$.40	☐	☐	☐	☐
25551	$.40	☐	☐	☐	☐
25552	$.40	☐	☐	☐	☐
25553	$.40	☐	☐	☐	☐
25554	$.40	☐	☐	☐	☐
25555	$.40	☐	☐	☐	☐
25556	$.40	☐	☐	☐	☐

#1035 3¢ LIBERTY Continued

		UL	UR	LL	LR
25557	$.40	☐	☐	☐	☐
25558	$1.00	☐	☐	☐	☐
25559	$1.00	☐	☐	☐	☐
25560	$.40	☐	☐	☐	☐
25561	$.40	☐	☐	☐	☐
25562	$.40	☐	☐	☐	☐
25563	$.40	☐	☐	☐	☐
25564	$.40	☐	☐	☐	☐
25581	$.40	☐	☐	☐	☐
25582	$.40	☐	☐	☐	☐
25583	$.40	☐	☐	☐	☐
25584	$.40	☐	☐	☐	☐
25587	$.40	☐	☐	☐	☐
25588	$.40	☐	☐	☐	☐
25607	$.40	☐	☐	☐	☐
25608	$.40	☐	☐	☐	☐
25609	$.40	☐	☐	☐	☐
25610	$.40	☐	☐	☐	☐
25661	$.40	☐	☐	☐	☐
25662	$.40	☐	☐	☐	☐
25671	$.40	☐	☐	☐	☐
25672	$.40	☐	☐	☐	☐
25716	$.40	☐	☐	☐	☐
25717	$.40	☐	☐	☐	☐
25731	$.40	☐	☐	☐	☐
25732	$.40	☐	☐	☐	☐
25733	$.40	☐	☐	☐	☐
25734	$.40	☐	☐	☐	☐
25792	$.40	☐	☐	☐	☐
25793	$.40	☐	☐	☐	☐
25794	$.40	☐	☐	☐	☐
25795	$.40	☐	☐	☐	☐
25810	$.40	☐	☐	☐	☐
25811	$.40	☐	☐	☐	☐
25813	$.40	☐	☐	☐	☐
25814	$.40	☐	☐	☐	☐
25815	$.40	☐	☐	☐	☐
25816	$.40	☐	☐	☐	☐
25819	$.40	☐	☐	☐	☐
25820	$.40	☐	☐	☐	☐
25821	$.40	☐	☐	☐	☐
25822	$.40	☐	☐	☐	☐
25827	$.40	☐	☐	☐	☐
25828	$.40	☐	☐	☐	☐
25829	$.40	☐	☐	☐	☐
25830	$.40	☐	☐	☐	☐
25831	$.40	☐	☐	☐	☐
25832	$.40	☐	☐	☐	☐
25833	$.40	☐	☐	☐	☐
25835	$.40	☐	☐	☐	☐
25836	$.40	☐	☐	☐	☐
25837	$.40	☐	☐	☐	☐
25838	$.40	☐	☐	☐	☐
25839	$.40	☐	☐	☐	☐
25840	$.40	☐	☐	☐	☐
25841	$.40	☐	☐	☐	☐
25842	$.40	☐	☐	☐	☐

1954 REGULAR ISSUE

#1035 3¢ LIBERTY Continued

		UL	UR	LL	LR
25849	$.40	☐	☐	☐	☐
25850	$.40	☐	☐	☐	☐
25851	$.40	☐	☐	☐	☐
25852	$.40	☐	☐	☐	☐
25873	$1.00	☐	☐	☐	☐
25874	$1.00	☐	☐	☐	☐
25880	$.40	☐	☐	☐	☐
25881	$.40	☐	☐	☐	☐
25885	$.40	☐	☐	☐	☐
25886	$.40	☐	☐	☐	☐
25895	$.40	☐	☐	☐	☐
25896	$.40	☐	☐	☐	☐
25906	$.40	☐	☐	☐	☐
25907	$.40	☐	☐	☐	☐
25914	$2.00	☐	☐	☐	☐
25915	$.40	☐	☐	☐	☐
25916	$1.00	☐	☐	☐	☐
25917	$1.00	☐	☐	☐	☐
25918	$.40	☐	☐	☐	☐
25919	$.40	☐	☐	☐	☐
25920	$.40	☐	☐	☐	☐
25921	$.40	☐	☐	☐	☐
25922	$.40	☐	☐	☐	☐
25926	$.40	☐	☐	☐	☐
25927	$.40	☐	☐	☐	☐
25928	$.40	☐	☐	☐	☐
25929	$.40	☐	☐	☐	☐
25933	$.40	☐	☐	☐	☐
25934	$.40	☐	☐	☐	☐
25935	$.40	☐	☐	☐	☐
25936	$.40	☐	☐	☐	☐
26362	$.40	☐	☐	☐	☐
26363	$.40	☐	☐	☐	☐
26378	$.40	☐	☐	☐	☐
26426	$.40	☐	☐	☐	☐
26427	$.40	☐	☐	☐	☐
26480	$.40	☐	☐	☐	☐
26509	$.40	☐	☐	☐	☐
26510	$.40	☐	☐	☐	☐
26545	$.40	☐	☐	☐	☐
26546	$.40	☐	☐	☐	☐
26571	$.40	☐	☐	☐	☐
26572	$.40	☐	☐	☐	☐
26583	$.40	☐	☐	☐	☐
26584	$.40	☐	☐	☐	☐
26595	$.40	☐	☐	☐	☐
26824	$.40	☐	☐	☐	☐
26825	$.40	☐	☐	☐	☐
26850	$.40	☐	☐	☐	☐
26851	$.40	☐	☐	☐	☐
27004	$.40	☐	☐	☐	☐
27005	$.40	☐	☐	☐	☐
27010	$.40	☐	☐	☐	☐
27011	$.40	☐	☐	☐	☐
27020	$.40	☐	☐	☐	☐
27021	$.40	☐	☐	☐	☐
27049	$.40	☐	☐	☐	☐
27050	$.40	☐	☐	☐	☐

#1035 3¢ LIBERTY Continued

		UL	UR	LL	LR
27051	$.40	☐	☐	☐	☐
27052	$.40	☐	☐	☐	☐
27054	$.40	☐	☐	☐	☐
27055	$.40	☐	☐	☐	☐
27056	$.40	☐	☐	☐	☐
27057	$.40	☐	☐	☐	☐
27058	$.40	☐	☐	☐	☐
27059	$.40	☐	☐	☐	☐
27163	$.40	☐	☐	☐	☐
27164	$.40	☐	☐	☐	☐
27165	$.40	☐	☐	☐	☐
27166	$.40	☐	☐	☐	☐
27271	$.40	☐	☐	☐	☐
27272	$.40	☐	☐	☐	☐
27273 o	$.40	☐	☐	☐	☐
27274 o	$.40	☐	☐	☐	☐
27280 o	$.40	☐	☐	☐	☐
27281 o	$.40	☐	☐	☐	☐
27323	$.40	☐	☐	☐	☐
27324	$.40	☐	☐	☐	☐

#1035 b 3¢ LIBERTY 4 Plates

Dry Printed — TAGGED

27273 o	$5.00	☐	☐	☐	☐
27274 o	$5.00	☐	☐	☐	☐
27280 o	$7.00	☐	☐	☐	☐
27281 o	$7.00	☐	☐	☐	☐

#1036 4¢ LINCOLN 4 Plates

Wet Printed

25075	$.50	☐	☐	☐	☐
25076	$.50	☐	☐	☐	☐
25081	$.50	☐	☐	☐	☐
25082	$.50	☐	☐	☐	☐

Dry Printed — UNTAGGED **199 Plates**

25445	$.50	☐	☐	☐	☐
25446	*$12.00*	☐	☐	☐	☐[2]
25447	$.50	☐	☐	☐	☐
25448	$.50	☐	☐	☐	☐
25449	$.50	☐	☐	☐	☐

o Issued both Tagged and Plain

1954 REGULAR ISSUE

#1036 4¢ LINCOLN Continued

		UL	UR	LL	LR
25450	$3.00	☐	☐	☐	☐
25451	$1.00	☐	☐	☐	☐
25452	$.50	☐	☐	☐	☐
25453	$.50	☐	☐	☐	☐
25454	$.50	☐	☐	☐	☐
25455	$.50	☐	☐	☐	☐
25456	$.50	☐	☐	☐	☐
25689	$.50	☐	☐	☐	☐
25690	$.50	☐	☐	☐	☐
25697	$.50	☐	☐	☐	☐
25698	$.50	☐	☐	☐	☐
25747	$.50	☐	☐	☐	☐
25748	$.50	☐	☐	☐	☐
25780	$.50	☐	☐	☐	☐
25781	$.50	☐	☐	☐	☐
25782	$.50	☐	☐	☐	☐
25783	$.50	☐	☐	☐	☐
25787	$.50	☐	☐	☐	☐
25788	$.50	☐	☐	☐	☐
25956	$.50	☐	☐	☐	☐
25957	$.50	☐	☐	☐	☐
26065	$.50	☐	☐	☐	☐
26066	$.50	☐	☐	☐	☐
26067	$.50	☐	☐	☐	☐
26068	$.50	☐	☐	☐	☐
26074	$.50	☐	☐	☐	☐
26075	$.50	☐	☐	☐	☐
26082	$.50	☐	☐	☐	☐
26083	$.50	☐	☐	☐	☐
26099	$.50	☐	☐	☐	☐
26100	$.50	☐	☐	☐	☐
26101	$.50	☐	☐	☐	☐
26102	$.50	☐	☐	☐	☐
26122	$.50	☐	☐	☐	☐
26123	$.50	☐	☐	☐	☐
26130	$.50	☐	☐	☐	☐
26131	$.50	☐	☐	☐	☐
26132	$.50	☐	☐	☐	☐
26133	$.50	☐	☐	☐	☐
26134	$.50	☐	☐	☐	☐
26135	$.50	☐	☐	☐	☐
26136	$.50	☐	☐	☐	☐
26137	$.50	☐	☐	☐	☐
26140	$.50	☐	☐	☐	☐
26141	$.50	☐	☐	☐	☐
26142	$.50	☐	☐	☐	☐
26143	$.50	☐	☐	☐	☐
26168	$.50	☐	☐	☐	☐
26169	$.50	☐	☐	☐	☐
26171	$.50	☐	☐	☐	☐
26172	$.50	☐	☐	☐	☐
26173	$.50	☐	☐	☐	☐
26174	$.50	☐	☐	☐	☐
26179	$.50	☐	☐	☐	☐
26180	$.50	☐	☐	☐	☐
26181	$.50	☐	☐	☐	☐
26183	$.50	☐	☐	☐	☐

#1036 4¢ LINCOLN Continued

		UL	UR	LL	LR
26184	$.50	☐	☐	☐	☐
26185	$.50	☐	☐	☐	☐
26186	$.50	☐	☐	☐	☐
26187	$.50	☐	☐	☐	☐
26188	$.50	☐	☐	☐	☐
26266	$.50	☐	☐	☐	☐
26267	$.50	☐	☐	☐	☐
26268	$.50	☐	☐	☐	☐
26293	$.50	☐	☐	☐	☐
26294	$.50	☐	☐	☐	☐
26295	$.50	☐	☐	☐	☐
26296	$.50	☐	☐	☐	☐
26311	$.50	☐	☐	☐	☐
26312	$.50	☐	☐	☐	☐
26313	$.50	☐	☐	☐	☐
26314	$.50	☐	☐	☐	☐
26330	$.50	☐	☐	☐	☐
26331	$.50	☐	☐	☐	☐
26332	$.50	☐	☐	☐	☐
26338	$.50	☐	☐	☐	☐
26339	$.50	☐	☐	☐	☐
26340	$.50	☐	☐	☐	☐
26341	$.50	☐	☐	☐	☐
26346	$.50	☐	☐	☐	☐
26347	$.50	☐	☐	☐	☐
26348	$.50	☐	☐	☐	☐
26349	$.50	☐	☐	☐	☐
26364	$.50	☐	☐	☐	☐
26365	$.50	☐	☐	☐	☐
26369	$.50	☐	☐	☐	☐
26370	$.50	☐	☐	☐	☐
26372	$.50	☐	☐	☐	☐
26373	$.50	☐	☐	☐	☐
26379	$.50	☐	☐	☐	☐
26380	$.50	☐	☐	☐	☐
26388	$.50	☐	☐	☐	☐
26389	$.50	☐	☐	☐	☐
26393	$.50	☐	☐	☐	☐
26394	$.50	☐	☐	☐	☐
26401	$.50	☐	☐	☐	☐
26402	$.50	☐	☐	☐	☐
26403	$.50	☐	☐	☐	☐
26421	$.50	☐	☐	☐	☐
26422	$.50	☐	☐	☐	☐
26473	$.50	☐	☐	☐	☐
26474	$.50	☐	☐	☐	☐
26490	$.50	☐	☐	☐	☐
26491	$.50	☐	☐	☐	☐
26496	$.50	☐	☐	☐	☐
26497	$.50	☐	☐	☐	☐
26503	$.50	☐	☐	☐	☐
26504	$.50	☐	☐	☐	☐
26526	$.50	☐	☐	☐	☐
26527	$.50	☐	☐	☐	☐
26559	$.50	☐	☐	☐	☐
26560	$.50	☐	☐	☐	☐
26573	$.50	☐	☐	☐	☐
26574	$.50	☐	☐	☐	☐

1954 REGULAR ISSUE

#1036 4¢ LINCOLN Continued

		UL	UR	LL	LR
26580	$.50	☐	☐	☐	☐
26581	$.50	☐	☐	☐	☐
26604	$.50	☐	☐	☐	☐
26605	$.50	☐	☐	☐	☐
26614	$.50	☐	☐	☐	☐
26615	$.50	☐	☐	☐	☐
26658	$.50	☐	☐	☐	☐
26659	$.50	☐	☐	☐	☐
26672	$.50	☐	☐	☐	☐
26673	$.50	☐	☐	☐	☐
26691	$.50	☐	☐	☐	☐
26701	$.50	☐	☐	☐	☐
26702	$.50	☐	☐	☐	☐
26727	$.50	☐	☐	☐	☐
26728	$.50	☐	☐	☐	☐
26765	$.50	☐	☐	☐	☐
26766	$.50	☐	☐	☐	☐
26808	$.50	☐	☐	☐	☐
26809	$.50	☐	☐	☐	☐
26810	$.50	☐	☐	☐	☐
26811	$.50	☐	☐	☐	☐
26837	$.50	☐	☐	☐	☐
26838	$.50	☐	☐	☐	☐
26854	$.50	☐	☐	☐	☐
26855	$.50	☐	☐	☐	☐
26868	$.50	☐	☐	☐	☐
26869	$.50	☐	☐	☐	☐
26883	$.50	☐	☐	☐	☐
26884	$.50	☐	☐	☐	☐
26887	$.50	☐	☐	☐	☐
26888	$.50	☐	☐	☐	☐
26889	$.50	☐	☐	☐	☐
26890	$.50	☐	☐	☐	☐
26920	$.50	☐	☐	☐	☐
26921	$.50	☐	☐	☐	☐
26931	$.50	☐	☐	☐	☐
26932	$.50	☐	☐	☐	☐
26939	$.50	☐	☐	☐	☐
26940	$.50	☐	☐	☐	☐
26945	$.50	☐	☐	☐	☐
26946	$.50	☐	☐	☐	☐
26960	$.50	☐	☐	☐	☐
26961	$.50	☐	☐	☐	☐
26966	$.50	☐	☐	☐	☐
26967	$.50	☐	☐	☐	☐
26980	$.50	☐	☐	☐	☐
26981	$.50	☐	☐	☐	☐
26982	$.50	☐	☐	☐	☐
26983	$.50	☐	☐	☐	☐
26996	$.50	☐	☐	☐	☐
26997	$.50	☐	☐	☐	☐
26998	$.50	☐	☐	☐	☐
26999	$.50	☐	☐	☐	☐
27008 o	$.50	☐	☐	☐	☐
27009 o	$.50	☐	☐	☐	☐
27037	$.50	☐	☐	☐	☐
27038	$.50	☐	☐	☐	☐
27102	$.50	☐	☐	☐	☐
27103	$.50	☐	☐	☐	☐

#1036 4¢ LINCOLN Continued

		UL	UR	LL	LR
27104	$.50	☐	☐	☐	☐
27105	$.50	☐	☐	☐	☐
27108 o	$.50	☐	☐	☐	☐
27109 o	$.50	☐	☐	☐	☐
27110	$.50	☐	☐	☐	☐
27111	$.50	☐	☐	☐	☐
27117	$.50	☐	☐	☐	☐
27118	$.50	☐	☐	☐	☐
27119 o	$.50	☐	☐	☐	☐
27120 o	$.50	☐	☐	☐	☐
27146 o	$.50	☐	☐	☐	☐
27168 o	$.50	☐	☐	☐	☐
27169	$.50	☐	☐	☐	☐
27980	$.50	☐	☐	☐	☐
27981	$.50	☐	☐	☐	☐
28004	$.50	☐	☐	☐	☐
28005	$.50	☐	☐	☐	☐
28006P	$20	☐	☐	☐	☐
28007P	$20	☐	☐	☐	☐
28221	$.50	☐	☐	☐	☐

#1036 b 4¢ LINCOLN

Dry Printed — TAGGED **8 Plates**

27008 o	$12.50	☐	☐	☐	☐
27009 o	$12.50	☐	☐	☐	☐
27108 o	$6.00	☐	☐	☐	☐
27109 o	$6.00	☐	☐	☐	☐
27119 o	$15.00	☐	☐	☐	☐
27120 o	$15.00	☐	☐	☐	☐
27146 o	$15.00	☐	☐	☐	☐
27168 o	$15.00	☐	☐	☐	☐

#1037 4½¢ HERMITAGE 4 Plates

Dry Printed

26264	$.75	☐	☐	☐	☐
26265	$.75	☐	☐	☐	☐
26269	$3.00	☐	☐	☐	☐
26270	$3.00	☐	☐	☐	☐

#1038 5¢ MONROE 16 Plates

Dry Printed

25087	$.65	☐	☐	☐	☐
25088	$.65	☐	☐	☐	☐
25090	$.65	☐	☐	☐	☐
25091	$.65	☐	☐	☐	☐
25858	$.65	☐	☐	☐	☐
25859	$.65	☐	☐	☐	☐
25865	$.65	☐	☐	☐	☐
25866	$.65	☐	☐	☐	☐

P These plate numbers have been reported only on precancelled stamps.

o Issued both Tagged and plain

1954 REGULAR ISSUE

#1038 5¢ MONROE Continued

Plate	Price	UL	UR	LL	LR
25924	$.65	□	□	□	□
25925	$.65	□	□	□	□
25930	$.65	□	□	□	□
25931	$.65	□	□	□	□
26710	$1.00	□	□	□	□
26711	$1.00	□	□	□	□
26720	$.65	□	□	□	□
26721	$.65	□	□	□	□

#1039 6¢ THEODORE ROOSEVELT

Wet Printed **2 Plates**

Plate	Price	UL	UR	LL	LR
25191	$1.75	□	□	□	□
25192	$1.75	□	□	□	□

Dry Printed **8 Plates**

Plate	Price	UL	UR	LL	LR
25427	$1.75	□	□	□	□
25428	$1.75	□	□	□	□
25843	$1.75	□	□	□	□
25844	$1.75	□	□	□	□
25853	$1.75	□	□	□	□
25854	$1.75	□	□	□	□
26004	$1.75	□	□	□	□
26005	$1.75	□	□	□	□

#1040 7¢ WILSON

Dry Printed **8 Plates**

Plate	Price	UL	UR	LL	LR
25299	$1.25	□	□	□	□
25300	$1.25	□	□	□	□
25304	$1.25	□	□	□	□
25305	$1.25	□	□	□	□
25309	$1.25	□	□	□	□
25310	$1.25	□	□	□	□
25313	$3.00	□	□	□	□
25314	$3.00	□	□	□	□

#1041 8¢ LIBERTY BICOLORED

Combination Plate Blocks of 4 Printed on both **flat** and **rotary** presses, the plate combinations appear in the same positions. Because of a new printing process, the rotary-press stamps appear to be identical with those from flat plates.

The centering of the issue, especially that of the earlier printings, has been so far below standard that near completion of all combinations in well centered condition has been impossible.

ROTARY PRESS

5 Frame Plates **2 Vignette Plates**

Frame -Vignette	Price	UL	UR	LL	LR
24923-24927	$3.50	□	□	□	□
24923-24938	$5.00	□	□	□	□
24924-24927	$4.00	□$_{2}$	□$_{5}$	□$_{2}$	□$_{2}$

#1041 8¢ LIBERTY Continued

Frame-Vignette	Price	UL	UR	LL	LR
24924-24938	$4.00	□$_{3}$	□$_{5}$	□$_{5}$	□$_{2}$
24928-24927	$3.50	□	□	□	□
24928-24938	$5.00	□	□	□	□
24940-24927	$3.50	□	□	□	□
24940-24938	$3.50	□	□	□	□
24942-24927	$6.00	□	□	□	□
24942-24938	$6.00	□	□	□	□

FLAT PRESS

9 Frame Plates **9 Vignette Plates**

Frame-Vignette	Price	UL	UR	LL	LR
24912-24916	$5.00	□	□	□	□
24912-24917	$5.00	□	□	□	□
24912-24918	$5.00	□	□	□	□
24912-24919	$5.00	□$_{2}$	□	□	□
24912-24935	$3.75	□	□	□	□
24912-24936	$3.75	□	□	□	□
24912-24937	$3.75	□	□	□	□
24912-24939	$3.75	□	□	□	□
24913-24916	$7.00	□	□	□	□
24913-24917	$7.00	□	□	□	□
24913-24918	$7.00	□	□	□	□
24913-24919	$7.00	□	□	□	□

Frame-Vignette	Price	UL	UR	LL	LR
24913-24920	$100	□	□	□	□
P 24913-24920	$40	□	□	□	□
24913-24935	$3.75	□	□	□	□
24913-24936	$3.75	□	□	□	□
24913-24937	$3.75	□	□	□	□
24913-24939	$3.75	□	□	□	□
24914-24916	$5.00	□	□	□	□
24914-24917	$2.00	□$_{4}$	□$_{3}$	□$_{3}$	□$_{3}$
24914-24918	$2.00	□$_{4}$	□$_{3}$	□$_{3}$	□$_{3}$
24914-24919	$2.00	□$_{5}$	□$_{3}$	□$_{3}$	□$_{3}$
24914-24935	$3.75	□	□	□	□
24914-24936	$3.75	□	□	□	□
24914-24937	$3.75	□	□	□	□
24914-24939	$3.75	□	□	□	□

P The combination also exists precancelled and is less difficult.

1954 REGULAR ISSUE

#1041 8¢ LIBERTY Continued

		UL	UR	LL	LR
24915-24916	$7.00	☐$_{2}$	☐	☐	☐
24915-24917	$10.00	☐$_{2}$	☐	☐	☐
24915-24918	$8.00	☐$_{4}$	☐	☐	☐
24915-24919	$5.00	☐$_{6}$	☐$_{5}$	☐$_{5}$	☐$_{5}$
24915-24920	$500.00	☐$_{8}$	☐$_{7}$	☐$_{7}$	☐$_{7}$
24915-24935	$3.75	☐	☐	☐	☐
24915-24936	$3.75	☐	☐	☐	☐
24915-24937	$3.75	☐	☐	☐	☐
24915-24939	$3.75	☐	☐	☐	☐
24926-24916	$25.00	☐$_{4}$	☐$_{6}$	☐$_{5}$	☐$_{4}$
24926-24917	$45.00	☐	☐	☐	☐
24926-24918	$30.00	☐	☐	☐	☐
24926-24919	$30.00	☐	☐	☐	☐
24929-24935	$6.00	☐	☐	☐	☐
24929-24936	$6.00	☐	☐	☐	☐
24929-24937	$6.00	☐	☐	☐	☐
24929-24939	$6.00	☐	☐	☐	☐
24930-24935	$6.00	☐	☐	☐	☐
24930-24936	$6.00	☐	☐	☐	☐
24930-24937	$6.00	☐	☐	☐	☐
24930-24939	$7.00	☐	☐	☐	☐
24932-24935	$6.00	☐	☐	☐	☐
24932-24936	$6.00	☐	☐	☐	☐
24932-24937	$6.00	☐	☐	☐	☐
24932-24939	$6.00	☐	☐	☐	☐
24933-24935	$6.00	☐	☐	☐	☐
24933-24936	$6.00	☐	☐	☐	☐
24933-24937	$7.00	☐	☐	☐	☐
24933-24939	$6.00	☐	☐	☐	☐

#1042 8¢ LIBERTY (GIORI) 12 Plates

ROTARY PRESS

		UL	UR	LL	LR
25932	$1.25	☐	☐	☐	☐
25937	$1.25	☐	☐	☐	☐
25950	$1.25	☐	☐	☐	☐
25955	$1.25	☐	☐	☐	☐
26221	$1.25	☐	☐	☐	☐
26224	$1.25	☐	☐	☐	☐
26230	$1.25	☐	☐	☐	☐
26231	$1.25	☐	☐	☐	☐
26242	$1.25	☐	☐	☐	☐
26524	$1.25	☐	☐	☐	☐
26525	$1.25	☐	☐	☐	☐
26821	$15.00	☐	☐	☐	☐

#1042A 8¢ PERSHING 4 Plates

Dry Printed

		UL	UR	LL	LR
27075	$1.25	☐	☐	☐	☐
27076	$1.25	☐	☐	☐	☐
27705	$1.25	☐	☐	☐	☐
27706	$1.25	☐	☐	☐	☐

#1043 9¢ ALAMO 6 Plates

Dry Printed

		UL	UR	LL	LR
25393	$1.40	☐	☐	☐	☐
25394	$1.40	☐	☐	☐	☐
25415	$1.40	☐	☐	☐	☐
25416	$1.40	☐	☐	☐	☐
26260	$1.40	☐	☐	☐	☐
26261	$1.40	☐	☐	☐	☐

#1044 10¢ INDEPENDENCE HALL

Dry Printed UNTAGGED 15 Plates

		UL	UR	LL	LR
25423	$1.25	☐	☐	☐	☐
25424	$1.25	☐	☐	☐	☐
25426	$3.50	☐	☐	☐	☐
25601	$1.25	☐	☐	☐	☐
25602	$1.25	☐	☐	☐	☐
25860	$1.25	☐	☐	☐	☐
25861	$1.25	☐	☐	☐	☐
25938	$1.25	☐	☐	☐	☐
25939	$1.25	☐	☐	☐	☐
26951	$1.25	☐	☐	☐	☐
26952	$1.25	☐	☐	☐	☐
27684 o	$1.65	☐	☐	☐	☐
27685 o	$1.65	☐	☐	☐	☐
27773 o	$1.65	☐	☐	☐	☐
27774 o	$1.65	☐	☐	☐	☐

#1044 b 10¢ INDEPENDENCE HALL

Dry Printed TAGGED 4 Plates

		UL	UR	LL	LR
27684 o	$15.00	☐	☐	☐	☐
27685 o	$15.00	☐	☐	☐	☐
27773 o	$12.00	☐	☐	☐	☐
27774 o	$12.00	☐	☐	☐	☐

#1044A 11¢ LIBERTY (GIORI)

Dry Printed UNTAGGED 4 Plates

		UL	UR	LL	LR
26976 o	$1.50	☐	☐	☐	☐
26978 o	$1.50	☐	☐	☐	☐
26979 o	$1.50	☐	☐	☐	☐
26986	$1.50	☐	☐	☐	☐

#1044A c 11¢ LIBERTY (GIORI)

Dry Printed TAGGED 3 Plates

		UL	UR	LL	LR
26976 o	$15.00	☐	☐	☐	☐
26978 o	$15.00	☐	☐	☐	☐
26979 o	$50.00	☐	☐	☐	☐

o Issued both Tagged and Plain

1954 REGULAR ISSUE

#1045 12¢ HARRISON

Dry Printed UNTAGGED **4 Plates**

		UL	UR	LL	LR
26281 o	$2.00	☐	☐	☐	☐
26282 o	$2.00	☐	☐	☐	☐
26283 o	$2.00	☐	☐	☐	☐
26284 o	$2.00	☐	☐	☐	☐

#1045 a 12¢ HARRISON

Dry Printed TAGGED **4 Plates**

26281 o	$4.00	☐	☐	☐	☐
26282 o	$4.00	☐	☐	☐	☐
26283 o	$4.00	☐	☐	☐	☐
26284 o	$4.00	☐	☐	☐	☐

#1046 15¢ JAY

Dry Printed UNTAGGED **4 Plates**

26138	$4.00	☐	☐	☐	☐
26139 o	$4.00	☐	☐	☐	☐
26165 o	$4.00	☐	☐	☐	☐
26166 o	$4.00	☐	☐	☐	☐

#1046 a 15¢ JAY

Dry Printed TAGGED **5 Plates**

26139 o	$8.50	☐	☐	☐	☐
26165 o	$8.50	☐	☐	☐	☐
26166 o	$12.50	☐	☐	☐	☐
27968	$3.50	☐	☐	☐	☐
27969	$3.50	☐	☐	☐	☐

#1047 20¢ MONTICELLO

Dry Printed **20 Plates**

25391	$2.50	☐	☐	☐	☐
25392	$2.50	☐	☐	☐	☐
25653	$2.50	☐	☐	☐	☐
25654	$2.50	☐	☐	☐	☐
25655	$2.50	☐	☐	☐	☐
25656	$2.50	☐	☐	☐	☐
25988	$2.50	☐	☐	☐	☐
25989	$2.50	☐	☐	☐	☐
26256	$2.50	☐	☐	☐	☐
26257	$2.50	☐	☐	☐	☐
26315	$2.50	☐	☐	☐	☐
26316	$2.50	☐	☐	☐	☐
26528	$2.50	☐	☐	☐	☐
26529	$2.50	☐	☐	☐	☐
27002	$2.50	☐	☐	☐	☐
27003	$2.50	☐	☐	☐	☐
28021	$2.50	☐	☐	☐	☐
28022	$2.50	☐	☐	☐	☐
28034	$7.00	☐	☐	☐	☐
28035	$7.00	☐	☐	☐	☐

#1048 25¢ REVERE

Dry Printed **4 Plates**

25962	$8.50	☐	☐	☐	☐
25963	$8.50	☐	☐	☐	☐
25964	$8.50	☐	☐	☐	☐
25965	$8.50	☐	☐	☐	☐

o Issued both Tagged and Plain

#1049 30¢ LEE

Wet Printed **2 Plates**

		UL	UR	LL	LR
25251	$5.00	☐	☐	☐	☐
25252	$5.00	☐	☐	☐	☐

Dry Printed **10 Plates**

25487	$5.00	☐	☐	☐	☐
25488	$5.00	☐	☐	☐	☐
25948	$5.00	☐	☐	☐	☐
25949	$5.00	☐	☐	☐	☐
26324	$5.00	☐	☐	☐	☐
26325	$5.00	☐	☐	☐	☐
26602	$5.00	☐	☐	☐	☐
26603	$5.00	☐	☐	☐	☐
29207	$5.00	☐	☐	☐	☐
29208	$5.00	☐	☐	☐	☐

#1050 40¢ MARSHALL

Wet Printed **2 Plates**

25249	$11.50	☐	☐	☐	☐
25250	$11.50	☐	☐	☐	☐

Dry Printed **6 Plates**

25571	$11.50	☐	☐	☐	☐
25572	$11.50	☐	☐	☐	☐
26203	$11.50	☐	☐	☐	☐
26204	$11.50	☐	☐	☐	☐
27814	$11.50	☐	☐	☐	☐
27815	$11.50	☐	☐	☐	☐

#1051 50¢ SUSAN ANTHONY

Wet Printed **4 Plates**

25231	$8.50	☐	☐	☐	☐
25232	$8.50	☐	☐	☐	☐
25237	$8.50	☐	☐	☐	☐
25238	$8.50	☐	☐	☐	☐

Dry Printed **6 Plates**

25897	$8.00	☐	☐	☐	☐
25898	$8.00	☐	☐	☐	☐
26205	$8.00	☐	☐	☐	☐
26206	$8.00	☐	☐	☐	☐
27957	$8.00	☐	☐	☐	☐
27958	$8.00	☐	☐	☐	☐

#1052 $1.00 PATRICK HENRY

Wet Printed **2 Plates**

25257	$35.00	☐	☐	☐	☐
25258	$35.00	☐	☐	☐	☐

Dry Printed **6 Plates**

25541	$35.00	☐	☐	☐	☐
25542	$35.00	☐	☐	☐	☐
26207	$35.00	☐	☐	☐	☐
26208	$35.00	☐	☐	☐	☐
27990	$55.00	☐	☐	☐	☐
27991	$55.00	☐	☐	☐	☐

#1053 $5.00 HAMILTON Dry Printed

FLAT PRESS Block of 4

25367	*$400.00*	☐	☐	☐	☐

1954 REGULAR ISSUE

BOOKLET PANE PLATES

ROTARY PRESS **PANES OF 6**

#1035 a 3¢ LIBERTY

Wet Printed **14 Plates**

24975	24976	24980	24981	25002
25003	25006	25007	25013	25014
25334	25335	25353	25354	

Dry Printed **22 Plates**

25355	25356	25357	25358	25363
25364	25372	25373	25417	25418
25567	25568	25569	25570	25743
25744	25757	25758	25774	25775
25789	25790			

#1036 a 4¢ LINCOLN 43 Plates

Dry Printed

26013	26014	26032	26033	26038
26039	26111	26112	26154	26155
26191	26192	26287	26288	26468
26469	26515	26516	26518	26519
26520	26521	26593	26594	26652
26653	*26689	26690	26699	26700
26817	26818	26819	26822	26823
26829	26830	26955	26956	27188
27189	27215	27216		

SIDE COIL PLATES

On the early 384 Subject coil plates the numbers were located further from the stamps than usual and consequently very few have been found. These wide-spaced plates are marked **w** in the following lists, after the plate number.

The plate numbers on the 432 subject plates are located under the first and last stamps in the bottom row only. Therefore these are collected in bottom strips of six stamps with a plate number from the companion plates on each side of the joint line.

SIDE COIL PLATES

#1054 1¢ WASHINGTON

Wet Printed **6 Plates**
170 Subject Plates **STRIPS OF 5**

25036	25037	25048	25049	25161
25162				

Dry Printed **8 Plates**
384 Subject Plates **STRIPS OF 5**

†25479**w**	†25480**w**	25721	25722	25868
25869	26006	26007		

432 Subject Plates **6 Plates**
STRIPS OF 6

26411	26412	26462	26463	†27043
†27044				

#1054A 1¼¢ SANTA FE

Dry Printed **2 Plates**
384 Subject Plates **STRIPS OF 5**

26670 26671

432 Subject Plates **6 Plates**
STRIPS OF 6

26621	26622	†26656	†26657	†28120
†28121				

#1055 2¢ JEFFERSON

Wet Printed **14 Plates**
170 Subject Plates **STRIPS OF 5**

25044	25045	25067	25068	25094
25095	25096	25097	25151	25152
25153	25157	25411	25412	

Dry Printed **14 Plates**
384 Subject Plates **STRIPS OF 5**

†25443**w**	†25444**w**	†25629**w**	†25630**w**	25673
25674	25759	25760	25951	25952
25968	25969	26008	26009	

432 Subject UNTAGGED **6 Plates**

†26360	†26361	26399**o**	26400**o**	27977
†27978				

#1055 a 2¢ JEFFERSON

432 Subject TAGGED **20 Plates**

26399**o**	26400**o**	32119	32120	†32129
†*32130*	*33487*	*33647*	†34353	†34354
35232	†35575	35773	†36208	†37602
†37603	†37612	†37613	37992	37993

#1056 2½¢ BUNKER HILL

Dry Printed **2 Plates**
384 Subject Plates **STRIPS OF 5**

26279 26280

432 Subject Plates **4 Plates**
STRIPS OF 6

†26436	†26437	†26449	†26450

1954 REGULAR ISSUE

SIDE COIL PLATES Continued

#1057 3¢ LIBERTY

Wet Printed **64 Plates**
170 Subject Plates **STRIPS OF 5**

24971 24972 24973 24974 24977
24978 24982 24983 24984 24985
24990 24991 24992 24993 24995
24996 25052 25053 25063 25064
25102 25103 25121 25122 25123
25124 25133 25134 25135 25136
25139 25140 25141 25142 25145
25146 25147 25148 25154 25155
25156 25159 25217 25218 25219
25220 25221 25222 25223 25224
25225 25226 25227 25228 25336
25337 25338 25339 25399 25400
25401 25402 25403 25404

Dry Printed **46 Plates**
384 Subject Plates **STRIPS OF 5**

†25433w †25434w †25435w †25436w 25481w
25482w †25575w †25576w †25577w †25578w
†25617w †25618w 25639 25640 25649
25650 †25663 25664 25665 †25666
25667 25668 25669 25670 25675
25676 25693 25694 25718 25719
25753 25754 25767 25768 25769
25770 25845 25846 25847 25848
25856 25857 26209 26210 26442
26443

432 Subject UNTAGGED **16 Plates**
STRIPS OF 6

25825 25826 †25899 †25900 25953
25954 †25975 †25976 27028 27029
†27030 †27031 27236o 27237o 27238
27239

432 Subject TAGGED **2 Plates**

27236o 27237o

#1058 4¢ LINCOLN

Wet Printed **2 Plates**
170 Subject Plates **STRIPS OF 5**

25098P 25099P

P These Plate numbers have been reported only on precancelled coils.

Dry Printed **42 Plates**
384 Subject Plates **STRIPS OF 5**

25705 25706 25709 25710 25755
25756 26040 26041 26072 26073
26084 26085 26086 26087 26089
26090 26093 26094 26109 26110
26144 26145 26146 26147 26150
26151 26152 26153 26232 26233
26258 26259 26383 26384 26395
26396 26404 26405 26650 26651
26663 26664

167 Plates
432 Subject Plates **STRIPS OF 6**

26015 26016 †26034 †26035 26113
26114 †26193 †26194 †26211 †26212

SIDE COIL PLATES Continued

#1058 4¢ LINCOLN Continued

†26213 †26214 26285 26286 26297
26298 26326 26327 26352 26353
†26478 †26479 †26484 †26485 26492
26493 †26505 †26506 †26513 †26514
†26538 †26539 †26547 †26548 †26585
†26586 26616 26617 26654 26655
†26703 †26704 26718 26719 †26732
†26733 †26748 †26749 26801 26802

†26812 †26813 †26835 †26836 †26839
†26840 26842 26843 26856 †26857
†26861 †26862 †26872 26873 †26876
†26877 †26879 †26880 †26881 †26882
†26891 †26892 †26893 †26894 †26902
†26903 26908 26909 †26918 †26919
†26922 †26923 †26924 †26925 †26933
†26934 †26941 †26942 †26947 †26948
†26949 †26950 †26953 †26954 †26957
†26958 †26962 †26963 †26968 †26969

†26973 †26974 †26984 †26985 27000
27001 27006 27007 †27012 †27013
†27018 †27019 †27022 †27023 27047
27048 †27069 †27070 †27077 †27078
†27084 †27085 †27094 †27095 †27097
†27098 †27100 †27101 †27123 †27124
27130 27131 27132 †27133 †27135
†27136 27137 27138 †27139 †27140
†27141 †27143 †27144 †27158 27159
27182 †27183 †27234 †27235 †27240

†27241 †27244 †27245 †27256 †27257
†27258 †27259 27267 27268 †27269
†27270 †27284 †27285 †27287 †27288
†27291 †27292

#1059 4½¢ HERMITAGE

Dry Printed **2 Plates**
384 Subject Plates **STRIPS OF 5**

26262 26263

432 Subject Plates **4 Plates**
STRIPS OF 6

†26374 †26375 †26381 †26382

#1059A 25¢ REVERE

Dry Printed
432 Subject Plates **STRIPS OF 6**
UNTAGGED **4 Plates**

28011 28012 30767o 30768o

#1059A b 25¢ REVERE

TAGGED **4 Plates**

30767o 30768o †37606 †37607

#1060-#1063 See Page 141

o Issued both Tagged and Plain

1955 COMMEMORATIVES

#1064 3¢ PENNSYLVANIA ACADEMY OF FINE ARTS 4 Plates

Plate	Price	UL	UR	LL	LR
25104	$.40	☐	☐	☐	☐
25105	$.40	☐	☐	☐	☐
25106	$.40	☐	☐	☐	☐
25107	$.40	☐	☐	☐	☐

#1065 3¢ LAND GRANT COLLEGES

4 Plates

Plate	Price	UL	UR	LL	LR
25117	$.40	☐	☐	☐	☐
25118	$.40	☐	☐	☐	☐
25119	$.40	☐	☐	☐	☐
25120	$.40	☐	☐	☐	☐

#1066 8¢ ROTARY CLUB 4 Plates

Plate	Price	UL	UR	LL	LR
25125	$1.25	☐	☐	☐	☐
25126	$1.25	☐	☐	☐	☐
25127	$1.25	☐	☐	☐	☐
25128	$1.25	☐	☐	☐	☐

#1067 3¢ ARMED FORCES RESERVE

4 Plates

Plate	Price	UL	UR	LL	LR
25175	$.40	☐	☐	☐	☐
25176	$.40	☐	☐	☐	☐
25177	$.40	☐	☐	☐	☐
25178	$.40	☐	☐	☐	☐

#1068 3¢ NEW HAMPSHIRE 4 Plates

Plate	Price	UL	UR	LL	LR
25183	$.40	☐	☐	☐	☐
25184	$.40	☐	☐	☐	☐
25185	$.40	☐	☐	☐	☐
25186	$.40	☐	☐	☐	☐

#1069 3¢ SOO LOCKS 6 Plates

Plate	Price	UL	UR	LL	LR
25193	$.40	☐	☐	☐	☐
25194	$.40	☐	☐	☐	☐
25195	$.40	☐	☐	☐	☐
25196	$.40	☐	☐	☐	☐
25197	$.40	☐	☐	☐	☐
25198	$.40	☐	☐	☐	☐

#1070 3¢ ATOMS FOR PEACE

4 Plates

Plate	Price	UL	UR	LL	LR
25207	$.50	☐	☐	☐	☐
25208	$.50	☐	☐	☐	☐
25209	$.50	☐	☐	☐	☐
25210	$.50	☐	☐	☐	☐

#1071 3¢ TICONDEROGA 4 Plates

Plate	Price	UL	UR	LL	LR
25245	$.40	☐	☐	☐	☐
25246	$.40	☐	☐	☐	☐
25247	$.40	☐	☐	☐	☐
25248	$.40	☐	☐	☐	☐

1955 COMMEMORATIVES

#1072 3¢ ANDREW MELLON

2 Plates

Dry Printed

Plate	Price	UL	UR	LL	LR
25301	$.40	☐	☐	☐	☐
25302	$.40	☐	☐	☐	☐

1956 COMMEMORATIVES

#1073 3¢ FRANKLIN 4 Plates

Plate	Price	UL	UR	LL	LR
25328	$.40	☐	☐	☐	☐
25329	$.40	☐	☐	☐	☐
25330	$.40	☐	☐	☐	☐
25331	$.40	☐	☐	☐	☐

#1074 3¢ BOOKER T. WASHINGTON

4 Plates

Plate	Price	UL	UR	LL	LR
25380	$.40	☐	☐	☐	☐
25381	$.40	☐	☐	☐	☐
25382	$.40	☐	☐	☐	☐
25383	$.40	☐	☐	☐	☐

#1075 3¢ FIPEX SHEET (Imperf.)

The plate numbers of this souvenir sheet were trimmed off after printing so no plate numbers were regularly issued.

#1076 3¢ FIPEX 4 Plates

Plate	Price	UL	UR	LL	LR
25374	$.40	☐	☐	☐	☐
25375	$.40	☐	☐	☐	☐
25386	$.40	☐	☐	☐	☐
25387	$.40	☐	☐	☐	☐

#1077 3¢ WILD TURKEY 4 Plates

Plate	Price	UL	UR	LL	LR
25395	$.50	☐	☐	☐	☐
25397	$.50	☐	☐	☐	☐
25398	$.50	☐	☐	☐	☐
25409	$.50	☐	☐	☐	☐

#1078 3¢ PRONGHORN ANTELOPE

4 Plates

Plate	Price	UL	UR	LL	LR
25429	$.50	☐	☐	☐	☐
25430	$.50	☐	☐	☐	☐
25431	$.50	☐	☐	☐	☐
25432	$.50	☐	☐	☐	☐

#1079 3¢ KING SALMON 4 Plates

Dry Printed

Plate	Price	UL	UR	LL	LR
25496	$.50	☐	☐	☐	☐
25497	$.50	☐	☐	☐	☐
25498	$.50	☐	☐	☐	☐
25499	$.50	☐	☐	☐	☐

#1080 3¢ PURE FOOD & DRUG LAWS

4 Plates

Plate	Price	UL	UR	LL	LR
25437	$.40	☐	☐	☐	☐
25438	$.40	☐	☐	☐	☐
25439	$.40	☐	☐	☐	☐
25440	$.40	☐	☐	☐	☐

1956 COMMEMORATIVES

All commemoratives are Dry Printed

#1081 3¢ WHEATLAND 4 Plates

Plate	Price	UL	UR	LL	LR
25475	$.40	☐	☐	☐	☐
25476	$.40	☐	☐	☐	☐
25477	$.40	☐	☐	☐	☐
25478	$.40	☐	☐	☐	☐

#1082 3¢ LABOR DAY 4 Plates

Plate	Price	UL	UR	LL	LR
25484	$.40	☐	☐	☐	☐
25485	$.40	☐	☐	☐	☐
25486	$.40	☐	☐	☐	☐
25489	$.40	☐	☐	☐	☐

#1083 3¢ NASSAU HALL 4 Plates

Plate	Price	UL	UR	LL	LR
25469	$.40	☐	☐	☐	☐
25470	$.40	☐	☐	☐	☐
25473	$.40	☐	☐	☐	☐
25474	$.40	☐	☐	☐	☐

#1084 3¢ DEVILS TOWER 4 Plates

Plate	Price	UL	UR	LL	LR
25500	$.40	☐	☐	☐	☐
25501	$.40	☐	☐	☐	☐
25502	$.40	☐	☐	☐	☐
25503	$.40	☐	☐	☐	☐

#1085 3¢ CHILDREN 4 Plates

Plate	Price	UL	UR	LL	LR
25533	$.40	☐	☐	☐	☐
25534	$.40	☐	☐	☐	☐
25535	$.40	☐	☐	☐	☐
25536	$.40	☐	☐	☐	☐

1957 COMMEMORATIVES

#1086 3¢ ALEXANDER HAMILTON 4 Plates

Plate	Price	UL	UR	LL	LR
25597	$.40	☐	☐	☐	☐
25598	$.40	☐	☐	☐	☐
25599	$.40	☐	☐	☐	☐
25600	$.40	☐	☐	☐	☐

#1087 3¢ POLIO 8 Plates

Plate	Price	UL	UR	LL	LR
25603	$.40	☐	☐	☐	☐
25604	$.40	☐	☐	☐	☐
25605	$.40	☐	☐	☐	☐
25606	$.40	☐	☐	☐	☐
25647	$.40	☐	☐	☐	☐
25648	$.40	☐	☐	☐	☐
25651	$.40	☐	☐	☐	☐
25652	$.40	☐	☐	☐	☐

#1088 3¢ GEODETIC SURVEY 4 Plates

Plate	Price	UL	UR	LL	LR
25621	$.40	☐	☐	☐	☐
25622	$.40	☐	☐	☐	☐
25623	$.40	☐	☐	☐	☐
25624	$.40	☐	☐	☐	☐

1957 COMMEMORATIVES

#1089 3¢ ARCHITECTS 4 Plates

Plate	Price	UL	UR	LL	LR
25625	$.40	☐	☐	☐	☐
25626	$.40	☐	☐	☐	☐
25627	$.40	☐	☐	☐	☐
25628	$.40	☐	☐	☐	☐

#1090 3¢ STEEL INDUSTRY 4 Plates

Plate	Price	UL	UR	LL	LR
25699	$.40	☐	☐	☐	☐
25700	$.40	☐	☐	☐	☐
25701	$.40	☐	☐	☐	☐
25702	$.40	☐	☐	☐	☐

#1091 3¢ NAVAL REVIEW 4 Plates

Plate	Price	UL	UR	LL	LR
25724	$.40	☐	☐	☐	☐
25725	$.40	☐	☐	☐	☐
25726	$.40	☐	☐	☐	☐
25730	$.40	☐	☐	☐	☐

#1092 3¢ OKLAHOMA 4 Plates

Plate	Price	UL	UR	LL	LR
25683	$.40	☐	☐	☐	☐
25684	$.40	☐	☐	☐	☐
25685	$.40	☐	☐	☐	☐
25686	$.40	☐	☐	☐	☐

#1093 3¢ TEACHERS 4 Plates

Plate	Price	UL	UR	LL	LR
25735	$.40	☐	☐	☐	☐
25736	$.40	☐	☐	☐	☐
25737	$.40	☐	☐	☐	☐
25738	$.40	☐	☐	☐	☐

#1094 4¢ U. S. FLAG 2 Plates

Plate	Price	UL	UR	LL	LR
25711	$.50	☐	☐	☐	☐
25712	$.50	☐	☐	☐	☐

#1095 3¢ SHIPBUILDING 4 Plates

Plate	Price	UL	UR	LL	LR
25776	$.40	☐	☐	☐	☐
25777	$.40	☐	☐	☐	☐
25778	$.40	☐	☐	☐	☐
25779	$.40	☐	☐	☐	☐

#1096 8¢ MAGSAYSAY

4 Combinations

2 Frame Plates 2 Vignette Plates

Plate	Price	UL	UR	LL	LR
25771-25805	$1.00	☐	☐	☐	☐
25771-25808	$1.00	☐	☐	☐	☐
25772-25805	$1.00	☐	☐	☐	☐
25772-25808	$1.00	☐	☐	☐	☐

#1097 3¢ LAFAYETTE BICENT. 4 Plates

Plate	Price	UL	UR	LL	LR
25798	$.40	☐	☐	☐	☐
25799	$.40	☐	☐	☐	☐
25800	$.40	☐	☐	☐	☐
25801	$.40	☐	☐	☐	☐

1957 COMMEMORATIVES

#1098 3¢ WHOOPING CRANE

6 Plates

		UL	UR	LL	LR
25862	$.40	☐	☐	☐	☐
25863	$.40	☐	☐	☐	☐
25864	$.40	☐	☐	☐	☐
25867	$.40	☐	☐	☐	☐
25879	$.40	☐	☐	☐	☐
25884	$.40	☐	☐	☐	☐

#1099 3¢ RELIGIOUS FREEDOM

4 Plates

25891	$.40	☐	☐	☐	☐
25892	$.40	☐	☐	☐	☐
25893	$.40	☐	☐	☐	☐
25905	$.40	☐	☐	☐	☐

1958 COMMEMORATIVES

#1100 3¢ GARDENING 4 Plates

		UL	UR	LL	LR
25942	$.40	☐	☐	☐	☐
25943	$.40	☐	☐	☐	☐
25944	$.40	☐	☐	☐	☐
25945	$.40	☐	☐	☐	☐

#1104 3¢ BRUSSELS EXHIBITION

4 Plates

25958	$.40	☐	☐	☐	☐
25959	$.40	☐	☐	☐	☐
25960	$.40	☐	☐	☐	☐
25961	$.40	☐	☐	☐	☐

#1105 3¢ MONROE BICENTENNIAL

4 Plates

25971	$.40	☐	☐	☐	☐
25972	$.40	☐	☐	☐	☐
25973	$.40	☐	☐	☐	☐
25974	$.40	☐	☐	☐	☐

#1106 3¢ MINNESOTA STATEHOOD

4 Plates

25994	$.40	☐	☐	☐	☐
25995	$.40	☐	☐	☐	☐
25996	$.40	☐	☐	☐	☐
25997	$.40	☐	☐	☐	☐

#1107 3¢ GEOPHYSICAL YEAR

5 Plates

25978	$.50	☐	☐	☐	☐
25985	$.50	☐	☐	☐	☐
25990	$.50	☐	☐	☐	☐
25993	$.50	☐	☐	☐	☐
26010	$.50	☐	☐	☐	☐

1958 COMMEMORATIVES

#1108 3¢ GUNSTON HALL

4 Plates

		UL	UR	LL	LR
26017	$.40	☐	☐	☐	☐
26018	$.40	☐	☐	☐	☐
26019	$.40	☐	☐	☐	☐
26020	$.40	☐	☐	☐	☐

#1109 3¢ MACKINAC BRIDGE

4 Plates

26028	$.40	☐	☐	☐	☐
26029	$.40	☐	☐	☐	☐
26030	$.40	☐	☐	☐	☐
26031	$.40	☐	☐	☐	☐

#1110 4¢ BOLIVAR 4 Plates

26057	$.45	☐	☐	☐	☐
26058	$.45	☐	☐	☐	☐
26059	$.45	☐	☐	☐	☐
26060	$.45	☐	☐	☐	☐

#1111 8¢ BOLIVAR

6 Combinations

2 Frame Plates 3 Vignette Plates

26056-26021	$2.00	☐	☐	☐	☐
26056-26026	$2.00	☐	☐	☐	☐
26061-26021	$2.00	☐	☐	☐	☐
26061-26026	$2.00	☐	☐	☐	☐
26062-26021	$2.00	☐	☐	☐	☐
26062-26026	$2.00	☐	☐	☐	☐

#1112 4¢ ATLANTIC CABLE

4 Plates

26076	$.45	☐	☐	☐	☐
26077	$.45	☐	☐	☐	☐
26078	$.45	☐	☐	☐	☐
26079	$.45	☐	☐	☐	☐

#1113 1¢ LINCOLN 4 Plates

26245	$.25	☐	☐	☐	☐
26246	$.25	☐	☐	☐	☐
26247	$.25	☐	☐	☐	☐
26248	$.25	☐	☐	☐	☐

#1114 3¢ LINCOLN 4 Plates

26251	$.45	☐	☐	☐	☐
26252	$.45	☐	☐	☐	☐
26253	$.45	☐	☐	☐	☐
26254	$.45	☐	☐	☐	☐

#1115 4¢ LINCOLN-DOUGLAS

4 Plates

26105	$.50	☐	☐	☐	☐
26106	$.50	☐	☐	☐	☐
26107	$.50	☐	☐	☐	☐
26108	$.50	☐	☐	☐	☐

1958 COMMEMORATIVES

#1116 4¢ LINCOLN 4 Plates

		UL	UR	LL	LR
26271	$.50	☐	☐	☐	☐
26272	$.50	☐	☐	☐	☐
26273	$.50	☐	☐	☐	☐
26274	$.50	☐	☐	☐	☐

#1117 4¢ KOSSUTH 4 Plates

26124	$.45	☐	☐	☐	☐
26125	$.45	☐	☐	☐	☐
26126	$.45	☐	☐	☐	☐
26127	$.45	☐	☐	☐	☐

#1118 8¢ KOSSUTH
12 Combinations
4 Frame Plates 4 Vignette Plates

26056-26098	$15.00	☐	☐	☐	☐
26056-26119	$1.75	☐	☐	☐	☐
26062-26098	$1.75	☐	☐	☐	☐
26062-26119	$15.00	☐	☐	☐	☐
26088-26092	$1.75	☐	☐	☐	☐
26088-26095	$1.75	☐	☐	☐	☐
26088-26098	$1.75	☐	☐	☐	☐
26088-26119	$1.75	☐	☐	☐	☐
26091-26092	$1.75	☐	☐	☐	☐
26091-26095	$1.75	☐	☐	☐	☐
26091-26098	$1.75	☐	☐	☐	☐
26091-26119	$1.75	☐	☐	☐	☐

#1119 4¢ FREEDOM OF PRESS
4 Plates

26115	$.45	☐	☐	☐	☐
26116	$.45	☐	☐	☐	☐
26117	$.45	☐	☐	☐	☐
26118	$.45	☐	☐	☐	☐

#1120 4¢ OVERLAND MAIL
4 Plates

26158	$.45	☐	☐	☐	☐
26159	$.45	☐	☐	☐	☐
26160	$.45	☐	☐	☐	☐
26161	$.45	☐	☐	☐	☐

1958 COMMEMORATIVES

#1121 4¢ NOAH WEBSTER

4 Plates		UL	UR	LL	LR
26103	$.45	☐	☐	☐	☐
26104	$.45	☐	☐	☐	☐
26120	$.45	☐	☐	☐	☐
26121	$.45	☐	☐	☐	☐

#1122 4¢ FOREST CONSERVATION
6 Plates

26149	$.45	☐	☐	☐	☐
26156	$.45	☐	☐	☐	☐
26157	$.45	☐	☐	☐	☐
26162	$.45	☐	☐	☐	☐
26167	$.45	☐	☐	☐	☐
26170	$.45	☐	☐	☐	☐

#1123 4¢ FORT DUQUESNE
4 Plates

26197	$.45	☐	☐	☐	☐
26198	$.45	☐	☐	☐	☐
26199	$.45	☐	☐	☐	☐
26200	$.45	☐	☐	☐	☐

1959 COMMEMORATIVES

#1124 4¢ OREGON STATEHOOD

4 Plates		UL	UR	LL	LR
26235	$.45	☐	☐	☐	☐
26236	$.45	☐	☐	☐	☐
26237	$.45	☐	☐	☐	☐
26243	$.45	☐	☐	☐	☐

#1125 4¢ SAN MARTIN 4 Plates

26238	$.45	☐	☐	☐	☐
26239	$.45	☐	☐	☐	☐
26240	$.45	☐	☐	☐	☐
26241	$.45	☐	☐	☐	☐

#1126 8¢ SAN MARTIN 2 Plates

26244	$1.00	☐	☐	☐	☐
26249	$1.00	☐	☐	☐	☐

#1127 4¢ NATO 4 Plates

26299	$.45	☐	☐	☐	☐
26300	$.45	☐	☐	☐	☐
26301	$.45	☐	☐	☐	☐
26302	$.45	☐	☐	☐	☐

#1128 4¢ ARCTIC EXPLORATION
4 Plates

26303	$.45	☐	☐	☐	☐
26304	$.45	☐	☐	☐	☐
26305	$.45	☐	☐	☐	☐
26306	$.45	☐	☐	☐	☐

1959 COMMEMORATIVES

#1129 8¢ WORLD PEACE 4 Plates

		UL	UR	LL	LR
26317	$1.00	☐	☐	☐	☐
26318	$1.00	☐	☐	☐	☐
26319	$1.00	☐	☐	☐	☐
26320	$1.00	☐	☐	☐	☐

#1130 4¢ SILVER CENTENNIAL
4 Plates

		UL	UR	LL	LR
26356	$.45	☐	☐	☐	☐
26357	$.45	☐	☐	☐	☐
26358	$.45	☐	☐	☐	☐
26359	$.45	☐	☐	☐	☐

#1131 4¢ ST. LAWRENCE SEAWAY
6 Plates

		UL	UR	LL	LR
26328	$.45	☐	☐	☐	☐
26333	$.45	☐	☐	☐	☐
26334	$.45	☐	☐	☐	☐
26335	$.45	☐	☐	☐	☐
26336	$.45	☐	☐	☐	☐
26343	$4500.00	☐	†	†	†

#1132 4¢ FLAG (49 STARS)
4 Plates

		UL	UR	LL	LR
26344	$.45	☐	☐	☐	☐
26354	$.45	☐	☐	☐	☐
26366	$.45	☐	☐	☐	☐
26368	$.45	☐	☐	☐	☐

#1133 4¢ SOIL CONSERVATION
6 Plates

		UL	UR	LL	LR
26406	$.45	☐	☐	☐	☐
26407	$.45	☐	☐	☐	☐
26410	$.45	☐	☐	☐	☐
26415	$.45	☐	☐	☐	☐
26423	$.45	☐	☐	☐	☐
26425	$.45	☐	☐	☐	☐

1959 COMMEMORATIVES

#1134 4¢ PETROLEUM 4 Plates

		UL	UR	LL	LR
26416	$.45	☐	☐	☐	☐
26417	$.45	☐	☐	☐	☐
26419	$.45	☐	☐	☐	☐
26431	$.45	☐	☐	☐	☐

#1135 4¢ DENTAL HEALTH
4 Plates

		UL	UR	LL	LR
26438	$.45	☐	☐	☐	☐
26439	$.45	☐	☐	☐	☐
26440	$.45	☐	☐	☐	☐
26441	$.45	☐	☐	☐	☐

#1136 4¢ REUTER 4 Plates

		UL	UR	LL	LR
26451	$.45	☐	☐	☐	☐
26452	$.45	☐	☐	☐	☐
26453	$.45	☐	☐	☐	☐
26454	$.45	☐	☐	☐	☐

#1137 8¢ REUTER 2 Plates

		UL	UR	LL	LR
26464	$1.00	☐	☐	☐	☐
26466	$1.00	☐	☐	☐	☐

#1138 4¢ MACDOWELL 4 Plates

		UL	UR	LL	LR
26498	$.45	☐	☐	☐	☐
26499	$.45	☐	☐	☐	☐
26500	$.45	☐	☐	☐	☐
26501	$.45	☐	☐	☐	☐

1960 COMMEMORATIVES

#1139 4¢ WASHINGTON CREDO
5 Plates

		UL	UR	LL	LR
26488	$.45	☐	☐	☐	☐
26489	$1.00	☐	☐	☐	☐
26494	$.45	☐	☐	☐	☐
26495	$.45	☐	☐	☐	☐
26508	$.45	☐	☐	☐	☐

1960 COMMEMORATIVES

#1140 4¢ FRANKLIN CREDO
4 Plates

Plate	Price	UL	UR	LL	LR
26582	$.45	☐	☐	☐	☐
26587	$.45	☐	☐	☐	☐
26589	$.45	☐	☐	☐	☐
26591	$.45	☐	☐	☐	☐

#1141 4¢ JEFFERSON CREDO
6 Plates

Plate	Price	UL	UR	LL	LR
26608	$.50	☐	☐	☐	☐
26611	$.50	☐	☐	☐	☐
26618	$.50	☐	☐	☐	☐
26623	$.50	☐	☐	☐	☐
26628	$.50	☐	☐	☐	☐
26629	$.50	☐	☐	☐	☐

#1142 4¢ FRANCIS SCOTT KEY CREDO 4 Plates

Plate	Price	UL	UR	LL	LR
26683	$.50	☐	☐	☐	☐
26693	$.50	☐	☐	☐	☐
26695	$.50	☐	☐	☐	☐
26696	$.50	☐	☐	☐	☐

#1143 4¢ LINCOLN CREDO
4 Plates

Plate	Price	UL	UR	LL	LR
26797	$.60	☐	☐	☐	☐
26803	$.60	☐	☐	☐	☐
26805	$.60	☐	☐	☐	☐
26806	$.60	☐	☐	☐	☐

#1144 4¢ PATRICK HENRY CREDO
4 Plates

Plate	Price	UL	UR	LL	LR
26738	$.60	☐	☐	☐	☐
26741	$.60	☐	☐	☐	☐
26747	$.60	☐	☐	☐	☐
26752	$.60	☐	☐	☐	☐

#1145 4¢ BOY SCOUTS 4 Plates

Plate	Price	UL	UR	LL	LR
26530	$.45	☐	☐	☐	☐
26531	$.45	☐	☐	☐	☐
26535	$.45	☐	☐	☐	☐
26536	$.45	☐	☐	☐	☐

#1146 4¢ WINTER GAMES 4 Plates

Plate	Price	UL	UR	LL	LR
26540	$.50	☐	☐	☐	☐
26541	$.50	☐	☐	☐	☐
26542	$.50	☐	☐	☐	☐
26550	$.50	☐	☐	☐	☐

#1147 4¢ MASARYK 4 Plates

Plate	Price	UL	UR	LL	LR
26552	$.45	☐	☐	☐	☐
26553	$.45	☐	☐	☐	☐
26554	$.45	☐	☐	☐	☐
26555	$.45	☐	☐	☐	☐

#1148 8¢ MASARYK 2 Plates

Plate	Price	UL	UR	LL	LR
26557	$1.25	☐	☐	☐	☐
26562	$1.25	☐	☐	☐	☐

#1149 4¢ REFUGEE YEAR
4 Plates

Plate	Price	UL	UR	LL	LR
26596	$.45	☐	☐	☐	☐
26597	$.45	☐	☐	☐	☐
26598	$.45	☐	☐	☐	☐
26599	$.45	☐	☐	☐	☐

#1150 4¢ WATER CONSERVATION
4 Plates

Plate	Price	UL	UR	LL	LR
26588	$.45	☐	☐	☐	☐
26590	$.45	☐	☐	☐	☐
26592	$.45	☐	☐	☐	☐
26600	$.45	☐	☐	☐	☐

#1151 4¢ SEATO 4 Plates

Plate	Price	UL	UR	LL	LR
26632	$.45	☐	☐	☐	☐
26633	$.45	☐	☐	☐	☐
26634	$.45	☐	☐	☐	☐
26638	$.45	☐	☐	☐	☐

#1152 4¢ AMERICAN WOMAN
4 Plates

Plate	Price	UL	UR	LL	LR
26643	$.45	☐	☐	☐	☐
26644	$.45	☐	☐	☐	☐
26645	$.45	☐	☐	☐	☐
26646	$.45	☐	☐	☐	☐

#1153 4¢ AMERICAN FLAG (50 STARS) 4 Plates

Plate	Price	UL	UR	LL	LR
26639	$.45	☐	☐	☐	☐
26640	$.45	☐	☐	☐	☐
26647	$.45	☐	☐	☐	☐
26648	$.45	☐	☐	☐	☐

#1154 4¢ PONY EXPRESS 4 Plates

Plate	Price	UL	UR	LL	LR
26624	$.45	☐	☐	☐	☐
26625	$.45	☐	☐	☐	☐
26626	$.45	☐	☐	☐	☐
26627	$.45	☐	☐	☐	☐

#1155 4¢ EMPLOY THE HANDICAPPED 4 Plates

Plate	Price	UL	UR	LL	LR
26679	$.45	☐	☐	☐	☐
26680	$.45	☐	☐	☐	☐
26681	$.45	☐	☐	☐	☐
26682	$.45	☐	☐	☐	☐

#1156 4¢ FORESTRY CONGRESS
4 Plates

Plate	Price	UL	UR	LL	LR
26685	$.45	☐	☐	☐	☐
26686	$.45	☐	☐	☐	☐
26687	$.45	☐	☐	☐	☐
26688	$.45	☐	☐	☐	☐

1960 COMMEMORATIVES

#1157 4¢ MEXICAN INDEPENDENCE
4 Plates

Plate	Price	UL	UR	LL	LR
26707	$.45	☐	☐	☐	☐
26713	$.45	☐	☐	☐	☐
26717	$.45	☐	☐	☐	☐
26722	$.45	☐	☐	☐	☐

#1158 4¢ U.S. - JAPAN AMITY
4 Plates

Plate	Price	UL	UR	LL	LR
26726	$.45	☐	☐	☐	☐
26729	$.45	☐	☐	☐	☐
26730	$.45	☐	☐	☐	☐
26731	$.45	☐	☐	☐	☐

#1159 4¢ PADEREWSKI 4 Plates

Plate	Price	UL	UR	LL	LR
26742	$.45	☐	☐	☐	☐
26743	$.45	☐	☐	☐	☐
26744	$.45	☐	☐	☐	☐
26745	$.45	☐	☐	☐	☐

#1160 8¢ PADEREWSKI 2 Plates

Plate	Price	UL	UR	LL	LR
26753	$1.25	☐	☐	☐	☐
26763	$1.25	☐	☐	☐	☐

#1161 4¢ ROBERT TAFT 4 Plates

Plate	Price	UL	UR	LL	LR
26759	$.45	☐	☐	☐	☐
26760	$.45	☐	☐	☐	☐
26761	$.45	☐	☐	☐	☐
26762	$.45	☐	☐	☐	☐

#1162 4¢ WHEELS OF FREEDOM
4 Plates

Plate	Price	UL	UR	LL	LR
26774	$.45	☐	☐	☐	☐
26775	$.45	☐	☐	☐	☐
26776	$.45	☐	☐	☐	☐
26777	$.45	☐	☐	☐	☐

#1163 4¢ BOYS' CLUBS 4 Plates

Plate	Price	UL	UR	LL	LR
26662	$.45	☐	☐	☐	☐
26665	$.45	☐	☐	☐	☐
26666	$.45	☐	☐	☐	☐
26669	$.45	☐	☐	☐	☐

#1164 4¢ AUTOMATED POST OFFICE 6 Plates

Plate	Price	UL	UR	LL	LR
26785	$.45	☐	☐	☐	☐
26787	$.45	☐	☐	☐	☐
26798	$.45	☐	☐	☐	☐
26799	$.45	☐	☐	☐	☐
26804	$.45	☐	☐	☐	☐
26807	$.45	☐	☐	☐	☐

#1165 4¢ MANNERHEIM 4 Plates

Plate	Price	UL	UR	LL	LR
26755	$.45	☐	☐	☐	☐
26756	$.45	☐	☐	☐	☐
26757	$.45	☐	☐	☐	☐
26758	$.45	☐	☐	☐	☐

1960 COMMEMORATIVES

#1166 8¢ MANNERHEIM 2 Plates

Plate	Price	UL	UR	LL	LR
26764	$1.25	☐	☐	☐	☐
26769	$1.25	☐	☐	☐	☐

#1167 4¢ CAMPFIRE GIRLS
6 Plates

Plate	Price	UL	UR	LL	LR
26740	$.45	☐	☐	☐	☐
26746	$.45	☐	☐	☐	☐
26751	$.45	☐	☐	☐	☐
26754	$.45	☐	☐	☐	☐
26816	$.45	☐	☐	☐	☐
26826	$.45	☐	☐	☐	☐

#1168 4¢ GARIBALDI 4 Plates

Plate	Price	UL	UR	LL	LR
26792	$.45	☐	☐	☐	☐
26793	$.45	☐	☐	☐	☐
26794	$.45	☐	☐	☐	☐
26795	$.45	☐	☐	☐	☐

#1169 8¢ GARIBALDI 3 Plates

Plate	Price	UL	UR	LL	LR
26779	$1.10	☐	☐	☐	☐
26788	$1.10	☐	☐	☐	☐
26790	$1.10	☐	☐	☐	☐

#1170 4¢ GEORGE 4 Plates

Plate	Price	UL	UR	LL	LR
26780	$.45	☐	☐	☐	☐
26781	$.45	☐	☐	☐	☐
26782	$.45	☐	☐	☐	☐
26783	$.45	☐	☐	☐	☐

#1171 4¢ CARNEGIE 4 Plates

Plate	Price	UL	UR	LL	LR
26674	$.45	☐	☐	☐	☐
26675	$.45	☐	☐	☐	☐
26676	$.45	☐	☐	☐	☐
26677	$.45	☐	☐	☐	☐

#1172 4¢ DULLES 4 Plates

Plate	Price	UL	UR	LL	LR
26770	$.45	☐	☐	☐	☐
26771	$.45	☐	☐	☐	☐
26772	$.45	☐	☐	☐	☐
26773	$.45	☐	☐	☐	☐

#1173 4¢ ECHO I 4 Plates

Plate	Price	UL	UR	LL	LR
26845	$1.50	☐	☐	☐	☐
26846	$1.50	☐	☐	☐	☐
26847	$1.50	☐	☐	☐	☐
26848	$1.50	☐	☐	☐	☐

1961 COMMEMORATIVES

#1174 4¢ GHANDI 4 Plates

Plate	Price	UL	UR	LL	LR
26864	$.45	☐	☐	☐	☐
26865	$.45	☐	☐	☐	☐
26866	$.45	☐	☐	☐	☐
26867	$.45	☐	☐	☐	☐

#1175 8¢ GHANDI 2 Plates

Plate	Price	UL	UR	LL	LR
26841	$1.25	☐	☐	☐	☐
26844	$1.25	☐	☐	☐	☐

1961-65 COMMEMORATIVES

#1176 4¢ RANGE CONSERVATION
6 Plates

		UL	UR	LL	LR
26849	$.45	☐	☐	☐	☐
26860	$.45	☐	☐	☐	☐
26870	$.45	☐	☐	☐	☐
26874	$.45	☐	☐	☐	☐
26901	$.45	☐	☐	☐	☐
26904	$.45	☐	☐	☐	☐

#1177 4¢ GREELEY 4 Plates

		UL	UR	LL	LR
26895	$.45	☐	☐	☐	☐
26896	$.45	☐	☐	☐	☐
26897	$.45	☐	☐	☐	☐
26898	$.45	☐	☐	☐	☐

#1178 4¢ FORT SUMTER 4 Plates

		UL	UR	LL	LR
26913	$.60	☐	☐	☐	☐
26914	$.60	☐	☐	☐	☐
26915	$.60	☐	☐	☐	☐
26916	$.60	☐	☐	☐	☐

#1179 4¢ SHILOH 4 Plates

		UL	UR	LL	LR
27178	$.55	☐	☐	☐	☐
27179	$.55	☐	☐	☐	☐
27180	$.55	☐	☐	☐	☐
27181	$.55	☐	☐	☐	☐

#1180 5¢ GETTYSBURG 6 Plates

		UL	UR	LL	LR
27477	$.65	☐	☐	☐	☐
27508	$.65	☐	☐	☐	☐
27510	$.65	☐	☐	☐	☐
27513	$.65	☐	☐	☐	☐
27519	$.65	☐	☐	☐	☐
27520	$.65	☐	☐	☐	☐

#1181 5¢ BATTLE OF THE WILDERNESS 6 Plates

		UL	UR	LL	LR
27763	$.65	☐	☐	☐	☐
27764	$.65	☐	☐	☐	☐
27765	$.65	☐	☐	☐	☐
27766	$.65	☐	☐	☐	☐
27771	$.65	☐	☐	☐	☐
27772	$.65	☐	☐	☐	☐

#1182 5¢ APPOMATTOX
6 Plates

		UL	UR	LL	LR
28064	$1.00	☐	☐	☐	☐
28067	$1.00	☐	☐	☐	☐
28068	$1.00	☐	☐	☐	☐
28073	$1.00	☐	☐	☐	☐
28074	$1.00	☐	☐	☐	☐
28075	$1.00	☐	☐	☐	☐

#1183 4¢ KANSAS 4 Plates

		UL	UR	LL	LR
26935	$.45	☐	☐	☐	☐
26936	$.45	☐	☐	☐	☐
26937	$.45	☐	☐	☐	☐
26938	$.45	☐	☐	☐	☐

1961 COMMEMORATIVES

#1184 4¢ NORRIS 4 Plates

		UL	UR	LL	LR
26990	$.45	☐	☐	☐	☐
26991	$.45	☐	☐	☐	☐
26992	$.45	☐	☐	☐	☐
26993	$.45	☐	☐	☐	☐

#1185 4¢ NAVAL AVIATION
4 Plates

		UL	UR	LL	LR
27014	$.45	☐	☐	☐	☐
27015	$.45	☐	☐	☐	☐
27016	$.45	☐	☐	☐	☐
27017	$.45	☐	☐	☐	☐

#1186 4¢ COMPENSATION LAW
4 Plates

		UL	UR	LL	LR
27024	$.45	☐	☐	☐	☐
27025	$.45	☐	☐	☐	☐
27026	$.45	☐	☐	☐	☐
27027	$.45	☐	☐	☐	☐

All of the LL & LR plate numbers of this commemorative are inverted.

#1187 4¢ REMINGTON 4 Plates

		UL	UR	LL	LR
27033	$.70	☐	☐	☐	☐
27034	$.70	☐	☐	☐	☐
27035	$.70	☐	☐	☐	☐
27036	$.70	☐	☐	☐	☐

#1188 4¢ SUN YAT-SEN
4 Plates

		UL	UR	LL	LR
27039	$.45	☐	☐	☐	☐
27040	$.45	☐	☐	☐	☐
27041	$.45	☐	☐	☐	☐
27042	$.45	☐	☐	☐	☐

#1189 4¢ BASKETBALL 4 Plates

		UL	UR	LL	LR
27060	$.50	☐	☐	☐	☐
27061	$.50	☐	☐	☐	☐
27062	$.50	☐	☐	☐	☐
27063	$.50	☐	☐	☐	☐

#1190 4¢ NURSING 12 Plates

		UL	UR	LL	LR
27081-27080	$.45	☐	☐	☐	☐
27081-27082	$.45	☐	☐	☐	☐
27081-27089	$.45	☐	☐	☐	☐
27081-27092	$.45	☐	☐	☐	☐
27083-27080	$.45	☐	☐	☐	☐
27083-27082	$.45	☐	☐	☐	☐
27083-27089	$.45	☐	☐	☐	☐
27096-27082	$.45	☐	☐	☐	☐
27096-27089	$.45	☐	☐	☐	☐
27096-27092	$.45	☐	☐	☐	☐
27099-27089	$7.00	☐	☐	☐	☐
27099-27092	$7.00	☐	☐	☐	☐

1962 COMMEMORATIVES

#1191 4¢ NEW MEXICO 4 Plates

		UL	UR	LL	LR
27107	$.45	☐	☐	☐	☐
27112	$.45	☐	☐	☐	☐
27113	$.45	☐	☐	☐	☐
27114	$.45	☐	☐	☐	☐

#1192 4¢ ARIZONA 4 Plates

		UL	UR	LL	LR
27125	$.45	☐	☐	☐	☐
27126	$.45	☐	☐	☐	☐
27127	$.45	☐	☐	☐	☐
27128	$.45	☐	☐	☐	☐

#1193 4¢ PROJECT MERCURY 6 Plates

		UL	UR	LL	LR
27064	$.50	☐	☐	☐	☐
27065	$.50	☐	☐	☐	☐
27066	$.50	☐	☐	☐	☐
27067	$.50	☐	☐	☐	☐
27068	$.50	☐	☐	☐	☐
27071	$.50	☐	☐	☐	☐

#1194 4¢ MALARIA 4 Plates

		UL	UR	LL	LR
27153	$.45	☐	☐	☐	☐
27154	$.45	☐	☐	☐	☐
27155	$.45	☐	☐	☐	☐
27157	$.45	☐	☐	☐	☐

#1195 4¢ HUGHES 4 Plates

		UL	UR	LL	LR
27171	$.45	☐	☐	☐	☐
27172	$.45	☐	☐	☐	☐
27173	$.45	☐	☐	☐	☐
27174	$.45	☐	☐	☐	☐

#1196 4¢ SEATTLE FAIR 7 Plates

		UL	UR	LL	LR
27167	$.45	☐	☐	☐	☐
27175	$.45	☐	☐	☐	☐
27176	$.45	☐	☐	☐	☐
27177	$.45	☐	☐	☐	☐
27198	$.45	☐	☐	☐	☐
27203	$.45	☐	☐	☐	☐
27204	$.45	☐	☐	☐	☐

#1197 4¢ LOUISIANA 6 Plates

		UL	UR	LL	LR
27184	$.45	☐	☐	☐	☐
27185	$.45	☐	☐	☐	☐
27186	$.45	☐	☐	☐	☐
27187	$.45	☐	☐	☐	☐
27205	$.45	☐	☐	☐	☐
27210	$.45	☐	☐	☐	☐

#1198 4¢ HOMESTEAD 4 Plates

		UL	UR	LL	LR
27147	$.45	☐	☐	☐	☐
27148	$.45	☐	☐	☐	☐
27149	$.45	☐	☐	☐	☐
27150	$.45	☐	☐	☐	☐

#1199 4¢ GIRL SCOUTS 4 Plates

		UL	UR	LL	LR
27217	$.45	☐	☐	☐	☐
27218	$.45	☐	☐	☐	☐
27219	$.45	☐	☐	☐	☐
27220	$.45	☐	☐	☐	☐

#1200 4¢ McMAHON 4 Plates

		UL	UR	LL	LR
27224	$.45	☐	☐	☐	☐
27225	$.45	☐	☐	☐	☐
27226	$.45	☐	☐	☐	☐
27227	$.45	☐	☐	☐	☐

#1201 4¢ APPRENTICE 4 Plates

		UL	UR	LL	LR
27247	$.45	☐	☐	☐	☐
27248	$.45	☐	☐	☐	☐
27249	$.45	☐	☐	☐	☐
27250	$.45	☐	☐	☐	☐

#1202 4¢ RAYBURN 6 Plates

		UL	UR	LL	LR
27255	$.45	☐	☐	☐	☐
27260	$.45	☐	☐	☐	☐
27262	$.45	☐	☐	☐	☐
27263	$.45	☐	☐	☐	☐
27264	$.45	☐	☐	☐	☐
27265	$.45	☐	☐	☐	☐

#1203 4¢ HAMMARSKJOLD 8 Plates

		UL	UR	LL	LR
27266-27275	$.45	☐	☐	☐	☐
27266-27277	$.45	☐	☐	☐	☐
27276-27275	$.45	☐	☐	☐	☐
27276-27277	$.45	☐	☐	☐	☐
27279-27278	$.45	☐	☐	☐	☐
27279-27282	$.45	☐	☐	☐	☐
27283-27278	$.45	☐	☐	☐	☐
27283-27282	$.45	☐	☐	☐	☐

#1204 4¢ HAMMARSKJOLD INVERT 8 Plates

		UL	UR	LL	LR
27266-27275	$1.25	☐	☐	☐	☐
27266-27277	$1.25	☐	☐	☐	☐
27276-27275	$1.25	☐	☐	☐	☐
27276-27277	$1.25	☐	☐	☐	☐
27279-27278	$1.25	☐	☐	☐	☐
27279-27282	$1.25	☐	☐	☐	☐
27283-27278	$1.25	☐	☐	☐	☐
27283-27282	$1.25	☐	☐	☐	☐

#1205 4¢ CHRISTMAS 1962 6 Plates

		UL	UR	LL	LR
27301	$.45	☐	☐	☐	☐
27306	$.45	☐	☐	☐	☐
27311	$.45	☐	☐	☐	☐
27314	$.45	☐	☐	☐	☐
27325	$.45	☐	☐	☐	☐
27330	$.45	☐	☐	☐	☐

1962 COMMEMORATIVES

#1206 4¢ HIGHER EDUCATION

8 Plates

		UL	UR	LL	LR
27286-27289	$.45				
27286-27295	$.45				
27290-27289	$.45				
27290-27295	$.45				
27293-27299	$.45				
27293-27300	$.45				
27296-27299	$.45				
27296-27300	$.45				

#1207 4¢ WINSLOW HOMER

6 Plates

		UL	UR	LL	LR
27362	$.50				
27374	$.50				
27379	$.50				
27380	$.50				
27381	$.50				
27386	$.50				

1963 REGULAR ISSUE

#1208 5¢ U.S. FLAG

UNTAGGED 26 Plates

		UL	UR	LL	LR
27392	$.50				
27393	$.50				
27398	$.50				
27403	$.50				
27408	$.50				
27411	$.50				
27558	$.50				
27559	$.50				
27561	$.50				
27568	$.50				
27569	$.50				
27572	$.50				
27716	$.50				
27718	$.50				
27725	$.50				
27732	$1.75				
27965	$.50				
27970	$.50				
28430	$1.75				
28431	$2.50				
28432	$1.75				
28433 o	$.75				
28442 o	$.75				
28445 o	$.75				
28449 o	$2.25				
28453 o	$2.25				

#1208 a 5¢ U.S. FLAG

TAGGED 16 Plates

		UL	UR	LL	LR
28433 o	$2.50				
28442 o	$2.50				
28445 o	$2.50				
28449 o	$15.00				
28453 o	$2.50				

1963 REGULAR ISSUE

#1208 a 5¢ U.S. FLAG Continued

		UL	UR	LL	LR
28631	$2.50				
28664	$2.50				
28681	$6.00				
28684	$4.00				
28685	$3.50				
28911	$1.25				
28914	$4.00				
28915	$2.50				
28918	$7.00				
28919	$7.00				
28921	$10.00				

#1209 1¢ JACKSON

UNTAGGED 18 Plates

		UL	UR	LL	LR
27382	$.25				
27383	$.25				
27387	$.25				
27388	$.25				
27459	$.25				
27460	$.25				
27464	$.25				
27465 o	$.25				
27473	$.25				
27474	$.25				
27695 o	$.25				
27696 o	$.25				
27779 o	$.25				
27780 o	$.25				
29184 o	$.25				
29185 o	$.25				
29389 o	$.25				
29390 o	$.25				

#1209 a 1¢ JACKSON

TAGGED 13 Plates

		UL	UR	LL	LR
27465 o	$1.00				
27695 o	$.50				
27696 o	$.50				
27779 o	$.50				
27780 o	$.50				
28062	$.25				
28063	$.25				
29182	$.25				
29183	$.25				
29184 o	$.50				
29185 o	$.50				
29389 o	$.50				
29390 o	$.50				

#1213 5¢ WASHINGTON

UNTAGGED 64 Plates

		UL	UR	LL	LR
27194	$.50				
27195	$.50				
27196	$.50				
27197	$.50				
27230	$.50				

1963 REGULAR ISSUE

#1213 5¢ WASHINGTON Continued

UNTAGGED

		UL	UR	LL	LR
27231	$.55	☐	☐	☐	☐
27232	$.55	☐	☐	☐	☐
27233	$.55	☐	☐	☐	☐
27297	$.55	☐	☐	☐	☐
27298	$.55	☐	☐	☐	☐
27307	$.55	☐	☐	☐	☐
27308	$.55	☐	☐	☐	☐
27315	$.55	☐	☐	☐	☐
27316	$.55	☐	☐	☐	☐
27317	$.55	☐	☐	☐	☐
27318	$.55	☐	☐	☐	☐
27326	$.55	☐	☐	☐	☐
27327	$.55	☐	☐	☐	☐
27328	$.55	☐	☐	☐	☐
27329	$.55	☐	☐	☐	☐
27337	$.55	☐	☐	☐	☐
27338	$.55	☐	☐	☐	☐
27339	$.55	☐	☐	☐	☐
27340	$.55	☐	☐	☐	☐
27341	$.55	☐	☐	☐	☐
27342	$.55	☐	☐	☐	☐
27343	$.55	☐	☐	☐	☐
27344	$.55	☐	☐	☐	☐
27425	$.55	☐	☐	☐	☐
27426	$.55	☐	☐	☐	☐
27478	$.55	☐	☐	☐	☐
27479	$.55	☐	☐	☐	☐
27486 o	$.55	☐	☐	☐	☐
27487	$.55	☐	☐	☐	☐
27493	$.55	☐	☐	☐	☐
27494	$.55	☐	☐	☐	☐
27501	$.55	☐	☐	☐	☐
27502	$.55	☐	☐	☐	☐
27517 o	$.55	☐	☐	☐	☐
27518 o	$.55	☐	☐	☐	☐
27553	$.55	☐	☐	☐	☐
27554	$.55	☐	☐	☐	☐
27555	$.55	☐	☐	☐	☐
27556	$.55	☐	☐	☐	☐
27597	$7.50	☐	☐	☐	☐
27598	$7.50	☐	☐	☐	☐
27701	$.55	☐	☐	☐	☐
27702	$.55	☐	☐	☐	☐
27703 o	$.55	☐	☐	☐	☐
27704 o	$.55	☐	☐	☐	☐
27727	$.55	☐	☐	☐	☐
27728	$.55	☐	☐	☐	☐
27748 o	$.55	☐	☐	☐	☐
27749 o	$.55	☐	☐	☐	☐
27864	$.55	☐	☐	☐	☐
27865	$.55	☐	☐	☐	☐
27866	$50.00	☐	☐	☐	☐
27867	$50.00	☐	☐	☐	☐
27873	$.55	☐	☐	☐	☐
27874	$.55	☐	☐	☐	☐
27961	$7.50	☐	☐	☐	☐
27962	$7.50	☐	☐	☐	☐
27993	$7.50	☐	☐	☐	☐
27994	$7.50	☐	☐	☐	☐

#1213 b 5¢ WASHINGTON

TAGGED — 7 Plates

		UL	UR	LL	LR
27486 o	$12.50	☐	☐	☐	☐
27517 o	$5.00	☐	☐	☐	☐
27518 o	$5.00	☐	☐	☐	☐
27703 o	$12.50	☐	☐	☐	☐
27704 o	$12.50	☐	☐	☐	☐
27748 o	$12.50	☐	☐	☐	☐
27749 o	$12.50	☐	☐	☐	☐

BOOKLET PLATES — PANES OF 5

#1213 a 5¢ WASHINGTON

UNTAGGED — 76 Plates

27347	27348	27349	27350	27351
27352	27357	27358	27412	27413
27435	27436	27438	27439	27498
27499	27503	27504	27505	27506
27523	27524	27525	27526	27546
27547	27563 o	27564 o	27565	27566
27650	27651	27669	27670	27671 o
27672	27675	27676	27678 o	27679 o
27723	27724	27734 o	27735 o	27736
27737	27738	27739	27827 o	27828
27829 o	27830	27833	27834	28013
28014	28039	28040	28080	28081 o
28084	28085	28090	28091 o	28214 o
28215 o	28216 o	28217 o	28338	28339 o
28345 o	28346	28440 o	28441 o	28471 o
28472 o				

#1213 c 5¢ WASHINGTON

TAGGED — 49 Plates

27563 o	27564 o	27671 o	27678 o	27679 o
27734 o	27735 o	27827 o	27829 o	28081 o
28091 o	28214 o	28215 o	28216 o	28217 o
28339 o	28345 o	28440 o	28441 o	28471 o
28472 o	28491	28492	28513	28514
28518	28538	28539	28567	28568
28569	28570	28619	28849	28850
28854	28904	28905	29053	29054
29058	29130	29131	29213	29214
29283	29284	29336	29337	

SIDE COIL PLATES

#1225 1¢ JACKSON

432 Subject Plates — STRIPS OF 6

UNTAGGED — 12 Plates

27384	†27385	†27419	†27420	27775 o
27776 o	28009 o	28010 o	29117	29118
29134	29135			

#1225 a 1¢ JACKSON

TAGGED — 4 Plates

27775 o 27776 o 28009 o 28010 o

o Issued both Tagged and Plain

SIDE COIL PLATES (Cont.)

#1229 5¢ WASHINGTON

432 Subject Plates — STRIPS OF 6
UNTAGGED — 223 Plates

27190	27191	27192	27193	27206
27207	†27208	†27209	27211	27212
†27302	†27303	27304	27305	†27309
†27310	†27319	†27320	†27321	†27322
27333	†27334	27335	†27336	†27394
†27395	†27396	†27397	†27399	†27400
†27404	†27405	†27406	†27407	†27421
†27422	†27423	†27424	†27429	†27430
†27440	†27441	†27442	†27443	†27444
†27445	†27448	†27449	†27451	†27452
†27470	†27471	†27480	†27481	†27495
†27496	†27531	†27532	†27533	†27534
†27536	†27537	†27538	†27539	†27542
†27543	†27544	†27545	†27549o	27550o
†27551	†27552	†27580o	†27581o	†27582
†27583o	†27617o	†27618o	†27619	†27620
†27628	†27629	27630o	†27631o	†27632o
†27633o	†27634o	†27635o	†27648o	27649o
27652o	27653o	†27665	†27666	†27667
†27668	†27690	†27691	†27708	†27709
†27710	†27711	†27712	†27713	†27729
†27730	†27752	†27753	†27755	†27756
†27757	†27758	†27759	†27760	†27761
†27762	†27767	†27768	†27769	†27770
†27781	†27782	†27783	27784	†27810
27811o	27816o	†27817	†27835	27836
†27837	27838	27855	27856	27858
27890	27894	27903o	27904o	27905o
27906o	†27907	†27908	27913	27914
27923	27924	†27938o	†27939o	27943
27944	27949	27950	27951o	27952o
27959	27960	†27963	†27964	†28052
†28053	28058	28059	28071	28072
28078	28079	†28125o	†28126o	28136
28137	28197	28198	†28199o	†28200o
28202	28203	28206	28207	28208
28209	†28288	†28289	28290	28291
28318	28319	28320	28321	28322
28323	28324	28325	28386	28387
†28388o	†28389o	28390o	28391o	28392
28393	28415o	28416o	28443o	28444o
†28446	†28447	†28454o	†28455o	28456o
28457o	†28464o	†28465o	†28477	†28489o
†28490o	†28502	†28503	†28504	†28534o
†28535o	28549o	28550o		

#1229 a 5¢ WASHINGTON

432 Subject Plates — STRIPS OF 6
TAGGED — 57 Plates

†27549o	27550o	†27580o	†27581o	†27583o
†27617o	†27618o	27630o	†27631o	†27632o
†27633o	†27634o	†27635o	†27648o	27649o
27652o	27653o	27811o	27816o	27903o
27904o	27905o	27906o	27938o	27939o
27951o	27952o	28125o	28126o	†28199o
†28200o	28388o	28389o	28390o	28391o
28415o	28416o	28443o	28444o	†28451
†28452	†28454o	†28455o	28456o	28457o
†28464o	†28465o	†28489o	†28490o	†28534o

SIDE COIL PLATES (Cont.)

#1229a 5¢ WASHINGTON Cont.

†28535 †28549o †28550o† 28551 †28552
†28555 †28556

SHEET STAMPS
1963 COMMEMORATIVES
Continued

#1230 5¢ NORTH CAROLINA

6 Plates		UL	UR	LL	LR
27428	$.50	☐	☐	☐	☐
27431	$.50	☐	☐	☐	☐
27432	$.50	☐	☐	☐	☐
27433	$.50	☐	☐	☐	☐
27434	$.50	☐	☐	☐	☐
27437	$.50	☐	☐	☐	☐

#1231 5¢ FOOD FOR PEACE

6 Plates

27482	$.50	☐	☐	☐	☐
27484	$.50	☐	☐	☐	☐
27485	$.50	☐	☐	☐	☐
27488	$.50	☐	☐	☐	☐
27489	$.50	☐	☐	☐	☐
27492	$.50	☐	☐	☐	☐

#1232 5¢ WEST VIRGINIA

6 Plates

27500	$.50	☐	☐	☐	☐
27507	$.50	☐	☐	☐	☐
27509	$.50	☐	☐	☐	☐
27511	$.50	☐	☐	☐	☐
27512	$.50	☐	☐	☐	☐
27514	$.50	☐	☐	☐	☐

#1233 5¢ EMANCIPATION 8 Plates

27453-27456	$.50	☐	☐	☐	☐
27453-27458	$.50	☐	☐	☐	☐
27455-27456	$.50	☐	☐	☐	☐
27455-27458	$.50	☐	☐	☐	☐
27457-27462	$.50	☐	☐	☐	☐
27457-27468	$.50	☐	☐	☐	☐
27461-27462	$.50	☐	☐	☐	☐
27461-27468	$.50	☐	☐	☐	☐

#1234 5¢ ALLIANCE FOR PROGRESS

6 Plates

27562	$.50	☐	☐	☐	☐
27567	$.50	☐	☐	☐	☐
27570	$.50	☐	☐	☐	☐
27571	$.50	☐	☐	☐	☐
27574	$.50	☐	☐	☐	☐
27576	$.50	☐	☐	☐	☐

#1235 5¢ CORDELL HULL

4 Plates

27613	$.50	☐	☐	☐	☐
27614	$.50	☐	☐	☐	☐
27615	$.50	☐	☐	☐	☐
27616	$.50	☐	☐	☐	☐

1963-64 COMMEMORATIVES

#1236 5¢ ELEANOR ROOSEVELT
4 Plates

		UL	UR	LL	LR
27604	$.50	☐	☐	☐	☐
27605	$.50	☐	☐	☐	☐
27606	$.50	☐	☐	☐	☐
27607	$.50	☐	☐	☐	☐

#1237 5¢ SCIENCE 6 Plates

		UL	UR	LL	LR
27623	$.50	☐	☐	☐	☐
27624	$.50	☐	☐	☐	☐
27626	$.50	☐	☐	☐	☐
27627	$.50	☐	☐	☐	☐
27636	$.50	☐	☐	☐	☐
27639	$.50	☐	☐	☐	☐

#1238 5¢ CITY DELIVERY
TAGGED **6 Plates**

		UL	UR	LL	LR
27596	$.50	☐	☐	☐	☐
27600	$.50	☐	☐	☐	☐
27611	$.50	☐	☐	☐	☐
27612	$.50	☐	☐	☐	☐
27621	$.50	☐	☐	☐	☐
27622	$.50	☐	☐	☐	☐

#1239 5¢ RED CROSS 8 Plates

		UL	UR	LL	LR
27641	$.50	☐	☐	☐	☐
27642	$.50	☐	☐	☐	☐
27654	$2.00	☐	☐	☐	☐
27656	$.50	☐	☐	☐	☐
27657	$.50	☐	☐	☐	☐
27658	$.50	☐	☐	☐	☐
27659	$.50	☐	☐	☐	☐
27660	$.50	☐	☐	☐	☐

#1240 5¢ CHRISTMAS 1963
UNTAGGED **17 Plates**

		UL	UR	LL	LR
27560	$.50	☐	☐	☐	☐
27573	$.50	☐	☐	☐	☐
27575	$1.25	☐	☐	☐	☐
27577	$.50	☐	☐	☐	☐
27578	$.50	☐	☐	☐	☐
27579	$.50	☐	☐	☐	☐
27587	$.50	☐	☐	☐	☐
27589 o	$.50	☐	☐	☐	☐
27591	$.50	☐	☐	☐	☐
27595	$.50	☐	☐	☐	☐
27599	$.50	☐	☐	☐	☐
27601 o	$.50	☐	☐	☐	☐
27602	$2.75	☐	☐	☐	☐
27608	$.50	☐	☐	☐	☐
27638	$.50	☐	☐	☐	☐
27640	$.50	☐	☐	☐	☐
27655	$.50	☐	☐	☐	☐

#1240 a 5¢ CHRISTMAS 1963
TAGGED **2 Plates**

		UL	UR	LL	LR
27589 o	$5.00	☐	☐	☐	☐
27601 o	$5.00	☐	☐	☐	☐

o Issued both Tagged and Plain

#1241 5¢ AUDUBON 6 Plates

		UL	UR	LL	LR
27586	$.50	☐	☐	☐	☐
27588	$.50	☐	☐	☐	☐
27590	$.50	☐	☐	☐	☐
27594	$.50	☐	☐	☐	☐
27603	$.50	☐	☐	☐	☐
27609	$.50	☐	☐	☐	☐

#1242 5¢ SAM HOUSTON 4 Plates

		UL	UR	LL	LR
27661	$.50	☐	☐	☐	☐
27662	$.50	☐	☐	☐	☐
27663	$.50	☐	☐	☐	☐
27664	$.50	☐	☐	☐	☐

#1243 5¢ C.M. RUSSELL 6 Plates

		UL	UR	LL	LR
27740	$.50	☐	☐	☐	☐
27741	$.50	☐	☐	☐	☐
27742	$.50	☐	☐	☐	☐
27747	$.50	☐	☐	☐	☐
27750	$.50	☐	☐	☐	☐
27751	$.50	☐	☐	☐	☐

#1244 5¢ N.Y. FAIR 4 Plates

		UL	UR	LL	LR
27743	$.50	☐	☐	☐	☐
27744	$.50	☐	☐	☐	☐
27745	$.50	☐	☐	☐	☐
27746	$.50	☐	☐	☐	☐

#1245 5¢ MUIR 4 Plates

		UL	UR	LL	LR
27687	$.50	☐	☐	☐	☐
27688	$.50	☐	☐	☐	☐
27692	$.50	☐	☐	☐	☐
27693	$.50	☐	☐	☐	☐

#1246 5¢ KENNEDY 12 Plates

		UL	UR	LL	LR
27800	$.50	☐	☐	☐	☐
27801	$.50	☐	☐	☐	☐
27802	$.50	☐	☐	☐	☐
27803	$.50	☐	☐	☐	☐
27804	$.50	☐	☐	☐	☐
27805	$.50	☐	☐	☐	☐
27806	$.50	☐	☐	☐	☐
27807	$.50	☐	☐	☐	☐
27808	$.50	☐	☐	☐	☐
27809	$.50	☐	☐	☐	☐
27818	$.50	☐	☐	☐	☐
27819	$.50	☐	☐	☐	☐

#1247 5¢ NEW JERSEY 4 Plates

		UL	UR	LL	LR
27786	$.50	☐	☐	☐	☐
27787	$.50	☐	☐	☐	☐
27788	$.50	☐	☐	☐	☐
27789	$.50	☐	☐	☐	☐

#1248 5¢ NEVADA 4 Plates

		UL	UR	LL	LR
27785	$.50	☐	☐	☐	☐
27790	$.50	☐	☐	☐	☐
27797	$.50	☐	☐	☐	☐
27798	$.50	☐	☐	☐	☐

1964 COMMEMORATIVES

#1249 5¢ REGISTER & VOTE
30 Plates

Plate	Price	UL	UR	LL	LR
27831	$.50	☐	☐	☐	☐
27832	$.50	☐	☐	☐	☐
27839	$.50	☐	☐	☐	☐
27840	$.50	☐	☐	☐	☐
27841	$.50	☐	☐	☐	☐
27847	$.50	☐	☐	☐	☐
28548	$.50	☐	☐	☐	☐
28554	$.50	☐	☐	☐	☐
28557	$.50	☐	☐	☐	☐
28560	$1.00	☐	☐	☐	☐
28561	$.50	☐	☐	☐	☐
28562	$.50	☐	☐	☐	☐
28571	$.50	☐	☐	☐	☐
28587	$.50	☐	☐	☐	☐
28591	$.50	☐	☐	☐	☐
28592	$.50	☐	☐	☐	☐
28598	$.50	☐	☐	☐	☐
28599	$.50	☐	☐	☐	☐
28602	$.50	☐	☐	☐	☐
28603	$.50	☐	☐	☐	☐
28604	$.50	☐	☐	☐	☐
28606	$.50	☐	☐	☐	☐
28609	$.50	☐	☐	☐	☐
28615	$.50	☐	☐	☐	☐
28616	$.50	☐	☐	☐	☐
28622	$.50	☐	☐	☐	☐
28623	$.50	☐	☐	☐	☐
28628	$.50	☐	☐	☐	☐
28680	$.50	☐	☐	☐	☐
28682	$1.75	☐	☐	☐	☐

#1250 5¢ SHAKESPEARE 4 Plates

Plate	Price	UL	UR	LL	LR
27842	$.50	☐	☐	☐	☐
27843	$.50	☐	☐	☐	☐
27844	$.50	☐	☐	☐	☐
27845	$.50	☐	☐	☐	☐

#1251 5¢ DOCTORS MAYO
4 Plates

Plate	Price	UL	UR	LL	LR
27869	$.50	☐	☐	☐	☐
27870	$.50	☐	☐	☐	☐
27871	$.50	☐	☐	☐	☐
27872	$.50	☐	☐	☐	☐

#1252 5¢ AMERICAN MUSIC
6 Plates

Plate	Price	UL	UR	LL	LR
27846	$.50	☐	☐	☐	☐
27848	$.50	☐	☐	☐	☐
27849	$.50	☐	☐	☐	☐
27852	$.50	☐	☐	☐	☐
27853	$.50	☐	☐	☐	☐
27854	$.50	☐	☐	☐	☐

#1253 5¢ HOMEMAKERS 6 Plates

Plate	Price	UL	UR	LL	LR
27917	$.50	☐	☐	☐	☐
27918	$.50	☐	☐	☐	☐
27919	$.50	☐	☐	☐	☐
27920	$.50	☐	☐	☐	☐

#1253 5¢ HOMEMAKERS Cont.

Plate	Price	UL	UR	LL	LR
27921	$.50	☐	☐	☐	☐
27922	$.50	☐	☐	☐	☐

#1254-7 5¢ CHRISTMAS 1964
UNTAGGED 29 Plates

Plate	Price	UL	UR	LL	LR
27875	$1.25	☐	☐	☐	☐
27876	$1.25	☐	☐	☐	☐
27878	$1.25	☐	☐	☐	☐
27879	$1.25	☐	☐	☐	☐
27880	$1.25	☐	☐	☐	☐
27883	$1.25	☐	☐	☐	☐
27884	$1.25	☐	☐	☐	☐
27885 o	$1.25	☐	☐	☐	☐
27888	$1.25	☐	☐	☐	☐
27889	$1.25	☐	☐	☐	☐
27892	$1.25	☐	☐	☐	☐
27893 o	$1.25	☐	☐	☐	☐
27896	$1.25	☐	☐	☐	☐
27897	$1.25	☐	☐	☐	☐
27902	$1.25	☐	☐	☐	☐
27909	$1.25	☐	☐	☐	☐
27910	$1.25	☐	☐	☐	☐
27911	$1.25	☐	☐	☐	☐
27915	$1.25	☐	☐	☐	☐
27925	$1.25	☐	☐	☐	☐
27926	$1.25	☐	☐	☐	☐
27929	$1.25	☐	☐	☐	☐
27930	$1.25	☐	☐	☐	☐
27931	$1.25	☐	☐	☐	☐
27932	$1.25	☐	☐	☐	☐
27953	$1.25	☐	☐	☐	☐
27954	$1.25	☐	☐	☐	☐
27955	$1.25	☐	☐	☐	☐
27956	$1.25	☐	☐	☐	☐

#1254 a-57 a 5¢ CHRISTMAS 1964
TAGGED 2 Plates

Plate	Price	UL	UR	LL	LR
27885 o	$5.00	☐	☐	☐	☐
27893 o	$5.00	☐	☐	☐	☐

#1258 5¢ VERRAZANO BRIDGE
4 Plates

Plate	Price	UL	UR	LL	LR
27945	$.50	☐	☐	☐	☐
27946	$.50	☐	☐	☐	☐
27947	$.50	☐	☐	☐	☐
27948	$.50	☐	☐	☐	☐

#1259 5¢ FINE ARTS 8 Plates

Plate	Price	UL	UR	LL	LR
27933-27936	$.50	☐	☐	☐	☐
27933-27941	$.50	☐	☐	☐	☐
27934-27936	$.50	☐	☐	☐	☐
27934-27941	$.50	☐	☐	☐	☐
27935-27937	$.50	☐	☐	☐	☐
27935-27942	$.50	☐	☐	☐	☐
27940-27937	$.50	☐	☐	☐	☐
27940-27942	$.50	☐	☐	☐	☐

1964-65 COMMEMORATIVES

#1260 5¢ AMATEUR RADIO

4 Plates

		UL	UR	LL	LR
27898	$.50	☐	☐	☐	☐
27899	$.50	☐	☐	☐	☐
27900	$.50	☐	☐	☐	☐
27901	$.50	☐	☐	☐	☐

#1261 5¢ NEW ORLEANS 6 Plates

		UL	UR	LL	LR
27982	$.50	☐	☐	☐	☐
27983	$.50	☐	☐	☐	☐
27984	$.50	☐	☐	☐	☐
27985	$.50	☐	☐	☐	☐
27987	$.50	☐	☐	☐	☐
27992	$.50	☐	☐	☐	☐

#1262 5¢ SOKOL 6 Plates

		UL	UR	LL	LR
27995	$.50	☐	☐	☐	☐
27996	$.50	☐	☐	☐	☐
27998	$.50	☐	☐	☐	☐
28002	$.50	☐	☐	☐	☐
28003	$.50	☐	☐	☐	☐
28008	$.50	☐	☐	☐	☐

#1263 5¢ CANCER CRUSADE

12 Plates

		UL	UR	LL	LR
28036-28038	$.50	☐	☐	☐	☐
28036-28044	$.50	☐	☐	☐	☐
28037-28038	$.50	☐	☐	☐	☐
28037-28044	$.50	☐	☐	☐	☐
28043-28048	$.50	☐	☐	☐	☐
28043-28049	$.50	☐	☐	☐	☐
28047-28048	$.50	☐	☐	☐	☐
28047-28049	$.50	☐	☐	☐	☐
28054-28057	$.50	☐	☐	☐	☐
28054-28060	$.50	☐	☐	☐	☐
28055-28057	$.50	☐	☐	☐	☐
28055-28060	$.50	☐	☐	☐	☐

#1264 5¢ CHURCHILL 4 Plates

		UL	UR	LL	LR
28104	$.50	☐	☐	☐	☐
28105	$.50	☐	☐	☐	☐
28106	$.50	☐	☐	☐	☐
28107	$.50	☐	☐	☐	☐

#1265 5¢ MAGNA CARTA 8 Plates

		UL	UR	LL	LR
28082-28088	$.50	☐	☐	☐	☐
28082-28089	$.50	☐	☐	☐	☐
28083-28088	$.50	☐	☐	☐	☐
28083-28089	$.50	☐	☐	☐	☐
28086-28092	$.50	☐	☐	☐	☐
28086-28093	$.50	☐	☐	☐	☐
28087-28092	$.50	☐	☐	☐	☐
28087-28093	$.50	☐	☐	☐	☐

#1266 5¢ U.N. COOPERATION

6 Plates

		UL	UR	LL	LR
28124	$.50	☐	☐	☐	☐
28127	$.50	☐	☐	☐	☐
28130	$.50	☐	☐	☐	☐
28131	$.50	☐	☐	☐	☐
28132	$.50	☐	☐	☐	☐
28133	$.50	☐	☐	☐	☐

#1267 5¢ SALVATION ARMY

6 Plates

		UL	UR	LL	LR
28113	$.50	☐	☐	☐	☐
28114	$.50	☐	☐	☐	☐
28117	$.50	☐	☐	☐	☐
28118	$.50	☐	☐	☐	☐
28122	$.50	☐	☐	☐	☐
28123	$.50	☐	☐	☐	☐

#1268 5¢ DANTE 4 Plates

		UL	UR	LL	LR
28108	$.50	☐	☐	☐	☐
28109	$.50	☐	☐	☐	☐
28110	$.50	☐	☐	☐	☐
28111	$.50	☐	☐	☐	☐

#1269 5¢ HOOVER 4 Plates

		UL	UR	LL	LR
28161	$.50	☐	☐	☐	☐
28162	$.50	☐	☐	☐	☐
28163	$.50	☐	☐	☐	☐
28164	$.50	☐	☐	☐	☐

#1270 5¢ FULTON 6 Plates

		UL	UR	LL	LR
28145	$.50	☐	☐	☐	☐
28148	$.50	☐	☐	☐	☐
28149	$.50	☐	☐	☐	☐
28151	$.50	☐	☐	☐	☐
28160	$.50	☐	☐	☐	☐
28168	$.50	☐	☐	☐	☐

#1271 5¢ FLORIDA 32 Plates

		UL	UR	LL	LR
28150-28155-28179	$.50	☐	☐	☐	☐
28150-28155-28183	$.50	☐	☐	☐	☐
28150-28159-28179	$.50	☐	☐	☐	☐
28150-28159-28183	$.50	☐	☐	☐	☐
28150-28166-28184	$.50	☐	☐	☐	☐
28150-28166-28185	$.50	☐	☐	☐	☐
28150-28169-28184	$.50	☐	☐	☐	☐
28150-28169-28185	$.50	☐	☐	☐	☐
28152-28155-28179	$.50	☐	☐	☐	☐
28152-28155-28183	$.50	☐	☐	☐	☐
28152-28159-28179	$.50	☐	☐	☐	☐
28152-28159-28183	$.50	☐	☐	☐	☐
28152-28166-28184	$.50	☐	☐	☐	☐
28152-28166-28185	$.50	☐	☐	☐	☐
28152-28169-28184	$.50	☐	☐	☐	☐
28152-28169-28185	$.50	☐	☐	☐	☐

1965 COMMEMORATIVES

#1271 5¢ FLORIDA Continued

		UL	UR	LL	LR
28153-28155-28179	$.50	☐	☐	☐	☐
28153-28155-28183	$.50	☐	☐	☐	☐
28153-28159-28179	$.50	☐	☐	☐	☐
28153-28159-28183	$.50	☐	☐	☐	☐
28153-28166-28184	$.50	☐	☐	☐	☐
28153-28166-28185	$.50	☐	☐	☐	☐
28153-28169-28184	$.50	☐	☐	☐	☐
28153-28169-28185	$.50	☐	☐	☐	☐
28158-28155-28179	$.50	☐	☐	☐	☐
28158-28155-28183	$.50	☐	☐	☐	☐
28158-28159-28179	$.50	☐	☐	☐	☐
28158-28159-28183	$.50	☐	☐	☐	☐
28158-28166-28184	$.50	☐	☐	☐	☐
28158-28166-28185	$.50	☐	☐	☐	☐
28158-28169-28184	$.50	☐	☐	☐	☐
25158-28169-28185	$.50	☐	☐	☐	☐

#1272 5¢ TRAFFIC 24 Plates

28187-28189	$.50	☐	☐	☐	☐
28187-28192	$.50	☐	☐	☐	☐
28187-28195	$.50	☐	☐	☐	☐
28187-28201	$.50	☐	☐	☐	☐
28188-28189	$1.25	☐	☐	☐	☐
28188-28192	$1.25	☐	☐	☐	☐
28188-28195	$1.25	☐	☐ 2	☐	☐
28188-28201	$1.25	☐	☐ 2	☐	☐
28190-28189	$.50	☐	☐	☐	☐
28190-28192	$.50	☐	☐	☐	☐
28190-28195	$.50	☐	☐	☐	☐
28190-28201	$.50	☐	☐	☐	☐
28191-28189	$.50	☐	☐	☐	☐
28191-28192	$.50	☐	☐	☐	☐
28191-28195	$.50	☐	☐	☐	☐
28191-28201	$.50	☐	☐	☐	☐
28193-28189	$2.25	☐	☐	☐	☐
28193-28192	$2.25	☐	☐	☐	☐
28193-28195	$2.00	☐	☐	☐	☐
28193-28201	$2.25	☐	☐	☐	☐
28194-28189	$1.00	☐ 2	☐ 5	☐ 4	☐ 3
28194-28192	$1.00	☐ 2	☐ 5	☐ 4	☐ 3
28194-28195	$2.00	☐	☐	☐	☐
28194-28201	$2.25	☐	☐	☐	☐

#1273 5¢ J.S. COPLEY 6 Plates

28210	$.50	☐	☐	☐	☐
28211	$.50	☐	☐	☐	☐
28212	$.50	☐	☐	☐	☐
28213	$.50	☐	☐	☐	☐
28218	$.50	☐	☐	☐	☐
28219	$.50	☐	☐	☐	☐

#1274 11¢ I.T.U. 4 Plates

28143-28139	$9.00	☐	☐	☐	☐
28143-28147	$9.00	☐	☐	☐	☐
28144-28139	$9.00	☐	☐	☐	☐
28144-28147	$9.00	☐	☐	☐	☐

1965 COMMEMORATIVES

#1275 5¢ STEVENSON 9 Plates

		UL	UR	LL	LR
28232	$.50	☐	☐	☐	☐
28233	$.50	☐	☐	☐	☐
28234	$2.00	☐	☐	☐	☐
28239	$.50	☐	☐	☐	☐
28240	$.50	☐	☐	☐	☐
28246	$.50	☐	☐	☐	☐
28258	$.50	☐	☐	☐	☐
28259	$.50	☐	☐	☐	☐
28281	$.50	☐	☐	☐	☐

#1276 5¢ CHRISTMAS 1965

Issued UNTAGGED 17 Plates

28172	$.50	☐	☐	☐	☐
28173	$.50	☐	☐	☐	☐
28174	$.50	☐	☐	☐	☐
28175	$.50	☐	☐	☐	☐
28176	$.50	☐	☐	☐	☐
28177	$.50	☐	☐	☐	☐
28178	$.50	☐	☐	☐	☐
28182	$.50	☐	☐	☐	☐
28224	$1.50	☐	☐	☐	☐
28230	$.50	☐	☐	☐	☐
28231	$.50	☐	☐	☐	☐
28235 o	$.50	☐	☐	☐	☐
28241 o	$.50	☐	☐	☐	☐
28251 o	$.50	☐	☐	☐	☐
28256 o	$.50	☐	☐	☐	☐
28275	$.50	☐	☐	☐	☐
28294	$.50	☐	☐	☐	☐

#1276 a 5¢ CHRISTMAS 1965

Issued TAGGED 4 Plates

28235 o	$7.50	☐	☐	☐	☐
28241 o	$7.50	☐	☐	☐	☐
28251 o	$7.50	☐	☐	☐	☐
28256 o	$7.50	☐	☐	☐	☐

1965 REGULAR ISSUE

ROTARY PRESS

#1278 1¢ JEFFERSON 32 Plates

Issued TAGGED Only

		UL	UR	LL	LR
29450	$.20	☐	☐	☐	☐
29451	$.20	☐	☐	☐	☐
29458	$.20	☐	☐	☐	☐
29459	$.20	☐	☐	☐	☐
29479	$.20	☐	☐	☐	☐
29480	$.20	☐	☐	☐	☐
29491	$.20	☐	☐	☐	☐
29492	$.20	☐	☐	☐	☐
29997	$.20	☐	☐	☐	☐
29998	$.20	☐	☐	☐	☐
30086	$.20	☐	☐	☐	☐
30087	$.20	☐	☐	☐	☐
30946	$.20	☐	☐	☐	☐
30947	$.20	☐	☐	☐	☐
30956	$.20	☐	☐	☐	☐
30987	$.20	☐	☐	☐	☐

1965 REGULAR ISSUE

#1278 1¢ JEFFERSON Continued

		UL	UR	LL	LR
30988	$.20	☐	☐	☐	☐
30989	$.20	☐	☐	☐	☐
30990	$.20	☐	☐	☐	☐
31006	$.20	☐	☐	☐	☐
31007	$.20	☐	☐	☐	☐
31008	$.20	☐	☐	☐	☐
31009	$.20	☐	☐	☐	☐
31301	$.20	☐	☐	☐	☐
31302	$.20	☐	☐	☐	☐
31303	$.20	☐	☐	☐	☐
31639	$.20	☐	☐	☐	☐
31640	$.20	☐	☐	☐	☐
31644	$.20	☐	☐	☐	☐
31645	$.20	☐	☐	☐	☐
37615	$.20	☐	☐	☐	☐
37616	$.20	☐	☐	☐	☐

#1279 1¼¢ GALLATIN 2 Plates

Issued UNTAGGED Only

		UL	UR	LL	LR
28930	$12.50	☐	☐	☐	☐
28931	$12.50	☐	☐	☐	☐

#1280 2¢ WRIGHT 22 Plates

Issued TAGGED Only

		UL	UR	LL	LR
28506	$.25	☐	☐	☐	☐
28507	$.25	☐	☐	☐	☐
28511	$.25	☐	☐	☐	☐
28512	$.25	☐	☐	☐	☐
29874	$.25	☐	☐	☐	☐
29875	$.25	☐	☐	☐	☐
32061	$.25	☐	☐	☐	☐
32062	$.25	☐	☐	☐	☐
32127	$.25	☐	☐	☐	☐
32128	$.25	☐	☐	☐	☐
32290	$.25	☐	☐	☐	☐
32291	$.25	☐	☐	☐	☐
32329	$.25	☐	☐	☐	☐
32330	$.25	☐	☐	☐	☐
32529	$.25	☐	☐	☐	☐
32574	$.25	☐	☐	☐	☐
32575	$.25	☐	☐	☐	☐
32576	$.25	☐	☐	☐	☐
33136	$.25	☐	☐	☐	☐
33137	$.25	☐	☐	☐	☐
37696	$.25	☐	☐	☐	☐
37697	$.25	☐	☐	☐	☐

#1281 3¢ PARKMAN 8 Plates

Issued TAGGED

		UL	UR	LL	LR
29258	$.40	☐	☐	☐	☐
29259	$.40	☐	☐	☐	☐
34243	$.40	☐	☐	☐	☐
34244	$.40	☐	☐	☐	☐
35775	$.40	☐	☐	☐	☐
35776	$.40	☐	☐	☐	☐
37623	$.40	☐	☐	☐	☐
37624	$.40	☐	☐	☐	☐

#1281 a 3¢ PARKMAN 4 Plates

Issued UNTAGGED

		UL	UR	LL	LR
36123 P	$5.00	☐	☐	☐	☐
36124 P	$5.00	☐	☐	☐	☐
37622 P	$25.00	☐	☐	☐	☐
37625 P	$25.00	☐	☐	☐	☐

#1282 4¢ LINCOLN 20 Plates

Issued UNTAGGED

		UL	UR	LL	LR
28242	$.50	☐	☐	☐	☐
28243	$.50	☐	☐	☐	☐
28244	$.50	☐	☐	☐	☐
28245	$.50	☐	☐	☐	☐
28247 o	$.50	☐	☐	☐	☐
28248 o	$.50	☐	☐	☐	☐
28303 o	$.50	☐	☐	☐	☐
28304 o	$.50	☐	☐	☐	☐
28305 o	$.50	☐	☐	☐	☐
28306 o	$.50	☐	☐	☐	☐
28312 o	$15.00	☐	☐	☐	☐
28313 o	$15.00	☐	☐	☐	☐
28314 o	$.50	☐	☐	☐	☐
28315 o	$.50	☐	☐	☐	☐
28329 o	$3.00	☐	☐	☐	☐
28330 o	$3.00	☐	☐	☐	☐
28331 o	$3.00	☐	☐	☐	☐
28332 o	$3.00	☐	☐	☐	☐
28600 o	$.50	☐	☐	☐	☐
28601 o	$.50	☐	☐	☐	☐

#1282 a 4¢ LINCOLN 27 Plates

Issued TAGGED

		UL	UR	LL	LR
28247 o	$1.50	☐	☐	☐	☐
28248 o	$1.50	☐	☐	☐	☐
28303 o	$.45	☐	☐	☐	☐
28304 o	$.45	☐	☐	☐	☐
28305 o	$.45	☐	☐	☐	☐
28306 o	$2.00	☐	☐	☐	☐
28307	$.45	☐	☐	☐	☐
28308	$.45	☐	☐	☐	☐
28312 o	$.45	☐	☐	☐	☐
28313 o	$.45	☐	☐	☐	☐
28314 o	$.45	☐	☐	☐	☐
28315 o	$.45	☐	☐	☐	☐
28329 o	$.45	☐	☐	☐	☐
28330 o	$.45	☐	☐	☐	☐
28331 o	$.45	☐	☐	☐	☐
28332 o	$.45	☐	☐	☐	☐
28600 o	$.45	☐	☐	☐	☐
28601 o	$.45	☐	☐	☐	☐
28831	$.45	☐	☐	☐	☐
28832	$.45	☐	☐	☐	☐

o Issued both Tagged and Plain

P These plate numbers have been reported only on precancelled stamps.

1965 REGULAR ISSUE

#1282 a 4¢ LINCOLN Continued

		UL	UR	LL	LR
28833	$.45	☐	☐	☐	☐
28834	$.45	☐	☐	☐	☐
28863	$.45	☐	☐	☐	☐
28868	$.45	☐	☐	☐	☐
28869	$.45	☐	☐	☐	☐
29407	$.45	☐	☐	☐	☐
29408	$.45	☐	☐	☐	☐

#1283 5¢ WASHINGTON 16 Plates

Issued UNTAGGED

		UL	UR	LL	LR
28349 o	$.60	☐	☐	☐	☐
28350 o	$.60	☐	☐	☐	☐
28351 o	$.60	☐	☐	☐	☐
28352 o	$.60	☐	☐	☐	☐
28353 o	$.60	☐	☐	☐	☐
28354 o	$.60	☐	☐	☐	☐
28355 o	$.60	☐	☐	☐	☐
28356 o	$.60	☐	☐	☐	☐
28357 o	$.60	☐	☐	☐	☐
28358 o	$.60	☐	☐	☐	☐
28360 o	$.60	☐	☐	☐	☐
28361 o	$.60	☐	☐	☐	☐
28363 o	$4.00	☐	☐	☐	☐
28364 o	$.60	☐	☐	☐	☐
28366 o	$4.00	☐	☐	☐	☐
28367 o	$4.00	☐	☐	☐	☐

#1283 a 5¢ WASHINGTON 38 Plates

Issued TAGGED

		UL	UR	LL	LR
28349 o	$.60	☐	☐	☐	☐
28350 o	$.60	☐	☐	☐	☐
28351 o	$.60	☐	☐	☐	☐
28352 o	$.60	☐	☐	☐	☐
28353 o	$.60	☐	☐	☐	☐
28354 o	$.60	☐	☐	☐	☐
28355 o	$.60	☐	☐	☐	☐
28356 o	$.60	☐	☐	☐	☐
28357 o	$.60	☐	☐	☐	☐
28358 o	$5.00	☐	☐	☐	☐
28359	$.60	☐	☐	☐	☐
28360 o	$10.00	☐	☐	☐	☐
28361 o	$.60	☐	☐	☐	☐
28362	$.60	☐	☐	☐	☐
28363 o	$.60	☐	☐	☐	☐
28364 o	$.60	☐	☐	☐	☐
28366 o	$.60	☐	☐	☐	☐
28367 o	$.60	☐	☐	☐	☐
28369	$.60	☐	☐	☐	☐
28370	$.60	☐	☐	☐	☐
28371	$.60	☐	☐	☐	☐
28372	$.60	☐	☐	☐	☐
28373	$.60	☐	☐	☐	☐
28374	$.60	☐	☐	☐	☐
28378	$.60	☐	☐	☐	☐
28379	$.60	☐	☐	☐	☐
28380	$.60	☐	☐	☐	☐

#1283 a 5¢ WASHINGTON Cont.

		UL	UR	LL	LR
28381	$.60	☐	☐	☐	☐
28382	$.60	☐	☐	☐	☐
28383	$.60	☐	☐	☐	☐
28384	$.60	☐	☐	☐	☐
28385	$.60	☐	☐	☐	☐
28651	$.60	☐	☐	☐	☐
28652	$.60	☐	☐	☐	☐
28675	$10.00	☐	☐	☐	☐
28676	$10.00	☐	☐	☐	☐
28678	$10.00	☐	☐	☐	☐
28679	$10.00	☐	☐	☐	☐

#1283B 5¢ WASHINGTON REDESIGNED

Issued TAGGED **30 Plates**

		UL	UR	LL	LR
29317		†	†	†	†
29318		†	†	†	†
29320	$.45	☐	☐	☐	☐
29323	$.45	☐	☐	☐	☐
29324	$.45	☐	☐	☐	☐
29356	$.45	☐	☐	☐	☐
29357	$.45	☐	☐	☐	☐
29362	$.45	☐	☐	☐	☐
29363	$.45	☐	☐	☐	☐
29371	$.45	☐	☐	☐	☐
38854	$.45	☐	☐	☐	☐
38855	$.45	☐	☐	☐	☐
39155	$1.50	☐	☐	☐	☐
39156	$1.50	☐	☐	☐	☐
39242	$.45	☐	☐	☐	☐
39312	$.45	☐	☐	☐	☐
39369	$1.00	☐	☐	☐	☐
39370	$1.00	☐	☐	☐	☐
39412	$.45	☐	☐	☐	☐
39413	$.45	☐	☐	☐	☐
39425	$.45	☐	☐	☐	☐
39426	$.45	☐	☐	☐	☐
39467	$.45	☐	☐	☐	☐
39468	$.45	☐	☐	☐	☐
39550	$.45	☐	☐	☐	☐
39551	$1.00	☐	☐	☐	☐
39556	$.45	☐	☐	☐	☐
39557	$.45	☐	☐	☐	☐
39584	$.45	☐	☐	☐	☐
39585	$.45	☐	☐	☐	☐

Please report any unlisted plate numbers or corrections to:

BUREAU ISSUES ASSOCIATION, Inc.
P.O. BOX 1047
BELLEVILLE, IL 62223-1047

1965 REGULAR ISSUE

#1284 6¢ F.D. ROOSEVELT
Issued UNTAGGED **6 Plates**

		UL	UR	LL	LR
28341o	$1.25	☐	☐	☐	☐
28342o	$1.25	☐	☐	☐	☐
28343o	$1.25	☐	☐	☐	☐
28344o	$1.25	☐	☐	☐	☐
30976P	$15.00	†	☐	☐	☐
31462P	$15.00	†	☐	☐	☐

#1284 6¢ F.D. ROOSEVELT
Issued TAGGED **57 Plates**

		UL	UR	LL	LR
28341o	$1.25	☐	☐	☐	☐
28342o	$1.25	☐	☐	☐	☐
28343o	$1.25	☐	☐	☐	☐
28344o	$1.25	☐	☐	☐	☐
29202	$3.00	☐	☐	☐	☐
29211	$.75	☐	☐	☐	☐
29212	$.75	☐	☐	☐	☐
29232	$.75	☐	☐	☐	☐
29233	$.75	☐	☐	☐	☐
29244	$.75	☐	☐	☐	☐
29254	$.75	☐	☐	☐	☐
29255	$.75	☐	☐	☐	☐
29481	$.75	☐	☐	☐	☐
29482	$.75	☐	☐	☐	☐
29487	$.75	☐	☐	☐	☐
29488	$.75	☐	☐	☐	☐
29496	$.75	☐	☐	☐	☐
29497	$.75	☐	☐	☐	☐
29526	$.75	☐	☐	☐	☐
29527	$4.00	☐	☐	☐	☐
29530	$.75	☐	☐	☐	☐
29531	$.75	☐	☐	☐	☐
29534	$.75	☐	☐	☐	☐
29535	$.75	☐	☐	☐	☐
29614	$.75	☐	☐	☐	☐
29615	$.75	☐	☐	☐	☐
29622	$.75	☐	☐	☐	☐
29623	$4.00	☐	☐	☐	☐
29631	$5.00	☐	☐	☐	☐
29632	$.75	☐	☐	☐	☐
29653	$.75	☐	☐	☐	☐
29654	$.75	☐	☐	☐	☐
29660	$.75	☐	☐	☐	☐
29694	$.75	☐	☐	☐	☐
30366	$.75	☐	☐	☐	☐
30367	$.75	☐	☐	☐	☐
30368	$.75	☐	☐	☐	☐
30369	$.70	☐	☐	☐	☐
30376	$.75	☐	☐	☐	☐
30377	$6.00	☐	☐	☐	☐
30400	$.75	☐	☐	☐	☐
30401	$.75	☐	☐	☐	☐
30455	$.75	☐	☐	☐	☐
30468	$10.00	☐ 15	☐	☐	☐
30469	$.75	☐	☐	☐	☐

#1284 6¢ F.D. ROOSEVELT Cont.

Issued TAGGED		UL	UR	LL	LR
30508	$.75	☐	☐	☐	☐
30509	$.75	☐	☐	☐	☐
30512	$.75	☐	☐	☐	☐
30513	$.75	☐	☐	☐	☐
30554	$.75	☐	☐	☐	☐
30555	$.75	☐	☐	☐	☐
31012	$.75	☐	☐	☐	☐
31013	$.75	☐	☐	☐	☐
31364	$.75	☐	☐	☐	☐
31365	$.75	☐	☐	☐	☐
31367	$.75	☐	☐	☐	☐
31368	$.75	☐	☐	☐	☐
30555	$.75	☐	☐	☐	☐
31012	$.75	☐	☐	☐	☐
31013	$.75	☐	☐	☐	☐
33422	$.75	☐	☐	☐	☐
33423	$.75	☐	☐	☐	☐
39870	$.75	☐	☐	☐	☐
39902	$.75	☐	☐	☐	☐

#1393D 7¢ FRANKLIN **6 Plates**
Issued TAGGED only

		UL	UR	LL	LR
33412	$1.00	☐	☐	☐	☐
33413	$1.00	☐	☐	☐	☐
33422	$1.00	☐	☐	☐	☐
33423	$1.00	☐	☐	☐	☐
39870	$1.00	☐	☐	☐	☐
39902	$1.00	☐	☐	☐	☐

#1285 8¢ EINSTEIN **4 Plates**
Issued UNTAGGED

		UL	UR	LL	LR
28398o	$1.50	☐	☐	☐	☐
28399o	$1.50	☐	☐	☐	☐
28400o	$2.50	☐	☐	☐	☐
28406o	$2.50	☐	☐	☐	☐
29341	$1.00	☐	☐	☐	☐
29342	$1.00	☐	☐	☐	☐
31896	$1.00	☐	☐	☐	☐
31913	$1.00	☐	☐	☐	☐
31914	$1.00	☐	☐	☐	☐
31915	$1.00	☐	☐	☐	☐
31916	$1.00	☐	☐	☐	☐
32048	$1.00	☐	☐	☐	☐
32049	$1.00	☐	☐	☐	☐
32117	—	†	†	†	†
32118	—	†	†	†	†
32179	$40.00	☐	☐	☐	☐
32180	$40.00	☐	☐	☐	☐
32201	$1.00	☐	☐	☐	☐

P Issued Precancelled only

o Issued both Tagged and Plain

† Unreported

1965 REGULAR ISSUE

#1286 10¢ JACKSON 12 Plates

Issued TAGGED

Plate	Price	UL	UR	LL	LR
28968	$1.00	☐	☐	☐	☐
28969	$1.00	☐	☐	☐	☐
29009	$1.00	☐	☐	☐	☐
29010	$1.00	☐	☐	☐	☐
30650	$1.00	☐	☐	☐	☐
30651	$1.00	☐	☐	☐	☐
30994	$1.00	☐	☐	☐	☐
30995	$1.00	☐	☐	☐	☐
34348	$1.00	☐	☐	☐	☐
34349	$1.00	☐	☐	☐	☐
34369	$1.00	☐	☐	☐	☐
34370	$1.00	☐	☐	☐	☐

#1286A 12¢ HENRY FORD 6 Plates

Issued TAGGED

Plate	Price	UL	UR	LL	LR
29548	$1.20	☐	☐	☐	☐
29549	$1.20	☐	☐	☐	☐
31266	$1.20	☐	☐	☐	☐
31267	$1.20	☐	☐	☐	☐
31911	$1.20	☐	☐	☐	☐
31912	$1.20	☐	☐	☐	☐

#1287 13¢ KENNEDY 4 Plates

Issued TAGGED

Plate	Price	UL	UR	LL	LR
29113	$1.30	☐	☐	☐	☐
29114	$1.30	☐	☐	☐	☐
29392	$1.30	☐	☐	☐	☐
29393	$1.30	☐	☐	☐	☐

#1397 14¢ LaGUARDIA 4 Plates

Issued TAGGED

Plate	Price	UL	UR	LL	LR
33457	$1.10	☐	☐	☐	☐
33458	$1.10	☐	☐	☐	☐
33469	$1.10	☐	☐	☐	☐
33470	$1.10	☐	☐	☐	☐

#1288 15¢ O.W. HOLMES (DIE I) 26 Plates

Issued TAGGED

Plate	Price	UL	UR	LL	LR
29602	$1.60	☐	☐	☐	☐
29603	$1.60	☐	☐	☐	☐
38152	$1.60	☐	☐	☐	☐
38160	$1.60	☐	☐	☐	☐
38618	$1.60	☐	☐	☐	☐
38619	$1.60	☐	☐	☐	☐
38623	$1.60	☐	☐	☐	☐
38624	$1.60	☐	☐	☐	☐
38631	$1.60	☐	☐	☐	☐
38641	$1.60	☐	☐	☐	☐
38642	$1.60	☐	☐	☐	☐
38643	$1.60	☐	☐	☐	☐
38644	$1.60	☐	☐	☐	☐
38676	$10.00	☐	☐	☐[2]	☐
38677	$1.60	☐	☐	☐	☐

#1288 15¢ O.W. HOLMES Cont.

Plate	Price	UL	UR	LL	LR
38678	$1.50	☐	☐	☐	☐
38902	$1.50	☐	☐	☐	☐
38904	$1.50	☐	☐	☐	☐
38936	$1.50	☐	☐	☐	☐
38937	—	†	†	†	†
38957	$1.50	☐	☐	☐	☐
38958	—	†	†	†	†
38959	$1.50	☐	☐	☐	☐
38960	$1.50	☐	☐	☐	☐
38972	$1.50	☐	☐	☐	☐
38973	$1.50	☐	☐	☐	☐

#1288 d 15¢ O.W. HOLMES (DIE II)

Issued TAGGED 10 Plates

Plate	Price	UL	UR	LL	LR
39023	$1.50	☐	☐	☐	☐
39024	$1.50	☐	☐	☐	☐
39025	$1.50	☐	☐	☐	☐
39026	$1.50	☐	☐	☐	☐
39043	$1.50	☐	☐	☐	☐
39044	$1.50	☐	☐	☐	☐
39069	$1.50	☐	☐	☐	☐
39070	$1.50	☐	☐	☐	☐
39105	—	†	†	†	†
39106	—	†	†	†	†

#1398 16¢ ERNIE PYLE 4 Plates

Issued TAGGED

Plate	Price	UL	UR	LL	LR
32886	$1.40	☐	☐	☐	☐
32887	$1.40	☐	☐	☐	☐
32888	$1.40	☐	☐	☐	☐
32889	$1.40	☐	☐	☐	☐

#1399 18¢ ELIZABETH BLACKWELL

Issued TAGGED 4 Plates

Plate	Price	UL	UR	LL	LR
34660	$1.50	☐	☐	☐	☐
34661	$1.50	☐	☐	☐	☐
34662	$1.50	☐	☐	☐	☐
34926	$1.50	☐	☐	☐	☐

#1289 20¢ MARSHALL 6 Plates

Issued UNTAGGED

Plate	Price	UL	UR	LL	LR
29261	$1.60	☐	☐	☐	☐
29262	$1.60	☐	☐	☐	☐
29425	$1.60	☐	☐	☐	☐
29426 o	$1.60	☐	☐	☐	☐
29773 o	$1.60	☐	☐	☐	☐
30918 o	$1.60	☐	☐	☐	☐

#1289 a 20¢ MARSHALL 13 Plates

Issued TAGGED

(See appendix A for gum and paper varieties)

Plate	Price	UL	UR	LL	LR
29426 o	$3.00	☐	☐	☐	☐
29773 o	$1.60	☐	☐	☐	☐
30918 o	$1.60	☐	☐	☐	☐
33964	$1.60	☐	☐	☐	☐
34103	$1.60	☐	☐	☐	☐

1965 REGULAR ISSUE

#1289 a 20¢ MARSHALL Continued

Plate	Price	UL	UR	LL	LR
35342	$1.60	☐	☐	☐	☐
35343	$1.60	☐	☐	☐	☐
38536	$1.60	☐	☐	☐	☐
38537	$1.60	☐	☐	☐	☐
38873	$1.60	☐	☐	☐	☐
38915	$1.60	☐	☐	☐	☐
38938	$1.60	☐	☐	☐	☐
38939	$1.60	☐	☐	☐	☐

#1400 21¢ GIANNINI 4 Plates

Issued TAGGED Only

Plate	Price	UL	UR	LL	LR
34180	$1.70	☐	☐	☐	☐
34184	$1.70	☐	☐	☐	☐
34185	$1.70	☐	☐	☐	☐
34201	$1.70	☐	☐	☐	☐

#1290 25¢ DOUGLASS 4 Plates

Issued UNTAGGED

Plate	Price	UL	UR	LL	LR
28940 o	$2.00	☐	☐	☐	☐
28946 o	$2.00	☐	☐	☐	☐
31289 o	$2.00	☐	☐	☐	☐
31290 o	$2.00	☐	☐	☐	☐

#1290 a 25¢ DOUGLASS 8 Plates

Issued TAGGED

(See appendix A for gum and paper varieties)

Plate	Price	UL	UR	LL	LR
28940 o	$4.00	☐	☐	☐	☐
28946 o	$4.00	☐	☐	☐	☐
31289 o	$2.00	☐	☐	☐	☐
31290 o	$2.00	☐	☐	☐	☐
37604	$2.00	☐	☐	☐	☐
37605	$2.00	☐	☐	☐	☐
39378	$2.00	☐	☐	☐	☐
39432	$2.00	☐	☐	☐	☐

#1291 30¢ JOHN DEWEY 4 Plates

Issued UNTAGGED

Plate	Price	UL	UR	LL	LR
30320 o	$3.50	☐	☐	☐	☐
30321 o	$3.50	☐	☐	☐	☐
31292 o	$3.50	☐	☐	☐	☐
31293 o	$3.50	☐	☐	☐	☐

#1291 a 30¢ JOHN DEWEY 4 Plates

Issued TAGGED

Plate	Price	UL	UR	LL	LR
30320 o	$2.50	☐	☐	☐	☐
30321 o	$2.50	☐	☐	☐	☐
31292 o	$2.50	☐	☐	☐	☐
31293 o	$3.50	☐	☐	☐	☐

#1292 40¢ THOMAS PAINE 4 Plates

Issued UNTAGGED

Plate	Price	UL	UR	LL	LR
29537 o	$3.25	☐	☐	☐	☐
29545 o	$3.25	☐	☐	☐	☐
31337 o	$3.25	☐	☐	☐	☐
31338 o	$3.25	☐	☐	☐	☐

#1292 a 40¢ THOMAS PAINE 8 Plates

Issued TAGGED

(See appendix A for gum and paper varieties)

Plate	Price	UL	UR	LL	LR
29537 o	$3.25	☐	☐	☐	☐
29545 o	$3.25	☐	☐	☐	☐
31337 o	$3.25	☐	☐	☐	☐
31338 o	$3.25	☐	☐	☐	☐
34074	$3.25	☐	☐	☐	☐
37044	$3.25	☐	☐	☐	☐
37045	$3.25	☐	☐	☐	☐
37046	$3.25	☐	☐	☐	☐

#1293 50¢ LUCY STONE 6 Plates

Issued UNTAGGED

Plate	Price	UL	UR	LL	LR
30133	$4.50	☐	☐	☐	☐
30134	$4.50	☐	☐	☐	☐
31588 o	$4.50	☐	☐	☐	☐
31589 o	$4.50	☐	☐	☐	☐
33077 o	$4.50	☐	☐	☐	☐
33079 o	$4.50	☐	☐	☐	☐

#1293 a 50¢ LUCY STONE 4 Plates

Issued TAGGED

Plate	Price	UL	UR	LL	LR
31588 o	$4.00	☐	☐	☐	☐
31589 o	$4.00	☐	☐	☐	☐
33077 o	$4.00	☐	☐	☐	☐
33079 o	$4.00	☐	☐	☐	☐

#1294 $1 O'NEILL 8 Plates

Issued UNTAGGED

Plate	Price	UL	UR	LL	LR
29105	$8.00	☐	☐	☐	☐
29264	$8.00	☐	☐	☐	☐
31613	$8.00	☐	☐	☐	☐
31614	$8.00	☐	☐	☐	☐
32847 o	$8.00	☐	☐	☐	☐
32848 o	$8.00	☐	☐	☐	☐
32902 o	$12.50	☐	☐	☐	☐
32903 o	$12.50	☐	☐	☐	☐

#1294 a $1 O'NEILL 8 Plates

Issued TAGGED

Plate	Price	UL	UR	LL	LR
32847 o	$8.00	☐	☐	☐	☐
32848 o	$8.00	☐	☐	☐	☐
32902 o	$12.50	☐	☐	☐	☐
32903 o	$12.50	☐	☐	☐	☐
37564	$8.00	☐	☐	☐	☐
37565	$8.00	☐	☐	☐	☐
37994	$8.00	☐	☐	☐	☐
37995	$8.00	☐	☐	☐	☐

#1295 $5 J.B. MOORE 2 Plates

Issued UNTAGGED

Plate	Price	UL	UR	LL	LR
28766 o	$40.00	☐	☐	☐	☐
28767 o	$40.00	☐	☐	☐	☐

1965 REGULAR ISSUE

#1295 a $5 J.B. MOORE 2 Plates

Issued TAGGED		UL	UR	LL	LR
28766 o	$30.00	☐	☐	☐	☐
28767 o	$30.00	☐	☐	☐	☐

BOOKLET PANE PLATES

#1278 a 1¢ JEFFERSON

PANES OF 8 Issued TAGGED

Plate numbers are located much further away from the stamps so no plate numbers were regularly issued.

#1278 b 1¢ JEFFERSON

PANES OF 4 Issued TAGGED

32904 32905 32906 32907

#1280 a 2¢ WRIGHT

PANES OF 5 Issued TAGGED

29558 29559 29561 29562

#1280 c 2¢ WRIGHT

PANES OF 6 Issued TAGGED

32966 32967 32996 32997 33985
34102 36882 36883 36884 36885

#1284 b 6¢ F.D. ROOSEVELT

PANES OF 8 Issued TAGGED

Plate numbers are located much further away from the stamps so no plate numbers were regularly issued.

BOOKLET PANE PLATES

#1284 c 6¢ F.D. ROOSEVELT

PANES OF 5 Issued TAGGED

29556 29557 29565 29566 31244

#1288 c 15¢ O.W. HOLMES

PANES OF 8 Issued TAGGED

Plate numbers are located much further away from the stamps so no plate numbers were regularly issued.

END COIL PLATES

PERF. 10 HORIZONTALLY

#1297 3¢ PARKMAN

432 Subject Plates **STRIPS OF 6**

Issued TAGGED **12 Plates**

35708 35709 35762 35763 36090
36091 36092 36093 †38423 †38483
†38492 38493

#1298 6¢ F.D. ROOSEVELT

432 Subject Plates **STRIPS OF 6**

Issued TAGGED **48 Plates**

†29138 †29139 29155 29166 29167
29168 †29171 †29172 †29175 †29176
†29178 †29179 †29188 29190 29191
29194 29195 29215 †29238 29533
†29554 †29555 29572 29573 29574
29575 †29577 †29578 29582 29583
†29584 †29585 †29606 †29607 29611
29612 29625 †29626 †29628 29629
29636 29637 29638 29639 29640
29641 29651 29652

SIDE COIL PLATES

PERF. VERTICALLY

#1299 1¢ JEFFERSON 30 Plates

432 Subject Plates **STRIPS OF 6**

Issued TAGGED

29452 29453 29460 29461 29483
29484 29489 29490 30974 30975
†32288 †32289 33404 33696 33903
33904 †37608 †37609 †37654 †37655
38427 38428 38495 38496 38550
38551 †38914 †39021 †39073 †39074

#1303 4¢ LINCOLN 14 Plates

432 Subject Plates **STRIPS OF 6**

Issued TAGGED

28271 28272 28273 28309 28699
28700 28902 28903 †28952 †28953
29024 29025 †29302 †29303

1966-81 SIDE COIL PLATE ISSUE

#1304 5¢ WASHINGTON

432 Subject Plates — STRIPS OF 6

Issued TAGGED Only — 145 Plates

†28546 †28547 28558 28559 †28563
28564 28565 †28566 28573 28574
†28583 †28584 †28585 †28586 28589
28590 28594 28595 †28596 †28597
28701 28702 28703 28704 28748
28749 28805 28806 †28811 †28812
28825 28826 28871 28872 28879
28880 †28886 †28887 †28891 †28892
28896 28897 28900 †28901 28906
†28907 28909 28910 28912 †28913

†28916 28917 28923 †28924 †28926
28927 †28928 28929 †28932 †28933
†28934 †28935 †28936 †28937 28938
†28939 28942 28943 28947 28948
28949 †28950 †28959 28960 28961
28962 28964 †28965 28973 †28974
29039 29040 29059 29060 29062
29063 29066 29067 29068 29069
29077 29078 29079 29080 29081
†29082 29083 29084 29088 28089

29108 29109 29119 29120 †29150
†29151 †29156 †29157 †29219 †29220
†29273 †29274 29281 29282 †29285
†29286 †29290 †29291 †29338 †29339
29347 29348 †29360 †29361 †29386
†29387 29402 29403 29404 29405
†29410 †29411 29415 29416 29422
29423 †39451 †39452 †39455 †39456
†39552 †39553 39555 39558 †39573

#1304C 5¢ WASHINGTON

432 Subject Plates — STRIPS OF 6

(clean shaven) — 2 Plates

Issued TAGGED Only

39479 39480

#1305 6¢ F.D. ROOSEVELT

432 Subject Plates — STRIPS OF 6

Issued TAGGED Only — 220 Plates

29663 29664 29665 29666 29667
29668 29669 29670 29671 29672
29685 29686 29687 29688 29689
29690 29696 29697 29708 29709
†29724 †29725 29734 29735 †29747
†29748 †29770 †29771 †29776 †29777
†29783 †29784 †29788 †29789 †29797
†29798 †29804 29805 †29812 †29813
†29815 29816 29828 29829 29840
29841 29848 29849 †29853 29854

29855 †29856 †29866 †29867 29883
29884 29916 29917 29937 29938
†29960 †29981 †29982 30029 †30030
30037 †30038 †30053 †30054 30066
†30067 30083 30084 †30090 †30091
†30107 †30108 †30118 †30119 30148

#1305 6¢ F.D. ROOSEVELT Cont.

†30149 30150 30151 †30158 †30159
30167 30168 30171 30172 30187
30188 30196 †30197 30214 30215
30264 30265 30292 30293 30352

30353 †30361 30362 30364 30390
†30391 30402 30403 30407 30408
†30429 †30430 30443 30444 30478
30479 30496 30497 30500 †30501
†30519 30520 30529 30530 30537
†30538 †30539 30540 30545 30546
†30549 30550 30568 †30569 †30584
†30585 30600 30601 †30639 †30640
†30661 30662 †30674 30675 30676
30677 30678 30679 30688 30689

30691 30692 30721 30722 30754
30755 30787 30788 30797 30798
30826 30827 30844 30845 †30860
30861 30869 30870 †30878 30879
30881 30882 30884 30885 †30890
†30891 †30902 †30903 †30919 †30920
30935 30936 30939 30940 30943
†30959 †30960 †30971 †30972 †31243
31342 31343 31348 31349 31362
31363 31379 31380 31421 31422

†31427 †31428 31434 31435 †31438
†31439 31445 31446 †31450 †31451
31466 31467 †31471 †31477 31535
31536 †31543 †31544 †31573 †31574

#1305E 15¢ O.W. HOLMES (DIE I)

432 Subject Plates — STRIPS OF 6

Issued TAGGED Only — 46 Plates

38625 38626 38628 38629 38645
38646 38647 38648 38679 38680
38690 38691 38760 38761 †38768
38769 38770 38775 38776 38780
38781 38782 38783 38784 †38785
38786 38814 38815 38816 38817
38818 †38819 38835 †38836 †38837
38838 38922 †38923 †38932 †38933
†38934 †38935 38961 38962 †38963
†38964

#1305 I 15¢ O.W. HOLMES (DIE II)

432 Subject Plates — STRIPS OF 6

Issued TAGGED Only — 30 Plates

38992 38993 38994 39027 †39028
†39029 †39030 39031 39041 39042
†39061 †39062 †39065 †39066 †39071
39103 39104 †39165 †39433 †39434
†39435 †39436 †39473 †39474 †39481
†39482 †39491 †39492 †39510 †39511

#1305C $1 O'NEILL — 2 Plates

432 Subject Plates — STRIPS OF 6

Issued TAGGED Only

33983 33984

1966 COMMEMORATIVES

#1306 5¢ MIGRATORY BIRDS

8 Plates

Plate	Price	UL	UR	LL	LR
28394-28395	$.50	☐	☐	☐	☐
28394-28401	$.50	☐	☐	☐	☐
28396-28395	$.50	☐	☐	☐	☐
28396-28401	$.50	☐	☐	☐	☐
28402-28408	$.50	☐	☐	☐	☐
28402-28409	$.50	☐	☐	☐	☐
28407-28408	$.50	☐	☐	☐	☐
28407-28409	$.50	☐	☐	☐	☐

#1307 5¢ HUMANE TREATMENT

9 Plates

Plate	Price	UL	UR	LL	LR
28413	$1.25	☐	☐	☐	☐
28417	$.50	☐	☐	☐	☐
28418	$.50	☐	☐	☐	☐
28419	$.50	☐	☐	☐	☐
28420	$.50	☐	☐	☐	☐
28425	$.50	☐	☐	☐	☐
28429	$.50	☐	☐	☐	☐
28462	$.50	☐	☐	☐	☐
28466	$.50	☐	☐	☐	☐

#1308 5¢ INDIANA 12 Plates

Plate	Price	UL	UR	LL	LR
28326-28365	$.50	☐	☐	☐	☐
28326-28368	$.50	☐	☐	☐	☐
28326-28375	$.50	☐	☐	☐	☐
28327-28365	$.50	☐	☐	☐	☐
28327-28368	$.50	☐	☐	☐	☐
28327-28375	$.50	☐	☐	☐	☐
28328-28334	$.50	☐	☐	☐	☐
28328-28347	$.50	☐	☐	☐	☐
28328-28348	$.50	☐	☐	☐	☐
28333-28334	$.50	☐	☐	☐	☐
28333-28347	$.50	☐	☐	☐	☐
28333-28348	$.50	☐	☐	☐	☐

#1309 5¢ CIRCUS 12 Plates

Plate	Price	UL	UR	LL	LR
28450-28460	$.50	☐	☐	☐	☐
28450-28461	$.50	☐	☐	☐	☐
28458-28460	$.50	☐	☐	☐	☐
28458-28461	$.50	☐	☐	☐	☐
28459-28460	$.50	☐	☐	☐	☐
28459-28461	$.50	☐	☐	☐	☐
28463-28467	$.50	☐	☐	☐	☐
28463-28473	$.50	☐	☐	☐	☐
28486-28467	$.50	☐	☐	☐	☐
28486-28473	$.50	☐	☐	☐	☐
28488-28467	$.50	☐	☐	☐	☐
28488-28473	$.50	☐	☐	☐	☐

#1310 5¢ SIPEX 6 Plates

Plate	Price	UL	UR	LL	LR
28468	$.50	☐	☐	☐	☐
28474	$.50	☐	☐	☐	☐
28479	$.50	☐	☐	☐	☐
28482	$.50	☐	☐	☐	☐
28522	$.50	☐	☐	☐	☐
28531	$.50	☐	☐	☐	☐

#1311 5¢ SIPEX SHEET (Imperf.)

The plate numbers of this souvenir sheet were trimmed off after printing so no plate numbers were regularly issued.

#1312 5¢ BILL OF RIGHTS

18 Plates

Plate	Price	UL	UR	LL	LR
28572-28580	$.50	☐	☐	☐	☐
28572-28582	$.50	☐	☐	☐	☐
28572-28588	$.50	☐	☐	☐	☐
28578-28580	$.50	☐	☐	☐	☐
28578-28582	$.50	☐	☐	☐	☐
28578-28588	$.50	☐	☐	☐	☐
28579-28580	$.50	☐	☐	☐	☐
28579-28582	$.50	☐	☐	☐	☐
28579-28588	$.50	☐	☐	☐	☐
28581-28593	$.50	☐	☐	☐	☐
28581-28618	$.50	☐	☐	☐	☐
28581-28621	$.50	☐	☐	☐	☐
28607-28593	$.50	☐	☐	☐	☐
28607-28618	$.50	☐	☐	☐	☐
28607-28621	$.50	☐	☐	☐	☐
28610-28593	$.50	☐	☐	☐	☐
28610-28618	$.50	☐	☐	☐	☐
28610-28621	$.50	☐	☐	☐	☐

#1313 5¢ POLISH MILLENNIUM

4 Plates

Plate	Price	UL	UR	LL	LR
28625	$.50	☐	☐	☐	☐
28626	$.50	☐	☐	☐	☐
28629	$.50	☐	☐	☐	☐
28630	$.50	☐	☐	☐	☐

#1314 5¢ NAT. PARK SERVICE

Issued UNTAGGED 6 Plates

Plate	Price	UL	UR	LL	LR
28632 o	$.50	☐	☐	☐	☐
28637 o	$.50	☐	☐	☐	☐
28642 o	$.50	☐	☐	☐	☐
28649 o	$.50	☐	☐	☐	☐
28668 o	$.50	☐	☐	☐	☐
28670 o	$.50	☐	☐	☐	☐

#1314 a 5¢ NAT. PARK SERVICE

Issued TAGGED 6 Plates

Plate	Price	UL	UR	LL	LR
28632 o	$2.00	☐	☐	☐	☐
28637 o	$10.00	☐	☐	☐	☐
28642 o	$2.00	☐	☐	☐	☐
28649 o	$2.00	☐	☐	☐	☐
28668 o	$2.00	☐	☐	☐	☐
28670 o	$4.50	☐	☐	☐	☐

#1315 5¢ MARINE CORPS RES.

Issued UNTAGGED 8 Plates

Plate	Price	UL	UR	LL	LR
28638 o	$.50	☐	☐	☐	☐
28639 o	$.50	☐	☐	☐	☐
28640 o	$.50	☐	☐	☐	☐
28646 o	$.50	☐	☐	☐	☐
28647 o	$.50	☐	☐	☐	☐

1966 COMMEMORATIVES

#1315 5¢ MARINE CORPS RES.

Issued UNTAGGED **Continued**

Plate	Price	UL	UR	LL	LR
28648 o	$.50	☐	☐	☐	☐
28720 o	$2.00	☐	☐	☐	☐
28721 o	$4.00	☐	☐	☐	☐

#1315 a 5¢ MARINE CORPS. RES.

Issued TAGGED **8 Plates**

Plate	Price	UL	UR	LL	LR
28638 o	$2.00	☐	☐	☐	☐
28639 o	$2.00	☐	☐	☐	☐
28640 o	$2.00	☐	☐	☐	☐
28646 o	$2.00	☐	☐	☐	☐
28647 o	$2.00	☐	☐	☐	☐
28648 o	$2.00	☐	☐	☐	☐
28720 o	$7.00	☐	☐	☐	☐
28721 o	$10.00	☐	☐	☐	☐

#1316 5¢ WOMEN'S CLUBS

Issued UNTAGGED **24 Plates**

Plate	Price	UL	UR	LL	LR
28705-28707 o	$.60	☐	☐	☐	☐
28705-28712 o	$.60	☐	☐	☐	☐
28705-28714 o	$.60	☐	☐	☐	☐
28706-28707 o	$.60	☐	☐	☐	☐
28706-28712 o	$.60	☐	☐	☐	☐
28706-28714 o	$.60	☐	☐	☐	☐
28708-28707 o	$.60	☐	☐	☐	☐
28708-28712 o	$.60	☐	☐	☐	☐
28708-28714 o	$.60	☐	☐	☐	☐
28711-28707 o	$.60	☐	☐	☐	☐
28711-28712 o	$.60	☐	☐	☐	☐
28711-28714 o	$.60	☐	☐	☐	☐
28713-28724 o	$.60	☐	☐	☐	☐
28713-28726 o	$.60	☐	☐	☐	☐
28713-28728 o	$.60	☐	☐	☐	☐
28715-28724 o	$.60	☐	☐	☐	☐
28715-28726 o	$.60	☐	☐	☐	☐
28715-28728 o	$.60	☐	☐	☐	☐
28722-28724 o	$.60	☐	☐	☐	☐
28722-28726 o	$.60	☐	☐	☐	☐
28722-28728 o	$.60	☐	☐	☐	☐
28723-28724 o	$.60	☐	☐	☐	☐
28723-28726 o	$.60	☐	☐	☐	☐
28723-28728 o	$.60	☐	☐	☐	☐

#1316 a 5¢ WOMEN'S CLUBS

Issued TAGGED **24 Plates**

Plate	Price	UL	UR	LL	LR
28705-28707 o	$7.50	☐	☐	☐	☐
28705-28712 o	$10.00	☐	☐	☐	☐
28705-28714 o	$2.00	☐	☐	☐	☐
28706-28707 o	$7.50	☐	☐	☐	☐
28706-28712 o	$10.00	☐	☐	☐	☐
28706-28714 o	$2.00	☐	☐	☐	☐
28708-28707 o	$7.50	☐	☐	☐	☐
28708-28712 o	$10.00	☐	☐	☐	☐
28708-28714 o	$2.00	☐	☐	☐	☐

#1316 a 5¢ WOMEN'S CLUBS Cont.

Plate	Price	UL	UR	LL	LR
28711-28707 o	$7.50	☐	☐	☐	☐
28711-28712 o	$10.00	☐	☐	☐	☐
28711-28714 o	$2.00	☐	☐	☐	☐
28713-28724 o	$2.00	☐	☐	☐	☐
28713-28726 o	$2.00	☐	☐	☐	☐
28713-28728 o	$2.00	☐	☐	☐	☐
28715-28724 o	$2.00	☐	☐	☐	☐
28715-28726 o	$2.00	☐	☐	☐	☐
28715-28728 o	$2.00	☐	☐	☐	☐
28722-28724 o	$2.00	☐	☐	☐	☐
28722-28726 o	$2.00	☐	☐	☐	☐
28722-28728 o	$2.00	☐	☐	☐	☐
28723-28724 o	$2.00	☐	☐	☐	☐
28723-28726 o	$2.00	☐	☐	☐	☐
28723-28728 o	$2.00	☐	☐	☐	☐

#1317 5¢ JOHNNY APPLESEED

Issued UNTAGGED **12 Plates**

Plate	Price	UL	UR	LL	LR
28669-28673 o	$.60	☐	☐	☐	☐
28669-28674 o	$.60	☐	☐	☐	☐
28669-28677 o	$.60	☐	☐	☐	☐
28671-28673 o	$.60	☐	☐	☐	☐
28671-28674 o	$.60	☐	☐	☐	☐
28671-28677 o	$.60	☐	☐	☐	☐
28672-28686 o	$.60	☐	☐	☐	☐
28672-28718 o	$.60	☐	☐	☐	☐
28672-28719 o	$.60	☐	☐	☐	☐
28683-28686 o	$.60	☐	☐	☐	☐
28683-28718 o	$.60	☐	☐	☐	☐
28683-28719 o	$.60	☐	☐	☐	☐

#1317 a 5¢ JOHNNY APPLESEED

Issued TAGGED **12 Plates**

Plate	Price	UL	UR	LL	LR
28669-28673 o	$5.00	☐	☐	☐	☐
28669-28674 o	$6.00	☐	☐	☐	☐
28669-28677 o	$2.00	☐	☐	☐	☐
28671-28673 o	$4.00	☐	☐	☐	☐
28671-28674 o	$4.50	☐	☐	☐	☐
28671-28677 o	$2.00	☐	☐	☐	☐
28672-28686 o	$2.00	☐	☐	☐	☐
28672-28718 o	$4.50	☐	☐	☐	☐
28672-28719 o	$5.00	☐	☐	☐	☐
28683-28686 o	$2.00	☐	☐	☐	☐
28683-28718 o	$4.50	☐	☐	☐	☐
28683-28719 o	$5.00	☐	☐	☐	☐

#1318 5¢ U.S. BEAUTIFICATION

Issued UNTAGGED **32 Plates**

Plate	Price	UL	UR	LL	LR
28727-28733 o	$.60	☐	☐	☐	☐
28727-28736 o	$.60	☐	☐	☐	☐
28727-28775 o	$.60	☐	☐	☐	☐
28727-28779 o	$.60	☐	☐	☐	☐
28727-28780	$.60	☐	☐	☐	☐
28727-28781	$.60	☐	☐	☐	☐

1966 COMMEMORATIVES

#1318 5¢ U. S. BEAUTIFICATION Continued

Plate	Price	UL	UR	LL	LR
28727-28786	$.60	☐	☐	☐	☐
28727-28788	$.60	☐	☐	☐	☐
28729-28733 o	$.60	☐	☐	☐	☐
28729-28736 o	$.60	☐	☐	☐	☐
28729-28775 o	$.60	☐	☐	☐	☐
28729-28779 o	$.60	☐	☐	☐	☐
28729-28780	$.60	☐	☐	☐	☐
28729-28781	$.60	☐	☐	☐	☐
28729-28786	$.60	☐	☐	☐	☐
28729-28788	$.60	☐	☐	☐	☐
28732-28733	$.60	☐	☐	☐	☐
28732-28736	$.60	☐	☐	☐	☐
28732-28775	$.60	☐	☐	☐	☐
28732-28779	$.60	☐	☐	☐	☐
28732-28780	$.60	☐	☐	☐	☐
28732-28781	$.60	☐	☐	☐	☐
28732-28786	$.60	☐	☐	☐	☐
28732-28788	$.60	☐	☐	☐	☐
28735-28733	$.60	☐	☐	☐	☐
28735-28736	$.60	☐	☐	☐	☐
28735-28775	$.60	☐	☐	☐	☐
28735-28779	$.60	☐	☐	☐	☐
28735-28780	$.60	☐	☐	☐	☐
28735-28781	$.60	☐	☐	☐	☐
28735-28786	$.60	☐	☐	☐	☐
28735-28788	$.60	☐	☐	☐	☐

#1318 a 5¢ U.S. BEAUTIFICATION

Issued TAGGED — 8 Plates

Plate	Price	UL	UR	LL	LR
28727-28733 o	$2.00	☐	☐	☐	☐
28727-28736 o	$2.00	☐	☐	☐	☐
28727-28775 o	$2.00	☐	☐	☐	☐
28727-28779 o	$2.00	☐	☐	☐	☐
28729-28733 o	$2.00	☐	☐	☐	☐
28729-28736 o	$2.00	☐	☐	☐	☐
28729-28775 o	$2.00	☐	☐	☐	☐
28729-28779 o	$2.00	☐	☐	☐	☐

#1319 5¢ GREAT RIVER ROAD

Issued UNTAGGED — 10 Plates

Plate	Price	UL	UR	LL	LR
28813	$.50	☐	☐	☐	☐
28816	$.50	☐	☐	☐	☐
28817	$.50	☐	☐	☐	☐
28820	$.50	☐	☐	☐	☐
28821 o	$.50	☐	☐	☐	☐
28828 o	$.50	☐	☐	☐	☐
28829 o	$.50	☐	☐	☐	☐
28840 o	$.50	☐	☐	☐	☐
28844	$.50	☐	☐	☐	☐
28884	$.50	☐	☐	☐	☐

#1319 a 5¢ GREAT RIVER ROAD

Issued TAGGED — 4 Plates

Plate	Price	UL	UR	LL	LR
28821 o	$2.00	☐	☐	☐	☐
28828 o	$2.00	☐	☐	☐	☐
28829 o	$2.00	☐	☐	☐	☐
28840 o	$2.00	☐	☐	☐	☐

#1320 5¢ SAVINGS BONDS

Issued UNTAGGED — 8 Plates

Plate	Price	UL	UR	LL	LR
28741 o	$.50	☐	☐	☐	☐
28752 o	$.50	☐	☐	☐	☐
28754 o	$.50	☐	☐	☐	☐
28759	$.50	☐	☐	☐	☐
28761	$.50	☐	☐	☐	☐
28763	$.50	☐	☐	☐	☐
28769 o	$.50	☐	☐	☐	☐
28772	$.50	☐	☐	☐	☐

#1320 a 5¢ SAVINGS BONDS

Issued TAGGED — 4 Plates

Plate	Price	UL	UR	LL	LR
28741 o	$2.00	☐	☐	☐	☐
28752 o	$2.00	☐	☐	☐	☐
28754 o	$2.00	☐	☐	☐	☐
28769 o	$2.00	☐	☐	☐	☐

#1321 5¢ CHRISTMAS 1966

Issued UNTAGGED — 29 Plates

Plate	Price	UL	UR	LL	LR
28739 o	$1.00	☐	☐	☐	☐
28740	$.50	☐	☐	☐	☐
28743 o	$.50	☐	☐	☐	☐
28745 o	$.50	☐	☐	☐	☐
28747	$2.00	☐	☐	☐	☐
28751 o	$1.00	☐	☐	☐	☐
28753 o	$.50	☐	☐	☐	☐
28756	$.50	☐	☐	☐	☐
28758 o	$.50	☐	☐	☐	☐
28760 o	$.50	☐	☐	☐	☐
28762	$.50	☐	☐	☐	☐
28768	$.50	☐	☐	☐	☐
28771	$.50	☐	☐	☐	☐
28808	$.50	☐	☐	☐	☐
28810	$.50	☐	☐	☐	☐
28815	$.50	☐	☐	☐	☐
28818	$.50	☐	☐	☐	☐
28822	$.50	☐	☐	☐	☐
28827	$.50	☐	☐	☐	☐
28830	$.50	☐	☐	☐	☐
28836	$.50	☐	☐	☐	☐
28839	$.50	☐	☐	☐	☐
28870	$.50	☐	☐	☐	☐
28875	$.50	☐	☐	☐	☐
28877	$.50	☐	☐	☐	☐
28883 o	$6.00	☐	☐	☐	☐
28889 o	$6.00	☐	☐	☐	☐
28890 o	$6.00	☐	☐	☐	☐
28893 o	$6.00	☐	☐	☐	☐

o Issued both Tagged and Plain

1966 COMMEMORATIVES

#1321 a 5¢ CHRISTMAS 1966
Issued TAGGED 11 Plates

		UL	UR	LL	LR
28739 o	$4.00	☐	☐	☐	☐
28743 o	$2.50	☐	☐	☐	☐
28745 o	$7.50	☐	☐	☐	☐
28751 o	$4.00	☐	☐	☐	☐
28753 o	$2.50	☐	☐	☐	☐
28758 o	$4.00	☐	☐	☐	☐
28760 o	$4.00	☐	☐	☐	☐
28883 o	$2.50	☐	☐	☐	☐
28889 o	$2.50	☐	☐	☐	☐
28890 o	$5.00	☐	☐	☐	☐
28893 o	$5.00	☐	☐	☐	☐

#1322 5¢ MARY CASSATT 12 Plates
Issued UNTAGGED

		UL	UR	LL	LR
28776-28793	$1.00	☐	☐	☐	☐
28776-28802	$1.00	☐	☐	☐	☐
28782-28793	$1.00	☐	☐	☐	☐
28782-28802	$1.00	☐	☐	☐	☐
28785-28793	$1.00	☐	☐	☐	☐
28785-28802	$1.00	☐	☐	☐	☐
28792-28807 o	$1.00	☐	☐	☐	☐
28792-28809 o	$1.00	☐	☐	☐	☐
28876-28807 o	$1.00	☐	☐	☐	☐
28876-28809 o	$1.00	☐	☐	☐	☐
28878-28807	$1.00	☐	☐	☐	☐
28878-28809	$1.00	☐	☐	☐	☐

#1322 a 5¢ MARY CASSATT
Issued TAGGED 4 Plates

		UL	UR	LL	LR
28792-28807 o	$4.50	☐	☐	☐	☐
28792-28809 o	$4.50	☐	☐	☐	☐
28876-28807 o	$4.50	☐	☐	☐	☐
28876-28809 o	$4.50	☐	☐	☐	☐

1967 COMMEMORATIVES

Issued TAGGED Only

#1323 5¢ NATIONAL GRANGE
8 Plates

		UL	UR	LL	LR
28951-28954	$.50	☐	☐	☐	☐
28951-28956	$.50	☐	☐	☐	☐
28955-28954	$.50	☐	☐	☐	☐
28955-28956	$.50	☐	☐	☐	☐
28957-28958	$.50	☐	☐	☐	☐
28957-28972	$.50	☐	☐	☐	☐
28963-28958	$.50	☐	☐	☐	☐
28963-28972	$.50	☐	☐	☐	☐

#1324 5¢ CANADA 42 Plates

		UL	UR	LL	LR
28979-29090	$.50	☐	☐	☐	☐
28979-29091	$.50	☐	☐	☐	☐
28979-29094	$.50	☐	☐	☐	☐
28979-29097	$.50	☐	☐	☐	☐

1967 COMMEMORATIVES

#1324 5¢ CANADA Continued

		UL	UR	LL	LR
28980-29090	$.50	☐	☐	☐	☐
28980-29091	$.50	☐	☐	☐	☐
28980-29094	$.50	☐	☐	☐	☐
28980-29097	$.50	☐	☐	☐	☐
28982-29090	$.50	☐	☐	☐	☐
28982-29091	$.50	☐	☐	☐	☐
28982-29094	$.50	☐	☐	☐	☐
28982-29097	$.50	☐	☐	☐	☐
28985-29090	$.50	☐	☐	☐	☐
28985-29091	$.50	☐	☐	☐	☐
28985-29094	$.50	☐	☐	☐	☐
28985-29097	$.50	☐	☐	☐	☐
28987-29074	$.50	☐	☐	☐	☐
28987-29075	$.50	☐	☐	☐	☐
28987-29076	$.50	☐	☐	☐	☐
28987-29086	$.50	☐	☐	☐	☐
28988-29074	$.50	☐	☐	☐	☐
28988-29075	$.50	☐	☐	☐	☐
28988-29076	$.50	☐	☐	☐	☐
28988-29086	$.50	☐	☐	☐	☐
28991-29074	$.50	☐	☐	☐	☐
28991-29075	$.50	☐	☐	☐	☐
28991-29076	$.50	☐	☐	☐	☐
28991-29086	$.50	☐	☐	☐	☐
28994-29074	$.50	☐	☐	☐	☐
28994-29075	$.50	☐	☐	☐	☐
28994-29076	$.50	☐	☐	☐	☐
28994-29086	$.50	☐	☐	☐	☐
29110-29137	$.50	☐	☐	☐	☐
29110-29146	$.50	☐	☐	☐	☐
29121-29147	$.50	☐	☐	☐	☐
29121-29153	$.50	☐	☐	☐	☐
29125-29137	$.50	☐	☐	☐	☐
29125-29146	$.50	☐	☐	☐	☐
29133-29147	$.50	☐	☐	☐	☐
29133-29153	$.50	☐	☐	☐	☐
29173-29137	$.50	☐	☐	☐	☐
29173-29146	$.50	☐	☐	☐	☐

#1325 5¢ ERIE CANAL 6 Plates

		UL	UR	LL	LR
28990	$.50	☐	☐	☐	☐
28995	$.50	☐	☐	☐	☐
28998	$.50	☐	☐	☐	☐
28999	$.50	☐	☐	☐	☐
29003	$.50	☐	☐	☐	☐
29008	$.50	☐	☐	☐	☐

#1326 5¢ SEARCH FOR PEACE
10 Plates

		UL	UR	LL	LR
29227	$.50	☐	☐	☐	☐
29239	$.50	☐	☐	☐	☐
29243	$.50	☐	☐	☐	☐
29246	$.50	☐	☐	☐	☐
29247	$.50	☐	☐	☐	☐

1967 COMMEMORATIVES

#1326 5¢ SEARCH FOR PEACE Cont.

		UL	UR	LL	LR
29248	$.50	☐	☐	☐	☐
29250	$.50	☐	☐	☐	☐
29256	$.50	☐	☐	☐	☐
29265	$.50	☐	☐	☐	☐
29266	$.50	☐	☐	☐	☐

#1327 5¢ THOREAU 8 Plates

29106	$.50	☐	☐	☐	☐
29129	$.50	☐	☐	☐	☐
29136	$.50	☐	☐	☐	☐
29140	$.50	☐	☐	☐	☐
29143	$.50	☐	☐	☐	☐
29144	$.50	☐	☐	☐	☐
29145	$.50	☐	☐	☐	☐
29148	$.50	☐	☐	☐	☐

#1328 5¢ NEBRASKA 8 Plates

29198	$.50	☐	☐	☐	☐
29199	$.50	☐	☐	☐	☐
29203	$.50	☐	☐	☐	☐
29206	$.50	☐	☐	☐	☐
29210	$.50	☐	☐	☐	☐
29216	$.50	☐	☐	☐	☐
29221	$.50	☐	☐	☐	☐
29223	$.50	☐	☐	☐	☐

#1329 5¢ VOICE OF AMERICA
4 Plates

29038	$.50	☐	☐	☐	☐
29043	$.50	☐	☐	☐	☐
29048	$.50	☐	☐	☐	☐
29052	$.50	☐	☐	☐	☐

#1330 5¢ DAVY CROCKETT 4 Plates

29222	$.50	☐	☐	☐	☐
29224	$.50	☐	☐	☐	☐
29235	$.50	☐	☐	☐	☐
29242	$.50	☐	☐	☐	☐

#1331-2 5¢ SPACE 5 Plates

29307	$4.00	☐	☐	☐	☐
29312	$4.00	☐	☐	☐	☐
29315	$4.00	☐	☐	☐	☐
29322	$4.00	☐	☐	☐	☐
29325	$4.00	☐	☐	☐	☐

#1333 5¢ URBAN RENEWAL
6 Plates

29349	$.50	☐	☐	☐	☐
29350	$.50	☐	☐	☐	☐
29359	$.50	☐	☐	☐	☐
29364	$.50	☐	☐	☐	☐
29367	$.50	☐	☐	☐	☐
29369	$.50	☐	☐	☐	☐

#1334 5¢ FINLAND 10 Plates

		UL	UR	LL	LR
29305	$.50	☐	☐	☐	☐
29306	$.50	☐	☐	☐	☐
29308	$.50	☐	☐	☐	☐
29311	$.50	☐	☐	☐	☐
29313	$.50	☐	☐	☐	☐
29314	$.50	☐	☐	☐	☐
29316	$.50	☐	☐	☐	☐
29321	$.50	☐	☐	☐	☐
29365	$.50	☐	☐	☐	☐
29366	$.50	☐	☐	☐	☐

#1335 5¢ EAKINS 12 Plates

This issue was printed at the Photogravure and Color Co. by the Gravure method.

29275-29276-29277-29278-29279-29280	$5.00	☐	☐	☐	☐
29275-29276-29277-29278-29333-29280	$1.00	☐	☐	☐	☐

#1336 5¢ CHRISTMAS 1967
42 Plates

29093	$.50	☐	☐	☐	☐
29095	$.50	☐	☐	☐	☐
29098	$.50	☐	☐	☐	☐
29099	$.50	☐	☐	☐	☐
29102	$.50	☐	☐	☐	☐
29107	$.50	☐	☐	☐	☐
29111	$.50	☐	☐	☐	☐
29149	$.50	☐	☐	☐	☐
29152	$.50	☐	☐	☐	☐
29158	$.50	☐	☐	☐	☐
29159	$.50	☐	☐	☐	☐
29162	$.50	☐	☐	☐	☐
29163	$.50	☐	☐	☐	☐
29164	$.50	☐	☐	☐	☐
29170	$.50	☐	☐	☐	☐
29174	$.50	☐	☐	☐	☐
29177	$.50	☐	☐	☐	☐
29193	$.50	☐	☐	☐	☐
29197	$.50	☐	☐	☐	☐
29200	$.50	☐	☐	☐	☐
29288	$.50	☐	☐	☐	☐
29289	$.50	☐	☐	☐	☐
29293	$.50	☐	☐	☐	☐
29296	$.50	☐	☐	☐	☐
29304	$2.00	☐	☐	☐	☐
29358	$.50	☐	☐	☐	☐
29396	$.50	☐	☐	☐	☐
29399	$.50	☐	☐	☐	☐
29400	$.50	☐	☐	☐	☐
29401	$.50	☐	☐	☐	☐
29412	$2.25	☐	☐	☐	☐
29413	$2.25	☐	☐	☐	☐
29414	$5.50	☐	☐	☐	☐

1967 COMMEMORATIVES

Issued TAGGED Only

#1336 5¢ CHRISTMAS 1967 Cont.

Plate	Price	UL	UR	LL	LR
29417	$2.25				
29418	$.50				
29419	$.50				
29430	$2.00				
29431	$.50				
29432	$.50				
29433	$.50				
29434	$.50				
29435	$3.00				

#1337 5¢ MISSISSIPPI 12 Plates

Plate	Price	UL	UR	LL	LR
29375-29376	$.50				
29375-29383	$.50				
29377-29376	$.50				
29377-29383	$.50				
29384-29388	$.50				
29384-29394	$.50				
29391-29388	$.50				
29391-29394	$.50				
29420-29424	$.50				
29420-29427	$.50				
29421-29424	$.50				
29421-29427	$.50				

1968-71 REGULAR ISSUE

Issued TAGGED Only

#1338 6¢ U. S. FLAG Perf. 11
118 Plates (Giori Printing)

Plate	Price	UL	UR	LL	LR
29604	$.60				
29605	$2.00				
29610	$.60				
29613	$2.00				
29616	$.60				
29617	$3.00				
29618	$.60				
29619	$.60				
29620	$.60				
29621	$3.00				
29624	$.60				
29630	$.60				
29633	$.60				
29634	$3.00				
29635	$.60				
29643	$2.50				
29649	$.60				
29655	$2.50				
29656	$.60				
29657	$.60				
29658	$2.50				
29659	$.60				
29662	$.60				

1968-71 REGULAR ISSUE Cont.

Issued TAGGED Only

#1338 6¢ U. S. FLAG Continued

Plate	Price	UL	UR	LL	LR
29702	$.60				
29707	$.60				
29715	$.60				
29717	$.60				
29718	$.60				
29722	$2.50				
29728	$.60				
29737	$.60				
29749	$3.00				
29757	$.60				
29794	$.60				
29795	$.60				
29801	$.60				
29807	$3.00				
29811	$.60				
29845	$.60				
29857	$.60				
30088	$.60				
30089	$.60				
30104	$.60				
30111	$.60				
30116	$.60				
30146	$.60				
30166	$.60				
30179	$.60				
30180	$3.00				
30195	$.60				
30213	$.60				
30223	$3.00				
30236	$.60				
30243	$.60				
30256	$.60				
30279	$.60				
30289	$.60				
30291	$3.00				
30302	$.60				
30312	$2.50				
30317	$3.50				
30322	$3.50				
30503	$.60				
30543	$.60				
30547	$4.00				
30548	$.60				
30551	$6.00				
30654	$3.00				
30681	$.60				
30685	$.60				
30687	$5.00				
30690	$.60				
30703	$.60				
30704	$.60				
30756	$3.00				
30793	$.60				
30799	$.60				
30804	$.60				
30806	$3.00				

1968-71 REGULAR ISSUE

Issued TAGGED Only

#1338 6¢ U. S. FLAG Perf. 11

		UL	UR	LL	LR
30815	$.60	□	□	□	□
30816	$.60	□	□	□	□
30836	$.60	□	□	□	□
30843	$7.50	□	□	□	□
30850	$.60	□	□	□	□
30859	$6.00	□	□	□	□
30862	$.60	□	□	□	□
30871	$.60	□	□	□	□
30954	$.60	□	□	□	□
30957	$.60	□	□	□	□
30958	$5.00	□	□	□	□
30964	$.60	□	□	□	□
30967	$5.00	□	□	□	□
30970	$.60	□	□	□	□
31138	$.60	□	□	□	□
31151	$.60	□	□	□	□
31245	$.60	□	□	□	□
31313	$.60	□	□	□	□
31315	$.60	□	□	□	□
31317	$.60	□	□	□	□
31339	$2.00	□	□	□	□
31340	$2.50	□	□	□	□
31341	$1.50	□	□	□	□
31468	$.60	□	□	□	□
31469	$.60	□	□	□	□
31470	$.60	□	□	□	□
31473	$.60	□	□	□	□
31476	$.60	□	□	□	□
31479	$.60	□	□	□	□
31637	$.60	□	□	□	□
31657	$.60	□	□	□	□
31660	$.60	□	□	□	□
31661	$3.00	□	□	□	□
31662	$5.00	□	□	□	□
31677	$.60	□	□	□	□
31755	$6.00	□	□	□	□
31762	$6.00	□	□	□	□
31871	$.60	□	□	□	□
31880	$.60	□	□	□	□

#1338 A 6¢ U. S. FLAG COIL
(Huck Printing)

Very few reported with enough of the plate number to identify.

#1338 D 6¢ U.S. FLAG
(Huck Printing) PERF. 11 x 10½

Positions T, B only **135 Plates**

Basic Price
Block of 20 (10 x 2) $2.50

HUCK PRESS PRINTING

It is possible to collect both the top and the bottom plate strips in four different combinations. Using Z to represent the Zip Code; M to represent Mail Early; N to represent the plate number and B to represent a Blank Tab, the following are the margin positions reading from left to right in a plate block of 20.

1) Z N B M Z N B M Z N
2) N B M Z N B M Z N B
3) B M Z N B M Z N B M
4) M Z N B M Z N B M Z

31816	31817	31818	31819	31820
31821	31828	31829	31830	*31831
31832	31833	31842	31843	31844
31845	31846	31847	31856	31857
31858	31859	31860	31861	31864
31866	31867	31868	31869	31874
31875	31876	31877	31878	31879
31882	31883	31884	31885	31886
31887	32065	32066	32067	32068
32069	32072	32073	32074	32075
32076	32077	32078	32079	32080
32081	32082	32083	32084	32085
32086	32087	32088	32089	32092
32093	32094	32095	32096	32098
32099	32100	32101	32102	32103
32110	32111	32112	32113	32114
32115	32121	32122	32123	32124
32125	32126	32132	32133	32134
32135	32136	32137	32139	*32140
32141	*32142	*32143	32144	*32156
32157	32158	32159	32160	*32161
32164	32165	32166	32167	*32168
†32169	32173	32174	*32175	32176
32177	*32178	32181	32182	32183
32184	32185	32186	32188	*32189
*32190	32191	32192	32193	*32195
32196	32197	*32198	*32199	32200

#1338 F 8¢ U. S. FLAG
(Huck Printing) PERF. 11 x 10½

Positions T, B only **145 Plates**

Basic Price
Block of 20 (10 x 2) $3.75

HUCK PRESS PRINTING

It is possible to collect both the top and the bottom plate strips in four different combinations. Using Z to represent the Zip Code; M to represent Mail Early; N to represent the Plate Number and B to represent a Blank Tab, the following are the margin positions reading from left to right in a plate block of 20.

1) Z N B M Z N B M Z N
2) N B M Z N B M Z N B
3) B M Z N B M Z N B M
4) M Z N B M Z N B M Z

1968-71 REGULAR ISSUE

#1338 F 8¢ U. S. FLAG Continued

32547	32548	32549	32550	32551
32552	32554	32555	32556	32557
32558	32559	32568	32569	32570
32571	32572	32573	32584	32585
32586	32587	32588	32589	32597
32598	32599	32600	32601	32602
32611	32612	32613	32614	32615
32616	32626	32627	32628	32629
32630	32631	32639	32640	32641
32642	32643	32644	32655	32656
32657	32658	32659	32660	32668
32669	32670	32671	32672	32673
32681	32682	32683	32684	32685
32686	32695	32696	32697	32698
32699	32700	32730	32731	32732
32733	32734	32735	32745	32746
32747	32748	32749	32750	32762
32763	32764	32765	32766	32767
32794	32795	32796	32797	32798
32799	32811	32812	32813	32814
32815	32816	32824	32825	32826
32827	32828	32829	†32839	32840
32841	32842	32843	32844	32861
32862	32863	32864	32865	32866
32878	32879	32880	32881	32882
32883	32896	32897	32898	32899
†32900	32901	33659	33660	33661
33662	†33663	†33664	33668	33669
†33670	33671	33672	33673	33676
†33677	*33678	33679	†33680	†33681
†33720	†33721	†33722	†33723	†33724
†33725	†33867	†33868	†33870	†33871
†33872	†33875	†33876	†33877	†33878
†33879				

#1338 G 8¢ U.S. FLAG COIL
(Huck Printing)

Very few reported with enough of the plate number to identify.

1968 COMMEMORATIVES

#1339 6¢ ILLINOIS 6 Plates

		UL	UR	LL	LR
29560	$.60	☐	☐	☐	☐
29570	$.60	☐	☐	☐	☐
29571	$.60	☐	☐	☐	☐
29576	$.60	☐	☐	☐	☐
29586	$.60	☐	☐	☐	☐
29590	$.60	☐	☐	☐	☐

1968 COMMEMORATIVES

#1340 6¢ HEMISFAIR 9 Plates

Issued TAGGED		UL	UR	LL	LR
29712	$.60	☐	☐	☐	☐
29716	$.60	☐	☐	☐	☐
29723	$.60	☐	☐	☐	☐
29731	$.60	☐	☐	☐	☐
29738	$.60	☐	☐	☐	☐
29742	$.60	☐	☐	☐	☐
29751	$.60	☐	☐	☐	☐
29753	$.60	☐	☐	☐	☐
29768	$.60	☐	☐	☐	☐

#1341 $1 AIRLIFT 8 Plates

Issued UNTAGGED

29761	*$13.50*	☐	☐	☐	☐
29762	*$13.50*	☐	☐	☐	☐
29763	*$13.50*	☐	☐	☐	☐
29766	*$13.50*	☐	☐	☐	☐
29769	*$13.50*	☐	☐	☐	☐
29774	*$13.50*	☐	☐	☐	☐
29779	*$13.50*	☐	☐	☐	☐
29781	*$13.50*	☐	☐	☐	☐

#1342 6¢ SUPPORT OUR YOUTH

Issued TAGGED **6 Plates**

29814	$.60	☐	☐	☐	☐
29817	$.60	☐	☐	☐	☐
29824	$.60	☐	☐	☐	☐
29830	$.60	☐	☐	☐	☐
29834	$.60	☐	☐	☐	☐
29837	$.60	☐	☐	☐	☐

#1343 6¢ LAW AND ORDER

Issued TAGGED **9 Plates**

29833	$.60	☐	☐	☐	☐
29835	$.60	☐	☐	☐	☐
29836	$.60	☐	☐	☐	☐
29839	$.60	☐	☐	☐	☐
29843	$.60	☐	☐	☐	☐
29846	$.60	☐	☐	☐	☐
29847	$.60	☐	☐	☐	☐
29851	$.60	☐	☐	☐	☐
29946	$.60	☐	☐	☐	☐

#1344 6¢ REGISTER & VOTE

Issued TAGGED **7 Plates**

29760	$.60	☐	☐	☐	☐
29764	$.60	☐	☐	☐	☐
29782	$.60	☐	☐	☐	☐
29786	$.60	☐	☐	☐	☐
29823	$.60	☐	☐	☐	☐
29996	$.60	☐	☐	☐	☐
30055	$.60	☐	☐	☐	☐

#1345-54 6¢ HISTORIC FLAGS

Issued TAGGED **10 Plates**

Block of 4

29995	$1.75	☐	☐	☐	☐
30028	$1.75	☐	☐	☐	☐

1968 COMMEMORATIVES

#1345-54 6¢ HISTORIC FLAGS Cont.

Block of 4		UL	UR	LL	LR
30045	$1.75	☐	☐	☐	☐
30052	$1.75	☐	☐	☐	☐
30074	$1.75	☐	☐	☐	☐
30085	$1.75	☐	☐	☐	☐
30306	$1.75	☐	☐	☐	☐
30311	$1.75	☐	☐	☐	☐
30705	$1.75	☐	☐	☐	☐
30706	$1.75	☐	☐	☐	☐

#1355 6¢ WALT DISNEY TAGGED

This issue was printed by the Achrovure Division of the Union-Camp Corp.

30006-30008-30009-30010-30012	$1.00	☐	☐	☐	☐
N 30006-30008-30009-30010-30012-	$1.00	☐	☐	☐	☐

#1356 6¢ FR. MARQUETTE

Issued TAGGED — 6 Plates

30120	$.60	☐	☐	☐	☐
30121	$.60	☐	☐	☐	☐
30123	$.60	☐	☐	☐	☐
30124	$.60	☐	☐	☐	☐
30135	$.60	☐	☐	☐	☐
30147	$.60	☐	☐	☐	☐

#1357 6¢ DANIEL BOONE

Issued TAGGED — 7 Plates

30257	$.60	☐	☐	☐	☐
30266	$.60	☐	☐	☐	☐
30280	$.60	☐	☐	☐	☐
30294	$.60	☐	☐	☐	☐
30301	$.60	☐	☐	☐	☐
30303	$.60	☐	☐	☐	☐
30341	$.60	☐	☐	☐	☐

#1358 6¢ ARKANSAS RIVER

Issued TAGGED — 8 Plates

30326	$.60	☐	☐	☐	☐
30327	$.60	☐	☐	☐	☐
30328	$.60	☐	☐	☐	☐
30329	$.60	☐	☐	☐	☐
30334	$.60	☐	☐	☐	☐
30337	$.60	☐	☐	☐	☐
30338	$.60	☐	☐	☐	☐
30339	$.60	☐	☐	☐	☐

#1359 6¢ ERIKSON — 8 Plates

Issued TAGGED

30435	$.60	☐	☐	☐	☐
30436	$.60	☐	☐	☐	☐
30445	$.60	☐	☐	☐	☐
30446	$.60	☐	☐	☐	☐
30447	$.60	☐	☐	☐	☐
30458	$.60	☐	☐	☐	☐
30471	$.60	☐	☐	☐	☐
30480	$.60	☐	☐	☐	☐

N With Hyphen After Plate Numbers

#1360 6¢ CHEROKEE STRIP

Issued TAGGED — 4 Plates

		UL	UR	LL	LR
30371	$.60	☐	☐	☐	☐
30372	$.60	☐	☐	☐	☐
30388	$.60	☐	☐	☐	☐
30389	$.60	☐	☐	☐	☐

#1361 6¢ TRUMBULL — 8 Plates

Issued TAGGED

30383	$.80	☐	☐	☐	☐
30385	$.80	☐	☐	☐	☐
30386	$.80	☐	☐	☐	☐
30387	$.80	☐	☐	☐	☐
30392	$.80	☐	☐	☐	☐
30393	$.80	☐	☐	☐	☐
30406	$.80	☐	☐	☐	☐
30415	$.80	☐	☐	☐	☐

#1362 6¢ WATERFOWL — 6 Plates

Issued TAGGED

30347	$1.00	☐	☐	☐	☐
30350	$1.00	☐	☐	☐	☐
30351	$1.00	☐	☐	☐	☐
30358	$1.00	☐	☐	☐	☐
30360	$1.00	☐	☐	☐	☐
30370	$1.00	☐	☐	☐	☐

#1363 6¢ CHRISTMAS 1968 (Huck)

Issued TAGGED and UNTAGGED

Positions L, R only

Basic Price
Block of 10 (2 x 5) LS, RS — $1.50

YELLOW PLATES — 30 plates

29868	29869	29870	29871	29872
29873	29893	29894	29895	29896
29910	29912	29913	29914	29915
29926	29950	29951	29952	29983
29984	29985	29986	29987	30022
30023	30024	30025	30026	30027

BLUE PLATES — 116 Plates

29897	29898	29899	†29923	29939
29940	29941	29942	29944	29962
29965	29966	29967	29975	29977
29979	29999	30000	30001	30002
30004	30031	30032	30033	30034
30035	30036	30056	30057	30058
30059	30060	30061	30077	30078
30079	30080	30081	30082	30098
30099	30100	30101	30102	30103
30127	30128	30129	30130	30131
30132	30152	30153	30154	30155
30156	30157	30173	30174	30175
30176	30177	30178	30189	30190
30191	30192	30193	30194	30207
30208	30209	30210	30211	30212

1968 COMMEMORATIVES

#1363 6¢ CHRISTMAS 1968 (Huck)

BLUE PLATES Continued

30217	30218	30219	30220	30221
30222	30230	30231	30232	30233
30234	30235	30244	*30245	30246
30247	30248	30249	30423	30424
30425	*30426	*30427	†30428	30437
30438	30439	30440	30441	30442
30472	30473	30475	30476	30477
30487	30488	30489	30490	†30491
30492				

BROWN PLATES **160 Plates**

29885	29886	29887	29888	29889
29890	29904	29905	29906	29907
29908	29909	29931	29932	29933
29934	29935	29936	29953	29954
29955	29956	29957	29958	29969
29970	29971	29972	29973	29974
29990	29991	30016	30017	30018
30019	30020	30021	30039	30040
30041	30042	30043	30044	30068
30069	30070	30071	30072	30073
30092	30093	30094	30095	30096
30097	30160	30161	30162	30181
30182	30183	30184	30185	30186
30224	30225	30226	30227	30228
30229	30237	30238	30239	30240
30241	30250	30251	30252	30253
30254	30255	30258	30259	30260
30261	30262	30263	30267	30268
30269	30270	30271	30272	30273
30274	30275	30276	30277	30278
30283	30284	30285	30286	30287
30288	30295	30296	30297	30298
30299	30300	30394	*30395	*30396
30397	30398	30399	*30416	30417
30418	30419	30420	*30421	30449
30450	30451	*30452	30453	30454
30460	30461	30462	30463	30464
30465	30523	30524	30525	30526
30527	30528	*30531	30532	30533
30534	30535	30536	30560	30561
30562	30563	*30564	30565	30577
*30578	*30579	30580	*30581	*30582

#1364 6¢ AMERICAN INDIAN

Issued TAGGED **6 Plates**

		UL	UR	LL	LR
30448	$1.00	☐	☐	☐	☐
30459	$1.00	☐	☐	☐	☐
30481	$1.00	☐	☐	☐	☐
30493	$1.00	☐	☐	☐	☐
30495	$1.00	☐	☐	☐	☐
30499	$1.00	☐	☐	☐	☐

1969 COMMEMORATIVES

Issued TAGGED Only

#1365-8 6¢ CIVIC BEAUTY 14 Plates

		UL	UR	LL	LR
30583	$3.00	☐	☐	☐	☐
30586	$3.00	☐	☐	☐	☐
30587	$3.00	☐	☐	☐	☐
30588	$3.00	☐	☐	☐	☐
30593	$3.00	☐	☐	☐	☐
30607	$3.00	☐	☐	☐	☐
30626	$3.00	☐	☐	☐	☐
30627	$3.00	☐	☐	☐	☐
30660	$3.00	☐	☐	☐	☐
30663	$3.00	☐	☐	☐	☐
30664	$3.00	☐	☐	☐	☐
30665	$3.00	☐	☐	☐	☐
30668	$3.00	☐	☐	☐	☐
30671	$3.00	☐	☐	☐	☐

#1369 6¢ AMERICAN LEGION

8 Plates

30759	$.60	☐	☐	☐	☐
30769	$.60	☐	☐	☐	☐
30782	$.60	☐	☐	☐	☐
30783	$.60	☐	☐	☐	☐
30786	$.60	☐	☐	☐	☐
30789	$.60	☐	☐	☐	☐
30790	$.60	☐	☐	☐	☐
30825	$.60	☐	☐	☐	☐

#1370 6¢ GRANDMA MOSES

10 Plates

30886	$.60	☐	☐	☐	☐
30889	$.60	☐	☐	☐	☐
30900	$.60	☐	☐	☐	☐
30901	$.60	☐	☐	☐	☐
30904	$.60	☐	☐	☐	☐
30921	$.60	☐	☐	☐	☐
30930	$.60	☐	☐	☐	☐
30933	$.60	☐	☐	☐	☐
30985	$.60	☐	☐	☐	☐
30986	$.60	☐	☐	☐	☐

#1371 6¢ APOLLO 8 8 Plates

30923	$.60	☐	☐	☐	☐
30931	$.60	☐	☐	☐	☐
30932	$.60	☐	☐	☐	☐
30934	$.60	☐	☐	☐	☐
30937	$.60	☐	☐	☐	☐
30938	$.60	☐	☐	☐	☐
30941	$.60	☐	☐	☐	☐
30945	$.60	☐	☐	☐	☐

#1372 6¢ W.C. HANDY 8 Plates

30707	$.60	☐	☐	☐	☐
30714	$.60	☐	☐	☐	☐
30725	$.60	☐	☐	☐	☐
30732	$.60	☐	☐	☐	☐
30735	$.60	☐	☐	☐	☐
30744	$.60	☐	☐	☐	☐
30751	$.60	☐	☐	☐	☐
30760	$.60	☐	☐	☐	☐

1969 COMMEMORATIVES

#1373 6¢ CALIFORNIA 10 Plates

		UL	UR	LL	LR
31016	$.60				
31030	$.60				
31043	$.60				
31064	$.60				
31078	$.60				
31095	$.60				
31105	$.60				
31124	$.60				
31262	$.60				
31268	$.60				

#1374 6¢ J.W. POWELL 8 Plates

31160	$.60				
31173	$.60				
31174	$.60				
31175	$.60				
31182	$.60				
31189	$.60				
31202	$.60				
31211	$.60				

#1375 6¢ ALABAMA 8 Plates

31275	$.60				
31276	$.60				
31277	$.60				
31288	$.60				
31291	$.60				
31300	$.60				
31304	$.60				
31312	$.60				

#1376-9 6¢ BOTANICAL CONGRESS 8 Plates

30973	$4.50				
30977	$4.50				
30983	$4.50				
30984	$4.50				
30993	$4.50				
30996	$4.50				
30997	$4.50				
31004	$4.50				

#1380 6¢ DANIEL WEBSTER 4 Plates

31056	$.60				
31057	$.60				
31079	$.60				
31080	$.60				

#1381 6¢ BASEBALL 9 Plates

31399	$1.50				
31402	$1.50				
31404	$1.50				
31407	$1.50				
31409	$1.50				

#1381 6¢ BASEBALL Continued

		UL	UR	LL	LR
31410	$1.50				
31413	$1.50				
31414	$1.50				
31436	$1.50				

#1382 6¢ FOOTBALL 8 Plates

31383	$1.00				
31386	$1.00				
31389	$1.00				
31391	$1.00				
31398	$1.00				
31403	$1.00				
31406	$1.00				
31408	$1.00				

#1383 6¢ EISENHOWER 8 Plates

31423	$.60				
31424	$.60				
31426	$.60				
31429	$.60				
31430	$.60				
31431	$.60				
31432	$.60				
31433	$.60				

#1384 6¢ CHRISTMAS 1969 (Huck)

Issued TAGGED

Basic Price	Positions T, B only
Block of 10 (5 x 2) T, B	$1.50

RED PLATES **65 plates**

31024	31025	31026	31027	31028
31029	31044	31045	31047	31048
31049	31050	31051	31052	31053
31054	31055	31066	31067	31068
31069	31070	31071	31083	31084
31085	31086	31087	31088	31096
31097	31098	31099	31100	31101
31145	31146	31147	31148	31149
31150	31161	31162	31163	31164
31165	31166	31176	31177	31178
31179	31180	31181	31190	31191
31192	31193	31194	31195	31205
31206	31207	31208	31209	31210

GREEN PLATES **119 Plates**

31031	31032	31033	31034	31035
31036	31037	31038	31039	31040
31041	31042	31058	31059	31060
31061	31062	31063	31072	31073
31074	31075	31076	31077	31089
31090	31091	31092	31093	31094
31106	31107	31108	31109	31110
31111	31112	31113	31114	31115
31117	31118	31119	31120	31121
31122	31123	31125	31126	31127
31128	31129	31130	31132	31133
31134	31135	31136	31137	31139
31140	31141	31142	31144	31152

1969 COMMEMORATIVES

#1384 6¢ CHRISTMAS 1969 (Huck)

GREEN PLATES Continued

31153	31154	31155	31156	31157
31167	31168	31169	31170	31171
31172	31183	31184	31185	31186
31187	31188	31196	31212	31213
31214	31215	31216	31217	31224
31225	31226	31227	31228	31229
31236	31237	31238	31239	31240
31241	31256	31257	31258	31259
31260	31261	31269	31270	31271
31272	31273	31274	31294	31295
31296	31297	31298	31299	

#1385 6¢ CRIPPLED CHILDREN

Blocks of 4		UL	UR	LL	LR
31447	$.60	☐	☐	☐	☐
31448	$.60	☐	☐	☐	☐
31449	$.60	☐	☐	☐	☐
31452	$.60	☐	☐	☐	☐
31455	$.60	☐	☐	☐	☐
31456	$.60	☐	☐	☐	☐
31461	$.60	☐	☐	☐	☐
31464	$.60	☐	☐	☐	☐

#1386 6¢ WILLIAM M. HARNETT

14 Plates

31486	$.60	☐	☐	☐	☐
31488	$.60	☐	☐	☐	☐
31489	$.60	☐	☐	☐	☐
31493	$.60	☐	☐	☐	☐
31494	$.60	☐	☐	☐	☐
31496	$.60	☐	☐	☐	☐
31502	$.60	☐	☐	☐	☐
31503	$.60	☐	☐	☐	☐
31505	$.60	☐	☐	☐	☐
31508	$.60	☐	☐	☐	☐
31509	$.60	☐	☐	☐	☐
31511	$.60	☐	☐	☐	☐
31512	$.60	☐	☐	☐	☐
31513	$.60	☐	☐	☐	☐

1970 COMMEMORATIVES

Issued TAGGED Only

#1387-90 6¢ NATURAL HISTORY

16 Plates		UL	UR	LL	LR
31678	$.75	☐	☐	☐	☐
31686	$.75	☐	☐	☐	☐
31702	$.75	☐	☐	☐	☐
31711	$.75	☐	☐	☐	☐
31720	$.75	☐	☐	☐	☐
31728	$.75	☐	☐	☐	☐
31729	$.75	☐	☐	☐	☐
31736	$.75	☐	☐	☐	☐
31834	$.75	☐	☐	☐	☐

1970 COMMEMORATIVES

#1387-90 6¢ NATURAL HISTORY

Continued		UL	UR	LL	LR
31848	$.75	☐	☐	☐	☐
31862	$.75	☐	☐	☐	☐
31870	$.75	☐	☐	☐	☐
31888	$.75	☐	☐	☐	☐
31889	$.75	☐	☐	☐	☐
31929	$1.75	☐	☐	☐	☐
31930	$1.75	☐	☐	☐	☐

#1391 6¢ MAINE 8 Plates

31951	$.60	☐	☐	☐	☐
31957	$.60	☐	☐	☐	☐
31958	$.60	☐	☐	☐	☐
31963	$.60	☐	☐	☐	☐
31968	$.60	☐	☐	☐	☐
31969	$.60	☐	☐	☐	☐
31983	$.60	☐	☐	☐	☐
31992	$.60	☐	☐	☐	☐

#1392 6¢ BUFFALO 4 Plates

31959	$.60	☐	☐	☐	☐
31960	$.60	☐	☐	☐	☐
31977	$.60	☐	☐	☐	☐
31978	$.60	☐	☐	☐	☐

1970-71 REGULAR ISSUE

Issued TAGGED Only

#1393 6¢ EISENHOWER 12 Plates

(See appendix regarding gum and paper varieties)

		UL	UR	LL	LR
31919	$.60	☐	☐	☐	☐
31920	$.60	☐	☐	☐	☐
31927	$.60	☐	☐	☐	☐
31928	$.60	☐	☐	☐	☐
31934	$.60	☐	☐	☐	☐
31935	$.60	☐	☐	☐	☐
31947	$.60	☐	☐	☐	☐
31948	$.60	☐	☐	☐	☐
32007	$.60	☐	☐	☐	☐
32008	$.60	☐	☐	☐	☐
32050	$.60	☐	☐	☐	☐
32051	$.60	☐	☐	☐	☐

#1393 D 7¢ FRANKLIN

See Page 169

#1394 8¢ EISENHOWER 68 Plates

32694	$.65	☐	☐	☐	☐
32701	$.65	☐	☐	☐	☐
32724	$.65	☐	☐	☐	☐
32725	$.65	☐	☐	☐	☐
32736	$.65	☐	☐	☐	☐
32743	$.65	☐	☐	☐	☐
32744	$.65	☐	☐	☐	☐
32751	$.65	☐	☐	☐	☐
32768	$.65	☐	☐	☐	☐
32769	$.65	☐	☐	☐	☐

1970-71 REGULAR ISSUE

#1394 8¢ EISENHOWER Continued

		UL	UR	LL	LR
32778	$.65	☐	☐	☐	☐
32779	$.65	☐	☐	☐	☐
32780	$.65	☐	☐	☐	☐
32781	$.65	☐	☐	☐	☐
32784	$.65	☐	☐	☐	☐
32785	$.65	☐	☐	☐	☐
32800	$.65	☐	☐	☐	☐
32817	$.65	☐	☐	☐	☐
32830	$.65	☐	☐	☐	☐
32845	$.65	☐	☐	☐	☐
32846	$.65	☐	☐	☐	☐
32867	$.65	☐	☐	☐	☐
32930	$.65	☐	☐	☐	☐
32933	$.65	☐	☐	☐	☐
33011	—	☐	☐	☐	☐
33026	$.65	☐	☐	☐	☐
33061	$.65	☐	☐	☐	☐
33063	*$17.50*	☐[2]	☐	☐	☐[2]
33071	$.65	☐	☐	☐	☐
33078	$.65	☐	☐	☐	☐
33135	$.65	☐	☐	☐	☐
33163	$.65	☐	☐	☐	☐
33230	$.65	☐	☐	☐	☐
33232	$.65	☐	☐	☐	☐
33373	*$12.00*	☐	☐	☐	☐[8]
33377	$.65	☐	☐	☐	☐
33381	$.65	☐	☐	☐	☐
33382	$.65	☐	☐	☐	☐
33385	$.65	☐	☐	☐	☐
33394	$.65	☐	☐	☐	☐
33400	*$12.00*	☐	☐	☐	☐
33445	*$13.50*	☐	☐	☐	☐
33446	*$22.00*	☐	☐	☐	☐
33490	$.65	☐	☐	☐	☐
33506	$.65	☐	☐	☐	☐
33507	$.65	☐	☐	☐	☐
33514	$.65	☐	☐	☐	☐
33515	$.65	☐	☐	☐	☐
33525		†	†	†	†
33531	$.65	☐	☐	☐	☐
33543	$.65	☐	☐	☐	☐
33553	$.65	☐	☐	☐	☐
33572	$.65	☐	☐	☐	☐
33581		†	†	†	†
33582	$.65	☐	☐	☐	☐
33598	$.65	☐	☐	☐	☐
33667	$.65	☐	☐	☐	☐
33674	$.65	☐	☐	☐	☐
33682	$.65	☐	☐	☐	☐
33685	$.65	☐	☐	☐	☐
33686	$.65	☐	☐	☐	☐
33687	$.65	☐	☐	☐	☐
33838	$2.00	☐	☐	☐	☐
34037	$.65	☐	☐	☐	☐
34073	$.65	☐	☐	☐	☐
34152	*$17.50*	☐	☐	☐	☐
38120	*$5.00*	☐	☐	☐	☐
38126	*$5.00*	☐	☐	☐	☐

BOOKLET PANES

#1393 a 6¢ EISENHOWER
PANES OF 8

Plate numbers are located much further away from the stamps. Only a few fold-overs have been reported.

#1393 b 6¢ EISENHOWER
PANES OF 5

31955 31956

#1395 a 8¢ EISENHOWER
PANES OF 8

Plate numbers are located much further away from the stamps. Only a few fold-overs have been reported.

#1395 b 8¢ EISENHOWER
PANES OF 6

32908 32909 32910 32911

#1395 c 8¢ EISENHOWER
PANES OF 4

Plate numbers are located much further away from the stamps.

Unreported

SHEET STAMPS

#1396 8¢ U.S. POSTAL SERVICE

Block of 12 (2 x 6)		UL	UR	LL	LR
32918-32919-32920-32921-32922-32923	$6.00	☐	☐	☐	☐
32924-32925-32926-32927-32928-32929	$6.00	☐	☐	☐	☐

#1397 14¢ LaGUARDIA

See page 173

#1398 16¢ ERNIE PYLE

See page 173

#1399 18¢ ELIZABETH BLACKWELL

See page 173

#1400 21¢ GIANNINI

See page 174

SIDE COIL PLATES

#1401 6¢ EISENHOWER

432 Subject Plates STRIPS OF 6

†31936 †31937 31949 31950 †31953
†31954 †31966 †31967 32036 †32037
†32339 †32372 †32373 †32395 †32396
†32470 †32471

1970-71 REGULAR ISSUE SIDE COIL PLATES Cont.

#1402 8¢ EISENHOWER

432 Subject Plates **STRIPS OF 6**

32714	32726	32727	32752	32753
32754	32755	32756	32757	32774
32775	32776	32777	32782	32783
32793	32801	32802	32803	32804
32831	32832	32849	32850	32857
32858	32859	†32860	32870	32871
†32884	†32885	33410	33435	33436
33437	†33455	33456	33516	33517
†33539	33540	33791	33792	†33873
†33889	33890	†33962	†33963	†34038
†34039	34052	34093	†34150	

1970 COMMEMORATIVES

Issued TAGGED Only

#1405 6¢ E.L. MASTERS 7 Plates

		UL	UR	LL	LR
31685	$.60	☐	☐	☐	☐
31687	$.60	☐	☐	☐	☐
31694	$.60	☐	☐	☐	☐
31701	$.60	☐	☐	☐	☐
31703	$.60	☐	☐	☐	☐
31712	$.60	☐	☐	☐	☐
31719	$.60	☐	☐	☐	☐

#1406 6¢ WOMAN SUFFRAGE

8 Plates

32131	$.60	☐	☐	☐	☐
32138	$.60	☐	☐	☐	☐
32155	$.60	☐	☐	☐	☐
32162	$.60	☐	☐	☐	☐
32163	$.60	☐	☐	☐	☐
32172	$.60	☐	☐	☐	☐
32187	$.60	☐	☐	☐	☐
32194	$.60	☐	☐	☐	☐

#1407 6¢ SOUTH CAROLINA

8 Plates

32012	$.60	☐	☐	☐	☐
32020	$.60	☐	☐	☐	☐
32027	$.60	☐	☐	☐	☐
32028	$.60	☐	☐	☐	☐
32029	$.60	☐	☐	☐	☐
32038	$.60	☐	☐	☐	☐
32047	$.60	☐	☐	☐	☐
32052	$.60	☐	☐	☐	☐

#1408 6¢ STONE MOUNTAIN

8 Plates

32246	$.60	☐	☐	☐	☐
32247	$.60	☐	☐	☐	☐
32248	$.60	☐	☐	☐	☐
32256	$.60	☐	☐	☐	☐
32259	$.60	☐	☐	☐	☐
32261	$.60	☐	☐	☐	☐
32262	$.60	☐	☐	☐	☐
32263	$.60	☐	☐	☐	☐

1970 COMMEMORATIVES

#1409 6¢ FORT SNELLING

8 Plates		UL	UR	LL	LR
32298	$.60	☐	☐	☐	☐
32302	$.60	☐	☐	☐	☐
32305	$.60	☐	☐	☐	☐
32311	$.60	☐	☐	☐	☐
32318	$.60	☐	☐	☐	☐
32320	$.60	☐	☐	☐	☐
32327	$.60	☐	☐	☐	☐
32331	$.60	☐	☐	☐	☐

#1410-13 6¢ ANTI-POLLUTION

Block of 10 (2 x 5)

32251-32252-32253-32254-32255	$4.00	☐	☐	☐	☐
32281-32282-32283-32284-32285	$4.00	☐	☐	☐	☐

#1414 6¢ CHRISTMAS-NATIVITY

Block of 8 (4 x 2)

31942-31939-31940-31941	$1.25	☐	☐	☐	☐
31942-32150-32151-32152	$1.25	☐	☐	☐	☐
31946-31939-31940-31941	$1.25	☐	☐	☐	☐
31946-31943-31944-31945	$1.25	☐	☐	☐	☐
31946-32150-32151-32152	$1.25	☐	☐	☐	☐
32332-31939-31940-31941	$1.25	☐	☐	☐	☐
32332-31943-31944-31945	$1.25	☐	☐	☐	☐

#1414 a 6¢ CHRISTMAS-NATIVITY (Precancelled)

Block of 8 (4 x 2)

32153-31939-31940-31941	$2.75	☐	☐	☐	☐
32153-31943-31944-31945	$2.75	☐	☐	☐	☐
32154-31939-31940-31941	$2.75	☐	☐	☐	☐
32154-31943-31944-31945	$2.75	☐	☐	☐	☐
32154-32150-32151-32152	$2.75	☐	☐	☐	☐

#1415-18 6¢ CHRISTMAS TOYS

Block of 8 (2 x 4)

31903-31900-31901-31902	$5.00	☐	☐	☐	☐
31903-31904-31905-31906	$5.00	☐	☐	☐	☐
31903-32145-32146-32147	$5.00	☐	☐	☐	☐

1970 COMMEMORATIVES

#1415-18 6¢ CHRISTMAS TOYS

Continued		UL	UR	LL	LR
31907-31900-31901-31902	$5.00	☐	☐	☐	☐
31907-31904-31905-31906	$5.00	☐	☐	☐	☐
31907-32145-32146-32147	$5.00	☐	☐	☐	☐

#1415 a-18 a 6¢ CHRISTMAS TOYS (Precancelled)

Blocks of 8 (2 x 4)

		UL	UR	LL	LR
32148-31900-31901-31902	$10.00	☐	☐	☐	☐
32148-31904-31905-31906	$10.00	☐	☐	☐	☐
32148-32145-32146-32147	$10.00	☐	☐	☐	☐
32149-31900-31901-31902	$10.00	☐	☐	☐	☐
32149-31904-31905-31906	$10.00	☐	☐	☐	☐
32149-32145-32146-32147	$20.00	☐	☐	☐	☐

#1419 6¢ UNITED NATIONS

Blocks of 4 **8 plates**

		UL	UR	LL	LR
32299	$.60	☐	☐	☐	☐
32300	$.60	☐	☐	☐	☐
32303	$.60	☐	☐	☐	☐
32306	$.60	☐	☐	☐	☐
32308	$.60	☐	☐	☐	☐
32310	$.60	☐	☐	☐	☐
32316	$.60	☐	☐	☐	☐
32317	$.60	☐	☐	☐	☐

#1420 6¢ PILGRIM LANDING

8 Plates

		UL	UR	LL	LR
32264	$.60	☐	☐	☐	☐
32269	$.60	☐	☐	☐	☐
32271	$.60	☐	☐	☐	☐
32272	$.60	☐	☐	☐	☐
32273	$.60	☐	☐	☐	☐
32279	$.60	☐	☐	☐	☐
32286	$.60	☐	☐	☐	☐
32287	$.60	☐	☐	☐	☐

#1421-22 6¢ DAV-POW 8 Plates

		UL	UR	LL	LR
32409	$2.00	☐	☐	☐	☐
32410	$2.00	☐	☐	☐	☐
32427	$2.00	☐	☐	☐	☐
32434	$2.00	☐	☐	☐	☐
32435	$2.00	☐	☐	☐	☐
32436	$2.00	☐	☐	☐	☐
32441	$2.00	☐	☐	☐	☐
32442	$2.00	☐	☐	☐	☐

1971 COMMEMORATIVES

Issued TAGGED Only

#1423 6¢ AMERICAN WOOL

8 Plates		UL	UR	LL	LR
32478	$.60	☐	☐	☐	☐
32485	$.60	☐	☐	☐	☐
32492	$.60	☐	☐	☐	☐
32501	$.60	☐	☐	☐	☐
32516	$.60	☐	☐	☐	☐
32523	$.60	☐	☐	☐	☐
32539	$.60	☐	☐	☐	☐
32541	$.60	☐	☐	☐	☐

#1424 6¢ GEN. MacARTHUR

8 Plates

		UL	UR	LL	LR
32301	$.60	☐	☐	☐	☐
32304	$.60	☐	☐	☐	☐
32307	$.60	☐	☐	☐	☐
32309	$.60	☐	☐	☐	☐
32319	$.60	☐	☐	☐	☐
32328	$.60	☐	☐	☐	☐
32340	$.60	☐	☐	☐	☐
32347	$.60	☐	☐	☐	☐

#1425 6¢ BLOOD DONORS

8 Plates

		UL	UR	LL	LR
32590	$.60	☐	☐	☐	☐
32603	$.60	☐	☐	☐	☐
32617	$.60	☐	☐	☐	☐
32632	$.60	☐	☐	☐	☐
32645	$.60	☐	☐	☐	☐
32661	$.60	☐	☐	☐	☐
32674	$.60	☐	☐	☐	☐
32687	$.60	☐	☐	☐	☐

#1426 8¢ MISSOURI

Block of 12 (2 x 6)

		UL	UR	LL	LR
32702-32703-32704-32705-32706-32707	$2.00	☐	☐	☐	☐
32708-32709-32710-32711-32712-32713	$2.00	☐	☐	☐	☐

#1427-30 8¢ WILDLIFE 10 Plates

		UL	UR	LL	LR
33032	$.80	☐	☐	☐	☐
33039	$.80	☐	☐	☐	☐
33045	$.80	☐	☐	☐	☐
33048	$.80	☐	☐	☐	☐
33050	$.80	☐	☐	☐	☐
33056	$.80	☐	☐	☐	☐
33060	$.80	☐	☐	☐	☐
33062	$.80	☐	☐	☐	☐
33080	$.80	☐	☐	☐	☐
33083	$.80	☐	☐	☐	☐

#1431 8¢ ANTARCTIC TREATY

9 Plates

		UL	UR	LL	LR
32940	$.80	☐	☐	☐	☐
32947	$.80	☐	☐	☐	☐
32954	$.80	☐	☐	☐	☐

1971 COMMEMORATIVES

Issued TAGGED Only

#1431 8¢ ANTARCTIC TREATY Cont.

		UL	UR	LL	LR
32955	$.80	☐	☐	☐	☐
32963	$.80	☐	☐	☐	☐
32969	$.80	☐	☐	☐	☐
32976	$.80	☐	☐	☐	☐
32978	$.80	☐	☐	☐	☐
33014	$.80	☐	☐	☐	☐

#1432 8¢ AMER. REVOLUTION

8 Plates

		UL	UR	LL	LR
33031	$1.00	☐	☐	☐	☐
33033	$1.00	☐	☐	☐	☐
33040	$1.00	☐	☐	☐	☐
33043	$1.00	☐	☐	☐	☐
33044	$1.00	☐	☐	☐	☐
33046	$1.00	☐	☐	☐	☐
33049	$1.00	☐	☐	☐	☐
33059	$1.00	☐	☐	☐	☐

#1433 8¢ JOHN SLOAN 10 Plates

		UL	UR	LL	LR
33102	$.80	☐	☐	☐	☐
33124	$.80	☐	☐	☐	☐
33125	$.80	☐	☐	☐	☐
33130	$.80	☐	☐	☐	☐
33131	$.80	☐	☐	☐	☐
33132	$.80	☐	☐	☐	☐
33133	$1.50	☐	☐	☐	☐
33134	$1.50	☐	☐	☐	☐
33168	$1.50	☐	☐	☐	☐
33169	$1.50	☐	☐	☐	☐

#1434-35 8¢ MOON ROVER

8 Plates

		UL	UR	LL	LR
33138	$.80	☐	☐	☐	☐
33147	$.80	☐	☐	☐	☐
33148	$.80	☐	☐	☐	☐
33153	$.80	☐	☐	☐	☐
33154	$.80	☐	☐	☐	☐
33155	$.80	☐	☐	☐	☐
33156	$.80	☐	☐	☐	☐
33162	$.80	☐	☐	☐	☐

#1436 8¢ EMILY DICKINSON

8 Plates

		UL	UR	LL	LR
33171	$.80	☐	☐	☐	☐
33173	$.80	☐	☐	☐	☐
33174	$.80	☐	☐	☐	☐
33175	$.80	☐	☐	☐	☐
33176	$.80	☐	☐	☐	☐
33196	$.80	☐	☐	☐	☐
33199	$.80	☐	☐	☐	☐
33200	$.80	☐	☐	☐	☐

#1437 8¢ SAN JUAN 8 Plates

		UL	UR	LL	LR
33201	$.80	☐	☐	☐	☐
33202	$.80	☐	☐	☐	☐
33203	$.80	☐	☐	☐	☐

#1437 8¢ SAN JUAN Continued

		UL	UR	LL	LR
33212	$.80	☐	☐	☐	☐
33213	$.80	☐	☐	☐	☐
33218	$.80	☐	☐	☐	☐
33219	$.80	☐	☐	☐	☐
33222	$.80	☐	☐	☐	☐

#1438 8¢ DRUG ABUSE

Block of 6 (3 x 2)

		UL	UR	LL	LR
33064-33065-33066	$1.00	☐	☐	☐	☐
33067-33068-33069	$1.00	☐	☐	☐	☐

#1439 8¢ CARE

Block of 8 (4 x 2)

		UL	UR	LL	LR
33139-33140-33141-33142	$1.50	☐	☐	☐	☐
33143-33144-33145-33146	$1.50	☐	☐	☐	☐

#1440-43 8¢ HISTORIC PRESERVATION 8 Plates

Block of 4

		UL	UR	LL	LR
33233	$.80	☐	☐	☐	☐
33234	$.80	☐	☐	☐	☐
33235	$.80	☐	☐	☐	☐
33236	$.80	☐	☐	☐	☐
33237	$.80	☐	☐	☐	☐
33238	$.80	☐	☐	☐	☐
33239	$.80	☐	☐	☐	☐
33247	$.80	☐	☐	☐	☐

#1444 8¢ NATIVITY

Block of 12 (6 x 2)

		UL	UR	LL	LR
33178-33179-33180-33181-33182-33183	$2.00	☐	☐	☐	☐
33184-33185-33186-33187-33188-33189	$2.00	☐	☐	☐	☐
33190-33191-33192-33193-33194-33195	$2.00	☐	☐	☐	☐

#1445 8¢ PARTRIDGE

Block of 12 (6 x 2)

		UL	UR	LL	LR
33106-33107-33108-33109-33110-33111	$2.00	☐	☐	☐	☐
33106-33107-33108-33109-33211-33111	$2.00	☐	☐	☐	☐
33112-33113-33114-33115-33116-33117	$2.00	☐	☐	☐	☐
33118-33119-33120-33121-33122-33123	$2.00	☐	☐	☐	☐

1972 COMMEMORATIVES

Issued TAGGED Only

#1446 8¢ LANIER — Block of 4

8 Plates

		UL	UR	LL	LR
33360	$.80	☐	☐	☐	☐
33361	$.80	☐	☐	☐	☐
33362	$.80	☐	☐	☐	☐
33364	$.80	☐	☐	☐	☐
33367	$.80	☐	☐	☐	☐
33374	$.80	☐	☐	☐	☐
33375	$.80	☐	☐	☐	☐
33376	$.80	☐	☐	☐	☐

#1447 8¢ PEACE CORPS

Block of 6 (3 x 2)

33223-33224-33225	$1.00	☐	☐	☐	☐
33226-33227-33228	$1.00	☐	☐	☐	☐

Blocks of 4

#1448-51 2¢ NATIONAL PARKS

8 Plates

33460	$.50	☐	☐	☐	☐
33462	$.50	☐	☐	☐	☐
33467	$.50	☐	☐	☐	☐
33482	$.50	☐	☐	☐	☐
33483	$.50	☐	☐	☐	☐
33488	$.50	☐	☐	☐	☐
33489	$.50	☐	☐	☐	☐
33499	$.50	☐	☐	☐	☐

#1452 6¢ NATIONAL PARKS

8 Plates

33603	$.60	☐	☐	☐	☐
33604	$.60	☐	☐	☐	☐
33618	$.60	☐	☐	☐	☐
33625	$.60	☐	☐	☐	☐
33632	$.60	☐	☐	☐	☐
33639	$.60	☐	☐	☐	☐
33646	$.60	☐	☐	☐	☐
33658	$.60	☐	☐	☐	☐

#1453 8¢ NATIONAL PARKS

8 Plates

33411	$.80	☐	☐	☐	☐
33415	$.80	☐	☐	☐	☐
33416	$.80	☐	☐	☐	☐
33417	$.80	☐	☐	☐	☐
33418	$.80	☐	☐	☐	☐
33421	$.80	☐	☐	☐	☐
33424	$.80	☐	☐	☐	☐
33427	$.80	☐	☐	☐	☐

#1454 15¢ NATIONAL PARKS

5 Plates

33717	$1.25	☐	☐	☐	☐
33719	$1.25	☐	☐	☐	☐

#1454 15¢ NATIONAL PARKS Cont.

		UL	UR	LL	LR
33726	$1.25	☐	☐	☐	☐
33727	$1.25	☐	☐	☐	☐
33728	$1.25	☐	☐	☐	☐

#1455 8¢ FAMILY PLANNING

8 Plates

33383	$.80	☐	☐	☐	☐
33384	$.80	☐	☐	☐	☐
33386	$.80	☐	☐	☐	☐
33392	$.80	☐	☐	☐	☐
33395	$.80	☐	☐	☐	☐
33396	$.80	☐	☐	☐	☐
33397	$.80	☐	☐	☐	☐
33399	$.80	☐	☐	☐	☐

#1456-59 8¢ COLONIAL CRAFTSMEN — 6 Plates

33580	$.80	☐	☐	☐	☐
33589	$.80	☐	☐	☐	☐
33590	$.80	☐	☐	☐	☐
33611	$.80	☐	☐	☐	☐
33665	$.80	☐	☐	☐	☐
33666	$.80	☐	☐	☐	☐

#1460 6¢ OLYMPICS

Block of 10 (2 x 5)

33312-33313-33314-33315-33316	$1.50	☐	☐	☐	☐

#1461 8¢ OLYMPICS

Block of 10 (2 x 5)

33327-33328-33329-33336-33331	$2.00	☐	☐	☐	☐
33333-33334-33335-33330-33337	$2.00	☐	☐	☐	☐

#1462 15¢ OLYMPICS

Block of 10 (2 x 5)

33317-33318-33319-33320-33321	$3.00	☐	☐	☐	☐

#1463 8¢ PARENT-TEACHER

33654-33655	$.80	☐	☐	☐	☐
33656-33657	$.40	☐$_2$	☐$_2$	☐$_2$	☐$_3$

The lower right position of yellow plate number 33656 is printed in reverse.

#1464-67 8¢ WILDLIFE CONSERVATION — 9 Plates

33729	$.80	☐	☐	☐	☐
33731	$.80	☐	☐	☐	☐
33738	$.80	☐	☐	☐	☐
33739	$.80	☐	☐	☐	☐
33757	$.80	☐	☐	☐	☐

1972 COMMEMORATIVES

#1464-67 8¢ WILDLIFE CONSERVATION Cont.

		UL	UR	LL	LR
33758	$.80	☐	☐	☐	☐
33759	$.80	☐	☐	☐	☐
33762	$.80	☐	☐	☐	☐
33805	$.80	☐	☐	☐	☐

#1468 8¢ MAIL ORDER

Block of 12 (2 x 6)

		UL	UR	LL	LR
33745-33746-33747-33748-33749-33750	$2.00	☐	☐	☐	☐
33751-33752-33753-33754-33755-33756	$2.00	☐	☐	☐	☐

#1469 8¢ OSTEOPATHIC MEDICINE

Block of 6 (3 x2)

		UL	UR	LL	LR
33784-33785-33786	$1.00	☐	☐	☐	☐
33787-33788-33789	$1.00	☐	☐	☐	☐

#1470 8¢ TOM SAWYER 10 Plates

		UL	UR	LL	LR
33809	$.80	☐	☐	☐	☐
33811	$.80	☐	☐	☐	☐
33815	$.80	☐	☐	☐	☐
33819	$.80	☐	☐	☐	☐
33820	$.80	☐	☐	☐	☐
33828	$.80	☐	☐	☐	☐
33833	$.80	☐	☐	☐	☐
33834	$.80	☐	☐	☐	☐
33911	$.80	☐	☐	☐	☐
33924	$.80	☐	☐	☐	☐

#1471 8¢ ST. LUCY LEGEND

Block of 12 (6 x 2)

		UL	UR	LL	LR
33554-33555-33556-33557-33558-33559	$2.00	☐	☐	☐	☐
33560-33561-33562-33563-33564-33565	$2.00	☐	☐	☐	☐
33566-33567-33568-33569-33570-33571	$2.00	☐	☐	☐	☐

#1472 8¢ SANTA CLAUS

Block of 12 (6 x 2)

		UL	UR	LL	LR
33698-33699-33700-33701-33702-33703	$2.00	☐	☐	☐	☐
33704-33705-33700-33707-33708-33709	$2.00	☐	☐	☐	☐
33704-33705-33706-33707-33708-33709	$2.00	☐	☐	☐	☐
33710-33711-33712-33713-33714-33715	$2.00	☐	☐	☐	☐

#1473 8¢ PHARMACY 8 Plates

		UL	UR	LL	LR
33808	$.80	☐	☐	☐	☐
33810	$.80	☐	☐	☐	☐

1972 COMMEMORATIVES

#1473 8¢ PHARMACY Continued

		UL	UR	LL	LR
33812	$.80	☐	☐	☐	☐
33813	$.80	☐	☐	☐	☐
33814	$.80	☐	☐	☐	☐
33816	$.80	☐	☐	☐	☐
33818	$.80	☐	☐	☐	☐
33856	$.80	☐	☐	☐	☐

#1474 8¢ STAMP COLLECTING

8 Plates

		UL	UR	LL	LR
33847	$.80	☐	☐	☐	☐
33850	$.80	☐	☐	☐	☐
33851	$.80	☐	☐	☐	☐
33852	$.80	☐	☐	☐	☐
33857	$.80	☐	☐	☐	☐
33858	$.80	☐	☐	☐	☐
33861	$.80	☐	☐	☐	☐
33866	$.80	☐	☐	☐	☐

1973 COMMEMORATIVES

Issued TAGGED Only

#1475 8¢ LOVE

Block of 6 (2 x 3)

		UL	UR	LL	LR
33931-33932-33933	$1.00	☐	☐	☐	☐
33934-33935-33937	$1.00	☐	☐	☐	☐

#1476 8¢ PAMPHLETEER 8 Plates

		UL	UR	LL	LR
34046	$.80	☐	☐	☐	☐
34047	$.80	☐	☐	☐	☐
34048	$.80	☐	☐	☐	☐
34049	$.80	☐	☐	☐	☐
34050	$.80	☐	☐	☐	☐
34051	$.80	☐	☐	☐	☐
34053	$.80	☐	☐	☐	☐
34054	$.80	☐	☐	☐	☐

#1477 8¢ BROADSIDE 8 Plates

		UL	UR	LL	LR
34116	$.80	☐	☐	☐	☐
34117	$.80	☐	☐	☐	☐
34119	$.80	☐	☐	☐	☐
34120	$.80	☐	☐	☐	☐
34121	$.80	☐	☐	☐	☐
34122	$.80	☐	☐	☐	☐
34123	$.80	☐	☐	☐	☐
34124	$.80	☐	☐	☐	☐

#1478 8¢ POSTRIDER 10 Plates

		UL	UR	LL	LR
34193	$.80	☐	☐	☐	☐
34196	$.80	☐	☐	☐	☐
34199	$.80	☐	☐	☐	☐
34200	$.80	☐	☐	☐	☐
34210	$.80	☐	☐	☐	☐
34211	$.80	☐	☐	☐	☐
34212	$.80	☐	☐	☐	☐
34226	$.80	☐	☐	☐	☐
34227	$.80	☐	☐	☐	☐
34229	$.80	☐	☐	☐	☐

1973 COMMEMORATIVES

Issued TAGGED Only

#1479 8¢ DRUMMER 8 Plates

		UL	UR	LL	LR
34288	$.80	☐	☐	☐	☐
34313	$.80	☐	☐	☐	☐
34345	$.80	☐	☐	☐	☐
34346	$.80	☐	☐	☐	☐
34347	$.80	☐	☐	☐	☐
34350	$.80	☐	☐	☐	☐
34351	$.80	☐	☐	☐	☐
34352	$.80	☐	☐	☐	☐

#1480-83 8¢ BOSTON TEA PARTY

8 Plates

34225	$.80	☐	☐	☐	☐
34230	$.80	☐	☐	☐	☐
34236	$.80	☐	☐	☐	☐
34247	$.80	☐	☐	☐	☐
34250	$.80	☐	☐	☐	☐
34252	$.80	☐	☐	☐	☐
34261	$.80	☐	☐	☐	☐
34272	$.80	☐	☐	☐	☐

#1484 8¢ GEORGE GERSHWIN

Block of 12 (2 x 6)

33950-33951-33952-33953-33960-33955
$2.00 ☐ ☐ ☐ ☐

33956-33957-33958-33959-33954-33961
$2.00 ☐ ☐ ☐ ☐

#1485 8¢ ROBINSON JEFFERS

Block of 12 (2 x 6)

34301-34302-34303-34304-34305-34306
$2.00 ☐ ☐ ☐ ☐

34307-34308-34309-34310-34311-34312
$2.00 ☐ ☐ ☐ ☐

#1486 8¢ HENRY O. TANNER

Block of 12 (2 x 6)

34315-34316-34317-34318-34319-34320
$2.00 ☐ ☐ ☐ ☐

34321-34322-34323-34324-34325-34326
$2.00 ☐ ☐ ☐ ☐

#1487 8¢ WILLA CATHER

Block of 12 (2 x 6)

34355-34356-34357-34358-34359-34366
$2.50 ☐ ☐ ☐ ☐

34361-34362-34363-34364-34365-34366
$2.50 ☐ ☐ ☐ ☐

#1488 8¢ COPERNICUS 9 Plates

34105	$.80	☐	☐	☐	☐
34106	$.80	☐	☐	☐	☐
34107	$2.00	☐	☐	☐	☐
34110	$.80	☐	☐	☐	☐
34111	$.80	☐	☐	☐	☐
34112	$.80	☐	☐	☐	☐

#1488 8¢ COPERNICUS Continued

		UL	UR	LL	LR
34114	$.80	☐	☐	☐	☐
34115	$.80	☐	☐	☐	☐
34118	$.80	☐	☐	☐	☐

#1489-98 8¢ POSTAL PEOPLE

Block of 20 (10 x 2)

34075-34076-34077-34078-34079
$3.25 ☐ ☐ ☐ ☐

34081-34082-34089-34084-34085
$3.25 ☐ ☐ ☐ ☐

34087-34088-34083-34090-34091
$3.25 ☐ ☐ ☐ ☐

Back Plate Numbers

†34080-†34086-*34092

#1499 8¢ HARRY S. TRUMAN

14 Plates

34153	$.80	☐	☐	☐	☐
34154	$.80	☐	☐	☐	☐
34155	$.80	☐	☐	☐	☐
34156	$.80	☐	☐	☐	☐
34159	$.80	☐	☐	☐	☐
34160	$.80	☐	☐	☐	☐
34161	$.80	☐	☐	☐	☐
34163	$.80	☐	☐	☐	☐
34164	$.80	☐	☐	☐	☐
34165	$.80	☐	☐	☐	☐
34167	$.80	☐	☐	☐	☐
34168	$.80	☐	☐	☐	☐
34169	$1.50	☐	☐	☐	☐
34177	$1.50	☐	☐	☐	☐

#1500 6¢ ELECTRONICS 6 Plates

34269	$.60	☐	☐	☐	☐
34270	$.60	☐	☐	☐	☐
34274	$.60	☐	☐	☐	☐
34275	$.60	☐	☐	☐	☐
34277	$.60	☐	☐	☐	☐
34278	$.60	☐	☐	☐	☐

#1501 8¢ ELECTRONICS 8 Plates

34233	$.80	☐	☐	☐	☐
34242	$.80	☐	☐	☐	☐
34249	$.80	☐	☐	☐	☐
34251	$.80	☐	☐	☐	☐
34260	$.80	☐	☐	☐	☐
34268	$.80	☐	☐	☐	☐
34273	$.80	☐	☐	☐	☐
34276	$.80	☐	☐	☐	☐

#1502 15¢ ELECTRONICS 5 Plates

34279	$1.50	☐	☐	☐	☐
34285	$1.50	☐	☐	☐	☐
34287	$1.50	☐	☐	☐	☐
34293	$1.50	☐	☐	☐	☐
34300	$1.50	☐	☐	☐	☐

1973-74 COMMEMORATIVES

#1503 8¢ LYNDON JOHNSON

Block of 12 (6 x 2)	UL	UR	LL	LR
34213-34214-34215-34216-34217-34218 $2.00	☐	☐	☐	☐
34219-34220-34221-34222-34223-34224 $2.00	☐	☐	☐	☐

#1504 8¢ ANGUS CATTLE

14 Plates

Plate	Price	UL	UR	LL	LR
34379	$.80	☐	☐	☐	☐
34380	$.80	☐	☐	☐	☐
34382	$.80	☐	☐	☐	☐
34383	$.80	☐	☐	☐	☐
34384	$.80	☐	☐	☐	☐
34385	$.80	☐	☐	☐	☐
34386	$.80	☐	☐	☐	☐
34387	$.80	☐	☐	☐	☐
34390	$.80	☐	☐	☐	☐
34391	$.80	☐	☐	☐	☐
34394	$.80	☐	☐	☐	☐
34395	$.80	☐	☐	☐	☐
34401	$.80	☐	☐	☐	☐
34404	$.80	☐	☐	☐	☐

#1505 10¢ CHAUTAUQUA

12 Plates

Plate	Price	UL	UR	LL	LR
35495	$1.00	☐	☐	☐	☐
35498	$1.00	☐	☐	☐	☐
35499	$1.00	☐	☐	☐	☐
35500	$1.00	☐	☐	☐	☐
35502	$1.00	☐	☐	☐	☐
35503	$1.00	☐	☐	☐	☐
35508	$1.00	☐	☐	☐	☐
35509	$1.00	☐	☐	☐	☐
35510	$1.00	☐	☐	☐	☐
35511	$1.00	☐	☐	☐	☐
35515	$1.00	☐	☐	☐	☐
35526	$1.00	☐	☐	☐	☐

#1506 10¢ KANSAS WHEAT

12 Plates

Plate	Price	UL	UR	LL	LR
35543	$1.00	☐	☐	☐	☐
35544	$1.00	☐	☐	☐	☐
35545	$1.00	☐	☐	☐	☐
35550	$1.00	☐	☐	☐	☐
35551	$1.00	☐	☐	☐	☐
35552	$1.00	☐	☐	☐	☐
35553	$1.00	☐	☐	☐	☐
35554	$1.00	☐	☐	☐	☐
35555	$1.00	☐	☐	☐	☐
35558	$1.00	☐	☐	☐	☐
35561	$1.00	☐	☐	☐	☐
35563	$1.00	☐	☐	☐	☐

1973-74 COMMEMORATIVES

#1507 8¢ CHRISTMAS MADONNA

Block of 12 (6 x 2)	UL	UR	LL	LR
34125-34126-34127-34128-34129-34130 $2.00	☐	☐	☐	☐
34131-34132-34133-34134-34135-34136 $2.00	☐	☐	☐	☐
34137-34138-34139-34140-34141-34142 $2.00	☐	☐	☐	☐

#1508 8¢ CHRISTMAS TREE

Block of 12 (6 x 2)				
34327-34328-34329-34330-34331-34332 $2.00	☐	☐	☐	☐
34333-34334-34335-34336-34337-34338 $2.00	☐	☐	☐	☐
34339-34340-34341-34342-34343-34344 $2.00	☐	☐	☐	☐

1974 REGULAR ISSUE

Issued TAGGED Only

#1509 10¢ CROSSED FLAGS (Huck)

Positions T, B only

Block of 20 (10 x 2)

On this issue it is possible to collect four different strips from the normal printing plus another four strips from the alternate printing. If we use the letter B to represent the blue plate printing; the letter R to represent the red plate number; M to represent the Mail Early and Z to represent Use Zip Code, the following are the margin positions reading from left to right:

NORMAL PRINTING

1) B R M Z B R M Z B R
2) R M Z B R M Z B R M
3) M Z B R M Z B R M Z
4) Z B R M Z B R M Z B

Basic Price $4.00

ALTERNATE PRINTING

1) R B Z M R B Z M R B
2) B Z M R B Z M R B Z
3) Z M R B Z M R B Z M
4) M R B Z M R B Z M R

Basic Price $8.00

BLUE PLATES

34641	34642	34643	34644	34645
34646	34663	34664	34665	34666
34667	34668	34669	34670	34671
34672	34673	34674	34687	34688
34689	34690	34691	34692	34699

1974 REGULAR ISSUE Issued TAGGED Only

#1509 10¢ CROSSED FLAGS (Huck)

BLUE PLATES Continued

34700 34701 34702 34703 34704
34705 34706 34707 34708 34709
34710 34723 34724 34725 34726
34727 34728 34744 34745 34746
34747 34748 34749 34876 34877

34878 34879 34880 34881 34892
34893 34894 34895 34896 34897
34908 34909 34910 34911 34912
34913 34943 34944 34945 34946
34947 34948 34960 34961 34962
34963 34964 34965 34972 34973
34974 34975 34976 34977 34986
34987 34988 34989 34990 34991
35179 35180 †35181 35183 35184

RED PLATES

34647 34648 34649 34650 34651
34652 34675 34676 34677 34678
34679 34680 34681 34682 34683
34684 34685 34686 34693 34694
34695 34696 34697 34711 34712
34713 34714 34715 34717 34718
34719 34720 34721 34722 34733
34734 34735 34736 34737 34738
34750 34751 34752 34753 34754
34755 34768 34769 34770 34771

34772 34773 34885 34886 34887
34888 34889 34890 34899 34900
34901 34902 34903 34904 34914
34915 34916 34917 34918 34919
34935 34936 34937 34938 34939
34940 34949 34950 †34951 †34952
34953 34954 34966 34967 34968
34969 34970 34971 34979 34980
34981 34982 34983 34984 34993
34994 34995 34996 34997 34998

35000 35001 *35002 35003 35004
35005 35006 35007 35008 35009
†35010 35011 35012 35013 35014
35015 35016 35017 35018 35019
†35020 35021 35022 35023 35030
35031 35032 35033 35034 35035
35173 35174 35175 35176 35177
35178 35185 35186 35187 *35188
35189 35190 35200 *35345 †35451
†35452 †35464 †35469 †35478 †35479

†35480 †35481 35881 *35882 *35883
*35884 *35885 *35886 35899 35900
35901 35902 35903 35910 35911
35912 35913 35914 35915 35923
35924 35925 35926 35927 35928
35935 35936 35937 35938 35939
35940 35954 35955 35956 35957
35958 35959 35969 †35970 35971
35972 35973 35978 35979 35980
†35981 35982 35983

#1510 10¢ JEFFERSON MEMORIAL

20 Plates		UL	UR	LL	LR
34591	$1.00	☐	☐	☐	☐
34592	$1.00	☐	☐	☐	☐
34593	$1.00	☐	☐	☐	☐
34594	$1.00	☐	☐	☐	☐
34595	$1.00	☐	☐	☐	☐
34596	$1.00	☐	☐	☐	☐
35042	$1.00	☐	☐	☐	☐
35043	$1.00	☐	☐	☐	☐
35191	$1.00	☐	☐	☐	☐
35192	$1.00	☐	☐	☐	☐
35680	$1.00	☐	☐	☐	☐
35681	$1.00	☐	☐	☐	☐
35766	$1.00	☐	☐	☐	☐
35767	$1.00	☐	☐	☐	☐
35781	$1.00	☐	☐	☐	☐
35782	$1.00	☐	☐	☐	☐
35783	$1.00	☐	☐	☐	☐
35784	$1.00	☐	☐	☐	☐
36003	$1.00	☐	☐	☐	☐
36004	$1.00	☐	☐	☐	☐

BOOKLET PANES

#1510 b 10¢ JEFFERSON MEMORIAL BOOKLET

PANES OF 5

34729 34730 34731 34732 34957
34958

#1510 c 10¢ JEFFERSON MEMORIAL BOOKLET

PANES OF 8

Plate numbers are located much further away from the stamps so no plate numbers were regularly issued.

#1510 d 10¢ JEFFERSON MEMORIAL BOOKLET

PANES OF 6

35211 35212

#1511 10¢ ZIP CODE

Block of 8 (2 x 4)		UL	UR	LL	LR
34415-34416-34417-34418	$1.90	☐	☐	☐	☐
34420-34421-34422-34423	$1.90	☐	☐	☐	☐

1974 REGULAR ISSUE

Issued TAGGED Only

SIDE COIL PLATES

PERF. 10 VERTICALLY

#1518 6.3¢ LIBERTY BELL COIL

432 Subject Plates — STRIPS OF 6

35612 35613 †35614 35615

#1519 10¢ CROSSED FLAGS COIL (Huck Printing)

Very few reported with enough of the plate number to identify.

#1520 10¢ JEFFERSON MEMORIAL COIL

432 Subject Plates — STRIPS OF 6

34388	34389	34413	34414	34497
34498	34654	34655	34656	†34657
†34658	†34659	†34924	†35280	35281
35323	†35504	†35505	†35506	†35507
†35547	†35548	†35549	†35560	†35570
†35624	†35625	†35626	†35627	†35695
†35696	†35697	†35698	†35699	†35700
†35701	†35702	†35705	†35706	†35758
35759	35760	35761	36008	†36012
36013	†36014	36087	†36088	†36119
36120	36205	†36206	†36207	†36359
†36360	36827	36828	†36849	36850
37122	37148	†37149	†37595	

1974 COMMEMORATIVES Cont.

#1525 10¢ VETERANS OF FOREIGN WARS

11 Plates

Plate	Price	UL	UR	LL	LR
34868	$1.00	☐	☐	☐	☐
34884	$1.00	☐	☐	☐	☐
34891	$1.00	☐	☐	☐	☐
34898	$1.00	☐	☐	☐	☐
34905	$1.00	☐	☐	☐	☐
34920	$1.00	☐	☐	☐	☐
34929	$2.50	☐	☐	☐	☐
34933	$1.00	☐	☐	☐	☐
34934	$1.00	☐	☐	☐	☐
34985	$1.00	☐	☐	☐	☐
34999	$1.00	☐	☐	☐	☐

#1526 10¢ ROBERT FROST 4 Plates

Plate	Price	UL	UR	LL	LR
34882	$1.00	☐	☐	☐	☐
34883	$1.00	☐	☐	☐	☐
34922	$1.00	☐	☐	☐	☐
34923	$1.00	☐	☐	☐	☐

#1527 10¢ EXPO '74

Block of 12 (2 x 6)

Plates	Price	UL	UR	LL	LR
34442-34443-34444-34445-34446-34447	$2.50	☐	☐	☐	☐
34448-34449-34450-34451-34452-34453	$2.50	☐	☐	☐	☐

1974 COMMEMORATIVES

Continued

#1528 10¢ HORSE RACING

Block of 12 (2 x 6)

Plates	Price	UL	UR	LL	LR
35108-35109-35110-35111-35112-35113	$2.50	☐	☐	☐	☐
35114-35115-35116-35117-35118-35119	$2.50	☐	☐	☐	☐

#1529 10¢ SKYLAB 12 Plates

Plate	Price	UL	UR	LL	LR
35213	$1.00	☐	☐	☐	☐
35214	$1.00	☐	☐	☐	☐
35215	$1.00	☐	☐	☐	☐
35216	$1.00	☐	☐	☐	☐
35217	$1.00	☐	☐	☐	☐
35218	$1.00	☐	☐	☐	☐
35219	$1.00	☐	☐	☐	☐
35220	$1.00	☐	☐	☐	☐
35221	$1.00	☐	☐	☐	☐
35222	$1.00	☐	☐	☐	☐
35227	$1.00	☐	☐	☐	☐
35256	$1.00	☐	☐	☐	☐

#1530-37 10¢ UNIVERSAL POSTAL UNION

Block of 10 (5 x 2)

Plates	Price	UL	UR	LL	LR
35263-35264-36265-35266-35267	$2.50	☐	☐	☐	☐
35268-35269-35270-35271-35272	$2.50	☐	☐	☐	☐

#1538-41 10¢ MINERAL HERITAGE

10 Plates

Plate	Price	UL	UR	LL	LR
35062	$1.00	☐	☐	☐	☐
35063	$1.00	☐	☐	☐	☐
35064	$1.00	☐	☐	☐	☐
35067	$1.00	☐	☐	☐	☐
35068	$1.00	☐	☐	☐	☐
35069	$1.00	☐	☐	☐	☐
35077	$1.00	☐	☐	☐	☐
35078	$1.00	☐	☐	☐	☐
35079	$1.00	☐	☐	☐	☐
35080	$1.00	☐	☐	☐	☐

#1542 10¢ FORT HARROD 12 Plates

Plate	Price	UL	UR	LL	LR
35245	$1.00	☐	☐	☐	☐
35246	$1.00	☐	☐	☐	☐
35248	$1.00	☐	☐	☐	☐
35255	$1.00	☐	☐	☐	☐
35258	$1.00	☐	☐	☐	☐
35259	$1.00	☐	☐	☐	☐
35260	$1.00	☐	☐	☐	☐
35261	$1.00	☐	☐	☐	☐
35262	$1.00	☐	☐	☐	☐
35273	$1.00	☐	☐	☐	☐
35279	$1.00	☐	☐	☐	☐
35284	$1.00	☐	☐	☐	☐

1974 COMMEMORATIVES Cont.

#1543-46 10¢ CONTINENTAL CONGRESS
16 Plates

Plate	Price	UL	UR	LL	LR
35308	$1.00	☐	☐	☐	☐
35309	$1.00	☐	☐	☐	☐
35310	$1.00	☐	☐	☐	☐
35311	$1.00	☐	☐	☐	☐
35312	$1.00	☐	☐	☐	☐
35313	$1.00	☐	☐	☐	☐
35314	$1.00	☐	☐	☐	☐
35315	$1.00	☐	☐	☐	☐
35325	$1.00	☐	☐	☐	☐
35326	$1.00	☐	☐	☐	☐
35335	$1.00	☐	☐	☐	☐
35336	$1.00	☐	☐	☐	☐
35350	$1.00	☐	☐	☐	☐
35358	$1.00	☐	☐	☐	☐
35394	$1.00	☐	☐	☐	☐
35401	$1.00	☐	☐	☐	☐

#1547 10¢ ENERGY 14 Plates

Plate	Price	UL	UR	LL	LR
35100	$1.00	☐	☐	☐	☐
35101	$1.00	☐	☐	☐	☐
35102	$1.00	☐	☐	☐	☐$_2$
35103	$1.00	☐	☐	☐	☐
35104	$1.00	☐	☐	☐	☐$_2$
35105	$1.00	☐	☐	☐	☐$_2$
35106	$1.00	☐	☐	☐	☐$_2$
35107	$1.00	☐	☐	☐	☐
35120	$1.00	☐	☐	☐	☐$_2$
35121	$1.00	☐	☐	☐	☐
35122	$1.00	☐	☐	☐	☐$_2$
35123	$1.00	☐	☐	☐	☐$_3$
35124	$1.00	☐	☐	☐	☐$_3$
35125	$1.00	☐	☐	☐	☐$_3$

#1548 10¢ SLEEPY HOLLOW
8 Plates

Plate	Price	UL	UR	LL	LR
35617	$1.00	☐	☐	☐	☐
35618	$1.00	☐	☐	☐	☐
35619	$1.00	☐	☐	☐	☐
35622	$1.00	☐	☐	☐	☐
35623	$1.00	☐	☐	☐	☐
35650	$1.00	☐	☐	☐	☐
35651	$1.00	☐	☐	☐	☐
35652	$1.00	☐	☐	☐	☐

#1549 10¢ RETARDED CHILDREN
8 Plates

Plate	Price	UL	UR	LL	LR
35496	$1.00	☐	☐	☐	☐
35497	$1.00	☐	☐	☐	☐
35501	$1.00	☐	☐	☐	☐
35514	$1.00	☐	☐	☐	☐
35525	$1.00	☐	☐	☐	☐
35528	$1.00	☐	☐	☐	☐
35529	$1.00	☐	☐	☐	☐
35535	$1.00	☐	☐	☐	☐

1974 COMMEMORATIVES

#1550 10¢ CHRISTMAS ANGEL
Block of 10 (5 x 2)

Plates	Price	UL	UR	LL	LR
35591-35592-35593-35594-35595	$2.00	☐	☐	☐	☐
35596-35597-35598-35599-35600	$2.00	☐	☐	☐	☐
35596-35597-35598-35599-35673	$2.00	☐	☐	☐	☐
35596-35597-35598-35599-35688	$2.00	☐	☐	☐	☐
35601-35602-35603-35604-35605	$2.00	☐	☐	☐	☐
35601-35602-35603-35604-35690	$2.00	☐	☐	☐	☐

#1551 10¢ CURRIER & IVES
Block of 12 (2 x 6)

Plates	Price	UL	UR	LL	LR
35408-35409-35410-35411-35412-35413	$2.50	☐	☐	☐	☐
35414-35415-35416-35417-35418-35419	$2.50	☐	☐	☐	☐
35420-35421-35422-35423-35424-35425	$2.50	☐	☐	☐	☐

Issued PLAIN Only

#1552 10¢ CHRISTMAS PEACE
Block of 12 (2 x 6)

Plates	Price	UL	UR	LL	LR
35634-35635-35636-35637-35638-35639	$3.00	☐	☐	☐	☐
35640-35641-35642-35643-35644-35645	$3.00	☐	☐	☐	☐

1975 COMMEMORATIVES
Issued TAGGED Only

#1553 10¢ BENJAMIN WEST
Block of 10 (5 x 2)

Plates	Price	UL	UR	LL	LR
35384-35385-35386-35387-35388	$2.00	☐	☐	☐	☐
35389-35390-35391-35392-35393	$2.00	☐	☐	☐	☐

#1554 10¢ P.L. DUNBAR
Block of 10 (5 x 2)

Plates	Price	UL	UR	LL	LR
36027-36028-36029-36030-36031	$2.00	☐	☐	☐	☐

#1555 10¢ D.W. GRIFFITH 12 Plates

Plate	Price	UL	UR	LL	LR
36037	$1.00	☐	☐	☐	☐
36039	$1.00	☐	☐	☐	☐
36040	$1.00	☐	☐	☐	☐
36045	$1.50	☐	☐	☐	☐
36046	$1.50	☐	☐	☐	☐
36047	$1.00	☐	☐	☐	☐
36048	$1.50	☐	☐	☐	☐
36050	$1.00	☐	☐	☐	☐

1975 COMMEMORATIVES

#1555 10¢ D.W. GRIFFITH Cont.

		UL	UR	LL	LR
36065	$1.00	☐	☐	☐	☐
36072	$1.00	☐	☐	☐	☐
36073	$1.00	☐	☐	☐	☐
36079	$1.00	☐	☐	☐	☐

#1556 10¢ JUPITER 14 Plates

35813	$1.00	☐	☐	☐	☐
35820	$1.00	☐	☐	☐	☐
35821	$1.00	☐	☐	☐	☐
35822	$1.00	☐	☐	☐	☐
35823	$1.00	☐	☐	☐	☐
35824	$1.00	☐	☐	☐	☐
35831	$1.00	☐	☐	☐	☐
35832	$1.00	☐	☐	☐	☐
35838	$1.00	☐	☐	☐	☐
35841	$1.00	☐	☐	☐	☐
35848	$1.00	☐	☐	☐	☐
35849	$1.00	☐	☐	☐	☐
35850	$1.00	☐	☐	☐	☐
35863	$1.00	☐	☐	☐	☐

#1557 10¢ MARINER 16 Plates

35947	$1.00	☐	☐	☐	☐
35966	$1.00	☐	☐	☐	☐
35967	$1.00	☐	☐	☐	☐
35968	$1.00	☐	☐	☐	☐
35975	$1.00	☐	☐	☐	☐
35976	$1.00	☐	☐	☐	☐
35977	$1.00	☐	☐	☐	☐
35984	$1.00	☐	☐	☐	☐
35985	$1.00	☐	☐	☐	☐
35989	$1.00	☐	☐	☐	☐
35990	$1.00	☐	☐	☐	☐
35991	$1.00	☐	☐	☐	☐
35992	$1.00	☐	☐	☐	☐
35993	$1.00	☐	☐	☐	☐
35997	$1.00	☐	☐	☐	☐
36002	$1.00	☐	☐	☐	☐

#1558 10¢ COLLECTIVE BARGAINING

Block of 8 (2 x 4)

35583-35584-35585-35586
$1.75 ☐ ☐ ☐ ☐

35587-35588-35589-35590
$1.75 ☐ ☐ ☐ ☐

#1559 8¢ S. LUDINGTON

Block of 10 (2 x 5)

35722-35723-35730-35725-35726
$1.60 ☐ ☐ ☐ ☐

†35727 Back Plate Number

#1560 10¢ SALEM POOR

Block of 10 (2 x 5)

35734-35735-35736-35737-35738
$2.00 ☐ ☐ ☐ ☐

*35739
Back Plate Number

#1561 10¢ HAYM SALOMON

Block of 10 (2 x 5) UL UR LL LR

35716-35711-35712-35719-35720
$2.00 ☐ ☐ ☐ ☐

†35715-†35721 Back Plate Number

35716-35717-35718-35719-35720
$2.00 ☐ ☐ ☐ ☐

#1562 18¢ PETER FRANCISCO

Block of 10 (2 x 5)

35746-35747-34748-34749-34750
$3.75 ☐ ☐ ☐ ☐

†35751 Back Plate Number

#1563 10¢ LEXINGTON

Block of 12 (2 x 6)

35789-35790-35791-35792-35793-35794
$2.50 ☐ ☐ ☐ ☐

35795-35796-35797-35798-35799-35800
$2.50 ☐ ☐ ☐ ☐

#1564 10¢ BUNKER HILL

Block of 12 (6 x 2)

36015-36016-36017-36018-36019-36020
$2.50 ☐ ☐ ☐ ☐

36015-36016-36017-36024-36019-36026
$2.50 ☐ ☐ ☐ ☐

#1565-68 10¢ MILITARY UNIFORMS

Block of 12 (6 x 2)

36053-36054-36055-36056-36057-36058
$2.50 ☐ ☐ ☐ ☐

36059-36060-36061-36062-36063-36064
$2.50 ☐ ☐ ☐ ☐

#1569-70 10¢ APOLLO-SOYUZ

Block of 12 (2 x 6)

36297-36298-36299-36306-36301-36302
$2.50 ☐ ☐ ☐ ☐

36297-36577-36299-36306-36301-36302
$2.50 ☐ ☐ ☐ ☐

36303-36304-36305-36300-36307-36308
$2.50 ☐ ☐ ☐ ☐

#1571 10¢ WOMEN'S YEAR

Block of 6 (2 x 3)

36431-36432-36433
$1.25 ☐ ☐ ☐ ☐

36434-36435-36436
$1.25 ☐ ☐ ☐ ☐

#1572-75 10¢ U.S.P.S. BICENT.

Block of 12 (2 x 6)

36331-36332-36333-36334-36335-36336
$2.50 ☐ ☐ ☐ ☐

36337-36338-36339-36340-36341-36342
$5.00 ☐ ☐ ☐ ☐

1975 COMMEMORATIVES

EXAMPLE OF IN-LINE PERFORATION

#1580 (10¢) CHRISTMAS CARD

Block of 12 (6 x 2)

In-Line Perforator 11.2 x 11.2

		UL	UR	LL	LR
36630-36631-36632-36633-36634-36635	$5.00	☐	☐	☐	☐
36636-36637-36638-36639-36640-36641	$2.60	☐	☐	☐	☐
36642-36643-36644-36645-36646-36647	$2.60	☐	☐	☐	☐
36886-36637-36638-36639-36640-36641	$2.60	☐	☐	☐	☐

EXAMPLE OF "L" PERFORATION

#1580 (10¢) CHRISTMAS CARD

Block of 12 (6 x 2)

"L" Perforator 10.9 x 10.9

		UL	UR	LL	LR
36630-36631-36632-36633-36634-36635	$5.00	☐	☐	☐	☐
36636-36637-36638-36639-36640-36641	$2.60	☐	☐	☐	☐
36642-36643-36644-36645-36646-36647	$2.60	☐	☐	☐	☐

EXAMPLE OF EE PERFORATION

#1580 b (10¢) CHRISTMAS CARD

Block of 12 (6 x 2)

EE Perforator 10.5 x 11.3

		UL	UR	LL	LR
36642-36643-36644-36645-36646-36647	$50.00	☐	☐	☐	☐
36886-36637-36638-36639-36640-36641	$15.00	☐	☐	☐	☐

NOTE:

"L" PERFORATION 10.9 x 10.9
HORIZONTAL & VERTICAL thru margins

EE PERFORATION 10.5 x 11.3
HORIZONTAL perfs thru side margin
VERTICAL perfs NOT thru side margin

IN-LINE PERFORATION 11.2 x 11.2
NO perforations thru margins

EUREKA Perforation 11.2 x 11.1

1975 COMMEMORATIVES

#1576 10¢ WORLD PEACE 16 Plates

		UL	UR	LL	LR
36467	$1.00	☐	☐	☐	☐
36487	$1.00	☐	☐	☐	☐
36488	$1.00	☐	☐	☐	☐
36489	$1.00	☐	☐	☐	☐
36496	$1.00	☐	☐	☐	☐
36497	$1.00	☐	☐	☐	☐
36506	$1.00	☐	☐	☐	☐
36513	$1.00	☐	☐	☐	☐
36514	$1.00	☐	☐	☐	☐
36515	$1.00	☐	☐	☐	☐
36526	$1.00	☐	☐	☐	☐
36527	$1.00	☐	☐	☐	☐
36528	$1.00	☐	☐	☐	☐
36535	$1.00	☐	☐	☐	☐
36538	$1.00	☐	☐	☐	☐
36552	$1.00	☐	☐	☐	☐

#1577-78 10¢ BANKING 14 plates

		UL	UR	LL	LR
36835	$1.25	☐	☐ 8	☐	☐
36843	$1.00	☐	☐	☐	☐
36844	$1.00	☐	☐	☐	☐
36845	$1.25	☐	☐ 8	☐	☐
36846	$1.00	☐	☐	☐	☐
36847	$1.25	☐	☐ 4	☐	☐
36848	$1.00	☐	☐	☐	☐
36852	$1.00	☐	☐	☐	☐
36864	$1.25	☐	☐ 4	☐	☐
36865	$1.00	☐	☐	☐	☐
36866	$1.00	☐	☐	☐	☐
36867	$1.00	☐	☐	☐	☐
36868	$1.00	☐	☐	☐	☐
36879	$1.00	☐	☐	☐	☐

#1579 (10¢) MADONNA (1975)

Block of 12 (6 x 2)

36741-36742-36743-36744-36745-36746	$2.60	☐	☐	☐	☐
36747-36748-36749-36750-36751-36752	$2.60	☐	☐	☐	☐
36753-36754-36755-36756-36757-36758	$5.00	☐	☐	☐	☐

1975 AMERICANA SERIES

Issued TAGGED Only

(See appendix A regarding gum and paper varieties)

#1581 1¢ ABILITY TO WRITE

10 Plates

		UL	UR	LL	LR
38251	$.25	☐	☐	☐	☐
38252	$.25	☐	☐	☐	☐
38255	$.25	☐	☐	☐	☐
38256	$.25	☐	☐	☐	☐
38257	$.25	☐	☐	☐	☐
38258	$.25	☐	☐	☐	☐
39423	$.25	☐	☐	☐	☐
39424	$.25	☐	☐	☐	☐
39682	$.25	☐	☐	☐	☐
39683	$.25	☐	☐	☐	☐

#1582 2¢ FREEDOM TO SPEAK OUT

14 Plates

38281	$.30	☐	☐	☐	☐
38282	$.30	☐	☐	☐	☐
38287	$.30	☐	☐	☐	☐
38288	$.30	☐	☐	☐	☐
38601	$.30	☐	☐	☐	☐
38602	$.30	☐	☐	☐	☐
38603	$.30	☐	☐	☐	☐
38604	$.30	☐	☐	☐	☐
38605	$.30	☐	☐	☐	☐
38606	$.30	☐	☐	☐	☐
39773	$.30	☐	☐	☐	☐
39774	$.30	☐	☐	☐	☐
39817	$.30	☐	☐	☐	☐
39818	$.30	☐	☐	☐	☐

#1584 3¢ TO CAST A FREE BALLOT

17 Plates

38277	$.35	☐	☐	☐	☐
38278	$.35	☐	☐	☐	☐
38279	$.35	☐	☐	☐	☐
38280	$.35	☐	☐	☐	☐
38290	$.35	☐	☐	☐	☐
39535	$.35	☐	☐	☐	☐
39536	$.35	☐	☐	☐	☐
39548	$.35	☐	☐	☐	☐
39549	$.35	☐	☐	☐	☐
39562	$.35	☐	☐	☐	☐

1975 AMERICANA SERIES

Issued TAGGED Only

#1584 3¢ TO CAST A FREE BALLOT Continued

		UL	UR	LL	LR
39563	$.35	☐	☐	☐	☐
39601	$.35	☐	☐	☐	☐
39602	$.35	☐	☐	☐	☐
39603	$.35	☐	☐	☐	☐
39604	$.35	☐	☐	☐	☐
39616	$.35	☐	☐	☐	☐
39617	$.35	☐	☐	☐	☐

#1585 4¢ A PUBLIC THAT READS

12 Plates

38283	$.45	☐	☐	☐	☐
38284	$.45	☐	☐	☐	☐
38291	$.45	☐	☐	☐	☐
38398	$.45	☐	☐	☐	☐
39457	$.45	☐	☐	☐	☐
39458	$.45	☐	☐	☐	☐
39524	$.45	☐	☐	☐	☐
39525	$.45	☐	☐	☐	☐
39586	$.45	☐	☐	☐	☐
39587	$.45	☐	☐	☐	☐
39591	$.45	☐	☐	☐	☐
39592	$.45	☐	☐	☐	☐

#1591 9¢ FREEDOM TO ASSEMBLE

12 Plates

36922	$.90	☐	☐	☐	☐
36923	$.90	☐	☐	☐	☐
36939	$.90	☐	☐	☐	☐
36940	$.90	☐	☐	☐	☐
36941	$.90	☐	☐	☐	☐
36942	$.90	☐	☐	☐	☐
37443	$.90	☐	☐	☐	☐
37444	$.90	☐	☐	☐	☐
38348	$.90	☐	☐	☐	☐
38349	$.90	☐	☐	☐	☐
38895	$.90	☐	☐	☐	☐
38896	$.90	☐	☐	☐	☐

#1592 10¢ RIGHT TO PETITION

12 Plates

37245	$1.00	☐	☐	☐	☐
37246	$1.00	☐	☐	☐	☐
37247	$1.00	☐	☐	☐	☐
37248	$1.00	☐	☐	☐	☐
37249	$1.00	☐	☐	☐	☐
37250	$1.00	☐	☐	☐	☐
37251	$1.00	☐	☐	☐	☐
37641	$1.00	☐	☐	☐	☐
39453	$1.00	☐	☐	☐	☐
39454	$1.00	☐	☐	☐	☐
39459	$1.00	☐	☐	☐	☐
39460	$1.00	☐	☐	☐	☐

#1593 11¢ FREEDOM OF PRESS

8 Plates		UL	UR	LL	LR
36915	$1.10	☐	☐	☐	☐
36916	$1.10	☐	☐	☐	☐
36924	$1.10	☐	☐	☐	☐
36925	$1.10	☐	☐	☐	☐
36929	$1.10	☐	☐	☐	☐
36935	$1.10	☐	☐	☐	☐
36936	$1.10	☐	☐	☐	☐
36943	$1.10	☐	☐	☐	☐

#1594 12¢ FREEDOM OF CONSCIENCE

6 Plates

37808	$1.50	☐	☐	☐	☐
37842	$1.50	☐	☐	☐	☐
37843	$1.50	☐	☐	☐	☐
37929	$1.50	☐	☐	☐	☐
37930	$1.50	☐	☐	☐	☐
37931	$1.50	☐	☐	☐	☐

#1596 13¢ AMERICAN EAGLE

Block of 12 (2 x 6) 29 Combinations

In Line Perforator 11.2 x 11.2

36309-36310-36311-36312-326313-36314	$3.00	☐	☐	☐	☐
36315-36316-36317-36318-36319-36320	$3.00	☐	☐	☐	☐
36315-37917-36317-37663-37664-37921	$3.00	☐	☐	☐	☐
36315-37918-38204-37920-37664-37921	$3.00	☐	☐	☐	☐
37231-37232-37233-37234-37235-37236	$3.00	☐	☐	☐	☐
37231-37232-37237-37234-37235-37236	$3.00	☐	☐	☐	☐
37347-37348-37349-37350-37351-37352	$3.00	☐	☐	☐	☐
37347-37460-37233-37919-36319-37921	$3.00	☐	☐	☐	☐
37347-37460-37349-37462-37351-37464	$3.00	☐	☐	☐	☐
37347-37666-37233-37920-37463-37921	$3.00	☐	☐	☐	☐
37347-37918-37233-37920-37463-37921	$3.00	☐	☐	☐	☐
37459-37460-37461-37462-37463-37464	$3.00	☐	☐	☐	☐
37459-37666-37461-37350-37463-37352	$3.00	☐	☐	☐	☐
37459-37666-37461-37350-37463-37464	$3.00	☐	☐	☐	☐
37459-37666-37461-37462-37463-37464	$20.00	☐	☐	☐	☐
37660-37661-37233-37663-37351-37464	$3.00	☐	☐	☐	☐
37660-37661-37233-37663-37664-37464	$3.00	☐	☐	☐	☐

1975 AMERICANA SERIES

Issued TAGGED only

#1596 13¢ AMERICAN EAGLE cont.

Plates	Price	UL	UR	LL	LR
37660-37661-37461-37350-36319-37464	$3.00	☐	☐	☐	☐
37660-37661-37461-37350-37351-37464	$3.00	☐	☐	☐	☐
37660-37661-36461-37663-37351-37464	$3.00	☐	☐	☐	☐
37660-37661-37662-37663-37664-37464	$3.00	☐	☐	☐	☐
37660-37661-37662-37663-37664-37665	$3.00	☐	☐	☐	☐
38195-37918-37349-38198-38199-38200	$15.00	☐	☐	☐	☐
38195-38203-37349-38198-38199-38200	$15.00	☐	☐	☐	☐
38202-38196-38197-38205-38206-38207	$3.00	☐	☐	☐	☐
38202-38203-38204-38205-38206-38207	$15.00	☐	☐	☐	☐
38271-38272-38273-38205-38206-38276	$3.00	☐	☐	☐	☐
38271-38272-38273-38205-38275-38276	$3.00	☐	☐	☐	☐
38271-38272-38273-38274-38275-38276	$3.00	☐	☐	☐	☐

#1597 15¢ FT. McHENRY FLAG

5 Plates **A Press (Intaglio)**

Blocks of 20 (2 x 10) will show one or two impressions of the plate number in the side margin.

Positions		L	R
38650	$6.00	☐	☐
38797	$6.00	☐	☐
39047	—	†	†
39365	$6.00	☐	☐
39380	$6.00	☐	☐

#1599 16¢ LIBERTY HEAD

6 Plates		UL	UR	LL	LR
38467	$1.60	☐	☐	☐	☐
38468	$1.60	☐	☐	☐	☐
38481	$1.60	☐	☐	☐	☐
38482	$1.60	☐	☐	☐	☐
38506	$1.60	☐	☐	☐	☐
38507	$1.60	☐	☐	☐	☐

#1603 24¢ OLD NORTH CHURCH

6 Plates

Plate	Price	UL	UR	LL	LR
36759	$2.50	☐	☐	☐	☐
36760	$2.50	☐	☐	☐	☐
36766	$2.50	☐	☐	☐	☐
36767	$2.50	☐	☐	☐	☐
36933	$2.50	☐	☐	☐	☐
36934	$2.50	☐	☐	☐	☐

#1604 28¢ FORT NISQUALLY

4 Plates		UL	UR	LL	LR
38772	$2.75	☐	☐	☐	☐
38773	$2.75	☐	☐	☐	☐
38778	$2.75	☐	☐	☐	☐
38779	$2.75	☐	☐	☐	☐

#1605 29¢ SANDY HOOK 4 Plates

Plate	Price	UL	UR	LL	LR
38485	$3.00	☐	☐	☐	☐
38486	$3.00	☐	☐	☐	☐
38499	$3.00	☐	☐	☐	☐
38500	$3.00	☐	☐	☐	☐

#1606 30¢ SCHOOLHOUSE 5 Plates

Plate	Price	UL	UR	LL	LR
39131	$3.00	☐	☐	☐	☐
39133	$3.00	☐	☐	☐	☐
39134	$3.00	☐	☐	☐	☐
39195	$3.00	☐	☐	☐	☐
39196	$3.00	☐	☐	☐	☐

#1608 50¢ IRON LAMP 6 Plates

Plate	Price	UL	UR	LL	LR
39146	$4.00	☐	☐	☐	☐
39149	$4.00	☐	☐	☐	☐
39157	$4.00	☐	☐	☐	☐
39159	$4.00	☐	☐	☐	☐
39588	$4.00	☐	☐	☐	☐
39589	$4.00	☐	☐	☐	☐

#1610 $1 CANDLE HOLDER

14 Plates

Plate	Price	UL	UR	LL	LR
39076	$8.00	☐	☐	☐	☐
39086	$8.00	☐	☐	☐	☐
39087	$8.00	☐	☐	☐	☐
39088	$8.00	☐	☐	☐	☐
40310	$8.00	☐	☐	☐	☐
40311	$8.00	☐	☐	☐	☐
40312	$8.00	☐	☐	☐	☐
40313	$8.00	☐	☐	☐	☐
40314	$8.00	☐	☐	☐	☐
40709	$8.00	☐	☐	☐	☐
40710	$8.00	☐	☐	☐	☐
40970	$8.00	☐	☐	☐	☐
47971	$8.00	☐	☐	☐	☐
41125	$8.00	☐	☐	☐	☐

#1611 $2 KEROSENE LAMP

5 Plates

Plate	Price	UL	UR	LL	LR
38900	$16.00	☐	☐	☐	☐
38905	$16.00	☐	☐	☐	☐
38906	$16.00	☐	☐	☐	☐
38907	$16.00	☐	☐	☐	☐
39075	$16.00	☐	☐	☐	☐

#1612 $5 RAILROAD LANTERN

9 Plates

Plate	Price	UL	UR	LL	LR
39135	$50.00	☐	☐	☐	☐
39141	$50.00	☐	☐	☐	☐
39142	$50.00	☐	☐	☐	☐
39143	$50.00	☐	☐	☐	☐
39164	$50.00	☐	☐	☐	☐
39169	$50.00	☐	☐	☐	☐
39172	—	†	†	†	†
39173	$32.00	☐	☐	☐	☐
39174	$32.00	☐	☐	☐	☐

1975 AMERICANA SERIES

BOOKLET PANES

#1595 a 13¢ LIBERTY BELL
PANES OF 6

36516 36517 36722 36723 36770
36771

#1595 b 13¢ LIBERTY BELL
PANES of 7

Plate numbers are located much further away from the stamps so no plate numbers were regularly issued.

#1595 c 13¢ LIBERTY BELL
PANES OF 8

Plate numbers are located much further away from the stamps so no plate numbers were regularly issued.

#1595 d 13¢ LIBERTY BELL
PANES OF 5

37253 37254 37255 37256 37258
37321 37327 37328 37345 37346
37374 37375 37376 37377 37572
37573

#1598 a 15¢ FT. HENRY FLAG
PANES OF 8

Plate numbers are located much further away from the stamps so no plate numbers were regularly issued.

SIDE COIL PLATES

PERF. 10 VERTICALLY

#1811 1¢ ABILITY TO WRITE
432 Subject Plates **STRIPS OF 6**

38253 38254 38259 38851 39342
39343

#1613 3.1¢ GUITAR
432 Subject Plates **STRIPS OF 6**

39181 39182 †39183 †39184

#1813 3.5¢ VIOLINS
432 Subject Plates **STRIPS OF 6**

39360 39361 †39366 †39367 †39943
†39955

#1614 7.7¢ SAXHORNS
432 Subject Plates **STRIPS OF 6**

37670 37671 37672 37673 †38351
†38352 †38396 †38397

#1615 7.9¢ DRUM
432 Subject Plates **STRIPS OF 6**

37275 37276 37278 37279 †37304
37305 †40011 40012 †40167 †40168

SIDE COIL PLATES

PERF. 10 VERTICALLY

#1615 C 8.4¢ GRAND PIANO
432 Subject Plates **STRIPS OF 6**

38715 38725 38726 †38747 38748
38751 38752 38832 †38893 †38894
†39344 †39345 †39414 †39415 †39449
†39450

#1616 9¢ FREEDOM TO ASSEMBLE
432 Subject Plates **STRIPS OF 6**

36984 36985 37152 37153 37166
37167 37168 †37169 †37536 †37537

#1617 10¢ RIGHT TO PETITION
432 Subject Plates **STRIPS OF 6**

38244 38245 38246 38247 38248
38249 †40222 †40223

#1816 12¢ FREEDOM OF CONSCIENCE
432 Subject Plates **STRIPS OF 6**

37810 37811 37844 37845 †37948
†37949

#1618 13¢ LIBERTY BELL
432 Subject Plates **STRIPS OF 6**

36193 36194 36195 36196 36273
36274 36800 36813 36814 36815
36816 †36817 †36853 †36854 36855
36856 36857 36858 36859 36860
37548 †37549 †37550 †37551 37559
37560 †37576 †37577 †37715 †37716
†37717 †37718 †37976 †37977 †37988
†37989 †38116 †38117 †38118 †38119
†38148 38149 †38182 †38183 †38184
†38185 38214 †38215 †38216 38217

†38228 †38229 †38230 †38231 †38261
†38262 †38263 †38264 †38342 †38343
†38345 †38420 †38456 †38457 †38458

#1618 C 15¢ FT. McHENRY FLAG
936 Subject Plates

†38692 †38759 †38850 †38877 †38996
†39048 ‡39199 †39283 †39399
Plate number not regularly issued.

#1619 16¢ LIBERTY HEAD
432 Subject Plates **STRIPS OF 6**

38429 38430 38460 38461 †38529
†38532

936 Subject Plates

†38563
Plate number not regularly issued.

1975 REGULAR ISSUE

#1622 13¢ U.S. FLAG (Huck)

PERF. 11 x 10½

297 Plates **Positions T, B only**

Block of 20 (10 x 2) $5.50

HUCK PRESS PRINTING

It is possible to collect both the top and the bottom plate strips in four different combinations. Using Z to represent the Zip Code; M to represent Mail Early; N to represent the plate number and B to represent a Blank Tab, the following are the margin positions reading from left to right in a plate block of 20.

1) Z N B M Z N B M Z N
2) N B M Z N B M Z N B
3) B M Z N B M Z N B M
4) M Z N B M Z N B M Z

36106	36107	36109	36117	36118
36125	36126	36127	36128	36129
36130	36136	36137	36138	36141
36144	36145	36146	36147	36148
36149	36150	36151	36152	36153
36154	36155	36168	36169	36170
36171	36172	36173	36174	36175
36176	36177	36178	36179	36180
36181	36182	36183	36184	36185
36215	36216	36217	36218	36219
36220	36227	36228	36229	36230
36231	36232	36239	36240	36241
36242	36243	36244	36251	†36252
36253	36254	*36255	36256	36776
36777	36778	36779	36780	36781
36794	36795	36796	36797	36798
36799	36801	36802	36803	36804
36805	36806	36807	36808	36809
36810	36811	36812	36821	36822
36823	36825	36829	36830	36831
36832	36833	36834	36837	36838
36839	36840	36841	36842	37005
37006	37007	37008	37009	37024
37025	37026	37027	37028	37029
37035	37036	37037	37038	37039
37040	37048	37050	37051	37052
37056	37057	37058	37059	37060
37061	37067	37068	37069	37070
37072	37074	37075	37076	37077
37078	37090	*37091	37092	37093
37095	37096	37097	37098	37099
37100	37101	37102	37103	37104
37105	37106	37107	37116	37117
37118	37119	37120	37123	37125
37126	37127	37128	37130	37131
37132	37133	37137	37138	37139
37143	37144	37145	37146	37147
37154	37155	37156	37157	37158
37159	37160	37161	37162	37163
*37164	37165	37170	37171	37172

1975 REGULAR ISSUE

Issued TAGGED Only

#1622 13¢ U.S. FLAG (Huck) **Cont.**

37173	37175	37176	37177	37178
37179	37180	37181	37182	37183
*37184	*37185	*37186	37187	37188
37189	37190	37191	37192	37193
37194	37195	37196	37197	37198
*37199	37200	37201	37202	37203
37204	37205	37206	37207	37208
37209	37210	37211	*37212	37213
37218	37219	*37220	37221	37222
37223	37225	37226	37227	37228
37229	37238	37239	37240	37241
37243	37700	37701	37702	*37703
*37704	37705	37746	37747	37748
37749	37750	37751	*37752	37753
*37754	37755	*37756	37757	37758
37759	37760	37761	37762	37763
37764	37765	37766	37767	37768
37769	†37786	37787	37788	*37789
37790	37791	*37798	37799	37800
37801	*37802	†37803		

#1622 c 13¢ U.S. FLAG

A Press (Intaglio) PERF. 11

Positions		**L**	**R**
39913	$75.00	☐	☐

These are the "Floating Plate Numbers" which move up and down in the right and left vertical margins. There are 23 different positions of the plate numbers on each side.

BOOKLET PANE

#1623 a 13¢ FLAG over CAPITOL
PANES OF 8

Plate numbers are located much further away from the stamps so no plate numbers were regularly issued.

SIDE COIL

#1625 13¢ U.S. FLAG COIL

Very few reported with enough of the plate number to identify.

1976 COMMEMORATIVES

#1629-31 13¢ SPIRIT OF 76

Block of 12 (6 x 2)		UL	UR	LL	LR
36946-36947-36948-36949-36950	$3.50	☐	☐	☐	☐
36951-36952-36953-36954-36955	$3.50	☐	☐	☐	☐

#1632 13¢ INTERPHIL 12 Plates

36958	$1.30	☐	☐	☐	☐
36960	$1.30	☐	☐	☐	☐
36975	$1.30	☐	☐	☐	☐
36978	$1.30	☐	☐	☐	☐
36980	$1.30	☐	☐	☐	☐

1976 COMMEMORATIVES

#1632 13¢ INTERPHIL Continued

		UL	UR	LL	LR
36982	$1.30	☐	☐	☐	☐
36987	$40.00	☐	☐	☐	☐
36990	$40.00	☐	☐	☐	☐
37003	$40.00	☐	☐	☐	☐
37011	$40.00	☐	☐	☐	☐
37141	$1.30	☐	☐	☐	☐
37150	$1.30	☐	☐	☐	☐

#1633-82 13¢ STATE FLAGS

Block of 12 (2 x 6)

36782-36783-36784-36785-36786-36787 $8.50	☐	☐	☐	☐
36782-36783-36784-36791-36786-36787 $4.00	☐	☐	☐	☐
36782-36783-36784-37244-36786-36787 $4.00	☐	☐	☐	☐
36782-36789-36784-36791-36786-36787 $8.50	☐	☐	☐	☐
36788-36789-36790-37244-36786-36787 $4.00	☐	☐	☐	☐
36788-36789-36790-37244-36792-36793 $4.00	☐	☐	☐	☐

#1683 13¢ TELEPHONE 16 Plates

37280	$1.30	☐	☐	☐	☐
37281	$1.30	☐	☐	☐	☐
37282	$1.30	☐	☐	☐	☐
37283	$1.30	☐	☐	☐	☐
37284	$1.30	☐	☐	☐	☐
37285	$1.30	☐	☐	☐	☐
37289	$1.30	☐	☐	☐	☐
37290	$1.30	☐	☐	☐	☐
37291	$1.30	☐	☐	☐	☐
37292	$1.30	☐	☐	☐	☐
37293	$1.30	☐	☐	☐	☐
37294	$1.30	☐	☐	☐	☐
37295	$1.30	☐	☐	☐	☐
37296	$1.30	☐	☐	☐	☐
37297	$1.30	☐	☐	☐	☐
37306	$1.30	☐	☐	☐	☐

#1684 13¢ COMMERCIAL AVIATION

Block of 10 (2 x 5)

36991-36992-36993-36994-36995 $3.00	☐	☐	☐	☐
36996-36997-36998-36999-37000 $3.00	☐	☐	☐	☐

#1685 13¢ CHEMISTRY

Block of 12 (2 x 6)

36963-36964-36965-36966-36967-36968 $3.25	☐	☐	☐	☐
36969-36970-36971-36972-36973-36974 $3.25	☐	☐	☐	☐

BICENTENNIAL ISSUE

SOUVENIR SHEETS

#1686 13¢ SURRENDER OF CORNWALLS

#1687 18¢ DECLARATION OF INDEPENDENCE

#1688 24¢ CROSSING THE DELAWARE

#1689 31¢ ARMY AT VALLEY FORGE

The plate numbers of these souvenir sheets were trimmed off after printing so no plate numbers were regularly issued.

#1690 13¢ BENJ. FRANKLIN

12 Plates		UL	UR	LL	LR
37338	$1.30	☐	☐	☐	☐
37339	$1.30	☐	☐	☐	☐
37343	$1.30	☐	☐	☐	☐
37353	$1.30	☐	☐	☐	☐
37354	$1.30	☐	☐	☐	☐
37355	$1.30	☐	☐	☐	☐
37356	$1.30	☐	☐	☐	☐
37357	$1.30	☐	☐	☐	☐
37364	$1.30	☐	☐	☐	☐
37365	$1.30	☐	☐	☐	☐
37366	$1.30	☐	☐	☐	☐
37395	$1.30	☐	☐	☐	☐

#1691-94 13¢ SIGNING THE DECLARATION

Block of 16 (8 x 2)

37480-37481-37482-37483-37484 $4.50	☐	☐	☐	☐
37486-37487-37488-37563-37490 $4.50	☐	☐	☐	☐

#1695-98 13¢ OLYMPIC GAMES

Block of 12 (6 x 2)

37429-37430-37431-37432-37433-37434 $7.50	☐	☐	☐	☐
37435-37430-37431-37438-37439-37440 $3.50	☐	☐	☐	☐

#1699 13¢ CLARA MAASS

Block of 12 (6 x 2)

37261-37262-37263-37264-37265-37266 $3.50	☐	☐	☐	☐
37267-37268-37269-37270-37271-37272 $3.50	☐	☐	☐	☐

1976 COMMEMORATIVES

#1700 13¢ ADOLPH OCHS

13 Plates		UL	UR	LL	LR
37592	$1.30	☐	☐	☐	☐
37593	$1.30	☐	☐	☐	☐
37594	$1.30	☐	☐	☐	☐
37596	$1.30	☐	☐	☐	☐
37597	$1.30	☐	☐	☐	☐
37598	$1.30	☐	☐	☐	☐
37599	$1.30	☐	☐	☐	☐
37610	$1.30	☐	☐	☐	☐
37626	$1.30	☐	☐	☐	☐
37627	$1.30	☐	☐	☐	☐
37628	$1.30	☐	☐	☐	☐
37629	$1.30	☐	☐	☐	☐
37632	$1.30	☐	☐	☐	☐

#1701 13¢ COPLEY'S NATIVITY

Block of 12 (2 x 6)

Plates	Price	UL	UR	LL	LR
37492-37493-37494-37495-37496-37497	$3.25	☐	☐	☐	☐
37498-37499-37500-37501-37502-37503	$3.25	☐	☐	☐	☐
37498-37499-37500-37501-37502-37640	$3.25	☐	☐	☐	☐
37504-37505-37506-37507-37508-37509	$3.25	☐	☐	☐	☐

#1702 13¢ CURRIER (Andreotti Press)

Block of 10 (2 x 5)

Plates	Price	UL	UR	LL	LR
37465-37466-37467-37468-37479	$3.00	☐	☐	☐	☐
37470-37471-37472-37473-37474	$3.00	☐	☐	☐	☐
37475-37476-37477-37478-37469	$3.00	☐	☐	☐	☐

#1703 13¢ CURRIER

A Press (Gravure) Positions L R only

Block of 20 (2 x 10)

These are the "Floating Plate Numbers" which move up and down in the right and left vertical margins. There are 23 different positions of the plate numbers on each side.

Plates	Price	L	R
37617-37618-37619-37620-37621	$5.00	☐	☐
37634-37635-37636-37637-37638	$5.00	☐	☐

#1704 13¢ WASHINGTON AT PRINCETON

Block of 10 (5 x 2)		UL	UR	LL	LR
37642-37643-37644-37645-37646	$3.00	☐	☐	☐	☐

1977 COMMEMORATIVES

Issued TAGGED Only

#1704 13¢ WASHINGTON AT PRINCETON Continued

Plates	Price	UL	UR	LL	LR
37647-37648-37649-37650-37651	$3.00	☐	☐	☐	☐

#1705 13¢ SOUND RECORDING

8 Plates

Plate	Price	UL	UR	LL	LR
37858	$1.30	☐	☐	☐	☐
37859	$1.30	☐	☐	☐	☐
37860	$1.30	☐	☐	☐	☐
37862	$1.30	☐	☐	☐	☐
37865	$1.30	☐	☐	☐	☐
37867	$1.30	☐	☐	☐	☐
37868	$1.30	☐	☐	☐	☐
37869	$1.30	☐	☐	☐	☐

#1706-09 13¢ PUEBLO ART

Block of 10 (5 x 2)

Plates	Price	UL	UR	LL	LR
37770-37771-37772-37773-37774	$3.00	☐	☐	☐	☐
37775-37776-37777-37778-37779	$3.00	☐	☐	☐	☐

#1710 13¢ LINDBERGH FLIGHT

Block of 12 (2 x 6)

Plates	Price	UL	UR	LL	LR
37933-37934-37935-37936-37937-37938	$3.50	☐	☐	☐	☐
37939-37940-37941-37942-37943-37944	$3.50	☐	☐	☐	☐

#1711 13¢ COLORADO

Block of 12 (6 x 2)

In Line Perforator 11.2 x 11.2

Plates	Price	UL	UR	LL	LR
37956-37957-37958-37959-37960-37961	$3.50	☐	☐	☐	☐
37956-37963-37964-37965-37966-37967	$3.50	☐	☐	☐	☐
37962-37963-37964-37965-37966-37967	$3.50	☐	☐	☐	☐

#1711 13¢ COLORADO

"L" Perforator 10.9 x 10.9

Plates	Price	UL	UR	LL	LR
37962-37963-37964-37965-37966-36969	$15.00	☐	☐	☐	☐

#1712-15 13¢ BUTTERFLIES

Block of 12 (2 x 6)

Plates	Price	UL	UR	LL	LR
37830-37831-37832-37833-37834-37835	$3.50	☐	☐	☐	☐
37836-37837-37838-37839-37840-37841	$3.50	☐	☐	☐	☐

#1716 13¢ LAFAYETTE 10 Plates

Plate	Price	UL	UR	LL	LR
37916	$1.30	☐	☐	☐	☐
37923	$1.30	☐	☐	☐	☐
37925	$1.30	☐	☐	☐	☐

1977 COMMEMORATIVES

#1716 13¢ LAFAYETTE Continued

		UL	UR	LL	LR
37928	$1.30	☐	☐	☐	☐
37945	$1.30	☐	☐	☐	☐
37952	$2.50	☐	☐	☐	☐
37954	$1.30	☐	☐	☐	☐
37968	$1.30	☐	☐	☐	☐
37978	$1.30	☐	☐	☐	☐
38269	*$150.00*	☐	☐	☐$_2$	☐

#1717-20 13¢ SKILLED HANDS

Block of 12 (2 x 6)

37812-37813-37814-37815-37816-37817	$3.50	☐	☐	☐	☐
37818-37919-37820-37821-37822-37823	$3.50	☐	☐	☐	☐

#1721 13¢ PEACE BRIDGE

4 Plates

38051	$1.30	☐	☐	☐	☐
38052	$1.30	☐	☐	☐	☐
38053	$1.30	☐	☐	☐	☐
38054	$1.30	☐	☐	☐	☐

#1722 13¢ ORISKANY

Block of 10 (2 x 5)

37682-37683-37684-37685-37686	$3.00	☐	☐	☐	☐
37687-37688-37689-37690-37691	$3.00	☐	☐	☐	☐

#1723-24 13¢ ENERGY

Block of 12 (2 x 6)

38088-38089-38090-38091-38092-38093	$3.50	☐	☐	☐	☐
38094-38095-38096-38097-38098-38099	$3.50	☐	☐	☐	☐

#1725 13¢ ALTA CALIFORNIA

8 Plates

38191	$1.30	☐	☐	☐	☐
38192	$1.30	☐	☐	☐	☐
38209	$1.30	☐	☐	☐	☐
38210	$1.30	☐	☐	☐	☐
38211	$1.30	☐	☐	☐	☐
38212	$1.30	☐	☐	☐	☐
38213	$1.30	☐	☐	☐	☐
38218	$1.30	☐	☐	☐	☐

#1726 13¢ CONFEDERATION

9 Plates

37875	$1.30	☐	☐	☐	☐
37890	$1.30	☐	☐	☐	☐
37914	$1.30	☐	☐	☐	☐
37915	$1.30	☐	☐	☐	☐
37922	$1.30	☐	☐	☐	☐
37924	$1.30	☐	☐	☐	☐

1977 COMMEMORATIVES

#1726 13¢ CONFEDERATION Cont.

		UL	UR	LL	LR
37926	$1.30	☐	☐	☐	☐
37932	$1.30	☐	☐	☐	☐
37951	$1.30	☐	☐	☐	☐

#1727 13¢ TALKING PICTURES

8 Plates

37991	$1.30	☐	☐	☐	☐
37996	$1.30	☐	☐	☐	☐
37997	$1.30	☐	☐	☐	☐
38000	$1.30	☐	☐	☐	☐
38001	$1.30	☐	☐	☐	☐
38014	$1.30	☐	☐	☐	☐
38021	$1.30	☐	☐	☐	☐
38034	$1.30	☐	☐	☐	☐

#1728 13¢ SARATOGA

Block of 10 (2 x 5)

38133-38134-38135-38136-38137	$3.00	☐	☐	☐	☐
38138-38139-38140-38141-38142	$3.00	☐	☐	☐	☐

#1729 13¢ VALLEY FORGE

A Press (Gravure)

Block of 20 (2 x 10) **Positions L R**

These are the "Floating Plate Numbers" which move up and down in the right and left vertical margins. There are 23 different positions of the plate numbers on each side.

		L	R
37892-37893-37894-37895-37896	$5.00	☐	☐
37898-37899-37900-37901-37902	$5.00	☐	☐
38121-38122-38123-38124-38125	$5.00	☐	☐

#1730 13¢ RURAL MAILBOX

Block of 10 (2 x 5)		UL	UR	LL	LR
37904-37905-37906-37907-37908	$3.00	☐	☐	☐	☐
37909-37910-37911-37912-37913	$6.00	☐	☐	☐	☐
38155-38156-38157-38158-38159	$3.00	☐	☐	☐	☐

1978 COMMEMORATIVES

Issued TAGGED Only

#1731 13¢ CARL SANDBURG

8 Plates		UL	UR	LL	LR
38317	$1.30	☐	☐	☐	☐
38330	$1.30	☐	☐	☐	☐
38332	$1.30	☐	☐	☐	☐
38334	$1.30	☐	☐	☐	☐

1978 COMMEMORATIVES

#1731 13¢ CARL SANDBURG Cont.

		UL	UR	LL	LR
38336	$1.30	☐	☐	☐	☐
38338	$1.30	☐	☐	☐	☐
38341	$1.30	☐	☐	☐	☐
38346	$1.30	☐	☐	☐	☐

#1732 13¢ CAPTAIN COOK

Portraits

Upper Left and Lower Left
Plate numbers only

13 Plates		UL	LL
38362	$1.30	☐	☐
38372	$1.30	☐	☐
38374	$1.30	☐	☐
38379	$1.30	☐	☐
38381	$2.50	☐	☐
38382	$1.30	☐	☐
38384	$1.30	☐	☐
38385	$1.30	☐	☐
38388	$1.30	☐	☐
38389	$1.30	☐	☐
38390	$1.30	☐	☐
38391	$1.30	☐	☐
38392	$1.30	☐	☐

#1733 13¢ CAPTAIN COOK

Ships

Lower Left and Lower Right
plate numbers only

13 Plates		LL	LR
38362	$1.30	☐	☐
38372	$1.30	☐	☐
38374	$1.30	☐	☐
38379	$1.30	☐	☐
38381	$2.50	☐	☐
38382	$1.30	☐	☐
38384	$1.30	☐	☐
38385	$1.30	☐	☐
38388	$1.30	☐	☐
38389	$1.30	☐	☐
38390	$1.30	☐	☐
38391	$1.30	☐	☐
38392	$1.30	☐	☐

#1734 13¢ INDIAN HEAD PENNY

150 subjects to the pane

8 Plates		UL	UR	LL	LR
38353	$1.50	☐	☐	☐	☐
38356	$1.50	☐	☐	☐	☐
38357	$1.50	☐	☐	☐	☐
38358	$1.50	☐	☐	☐	☐
38360	$1.50	☐	☐	☐	☐
38363	$1.50	☐	☐	☐	☐
38373	$1.50	☐	☐	☐	☐
38376	$1.50	☐	☐	☐	☐

1978-80 REGULAR ISSUE

Issued TAGGED Only

#1735 (15¢) "A" EAGLE 4 Plates

In Line Perforator 11.2 x 11.2

		UL	UR	LL	LR
35768	$1.50	☐	☐	☐	☐
35769	$1.50	☐	☐	☐	☐
35770	$1.50	☐	☐	☐	☐
35771	$1.50	☐	☐	☐	☐

#1735 (15¢ "A" EAGLE 2 Plates

"L" Perforator 10.9 x 10.9

		UL	UR	LL	LR
35768	$3.00	☐	☐	☐	☐
35769	$3.00	☐	☐	☐	☐

BOOKLET PANES

#1736 a (15¢) "A" EAGLE

PANES OF 8

Plate numbers are located much further away from the stamps so no plate numbers were regularly issued.

#1737 a 15¢ ROSES

PANES OF 8

Plate numbers are located much further away from the stamps so no plate numbers were regularly issued.

#1738 a - 42 a 15¢ WIND-MILLS

PANES OF 8

Plate numbers are located much further away from the stamps so no plate numbers were regularly issued.

SIDE COIL PLATES

PERF. 10 VERTICALLY

#1743 (15¢) "A" EAGLE

432 Subject Plates **STRIPS OF 6**

35840	†35858	35859	35860	†35861
35862	35875	35876	†35877	35878

1978 COMMEMORATIVES

Continued

#1744 13¢ HARRIET TUBMAN

Block of 12 (6 x 2)		UL	UR	LL	LR
38294-38295-38296-38297-38298-38299	$3.50	☐	☐	☐	☐
38300-38301-38302-38303-38304-38305	$3.50	☐	☐	☐	☐

#1745-48 13¢ QUILTS

Block of 12 (2 x 6)		UL	UR	LL	LR
38318-38319-38320-38321-38322-38323	$3.50	☐	☐	☐	☐
38324-38325-38326-38327-38328-38329	$3.50	☐	☐	☐	☐

1978 COMMEMORATIVES

#1749-52 13¢ AMERICAN DANCE

Block of 12 (2 x 6)		UL	UR	LL	LR
38443-38444-38445-38446-38447-38448	$3.50	☐	☐	☐	☐
38449-38450-38451-38452-38453-38454	$3.50	☐	☐	☐	☐

#1753 13¢ FRENCH ALLIANCE
11 Plates

Plate	Price	UL	UR	LL	LR
38497	$1.30	☐	☐	☐	☐
38509	$1.30	☐	☐	☐	☐
38510	$1.30	☐	☐	☐	☐
38511	$1.30	☐	☐	☐	☐
38512	$1.30	☐	☐	☐	☐
38513	$1.30	☐	☐	☐	☐
38514	$1.30	☐	☐	☐	☐
38535	$1.30	☐	☐	☐	☐
38538	$1.30	☐	☐	☐	☐
38539	$1.30	☐	☐	☐	☐
38543	$1.30	☐	☐	☐	☐

#1754 13¢ CANCER DETECTION
4 Plates

Plate	Price	UL	UR	LL	LR
38238	$1.30	☐	☐	☐	☐
38239	$1.30	☐	☐	☐	☐
38240	$1.30	☐	☐	☐	☐
38241	$1.30	☐	☐	☐	☐

#1755 13¢ JIMMIE RODGERS

Block of 12 (6 x 2)		UL	UR	LL	LR
38475-38476-38477-38478-38479-38480	$3.50	☐	☐	☐	☐

#1756 15¢ GEORGE M. COHAN

Block of 12 (6 x 2)		UL	UR	LL	LR
38406-38407-38408-38709-38410-38584	$3.75	☐	☐	☐	☐
38412-38413-38414-38710-38416-38585	$3.75	☐	☐	☐	☐

#1757 13¢ CAPEX SHEET 8 Plates

Individual panes showing the plate number.

Plate	Price	UL	UR	LL	LR
38615	$2.25	☐	☐	☐	☐
38617	$2.25	☐	☐	☐	☐
38620	$2.25	☐	☐	☐	☐
38621	$2.25	☐	☐	☐	☐
38622	$2.25	☐	☐	☐	☐
38627	$2.25	☐	☐	☐	☐
38638	$2.25	☐	☐	☐	☐
38649	$2.25	☐	☐	☐	☐

#1758 15¢ PHOTOGRAPHY

Block of 12 (6 x 2)		UL	UR	LL	LR
38515-38516-38517-38518-38519-38583	$3.75	☐	☐	☐	☐
38522-38523-38524-38525-38526-38582	$3.75	☐	☐	☐	☐

1978 COMMEMORATIVES

#1759 15¢ VIKING 9 Plates

Plate	Price	UL	UR	LL	LR
38712	$1.35	☐	☐	☐	☐
38713	$1.35	☐	☐	☐	☐
38714	$1.35	☐	☐	☐	☐
38717	$1.35	☐	☐	☐	☐
38727	$1.35	☐	☐	☐	☐
38728	$1.35	☐	☐	☐	☐
38729	$1.35	☐	☐	☐	☐
38730	$1.35	☐	☐	☐	☐
38743	$1.35	☐	☐	☐	☐

#1760-63 15¢ AMERICAN OWLS
8 Plates

Plate	Price	UL	UR	LL	LR
38792	$1.35	☐	☐	☐	☐
38793	$1.35	☐	☐	☐	☐
38794	$1.35	☐	☐	☐	☐
38796	$1.35	☐	☐	☐	☐
38798	$1.35	☐	☐	☐	☐
38799	$1.35	☐	☐	☐	☐
38800	$1.35	☐	☐	☐	☐
38806	$1.35	☐	☐	☐	☐

#1764-67 15¢ AMERICAN TREES

Block of 12 (2 x 6)		UL	UR	LL	LR
38808-38809-38810-38811-38812-38813	$4.00	☐	☐	☐	☐

#1768 15¢ MADONNA (1978)

Block of 12 (2 x 6)		UL	UR	LL	LR
38731-38732-38733-38734-38735-38736	$3.75	☐	☐	☐	☐
38737-38738-38739-38740-38741-38742	$3.75	☐	☐	☐	☐

#1769 15¢ HOBBY HORSE

Block of 12 (2 x 6)		UL	UR	LL	LR
38662-38663-38664-38665-38666-38667	$3.75	☐	☐	☐	☐
38668-38669-38670-38671-38672-38673	$3.75	☐	☐	☐	☐

1979 COMMEMORATIVES

Issued TAGGED Only

#1770 15¢ ROBERT KENNEDY
8 Plates

Plate	Price	UL	UR	LL	LR
38916	$1.35	☐	☐	☐	☐
38917	$1.35	☐	☐	☐	☐
38918	$1.35	☐	☐	☐	☐
38919	$1.35	☐	☐	☐	☐
38920	$1.35	☐	☐	☐	☐
38921	$1.35	☐	☐	☐	☐
38926	$1.35	☐	☐	☐	☐
38927	$1.35	☐	☐	☐	☐

1979 COMMEMORATIVES

#1771 15¢ MARTIN LUTHER KING

Block of 12 (6 x 2)		UL	UR	LL	LR
38820-38821-38822-38823-38824-38825	$3.75	☐	☐	☐	☐

#1772 15¢ YEAR OF THE CHILD

8 Plates

Plate	Price	UL	UR	LL	LR
38976	$1.35	☐	☐	☐	☐
38977	$1.35	☐	☐	☐	☐
38978	$1.35	☐	☐	☐	☐
38979	$1.35	☐	☐	☐	☐
38980	$1.35	☐	☐	☐	☐
38981	$1.35	☐	☐	☐	☐
38984	$1.35	☐	☐	☐	☐
38985	$1.35	☐	☐	☐	☐

#1773 15¢ JOHN STEINBECK

4 Plates

Plate	Price	UL	UR	LL	LR
38940	$1.35	☐	☐	☐	☐
38941	$1.35	☐	☐	☐	☐
38942	$1.35	☐	☐	☐	☐
38943	$1.35	☐	☐	☐	☐

#1774 15¢ ALBERT EINSTEIN

4 Plates		UL	UR	LL	LR
38966	$1.35	☐	☐	☐	☐
38967	$1.35	☐	☐	☐	☐
38968	$1.35	☐	☐	☐	☐
38969	$1.35	☐	☐	☐	☐

#1775-78 15¢ AMERICAN FOLK ART

Block of 10 (5 x 2)		UL	UR	LL	LR
38997-38998-38999-39000-39001	$3.50	☐	☐	☐	☐

#1779-82 15¢ ARCHITECTURE

8 Plates

Plate	Price	UL	UR	LL	LR
39035	$1.50	☐	☐	☐	☐
39036	$1.50	☐	☐	☐	☐
39038	$1.50	☐	☐	☐	☐
39039	$1.50	☐	☐	☐	☐
39040	$1.50	☐	☐	☐	☐
39055	$1.50	☐	☐	☐	☐
39056	$1.50	☐	☐	☐	☐
39058	$1.50	☐	☐	☐	☐

Perf. 12 x 12

1979-80 COMMEMORATIVES

#1783-86 15¢ ENDANGERED FLORA

Block of 12 (6 x 2) UL UR LL LR

39049-39050-39051-39052-39053-39054
$3.75 ☐ ☐ ☐ ☐

#1787 15¢ SEEING EYE DOGS

A Press (Gravure)
Positions T B only

These are the "Floating Plate Numbers" which move in the margins.

Block of 20 (10 x 2) T B

38986-38987-38988-38989-39037
$6.00 ☐ ☐

#1788 15¢ SPECIAL OLYMPICS

Block of 10 (5 x 2) UL UR LL LR

39096-39097-39098-39099-39100
$3.50 ☐ ☐ ☐ ☐

#1789 15¢ JOHN PAUL JONES

This issue was printed by the American Banknote Co.

Block of 10 (2 x 5)

Perf. 11 x 11
A0006-A0007-A0008-A0009-A0010
$3.50 ☐ ☐ ☐ ☐

Perf. 11 x 12
A0001-A0002-A0003-A0004-A0005
$3.50 ☐ ☐ ☐ ☐

Perf 11 x 12
A0006-A0007-A0008-A0009-A0010
$3.50 ☐ ☐ ☐ ☐

Perf. 12 x 12
A0001-A0002-A0003-A0004-A0005
— ☐ † ☐ †

#1790 10¢ OLYMPICS

Block of 12 (6 x 2)

39111-39112-39113-39114-39115-39116
$3.50 ☐ ☐ ☐ ☐

#1791-94 15¢ SUMMER OLYMPICS

Block of 12 (2 x 6)

39089-39090-39091-39092-39093-39094
$3.75 ☐ ☐ ☐ ☐

#1795-98 15¢ WINTER OLYMPICS

Block of 12 (2 x 6)

In Line Perforator 11.2 x 11.2

PERF. 11 x 10½
39204-39205-39206-39207-39208-39209
$17.50 ☐ ☐ ☐ ☐

EE Perforator 11.3 x 10.5
39204-39205-39206-39207-39208-39209
$5.25 ☐ ☐ ☐ ☐

#1799 15¢ MADONNA (DAVID)

Block of 12 (2 x 6) UL UR LL LR

38944-38945-38946-38947-38948-38949
$3.75 ☐ ☐ ☐ ☐

38950-38951-38952-38953-38954-38955
$3.75 ☐ ☐ ☐ ☐

#1800 15¢ SANTA CLAUS

Block of 12 (2 x 6)

38880-38881-38882-38883-38884-38885
$3.75 ☐ ☐ ☐ ☐

38886-38887-38888-38889-38890-38891
$3.75 ☐ ☐ ☐ ☐

#1801 15¢ WILL ROGERS

Block of 12 (6 x 2)

39080-39081-39082-39083-39084-39085
$3.75 ☐ ☐ ☐ ☐

#1802 15¢ VIETNAM VETERANS

Block of 10 (2 x 5)

39150-39151-39152-39153-39154
$3.25 ☐ ☐ ☐ ☐

#1803 15¢ W.C. FIELDS

Block of 12 (6 x 2)

39219-39220-39221-39222-39223-39224
$3.75 ☐ ☐ ☐ ☐

#1804 15¢ BENJ. BANNEKER

This issue was printed by the American Banknote Co.

Block of 12 (6 x 2)

A0011-A0012-A0013-A0014-A0015-A0016
$3.75 ☐ ☐ ☐ ☐

A0017-A0018-A0019-A0020-A0021-A0022
$3.75 ☐ ☐ ☐ ☐

#1805-10 15¢ LETTER WRITING

Block of 36 (6 x 6)

39231-39232-39233-39234-39235-39236
$12.00 ☐ ☐ ☐ ☐

1975 AMERICAN SERIES SIDE COIL PLATES

PERF. 10 VERTICALLY

#1811 1¢ ABILITY TO WRITE

See page 201

#1813 3.5¢ VIOLINS

See page 201

#1816 12¢ FREEDOM OF CONSCIENCE

See Page 201

NON-DENOMINATED 1980 REGULAR ISSUES

#1818 (18¢) B and EAGLE SHEET STAMP

3 Plates		UL	UR	LL	LR
36470	$1.80	☐	☐	☐	☐
36471	$1.80	☐	☐	☐	☐
36472	$1.80	☐	☐	☐	☐

#1819 (18¢) B and EAGLE BOOKLET PANE

Plate numbers are located much further away from the stamps so no plate numbers were regularly issued.

#1820 (18¢) B and EAGLE COIL STAMP

PERF. 10 VERTICALLY

*36569 *36761 *36762 *39033 *39247
*39248 *39249 *39250 *39276 *39277
†39288 †39289 †39291 †39292 †39300
†39315 †39346 †39347 †39373 †39374

1980 COMMEMORATIVES

Continued

#1821 15¢ FRANCES PERKINS

4 Plates		UL	UR	LL	LR
39270	$1.50	☐	☐	☐	☐
39271	$1.50	☐	☐	☐	☐
39272	$1.50	☐	☐	☐	☐
39273	$1.50	☐	☐	☐	☐

#1822 15¢ DOLLEY MADISON

5 Plates

39293	$1.75	☐	☐	☐	☐
39294	$1.75	☐	☐	☐	☐
39295	$1.75	☐	☐	☐	☐
39296	$1.75	☐	☐	☐	☐
39297	$1.75	☐	☐	☐	☐

#1823 15¢ EMILY BISSELL

8 Plates

39278	$1.35	☐	☐	☐	☐
39279	$1.35	☐	☐	☐	☐
39280	$1.35	☐	☐	☐	☐
39281	$1.35	☐	☐	☐	☐
39284	$1.35	☐	☐	☐	☐
39285	$1.35	☐	☐	☐	☐
39286	$1.35	☐	☐	☐	☐
39287	$1.35	☐	☐	☐	☐

#1824 15¢ HELEN KELLER

10 Plates

39313	$1.35	☐	☐	☐	☐
39314	$1.35	☐	☐	☐	☐
39316	$1.35	☐	☐	☐	☐
39340	$1.35	☐	☐	☐	☐
39341	$1.35	☐	☐	☐	☐

1980 COMMEMORATIVES

Continued

#1824 15¢ HELEN KELLER Cont.

		UL	UR	LL	LR
39348	$1.35	☐	☐	☐	☐
39349	$1.35	☐	☐	☐	☐
39350	$1.35	☐	☐	☐	☐
39352	$1.35	☐	☐	☐	☐
39383	$1.35	☐	☐	☐	☐

#1825 15¢ VETERANS ADMIN.

This issue was printed by the American Banknote Co.,

Block of 4

A0023 A0024	$1.35	☐	☐	☐	☐
A0025 A0026	$1.35	☐	☐	☐	☐

#1826 15¢ GENERAL GALVEZ

7 Plates

39359	$1.35	☐	☐	☐	☐
39364	$1.35	☐	☐	☐	☐
39368	$1.35	☐	☐	☐	☐
39381	$1.35	☐	☐	☐	☐
39382	$1.35	☐	☐	☐	☐
39391	$1.35	☐	☐	☐	☐
39397	$1.35	☐	☐	☐	☐

#1827-30 15¢ CORAL REEFS

Block of 12 (6 x 2)

39385-39386-39387-39388-39389-39390
$4.50 ☐ ☐ ☐ ☐

#1831 15¢ ORGANIZED LABOR

Block of 12 (6 x 2)

39405-39406-39407-39408-39409-39410
$4.25 ☐ ☐ ☐ ☐

#1832 15¢ EDITH WHARTON

4 Plates

39393	$1.35	☐	☐	☐	☐
39394	$1.35	☐	☐	☐	☐
39395	$1.35	☐	☐	☐	☐
39396	$1.35	☐	☐	☐	☐

#1833 15¢ EDUCATION

This issue was printed by the American Banknote Co.

Block of 6 (3 x 2)

A0027-A0028-A0029
$2.00 ☐ ☐ ☐ ☐

A0030-A0031-A0032
$2.00 ☐ ☐ ☐ ☐

#1834-37 15¢ INDIAN MASKS

Block of 10 (5 x 2)

39265-39266-39267-39268-39269
$3.75 ☐ ☐ ☐ ☐

1980 COMMEMORATIVES

#1838-41 15¢ ARCHITECTURE

8 Plates		UL	UR	LL	LR
39417	$1.35	☐	☐	☐	☐
39421	$1.35	☐	☐	☐	☐
39422	$1.35	☐	☐	☐	☐
39427	$1.35	☐	☐	☐	☐
39428	$2.00	☐	☐	☐	☐
39429	$1.35	☐	☐	☐	☐
39430	$1.35	☐	☐	☐	☐
39431	$1.35	☐	☐	☐	☐

#1842 15¢ XMAS STAINED GLASS

Block of 12 (6 x 2)

Plates	Price				
39327-39328-39329-39330-39331-39332	$3.75	☐	☐	☐	☐
39333-39334-39335-39336-39337-39338	$3.75	☐	☐	☐	☐

#1843 15¢ XMAS WREATH
A Press (Gravure)

Block of 20 (10 x 2)

These are the "Floating Plate Numbers" which move in the margins.

Plates	Price	T	B
39317-39318-39319-39320-39321	$6.50	☐	☐
39322-39323-39324-39325-39326	$6.50	☐	☐

THE NEW PLATE NUMBERING SYSTEM

Starting in 1981 with the Everett Dirksen commemorative, the plate numbering system was changed. Where formerly the plate numbers consisted of five digit numbers for each of the plates used irrespective of whether they were intaglio, gravure or offset plates, a new method of designating the printing plate was introduced. The old five digit numbering was continued for record purposes but the number was placed in an area where it would not appear on the finished product. In its place a single digit was used that would appear on the face. The intent was to start each type of plate with the digit 1 and continue with consecutive numbers to represent the additional identical plates used to print the stamp. Since more than one method of printing is used and also more than one type of press for similar printing methods is used, we encounter different formats of numbers in the selvedge of sheets of stamps that are issued.

Another question that must be addressed is what is considered to be a PLATE BLOCK. We will define a plate block to mean a minimum quantity of stamps which maintains the intended design and at the same time to show all of the plate numbers involved in an aesthetically pleasing block format.

The product of the current intaglio presses will result in a plate block of four stamps similar to the former rotary press product with selvedge on two adjacent sides.

The product of the use of both an offset press in one operation and an intaglio press in another operation will also be a plate block of four with selvedge on two adjacent sides.

The product of the current gravure presses will result in a plate block of four with selvedge on two adjacent sides.

The product of the A press, which creates the "floating" plate numbers will result in two different collecting forms depending upon whether only one section is used or both the intaglio and gravure sections are used. In the case of only one section, a plate block will be identical to the old flat plate format where there is one stamp with blank selvedge at either side of the plate number. This is a block of SIX. In the case where both printing sections are used, the plate block will be a block of FOUR, with the intaglio numbers adjacent to one stamp and the gravure numbers adjacent to the other stamp.

Where a plate block consists of more than four stamps, we will list the quantity of stamps in the plate block in the heading of the issue.

The changeover in the numbering system has also resulted in a change in the status of coil stamps and booklet pane stamps. Since the introduction of the rotary press method of printing, the plate numbers had been placed in a position where they were intended to be trimmed off in the manufacturing process. Where formerly a partial plate number might be found by accident, now the plate number is an INTEGRAL part of the design of the stamps in one row of each printing plate used for coil stamps. The booklet panes have the number in the selvedge adjacent to the stamps.

We will define a plate strip of coil stamps as having five stamps with the plate number on the middle stamp.

We will define a plate number pane of booklet stamps as the full pane as issued with the plate number in the selvedge.

1980 REGULAR ISSUES GREAT AMERICANS

#1844 $.01 DOROTHEA DIX
A Press (intaglio)
In-line Perforator 11.2 x 11.1

		L	R
1	.15	☐	☐

"L" Perforator 10.8 x 10.9

		L	R
1	.15	☐	☐
2	.15	☐	☐

#1845 $.02 IGOR STRAVINSKY
Cottrell Press
EE Perforator 11.2 x 10.5

		UL	UR	LL	LR
1	.25	☐	☐	☐	☐
2	.25	☐	☐	☐	☐
3	.25	☐	☐	☐	☐
4	.25	☐	☐	☐	☐
5	.25	☐	☐	☐	☐
6	.25	☐	☐	☐	☐

#1846 $.03 HENRY CLAY
Cottrell Press
EE Perforator 11.2 x 10.5

1	$.30	☐	☐	☐	☐
2	$.30	☐	☐	☐	☐

#1847 $.04 CARL SCHURZ
Cottrell Press
EE Perforator 11.2 x 10.5

1	1$.40	☐	☐	☐	☐
2	$.40	☐	☐	☐	☐
3	$.40	☐	☐	☐	☐
4	$.40	☐	☐	☐	☐

#1848 $.05 PEARL BUCK
Cottrell Press
EE Perforator 11.2 x 10.5

1	$.50	☐	☐	☐	☐
2	$.50	☐	☐	☐	☐
3	$.50	☐	☐	☐	☐
4	$.50	☐	☐	☐	☐

#1849 $.06 WALTER LIPPMANN
A Press (intaglio)
"L" Perforator 10.8 x 10.9

		L	R
1	.60	☐	☐

#1850 $.07 ABRAHAM BALDWIN
A Press (intaglio)
"L" Perforator 10.8 x 10.9

		L	R
1	.70	☐	☐

#1851 $.08 HENRY KNOX
I-8 Press
"L" Perforator 10.9 x 10.9

3	$.80	☐	☐	☐	☐
4	$.80	☐	☐	☐	☐
5	$.80	☐	☐	☐	☐
6	$.80	☐	☐	☐	☐

#1852 $.09 SYLVANUS THAYER
A Press (intaglio)
"L" Perforator 10.8 x 10.9

		L	R
1	.90	☐	☐

#1853 $.10 RICHARD RUSSELL
A Press (intaglio)
"L" Perforator 10.8 x 10.9

		L	R
1	$1.00	☐	☐

#1854 $.11 ALLEN PARTRIDGE
I-8 Press
"L" Perforator 10.9 x 10.8

		UL	UR	LL	LR
2	$1.10	☐	☐	☐	☐
3	$1.10	☐	☐	☐	☐
4	$1.10	☐	☐	☐	☐
5	$1.10	☐	☐	☐	☐

#1855 $.13 CRAZY HORSE
Cottrell Press
EE Perforator 11.2 x 10.5

1	$1.30	☐	☐	☐	☐
2	$1.30	☐	☐	☐	☐
3	$1.30	☐	☐	☐	☐
4	$1.30	☐	☐	☐	☐

#1856 $.14 SINCLAIR LEWIS
A Press (Intaglio)
"L" Perforator 10.8 x 10.9

		L	R
1	$1.40	☐	☐

1980 REGULAR ISSUES GREAT AMERICANS Cont.

#1857 17¢ RACHEL CARSON

		UL	UR	LL	LR
1	$1.70	□	□	□	□
2	$1.70	□	□	□	□
3	$1.70	□	□	□	□
4	$1.70	□	□	□	□
13	$1.70	□	□	□	□
14	$1.70	□	□	□	□
15	$1.70	□	□	□	□
16	$1.70	□	□	□	□

#1858 $.18 GEORGE MASON

Cottrell Press

EE Perforator 11.2 x 10.5

1	$1.80	□	□	□	□
2	$1.80	□	□	□	□
3	$1.80	□	□	□	□
4	$1.80	□	□	□	□
5	$1.80	□	□	□	□
6	$1.80	□	□	□	□

#1859 $.19 SEQUOYAH

Cottrell Press

EE Perforator 11.2 x 10.5

39529	$1.90	□	□	□	□
39530	$1.90	□	□	□	□

#1860 $.20 RALPH BUNCHE

Cottrell Press

EE Perforator 11.2 x 10.5

1	$1.75	□	□	□	□
2	$1.75	□	□	□	□
3	$1.75	□	□	□	□
4	$1.75	□	□	□	□
5	$1.75	□	□	□	□
6	$1.75	□	□	□	□
7	$1.75	□	□	□	□
8	$1.75	□	□	□	□
10	$1.75	□	□	□	□
11	$1.75	□	□	□	□
13	$1.75	□	□	□	□

#1861 $.20 THOMAS H. GALLAUDET

Cottrell Press

EE Perforator 11.2 x 10.5

1	$1.75	□	□	□	□
2	$1.75	□	□	□	□
3	—	†	†	†	†
4	—	†	†	†	†
5	$1.75	□	□	□	□
6	$1.75	□	□	□	□
8	$2.75	□	□	□	□
9	$2.75	□	□	□	□

#1862 $.20 HARRY S. TRUMAN

A Press (Intaglio)

"L" Perforator 10.8 x 10.9

		L	R
1	$.75	□	□

A Press (revised)

Eureka Perforator 11.2 x 11.1

		UL	UR	LL	LR
2	$1.75	□	□	□	□

#1863 $.22 JOHN J. AUDUBON

A Press (Intaglio)

"L" Perforator 10.8 x 10.9

		L	R
1	$1.80	□	□

A Press (revised)

Eureka Perforator 10.8 x 10.9

		UL	UR	LL	LR
3	$1.80	□	□	□	□

#1864 $.30 FRANK C. LAUBACH

A Press (intaglio)

"L" Perforator 10.8 x 10.9

		L	R
1	$2.50	□	□

A Press (revised)

Eureka Perforator 11.2 x 11.1

2	$2.50	□	□	□	□

#1865 $.35 CHARLES R. DREW

Cottrell Press

EE Perforator 11.2 x 10.5

		UL	UR	LL	LR
1	$3.00	□	□	□	□
2	$3.00	□	□	□	□
3	$3.00	□	□	□	□
4	$3.00	□	□	□	□

#1866 $.37 ROBERT MILLIKAN

Cottrell Press

EE Perforator 11.2 x 10.5

1	$3.25	□	□	□	□
2	$3.25	□	□	□	□
3	$3.25	□	□	□	□
4	$3.25	□	□	□	□

#1867 $.39 GRENVILLE CLARK

A Press (intaglio)

"L" Perforator 10.8 x 10.9

		L	R
1	$3.35	□	□

A Press (revised)

Eureka Perforator 11.2 x 11.1

2	$3.35	□	□	□	□

1980 REGULAR ISSUES GREAT AMERICANS, Cont.

#1968 $.40 LILLIAN M. GILBRETH

A Press (intaglio)

"L" Perforator 10.8 x 10.9

		L	R
1	$3.50	☐	☐

#A Press (revised)

Eureka Perforator 11.2 x 11.1

2	$3.50	☐	☐	☐	☐

#1869 $.50 CHESTER W. NIMITZ

I-8 Press

"L" Perforator 10.9 x 10.8

1	$3.50	☐	☐	☐	☐
2	$3.50	☐	☐	☐	☐
3	$3.50	☐	☐	☐	☐
4	$3.50	☐	☐	☐	☐

A Press (revised)

Eureka Perforator 11.2 x 11.1

1	$3.50	☐	☐	☐	☐
2	$3.50	☐	☐	☐	☐

EXAMPLE OF EUREKA PERFORATION

See page 201 for illustrations of EE perforation, In-Line perforation, and "L" perforation.

1981 COMMEMORATIVES

Issued TAGGED Only

#1874 15¢ EVERETT DIRKSEN

8 Plates		UL	UR	LL	LR
1	$1.35	☐	☐	☐	☐
2	$1.35	☐	☐	☐	☐
3	$1.35	☐	☐	☐	☐
4	$1.35	☐	☐	☐	☐
5	$1.35	☐	☐	☐	☐
6	$1.35	☐	☐	☐	☐
7	$1.35	☐	☐	☐	☐
8	$1.35	☐	☐	☐	☐

1981COMMEMORATIVES

#1875 15¢ WHITNEY YOUNG

111111	$1.35	☐	☐	☐	☐

#1876-79 18¢ FLOWERS

111111	$1.60	☐	☐	☐	☐

Continued on page 226

1981 REGULAR ISSUE

BOOKLETS

#1889a $3.60 WILDLIFE BOOKET

2 PANES OF 10 STAMPS #at top

1	$25.00	☐
2	$25.00	☐
3	$25.00	☐
4	$25.00	☐
5	$25.00	☐
6	$25.00	☐
7	$25.00	☐
8	$25.00	☐
9	$25.00	☐
10	$25.00	☐
11	$40.00	☐
12	$40.00	☐
13	$40.00	☐
14	$30.00	☐
15	$30.00	☐
16	$30.00	☐

1981 FLAG and ANTHEM ISSUES

#1890 $.18 FLAG AND "AMBER" WAVES

A Press (Intaglio)

In-line Perforator 11.2 x 11.2

		L	R
1	$1.80	☐	☐
2	$1.80	☐	☐

#1891 $.18 COIL FLAG & "FROM SEA"

B Press	Strips of 5	Bottom
1	$500.	☐
2	$40.	☐
3	$500.	☐
4	$11.	☐
5	$6.	☐
6	$1800.	☐
7	$30.	☐

#1892-93 $1.20 BOOKLET

1 Pane of 2-$.06 6-$.18 TOP

1	$3.00	☐

1981 FLAG OVER SUPREME COURT ISSUES

#1894 .20 SHEET STAMP
A Press (Intaglio)
In-Line Perforator 11.2 x 11.2

		L	R
2	$2.00	☐	☐
3	$2.00	☐	☐
4	$2.00	☐	☐

"L" Perforator 10.9 x 10.9

		L	R
2	$2.00	☐	☐
3	$2.00	☐	☐
4	$2.00	☐	☐

#1895 $.20 COIL STAMP
B Press

		B
1	$80.00	☐
2	$12.00	☐
3	$6.00	☐
5	$6.00	☐
11	$10.00	☐

#1895 20¢ COIL STAMP Continued
B Press Continued

		B
13	$6.00	☐
14	$6.00	☐

C Press

4	$300.00	☐
5	$80.00	☐
6	$24.00	☐
9	$6.00	☐
10	$6.00	☐
12	$6.00	☐

#1896a $1.20 FLAG & SUPREME COURT BOOKLET
1 PANE OF 6 STAMPS # at top

1	$2.50	☐

#1896b $2.00 FLAG & SUPREME COURT BOOKLET
2 PANES OF 10 STAMPS # at top

2	$8.00	☐
3	$8.00	☐
4	$8.00	☐

PRECANCEL STYLES

Style 1
Un-precancelled version

Style 2

Style 3

Style 4

Style 5C

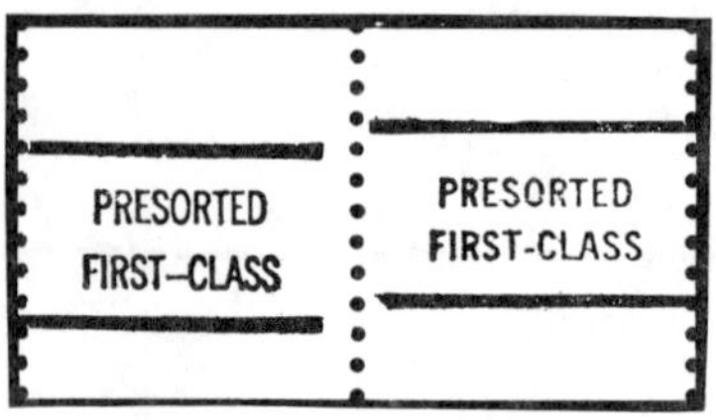

Style 5B *Style 5A*

Style 6
Assigned, but not issued

Style 7

Style 8

Style 9

Style 10

***Style 11**

***Style 12**

***Style 13A**

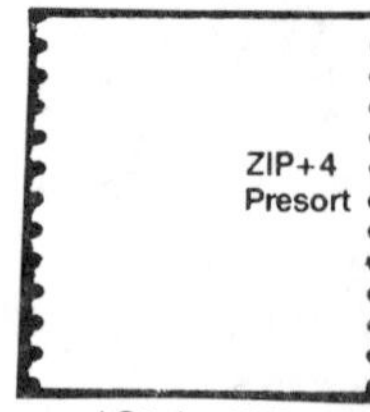

***Style 13B**

Style 14

Style 15

***Style 16**

***Style 17**

***Style 18**

***Style 19**

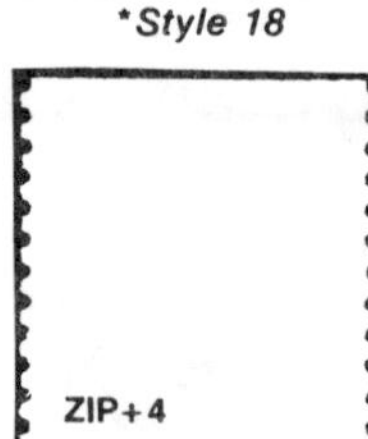

***Style 20**

***Style 21**

* These styles are part of the sleeve but printed in another color.

TRANSPORTATION COIL ISSUES
STRIPS OF FIVE

#1897 1¢ OMNIBUS

Cottrell Press

1 $.75 ☐
2 $.75 ☐
3 $.75 ☐
4 $.75 ☐
5 $.75 ☐
6 $.75 ☐

#2225 1¢ OMNIBUS COIL (revised)

B Press

1 $.75 ☐
2 $.75 ☐

#1897A 2¢ LOCOMOTIVE

Cottrell Press

2 $.80 ☐
3 $.80 ☐
4 $.80 ☐
6 $.80 ☐
8 $.80 ☐
10 $.80 ☐

#2226 2¢ LOCOMOTIVE COIL (revised)

B Press

1 $.75 ☐

#1898 3¢ HARDCAR

Cottrell Press

1 $1.25 ☐
2 $1.25 ☐
3 $1.25 ☐
4 $1.25 ☐

#2252 3¢ CONESTOGA WAGON

B Press

1 $1.25 ☐

#2123 3.4¢ SCHOOL BUS

Cottrell Press

1 $1.50 ☐
2 $1.50 ☐

#2123a 3.4¢ SCHOOL BUS (Style 3)

Cottrell Press PRECANCEL

1 $1.75 ☐
2 $1.75 ☐

#1898A 4¢ STAGECOACH

Cottrell Press

1 $2.00 ☐
2 $2.00 ☐
3 $2.00 ☐

#1898A 4¢ STAGECOACH Cont.

4 $2.00 ☐
5 $2.00 ☐
6 $2.00 ☐

#1898Ab 4¢ STAGECOACH

Cottrell Press PRECANCEL

3 $3.00 ☐
4 $3.00 ☐
5 $3.00 ☐
6 $3.00 ☐

#2228 4¢ STAGECOACH (revised)

B Press

1 $1.50 ☐

#2124 4.9¢ BUCKBOARD

Cottrell Press

3 $1.75 ☐
4 $1.75 ☐

#2124a $.049 BUCKBOARD (Style 4)

1 $2.50 ☐
2 $2.50 ☐
3 $2.50 ☐
4 $2.50 ☐
5 $2.50 ☐
6 $2.50 ☐

#1899 5¢ POPE MOTORCYCLE

Cottrell Press

1 $1.50 ☐
2 $1.50 ☐
3 $1.50 ☐
4 $1.50 ☐

#2253 5¢ MILK WAGON

B Press

1 $1.50 ☐

#1900 5.2¢ SLEIGH

Cottrell Press

1 $15.00 ☐
2 $15.00 ☐
3 $15.00 ☐
5 $15.00 ☐

#1900a 5.2¢ SLEIGH (Style 2)

Cottrell Press PRECANCEL

1 $12.00 ☐
2 $12.00 ☐
3 $12.00 ☐
4 $15.00 ☐
5 $12.00 ☐
6 $15.00 ☐

TRANSPORTATION COILS Cont.

#2254 5.3¢ ELEVATOR (Style 19)
B Press **PRECANCEL**
1 $1.50 ☐

#2125 5.5¢ STAR ROUTE TRUCK
B Press
1 $2.00 ☐ ☐

#2125a 5.5¢ STAR ROUTE TRUCK (Style 11)
B Press **PRECANCEL**
1 $2.50 ☐
2 $2.50 ☐

#1901 5.9¢ BICYCLE
Cottrell Press
3 $20.00 ☐
4 $20.00 ☐

#1901a 5.9¢ BICYCLE (Style 2)
Cottrell Press **PRECANCEL**
3 $20.00 ☐
4 $20.00 ☐
5 $75.00 ☐
6 $75.00 ☐

#2126 6¢ TRICYCLE
B Press
1 $2.00 ☐

#2126a 6¢ TRICYCLE
B Press **PRECANCEL**
1 $3.00 ☐
2 $7.00 ☐

#2127 7.1¢ TRACTOR
B Press
1 $3.00 ☐

#2127a 7.1¢ TRACTOR (Style 12)
B Press **PRECANCEL**
1 $3.00 ☐

#2127a 7.1¢ TRACTOR (Style 21)
B Press **PRECANCEL**
1 $2.50 ☐

#1902 7.4¢ BABY BUGGY
B Press
2 $15.00 ☐

#1902a 7.4¢ BABY BUGGY (Style 7)
B Press **PRECANCEL**
2 $4.00 ☐

#2255 7.6¢ CARRETA (Style 17)
B Press **PRECANCEL**
1 $3.00 ☐
2 $3.00 ☐
3 $3.00 ☐ ☐

#2128 8.3¢ AMBULANCE
Cottrell Press
1 $2.50 ☐
2 $2.50 ☐

#2128a 8.3¢ AMBULANCE
Cottrell Press **PRECANCEL**
1 $2.50 ☐
2 $2.50 ☐
3 $4.00 ☐
4 $4.00 ☐

#2231 8.3¢ AMBULANCE
B Press **PRECANCEL**
1 $4.50 ☐
2 $4.50 ☐

#2256 8.4¢ WHEELCHAIR (Style 17)
B Press **PRECANCEL**
1 $3.50 ☐

#2256 8.4¢ WHEELCHAIR (Style 17)
C Press **PRECANCEL**
2 $3.50 ☐
3 $3.50 ☐

#2129 8.4¢ TOW TRUCK
B Press
1 $3.50 ☐

#2129a 8.5¢ TOW TRUCK
B Press **PRECANCEL**
1 $4.00 ☐
2 $4.00 ☐

TRANSPORTATION COIL ISSUES Cont.

#1903 9.3¢ MAIL WAGON
Cottrell Press

1 $15.00 ☐
2 $15.00 ☐
3 $40.00 ☐
4 $40.00 ☐
5 $250.00 ☐
6 $250.00 ☐

#1903a 9.3¢ MAIL WAGON (Style 2)
Cottrell Press PRECANCEL

1 $15.00 ☐
2 $15.00 ☐
3 $25.00 ☐
4 $25.00 ☐
5 $5.00 ☐
6 $5.00 ☐
8 $150.00 ☐

#2257 10¢ CANAL BOAT
B Press

1 $2.50 ☐

#2130 10.1¢ OIL WAGON
B Press

1 $3.50 ☐

#2130a 10.1¢ OIL WAGON (Style 8)
B Press PRECANCEL

1 $4.50 ☐
2 $4.50 ☐

#2130a 10.1¢ OIL WAGON (Style 15)
B Press PRECANCEL

2 $4.00 ☐
3 $4.00 ☐

#1904 10.9¢ HANSOM CAB
Cottrell Press

1 $40.00 ☐
2 $40.00 ☐
☐

#1904a 10.9¢ HANSOM CAB (Style 2)
Cottrell Press PRECANCEL

1 $30.00 ☐
2 $30.00 ☐
3 $400.00 ☐
4 $400.00 ☐

#1905 11¢ RAILROAD CABOOSE
B Press

1 $6.00 ☐

#1905a 11¢ RAILROAD CABOOSE (Style 2)
B Press PRECANCEL

1 $4.50 ☐

#2131 11¢ STUTZ BEARCAT
Cottrell Press

1 $4.00 ☐
2 $4.00 ☐
3 $2.50 ☐
4 $2.50 ☐

#2132 12¢ STANLEY STEAMER
Cottrell Press

1 $2.50 ☐
2 $2.50 ☐

#2132a 12¢ STANELY STEAMER (Style 5)
Cottrell Press PRECANCEL

1 $3.50 ☐
2 $3.50 ☐

B Press PRECANCEL

1 $5.00 ☐

#2133 12.5¢ PUSHCART
B Press

1 $3.00 ☐
2 $5.00 ☐

#2133a 12.5¢ PUSHCART (Style 8)
B Press PRECANCEL

1 $4.50 ☐
2 $4.50 ☐

#2258 13¢ POLICE PATROL (Style 18)
B Press PRECANCEL

1 $3.50 ☐

#2259 13.2¢ RR COAL CAR (Style 16)
B Press PRECANCEL

1 $3.50 ☐
2 $3.50 ☐

#2134 14¢ ICEBOAT
Cottrell Press

1 $2.50 ☐
2 $2.50 ☐
3 $2.50 ☐
4 $2.50 ☐

TRANSPORTATION COIL ISSUES Cont.

#2134 14¢ ICEBOAT

B Press

2	$3.50	☐

#2260 15¢ TUGBOAT

B Press

1	$4.00	☐
2	$4.00	☐

#2261 16.7¢ POPCORN WAGON (Style 16)

B Press PRECANCEL

1	$5.00	☐
2	$5.00	☐

#1906 17¢ ELECTRIC AUTO

Cottrell Press

1	$4.00	☐
2	$4.00	☐
3	$4.00	☐
4	$4.00	☐
5	$4.00	☐
6	$20.00	☐
7	$7.50	☐

#1906a 17¢ ELECTRIC AUTO (Style 5-A)

"Presorted" is 11 mm long

Cottrell Press PRECANCEL

3	$7.00	☐
4	$7.00	☐
5	$7.00	☐
6	$12.50	☐
7	$12.50	☐

#1906a 17¢ ELECTRIC AUTO (Style 5-B)

"Presorted" is 12.5 mm long

Cottrell Press PRECANCEL

3	$30.00	☐
4	$30.00	☐
5	$12.00	☐
6	$12.00	☐

#1906a 17¢ ELECTRIC AUTO (Style 5-C)

"Presorted" is 13.5 mm long

Cottrell Press PRECANCEL

1	$10.00	☐
2	$10.00	☐
3	$12.50	☐
4	$12.50	☐
5	$25.00	☐
7	$25.00	☐

#2135 17¢ DOG SLED

B Press

2	$3.00	☐

#2262 17.5¢ RACING CAR

B Press

1	$5.00	☐

#2262a 17.5¢ RACING CAR (Style 13)

B Press PRECANCEL

1	$5.00	☐

#1907 18¢ SURREY

Cottrell Press

1	$80.00	☐
2	$5.00	☐
3	$50.00	☐
4	$50.00	☐
5	$5.00	☐
6	$5.00	☐
7	$30.00	☐
8	$5.00	☐
9	$5.00	☐
10	$5.00	☐
11	$10.00	☐
12	$10.00	☐
13	$7.00	☐
14	$7.00	☐
15	$7.00	☐
16	$7.00	☐
17	$7.00	☐
18	$7.00	☐

#1908 20¢ FIRE PUMPER

Cottrell Press

1	$175.00	☐
2	$1000.00	☐
3	$6.00	☐
4	$6.00	☐
5	$4.00	☐
6	$8.00	☐
7	$125.00	☐
8	$125.00	☐
9	$4.00	☐
10	$4.00	☐
11	$65.00	☐
12	$15.00	☐
13	$6.00	☐
14	$15.00	☐
15	$6.00	☐
16	$6.00	☐

#2263 20¢ CABLE CAR

C Press

1	$5.00	☐
2	$5.00	☐

TRANSPORTATION COIL ISSUES Cont.

#2264 20.5¢ FIRE ENGINE (Style 13)

B Press **PRECANCEL**

1 $4.50 ☐

#2265 21¢ RR MAIL CAR (Style 18)

B Press **PRECANCEL**

1 $4.50 ☐

#2265 21¢ RR MAIL CAR (Style 18)

C Press **PRECANCEL**

2 $4.50 ☐

#2266 24.1¢ TANDEM BICYCLE (Style 18)

B Press **PRECANCEL**

1 $5.50 ☐

#2136 25¢ BREADWAGON

B PRESS

1 $5.00 ☐
5 $6.00 ☐

#2136 25¢ BREADWAGON

C/D Press

2 $5.00 ☐
3 $5.00 ☐
4 $5.00 ☐

EXPRESS MAIL ISSUE

continued from page 218

#1909a $28.05 EAGLE BOOKLET

1 PANE OF 3 STAMPS		#at top
1111	$70.00	☐

1981 COMMEMORATIVES

Continued

#1910 18¢ AMERICAN RED CROSS

		UL	UR	LL	LR
111111	$1.60	☐	☐	☐	☐

#1911 18¢ SAVINGS & LOAN

111111	$1.60	☐	☐	☐	☐

#1912-19 18¢ SPACE ACHIEVEMENTS
(Block of 8)

111111	$3.50	☐	☐	☐	☐
222222	$3.50	☐	☐	☐	☐

#1920 18¢ PROFESSIONAL MANAGEMENT

11	$1.60	☐	☐	☐	☐

#1921-24 18¢ WILDLIFE HABITAT

11111	$1.60	☐	☐	☐	☐

#1925 18¢ DISABLED PERSONS

111111	$1.60	☐	☐	☐	☐

#1926 18¢ EDNA ST. VINCENT MILLAY

		UL	UR	LL	LR
111111-4	$1.60	☐	☐	☐	☐
111111-6	$1.60	☐	☐	☐	☐
111111-7	$1.60	☐	☐	☐	☐
111111-8	$1.60	☐	☐	☐	☐

#1927 18¢ ALCOHOLISM

A Press (Gravure)		L	R
1	$15.00	☐	☐

#1928-31 18¢ ARCHITECTURE

		UL	UR	LL	LR
1	$1.80	☐	☐	☐	☐
2	$1.80	☐	☐	☐	☐
3	$1.80	☐	☐	☐	☐
4	$1.80	☐	☐	☐	☐
5	$1.80	☐	☐	☐	☐
6	$1.80	☐	☐	☐	☐
7	$1.80	☐	☐	☐	☐
8	$1.80	☐	☐	☐	☐

#1932 18¢ BABE ZAHARIAS

1	$1.80	☐	☐	☐	☐
2	$1.80	☐	☐	☐	☐
3	$1.80	☐	☐	☐	☐
4	$1.80	☐	☐	☐	☐

1981 COMMEMORATIVES

Continued

#1933 18¢ BOBBY JONES

		UL	UR	LL	LR
1	$1.80	☐	☐	☐	☐
2	$1.80	☐	☐	☐	☐
3	$1.80	☐	☐	☐	☐
4	$1.80	☐	☐	☐	☐

#1934 18¢ REMINGTON

11-1	$1.60	☐	☐	☐	☐
11-2	$1.60	☐	☐	☐	☐
11-3	$1.60	☐	☐	☐	☐
11-4	$1.60	☐	☐	☐	☐
11-5	$1.60	☐	☐	☐	☐
11-6	$1.60	☐	☐	☐	☐
11-7	$1.60	☐	☐	☐	☐
11-8	$1.60	☐	☐	☐	☐
12-3	$1.60	☐	☐	☐	☐
12-6	$1.60	☐	☐	☐	☐
12-7	$1.60	☐	☐	☐	☐
12-8	$1.60	☐	☐	☐	☐

#1935 18¢ HOBAN

111111	$1.60	☐	☐	☐	☐

#1936 20¢ HOBAN

111112	$1.75	☐	☐	☐	☐

#1937-38 18¢ YORKTOWN-CAPES

111111-1	$1.80	☐	☐	☐	☐
111111-2	$1.80	☐	☐	☐	☐
111111-3	$1.80	☐	☐	☐	☐
111111-4	$1.80	☐	☐	☐	☐
111111-5	$1.80	☐	☐	☐	☐
111111-6	$1.80	☐	☐	☐	☐
111111-7	$1.80	☐	☐	☐	☐
111111-8	$1.80	☐	☐	☐	☐
211111-1	$1.80	☐	☐	☐	☐
211111-5	—	†	☐	†	†
211111-6	$1.80	☐	☐	☐	☐
211111-7	$1.80	☐	☐	☐	☐
211111-8	$1.80	☐	☐	☐	☐
211112-1	—	†	†	☐	☐
211112-6	—	†	†	☐	☐
211112-7	—	†	†	☐	☐
211112-8	—	☐	†	☐	☐
212112-1	$1.80	☐	☐	☐	☐
212112-2	$1.80	☐	☐	☐	☐
212112-3	$1.80	☐	☐	☐	☐
212112-4	$1.80	☐	☐	☐	☐
212112-5	—	☐	†	☐	☐
212112-6	$1.80	☐	☐	☐	☐
212112-7	$1.80	☐	☐	☐	☐
212112-8	$1.80	☐	☐	☐	☐

1981COMMEMORATIVES Cont.

#1937-38 18¢ YORKTOWN-CAPES Continued

Plate	Price	UL	UR	LL	LR
212122-2	$1.80	☐	☐	☐	☐
212122-3	$1.80	☐	☐	☐	☐
212122-4	$1.80	☐	☐	☐	☐
212122-5	$1.80	☐	☐	☐	☐
212222-2	$1.80	☐	☐	☐	☐
212222-3	$1.80	☐	☐	☐	☐
212222-4	$1.80	☐	☐	☐	☐
212222-5	$1.80	☐	☐	☐	☐
222222-2	$1.80	☐	☐	☐	☐
222222-3	$1.80	☐	☐	☐	☐
222222-4	$1.80	☐	☐	☐	☐
222222-5	$1.80	☐	☐	☐	☐
223222-2	$2.00	☐	☐	☐	☐
223222-3	$2.00	☐	☐	☐	☐
223222-4	$2.00	☐	☐	☐	☐
223222-5	$2.00	☐	☐	☐	☐
223223-2	$2.00	☐	☐	☐	☐
223223-3	$2.00	☐	☐	☐	☐
223223-4	$2.00	☐	☐	☐	☐
223223-5	$2.00	☐	☐	☐	☐
323223-2	$2.00	☐	☐	☐	☐
323223-3	$2.00	☐	☐	☐	☐
323223-4	$2.00	☐	☐	☐	☐
323223-5	$2.00	☐	☐	☐	☐

#1939 (20¢) ART MASTERPIECE

Plate	Price	UL	UR	LL	LR
111111	$1.60	☐	☐	☐	☐
222222	$1.60	☐	☐	☐	☐

#1940 (20¢) TEDDY BEAR

Plate	Price	UL	UR	LL	LR
11111	$1.60	☐	☐	☐	☐
12222	$1.60	☐	☐	☐	☐
22222	$1.60	☐	☐	☐	☐

#1941 20¢ JOHN HANSON

Plate	Price	UL	UR	LL	LR
11111	$1.60	☐	☐	☐	☐

#1942-45 20¢ DESERT PLANTS

Plate	Price	UL	UR	LL	LR
111111-1	$2.00	☐	☐	☐	☐
111111-2	$2.00	☐	☐	☐	☐
111111-3	$2.00	☐	☐	☐	☐
111111-4	$2.00	☐	☐	☐	☐
111111-5	$2.00	☐	☐	☐	☐
111111-6	$2.00	☐	☐	☐	☐
111111-7	$2.00	☐	☐	☐	☐
111111-8	$2.00	☐	☐	☐	☐
111112-1	$2.00	☐	☐	☐	☐
111112-3	$2.00	☐	☐	☐	☐
111112-5	$2.00	☐	☐	☐	☐
111112-7	$2.00	☐	☐	☐	☐

#1942-45 20¢ DESERT PLANTS Continued

Plate	Price	UL	UR	LL	LR
121112-1	$2.00	☐	☐	☐	☐
121112-3	$2.00	☐	☐	☐	☐
121112-5	$2.00	☐	☐	☐	☐
121112-7	$2.00	☐	☐	☐	☐
121113-1	$2.00	☐	☐	☐	☐
121113-3	$2.00	☐	☐	☐	☐
121113-5	$2.00	☐	☐	☐	☐
121113-7	$2.00	☐	☐	☐	☐
221113-1	$2.00	☐	☐	☐	☐
221113-3	$2.00	☐	☐	☐	☐
221113-5	$2.00	☐	☐	☐	☐
221113-7	$2.00	☐	☐	☐	☐
221123-1	$2.00	☐	☐	☐	☐
221123-3	$2.00	☐	☐	☐	☐
221123-5	$2.00	☐	☐	☐	☐
221123-7	$2.00	☐	☐	☐	☐

1981 REGULAR ISSUES

#1946 (20¢) "C" & EAGLE SHEET STAMP

Plate	Price	UL	UR	LL	LR
39566	$1.60	☐	☐	☐	☐
39567	$1.60	☐	☐	☐	☐
39568	$1.60	☐	☐	☐	☐

#1947 (20¢) "C" & EAGLE COIL STAMP

†39437	†39438	†39439	†39440	†39441
†39442	†39443	†39444	†39445	†39446
†39447	†39448	†39564	*39569	†39570
†39571	†39572	†39575	†39576	*39577
†39578	†39583	†39614	†39615	

#1948 a (20¢) "C" & EAGLE BOOKLET PANE

Plate numbers are located much further away from the stamps so no plate numbers were regularly issued.

1982 REGULAR ISSUE

#1949a $4.00 BIGHORN SHEEP BOOKLET

2 PANES OF 10 STAMPS		# at top
1	$20.00	☐
2	$20.00	☐
3	$20.00	☐
4	$20.00	☐
5	$20.00	☐
6	$20.00	☐
9	$30.00	☐
10	$25.00	☐
11	$30.00	☐
12	$40.00	☐

BOOKLET PANE Cont.

#1949a $4.00 BIGHORN SHEEP Continued

14	$25.00	☐
15	$25.00	☐
16	$40.00	☐
17	$30.00	☐
18	$30.00	☐
19	$25.00	☐
20	—	☐
21	—	☐
22	—	☐
23	—	☐
24	—	☐
25	—	☐
26	—	☐
28	—	☐
29	—	☐
34	$20.00	☐

1982 COMMEMORATIVES

Issued TAGGED Only

#1950 20¢ ROOSEVELT

I-8 Press

		UL	UR	LL	LR
1	$2.00	☐	☐	☐	☐
2	$2.00	☐	☐	☐	☐
3	$2.00	☐	☐	☐	☐
4	$2.00	☐	☐	☐	☐

#1951 20¢ LOVE

Andreotti Gravure

"EE" Perforator 11.3 x 10.5

11111	$3.00	☐	☐	☐	☐

In Line Perforator 11.2 x 11.2

11111	$1.75	☐	☐	☐	☐
22222	$1.75	☐	☐	☐	☐

#1952 20¢ WASHINGTON

Andreotti Gravure

111111	$1.60	☐	☐	☐	☐

#1953-2002 20¢ STATE BIRDS AND FLOWERS (sheet 50)

Andreotti Gravure

		UL	UR	LL	LR
"EE" Perforator 10.5 x 11.3					
11111	$17.50	☐	☐	☐	☐
22222	$17.50	☐	☐	☐	☐
In Line Perforator 11.2 x 11.2					
11111	$20.00	☐	☐	☐	☐
22222	$20.00	☐	☐	☐	☐

#2003 20¢ NETHERLANDS

A Press (Gravure		L	R
111	$1.60	☐	☐

#2004 20¢ LIBRARY OF CONGRESS

I-8 Press

		UL	UR	LL	LR
1	$1.60	☐	☐	☐	☐
2	$1.60	☐	☐	☐	☐
3	$1.60	☐	☐	☐	☐
4	$1.60	☐	☐	☐	☐

#2005 20¢ CONSUMER EDUCATION Coil

STRIP OF 5 **4 Plates** Bottom Only

Cottrell Press

		B
1	$190.00	☐
2	$190.00	☐
3	$140.00	☐
4	$140.00	☐

#2006-09 20¢ KNOXVILLE FAIR

Andreotti Gravure

		UL	UR	LL	LR
111111	$1.75	☐	☐	☐	☐

#2010 20¢ HORATIO ALGER

I-8 Press

1	$1.60	☐	☐	☐	☐
2	$1.60	☐	☐	☐	☐
3	$1.60	☐	☐	☐	☐
4	$1.60	☐	☐	☐	☐

#2011 20¢ AGING

I-8 Press

		UL	UR	LL	LR
1	$1.60	☐	☐	☐	☐
2	$1.60	☐	☐	☐	☐
3	$1.60	☐	☐	☐	☐
4	$1.60	☐	☐	☐	☐

#2012 20¢ THE BARRYMORES

Andreotti Gravure

111111	$1.60	☐	☐	☐	☐

#2013 20¢ DR. MARY WALKER

Andreotti Gravure

111111	$1.60	☐	☐	☐	☐

#2014 20¢ PEACE GARDEN

Miller Offset and I-8 Press

1111-1	$2.00	☐	☐	☐	☐
1111-2	$2.00	☐	☐	☐	☐
1111-3	$2.00	☐	☐	☐	☐
1111-4	$2.00	☐	☐	☐	☐
1211-1	$2.00	☐	☐	☐	☐
1211-2	$2.00	☐	☐	☐	☐
1211-3	$2.00	☐	☐	☐	☐
1211-4	$2.00	☐	☐	☐	☐

1982 COMMEMORATIVES

#2014 20¢ PEACE GARDEN Cont.

		UL	UR	LL	LR
1221-1	$2.00	☐	☐	☐	☐
1221-2	$2.00	☐	☐	☐	☐
1221-3	$2.00	☐	☐	☐	☐
1221-4	$2.00	☐	☐	☐	☐
1321-1	$2.00	☐	☐	☐	☐
1321-2	$2.00	☐	☐	☐	☐
1321-3	$2.00	☐	☐	☐	☐
1321-4	$2.00	☐	☐	☐	☐
1322-1	$2.00	☐	☐	☐	☐
1322-2	$2.00	☐	☐	☐	☐
1322-3	$2.00	☐	☐	☐	☐
1322-4	$2.00	☐	☐	☐	☐
2322-1	$2.00	☐	☐	☐	☐
2322-2	$2.00	☐	☐	☐	☐
2322-3	$2.00	☐	☐	☐	☐
2322-4	$2.00	☐	☐	☐	☐
2422-1	$2.00	☐	☐	☐	☐
2422-2	$2.00	☐	☐	☐	☐
2422-3	$2.00	☐	☐	☐	☐
2422-4	$2.00	☐	☐	☐	☐
2432-1	$2.00	☐	☐	☐	☐
2432-2	$2.00	☐	☐	☐	☐
2432-3	$2.00	☐	☐	☐	☐
2432-4	$2.00	☐	☐	☐	☐
2532-1	$2.00	☐	☐	☐	☐
2532-2	$2.00	☐	☐	☐	☐
2532-3	$2.00	☐	☐	☐	☐
2532-4	$2.00	☐	☐	☐	☐
3532-1	$2.00	☐	☐	☐	☐
3532-2	$2.00	☐	☐	☐	☐
3532-3	$2.00	☐	☐	☐	☐
3532-4	$2.00	☐	☐	☐	☐
3632-1	$5.00	☐	☐	☐	☐
3632-2	$5.00	☐	☐	☐	☐
3632-3	$5.00	☐	☐	☐	☐
3632-4	$5.00	☐	☐	☐	☐
3633-1	$2.00	☐	☐	☐	☐
3633-2	$2.00	☐	☐	☐	☐
3633-3	$2.00	☐	☐	☐	☐
3633-4	$2.00	☐	☐	☐	☐
3733-1	$2.00	☐	☐	☐	☐
3733-2	$2.00	☐	☐	☐	☐
3733-3	$2.00	☐	☐	☐	☐
3733-4	$2.00	☐	☐	☐	☐
3734-1	$2.00	☐	☐	☐	☐
3734-2	$2.00	☐	☐	☐	☐
3734-3	$2.00	☐	☐	☐	☐
3734-4	$2.00	☐	☐	☐	☐
3744-1	$2.00	☐	☐	☐	☐
3744-2	$2.00	☐	☐	☐	☐
3744-3	$2.00	☐	☐	☐	☐
3744-4	$2.00	☐	☐	☐	☐
3844-1	$2.00	☐	☐	☐	☐
3844-2	$2.00	☐	☐	☐	☐
3844-3	$2.00	☐	☐	☐	☐
3844-4	$2.00	☐	☐	☐	☐

#2015 20¢ LIBRARIES OF AMERICA

I-8 Press

1	$1.60	☐	☐	☐	☐
2	$1.60	☐	☐	☐	☐
3	$1.60	☐	☐	☐	☐
4	$1.60	☐	☐	☐	☐
5	$1.60	☐	☐	☐	☐

#2016 20¢ JACKIE ROBINSON

Andreotti Gravure

11111	$1.60	☐	☐	☐	☐

#2017 20¢ TOURO SYNAGOGUE

A Press (Gravure and Intaglio)

		L	R
11111-1	$1.60	☐	☐

#2018 20¢ WOLF TRAP FARM PARK

Andreotti Gravure

		UL	UR	LL	LR
11111	$1.60	☐	☐	☐	☐

#2019-22 20¢ ARCHITECTURE

I-8 Press

1	$1.60	☐	☐	☐	☐
2	$1.60	☐	☐	☐	☐
3	$1.60	☐	☐	☐	☐
4	$1.60	☐	☐	☐	☐
5	$1.60	☐	☐	☐	☐
6	$1.60	☐	☐	☐	☐

#2023 20¢ ST. FRANCIS OF ASSISI

Printed by American Bank Note Co. and J.W. Fergusson and Sons.

A111111	$1.60	☐	☐	☐	☐

#2024 20¢ PONCE DE LEON

A Press (Gravure)

		L	R
11111	$1.60	☐	☐
22222	$1.60	☐	☐

#2025 13¢ KITTEN & PUPPY

Andreotti Gravure

		UL	UR	LL	LR
1111	$1.10	☐	☐	☐	☐
1121	$1.10	☐	☐	☐	☐
2222	$1.10	☐	☐	☐	☐

1982 COMMEMORATIVES

#2026 20¢ TIEPOLO CHRISTMAS

Andreotti Gravure

		T	B
11111	$1.60	☐	☐
13131	$1.60	☐	☐
13233	$1.60	☐	☐
13243	$1.60	☐	☐
22222	$1.60	☐	☐
24243	$1.60	☐	☐
35354	$1.60	☐	☐
44265	$1.60	☐	☐
44465	$1.60	☐	☐
45266	$1.60	☐	☐
45364	$1.60	☐	☐
45365	$1.60	☐	☐
45366	$1.60	☐	☐
46365	$1.60	☐	☐
46465	$1.60	☐	☐

#2027-2030 20¢ SNOW SCENES

Andreotti Gravure

		UL	UR	LL	LR
1111	$1.60	☐	☐	☐	☐
1311	$1.60	☐	☐	☐	☐
2111	$1.60	☐	☐	☐	☐
2122	$1.60	☐	☐	☐	☐
2222	$1.60	☐	☐	☐	☐

1983 COMMEMORATIVES

#2031 20¢ SCIENCE & INDUSTRY

Miller Offset and I-8 Presses

		UL	UR	LL	LR
658-5	$1.60	☐	☐	☐	☐
658-6	$1.60	☐	☐	☐	☐
658-7	$1.60	☐	☐	☐	☐
658-8	$1.60	☐	☐	☐	☐
777-1	—	†	†	☐	†
777-3	—	☐	†	☐	†
777-5	$1.60	☐	☐	☐	☐
777-6	$1.60	☐	☐	☐	☐
777-7	$1.60	☐	☐	☐	☐
777-8	$1.60	☐	☐	☐	☐
779-5	$1.60	☐	☐	☐	☐
779-6	$1.60	☐	☐	☐	☐
779-7	$1.60	☐	☐	☐	☐
779-8	$1.60	☐	☐	☐	☐
788-5	$1.60	☐	☐	☐	☐
788-6	$1.60	☐	☐	☐	☐
788-7	$1.60	☐	☐	☐	☐
788-8	$1.60	☐	☐	☐	☐
798-5	$1.60	☐	☐	☐	☐
798-6	$1.60	☐	☐	☐	☐
798-7	$1.60	☐	☐	☐	☐
798-8	$1.60	☐	☐	☐	☐
799-5	$1.60	☐	☐	☐	☐
799-6	$1.60	☐	☐	☐	☐
799-7	$1.60	☐	☐	☐	☐
799-8	$1.60	☐	☐	☐	☐

1983 COMMEMORATIVES

#2031 20¢ SCIENCE & INDUSTRY Cont.

		UL	UR	LL	LR
855-5	$1.60	☐	☐	☐	☐
855-6	$1.60	☐	☐	☐	☐
855-7	$1.60	☐	☐	☐	☐
855-8	$1.60	☐	☐	☐	☐
858-5	$1.60	☐	☐	☐	☐
858-6	$1.60	☐	☐	☐	☐
858-7	$1.60	☐	☐	☐	☐
858-8	$1.60	☐	☐	☐	☐
884-5	$1.60	☐	☐	☐	☐
884-6	$1.60	☐	☐	☐	☐
884-7	$1.60	☐	☐	☐	☐
884-8	$1.60	☐	☐	☐	☐
885-5	$1.60	☐	☐	☐	☐
885-6	$1.60	☐	☐	☐	☐
885-7	$1.60	☐	☐	☐	☐
885-8	$1.60	☐	☐	☐	☐
886-5	$1.60	☐	☐	☐	☐
886-6	$1.60	☐	☐	☐	☐
886-7	$1.60	☐	☐	☐	☐
886-8	$1.60	☐	☐	☐	☐
888-5	$1.60	☐	☐	☐	☐
888-6	$1.60	☐	☐	☐	☐
888-7	$1.60	☐	☐	☐	☐
888-8	$1.60	☐	☐	☐	☐

#2032-35 20¢ BALLOONS

Andreotti Gravure

11112	$1.60	☐	☐	☐	☐
11132	$1.60	☐	☐	☐	☐
11142	$1.60	☐	☐	☐	☐
22141	$1.60	☐	☐	☐	☐
22221	$1.60	☐	☐	☐	☐
22222	$1.60	☐	☐	☐	☐
22241	$1.60	☐	☐	☐	☐
22242	$3.25	☐	☐	☐	☐

#2036 20¢ AMITY AND COMMERCE

I-8 Press

		UL	UR	LL	LR
1	$1.60	☐	☐	☐	☐
2	$1.60	☐	☐	☐	☐
3	$1.60	☐	☐	☐	☐
4	$1.60	☐	☐	☐	☐
9	$1.60	☐	☐	☐	☐
10	$1.60	☐	☐	☐	☐

#2037 20¢ CCC

Andreotti Gravure

111111	$1.60	☐	☐	☐	☐

#2038 20¢ JOSEPH PRIESTLEY

Printed by American Bank Note Co. and J.W. Fergusson and Sons.

A111111	$1.60	☐	☐	☐	☐

1983 COMMEMORATIVES

#2039 20¢ VOLUNTARISM

A Press (Gravure)		L	R
3	$1.60	☐	☐

#2040 20¢ CONCORD

I-8 Press		UL	UR	LL	LR
1	$1.60	☐	☐	☐	☐
2	$1.60	☐	☐	☐	☐
3	$1.60	☐	☐	☐	☐
4	$1.60	☐	☐	☐	☐

#2041 20¢ BROOKLYN BRIDGE

I-8 Press

1	$1.60	☐	☐	☐	☐
4	$1.60	☐	☐	☐	☐
5	$1.60	☐	☐	☐	☐
6	$1.60	☐	☐	☐	☐

#2042 20¢ TVA

A Press (Gravure and Intaglio)

		L	R
1111-1	$1.60	☐	☐
1121-1	$1.60	☐	☐

#2043 20¢ PHYSICAL FITNESS

A Press (Gravure)

1111	$1.60	☐	☐

#2044 20¢ SCOTT JOPLIN

Andreotti Gravure

		UL	UR	LL	LR
111111	$1.60	☐	☐	☐	☐
121111	—	†	†	†	†

#2045 20¢ MEDAL OF HONOR

Miller Offset and I-8 Presses

1111-1	$1.60	☐	☐	☐	☐
1111-2	$1.60	☐	☐	☐	☐
1111-3	$1.60	☐	☐	☐	☐
1111-5	$1.60	☐	☐	☐	☐
2121-1	$1.60	☐	☐	☐	☐
2121-2	$1.60	☐	☐	☐	☐
2121-3	$1.60	☐	☐	☐	☐
2121-5	$1.60	☐	☐	☐	☐
2122-1	$1.60	☐	☐	☐	☐
2122-2	$1.60	☐	☐	☐	☐
2122-3	$1.60	☐	☐	☐	☐
2122-5	$1.60	☐	☐	☐	☐
2222-1	$1.60	☐	☐	☐	☐
2222-2	$1.60	☐	☐	☐	☐
2222-3	$1.60	☐	☐	☐	☐
2222-5	$1.60	☐	☐	☐	☐
2223-1	$1.60	☐	☐	☐	☐
2223-2	$1.60	☐	☐	☐	☐
2223-3	$1.60	☐	☐	☐	☐
2223-5	$1.60	☐	☐	☐	☐

1983 COMMEMORATIVES

#2045 20¢ MEDAL OF HONOR
Continued

3223-1	$1.60	☐	☐	☐	☐
3223-2	$1.60	☐	☐	☐	☐
3223-3	$1.60	☐	☐	☐	☐
3223-5	$1.60	☐	☐	☐	☐

#2046 20¢ BABE RUTH

Cottrell Press

1	—	†	†	†	†
2	$1.60	☐	☐	☐	☐
3	$1.60	☐	☐	☐	☐
4	$1.60	☐	☐	☐	☐
5	$1.60	☐	☐	☐	☐

#2047 20¢ NATHANIEL HAWTHORNE

Andreotti Gravure

1111	$1.60	☐	☐	☐	☐

#2048-51 13¢ OLYMPIC GAMES

Andreotti Gravure

		UL	UR	LL	LR
1111	$1.25	☐	☐	☐	☐

#2052 20¢ TREATY OF PARIS

Andreotti Gravure

1111	$1.60	☐	☐	☐	☐

#2053 20¢ CIVIL SERVICE

A Press (Intaglio and Gravure)

		L	R
1-1	$1.60	☐	☐

#2054 20¢ METROPOLITAN OPERA

Offset and I-8 Presses

		UL	UR	LL	LR
1-1	$1.60	☐	☐	☐	☐
1-2	$1.60	☐	☐	☐	☐
1-3	$1.60	☐	☐	☐	☐
1-4	$1.60	☐	☐	☐	☐
2-1	$1.60	☐	☐	☐	☐
2-2	$1.60	☐	☐	☐	☐
2-3	$1.60	☐	☐	☐	☐
2-4	$1.60	☐	☐	☐	☐

#2055-58 20¢ INVENTORS

Offset and I-8 Presses

3-1	$1.60	☐	☐	☐	☐
3-2	$1.60	☐	☐	☐	☐
3-4	$1.60	☐	☐	☐	☐
3-5	$1.60	☐	☐	☐	☐
3-6	$1.60	☐	☐	☐	☐
4-1	$1.60	☐	☐	☐	☐
4-2	$1.60	☐	☐	☐	☐
4-4	$1.60	☐	☐	☐	☐
4-5	$1.60	☐	☐	☐	☐

1983 COMMEMORATIVES

#2055-58 20¢ INVENTORS Cont.

		UL	UR	LL	LR
5-1	$1.60	☐	☐	☐	☐
5-2	$1.60	☐	☐	☐	☐
5-4	$1.60	☐	☐	☐	☐
5-5	$1.60	☐	☐	☐	☐
6-1	$1.60	☐	☐	☐	☐
6-2	$1.60	☐	☐	☐	☐
6-4	$1.60	☐	☐	☐	☐
6-5	$1.60	☐	☐	☐	☐
6-6	$1.60	☐	☐	☐	☐
7-2	$1.60	☐	☐	☐	☐
7-4	$1.60	☐	☐	☐	☐
7-5	$1.60	☐	☐	☐	☐
7-6	$1.60	☐	☐	☐	☐
8-2	$1.60	☐	☐	☐	☐
8-4	$1.60	☐	☐	☐	☐
8-5	$1.60	☐	☐	☐	☐
8-6	$1.60	☐	☐	☐	☐
9-2	$1.60	☐	☐	☐	☐
9-4	$1.60	☐	☐	☐	☐
9-5	$1.60	☐	☐	☐	☐
9-6	$1.60	☐	☐	☐	☐
10-2	$1.60	☐	☐	☐	☐
10-4	$1.60	☐	☐	☐	☐
10-5	$1.60	☐	☐	☐	☐
10-6	$1.60	☐	☐	☐	☐
11-2	—	☐	☐	☐	☐
11-4	—	☐	☐	☐	☐
11-5	—	☐	☐	☐	☐
11-6	—	†	†	†	†
12-2	$1.60	☐	☐	☐	☐
12-4	$1.60	☐	☐	☐	☐
12-5	$1.60	☐	☐	☐	☐
12-6	$1.60	☐	☐	☐	☐

#2059-62 20¢ STREETCARS

Miller Offset and I-8 Presses

		UL	UR	LL	LR
1111-1	$1.60	☐	☐	☐	☐
1111-2	$1.60	☐	☐	☐	☐
1111-3	$1.60	☐	☐	☐	☐
1111-4	$1.60	☐	☐	☐	☐
2222-1	$1.60	☐	☐	☐	☐
2222-2	$1.60	☐	☐	☐	☐
2222-3	$1.60	☐	☐	☐	☐
2222-4	$1.60	☐	☐	☐	☐
3333-1	—	☐	☐	☐	☐
3333-2	—	☐	☐	☐	☐
3333-3	—	☐	☐	☐	☐
3333-4	—	☐	☐	☐	☐

#2063 20¢ RAPHAEL CHRISTMAS

Andreotti Gravure

#2063 20¢ RAPHAEL CHRISTMAS Continued

		UL	UR	LL	LR
11111	$1.60	☐	☐	☐	☐
11112	$1.60	☐	☐	☐	☐
12111	$1.60	☐	☐	☐	☐
12112	$1.60	☐	☐	☐	☐
21222	$1.60	☐	☐	☐	☐
22112	$1.60	☐	☐	☐	☐
32111	$1.60	☐	☐	☐	☐

#2064 20¢ SANTA CLAUS

A Press (Gravure)

		L	R
11211	$1.60	☐	☐
22322	$1.60	☐	☐

#2065 20¢ MARTIN LUTHER

Printed by American Bank Note Co. and J.W. Fergusson and Sons.

		UL	UR	LL	LR
A11111	$1.60	☐	☐	☐	☐

1984 COMMEMORATIVES

#2066 20¢ ALASKA STATEHOOD

Printed by American Bank Note Co.

		UL	UR	LL	LR
A11111	$1.60	☐	☐	☐	☐

#2067-70 20¢ WINTER OLYMPICS

Andreotti Gravure

		UL	UR	LL	LR
1111	$2.00	☐	☐	☐	☐

#2071 20¢ FEDERAL DEPOSIT INSURANCE

This issue was part of a quadrant printing. See also #2074, #2075 and #2081 for the other stamps. Only one position of the plate number exists.

Andreotti Gravure

		UL	UR	LL	LR
122221	$1.60	☐	‡	‡	‡
122222	$1.60	☐	‡	‡	‡
222221	$1.60	☐	‡	‡	‡
222222	$1.60	☐	‡	‡	‡

#2072 20¢ LOVE

A Press (Gravure and Intaglio)

		T	B
1-11111	$1.60	☐	☐
2-11111	$1.60	☐	☐
2-11112	$3.25	☐	☐
2-12222	$3.25	☐	☐
2-22221	$1.60	☐	☐
2-22222	$1.60	☐	☐
2-22223	$1.60	☐	☐

1984 COMMEMORATIVES

#2073 20¢ CARTER G. WOODSON

Printed by American Bank Note Co.

		UL	UR	LL	LR
A111111	$1.60	□	□	□	□

#2074 20¢ SOIL AND WATER CONSERVATION

This issue was part of a quadrant printing. See also #2071, #2075 and #2081 for the other stamps. Only one position of the plate number exists.

Andreotti Gravure

		UL	UR	LL	LR
122221	$1.60	‡	□	‡	‡
122222	$1.60	‡	□	‡	‡
222221	$1.60	‡	□	‡	‡
222222	$1.60	‡	□	‡	‡

#2075 20¢ CREDIT UNION

This printing was part of a quadrant printing. See also #2071, #2074 and #2081 for the other stamps. Only one position of the plate number exists.

Andreotti Gravure

		UL	UR	LL	LR
122221	$1.60	‡	‡	‡	□
122222	$1.60	‡	‡	‡	□
222221	$1.60	‡	‡	‡	□
222222	$1.60	‡	‡	‡	□

#2076-79 20¢ ORCHIDS

Andreotti Gravure

		UL	UR	LL	LR
11111	$1.60	□	□	□	□
11121	$1.60	□	□	□	□
11122	$1.60	□	□	□	□

#2080 20¢ HAWAII STATEHOOD

Printed by the American Bank Note Co.

		UL	UR	LL	LR
A11111	$1.60	□	□	□	□

#2081 20¢ NATIONAL ARCHIVES

This issue was part of a quadrant printing. See also #2071, #2074 and #2075 for the other stamps. Only one position of the plate number exists.

Andreotti Gravure

		UL	UR	LL	LR
122221	$1.60	‡	‡	□	‡
122222	$1.60	‡	‡	□	‡
222221	$1.60	‡	‡	□	‡
222222	$1.60	‡	‡	□	‡

#2082-85 20¢ SUMMER OLYMPICS

Andreotti Gravure

		UL	UR	LL	LR
1111	$1.60	□	□	□	□
1121	$1.60	□	□	□	□
1131	$1.60	□	□	□	□
1141	$1.60	□	□	□	□

#2086 20¢ LOUISIANA WORLD EXPOSITION

Andreotti Gravure

		UL	UR	LL	LR
11111	$1.60	□	□	□	□

#2087 20¢ HEALTH RESEARCH

Printed by the American Bank Note Co.

		UL	UR	LL	LR
A11111	$1.60	□	□	□	□

#2088 20¢ DOUGLAS FAIRBANKS

A Press (Gravure and Intaglio)

		T	B
1-1111	$1.60	□	□
2-1111	$1.60	□	□

#2089 20¢ JIM THORPE

I-8 Press

		UL	UR	LL	LR
1	—	†	†	†	†
2	—	†	†	†	†
3	$1.60	□	□	□	□
4	$1.60	□	□	□	□
5	—	†	†	†	†
6	—	†	†	†	†
7	$1.60	□	□	□	□
9	$3.25	□	□	□	□
10	$1.60	□	□	□	□
11	$1.60	□	□	□	□
12	$1.60	□	□	□	□
13	$1.60	□	□	□	□
14	$1.60	□	□	□	□
17	$1.60	□	□	□	□
18	$1.60	□	□	□	□
19	$1.60	□	□	□	□
20	$1.60	□	□	□	□
22	$1.60	□	□	□	□
25	$1.60	□	□	□	□
26	$1.60	□	□	□	□
27	$1.60	□	□	□	□

#2090 20¢ JOHN McCORMACK

Andreotti Gravure

		UL	UR	LL	LR
11111	$1.60	□	□	□	□

#2091 20¢ ST. LAWRENCE SEAWAY

Printed by the American Bank Note Co.

		UL	UR	LL	LR
A1111	$1.60	□	□	□	□

#2092 20¢ MIGRATORY BIRD HUNTING

I-8 Press

		UL	UR	LL	LR
1	—	†	†	†	†
6	—	†	†	†	†
18	$1.60	□	□	□	□
19	$1.60	□	□	□	□

1984 COMMEMORATIVES

#2092 20¢ MIGRATORY BIRD HUNTING Continued

		UL	UR	LL	LR
20	$1.60	☐	☐	☐	☐
21	$1.60	☐	☐	☐	☐
22	$1.60	☐	☐	☐	☐
23	$1.60	☐	☐	☐	☐
24	$1.60	☐	☐	☐	☐
25	$1.60	☐	☐	☐	☐

#2093 20¢ ROANOKE VOYAGERS

Printed by the American Bank Note Co.

A11111	$1.60	☐	☐	☐	☐

#2094 20¢ HERMAN MELVILLE

I-8 Press

14	$1.60	☐	☐	☐	☐
15	$1.60	☐	☐	☐	☐
16	$1.60	☐	☐	☐	☐
17	$1.60	☐	☐	☐	☐

#2095 20¢ HORACE A. MOSES

A Press (Intaglio)

		T	B
1	$2.00	☐	☐

#2096 20¢ SMOKEY THE BEAR

D Press (Offset and Intaglio)

		UL	UR	LL	LR
1121-3	$2.00	☐	☐	☐	☐
1221-3	—	†	†	☐	†
1313-3	$2.00	☐	☐	☐	☐
1321-3	$2.00	☐	☐	☐	☐
1323-3	—	☐	☐	†	☐
2232-3	$2.00	☐	☐	☐	☐
3232-3	$2.00	☐	☐	☐	☐
5656-3	$2.00	☐	☐	☐	☐
6667-3	$2.00	☐	☐	☐	☐
6868-3	$2.00	☐	☐	☐	☐
6888-3	$2.00	☐	☐	☐	☐
8888-3	$2.00	☐	☐	☐	☐
8989-3	$2.00	☐	☐	☐	☐
8999-3	$2.00	☐	☐	☐	☐
9212-3	$2.00	☐	☐	☐	☐
9213-3	$4.25	☐	☐	☐	☐
9991-3	$2.00	☐	☐	☐	☐
10101010-3	—	☐	☐	†	†
10111010-3	$2.00	☐	☐	☐	☐
10111110-3	$2.00	☐	☐	☐	☐
10111111-3	—	†	†	†	☐
10141411-3	$2.00	☐	☐	☐	☐
11141414-3	$2.00	☐	☐	☐	☐
13131212-3	$2.00	☐	☐	☐	☐
13131213-3	$2.00	☐	☐	☐	☐
14151515-3	$2.00	☐	☐	☐	☐
14151516-3	$2.00	☐	☐	☐	☐
14161616-3	$2.00	☐	☐	☐	☐
17171717-3	$2.00	☐	☐	☐	☐

#2097 20¢ ROBERTO CLEMENTE

Andreotti Gravure

111111	$1.60	☐	☐	☐	☐
111211	—	†	†	†	†

#2098-2101 20¢ DOGS

Andreotti Gravure

1111	$1.60	☐	☐	☐	☐
1112	$1.60	☐	☐	☐	☐

#2102 20¢ CRIME PREVENTION

Printed by the American Bank Note Co.

A1111	$1.60	☐	☐	☐	☐

#2103 20¢ HISPANIC AMERICANS

Andreotti Gravure

111111	$1.60	☐	☐	☐	☐
122211	$1.60	☐	☐	☐	☐

#2104 20¢ FAMILY UNITY

A Press (Gravure and Intaglio)

		T	B
12-2	$1.60	☐	☐
21-2	$1.60	☐	☐
22-2	$1.60	☐	☐

#2105 20¢ ELEANOR ROOSEVELT

I-8 Press

		UL	UR	LL	LR
2	$1.60	☐	☐	☐	☐
3	$1.60	☐	☐	☐	☐
4	$1.60	☐	☐	☐	☐
6	$1.60	☐	☐	☐	☐
8	$1.60	☐	☐	☐	☐
9	$1.60	☐	☐	☐	☐
11	$1.60	☐	☐	☐	☐
12	$1.60	☐	☐	☐	☐

#2106 20¢ A NATION OF READERS

I-8 Press

1	$1.60	☐	☐	☐	☐
2	$1.60	☐	☐	☐	☐
3	$1.60	☐	☐	☐	☐
4	$1.60	☐	☐	☐	☐
5	$1.60	☐	☐	☐	☐
6	$1.60	☐	☐	☐	☐
7	$1.60	☐	☐	☐	☐
8	$1.60	☐	☐	☐	☐

#2107 20¢ LIPPI CHRISTMAS MADONNA

Andreotti Gravure

11111	$1.60	☐	☐	☐	☐
22222	$1.60	☐	☐	☐	☐

1984 COMMEMORATIVES

#2108 20¢ CONTEMPORARY CHRISTMAS

Andreotti Gravure

		UL	UR	LL	LR
11111	$1.60				
22222	$1.60				

#2109 20¢ VIET-NAM VETERANS

I-8 Press

		UL	UR	LL	LR
2	$1.60				
3	$1.60				
4	$1.60				
6	$1.60				
7	$1.60				
8	$1.60				
9	$1.60				
10	$1.60				

1985 COMMEMORATIVES

#2110 22¢ JEROME KERN

Printed by American Bank Note Company.

		UL	UR	LL	LR
A11111	$1.75				

#2137 22¢ MARY McLEOD BETHUNE

Printed by American Bank Note Company.

		UL	UR	LL	LR
A111111	$1.75				

#2138-41 22¢ DUCK DECOYS

Printed by American Bank Note Company.

		UL	UR	LL	LR
A11111	$1.75				

#2142 22¢ WINTER SPECIAL OLYMPICS

Andreotti Gravure

		UL	UR	LL	LR
111111	$1.75				
112121	$1.75				

#2143 22¢ LOVE

Andreotti Gravure

		UL	UR	LL	LR
111312	$1.75				
112111	$1.75				
112211	$1.75				
112212	$1.75				
221221	$1.75				
222221	$1.75				

1985 COMMEMORATIVES

#2144 22¢ R.E.A.

A Press (Gravure and Intaglio)

		L	R
1-1111	$1.75		
1-1131	$1.75		

#2145 22¢ AMERIPEX

Miller Offset and I-8 Presses

		UL	UR	LL	LR
11-1	$1.75				
11-2	—				
11-3	$1.75				
11-4	$1.75				
11-5	$1.75				
13-1	$1.75				
13-3	$1.75				
13-4	$1.75				
13-5	$1.75				
22-1	$1.75				
22-3	$1.75				
22-4	$1.75				
22-5	$1.75				
24-1	$1.75				
24-3	$1.75				
24-4	$1.75				
24-5	$1.75				
33-1	$1.75				
33-3	$1.75				
33-4	$1.75				
33-5	$1.75				
35-1	$1.75				
35-3	$1.75				
35-4	$1.75				
35-5	$1.75				
44-1	$1.75				
44-3	$1.75				
44-4	$1.75				
44-5	$1.75				
46-1	$1.75				
46-3	$1.75				
46-4	$1.75				
46-5	$1.75				
55-1	$1.75				
55-3	$1.75				
55-4	$1.75				
55-5	$1.75				
65-1	$1.75				
65-3	$1.75				
65-4	$1.75				
65-5	$1.75				
99-1	$1.75				
99-3	$1.75				
99-4	$1.75				
99-5	$1.75				

1985 COMMEMORATIVES

#2145 22¢ AMERIPEX Continued

		UL	UR	LL	LR
1010-1	$1.75	☐	☐	☐	☐
1010-3	$1.75	☐	☐	☐	☐
1010-4	$1.75	☐	☐	☐	☐
1010-5	$1.75	☐	☐	☐	☐
1109-1	$1.75	☐	☐	☐	☐
1109-3	$1.75	☐	☐	☐	☐
1109-4	$1.75	☐	☐	☐	☐
1109-5	$1.75	☐	☐	☐	☐
1210-1	$1.75	☐	☐	☐	☐
1210-3	$1.75	☐	☐	☐	☐
1210-4	$1.75	☐	☐	☐	☐
1210-5	$1.75	☐	☐	☐	☐
1309-1	$1.75	☐	☐	☐	☐
1309-3	$1.75	☐	☐	☐	☐
1309-4	$1.75	☐	☐	☐	☐
1309-5	$1.75	☐	☐	☐	☐
1311-1	$1.75	☐	☐	☐	☐
1311-3	$1.75	☐	☐	☐	☐
1311-4	$1.75	☐	☐	☐	☐
1311-5	$1.75	☐	☐	☐	☐
1410-1	$1.75	☐	☐	☐	☐
1410-3	$1.75	☐	☐	☐	☐
1410-4	$1.75	☐	☐	☐	☐
1410-5	$1.75	☐	☐	☐	☐
1412-1	$1.75	☐	☐	☐	☐
1412-3	$1.75	☐	☐	☐	☐
1412-4	$1.75	☐	☐	☐	☐
1412-5	$1.75	☐	☐	☐	☐
1511-1	$1.75	☐	☐	☐	☐
1511-3	$1.75	☐	☐	☐	☐
1511-4	$1.75	☐	☐	☐	☐
1511-5	$1.75	☐	☐	☐	☐
1612-1	$1.75	☐	☐	☐	☐
1612-3	$1.75	☐	☐	☐	☐
1612-4	$1.75	☐	☐	☐	☐
1612-5	$1.75	☐	☐	☐	☐
1711-1	$1.75	☐	☐	☐	☐
1711-3	$1.75	☐	☐	☐	☐
1711-4	$1.75	☐	☐	☐	☐
1711-5	$1.75	☐	☐	☐	☐

#2146 22¢ ABIGAIL ADAMS

Andreotti Gravure

1111	$1.75	☐	☐	☐	☐

#2147 22¢ BARTHOLDI

D Press (Offset and Intaglio)

1111-1	$1.75	☐	☐	☐	☐
2222-1	$1.75	☐	☐	☐	☐
2242-1	$1.75	☐	☐	☐	☐
2252-1	$1.75	☐	☐	☐	☐
3535-1	$1.75	☐	☐	☐	☐
3555-1	$1.75	☐	☐	☐	☐

#2152 22¢ KOREAN WAR VETERANS

I-8 Press

		UL	UR	LL	LR
1	$1.75	☐	☐	☐	☐
2	$1.75	☐	☐	☐	☐
3	$1.75	☐	☐	☐	☐
4	$1.75	☐	☐	☐	☐
5	$1.75	☐	☐	☐	☐

#2153 22¢ SOCIAL SECURITY ACT

Printed by American Bank Note Company

A11	$1.75	☐	☐	☐	☐

#2154 22¢ WORLD WAR I VETERANS

I-8 Press

1	$1.75	☐	☐	☐	☐
2	$1.75	☐	☐	☐	☐
3	$1.75	☐	☐	☐	☐
4	$1.75	☐	☐	☐	☐

#2155-58 22¢ HORSES

Gravure Press

11111	$1.75	☐	☐	☐	☐

#2159 22¢ PUBLIC EDUCATION

Printed by American Bank Note Company

A11111	$1.75	☐	☐	☐	☐

#2160-63 22¢ INTERNATIONAL YOUTH YEAR

Printed by American Bank Note Company

A11111	$1.75	☐	☐	☐	☐

#2164 22¢ HELP END HUNGER

Printed by American Bank Note Company

A111111	$2.20	☐	☐	☐	☐

#2165 22¢ MADONNA & CHILD CHRISTMAS

Gravure Press

1111	$1.75	☐	☐	☐	☐
1112	$1.75	☐	☐	☐	☐
2222	$1.75	☐	☐	☐	☐

#2166 22¢ POINSETTIA CHRISTMAS

Gravure Press

11111	$1.75	☐	☐	☐	☐
12111	$1.75	☐	☐	☐	☐
21222	$1.75	☐	☐	☐	☐
22222	$1.75	☐	☐	☐	☐

1985 REGULAR ISSUES

#2111 (22¢) "D" & EAGLE SHEET STAMP

A Press (Gravure)		L	R
1	$1.75	☐	☐
2	$1.75	☐	☐
3	$1.75	☐	☐
4	$1.75	☐	☐

#2112 (22¢) "D" & EAGLE COIL STAMP

STRIP OF FIVE		# at bottom
1	$7.00	☐
2	$7.00	☐

#2113a $4.40 "D" BOOKLET

2 PANES OF 10 STAMPS		# at top
1	$12.50	☐
3	$20.00	☐
4	$15.00	☐

#2114 $.22 FLAG & CAPITOL

A Press (revised)

Eureka Perforator 11.2 x 11.1

		UL	UR	LL	LR
1	$1.80	☐	☐	☐	☐
1	$1.80	☐	☐	☐	☐
3	$1.80	☐	☐	☐	☐
4	$1.80	☐	☐	☐	☐
5	$1.80	☐	☐	☐	☐
6	$1.80	☐	☐	☐	☐

#2115 22¢ FLAG OVER CAPITOL

STRIP OF 5 **# at bottom**

B Press

2	$5.00	☐
4	$5.00	☐
6	$10.00	☐
10	$5.00	☐
13	$8.50	☐
15	$5.00	☐
16	$5.00	☐

C or D Press

1	$15.00	☐
3	$50.00	☐
5	$5.00	☐
7	$12.50	☐
8	$5.00	☐
11	$7.50	☐
12	$5.00	☐
17	$7.50	☐
18	$6.00	☐
19	$6.00	☐
20	$6.00	☐
21	$5.00	☐
22	$5.00	☐

#2115b 22¢ FLAG OVER CAPITOL (TEST COIL)

C Press

T1	$6.50	☐

#2116a $1.10 FLAG OVER CAPITOL BOOKLET

1 PANE OF 5 STAMPS		# at top
1	$2.25	☐
3	$2.25	☐

#2116a $2.20 FLAG OVER CAPITOL BOOKLET

2 PANES OF 5 STAMPS		# at top
1	$4.50	☐
3	$3.50	☐

#2121a $4.40 SEASHELLS BOOKLET

2 PANES OF 10 STAMPS		# at top
1	$8.50	☐
2	$8.50	☐
3	$8.50	☐
5	$8.50	☐
6	$8.50	☐
7	$8.50	☐
8	$8.50	☐
10	$8.50	☐

#2122a $32.25 EAGLE BOOKLET

1 PANE OF 3 STAMPS		# at top
1111	$40.00	☐
2222	$40.00	☐

BOTTOM STRIP OF 5 ONLY

#2149 18¢ WASHINGTON & WASHINGTON MONUMENT COIL

Andreotti Gravure

1112	$4.00	☐
3333	$4.00	☐

#2149a 18¢ WASHINGTON & WASHINGTON MONUMENT COIL PRECANCEL Style 9

Andreotti Gravure

11121	$7.00	☐
33333	$4.00	☐
43444	$7.00	☐

#2150 21.1¢ LETTERS

Andreotti Gravure

111111	$5.00	☐
111121	$6.00	☐

#2150a 21.1¢ LETTERS PRECANCEL Style 10

Andreotti Gravure

111111	$5.00	☐
111121	$6.00	☐

1986 REGULAR ISSUES GREAT AMERICANS

#2168 1¢ MARGARET MITCHELL
A Press (revised)
Eureka perforator 11.2 x 11.1

		UL	UR	LL	LR
1	15¢	☐	☐	☐	☐

#2169 2¢ MARY LYON
A Press (revised)
Eureka perforator 11.2 x 11.1

1 25¢ ☐ ☐ ☐ ☐
2 25¢ ☐ ☐ ☐ ☐

#2170 3¢ PAUL DUDLEY WHITE
A Press (revised)
Eureka perforator 11.2 x 11.1

1 30¢ ☐ ☐ ☐ ☐
2 30¢ ☐ ☐ ☐ ☐
3 30¢ ☐ ☐ ☐ ☐

#2171 4¢ FATHER FLANAGAN
A Press (revised)
Eureka perforator 11.2 x 11.1

1 40¢ ☐ ☐ ☐ ☐

#2172 5¢ HUGO L. BLACK
A Press (revised)
Eureka perforator 11.2 x 11.1

1 50¢ ☐ ☐ ☐ ☐
2 50¢ ☐ ☐ ☐ ☐

#2176 10¢ RED CLOUD
A Press (revised)
Eureka perforator 11.2 x 11.1

1 $1.00 ☐ ☐ ☐ ☐

#2177 14¢ JULIA WARD HOWE
A Press (revised)
Eureka perforator 11.2 x 11.1

1 $1.40 ☐ ☐ ☐ ☐
2 $1.40 ☐ ☐ ☐ ☐

#2178 15¢ BUFFALO BILL CODY
A Press (revised)
Eureka perforator 11.2 x 11.1

1 $1.50 ☐ ☐ ☐ ☐

"D" Press
Eureka perforator 11.2 x 11.1

2 $1.50 ☐ ☐ ☐ ☐

#2179 17¢ BELVA LOCKWOOD
A Press (revised)
Eureka perforator 11.2 x 11.1

1 $1.70 ☐ ☐ ☐ ☐
2 $1.70 ☐ ☐ ☐ ☐

#2180 21¢ CARLSON
A Press (revised)
Eureka perforator 11.2 x 11.1

1 $1.75 ☐ ☐ ☐ ☐

#2182 23¢ MARY CASSATT
A Press (revised)
Eureka perforator 11.2 x 11.1

1 $1.85 ☐ ☐ ☐ ☐

#2183 25¢ JACK LONDON
A Press (revised)
Eureka perforator 11.2 x 11.1

1 $2.00 ☐ ☐ ☐ ☐
2 $2.00 ☐ ☐ ☐ ☐

#2184 28¢ SITTING BULL
Eureka perforator 11.2 x 11.1

1 $2.25 ☐ ☐ ☐ ☐

#2188 45¢ HARVEY CUSHING
A Press (revised)
Eureka perforator 11.2 x 11.1

1 $3.75 ☐ ☐ ☐ ☐

#2191 56¢ JOHN HARVARD
A Press (revised)
Eureka perforator 11.2 x 11.1

1 $4.50 ☐ ☐ ☐ ☐

#2192 65¢ "HAP" ARNOLD
A Press (revised)
Eureka perforator 11.2 x 11.1

1 $5.00 ☐ ☐ ☐ ☐

#2194 $1.00 BERNARD REVEL
A Press (revised)
Eureka perforator 11.2 x 11.1

1 $7.00 ☐ ☐ ☐ ☐

#2194A $1.00 JOHNS HOPKINS
A Press (revised)
Eureka perforator 11.2 x 11.1

1 $7.00 ☐ ☐ ☐ ☐

#2195 $2.00 WILLIAM JENNINGS BRYAN
A Press (revised)
Eureka perforator 11.2 x 11.1

2 $15.00 ☐ ☐ ☐ ☐

#2196 $5.00 BRET HARTE
A Press (revised)
Eureka perforator 11.2 x 11.1

1 $32.50 ☐ ☐ ☐ ☐

1986 REGULAR ISSUES

#2183a $5.00 JACK LONDON BOOKLET

2 PANES OF 10 STAMPS # at top

1	$9.50	☐
2	$9.50	☐

#2197a $1.50 JACK LONDON BOOKLET

1 PANE OF 6 STAMPS # at top

1	$2.50	☐

#2197a $3.00 JACK LONDON BOOKLET

2 PANES OF 6 STAMPS # at top

1	$5.00	☐

#2201a $1.76 STAMP COL-LECTING BOOKLET

2 PANES OF 4 STAMPS # at left

1	$4.00	☐

#2209a $2.20 FISH BOOKLET

2 PANES OF 6 STAMPS # at top

11111	$4.50	☐
22222	$4.50	☐

1986 COMMEMORATIVES

#2167 22¢ ARKANSAS STATEHOOD

		UL	UR	LL	LR
A111111	$1.75	☐	☐	☐	☐

#2202 22¢ LOVE (PUPPY) 1986

11112	$1.75	☐	☐	☐	☐
12221	$1.75	☐	☐	☐	☐
21112	$1.75	☐	☐	☐	☐

#2203 22¢ SOJOURNER TRUTH

A11111	$1.75	☐	☐	☐	☐

#2204 22¢ REPUBLIC OF TEXAS

A111	$1.75	☐	☐	☐	☐

#2210 22¢ PUBLIC HOSPITALS

A11111	$1.75	☐	☐	☐	☐

#2211 22¢ "DUKE" ELLINGTON

A111111	$1.75	☐	☐	☐	☐
A222222	$1.75	☐	☐	☐	☐

#2216-2219 $1.98 Souvenir Sheets (4) issued without plate numbers

1986 COMMEMORATIVES
Continued

#2220-23 22¢ POLAR EXPLORERS

		UL	UR	LL	LR
A11111	$1.75	☐	☐	☐	☐

#2224 22¢ STATUE OF LIBERTY

1	$1.75	☐	☐	☐	☐

#2235-38 22¢ NAVAJO ART

1111-1	$1.75	☐	☐	☐	☐
1211-1	$1.75	☐	☐	☐	☐
2211-1	$1.75	☐	☐	☐	☐
2222-1	$1.75	☐	☐	☐	☐
2322-1	$1.75	☐	☐	☐	☐

#2239 22¢ T.S. ELIOT

2	$1.75	☐	☐	☐	☐

#2240-43 22¢ WOODCARVED FIGURINES

A11111	$1.75	☐	☐	☐	☐

#2244 22¢ MADONNA (1986)

22222	$1.75	☐	☐	☐	☐

#2245 22¢ VILLAGE SCENE

111121	$1.75	☐	☐	☐	☐
111122	$15.00	☐	☐	☐	☐

1987 COMMEMORATIVES

#2246 22¢ MICHIGAN STATEHOOD

11111	$1.75	☐	☐	☐	☐

#2247 22¢ PAN AMERICAN GAMES

11111	$1.75	☐	☐	☐	☐

#2248 22¢ LOVE

11111	$1.75	☐	☐	☐	☐
11121	$1.75	☐	☐	☐	☐
11131	$1.75	☐	☐	☐	☐
11231	$1.75	☐	☐	☐	☐
12222	—	☐	☐	☐	☐
12232	—	☐	☐	☐	☐

#2249 22¢ JEAN BAPTISTE

111111	$1.75	☐	☐	☐	☐

#2250 22¢ CARUSO

A1111	$1.75	☐	☐	☐	☐

#2251 22¢ GIRL SCOUTS

11111-1	$1.75	☐	☐	☐	☐
11112-1	$1.75	☐	☐	☐	☐
22223-1	$1.75	☐	☐	☐	☐

MISCELLANEOUS ISSUES

#2274a $2.20 GREETINGS BOOKLET

2 PANES OF 4 STAMPS **# at top**

11111	$4.50	☐
22222	$4.50	☐

#2275 22¢ UNITED WAY

		UL	UR	LL	LR
21211-1	$1.75	☐	☐	☐	☐
21221-1	$1.75	☐	☐	☐	☐
21222-1	$1.75	☐	☐	☐	☐
21322-1	$1.75	☐	☐	☐	☐
22332-1	$1.75	☐	☐	☐	☐
32432-1	$1.75	☐	☐	☐	☐
32442-1	$1.75	☐	☐	☐	☐

#2276 $.22 FLAG WITH FIREWORKS

Andreotti Press

Eureka Perforator 11.2 x 11.1

1111	$2.00	☐	☐	☐	☐
2222	$2.00	☐	☐	☐	☐

#2276a $4.40 FLAG & FIREWORKS BOOKLET

...prepared from sheet stamps

1 PANE OF 20 STAMPS

1111	$10.00	☐	†	☐	†
2122	$20.00	☐	†	☐	†
2222	$12.50	☐	†	☐	†

#2277 E ($.25) Sheet

Eureka Perforator 11.2 x 11.1

1111	$2.00	☐	☐	☐	☐

#2278a 25¢ FLAG WITH CLOUDS

Eureka Perforator 11.1 x 11.2

1111	$2.00	☐	☐	☐	☐
1222	$2.00	☐	☐	☐	☐
2131	$2.00	☐	☐	☐	☐
2222	$2.00	☐	☐	☐	☐
2231	$2.00	☐	☐	☐	☐
2232	$2.00	☐	☐	☐	☐

#2279 E($.25) COIL

STRIP OF 5 **# at bottom**

1111	$4.00	☐
1211	$6.00	☐
1222	$4.00	☐
2222	$7.00	☐

#2280 $.25 FLAG OVER YOSEMITE COIL

 # at bottom

1	$6.00	☐
2	$6.00	☐
3	$6.00	☐
4	$5.00	☐
5	$5.00	☐
6	$6.00	☐
7	$5.00	☐
8	$5.00	☐
9	$5.00	☐
10	$5.00	☐
11	$5.00	☐
13	$4.00	☐
14	$4.00	☐

(The above exist on either block tagged or pre-phosphored paper or both)

#2281 $.25 HONEYBEE COIL

1	$5.00	☐
2	$5.00	☐

#2282a $5.00 "E" BOOKLET

2 PANES OF 10 STAMPS **# at top**

1111	$12.50	☐
2122	$20.00	☐
2222	$12.50	☐

#2283a $5.00 PHEASANT BOOKLET

2 PANES OF 10 STAMPS **# at left**

A1111	$8.00	☐
A3111	$8.00	☐
A3222	$8.00	☐

#2285b $5.00 OWL & GROSBEAK BOOKLET

2 PANES OF 10 STAMPS **# at top**

1111	$8.00	☐
1112	$8.00	☐
1133	$8.00	☐
1211	$8.00	☐
1433	$8.00	☐
2111	$8.00	☐
2121	$8.00	☐
2122	$8.00	☐
2221	$8.00	☐
2222	$8.00	☐
2321	$8.00	☐
3133	$8.00	☐
3233	$8.00	☐
3333	$8.00	☐
3512	$8.00	☐
3521	$8.00	☐
4642	$8.00	☐
4644	$8.00	☐

MISCELLANEOUS ISSUES Cont.

#2285Ac $3.00 FLAG & CLOUDS BOOKLET

2 PANES OF 6 STAMPS **# at left**

1111	$5.00	☐

#2286-2335 22¢ WILDLIFE

		UL	UR	LL	LR
1111	$1.75	☐	☐	☐	☐

RATIFICATION OF THE CONSTITUTION BICENTENNIAL 13 States

#2336 22¢ DELAWARE

		UL	UR	LL	LR
1111-1	$1.75	☐	☐	☐	☐
2122-1	$1.75	☐	☐	☐	☐
2132-1	$1.75	☐	☐	☐	☐
3243-1	$1.75	☐	☐	☐	☐
3253-1	$1.75	☐	☐	☐	☐
4254-1	$1.75	☐	☐	☐	☐
6666-1	$1.75	☐	☐	☐	☐
7666-1	—	☐	☐	☐	☐
8666-1	$1.75	☐	☐	☐	☐
8676-1	$1.75	☐	☐	☐	☐

#2337 22¢ PENNSYLVANIA

		UL	UR	LL	LR
A11111	$1.75	☐	☐	☐	☐

#2338 22¢ NEW JERSEY

		UL	UR	LL	LR
A11111	$1.75	☐	☐	☐	☐

#2339 22¢ GEORGIA

		UL	UR	LL	LR
A1111	$1.75	☐	☐	☐	☐

#2340 22¢ CONNECTICUT

		UL	UR	LL	LR
1111-1	$1.75	☐	☐	☐	☐
1112-1	$1.75	☐	☐	☐	☐
1113-1	$1.75	☐	☐	☐	☐
1213-1	$1.75	☐	☐	☐	☐
2223-1	$1.75	☐	☐	☐	☐
2224-1	$1.75	☐	☐	☐	☐
2225-1	$1.75	☐	☐	☐	☐
2325-1	$1.75	☐	☐	☐	☐
2335-1	$1.75	☐	☐	☐	☐
2336-1	$1.75	☐	☐	☐	☐
2337-1	$1.75	☐	☐	☐	☐
2438-1	$1.75	☐	☐	☐	☐

#2341 22¢ MASSACHUSETTS

		UL	UR	LL	LR
1	$1.75	☐	☐	☐	☐

#2342 22¢ MARYLAND

		UL	UR	LL	LR
11111-1	$1.75	☐	☐	☐	☐
11211-1	$1.75	☐	☐	☐	☐

RATIFICATION OF THE CONSTITUTION BICENTENNIAL Continued

#2343 25¢ SOUTH CAROLINA

		UL	UR	LL	LR
A11111	$2.00	☐	☐	☐	☐

#2344 25¢ NEW HAMPSHIRE

		UL	UR	LL	LR
A1111	$2.00	☐	☐	☐	☐

#2345 25¢ VIRGINIA STATEHOOD

		UL	UR	LL	LR
1111-1	$2.00	☐	☐	☐	☐
2222-1	$2.00	☐	☐	☐	☐
2223-1	$2.00	☐	☐	☐	☐
3223-1	$2.00	☐	☐	☐	☐
3323-1	$2.00	☐	☐	☐	☐
3333-1	$2.00	☐	☐	☐	☐

#2346 25¢ NEW YORK

		UL	UR	LL	LR
1111-1	$2.00	☐	☐	☐	☐
2111-1	$2.00	☐	☐	☐	☐
2131-1	$2.00	☐	☐	☐	☐
2232-1	$2.00	☐	☐	☐	☐
2242-1	$2.00	☐	☐	☐	☐

#2347 25¢ NORTH CAROLINA

		UL	UR	LL	LR
A11111	$2.00	☐	☐	☐	☐

#2348 25¢ RHODE ISLAND

		UL	UR	LL	LR
....		☐	☐	☐	☐
....		☐	☐	☐	☐

1987 MISCELLANEOUS ISSUES

#2349 22¢ MOROCCO TREATY

		UL	UR	LL	LR
1-1	$1.75	☐	☐	☐	☐
2-1	—	☐	☐	☐	☐
3-1	$1.75	☐	☐	☐	☐
4-1	$1.75	☐	☐	☐	☐
5-1	$1.75	☐	☐	☐	☐

#2350 22¢ WILLIAM FAULKNER

		UL	UR	LL	LR
1	$1.75	☐	☐	☐	☐

#2351-2354 22¢ LACEMAKING

		UL	UR	LL	LR
111-1	$1.75	☐	☐	☐	☐
112-1	$1.75	☐	☐	☐	☐
122-1	$1.75	☐	☐	☐	☐
123-1	$1.75	☐	☐	☐	☐
123-2	$1.75	☐	☐	☐	☐
124-1	$1.75	☐	☐	☐	☐
124-2	$1.75	☐	☐	☐	☐
224-2	$1.75	☐	☐	☐	☐
225-2	$1.75	☐	☐	☐	☐
235-1	$1.75	☐	☐	☐	☐
235-2	$1.75	☐	☐	☐	☐
236-2	$1.75	☐	☐	☐	☐

1987 MISCELLANEOUS ISSUES Continued

#2359a $4.40 CONSTITUTION BOOKLET

4 PANES OF 5 STAMPS # at top

Plate	Price	
1111	$8.50	☐
1112	$8.50	☐

#2360 22¢ CONSTITUTION

Plate	Price	UL	UR	LL	LR
12111-1	$1.75	☐	☐	☐	☐
12311-1	$1.75	☐	☐	☐	☐
12311-1	$1.75	☐	☐	☐	☐
12312-1	$1.75	☐	☐	☐	☐
22322-1	$1.75	☐	☐	☐	☐
23322-1	$1.75	☐	☐	☐	☐
33322-1	$1.75	☐	☐	☐	☐

#2361 22¢ C.P.A.

Plate	Price				
1111-1	$1.75	☐	☐	☐	☐
1112-1	$1.75	☐	☐	☐	☐
1113-1	$1.75	☐	☐	☐	☐
1124-1	$1.75	☐	☐	☐	☐

#2366a $4.40 LOCOMOTIVE BOOKLET

4 PANES OF 5 STAMPS # at top

Plate	Price	
1	$8.50	☐
2	$9.00	☐

#2367 22¢ CHRISTMAS (Madonna)

Plate	Price	UL	UR	LL	LR
111111	$1.75	☐	☐	☐	☐
121112	$1.75	☐	☐	☐	☐

#2368 22¢ CHRISTMAS (Tree)

Plate	Price				
111111	$1.75	☐	☐	☐	☐

1988 MISCELLANEOUS ISSUES

#2369 22¢ WINTER OLYMPICS

Plate	Price				
A1111	$1.75	☐	☐	☐	☐

#2370 22¢ AUSTRALIA

Plate	Price				
11111	$1.75	☐	☐	☐	☐
12111	$1.75	☐	☐	☐	☐

#2371 22¢ JAMES JOHNSON

Plate	Price				
A11111	$1.75	☐	☐	☐	☐

#2372-75 22¢ CATS

Plate	Price				
A11111	$1.75	☐	☐	☐	☐

#2376 22¢ KNUTE ROCKNE

Plate	Price				
111111-1	$1.75	☐	☐	☐	☐

#2377 25¢ FRANCIS OUIMET

Plate	Price				
A11111	$2.00	☐	☐	☐	☐

1988 MISCELLANEOUS ISSUES Continued

#2378 25¢ LOVE

Plate	Price	UL	UR	LL	LR
11111	$2.00	☐	☐	☐	☐

#2379 45¢ LOVE

Plate	Price				
1111	$2.75	☐	☐	☐	☐

#2380 25¢ SUMMER OLYMPICS

Plate	Price				
12111	$2.00	☐	☐	☐	☐

#2385a $5.00 CLASSIC AUTO BOOKLET

4 PANES OF 5 STAMPS # at top

Plate	Price	
1	$9.00	☐

#2386-89 25¢ EXPLORERS

Plate	Price	UL	UR	LL	LR
A111111	$2.00	☐	☐	☐	☐

#2390-2393 25¢ CAROUSEL ANIMALS

Plate	Price				
111111-1	$2.00	☐	☐	☐	☐
111121-1	$2.00	☐	☐	☐	☐
222232-1	$2.00	☐	☐	☐	☐
323232-1	$2.00	☐	☐	☐	☐
323243-1	$2.00	☐	☐	☐	☐

#2394 $8.75 EXPRESS MAIL

Eureka Perforator 11.1 x 11.2

Plate	Price				
1-11111	$45.00	☐	☐	☐	☐

#2396a & 2398a $3.00 BOOKLET

2 PANES OF 6 STAMPS # in middle

Plate	Price	
A1111	$6.00	☐

#2399 25¢ TRADITIONAL CHRISTMAS

Plate	Price	UL	UR	LL	LR	CUL	CUR
11111-1	$2.00	☐	☐	☐	☐	☐	☐
22222-2	$2.00	☐	☐	☐	☐	☐	☐
22323-2	$2.00	☐	☐	☐	☐	☐	☐
22333-2	$2.00	☐	☐	☐	☐	☐	☐
32333-2	$2.00	☐	☐	☐	☐	☐	☐
32433-2	$2.00	☐	☐	☐	☐	☐	☐
42433-2	$2.00	☐	☐	☐	☐	☐	☐
42443-2	$2.00	☐	☐	☐	☐	☐	☐
42444-2	$2.00	☐	☐	☐	☐	☐	☐
43444-2	$2.00	☐	☐	☐	☐	☐	☐
43454-1	$2.00	☐	☐	☐	☐	☐	☐
53454-1	$2.00	☐	☐	☐	☐	☐	☐
53554-1	$2.00	☐	☐	☐	☐	☐	☐
63554-1	$2.00	☐	☐	☐	☐	☐	☐
63554-2	$2.00	☐	☐	☐	☐	☐	☐
63565-2	$2.00	☐	☐	☐	☐	☐	☐
63665-2	$2.00	☐	☐	☐	☐	☐	☐

1988 MISCELLANEOUS ISSUES Continued

#2400 25¢ CONTEMPORARY CHRISTMAS

		UL	UR	LL	LR	CUL	CUR
111111	$2.00	□	□	□	□	□	□

1989 MISCELLANEOUS ISSUES

#2401 25¢ MONTANA STATEHOOD

1111-1	$2.00	□	□	□	□
1211-1	$2.00	□	□	□	□
2211-1	—	†	□	†	□
2222-1	$2.00	□	□	□	□
2232-1	$2.00	□	□	□	□
3332-1	$2.00	□	□	□	□
4332-1	$2.00	□	□	□	□
4352-1	$2.00	□	□	□	□
5352-1	$2.00	□	□	□	□
5362-1	$2.00	□	□	□	□
6362-1	$2.00	□	□	□	□
6363-1	$2.00	□	□	□	□
6463-1	$2.00	□	□	□	□
6473-1	$2.00	□	□	□	□
6483-1	$2.00	□	□	□	□
6494-1	$2.00	□	□	□	□

#2402 25¢ RANDOLPH

11111	$2.00	□	□	□	□
12111	$2.00	□	□	□	□

#2403 25¢ NORTH DAKOTA STATEHOOD

A1111	$2.00	□	□	□	□

#2404 25¢ WASHINGTON STATEHOOD

A1111	$2.00	□	□	□	□

#2409a $5.00 STEAMBOAT BOOKLET

4 PANES OF 5 STAMPS **# at top**

1	$9.00	□
2	$9.00	□

#2410 25¢ WORLD STAMP EXPO

111-1	$2.00	□	□	□	□
212-1	$2.00	□	□	□	□

#2411 25¢ ARTURO TOSCANINI

A11111	$2.00	□	□	□	□

1989 MISCELLANEOUS ISSUES Continued

#2412 25¢ HOUSE OF REPRESENTATIVES

111-1	$2.00	□	□	□	□
211-1	$2.00	□	□	□	□
221-1	—	□	†	□	†
321-1	$2.00	□	□	□	□
422-1	$2.00	□	□	□	□
522-1	$2.00	□	□	□	□
622-1	$2.00	□	□	□	□
722-1	$2.00	□	□	□	□
723-1	—	□	□	□	†
724-1	$2.00	□	□	□	□
823-1	$2.00	□	□	□	□

#2413 25¢ SENATE

		UL	UR	LL	LR
111-1	$2.00	□	□	□	□
211-1	$2.00	□	□	□	□
212-1	$2.00	□	□	□	□
213-1	$2.00	□	□	□	□
313-1	$2.00	□	□	□	□
314-1	$2.00	□	□	□	□
315-1	$2.00	□	□	□	□
414-1	$2.00	□	□	□	□
514-1	$2.00	□	□	□	□
615-1	$2.00	□	□	□	□
715-1	$2.00	□	□	□	□

#2414 25¢ EXECUTIVE BRANCH

111-1	$2.00	□	□	□	□
211-1	$2.00	□	□	□	□
312-1	$2.00	□	□	□	□

#2416 25¢ SOUTH DAKOTA

A1111	$2.00	□	□	□	□

#2417 25¢ LOU GEHRIG

A111111	$2.00	□	□	□	□

#2418 25¢ ERNEST HEMINGWAY

A11111-1	$2.00	□	□	□	□

#2419 $2.40 MOON LANDING

11111-1	$5.00	□	□	□	□
11112-1	$5.00	□	□	□	□
11113-1	$5.00	□	□	□	□
11114-1	$5.00	□	□	□	□
11124-1	$5.00	□	□	□	□
11211-1	$5.00	□	□	□	□
33437-1	$5.00	□	□	□	□

#2420 25¢ LETTER CARRIERS

A111111	$2.00	□	□	□	□

1989 MISCELLANEOUS ISSUES
Continued

#2421 25¢ BILL OF RIGHTS

		UL	UR	LL	LR
111-1	$2.00	☐	☐	☐	☐
112-1	$2.00	☐	☐	☐	☐
122-1	$2.00	☐	☐	☐	☐
123-1	—	☐	☐	☐	☐
223-1	$2.00	☐	☐	☐	☐
234-1	$2.00	☐	☐	☐	☐
235-1	$2.00	☐	☐	☐	☐
376-1	$2.00	☐	☐	☐	☐
377-1	$2.00	☐	☐	☐	☐
446-1	$2.00	☐	☐	☐	☐
456-1	$2.00	☐	☐	☐	☐
466-1	—	☐	☐	☐	☐
467-1	$2.00	☐	☐	☐	☐
477-1	$2.00	☐	☐	☐	☐
676-1	$2.00	☐	☐	☐	☐

#2422-25 25¢ DINOSAURS

		UL	UR	LL	LR
11111-1	$2.00	☐	☐	☐	☐
12111-1	$2.00	☐	☐	☐	☐
12121-1	$2.00	☐	☐	☐	☐
12122-1	$2.00	☐	☐	☐	☐
12232-1	$2.00	☐	☐	☐	☐
27367-1	$2.00	☐	☐	☐	☐
28367-1	$2.00	☐	☐	☐	☐
29367-1	$2.00	☐	☐	☐	☐
29368-1	$2.00	☐	☐	☐	☐
29668-1	$2.00	☐	☐	☐	☐
29669-1	$2.00	☐	☐	☐	☐
44443-1	$2.00	☐	☐	☐	☐
44444-1	$2.00	☐	☐	☐	☐
44445-1	$2.00	☐	☐	☐	☐
44455-1	$2.00	☐	☐	☐	☐
45555-1	$2.00	☐	☐	☐	☐
45556-1	$2.00	☐	☐	☐	☐
46556-1	$2.00	☐	☐	☐	☐

#2426 25¢ AMERICAS ISSUE

		UL	UR	LL	LR
A11111	$2.00	☐	☐	☐	☐

#2427 25¢ TRADITIONAL CHRISTMAS

		UL	UR	LL	LR	CUL	CUR
1111-1	$2.00	☐	☐	☐	☐	☐	☐
2211-1	—	†	†	☐	†	†	☐
2221-1	$2.00	☐	☐	☐	☐	☐	☐
3342-1	$2.00	☐	☐	☐	☐	☐	☐
4453-1	$2.00	☐	☐	☐	☐	☐	☐
5564-1	$2.00	☐	☐	☐	☐	☐	☐
6675-1	$2.00	☐	☐	☐	☐	☐	☐

#2427a $5.00 CHRISTMAS BOOKLET

2 PANES OF 10 STAMPS **# at left**

	# at left
1	☐

1989 MISCELLANEOUS ISSUES
Continued

#2428 25¢ CONTEMPORARY CHRISTMAS

		UL	UR	LL	LR	CUL	CUR
A11111	$2.00	☐	☐	☐	☐	☐	☐

#2428a $5.00 CHRISTMAS BOOKLET

2 PANES OF 10 STAMPS **# at top**

	# at top
A1111	☐
A2111	☐

1990 ISSUES
LISTED IN ORDER ISSUED

#2439 25¢ IDAHO STATEHOOD

		UL	UR	LL	LR
A11111	$2.00	☐	☐	☐	☐

#2440 25¢ LOVE (Sheet Stamp)

		UL	UR	LL	LR	CUL	CLL
U1111	$2.00	☐	☐	☐	☐	☐	☐
U2222	$2.00	☐	☐	☐	☐	☐	☐
U3223	$2.00	☐	☐	☐	☐	☐	☐
U3323	$2.00	☐	☐	☐	☐	☐	☐
U3333	$2.00	☐	☐	☐	☐	☐	☐
U3353	$2.00	☐	☐	☐	☐	☐	☐

#2441 $5.00 LOVE (Booklet)

2 PANES OF 10 STAMPS **# at left**

		# at left
1211	$7.50	☐
2111	$7.50	☐
2211	$7.50	☐
2222	$7.50	☐

#2442 25¢ IDA B. WELLS

		UL	UR	LL	LR
A11111	$2.00	☐	☐	☐	☐

#2415 $.25 U.S. SUPREME COURT

211-1	$2.00	☐	☐	☐	☐
212-1	$2.00	☐	☐	☐	☐
214-1	$2.00	☐	☐	☐	☐

#2443 $3.00 BEACH UMBRELLA BOOKLET

4 PANES OF 5 STAMPS **# at top**

		# at top
111111	$4.50	☐

#2173 5¢ LUIS MUNOZ MARIN

1	$.40	☐	☐	☐	☐

#2444 25¢ WYOMING STATEHOOD

1112-1	$2.00	☐	☐	☐	☐
1122-1	$2.00	☐	☐	☐	☐
1132-1	$2.00	☐	☐	☐	☐
1142-1	$2.00	☐	☐	☐	☐

#2444 25¢ WYOMING Cont.

		UL	UR	LL	LR
1152-1	$2.00	☐	☐	☐	☐
2251-1	$2.00	☐	☐	☐	☐
2261-1	$2.00	☐	☐	☐	☐
2363-1	$2.00	☐	☐	☐	☐

#2445-48 25¢ CLASSIC FILMS

A1111	$2.00	☐	☐	☐	☐

#2449 25¢ MARIANNE MOORE

A111	$2.00	☐	☐	☐	☐

#2468 $1.00 SEAPLANE

Strip of 5 **# at bottom**

1	$7.50	☐

#2470-74 $5.00 LIGHTHOUSES BOOKLET

4 PANES OF 5 STAMPS **# at left**

1	$7.50	☐
2	$7.50	☐
3	$7.50	☐
4	$7.50	☐
5	$7.50	☐

ADDITIONAL ISSUES

.... ☐ ☐ ☐ ☐
.... ☐ ☐ ☐ ☐
.... ☐ ☐ ☐ ☐
.... ☐ ☐ ☐ ☐
.... ☐ ☐ ☐ ☐
.... ☐ ☐ ☐ ☐
.... ☐ ☐ ☐ ☐
.... ☐ ☐ ☐ ☐
.... ☐ ☐ ☐ ☐
.... ☐ ☐ ☐ ☐
.... ☐ ☐ ☐ ☐
.... ☐ ☐ ☐ ☐
.... ☐ ☐ ☐ ☐
.... ☐ ☐ ☐ ☐
.... ☐ ☐ ☐ ☐
.... ☐ ☐ ☐ ☐
.... ☐ ☐ ☐ ☐
.... ☐ ☐ ☐ ☐
.... ☐ ☐ ☐ ☐
.... ☐ ☐ ☐ ☐
.... ☐ ☐ ☐ ☐
.... ☐ ☐ ☐ ☐
.... ☐ ☐ ☐ ☐
.... ☐ ☐ ☐ ☐
.... ☐ ☐ ☐ ☐
.... ☐ ☐ ☐ ☐
.... ☐ ☐ ☐ ☐
.... ☐ ☐ ☐ ☐
.... ☐ ☐ ☐ ☐
.... ☐ ☐ ☐ ☐
.... ☐ ☐ ☐ ☐
.... ☐ ☐ ☐ ☐

ADDITIONAL ISSUES

.... ☐ ☐ ☐ ☐
.... ☐ ☐ ☐ ☐
.... ☐ ☐ ☐ ☐
.... ☐ ☐ ☐ ☐
.... ☐ ☐ ☐ ☐
.... ☐ ☐ ☐ ☐
.... ☐ ☐ ☐ ☐
.... ☐ ☐ ☐ ☐
.... ☐ ☐ ☐ ☐
.... ☐ ☐ ☐ ☐
.... ☐ ☐ ☐ ☐
.... ☐ ☐ ☐ ☐
.... ☐ ☐ ☐ ☐
.... ☐ ☐ ☐ ☐
.... ☐ ☐ ☐ ☐
.... ☐ ☐ ☐ ☐
.... ☐ ☐ ☐ ☐
.... ☐ ☐ ☐ ☐
.... ☐ ☐ ☐ ☐
.... ☐ ☐ ☐ ☐
.... ☐ ☐ ☐ ☐
.... ☐ ☐ ☐ ☐
.... ☐ ☐ ☐ ☐
.... ☐ ☐ ☐ ☐
.... ☐ ☐ ☐ ☐
.... ☐ ☐ ☐ ☐
.... ☐ ☐ ☐ ☐
.... ☐ ☐ ☐ ☐
.... ☐ ☐ ☐ ☐
.... ☐ ☐ ☐ ☐
.... ☐ ☐ ☐ ☐
.... ☐ ☐ ☐ ☐
.... ☐ ☐ ☐ ☐
.... ☐ ☐ ☐ ☐
.... ☐ ☐ ☐ ☐
.... ☐ ☐ ☐ ☐
.... ☐ ☐ ☐ ☐
.... ☐ ☐ ☐ ☐
.... ☐ ☐ ☐ ☐
.... ☐ ☐ ☐ ☐
.... ☐ ☐ ☐ ☐
.... ☐ ☐ ☐ ☐
.... ☐ ☐ ☐ ☐
.... ☐ ☐ ☐ ☐
.... ☐ ☐ ☐ ☐
.... ☐ ☐ ☐ ☐
.... ☐ ☐ ☐ ☐
.... ☐ ☐ ☐ ☐
.... ☐ ☐ ☐ ☐
.... ☐ ☐ ☐ ☐
.... ☐ ☐ ☐ ☐
.... ☐ ☐ ☐ ☐
.... ☐ ☐ ☐ ☐
.... ☐ ☐ ☐ ☐
.... ☐ ☐ ☐ ☐
.... ☐ ☐ ☐ ☐
.... ☐ ☐ ☐ ☐
.... ☐ ☐ ☐ ☐
.... ☐ ☐ ☐ ☐
.... ☐ ☐ ☐ ☐
.... ☐ ☐ ☐ ☐
.... ☐ ☐ ☐ ☐
.... ☐ ☐ ☐ ☐
.... ☐ ☐ ☐ ☐

AIR MAIL ISSUES

1918 ISSUE

FLAT PRESS PERF. 11

#C1 6¢ CURTISS "JENNY"

Plate and Arrow Block of 6

9155 Top position only ☐ $1,000

#C2 16¢ CURTISS "JENNY"

Plate and Arrow Block of 6

8900 Top position only ☐ $2,500

#C3 24¢ CURTISS "JENNY" BICOLORED

Top Position only
Plate Combination 8493-8492
Block of 8 with plates and arrow ☐ $1,500

Block of 12 with plates and arrow plus blue TOP and red TOP ☐ $2,750

Block of 12 with plates and arrow plus blue TOP only Very scarce ☐ $9,500

1923 ISSUE

FLAT PRESS PERF.11

#C4 8¢ PROPELLER Block of 6

4 Plates		TL	TR	L	R	B
14824	$600	☐	☐	☐	☐	☐
14825	$600	☐	☐	☐	☐	☐
14826	$600	☐	☐	☐	☐	☐
14827	$600	☐	☐	☐	☐	☐

#C5 16¢ AIR SERVICE INSIGNIA

4 Plates						
14828	$3,500	☐	☐	☐	☐	☐
14829	$3,500	☐	☐	☐	☐	☐
14830	$3,500	☐	☐	☐	☐	☐
14831	$3,500	☐	☐	☐	☐	☐

1923 ISSUE Continued

#C6 24¢ DE HAVILAND BIPLANE

4 Plates		TL	TR	L	R	B
14840	$4,250	☐	☐	☐	☐	☐
14841	$4,250	☐	☐	☐	☐	☐
14842	$4,250	☐	☐	☐	☐	☐
14843	$4,250	☐	☐	☐	☐	☐

1926-27 ISSUE

FLAT PRESS PERF. 11

#C7 10¢ MAP Block of 6

8 Plates		TL	TR	L	R	B
18246	$60	☐	☐	☐	☐	☐
18247	$60	☐	☐	☐	☐	☐
18248	$60	☐	☐	☐	☐	☐
18249	$60	☐	☐	☐	☐	☐
18250	$75	☐	☐	☐	☐	☐
18903	$75	☐	☐	☐	☐	☐
18904	$75	☐	☐	☐	☐	☐
18905	$75	☐	☐	☐	☐	☐

#C8 15¢ MAP **4 Plates**

18745	$75	☐	☐	☐	☐	☐
18746	$75	☐	☐	☐	☐	☐
18747	$75	☐	☐	☐	☐	☐
18748	$75	☐	☐	☐	☐	☐

AIR MAIL ISSUES

1926-27 ISSUE Continued

#C9 20¢ MAP **8 Plates**

		TL	TR	L	R	B
18890	$175	□	□ Z_1	□	□	□
18891	$175	□	□	□	□	□
18892	$175	□	□ Z_2	□	□	□
18893	$175	□	□	□	□	□
18894	$175	□	□	□	□	□
18897	$175	□	□	□	□	□
18898	$175	□	□	□	□	□
18899	$175	□	□	□	□	□

Z_1 The letter F is not on the TR position. It appears on the left side bottom plate inverted with respect to the plate number.

Z_2 The letter F appears in the TR position and also appears on the left side bottom plate inverted with respect to the plate number.

1927 ISSUE

FLAT PRESS PERF. 11

#C10 10¢ LINDBERGH **12 Plates**

18997	$225	□	□	□	□	□
18998	$225	□	□	□	□	□
18999	$225	□	□	□	□	□
19000	$225	□	□	□	□	□
19001	$225	□	□	□	□	□
19002	$225	□	□	□	□	□
19003	$225	□	□	□	□	□
19004	$225	□	□	□	□	□
19005	$225	□	□	□	□	□
19006	$225	□	□	□	□	□
19007	$225	□	□	□	□	□
19008	$225	□	□	□	□	□

#C10 a 10¢ LINDBERGH BOOKLET
PANES OF 3 **4 Plates**

*19414 *19425 *19426 *19427

1928 ISSUE

FLAT PRESS PERF. 11

#C11 5¢ BEACON BICOLORED

Plate Combination Blocks of 6

Basic Prices: **Positions TL, TR**

With TOP (red or blue)	$65.00
Without TOP	$250.00
With Double TOP (red and blue)	$200.00

40 BLUE (Vignette) Plates

19545	19546	19547	19548	19573
19574	19575	19576	19577	19578
19579	19580	19597	19598	19599
19600	19608	19609	19610	19611
19616	19617	19618	19619	*19639 N
19666	19667	19668	19669	19674
19675	19676	19677	19688	19689
19690	19691	19692	19693	19694

1928 ISSUE Continued

#C11 5¢ BEACON BICOLORED Continued

55 Red (Frame) Plates

19549	19550	19551	19552	19565
19566	19567	19568	19569	19570
19571	19572	19585	19586	19587
19588	19589	19590	19591	19592
19605	19606	19607	19612	19613
19614	19615	19620	19621	19622
19623	19624	19625	19626	19627
19628	19629	19630	19631	19632
19633	19634	19635	19670	19671
19672	19673	19696	19697	19698
19699	19700	19701	19702	19703

Although between 1,000 and 1,100 number combinations have been recorded, no one plate exists in combination with all others.

The standard plate number plus TOP arrangement is:

Left Pane

RED	BLUE	RED
Plate #	**Plate #**	**TOP**

Right Pane

BLUE	BLUE	RED
TOP	**F Plate #**	**F Plate #**

Through error the inscription TOP was entered on the left pane of vignette plate 19597. Therefore, all combinations containing that number have the following arrangement.

Left Pane

RED	BLUE	RED & BLUE
Plate #	**Plate #**	**Double TOP**

Right Pane

	BLUE	RED
No Top	**F Plate #**	**F Plate #**

The F placement on frame plate 19605 is an exception to the rule. On this plate the F is on the **left** pane.

Scattered through the issue there are undoubtedly many scarce to rare plate-number combinations, but no one has studied the issue seriously enough to establish their identity. A large showing of Beacon Air Mail combinations, with fine centering throughout, is unheard of.

N Four special vignette plates - 19636 19637 19638 19639 - were used for an experimental printing. There were 100 impressions from each plate. It is said that most of the sheets were never distributed. The question has been raised as to whether any of the plates were placed on general sale. We know the existence of only one of them — F19639-19605 in a strip of 3.

5¢ BEACON AIRMAIL of 1928

RED PLATES listed Vertically
BLUE PLATES listed Horizontally

	19545	F19545	19546	F19546	19547	F19547	19548	F19548	19573	F19573	19574	F19574	19575	F19575	19576	F19576	19577	F19577	19578	F19578	19579	F19579	19580	F19580	19597	F19597	19598	F19598	19599	F19599	19600	F19600	19608	F19608	19609	F19609	19610	F19610	19611	F19611
19549	●	●	●	●	●	●	●	●	●	●	●	●	●	●	●	●	●	●	●	●	●	●	●	●																
19550	●	●	●	●	●	●	●	●	●	●	●	●	●	●	●	●	●	●	●	●	●	●	●	●																
19551	●	●	●	●	●	●	●	●	●	●	●	●	●	●	●	●	●	●	●	●	●	●	●	●																
19552	●	●	●	●	●	●	●	●	●	●	●	●	●	●	●	●	●	●	●	●	●	●	●	●																
19565	●	●	●	●	●	●	●	●	●	●	●	●	●	●	●	●	●	●	●	●	●	●	●	●																
19566	●	●	●	●	●	●	●	●	●	●	●	●	●	●	●	●	●	●	●	●	●	●	●	●																
19567	●	●	●	●	●	●	●	●	●	●	●	●	●	●	●	●	●	●	●	●	●	●	●	●																
19568	●	●	●	●	●	●	●	●	●	●	●	●	●	●	●	●	●	●	●	●	●	●	●	●																
19569	●	●	●	●	●	●	●	●	●	●	●	●	●	●	●	●	●	●	●	●	●	●	●	●																
19570	●	●	●	●	●	●	●	●	●	●	●	●	●	●	●	●	●	●	●	●	●	●	●	●																
19571	●	●	●	●	●	●	●	●	●	●	●	●	●	●	●	●	●	●	●	●	●	●	●	●	●	●	●	●												
19572	●	●	●	●	●	●	●	●	●	●	●	●	●	●	●	●	●	●	●	●	●	●	●	●																
19585	●	●	●	●	●	●	●	●	●	●	●	●	●	●	●	●	●	●	●	●	●	●	●	●	●	●	●	●	●	●	●	●	●	●	●	●	●	●	●	●
19586	●	●	●	●	●	●	●	●	●	●	●	●	●	●	●	●	●	●	●	●	●	●	●	●	●	●	●	●	●	●	●	●	●	●	●	●	●	●	●	●
19587	●	●	●	●	●	●	●	●	●	●	●	●	●	●	●	●	●	●	●	●	●	●	●	●	●	●	●	●	●	●	●	●	●	●	●	●	●	●	●	●
19588	●	●	●	●	●	●	●	●	●	●	●	●	●	●	●	●	●	●	●	●	●	●	●	●	●	●	●	●	●	●	●	●	●	●	●	●	●	●		
19589	●	●	●	●	●	●	●	●	●	●	●	●	●	●	●	●	●	●	●	●	●	●	●	●	●	●	●	●												
19590	●	●	●	●	●	●	●	●	●	●	●	●	●	●	●	●	●	●	●	●	●	●	●	●	●	●	●	●	●	●	●	●	●	●	●	●	●	●	●	●
19591	●	●	●	●	●	●	●	●	●	●	●	●	●	●	●	●	●	●	●	●	●	●	●	●	●	●	●	●	●	●	●	●	●	●	●	●	●	●		
19592	●	●	●	●	●	●	●	●	●	●	●	●	●	●	●	●	●	●	●	●	●	●	●	●	●	●	●	●	●	●										
19605	●	●	●	●	●	●	●	●	●	●	●	●	●	●	●	●	●	●	●	●	●	●	●	●	●	●	●	●	●	●	●	●	●	●	●	●	●	●	●	●
19606	●	●	●	●	●	●	●	●	●	●	●	●	●	●	●	●	●	●	●	●	●	●			●	●	●	●	●	●	●	●	●	●	●	●	●	●	●	●
19607	●	●	●	●	●	●	●	●	●	●	●	●	●	●	●	●									●	●	●	●	●	●	●	●	●	●	●	●	●	●	●	●
19612									●	●			●	●	●	●									●	●	●	●	●	●	●	●	●	●	●	●	●	●	●	●
19613					●	●	●	●	●	●	●	●	●	●	●	●					●	●			●	●	●	●	●	●	●	●	●	●	●	●	●	●	●	●
19614	●	●	●	●	●	●	●	●	●	●			●	●	●	●									●	●	●	●	●	●	●	●	●	●	●	●	●	●	●	●
19615					●	●			●	●	●	●	●	●							●	●			●	●	●	●	●	●	●	●	●	●	●	●	●	●	●	●
19620					●	●	●	●	●	●	●	●	●	●	●	●					●	●			●	●	●	●	●	●	●	●	●	●	●	●	●	●	●	●
19621							●	●			●	●			●	●					●	●			●	●	●	●	●	●	●	●	●	●	●	●	●	●	●	●
19622									●	●					●	●									●	●	●	●	●	●	●	●	●	●	●	●	●	●	●	●
19623									●	●			●	●	●	●									●	●	●	●	●	●	●	●	●	●	●	●	●	●	●	●
19624					●	●			●	●			●	●	●	●									●	●	●	●	●	●	●	●	●	●	●	●	●	●	●	●
19625									●	●			●	●	●	●									●	●	●	●	●	●	●	●	●	●	●	●	●	●	●	●
19626									●	●	●	●	●	●	●	●									●	●	●	●	●	●	●	●	●	●	●	●	●	●	●	●
19627									●	●			●	●	●	●									●	●	●	●	●	●	●	●	●	●	●	●	●	●	●	●
19628									●	●			●	●	●	●									●	●	●	●	●	●	●	●	●	●	●	●			●	●
19629									●	●			●	●	●	●									●	●	●	●	●	●	●	●	●	●	●	●			●	●
19630									●	●	●	●	●	●	●	●									●	●	●	●			●	●	●	●	●	●			●	●
19631									●	●			●	●	●	●									●	●	●	●			●	●	●	●	●	●			●	●
19632																									●	●	●	●					●	●	●	●			●	●
19633																									●	●	●	●					●	●	●	●			●	●
19634																									●	●	●	●					●	●	●	●			●	●
19635																									●	●	●	●					●	●	●	●			●	●
19670																									●	●	●	●					●	●					●	●
19671																									●	●	●	●					●	●					●	●
19672																									●	●	●	●					●	●					●	●
19673																									●	●	●	●											●	●
19696																																								
19697																																								
19698																																								
19699																									●	●	●	●											●	●
19700																																								
19701																									●	●	●	●											●	●
19702																																								
19703																																								

5¢ BEACON AIRMAIL of 1928

RED PLATES listed Vertically
BLUE PLATES listed Horizontally

	19616	F19616	19617	F19617	19618	F19618	19619	F19619	19639	F19639	19666	F19666	19667	F19667	19668	F19668	19669	F19669	19674	F19674	19675	F19675	19676	F19676	19677	F19677	19688	F19688	19689	F19689	19690	F19690	19691	F19691	19692	F19692	19693	F19693	19694	F19694	
19549																																									19549
19550																																									19550
19551																																									19551
19552																																									19552
19565																																									19565
19566																																									19566
19567																																									19567
19568																																									19568
19569																																									19569
19570																																									19570
19571																																									19571
19572																																									19572
19585	●	●	●	●	●	●	●	●																																	19585
19586	●	●	●	●	●	●	●	●																																	19586
19587	●	●	●	●	●	●	●	●																																	19587
19588	●	●	●	●	●	●																																			19588
19589																																									19589
19590	●	●	●	●	●	●	●	●																																	19590
19591	●	●			●	●	●	●																																	19591
19592																																									19592
19605	●	●	●	●	●	●	●	●		●																															19605
19606	●	●	●	●	●	●	●	●			●	●	●	●			●	●																							19606
19607	●	●	●	●	●	●	●	●			●	●	●	●	●	●	●	●	●	●	●	●	●	●	●	●	●	●													19607
19612	●	●	●	●	●	●	●	●			●	●	●	●			●	●	●	●	●	●	●	●	●	●	●	●													19612
19613	●	●	●	●	●	●	●	●																																	19613
19614	●	●	●	●	●	●	●	●			●	●	●	●	●	●	●	●	●	●	●	●	●	●	●	●	●	●													19614
19615	●	●	●	●	●	●	●	●			●	●	●	●	●	●	●	●	●	●	●	●	●	●	●	●	●	●													19615
19620	●	●	●	●	●	●	●	●			●	●	●	●	●	●	●	●	●	●	●	●	●	●	●	●	●	●													19620
19621	●	●	●	●	●	●	●	●																																	19621
19622	●	●	●	●	●	●	●	●																																	19622
19623	●	●	●	●	●	●	●	●			●	●	●	●	●	●	●	●	●	●	●	●	●	●	●	●	●	●													19623
19624	●	●	●	●	●	●	●	●			●	●	●	●			●	●	●	●	●	●					●	●													19624
19625	●	●	●	●	●	●	●	●			●	●	●	●	●	●	●	●	●	●	●	●	●	●	●	●	●	●													19625
19626	●	●	●	●	●	●	●	●			●	●	●	●	●	●	●	●	●	●	●	●	●	●	●	●	●	●													19626
19627	●	●	●	●	●	●	●	●			●	●	●	●	●	●	●	●	●	●	●	●	●	●	●	●	●	●													19627
19628	●	●	●	●	●	●	●	●			●	●	●	●			●	●	●	●	●	●	●	●	●	●	●	●													19628
19629	●	●	●	●	●	●	●	●			●	●	●	●	●	●	●	●	●	●	●	●	●	●	●	●	●	●													19629
19630	●	●	●	●	●	●	●	●			●	●	●	●	●	●	●	●	●	●	●	●	●	●	●	●	●	●													19630
19631	●	●	●	●	●	●	●	●			●	●	●	●	●	●	●	●	●	●	●	●	●	●	●	●	●	●													19631
19632	●	●	●	●	●	●	●	●			●	●	●	●	●	●	●	●	●	●	●	●	●	●	●	●	●	●	●	●	●	●	●	●	●	●	●	●	●	●	19632
19633	●	●	●	●	●	●	●	●			●	●	●	●	●	●	●	●	●	●	●	●	●	●	●	●	●	●	●	●	●	●	●	●	●	●	●	●	●	●	19633
19634	●	●	●	●	●	●	●	●			●	●	●	●	●	●	●	●	●	●	●	●	●	●	●	●	●	●	●	●	●	●	●	●	●	●	●	●	●	●	19634
19635	●	●	●	●	●	●	●	●			●	●	●	●	●	●	●	●	●	●	●	●	●	●	●	●	●	●	●	●	●	●	●	●	●	●	●	●	●	●	19635
19670	●	●	●	●	●	●	●	●			●	●	●	●	●	●	●	●	●	●	●	●	●	●	●	●	●	●	●	●	●	●	●	●	●	●	●	●	●	●	19670
19671	●	●	●	●	●	●	●	●			●	●	●	●	●	●	●	●	●	●	●	●	●	●	●	●	●	●	●	●	●	●	●	●	●	●	●	●	●	●	19671
19672	●	●	●	●	●	●	●	●			●	●	●	●	●	●	●	●	●	●	●	●	●	●	●	●	●	●	●	●	●	●	●	●	●	●	●	●	●	●	19672
19673	●	●	●	●	●	●	●	●			●	●	●	●	●	●	●	●	●	●	●	●	●	●	●	●	●	●	●	●	●	●	●	●	●	●	●	●	●	●	19673
19696											●	●			●	●			●	●	●	●	●	●	●	●	●	●	●	●	●	●	●	●	●	●	●	●	●	●	19696
19697											●	●			●	●			●	●	●	●	●	●	●	●	●	●	●	●	●	●	●	●	●	●	●	●	●	●	19697
19698											●	●			●	●			●	●	●	●	●	●	●	●	●	●	●	●	●	●	●	●	●	●	●	●	●	●	19698
19699	●	●	●	●	●	●	●	●			●	●	●	●	●	●	●	●	●	●	●	●	●	●	●	●	●	●	●	●	●	●	●	●	●	●	●	●	●	●	19699
19700											●	●			●	●			●	●	●	●	●	●	●	●	●	●	●	●	●	●	●	●	●	●	●	●	●	●	19700
19701	●	●	●	●	●	●	●	●			●	●	●	●	●	●	●	●	●	●	●	●	●	●	●	●	●	●	●	●	●	●	●	●	●	●	●	●	●	●	19701
19702											●	●			●	●			●	●	●	●	●	●	●	●	●	●	●	●	●	●	●	●	●	●	●	●	●	●	19702
19703											●	●			●	●			●	●	●	●	●	●	●	●	●	●	●	●	●	●	●	●	●	●	●	●	●	●	19703
	19616	F19616	19617	F19617	19618	F19618	19619	F19619	19639	F19639	19666	F19666	19667	F19667	19668	F19668	19669	F19669	19674	F19674	19675	F19675	19676	F19676	19677	F19677	19688	F19688	19689	F19689	19690	F19690	19691	F19691	19692	F19692	19693	F19693	19694	F19694	

AIR MAIL ISSUES

1930 ISSUE

FLAT PRESS PERF. 11
Block of 6

#C12 5¢ WINGED GLOBE

13 Plates

Plate	Price	TL	TR	L	R	B
19941	$250	☐	☐	☐	☐	☐
19942	$250	☐	☐	☐	☐	☐
19943	$250	☐	☐	☐	☐	☐
19944	$250	☐	☐	☐	☐	☐
19945	$250	☐	☐	☐	☐	☐
19946	$250	☐	☐	☐	☐	☐
19947	$250	☐	☐	☐	☐	☐
19948	$250	☐	☐	☐	☐	☐
20187	$450	☐	☐	‡	‡	☐
20188	$450	☐	☐	‡	‡	☐
20189	$450	☐	☐	‡	‡	☐
20190	$450	☐	☐	‡	‡	☐
20323	$500	☐	☐	‡	‡	☐

#C13 65¢ ZEPPELIN

Plate	Price	TL	TR	L	R	B
20077	$4,000	☐	☐	☐	☐	☐
20078	$4,000	☐	☐	☐	☐	☐
20079	$4,000	☐	☐	☐	☐	☐
20080	$4,000	☐	☐	☐	☐	☐

#C14 $1.30 ZEPPELIN

Plate	Price	TL	TR	L	R	B
20085	$7,500	☐	☐	☐	☐	☐
20086	$7,500	☐	☐	☐	☐	☐
20087	$7,500	☐	☐	☐	☐	☐
20088	$7,500	☐	☐	☐	☐	☐

1930 ISSUE

#C15 $2.60 ZEPPELIN 4 Plates

Plate	Price	TL	TR	L	R	B
20090	$12,500	☐	☐	☐	☐	☐
20091	$12,500	☐	☐	☐	☐	☐
20092	$12,500	☐	☐	☐	☐	☐
20095	$12,500	☐	☐	☐	☐	☐

1931-32 ISSUE

ROTARY PRESS PERF. 10½ x 11
Block of 4

#C16 5¢ WINGED GLOBE 2 Plates

Plate	Price	UL	UR	LL	LR
20606	$150.00	☐	☐	☐	☐
20607	$150.00	☐	☐	☐	☐

#C17 8¢ WINGED GLOBE 6 Plates

Plate	Price	UL	UR	LL	LR
21028	$50.00	☐	☐	☐	☐
21029	$50.00	☐	☐	☐	☐
21030	$50.00	☐	☐	☐	☐
21031	$50.00	☐	☐	☐	☐
21032	$50.00	☐	☐	☐	☐
21033	$50.00	☐	☐	☐	☐

1933 ISSUE

FLAT PRESS PERF. 11

#C18 50¢ GRAF ZEPPELIN 4 Plates

Block of 6

Plate	Price	T	B
21171	$1,100	☐	☐
21172	$1,100	☐	☐
21177	$1,100	☐	☐
21178	$1,100	☐	☐

AIR MAIL ISSUES

1934 ISSUE

ROTARY PRESS PERF. 10½ x 11

Block of 4

#C19 6¢ WINGED GLOBE

6 Plates		UL	UR	LL	LR
21234	$32.50	□	□	□	□
21235	$32.50	□	□	□	□
21236	$32.50	□	□	□	□
21237	$32.50	□	□	□	□
21598	$32.50	□	□	□	□
21599	$32.50	□	□	□	□

1935-37 ISSUE

FLAT PRESS Block of 6 PERF 11

#C20 25¢ CHINA CLIPPER

4 Plates		TL	TR	L	R	B
21473	$30.00	□	□	‡	‡	□

1935-37 ISSUE

#C20 25¢ CHINA CLIPPER Cont.

		TL	TR	L	R	B
21474	$30.00	□	□	‡	‡	□
21475	$30.00	□	□	‡	‡	□
21476	$30.00	□	□	‡	‡	□

#C21 20¢ CHINA CLIPPER

4 Plates		TL	TR	L	R	B
21622	$150.00	□	□	‡	‡	□
21623	$150.00	□	□	‡	‡	□
21626	$150.00	□	□	‡	‡	□
21627	$150.00	□	□	‡	‡	□

#C22 50¢ CHINA CLIPPER

4 Plates		TL	TR	L	R	B
21624	$140.00	□	□	‡	‡	□
21625	$140.00	□	□	‡	‡	□
21628	$140.00	□	□	‡	‡	□
21629	$140.00	□	□	‡	‡	□

1933 ISSUE

6¢ EAGLE BICOLORED AIR MAIL

Compiled and edited by Albert L. Goldman from the original Durland notes and later information.

#C23 6¢ EAGLE

The frame plates contained 100 subjects, divided into left and right panes of 50, with **top** plate numbers **only.** The **F** was not placed consistently on right panes.

Plates 22186 and 22192 had no **F** but the positions can be identified by differences in the registration markings. (See "THE UNITED STATES SPECIALIST", pages 253-254, May 1976).

The vignette plates were single panes of 50 subject with plate numbers at top. The first 18 numbers are preceded by an **F** and the remaining 20 are plain.

The plate-number combinations fall into two **major** classifications, those **with** and those **without** arrow.

All of the early printings are **with arrow.**

With-arrow combinations containing vignette plates 21918, 21919, 21920 are very scarce, and we have not seen any containing 21921, or 21922.

Vignette plate 21909 occurs only in **with** arrow combinations.

All late printings are **without arrow**.

No arrows exist on any combinations containing vignette plates 22197, 22198, 22199, 22200, or frame plates 22185, 22186, 22191, 22192.

FLAT PRESS PERF. 11

22192 is the scarcest frame plate. All vignette plates from 21920 to 22200 are scarce.

Some combinations are common with arrow and scarce without, and vice versa. There are also combinations where one pane is much scarcer than the other.

1933 ISSUE

#C23 1983 6¢ EAGLE BICOLORED Continued

Of the positions for which there is no designated value, some do not exist and others are unreported.

The lack of a value designation for such positions is not necessarily an indication of relative scarcity.

Blocks of 4

WITH ARROW

16 Frame Plates

Vignette Plates		F21835	21835	F21836	21836	F21837	21837	F21838	21838	F21855	21855	F21856	21856	F21857	21857	F21858	21858	21948	F21948	21949	F21949	21950	F21950	21951	F21951	22185	F22185	22186	22186	22191	F22191	22192	22192
		L	R	L	R	L	R	L	R	L	R	L	R	L	R	L	R	L	R	L	R	L	R	L	R	L	R	L	R	L	R	L	R
18 Vignette Plates with F	F21839	A	B	A	C	B	E	E	E	E	E	E	A	E	D	E	B	K	P	T	T	T	V	X	Y								
	F21840	E	E	A	B	E	E	E	E	E	E	C	D	C	C	E	B	D	D	V	V	S	V	S	V								
	F21841	E	B	E	E	E	C	C	B	E	D	S	B	K	E	D	E	K	T	P	X	D	X	T	T								
	F21842	E	E	E	C	E	B	E	C	E	E	B	C	B	E	E	B	Y	X	Y	X	V	Y	N	X								
	F21843	E	C	E	E	B	B	E	A	T	B	H	B	Y	B	X	B	T	T	X	Y	V	N	T									
	F21844	N	E	K	B	B	B	E	E	E	B	Y	B	X	E	E	B	X	T	P	T	T	T	T	T								
	F21845	E	E	E	B	K	B	A	B	K	B	K	B	V	B	P	B																
	F21846	N	B	H	E	N	E	K	B	C	E	H	E	H	E	X	E	S															
	F21847	P	E	T	E	N	E	H	B		B		B		B		B	S	Y	T	P	P	H	T	P								
	F21848	B	N	B	B	E	H	K	K	B		B	Y	B		B	B	S	Y	N	S	K	P	H	N								
	F21849	X	E	X	E	P	E	C	E		B		B		S	X	E	V	Y	H	H	P	Y	K	X								
	F21850	X	D	X	B	X	B		C		C		E		B		B																
	F21851		E		B	K	E		E		B		E		A		B																
	F21852	K	P	K	P	K	T	T	T	K	K	P		S	Y	S		Y	S	P	P	X	S	X	X								
	F21853	P	P	B	X	B	N	E	N	B		B	S	B	T	E	S	V	P	T	P	V	V	V	V								
	F21854	E	X	B	T	E	V	E	Y	B		B	X	E	X	B	S	Y	P	S	X	X	X	T	T								
	F21901	E	V	E	P	E	X	E	X	B	X	E	S	E	S	B	X	X	Y	T	P	T	X	T	X								
	F21902	N	N	E	N	E	C	E	E	E	T	E	P	E	X	E	X	T	T	V	S	K	T	S	X								
20 Vignette Plates without F	21903	E	B	E	S	C	H	E	T	E	P	E	K	E	T	E	X	K	T	P	S	N	S	N	T								
	21904	E	B	E	X	B	H	E	P	E		E		E		E	P	T	X	X	P	Z	S	N	N								
	21909	K	P	H	T	K	T	H	X	K	T	H	T	H	X	H	X																
	21910	E	B	E	H	E	P	E	K	C	S	E	V	E	S	E	P	X		Y		X		Z	X								
	21911		E		E		E		E		E		B		B		E																
	21912		E		E		E		D		E		N		B		H																
	21913		E		E		E		E		E		B		E		E																
	21914		E		E		E		B		E		E		E		D																
	21915	C	P	E	P	E	X	E		D	P	E	P	E	X	E																	
	21916	E	P	B	P	E	P	A		B	P	E		E	P	B	X																
	21917	B		K	X	E		T	T	S	X	K	P	K	V	N	X																
	21918								Z																								
	21919				Z		Z		Z																								
	21920		Z				Y																										
	21921																																
	21922																																
	22197																																
	22198																																
	22199																																
	22200																																

1933 ISSUE

#C23 1938 6¢ EAGLE BICOLORED Continued

KEY TO VALUATIONS

E.....11.00	D 14.00	P.....27.50	X.....52.50
A.....11.50	H 16.00	S.....30.00	Y.....62.50
B.....12.25	K.....18.00	T.....38.50	Z....105.00
C 13.50	N 22.00	V.....45.00	

Blocks of 4
WITHOUT ARROW

16 Frame Plates

		F21835 L	21835 R	F21836 L	21836 R	F21837 L	21837 R	F21838 L	21838 R	F21855 L	21855 R	F21856 L	21856 R	F21857 L	21857 R	F21858 L	21858 R	21948 L	F21948 R	21949 L	F21949 R	21950 L	F21950 R	21951 L	F21951 R	22185 L	F22185 R	22186 L	22186 R	22191 L	F22191 R	22192 L	22192 R
18 Vignette Plates with F	F21839	E	E	E	E	E	E	E	E	E	E	E	E	E	E	E	E	E	E	E	E	E	E	E	E	H	H	K	T	K	H	Y	
	F21840	E	E	E	E	E	E	E	E	E	A	E	E	E	E	E	E	D	E	E	E	E	E	E	A	N	X						
	F21841	C	E	E	E	E	E	E	E	E	E	E	K	E	B	E	E	E	E	E	E	E	E	E	E	Y	Y						
	F21842	E	E	E	E	E	E	E	E	E	E	E	E	E	E	E	E	E	E	E	E	E	E	E	E	V	V						
	F21843	E	E	E	E	E	E	E	E	E	E	E	E	E	E	E	E	E	E	E	E	E	E	E	E	N	V	N	N	K	N	X	
	F21844	E	E	E	E	E	E	E	E	E	E	E	E	E	E	E	E	E	E	E	E	E	E	E	E	H	T	N	N	S	N	X	X
	F21845	D	C	C	T	K	N	D	C	C	C	C	D	D	C	E	E	E	E	E	E	E	E	E	E	H	N	S	N	K	K	Y	Y
	F21846	B	X	A	D	E	B	P	E	E	D	E	E	E	E	C	C	E	E	B	C	B	E	C	E	H	K	H	H	K	K	Y	Y
	F21847	E	E	E	D	E	E	D	E	E	T	E	N	E	N	E	E	E	E	E	E	E	E	E	E	H	H	K	H	H	H	T	X
	F21848	E	E	E	E	E	E	E	E	E	E	E	E	E	E	E	E	E	E	E	E	E	E	E	E	H	H	K	K	H	H	T	T
	F21849	E	E	E	E	E	E	E	E	E	Y	E	E	E	E	E	E	E	E	E	E	E	E	E	E	Y		K	K	X	X		
	F21850	E	K	E	E	E	B	E	E	E	C	E	E	C	K	E	T	E	E	C	B	C	E	D	B	S	S	K	S	X	X		
	F21851	E	E	E	E	E	E	E	E	E	D	E	H	E	B	E	E	E	E	E	E	E	E	E	E	K	K	K	K	K	K	Y	
	F21852	E	E	E	E	E	E	E	E	E	E	B	E	E	E	E	E	E	B	E	E	E	E	E	E	H	H	K	N	P	P		
	F21853	K	T	K	H	K	H	K	V	H	S	H	K	B	K	D	D	N	D	Y	Y	T	S	K	T		Y						
	F21854	C	E	E	N	E	E	E	E	C	B	K	C	C	B	E	E	E	E	E	E	E	E	E	E	H	H	K	K	H	H		
	F21901	C	C	P	C	E	P	B	N	B	H	C	H	C	C	E	A	S	E	S	K	S	E	S	D	X	X						
	F21902	E	D	C	X	E	D	B	N	B	C	N	N	E	K	K	E	E	B	E	E	C	E	B	E	K	X	K	K	P	T		
20 Vignette Plates without F	21903	E	E	B	B	D	E	B	E	K	C	S	C	D	D	B	E	E	E	E	E	E	E	E	E	K	K	K	K	K	K	X	X
	21904	T	T	K	S	S	T	T	S	D	T	H	T	K	T	K	Y	P	K	K	K	K	H	K	K	Z	Y						
	21909																																
	21910	K	B	E	E	E	E	E	E	B	B	D	C	B	C	E	E	E	E	E	E	E	E	E	E	P	P	K	K	K	K	X	T
	21911	E	D	E	E	E	E	E	E	E	E	B	K	K	T	E	E	E	E	E	E	E	E	E	E	H	H	K	K	K	H	P	V
	21912	B	E	E	A	B	B	B	D	E	E	C	D	C	X	C	K	E	E	E	B	E	E	E	H	Z	X	H	K	K	N		X
	21913	T	X	T	C	C	T	N	D	B	V	C	S	H	S	D	T	T	C	E	X	T	C	N	C		X						
	21914	C	P	C	B	D	C	D	D	E	D	D	T	B	D	E	D	E	E	B	E	B	B	K	E	Y		P	X	X	X		
	21915	K	D	T	B	P	V	T	H	P	T	D	B	N	T	T	N	B	B	C	D	B	B	B	C								
	21916	B	C	D	E	B	S	C	E	N	D	D	D	B	C	B	E	E	C	E	H	E	E	E	C	H	K	N	P	P	P		
	21917	K	E	D	E	T	E	B	B	E	E	D	C	D	D	D	C	E	B	D	K	B	C	E	E	Y	X		Z	X			
	21918	D	T	D	D	T	D	C	K	P	Y	T	V	X	K	P	X	B	B	P	C	T	T	K	T								
	21919	D	D	C	E	B	E	C	E	K	K	E	T	E	K	D	C	N	N	X	C	B	E	D	D	X	V		S	P	P		
	21920	V		V		V	Y	X	Y	Y	Y	Y	X	X	V	T	X	X	N	T	T	P	T	X	X								
	21921	T	X	V		V		K		X	X	V	X	X	X	X	S	T	T	P	P	V	V	K	T								
	21922	V	P	K	T	V	N	K	K	T	X	P	X	S	S	K	S	P	P	N	T	K	S	S	T	Y	P				Z		
	22197	X	X	T	X	Y	Y	S	Y	K	X	Z	N	N	T	X	T	P	K	T	T	K	K	P	N	P			Z		Z		
	22198	X	Y	Y		X	T	T	Z	S	S	V	X	V	P	Y	Y	T	P	S	V	X	V	V	S	T	T						
	22199	X	P		Y	X			T	S	X	S	X	Y	Y	N	X	V	S	S	S	V	V	V	Y	V							
	22200	X		X	Y	Y			T	P	Y	X	P	T	X	S	X	X	P	X	T	X	P	X	P	Z							

AIR MAIL ISSUES

1939 ISSUE

FLAT PRESS PERF. 11

#C24 30¢ TRANS ATLANTIC WINGED GLOBE Block of 6

4 Plates		TL	TR	L	R	B
22381	$225	☐	☐	‡	‡	☐
22382	$225	☐	☐	‡	‡	☐
22383	$225	☐	☐	‡	‡	☐
22384	$225	☐	☐	‡	‡	☐

1941-44 ISSUES

ROTARY PRESS PERF. 11 x 10½

#C25 6¢ TRANSPORT Block of 4

40 Plates		UL	UR	LL	LR
22752	$1.00	☐	☐	☐	☐
22753	$1.00	☐	☐	☐	☐
22754	$1.00	☐	☐	☐	☐
22755	$1.00	☐	☐	☐	☐
22888	$1.00	☐	☐	☐	☐
22889	$1.00	☐	☐	☐	☐
22890	$2.50	☐	☐$_2$	☐	☐
22891	$2.50	☐	☐$_2$	☐	☐
23043	$1.00	☐	☐	☐	☐
23044	$1.00	☐	☐	☐	☐
23049	$1.00	☐	☐	☐	☐
23052	$1.00	☐	☐	☐	☐
23109	$1.00	☐	☐	☐	☐
23110	$1.00	☐	☐	☐	☐
23111	$1.00	☐	☐	☐	☐
23112	$1.00	☐	☐	☐	☐
23113	$1.00	☐	☐	☐	☐
23114	$1.00	☐	☐	☐	☐
23165	$1.00	☐	☐	☐	☐
23166	$1.00	☐	☐	☐	☐
23174	$2.00	☐	☐	☐	☐
23175	$2.00	☐	☐	☐	☐
23252	$1.00	☐	☐	☐	☐
23253	$1.00	☐	☐	☐	☐
23268	$1.00	☐	☐	☐	☐
23269	$1.00	☐	☐	☐	☐
23270	$1.00	☐	☐	☐	☐
23271	$1.00	☐	☐	☐	☐

1941-44 ISSUES

#C25 6¢ TRANSPORT Continued

		UL	UR	LL	LR
23272	$1.50	☐	☐	☐	☐
23273	$1.50	☐	☐	☐	☐
23274	$1.50	☐	☐	☐	☐
23275	$1.50	☐	☐	☐	☐
23277	$1.50	☐	☐	☐	☐
23278	$1.50	☐	☐	☐	☐
23279	$1.50	☐	☐	☐	☐
23280	$1.50	☐	☐	☐	☐
23281	$1.50	☐	☐	☐	☐
23282	$1.50	☐	☐	☐	☐
23348	$1.50	☐	☐	☐	☐
23349	$1.50	☐	☐	☐	☐

#C25 a 6¢ TRANSPORT PLANE

BOOKLET PANES OF 3

22979	22980	22981	22982	23028
23029	23048	23072	23258	23259

#C26 8¢ TRANSPORT 22 Plates

		UL	UR	LL	LR
23121	$1.50	☐	☐	☐	☐
23122	$1.50	☐	☐	☐	☐
23123	$1.50	☐	☐	☐	☐
23124	$1.50	☐	☐	☐	☐
23125	$1.50	☐	☐	☐	☐
23126	$1.50	☐	☐	☐	☐
23127	$1.50	☐	☐	☐	☐
23128	$1.50	☐	☐	☐	☐
23129	$1.50	☐	☐	☐	☐
23130	$1.50	☐	☐	☐	☐
23131	$1.50	☐	☐	☐	☐
23132	$1.50	☐	☐	☐	☐
23135	$1.50	☐	☐	☐	☐
23136	$1.50	☐	☐	☐	☐
23137	$1.50	☐	☐	☐	☐
23138	$1.50	☐	☐	☐	☐
23328	$5.00	☐$_5$	☐$_4$	☐$_5$	☐$_4$
23329	$5.00	☐$_6$	☐$_5$	☐$_6$	☐$_5$
23351	$10.00	☐	☐	☐	☐
23352	$10.00	☐	☐	☐	☐
23356	$5.00	☐	☐	☐	☐
23557	$5.00	☐	☐	☐	☐

AIR MAIL ISSUES

1941-44 ISSUES

#C27 10¢ TRANSPORT 4 Plates

Plate	Price	UL	UR	LL	LR
22756	$11.50	☐	☐	☐	☐
22757	$11.50	☐	☐	☐	☐
22758	$12.50	☐$_{2}$	☐$_{5}$	☐$_{2}$	☐$_{5}$
22759	$12.50	☐$_{2}$	☐$_{5}$	☐$_{2}$	☐$_{5}$

#C28 15¢ TRANSPORT 4 Plates

Plate	Price	UL	UR	LL	LR
22764	$15.00	☐	☐	☐	☐
22765	$15.00	☐	☐	☐	☐
22766	$30.00	☐	☐	☐	☐
22767	$30.00	☐	☐	☐	☐

1941-44 ISSUES

#C29 20¢ TRANSPORT 2 Plates

Plate	Price	UL	UR	LL	LR
22760	$13.00	☐	☐	☐	☐
22761	$13.00	☐	☐	☐	☐

#C30 30¢ TRANSPORT 2 Plates

Plate	Price	UL	UR	LL	LR
22774	$15.00	☐	☐	☐	☐
22775	$15.00	☐	☐	☐	☐

#C31 50¢ TRANSPORT 2 Plates

Plate	Price	UL	UR	LL	LR
22778	$100.00	☐	☐	☐	☐
22779	$100.00	☐	☐	☐	☐

1946 ISSUE

#C32 5¢ SKYMASTER (LARGE)

32 Plates

Plate	Price	UL	UR	LL	LR
23483	$.50	☐	☐	☐	☐
23484	$.50	☐	☐	☐	☐
23485	$.50	☐	☐	☐	☐
23486	$.50	☐	☐	☐	☐
23487	$.50	☐	☐	☐	☐
23488	$.50	☐	☐	☐	☐
23489	$.50	☐	☐	☐	☐
23490	$.50	☐	☐	☐	☐
23491	$.50	☐	☐	☐	☐
23492	$.50	☐	☐	☐	☐
23493	$.50	☐	☐	☐	☐
23494	$.50	☐	☐	☐	☐
23495	$.50	☐	☐	☐	☐
23496	$.50	☐	☐	☐	☐
23497	$.50	☐	☐	☐	☐
23498	$.50	☐	☐	☐	☐
23503	$.50	☐	☐	☐	☐
23504	$1.50	☐$_{3}$	☐	☐$_{3}$	☐
23505	$.50	☐	☐	☐	☐
23506	$1.00	☐	☐	☐	☐
23507	$1.00	☐	☐	☐	☐
23508	$1.00	☐	☐	☐$_{2}$	☐
23509	$1.00	☐	☐	☐$_{2}$	☐
23510	$.50	☐	☐	☐	☐
23515	$.50	☐	☐	☐	☐
23516	$.50	☐	☐	☐	☐
23517	$.50	☐	☐	☐	☐
23518	$.50	☐	☐	☐	☐
23523	$.50	☐	☐	☐	☐

1946 ISSUE

#C32 5¢ SKYMASTER Cont.

Plate	Price	UL	UR	LL	LR
23524	$1.00	☐$_{3}$	☐$_{4}$	☐$_{3}$	☐$_{4}$
23525	$1.00	☐$_{3}$	☐$_{4}$	☐$_{3}$	☐$_{4}$
23526	$.50	☐	☐	☐	☐

1947 ISSUES

#C33 5¢ SKYMASTER (SMALL)

8 Plates

Plate	Price	UL	UR	LL	LR
23580	$.60	☐	☐	☐	☐
23581	$.60	☐	☐	☐	☐
23582	$.60	☐	☐	☐	☐
23583	$.60	☐	☐	☐	☐
23586	$.60	☐	☐	☐	☐
23588	$.60	☐	☐	☐	☐
23590	$1.25	☐	☐	☐	☐
23591	$1.25	☐	☐	☐	☐

#C34 10¢ PAN-AM UNION BLDG.

Wet Printed **4 Plates**

Plate	Price	UL	UR	LL	LR
23693	$1.60	☐	☐	☐	☐
23694	$1.60	☐	☐	☐	☐
24898	$30.00	☐	☐$_{3}$	☐	☐
24899	$30.00	☐	☐$_{3}$	☐	☐

Dry printed **2 Plates**

Plate	Price	UL	UR	LL	LR
25613	$1.60	☐	☐	☐	☐
25614	$1.60	☐	☐	☐	☐

#C35 15¢ NEW YORK SKY LINE

Wet Printed **6 Plates**

Plate	Price	UL	UR	LL	LR
23683	$1.75	☐	☐	☐	☐
23684	$1.75	☐	☐	☐	☐
23685	$1.75	☐	☐	☐	☐
24505	$1.75	☐	☐	☐	☐
24584	$1.75	☐	☐	☐	☐
24585	$1.75	☐	☐	☐	☐

Dry Printed **6 Plates**

Plate	Price	UL	UR	LL	LR
25492	$6.00	☐	☐	☐	☐
25493	$6.00	☐	☐	☐	☐
25889	$6.00	☐	☐	☐	☐
25890	$6.00	☐	☐	☐	☐
25940	$2.00	☐	☐	☐	☐
25941	$2.00	☐	☐	☐	☐

#C36 25¢ OAKLAND BAY BRIDGE

Wet Printed **8 Plates**

Plate	Price	UL	UR	LL	LR
23667	$5.00	☐	☐	☐	☐
23668	$5.00	☐	☐	☐	☐
23669	$5.00	☐	☐	☐	☐
23670	$5.00	☐	☐	☐	☐
23671	$18.00	☐	☐	☐	☐
23672	$18.00	☐	☐	☐	☐
23681	$20.00	☐	☐	☐	☐
23682	$20.00	☐	☐	☐	☐

Dry Printed **2 Plates**

Plate	Price	UL	UR	LL	LR
25615	$5.00	☐	☐	☐	☐
25616	$5.00	☐	☐	☐	☐

AIR MAIL ISSUES

1948 ISSUES

#C37 5¢ SKYMASTER (SMALL) COIL

170 Subject Plates STRIPS OF 5

23716 23717

#C38 5¢ NEW YORK COMMEM.

2 Plates		UL	UR	LL	LR
23846	$6.00	☐	☐	☐	☐
23851	$6.00	☐	☐	☐	☐

1949 ISSUES

#C39 6¢ SKYMASTER (SMALL)

Wet Printed **16 Plates**

Plate	Price	UL	UR	LL	LR
23973	$.60	☐	☐	☐	☐
23974	$.60	☐	☐	☐	☐
23975	$.60	☐	☐	☐	☐
23976	$.60	☐	☐	☐	☐
23977	$.60	☐	☐	☐	☐
23978	$.60	☐	☐	☐	☐
23979	$.60	☐	☐	☐	☐
23985	$.60	☐	☐	☐	☐
23986	$.60	☐	☐	☐	☐
24031	$.60	☐	☐	☐	☐
24042	$.60	☐	☐	☐	☐
24043	$.60	☐	☐	☐	☐
24550	$.60	☐	☐	☐	☐
24551	$.60	☐	☐	☐	☐
24859	$.60	☐	☐	☐	☐
24860	$.60	☐	☐	☐	☐

Dry Printed **6 plates**

Plate	Price	UL	UR	LL	LR
25340	$.60	☐	☐	☐	☐
25341	$.60	☐	☐	☐	☐
25413	$1.25	☐	☐	☐	☐
25414	$1.25	☐	☐	☐	☐
25421	*$15.00*	☐	☐	☐	☐
25422	*$15.00*	☐	☐	☐	☐

#C39 a 6¢ SKYMASTER (SMALL) BOOKLET PANES OF 6

Wet Printed

24141 24142 24263 24264 24564
24565 24908 24909

Dry Printed

25359 25360 25376 *25377

#C40 6¢ ALEXANDRIA BICENTENNIAL ISSUE

6 Plates		UL	UR	LL	LR
24083	$.50	☐	☐	☐	☐
24084	$.50	☐	☐	☐	☐
24085	$.50	☐	☐	☐	☐
24086	$.50	☐	☐	☐	☐
24087	$.50	☐	☐	☐	☐
24088	$.50	☐	☐	☐	☐

1949 ISSUES

#C41 6¢ SKYMASTER (SMALL) COIL

STRIPS OF 5

24116 24117 24122 24123 25169
25170 †25171 †25172 25173 25174

UNIVERSAL POSTAL UNION ISSUE

#C42 10¢ P.O.D. BUILDING

2 Plates		UL	UR	LL	LR
24151	$1.25	☐	☐	☐	☐
24155	$1.25	☐	☐	☐	☐

#C43 15¢ GLOBE & DOVES

4 Plates		UL	UR	LL	LR
24147	$1.25	☐	☐	☐	☐
24148	$1.25	☐	☐	☐	☐
24149	$1.25	☐	☐	☐	☐
24150	$1.25	☐	☐	☐	☐

#C44 25¢ GLOBE & PLANE

2 Plates		UL	UR	LL	LR
24153	$8.00	☐	☐	☐	☐
24154	$8.00	☐	☐	☐	☐

#C45 6¢ WRIGHT BROTHERS

4 Plates		UL	UR	LL	LR
24156	$.70	☐	☐	☐	☐
24157	$.70	☐	☐	☐	☐
24158	$.70	☐	☐	☐	☐
24159	$.70	☐	☐	☐	☐

1952 ISSUE

#C46 80¢ HAWAII 3 Plates

Plate	Price	UL	UR	LL	LR
24592	$30.00	☐	☐	☐	☐
24593	$30.00	☐	☐	☐	☐
24594	$37.50	☐	☐	☐	☐

1953 ISSUE

#C47 6¢ 50th ANNIVERSARY

6 Plates		UL	UR	LL	LR
24781	$.60	☐	☐	☐	☐
24782	$.60	☐	☐	☐	☐
24783	$.60	☐	☐	☐	☐
24784	$.60	☐	☐	☐	☐
24785	$.60	☐	☐	☐	☐
24786	$.60	☐	☐	☐	☐

1954 ISSUE

#C48 4¢ EAGLE IN FLIGHT

4 Plates		UL	UR	LL	LR
25034	$2.00	☐	☐	☐	☐
25035	$2.00	☐	☐	☐	☐
25040	$7.00	☐	☐	☐	☐
25041	$7.00	☐	☐	☐	☐

AIR MAIL ISSUES

1957 ISSUE

#C49 6¢ U.S. AIR FORCE 4 plates

		UL	UR	LL	LR
25761	$.60	☐	☐	☐	☐
25762	$.60	☐	☐	☐	☐
25763	$.60	☐	☐	☐	☐
25764	$.60	☐	☐	☐	☐

1958 ISSUES

#C50 5¢ EAGLE IN FLIGHT

4 Plates

26052	$1.75	☐	☐	☐	☐
26053	$1.75	☐	☐	☐	☐
26215	$6.00	☐	☐	☐	☐
26216	$6.00	☐	☐	☐	☐

#C51 7¢ JET PLANE Blue

10 Plates

26044	$.65	☐	☐	☐	☐
26045	$.65	☐	☐	☐	☐
26046	$.65	☐	☐	☐	☐
26047	$.65	☐	☐	☐	☐
26177	$.65	☐	☐	☐	☐
26178	$.65	☐	☐	☐	☐
26385	$.65	☐	☐	☐	☐
26386	$.65	☐	☐	☐	☐
26444	$.65	☐	☐	☐	☐
26445	$.65	☐	☐	☐	☐

#C51 a 7¢ JET PLANE Blue

BOOKLET PANES OF 6

26042 26043 26175 26176 26458
26459

#C52 7¢ JET PLANE COIL Blue

384 Subject Plates STRIPS OF 5

26048 26054 26055 26069

432 Subject Plates STRIPS OF 6

26446 26447

1959 ISSUES

#C53 7¢ ALASKA 4 Plates

26225	$.65	☐	☐	☐	☐
26226	$.65	☐	☐	☐	☐
26227	$.65	☐	☐	☐	☐
26228	$.65	☐	☐	☐	☐

#C54 7¢ JUPITER 4 Plates

26390	$.65	☐	☐	☐	☐
26391	$.65	☐	☐	☐	☐
26392	$.65	☐	☐	☐	☐
26397	$.65	☐	☐	☐	☐

#C55 7¢ HAWAII 4 Plates

26432	$.65	☐	☐	☐	☐
26433	$.65	☐	☐	☐	☐
26434	$.65	☐	☐	☐	☐
26435	$.65	☐	☐	☐	☐

1959 ISSUES

#C56 10¢ PAN AMERICAN GAMES

2 Plates		UL	UR	LL	LR
26413	$1.75	☐	☐	☐	☐
26414	$1.75	☐	☐	☐	☐

1959-60 ISSUES

#C57 10¢ LIBERTY BELL

3 Plates

26630	$7.50	☐	☐	☐	☐
26635	$7.50	☐	☐	☐	☐
26636	$7.50	☐	☐	☐	☐

#C58 15¢ STATUE OF LIBERTY

4 Plates

26482	$1.75	☐	☐	☐	☐
26483	$1.75	☐	☐	☐	☐
26486	$1.75	☐	☐	☐	☐
26487	$7.00	☐	☐	☐	☐

#C59 25¢ LINCOLN

Issued UNTAGGED 3 Plates

26563o	$2.50	☐	☐	☐	☐
26570	$2.50	☐	☐	☐	☐
26576	$2.50	☐	☐	☐	☐

#C59 a 25¢ LINCOLN

Issued TAGGED 9 plates

26563o	$5.00	☐	☐	☐	☐
28536	$2.25	☐	☐	☐	☐
28543	$2.25	☐	☐	☐	☐
30638	$15.00	☐	☐	☐	☐
30649	$7.00	☐	☐	☐	☐
31603	$12.00	☐	☐	☐	☐
31604	$6.00	☐	☐	☐	☐
31615	$30.00	☐$_2$	☐$_2$	☐	☐$_2$
31648	$30.00	☐$_2$	☐$_2$	☐	☐$_2$

1960 ISSUES

#C60 7¢ JET PLANE Red

14 Plates

26385	$.65	☐	☐	☐	☐
26386	$.65	☐	☐	☐	☐
26444	$.65	☐	☐	☐	☐
26445	$.65	☐	☐	☐	☐
26667	$.65	☐	☐	☐	☐
26668	$.65	☐	☐	☐	☐
26714	$.65	☐	☐	☐	☐
26715	$.65	☐	☐	☐	☐
26899	$.65	☐	☐	☐	☐
26900	$.65	☐	☐	☐	☐
27213	$.65	☐	☐	☐	☐
27214	$.65	☐	☐	☐	☐
27242	$2.00	☐	☐	☐	☐
27243	$2.00	☐	☐	☐	☐

AIR MAIL ISSUES

1960 ISSUES

#C60 a 7¢ JET PLANE Red

BOOKLET PANES OF 6

26458 26459 26475 26476

#C61 7¢ JET PLANE COIL Red

432 Subject Plates **STRIPS OF 6**

26446 26447 †26455 †26456

1961 ISSUES

#C62 13¢ LIBERTY

Issued UNTAGGED **8 Plates**

		UL	UR	LL	LR
26965 o	$1.75	☐	☐	☐	☐
26970 o	$1.75	☐	☐	☐	☐
26975	$1.75	☐	☐	☐	☐
26977	$1.75	☐	☐	☐	☐
28608	$1.75	☐	☐	☐	☐
28611	$1.75	☐	☐	☐	☐
28617	$1.75	☐	☐	☐	☐
28620	$1.75	☐	☐	☐	☐

#C62 a 13¢ LIBERTY BELL

Issued TAGGED **2 Plates**

		UL	UR	LL	LR
26965 o	$7.50	☐	☐	☐	☐
26970 o	$7.50	☐	☐	☐	☐

#C63 15¢ STATUE OF LIBERTY REDESIGNED

Issued UNTAGGED **13 Plates**

		UL	UR	LL	LR
26875	$1.25	☐	☐	☐	☐
26878	$1.25	☐	☐	☐	☐
26885	$1.25	☐	☐	☐	☐
26886	$1.25	☐	☐	☐	☐
28033 o	$1.75	☐	☐	☐	☐
28335 o	$1.75	☐	☐	☐	☐
28336 o	$5.00	☐	☐	☐	☐
28340 o	$5.00	☐	☐	☐	☐
28644	$1.25	☐	☐	☐	☐
28645	$1.25	☐	☐	☐	☐
28655	$1.25	☐	☐	☐	☐
28657	$17.50	☐	☐	☐	☐
28659	$1.25	☐	☐	☐	☐

#C63 a 15¢ STATUE OF LIBERTY REDESIGNED

Issued TAGGED **10 Plates**

		UL	UR	LL	LR
28033 o	$2.50	☐	☐	☐	☐
28051	$1.25	☐	☐	☐	☐
28335 o	$2.50	☐	☐	☐	☐
28336 o	$2.50	☐	☐	☐	☐
28340 o	$2.50	☐	☐	☐	☐
31551	$1.25	☐	☐	☐	☐
31558	$1.25	☐	☐	☐	☐
31559	$1.25	☐	☐	☐	☐
31892	$1.25	☐	☐	☐	☐
31893	$1.25	☐	☐	☐	☐

1962 ISSUES

#C64 8¢ CAPITOL

Issued UNTAGGED **10 Plates**

		UL	UR	LL	LR
27365 o	$1.00	☐	☐	☐	☐
27366 o	$1.00	☐	☐	☐	☐
27377	$.65	☐	☐	☐	☐
27378	$.65	☐	☐	☐	☐
27593 o	$1.00	☐	☐	☐	☐
27625 o	$1.00	☐	☐	☐	☐
27680 o	$1.00	☐	☐	☐	☐
27681 o	$1.00	☐	☐	☐	☐
27682 o	$3.00	☐	☐	☐	☐
27683 o	$3.00	☐	☐	☐	☐

#C64 a 8¢ CAPITOL

Issued TAGGED **22 Plates**

		UL	UR	LL	LR
27365 o	$4.00	☐	☐	☐	☐
27366 o	$4.00	☐	☐	☐	☐
27593 o	$2.00	☐	☐	☐	☐
27625 o	$2.00	☐	☐	☐	☐
27680 o	$2.00	☐	☐	☐	☐
27681 o	$2.00	☐	☐	☐	☐
27682 o	$2.00	☐	☐	☐	☐
27683 o	$2.00	☐	☐	☐	☐
28024	$.65	☐	☐	☐	☐
28025	$.65	☐	☐	☐	☐
28041	$.65	☐	☐	☐	☐
28042	$.65	☐	☐	☐	☐
28423	$.65	☐	☐	☐	☐
28424	$.65	☐	☐	☐	☐
28475	$.65	☐	☐	☐	☐
28476	$.65	☐	☐	☐	☐
28484	$.65	☐	☐	☐	☐
28485	$.65	☐	☐	☐	☐
28612	$5.00	☐	☐	☐	☐
28613	$5.00	☐	☐	☐	☐
29029	$20.00	☐	☐	☐	☐
29030	$20.00	☐	☐	☐	☐

#C64 b 8¢ CAPITOL

BOOKLET PANES OF 5

Issued UNTAGGED **12 Plates**

27371 27372 27375 27376 27515
27516 27646o 27673o 27674o 27677o
27697o 27698o

#C64 c 8¢ CAPITOL

Issued TAGGED **24 Plates**

27646o 27673o 27674o 27677o 27697o
27698o 28030 28031 28032 28050
28115 28116 28317 28403 28404
28405 28469 28470 28480 28481
28496 28497 28575 28576

o Issued both Tagged and Plain

AIR MAIL ISSUES

1962 ISSUES

#C65 8¢ CAPITOL COIL

432 Subject Plates STRIPS OF 6

Issued UNTAGGED 4 Plates

†27367 †27368 27369o 27370o

#C65 a 8¢ CAPITOL COIL

Issued TAGGED 6 Plates

27369o 27370o †27699 †27700 †28045 †28280

1963 ISSUES

#C66 15¢ BLAIR 2 Plates

		UL	UR	LL	LR
27463	$3.50	☐	☐	☐	☐
27466	$3.50	☐	☐	☐	☐

#C67 6¢ EAGLE

Issued UNTAGGED 2 Plates

		UL	UR	LL	LR
27390 o	$2.00	☐	☐	☐	☐
27391 o	$2.00	☐	☐	☐	☐

#C67 a 6¢ EAGLE

Issued TAGGED 2 Plates

		UL	UR	LL	LR
27390 o	$50.00	☐	☐	☐	☐
27391 o	$50.00	☐	☐	☐	☐

#C68 8¢ EARHART 4 Plates

		UL	UR	LL	LR
27497	$1.25	☐	☐	☐	☐
27529	$1.25	☐	☐	☐	☐
27541	$1.25	☐	☐	☐	☐
27548	$1.25	☐	☐	☐	☐

1964 ISSUE

Issued TAGGED Only

#C69 8¢ GODDARD 4 Plates

		UL	UR	LL	LR
27860	$2.00	☐	☐	☐	☐
27861	$2.00	☐	☐	☐	☐
27862	$2.00	☐	☐	☐	☐
27863	$2.00	☐	☐	☐	☐

1967 ISSUES

Issued TAGGED Only

#C70 8¢ ALASKA PURCHASE

4 Plates

		UL	UR	LL	LR
29013	$1.75	☐	☐	☐	☐
29019	$1.75	☐	☐	☐	☐
29022	$1.75	☐	☐	☐	☐
29026	$1.75	☐	☐	☐	☐

#C71 20¢ AUDUBON 5 Plates

		UL	UR	LL	LR
29073	$4.00	☐	☐	☐	☐
29087	$4.00	☐	☐	☐	☐
29092	$4.00	☐	☐	☐	☐
29096	$4.00	☐	☐	☐	☐
29542	$4.00	☐	☐	☐	☐

1968 ISSUES

Issued TAGGED Only

#C72 10¢ STAR RUNWAY

16 plates

		UL	UR	LL	LR
29467	$1.00	☐	☐	☐	☐
29468	$1.00	☐	☐	☐	☐
29475	$1.00	☐	☐	☐	☐
29476	$1.00	☐	☐	☐	☐
29494	$1.00	☐	☐	☐	☐
29495	$1.00	☐	☐	☐	☐
29517	$1.00	☐	☐	☐	☐
29518	$1.00	☐	☐	☐	☐
30733	$1.00	☐	☐	☐	☐
30734	$1.00	☐	☐	☐	☐
30757	$1.00	☐	☐	☐	☐
30758	$1.00	☐	☐	☐	☐
31894	$1.00	☐	☐	☐	☐
31895	$1.00	☐	☐	☐	☐
31990	$3.00	☐	☐	☐	☐
32039	$3.00	☐	☐	☐	☐

#C72 b 10¢ STAR RUNWAY

BOOKLET PANES OF 8

Plate numbers are located much further away from the stamps so no plate numbers were regularly issued.

#C72 c 10¢ STAR RUNWAY

BOOKLET PANES OF 5

29563 29564 29567 29568

#C73 10¢ STAR RUNWAY COIL

432 Subject Plates STRIPS OF 6

29472 29473 29474 29500 29501
29514 29519 29520 †31908 †31909

#C74 10¢ 50th ANN. AIR MAIL

4 Plates

		UL	UR	LL	LR
29673	$2.75	☐	☐	☐	☐
29678	$2.75	☐	☐	☐	☐
29679	$2.75	☐	☐	☐	☐
29684	$2.75	☐	☐	☐	☐

#C75 20¢ USA AIR MAIL

11 Plates

		UL	UR	LL	LR
30494	$2.50	☐	☐	☐	☐
30498	$2.50	☐	☐	☐	☐
30502	$2.50	☐	☐	☐	☐
30510	$2.50	☐	☐	☐	☐
30511	$7.00	☐	☐	☐	☐
30518	$8.00	☐	☐	☐	☐
30602	$2.50	☐	☐	☐	☐
30606	$2.50	☐	☐	☐	☐
31566	$2.50	☐	☐	☐	☐
31581	$2.50	☐	☐	☐	☐
31590	$2.50	☐	☐	☐	☐

o Issued both Tagged and Plain

AIR MAIL ISSUES

1969 ISSUES

Issued TAGGED Only

#C76 10¢ MOON LANDING

15 Plates

Plate	Price	UL	UR	LL	LR
31371	$1.25	☐	☐	☐	☐
31374	$1.25	☐	☐	☐	☐
31375	$1.25	☐	☐	☐	☐
31376	$1.25	☐	☐	☐	☐
31378	$1.25	☐	☐	☐	☐
31381	$1.25	☐	☐	☐	☐
31382	$1.25	☐	☐	☐	☐
31384	$1.25	☐	☐	☐	☐
31387	$1.25	☐	☐	☐	☐
31388	$1.25	☐	☐	☐	☐
31390	$1.25	☐	☐	☐	☐
31392	$1.25	☐	☐	☐	☐
31400	$1.25	☐	☐	☐	☐
31401	$1.25	☐	☐	☐	☐
31405	$1.25	☐	☐	☐	☐

1971-73 ISSUES

Issued TAGGED Only

#C77 9¢ AIR MAIL **2 Plates**

Plate	Price	UL	UR	LL	LR
32945	$.75	☐	☐	☐	☐
32946	$.75	☐	☐	☐	☐

#C78 11¢ AIR MAIL **8 Plates**

Plate	Price	UL	UR	LL	LR
32941	$.90	☐	☐	☐	☐
32942	$.90	☐	☐	☐	☐
32998	$.90	☐	☐	☐	☐
32999	$.90	☐	☐	☐	☐
33019	$.90	☐	☐	☐	☐
33020	$.90	☐	☐	☐	☐
33887	$6.50	☐	☐	☐	☐
33888	$6.50	☐	☐	☐	☐

#C78 a 11¢ AIR MAIL

BOOKLET PANES OF 4

32964 32965 32994 32995 33485
33486

#C79 13¢ AIR MAIL (SMALL)

6 Plates

Plate	Price	UL	UR	LL	LR
34557	$1.00	☐	☐	☐	☐
34558	$1.00	☐	☐	☐	☐
34584	$1.00	☐	☐	☐	☐
34653	$1.00	☐	☐	☐	☐
35579	$1.00	☐	☐	☐	☐
35580	$1.00	☐	☐	☐	☐

#C79 a 13¢ AIR MAIL (SMALL)

BOOKLET PANES OF 5

34795 34796 34843 34844 35338
35339

1971-73 ISSUES

#C80 17¢ AIR MAIL **8 Plates**

Plate	Price	UL	UR	LL	LR
33092	$1.70	☐	☐	☐	☐
33093	$1.70	☐	☐	☐	☐
33094	$1.70	☐	☐	☐	☐
33096	$1.70	☐	☐	☐	☐
33097	$1.70	☐	☐	☐	☐
33098	$1.70	☐	☐	☐	☐
33099	$1.70	☐	☐	☐	☐
33100	$1.70	☐	☐	☐	☐

#C81 21¢ AIR MAIL **19 plates**

Plate	Price	UL	UR	LL	LR
33003	$1.50	☐	☐	☐	☐
33005	$1.50	☐	☐	☐	☐
33007	$1.50	☐	☐	☐	☐
33009	$1.50	☐	☐	☐	☐
33012	$4.00	☐	☐	☐	☐
33013	$4.00	☐	☐	☐	☐
33017	$1.50	☐	☐	☐	☐
33018	$4.00	☐	☐	☐	☐
33027	$4.00	☐	☐	☐	☐
33029	$4.00	☐	☐	☐	☐
33030	$4.00	☐	☐	☐	☐
33242	$1.50	☐	☐	☐	☐
33246	$1.50	☐	☐	☐	☐
33248	$1.50	☐	☐	☐	☐
33279	$1.50	☐	☐	☐	☐
33332	$1.50	☐	☐	☐	☐
33550	$1.50	☐	☐	☐	☐
35128	$1.50	☐	☐	☐	☐
35704	$1.50	☐	☐	☐	☐

#C82 11¢ AIR MAIL COIL

432 Subject Plates **STRIPS OF 6**

32943 32944 33000 33001 33244
33697

#C83 13¢ AIR MAIL COIL (SMALL)

432 Subject Plates **STRIPS OF 6**

34739 34740 †34741 †34742 35565
35566 †35670 †35671

1972 ISSUES

Issued TAGGED Only

#C84 11¢ NATIONAL PARKS

8 Plates

Plate	Price	UL	UR	LL	LR
33454	$.90	☐	☐	☐	☐
33459	$.90	☐	☐	☐	☐
33461	$.90	☐	☐	☐	☐
33463	$.90	☐	☐	☐	☐
33465	$.90	☐	☐	☐	☐
33466	$.90	☐	☐	☐	☐
33468	$.90	☐	☐	☐	☐
33481	$.90	☐	☐	☐	☐

#C85 11¢ OLYMPICS

Block of 10 (2 x 5)

33322 33323 33324 33325 33326

Price	UL	UR	LL	LR
$2.25	☐	☐	☐	☐

AIR MAIL ISSUES

1973 ISSUE

Issued TAGGED Only

#C86 11¢ ELECTRONICS 6 Plates

		UL	UR	LL	LR
34190	$.90	☐	☐	☐	☐
34191	$.90	☐	☐	☐	☐
34192	$.90	☐	☐	☐	☐
34197	$.90	☐	☐	☐	☐
34232	$.90	☐	☐	☐	☐
34235	$.90	☐	☐	☐	☐

1974 ISSUES

Issued TAGGED Only

#C87 18¢ STATUE OF LIBERTY

		UL	UR	LL	LR
34932-34928	$1.50	☐	☐	☐	☐
34932-34931	$1.50	☐	☐	☐	☐
34932-34941	$1.50	☐	☐	☐	☐
34932-34955	$1.50	☐	☐	☐	☐
34942-34928	$1.50	☐	☐	☐	☐
34942-34931	$1.50	☐	☐	☐	☐
34942-34941	$1.50	☐	☐	☐	☐
34942-34955	$1.50	☐	☐	☐	☐
34956-34928	$1.50	☐	☐	☐	☐
34956-34931	$1.50	☐	☐	☐	☐
34956-34941	$1.50	☐	☐	☐	☐
34956-34955	$1.50	☐	☐	☐	☐
34959-34928	$4.00	☐	☐	☐	☐
34959-34931	$4.00	☐	☐	☐	☐
34959-34941	$35.00	☐	☐	☐	☐
34959-34955	$4.00	☐	☐	☐	☐

#C88 26¢ MOUNT RUSHMORE
8 Plates

		UL	UR	LL	LR
34774	$2.00	☐	☐	☐	☐
34851	$2.00	☐	☐	☐	☐
34853	$2.00	☐	☐	☐	☐
34860	$2.00	☐	☐	☐	☐
34867	$2.00	☐	☐	☐	☐
34875	$2.00	☐	☐	☐	☐
34907	$2.00	☐	☐	☐	☐
34927	$2.00	☐	☐	☐	☐

1975 ISSUES

Issued TAGGED Only

#C89 25¢ AIR MAIL 7 Plates

		UL	UR	LL	LR
36956	$2.00	☐	☐	☐	☐
36957	$2.00	☐	☐	☐	☐
36959	$2.00	☐	☐	☐	☐
36976	$2.00	☐	☐	☐	☐
36979	$2.00	☐	☐	☐	☐
36988	$2.00	☐	☐	☐	☐
37001	$5.00	☐	☐ 3	☐	☐

1975 ISSUES

#C90 31¢ AIR MAIL 16 Plates

		UL	UR	LL	LR
36977	$2.50	☐	☐	☐	☐
36981	$2.50	☐	☐	☐	☐
36989	$2.50	☐	☐	☐	☐
37002	$2.50	☐	☐	☐	☐
37014	$2.50	☐	☐	☐	☐
37034	$2.50	☐	☐	☐	☐
37344	$2.50	☐	☐	☐	☐
37402	$2.50	☐	☐	☐	☐
37614	$2.50	☐	☐	☐	☐
37927	$2.50	☐	☐	☐	☐
37950	$2.50	☐	☐	☐	☐
38309	$2.50	☐	☐	☐	☐
38310	$2.50	☐	☐	☐	☐
38312	$2.50	☐	☐	☐	☐
38313	$2.50	☐	☐	☐	☐
38314	$2.50	☐	☐	☐	☐

1978 ISSUE

Issued TAGGED Only

#C91-C92 31¢ WRIGHT BROTHERS
9 Plates

		UL	UR	LL	LR
38844	$2.50	☐	☐	☐	☐
38845	$2.50	☐	☐	☐	☐
38853	$2.50	☐	☐	☐	☐
38856	$2.50	☐	☐	☐	☐
38857	$2.50	☐	☐	☐	☐
38858	$2.50	☐	☐	☐	☐
38859	$2.50	☐	☐	☐	☐
38860	$2.50	☐	☐	☐	☐
38861	$2.50	☐	☐	☐	☐

1979 ISSUES

Issued TAGGED Only

#C93-C94 21¢ OCTAVE CHANUTE
8 Plates

		UL	UR	LL	LR
39007	$4.00	☐	☐	☐	☐
39008	$4.00	☐	☐	☐	☐
39014	$4.00	☐	☐	☐	☐
39015	$4.00	☐	☐	☐	☐
39017	$15.00	☐	☐	☐	☐
39018	$15.00	☐	☐	☐	☐
39019	$15.00	☐	☐	☐	☐
39020	$15.00	☐	☐	☐	☐

#C95-C96 25¢ WILEY POST 4 Plates

		UL	UR	LL	LR
39193	$10.00	☐	☐	☐	☐
39197	$10.00	☐	☐	☐	☐
39198	$10.00	☐	☐	☐	☐
39210	$10.00	☐	☐	☐	☐

#C97 31¢ SUMMER OLYMPICS

Block of 12 (6 x 2)

39117-39118-39119-39120-39121-39122

		UL	UR	LL	LR
	$10.00	☐	☐	☐	☐

AIR MAIL ISSUES

1980 ISSUES

Issued TAGGED Only

#C98 40¢ PHILIP MAZZEI

		UL	UR	LL	LR
Block of 12 (6 x 2)					
"EE" Perforator 10.5 x 11.3					
39461-39462-39463-39464-39465-39466	$13.50	☐	☐	☐	☐
In Line Perforator 11.2 x 11.2					
39461-39462-39463-39464-39465-39466	$9.00	☐	☐	☐	☐
40518-40519-40520-40521-40522-40523	$9.00	☐	☐	☐	☐

#C99 28¢ BLANCHE SCOTT

Block of 12 (2 x 6)

		UL	UR	LL	LR
39537-39538-39539-39540-39541-39542	$7.00	☐	☐	☐	☐

#C100 35¢ GLENN CURTISS

Block of 12 (2 x 6)

		UL	UR	LL	LR
39502-39503-39504-39505-39506-39507	$8.00	☐	☐	☐	☐

1983 ISSUES

#C101-C104 28¢ OLYMPIC GAMES

Gravure Press

		UL	UR	LL	LR
2222	$3.50	☐	☐	☐	☐

#C105-C108 40¢ OLYMPIC GAMES

Gravure Press

In Line Perforator 11.2 x 11.2

		UL	UR	LL	LR
2222	$3.25	☐	☐	☐	☐

"L" Perforator 10.9 x 10.9

		UL	UR	LL	LR
2222	$3.25	☐	☐	☐	☐

#C109-C112 35¢ OLYMPIC GAMES

Gravure Press

		UL	UR	LL	LR
1111	$6.00	☐	☐	☐	☐

1985 ISSUES

#C113 33¢ ALFRED V. VERVILLE

Andreotti Gravure (combined with C114)

		UL	UR	LL	LR
11111	$2.50	☐	‡	‡	☐
12111	$2.50	☐	‡	‡	☐

#C114 39¢ LAWRENCE & ELMER SPERRY AIRMAIL

Andreotti Gravure (combined with C113)

		UL	UR	LL	LR
11111	$3.75	☐	☐	☐	☐
12111	$3.75	☐	☐	☐	☐
(New printing of our position stock-C-114 only)					
1111	$3.75	☐	☐	☐	☐

1985 ISSUES

Continued

#C115 44¢ TRANSPACIFIC AIRMAIL

Andreotti Gravure

		UL	UR	LL	LR
1111	$3.50	☐	☐	☐	☐
1112	$4.00	☐	☐	☐	☐

#C116 44¢ FR. JUNIPERO SERRA

Andreotti Gravure

		UL	UR	LL	LR
1111	$5.00	☐	☐	☐	☐

1988 ISSUES

#C117 44¢ SWEDEN AIRMAIL

		UL	UR	LL	LR
1111-1	$6.00	☐	☐	☐	☐

#C118 45¢ LANGLEY AIRMAIL

		UL	UR	LL	LR
111111-1	$4.00	☐	☐	☐	☐
111121-1	$4.00	☐	☐	☐	☐
111131-1	$4.00	☐	☐	☐	☐
111231-1	$4.00	☐	☐	☐	☐
111232-1	$4.00	☐	☐	☐	☐
121232-1	$4.00	☐	☐	☐	☐
222232-1	$4.00	☐	☐	☐	☐
223232-1	$4.00	☐	☐	☐	☐
224232-1	$4.00	☐	☐	☐	☐
224233-1	$4.00	☐	☐	☐	☐
324233-1	$4.00	☐	☐	☐	☐
324343-1	$4.00	☐	☐	☐	☐
334344-1	$4.00	☐	☐	☐	☐
335344-1	$4.00	☐	☐	☐	☐
435344-1	$4.00	☐	☐	☐	☐
435364-1	$4.00	☐	☐	☐	☐
435464-1	$4.00	☐	☐	☐	☐
445564-1	$4.00	☐	☐	☐	☐
446564-1	$4.00	☐	☐	☐	☐
447564-1	$4.00	☐	☐	☐	☐
447565-1	$4.00	☐	☐	☐	☐
647565-1	$4.00	☐	☐	☐	☐
779898-1	$4.00	†	†	☐	†
979898-1	$4.00	†	†	†	☐
979899-1	$4.00	†	☐	†	☐

#C119 36¢ SIKORSKY AIRMAIL

		UL	UR	LL	LR
11111-1	$2.75	☐	☐	☐	☐
12112-1	$2.75	☐	☐	☐	☐
21111-1	$2.75	☐	☐	☐	☐
21112-1	$2.75	☐	☐	☐	☐
22112-1	$2.75	☐	☐	☐	☐
32211-1	$2.75	☐	☐	☐	☐
42211-1	$2.75	☐	☐	☐	☐

#C120 45¢ FRENCH REVOLUTION

		UL	UR	LL	LR
111-1	$3.75	☐	☐	☐	☐
121-1	$3.75	☐	☐	☐	☐
222-1	$3.75	☐	☐	☐	☐

#C121 45¢ AMERICA ISSUE

		UL	UR	LL	LR
1111	$3.75	☐	☐	☐	☐

1988 ISSUES Cont.

#C122-25 45¢ FUTURE MAIL TRANSPORTATION

		UL	UR	LL	LR
1111-1	$3.75	☐	☐	☐	☐
1112-1	$3.75	☐	☐	☐	☐
2223-1	$3.75	☐	☐	☐	☐
2233-1	—	†	☐	†	☐
2243-1	$3.75	☐	☐	☐	☐
2263-1	$3.75	☐	☐	☐	☐

#C126 $1.80 SOUVENIR SHEET

No Plate Numbers

ADDITIONAL ISSUES

....	☐	☐	☐	☐
....	☐	☐	☐	☐
....	☐	☐	☐	☐
....	☐	☐	☐	☐
....	☐	☐	☐	☐
....	☐	☐	☐	☐
....	☐	☐	☐	☐
....	☐	☐	☐	☐
....	☐	☐	☐	☐
....	☐	☐	☐	☐
....	☐	☐	☐	☐
....	☐	☐	☐	☐
....	☐	☐	☐	☐
....	☐	☐	☐	☐
....	☐	☐	☐	☐
....	☐	☐	☐	☐
....	☐	☐	☐	☐
....	☐	☐	☐	☐
....	☐	☐	☐	☐
....	☐	☐	☐	☐
....	☐	☐	☐	☐
....	☐	☐	☐	☐
....	☐	☐	☐	☐
....	☐	☐	☐	☐
....	☐	☐	☐	☐
....	☐	☐	☐	☐
....	☐	☐	☐	☐
....	☐	☐	☐	☐
....	☐	☐	☐	☐
....	☐	☐	☐	☐
....	☐	☐	☐	☐
....	☐	☐	☐	☐
....	☐	☐	☐	☐
....	☐	☐	☐	☐
....	☐	☐	☐	☐
....	☐	☐	☐	☐
....	☐	☐	☐	☐
....	☐	☐	☐	☐
....	☐	☐	☐	☐
....	☐	☐	☐	☐
....	☐	☐	☐	☐
....	☐	☐	☐	☐
....	☐	☐	☐	☐
....	☐	☐	☐	☐

ADDITIONAL ISSUES

....	☐	☐	☐	☐
....	☐	☐	☐	☐
....	☐	☐	☐	☐
....	☐	☐	☐	☐
....	☐	☐	☐	☐
....	☐	☐	☐	☐
....	☐	☐	☐	☐
....	☐	☐	☐	☐
....	☐	☐	☐	☐
....	☐	☐	☐	☐
....	☐	☐	☐	☐
....	☐	☐	☐	☐
....	☐	☐	☐	☐
....	☐	☐	☐	☐
....	☐	☐	☐	☐
....	☐	☐	☐	☐
....	☐	☐	☐	☐
....	☐	☐	☐	☐
....	☐	☐	☐	☐
....	☐	☐	☐	☐
....	☐	☐	☐	☐
....	☐	☐	☐	☐
....	☐	☐	☐	☐
....	☐	☐	☐	☐
....	☐	☐	☐	☐
....	☐	☐	☐	☐
....	☐	☐	☐	☐
....	☐	☐	☐	☐
....	☐	☐	☐	☐
....	☐	☐	☐	☐
....	☐	☐	☐	☐
....	☐	☐	☐	☐
....	☐	☐	☐	☐
....	☐	☐	☐	☐
....	☐	☐	☐	☐
....	☐	☐	☐	☐
....	☐	☐	☐	☐
....	☐	☐	☐	☐
....	☐	☐	☐	☐
....	☐	☐	☐	☐
....	☐	☐	☐	☐
....	☐	☐	☐	☐
....	☐	☐	☐	☐
....	☐	☐	☐	☐
....	☐	☐	☐	☐
....	☐	☐	☐	☐
....	☐	☐	☐	☐
....	☐	☐	☐	☐
....	☐	☐	☐	☐
....	☐	☐	☐	☐
....	☐	☐	☐	☐
....	☐	☐	☐	☐
....	☐	☐	☐	☐
....	☐	☐	☐	☐
....	☐	☐	☐	☐
....	☐	☐	☐	☐
....	☐	☐	☐	☐
....	☐	☐	☐	☐
....	☐	☐	☐	☐
....	☐	☐	☐	☐
....	☐	☐	☐	☐
....	☐	☐	☐	☐
....	☐	☐	☐	☐
....	☐	☐	☐	☐

AIR MAIL SPECIAL DELIVERY

FLAT PRESS

1934 FIRST ISSUE

#CEI 16¢ BLUE 4 Plates

		TL	TR	L	R	B
21312	$22.50	□	□	‡	‡	□
21313	$22.50	□	□	‡	‡	□
21314	$22.50	□	□	‡	‡	□
21315	$22.50	□	□	‡	‡	□

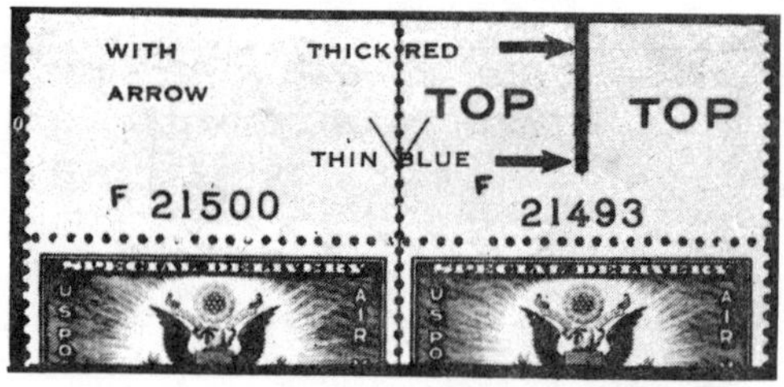

TYPE 2

THICK RED THIN BLUE
RELATIVE SCARCITY GRADES FOR TYPE 2

	F21495	F21496	F21497	F21498	F21499	F21500	F21501	F21502
21491	X	X	V	T	Z	Z	†	Y
F21491	Y	Z	Z	Z	V	S	T	S
21492	V	S	T	N	Z	Z	Z	Z
F21492	†	Y	Y	Z	T	N	T	S
21493	S	S	T	T	Z	Z	Z	Z
F21493	Z	Z	Z	Z	S	S	T	P
21494	S	T	P	X	Z	Y	Z	†
F21494	Z	Y	Z	Z	T	T	P	V

1936 SECOND ISSUE

#CE2 16¢ BICOLORED

The Prices for the Letter Value are as shown below

E	$8.50	P	$25.00
A	$9.00	S	$30.00
B	$9.50	T	$35.00
C	$10.00	V	$40.00
D	$12.00	X	$60.00
H	$14.00	Y	$65.00
K	$18.00	Z	$75.00
N	$20.00		

TYPE 1

THIN RED THIN BLUE
RELATIVE SCARCITY GRADES FOR TYPE 1

	F21495	F21496	F21497	F21498	F21499	F21500	F21501	F21502
21491	E	A	E	E	A	B	E	C
F21491	E	A	A	E	B	A	B	C
21492	E	E	E	E	E	B	A	B
F21492	E	E	E	E	E	A	B	B
21493	E	E	E	E	E	A	E	A
F21493	E	E	E	E	A	B	C	C
21494	E	E	E	E	E	B	B	A
F21494	E	E	E	E	E	E	B	B

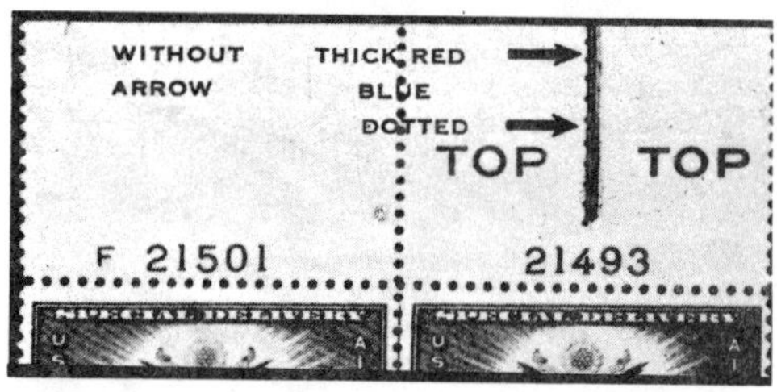

TYPE 3

THICK RED DOTTED BLUE
RELATIVE SCARCITY GRADES FOR TYPE 3

	F21495	F21496	F21497	F21498	F21499	F21500	F21501	F21502
21491	X	Y	X	Y	Y	Y	Z	Z
F21491	Z	Y	Y	Z	Z	Z	X	Z
21492	Z	X	Z	X	Z	Y	Z	X
F21492	Y	Z	Z	X	Y	X	Y	Z
21493	Y	Y	Y	Y	Y	Z	Z	Z
F21493	Z	Y	Z	Y	Z	Y	Z	Y
21494	Y	Z	X	Y	Z	Y	Y	Z
F21494	Y	Y	Y	X	Y	Y	Z	Z

AIR MAIL SPECIAL DELIVERY
Continued

1934 SECOND ISSUE

#CE2 16¢ BICOLORED Cont.

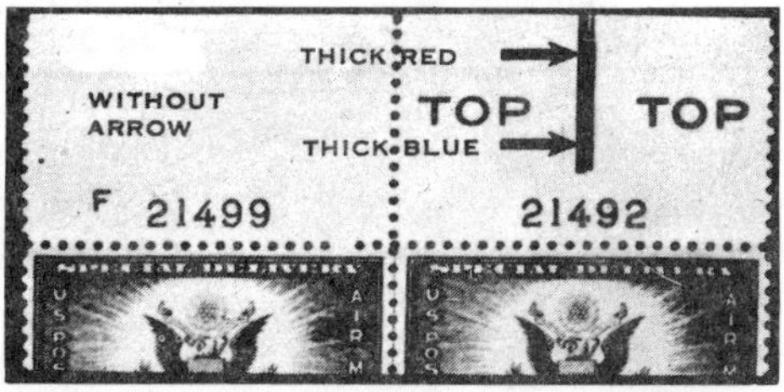

TYPE 4

THICK RED THICK BLUE
RELATIVE SCARCITY GRADES FOR TYPE 4

	F21495	F21496	F21497	F21498	F21499	F21500	F21501	F21502
21491	D	C	C	D	K	D	K	N
F21491	B	D	B	B	H	K	H	D
21492	C	C	C	C	N	K	K	H
F21492	C	C	C	C	K	K	N	K
21493	H	D	B	D	N	K	H	H
F21493	B	B	B	B	N	D	H	H
21494	D	D	D	C	H	K	D	H
F21494	C	D	C	B	D	D	H	D

SPECIAL DELIVERY ISSUES

1894 ISSUE
FLAT PRESS Perf. 12
Unwatermarked

#E4 10¢ SPECIAL DELIVERY

Imprint Strip of 3, **T** or **B** $3,250
Imprint Block of 6, **T** or **B** $16,500

Imprint III

77

1895 ISSUE
Double Line Wmk. Perf. 12

#E5 10¢ SPECIAL DELIVERY

Basic Prices:

Imprint Strip of 3, **T** or **B** $700
Imprint Block of 6, **T** or **B** $5,000

Imprint III

77

Imprint VI

257

Imprint VII

381	492	880	881	882
883	*1257	*1258	*1259	*1260

Much of our plate number information stems from studies made by members of the Bureau Issues Association and published in their magazine. Serious plate number collectors should join this organization. For further information write to:

Mr. George V.H. Godin, Exec. Sec.
P.O. 1047, Belleville, IL 62223-1047

SPECIAL DELIVERY ISSUES

1902 ISSUE

Double Line Wmk. Perf. 12

#E6 10¢ SPECIAL DELIVERY

Basic Prices:

Imprint Strip of 3, T or B $425
Imprint Block of 6, T or B $3,250

Imprint VII

1481 1482 1483 1484 1773
1774 1775 1776 *5240 *5243
*5244 *5245

#E6 1909 REISSUE

Basic Prices:

Imprint Strip of 3, T or B $400
Imprint Block of 6, T or B $3,000

Imprint VII

5240-09 5243-09 5244-09 5245-09

1908 ISSUE

Double Line Wmk. Perf. 12

#E7 10¢ SPECIAL DELIVERY

Basic Prices:

Imprint Block of 6, T $1,000
Imprint Block of 6, L, R, B $950

Imprint V

4916 4917 4920 4921

1911 ISSUE

Single Line Wmk. Perf. 12

#E8 10¢ SPECIAL DELIVERY

Basic Prices:

Imprint Block of 6, T $2,500
Imprint Block of 6, L, R, B $2,400

Imprint VII

5513 5514 *5520 5535 5539

Basic Prices:

Block of 6, T $2,750
Block of 6, L, R, B $2,650

Imprint IX

5854 5857 5860 5863

1914 ISSUE

Single Line Wmk. Perf. 10

#E9 10¢ SPECIAL DELIVERY

Imprint Block of 6, T $5,250
Imprint Block of 6, L, R, B $5,000

Imprint VII

5520

Basic Prices:

Block of 6, T $4,500
Block of 6, L, R, B $4,250

Imprint IX

5854 5857 5860 5863 6043
6046 6049

1916 ISSUE

Unwmkd. Perf. 10

#E10 10¢ SPECIAL DELIVERY

Imprint Block of 6, T $6,250
Imprint Block of 6, L, R, B $6,000

Imprint VII

5520

Basic Prices:

Block of 6, T $5,750
Block of 6, L, R, B $5,500

Imprint IX

6043 6046 6049

1917 ISSUE

Unwmkd. Perf. 11

#E11 10¢ SPECIAL DELIVERY

Imprint Block of 6, T $800
Imprint Block of 6, L, R, B $750

Imprint VII

5520

Basic Prices:

Block of 6, T (TL, TR) $250
Block of 6, L, R, B $225

Imprint IX

6043 6046 6049 7642 7643
7648 7653

Positions TL, TR, L, R, B

8506 8507 8508 8509 10274
10275 10276 10277 10631 10632
10634 *10653 11814 11815 11816
11817 13391 13392 13393 13394
13552 13553 13554 13555 13816
13817 *13818 *13819

1922 ISSUE

Unwmkd. Perf. 11

#E12 10¢ SPECIAL DELIVERY

69 Plates

Basic Price TL, TR $450
Basic Price L, R, B $425

13916 13917 13918 13919 13920
13921 13922 13923 14262 14263
14264 14265 14328 14329 14330
14331 *14579 14614 14615 14616
14617 15101 15102 15103 15104
15231 15232 15233 15234 16091
16092 16093 16094 *16119 16120
16121 16122 17223 17224 17225
17226 17239 17240 17241 17242
17513 17514 17515 17516 17564
17565 17566 17567 17625 17626
17627 17628 17637 17638 17639
17640 *17641 17642 17643 *17644
*18683 18684 *18685 18686

SPECIAL DELIVERY ISSUES

1925 ISSUE

Unwmkd. Perf. 11

#E13 15¢ SPECIAL DELIVERY

8 Plates

Basic Price TL, TR $325.00
Basic Price L, R, B $300.00

16833 16834 16835 16836 16857
*16858 16859 *16860

#E14 20¢ SPECIAL DELIVERY

16 Plates

Basic Price TL, TR $55.00
Basic Price L, R, B $50.00

17175 17176 17177 17178 17183
17184 17185 17186 17191 17192
17193 17199 *17206 *17211 *17213
*17214

1927 ISSUE

Unwmkd. Perf. 11 x 10½

ROTARY PRESS Plate Block of 4

#E15 10¢ SPECIAL DELIVERY

16 Plates

Plate	Price	UL	UR	LL	LR
18919	$7.00	☐	☐	☐	☐
18920	$7.00	☐	☐	☐	☐
19248	$7.00	☐	☐	☐	☐
19249	$7.00	☐	☐	☐	☐
19260	—	☐	☐	☐	☐
19261	$7.00	☐	☐	☐	☐
19280	$7.00	☐	☐	☐	☐
19281	$7.00	☐	☐	☐	☐
19282	$7.00	☐	☐	☐	☐
19283	$7.00	☐	☐	☐	☐
22738	$7.00	☐	☐	☐	☐
22739	$7.00	☐	☐	☐	☐
22841	$15.00	☐	☐	☐	☐
22842	$15.00	☐	☐	☐	☐
23105	$20.00	☐	☐	☐	☐
23106	$20.00	☐	☐	☐	☐

1931 ISSUE

Unwmkd. Perf. 11 x 10½

#E16 15¢ SPECIAL DELIVERY

4 Plates

Plate	Price	UL	UR	LL	LR
20595	$5.00	☐	☐	☐	☐
20596	$5.00	☐	☐	☐	☐
23034	$5.00	☐	☐	☐	☐
23035	$5.00	☐	☐	☐	☐

1944 ISSUE

#E17 13¢ SPECIAL DELIVERY

6 Plates

Plate	Price	UL	UR	LL	LR
23170	$3.75	☐	☐	☐	☐
23171	$3.75	☐	☐	☐	☐
23172	$3.75	☐	☐	☐	☐

1944 ISSUE

#E17 13¢ SPECIAL DELIVERY Cont.

Plate	Price	UL	UR	LL	LR
23173	$3.75	☐	☐	☐	☐
23720	$3.75	☐	☐	☐	☐
23721	$3.75	☐	☐	☐	☐

#E18 17¢ SPECIAL DELIVERY

2 Plates

Plate	Price	UL	UR	LL	LR
23168	$27.50	☐	☐	☐	☐
23169	$27.50	☐	☐	☐	☐

1951 ISSUE

#E19 20¢ SPECIAL DELIVERY

4 Plates

Plate	Price	UL	UR	LL	LR
24552	$8.50	☐	☐	☐	☐
24553	$8.50	☐	☐	☐	☐
24554	$8.50	☐	☐	☐	☐
24555	$8.50	☐	☐	☐	☐

1954 ISSUE

#E20 20¢ SPECIAL DELIVERY

6 Plates

Plate	Price	UL	UR	LL	LR
25054	$3.00	☐	☐	☐	☐
25055	$3.00	☐	☐	☐	☐
25059	$3.00	☐	☐	☐	☐
25060	$3.00	☐	☐	☐	☐
25065	$5.00	☐	☐	☐	☐
25066	$5.00	☐	☐	☐	☐

1957 ISSUE

#E21 30¢ SPECIAL DELIVERY

8 Plates

Plate	Price	UL	UR	LL	LR
25796	$3.25	☐	☐	☐	☐
25797	$3.25	☐	☐	☐	☐
25806	$3.25	☐	☐	☐	☐
25807	$3.25	☐	☐	☐	☐
27812	$3.25	☐	☐	☐	☐
27813	$3.25	☐	☐	☐	☐
28410	*$3.75*	☐	☐	☐	☐
28411	*$3.75*	☐	☐	☐	☐

1969 ISSUE

#E22 45¢ SPECIAL DELIVERY

9 Plates

Plate	Price	UL	UR	LL	LR
31484	$8.00	☐	☐	☐	☐
31485	$8.00	☐	☐	☐	☐
31487	$8.00	☐	☐	☐	☐
31492	$17.50	☐	☐	☐	☐
31495	$8.00	☐	☐	☐	☐
31504	$8.00	☐	☐	☐	☐
31506	$8.00	☐	☐	☐	☐
31507	$8.00	☐	☐	☐	☐
31510	$8.00	☐	☐	☐	☐

SPECIAL DELIVERY ISSUES

ROTARY PRESS Block of 4

1971 ISSUE

Unwmkd. Perf. 11 x 10½

#E23 60¢ SPECIAL DELIVERY

8 Plates		UL	UR	LL	LR
32962	$5.00	☐	☐	☐	☐
32977	$5.00	☐	☐	☐	☐
32985	$5.00	☐	☐	☐	☐
32986	$5.00	☐	☐	☐	☐
33002	$5.00	☐	☐	☐	☐
33004	$5.00	☐	☐	☐	☐
33006	$5.00	☐	☐	☐	☐
33008	$5.00	☐	☐	☐	☐

REGISTRATION STAMP

FLAT PRESS Block of 6

1911 ISSUE

Single Line Wmk. Perf. 12

#F1 10¢ REGISTRY

Imprint XII

4 Plates		T	L	R	B
5720	$2,000	☐	☐	☐	☐
5723	$2,000	☐	☐	☐	☐
5726	$2,000	☐	☐	☐	☐
5729	$2,000	☐	☐	☐	☐

CERTIFIED MAIL

ROTARY PRESS Block of 4

1955 ISSUE

Unwmkd. Perf. 10½ x 11

#FA1 15¢ CERTIFIED MAIL

2 Plates		UL	UR	LL	LR
25179	$6.00	☐	☐	☐	☐
25180	$6.00	☐	☐	☐	☐

POSTAGE DUE ISSUES

FLAT PRESS Block of 6

1894 ISSUE

Unwmkd. Perf. 12

#J29 1¢ POSTAGE DUE

Imprint Strip of 3, T or B	$1,500.00
Imprint Block of 6, T or B	$5,000.00

Imprint I

57

POSTAGE DUE ISSUES

1894 ISSUE

#J30 2¢ POSTAGE DUE

Imprint Strip of 3, T or B	$700.00
Imprint Block of 6, T or B	$2,250.00

Imprint I

34

#J31 1¢ POSTAGE DUE

Basic Prices:

Imprint Strip of 3, T	$100.00
Imprint Strip of 3, B	$75.00
Imprint Block of 6, T	$375.00
Imprint Block of 6, B	$325.00

Imprint I

57

Imprint II

147

#J32 2¢ POSTAGE DUE

Basic Prices:

Imprint Strip of 3, T	$70.00
Imprint Strip of 3, B	$35.00
Imprint Block of 6, T	$325.00
Imprint Block of 6, B	$300.00

Imprint I

60 159

#J33 3¢ POSTAGE DUE

Imprint Strip of 3, T	$650.00
Imprint Strip of 3, B	$250.00
Imprint Block of 6, T	$1,750.00
Imprint Block of 6, B	$850.00

Imprint I

70

#J34 5¢ POSTAGE DUE

Imprint Strip of 3, T	Rare
Imprint Strip of 3, B	$300.00
Imprint Block of 6, T	Rare
Imprint Block of 6, B	$950.00

Imprint I

71

#J35 10¢ POSTAGE DUE

Imprint Strip of 3, T or B	$200.00
Imprint Block of 6, T or B	$850.00

Imprint I

72

#J36 30¢ POSTAGE DUE

Imprint Strip of 3, T or B	$650.00
Imprint Block of 6, T or B	$2,350.00

Imprint I

73

#J37 50¢ POSTAGE DUE

Imprint Strip of 3, T or B	$1,500.00
Imprint Block of 6, T or B	$5,000.00

Imprint II

74

POSTAGE DUE ISSUES
1895 ISSUE
Double Line Wmk. Perf. 12

#J38 1¢ POSTAGE DUE
Basic Prices:

Imprint Strip of 3, T or B	$20.00
Imprint Block of 6, T or B	$175.00

Imprint I

57

Imprint II

147

Imprint IV

246 267

Imprint V

*1632 *1777 *1778 *1779 *1780

#J39 2¢ POSTAGE DUE
Basic Prices:

Imprint Strip of 3, T or B	$40.00
Imprint Block of 6, T or B	$175.00

Imprint I

60 159

Imprint IV

247 268

Imprint V

*1099 *1242 *1243 *1244 *1245
*1783 *1784 *1785 *1786

#J40 3¢ POSTAGE DUE
Basic Prices:

Imprint Strip of 3, T or B	$100.00
Imprint Block of 6, T or B	$400.00

Imprint I

70

Imprint IV

*254

Imprint V

*1631 *1787

#J41 5¢ POSTAGE DUE
Basic Prices:

Imprint Strip of 3, T or B	$125.00
Imprint Block of 6, T or B	$450.00

Imprint I

71

Imprint V

255 *1642 *1792

#J42 10¢ POSTAGE DUE
Basic Prices:

Imprint Strip of 3, T or B	$140.00
Imprint Block of 6, T or B	$550.00

Imprint I

72

Imprint IV

256

Imprint V

*1633 *1781 *1782

POSTAGE DUE ISSUES
1895 ISSUE

#J43 30¢ POSTAGE DUE
Basic Prices:

Imprint Strip of 3, T or B	$1,000.00
Imprint Block of 6, T or B	$3,750.00

Imprint I

73

#J44 50¢ POSTAGE DUE
Basic Prices:

Imprint Strip of 3, T or B	$650.00
Imprint Block of 6, T or B	$2,250.00

Imprint II

74

1910-12 ISSUE
Single Line Wmk. Perf. 12

#J45 1¢ POSTAGE DUE
Basic Prices:

Imprint Block of 6, T	$400.00
Imprint Block of 6, L, R, B	$375.00

Imprint X

5510 *5522 *5534 *5541

#J46 2¢ POSTAGE DUE
Basic Prices:

Imprint Block of 6, T	$350.00
Imprint Block of 6, L, R, B	$325.00

Imprint X

5511 5519 5530 5538

Basic Prices:

Block of 6, T	$375.00
Block of 6, L, R, B	$350.00

Imprint IX

6703 6704 *6705 6706

#J47 3¢ POSTAGE DUE
Basic Prices:

Imprint Block of 6, T	$3,750.00
Imprint Block of 6, L, R, B	$3,650.00

Imprint X

*5523 5529

#J48 5¢ POSTAGE DUE
Basic Prices:

Imprint Block of 6, T	$550.00
Imprint Block of 6, L, R, B	$525.00

Imprint X

5524 *5531

#J49 10¢ POSTAGE DUE
Basic Prices:

Imprint Block of 6, T	$1,000.00
Imprint Block of 6, L, R, B,	$950.00

Imprint X

5525 *5532 *5540 *6555

POSTAGE DUE ISSUES

1910-12 ISSUE

Single Line Wmk. Perf. 12

#J50 50¢ POSTAGE DUE

Imprint Block of 6, **T** $6,000.00
Imprint Block of 6, **L, R, B** $5,750.00

Imprint X

5527

1914-15 ISSUE

Single Line Wmk. Perf. 10

#J52 1¢ POSTAGE DUE

Basic Prices:
Imprint Block of 6, **T** $550.00
Imprint Block of 6, **L, R, B** $525.00

Imprint X

5510 *5522 *5534 *5541

#J53 2¢ POSTAGE DUE

Basic Price **T** $325.00
Basic Price **L, R, B** $300.00

Imprint IX

6703 6704 6705 6706

#J54 3¢ POSTAGE DUE

Basic Prices:
Imprint Block of 6, **T** $4,000.00
Imprint Block of 6, **L, R, B** $3,750.00

Imprint X

5523 5529

#J55 5¢ POSTAGE DUE

Basic Prices:
Imprint Block of 6, **T** $275.00
Imprint Block of 6, **L, R, B** $250.00

Imprint X

5524 5531

#J56 10¢ POSTAGE DUE

Basic Prices:
Imprint Block of 6, **T** $650.00
Imprint Block of 6, **L, R, B** $600.00

Imprint X

*5525 5532 *5540 6555

#J57 30¢ POSTAGE DUE

Basic Prices:
Imprint Block of 6, **T** $2,250.00
Imprint Block of 6, **L, R, B** $2,000.00

Imprint X

5526

#J58 50¢ POSTAGE DUE

Basic Prices:
Imprint Block of 6, **T** $35,000.00
Imprint Block of 6, **L,R,B** $35,000.00

Imprint X

5527

POSTAGE DUE ISSUES

1916 ISSUE

Unwmkd. Perf. 10

#J59 1¢ POSTAGE DUE

Basic Prices:
Imprint Block of 6, **T** $10,000.00
Imprint Block of 6, **L, R, B,** $7,250.00

Imprint X

5510 5522 5541

#J60 2¢ POSTAGE DUE

Basic Price **T** $700.00
Basic Price **L, R, B** $650.00

Imprint IX

6703 6704 6705 6706

1917-23 ISSUE

Unwmkd. Perf. 11

#J61 1¢ POSTAGE DUE

Basic Prices:
Imprint Block of 6, **T** $85.00
Imprint Block of 6, **L, R, B** $80.00

Imprint X

5510 *5522 *5534 *5541

Basic Prices:
Block of 6, **T (TL, TR)** $40.00
Block of 6, **L, R, B** $37.50

Imprint IX

7122 7129 7132 7141 8211
8212 8213 8214

Positions TL, TR, L, R, B

13844 13845 13846 13847**N** *14034
*14035 *14036 *14037

N Inverted F on One Bottom Position

#J62 2¢ POSTAGE DUE

Basic Prices:
Block of 6, **T (TL, TR)** $35.00
Block of 6, **L, R, B** $32.50

Imprint IX

6703 6704 6705 6706 7121
7126 7130 7134

Positions TL, TR, L, R, B

10335 10336 10337 10338 14026
14027 14028 14029 14596 14597
14598 14599 15828 *15829 19076
19077 19078 19079 19082 *19083
*19084 *19085

#J63 3¢ POSTAGE DUE

Basic Prices:
Imprint Block of 6, **T** $100.00
Imprint Block of 6, **L, R, B** $95.00

Imprint X

5523 5529

POSTAGE DUE ISSUES

1917-23 ISSUE

#J63 3¢ POSTAGE DUE Cont.

Basic Prices:

Block of 6, **TL, TR** $85.00
Block of 6, **L, R, B** $80.00

Imprint IX

8477 8478 8479 8480

With no side plate numbers

*20069 *20070 *20071 *20072

#J64 5¢ POSTAGE DUE

Basic Prices:

Imprint Block of 6, **T** $100.00
Imprint Block of 6, **L, R, B** $90.00

Imprint X

5524 5531

Basic Prices:

Block of 6, **TL, TR** $100.00
Block of 6, **L, R, B** $90.00

Imprint IX

15854 15855 15856 15857 *19469
*19470 *19877 *19878

#J65 10¢ POSTAGE DUE

Basic Prices:

Imprint Block of 6, **T** $140.00
Imprint Block of 6, **L, R, B** $130.00

Imprint X

5525 5532 5540 6555 6556

Basic Prices:

Block of 6, **TL, TR** $150.00
Block of 6, **L, R, B,** $140.00

Imprint IX

15860 *15861 *15862 15863 18724
18725 18726 18727

#J66 30¢ POSTAGE DUE

Basic Prices

Imprint Block of 6, **T** $575.00
Imprint Block of 6, **L, R, B** $550.00

Imprint X

5526 5537

Basic Prices:

Block of 6, **TL, TR** $550.00
Block of 6, **L, R, B** $525.00

Imprint IX

*15876 15877 *19881 *19882 *19883
*19884

#J67 50¢ POSTAGE DUE

Basic Prices:

Imprint Block of 6, **T** $700.00
Imprint Block of 6, **L, R, B** $650.00

Imprint X

5527 5533

1917-23 ISSUE

#J67 50¢ POSTAGE DUE Cont.

Basic Prices:

Block of 6, **TL, TR** $650.00
Block of 6, **L, R, B** $600.00

Imprint IX

15886 15887

With no side plate numbers

20035 20036

1925 ISSUE

Unwmkd. Perf. 11

#J68 ½¢ POSTAGE DUE 5 Plates

		TL	TR	L	R	B
17127	$12.00	☐	☐	☐	☐	☐
17128	$12.00	☐	☐	☐	☐	☐
17129	$12.00	☐	☐	☐	☐	☐
17130	$12.00	☐	☐	☐	☐	☐
17131	$12.00	☐	☐	☐	☐	☐

1930-31 ISSUE

Unwmkd. Perf. 11

#J69 ½¢ POSTAGE DUE 4 Plates

		TL	TR	L	R	B
20239	$35.00	☐	☐	‡	‡	☐
20240	$35.00	☐	☐	‡	‡	☐
20241	$35.00	☐	☐	‡	‡	☐
20242	$35.00	☐	☐	‡	‡	☐

#J70 1¢ POSTAGE DUE 4 Plates

		TL	TR	L	R	B
20162	$30.00	☐	☐	‡	‡	☐
20163	$30.00	☐	☐	‡	‡	☐
20164	$30.00	☐	☐	‡	‡	☐
20165	$30.00	☐	☐	‡	‡	☐

#J71 2¢ POSTAGE DUE 8 Plates

		TL	TR	L	R	B
20217	$45.00	☐	☐	‡	‡	☐
20218	$45.00	☐	☐	‡	‡	☐
20219	$45.00	☐	☐	‡	‡	☐
20220	$45.00	☐	☐	‡	‡	☐
20251	$225.00	☐	☐	‡	‡	☐
20252	$225.00	☐	☐	‡	‡	☐
20253	$225.00	☐	☐	‡	‡	☐
20254	$225.00	☐	☐	‡	‡	☐

#J72 3¢ POSTAGE DUE 4 Plates

		TL	TR	L	R	B
20213	$235.00	☐	☐	‡	‡	☐
20214	$235.00	☐	☐	‡	‡	☐
20215	$235.00	☐	☐	‡	‡	☐
20216	$235.00	☐	☐	‡	‡	☐

#J73 5¢ POSTAGE DUE 4 Plates

		TL	TR	L	R	B
20209	$225.00	☐	☐	‡	‡	☐
20210	$225.00	☐	☐	‡	‡	☐
20211	$225.00	☐	☐	‡	‡	☐
20212	$225.00	☐	☐	‡	‡	☐

POSTAGE DUE ISSUES

1930-31 ISSUE Continued

#J74 10¢ POSTAGE DUE 4 Plates

Plate	Price	TL	TR	L	R	B
20235	$375.00	☐	☐	‡	‡	☐
20236	$375.00	☐	☐	‡	‡	☐
20237	$375.00	☐	☐	‡	‡	☐
20238	$375.00	☐	☐	‡	‡	☐

#J75 30¢ POSTAGE DUE 4 Plates

Plate	Price	TL	TR	L	R	B
20225	$2,000	☐	☐	‡	‡	☐
20226	$2,000	☐	☐	‡	‡	☐
20227	$2,000	☐	☐	‡	‡	☐
20228	$2,000	☐	☐	‡	‡	☐

#J76 50¢ POSTAGE DUE 4 Plates

Plate	Price	TL	TR	L	R	B
20229	$1,150	☐	☐	‡	‡	☐
20230	$1,150	☐	☐	‡	‡	☐
20231	$1,150	☐	☐	‡	‡	☐
20232	$1,150	☐	☐	‡	‡	☐

#J77 $1 POSTAGE DUE 4 Plates

Plate	Price	TL	TR	L	R	B
20130	$275.00	☐	☐	‡	‡	☐
20131	$275.00	☐	☐	‡	‡	☐
20132	$275.00	☐	☐	‡	‡	☐
20133	$275.00	☐	☐	‡	‡	☐

#J78 $5 POSTAGE DUE

Wet Printed 4 Plates

Plate	Price	TL	TR	L	R	B
20158	$425.00	☐	☐	‡	‡	☐
20159	$425.00	☐	☐	‡	‡	☐
20160	$425.00	☐	☐	‡	‡	☐
20161	$425.00	☐	☐	‡	‡	☐

Dry Printed 4 Plates

Plate	Price	TL	TR	L	R	B
20158	$525.00	☐	☐	‡	‡	☐
20159	$525.00	☐	☐	‡	‡	☐
20160	$525.00	☐	☐	‡	‡	☐
20161	$525.00	☐	☐	‡	‡	☐

1931-32 ISSUE

Unwmkd. Perf. 11 x 10½

ROTARY PRESS Blocks of 4

#J79 ½¢ POSTAGE DUE

Wet Printed 4 Plates

Plate	Price	UL	UR	LL	LR
20571	$20.00	☐	☐	☐	☐
20572	$20.00	☐	☐	☐	☐
22805	$20.00	☐	☐	☐	☐
22806	$20.00	☐	☐	☐	☐

#J80 1¢ POSTAGE DUE

Wet Printed 4 Plates

Plate	Price	UL	UR	LL	LR
20579	$2.00	☐	☐	☐	☐
20580	$2.00	☐	☐	☐	☐
22807	$2.00	☐	☐	☐	☐
22808	$2.00	☐	☐	☐	☐

Dry Printed 2 Plates

Plate	Price	UL	UR	LL	LR
25635	$2.00	☐	☐	☐	☐
25636	$2.00	☐	☐	☐	☐

1931-32 ISSUE Continued

#J81 2¢ POSTAGE DUE

Wet Printed 8 Plates

Plate	Price	UL	UR	LL	LR
20610	$2.00	☐	☐	☐	☐
20611	$2.00	☐	☐	☐	☐
20674	$2.00	☐	☐	☐	☐
20675	$2.00	☐	☐	☐	☐
22809	$2.00	☐	☐	☐	☐
22810	$2.00	☐	☐	☐	☐
23156	$2.00	☐	☐	☐	☐
23157	$2.00	☐	☐	☐	☐

Dry printed 2 Plates

Plate	Price	UL	UR	LL	LR
25637	$2.00	☐	☐	☐	☐
25638	$2.00	☐	☐	☐	☐

#J82 3¢ POSTAGE DUE

Wet Printed 10 Plates

Plate	Price	UL	UR	LL	LR
20612	$3.00	☐	☐	☐	☐
20613	$3.00	☐	☐	☐	☐
20676	$3.00	☐	☐	☐	☐
20677	$3.00	☐	☐	☐	☐
22811	$3.00	☐	☐	☐	☐
22812	$3.00	☐	☐	☐	☐
22963	$3.00	☐	☐	☐	☐
22964	$3.00	☐	☐	☐	☐
23644	$3.00	☐	☐	☐	☐
23645	$3.00	☐	☐	☐	☐

Dry Printed 2 Plates

Plate	Price	UL	UR	LL	LR
25641	$3.25	☐	☐	☐	☐
25642	$3.25	☐	☐	☐	☐

#J83 5¢ POSTAGE DUE

Wet Printed 6 Plates

Plate	Price	UL	UR	LL	LR
20615	$4.00	☐	☐	☐	☐
20616	$4.00	☐	☐	☐	☐
22813	$4.00	☐	☐	☐	☐
22814	$4.00	☐	☐	☐	☐
23148	$4.00	☐	☐	☐	☐
24058	$4.00	☐	☐	☐	☐

Dry Printed 2 Plates

Plate	Price	UL	UR	LL	LR
25643	$4.25	☐	☐	☐	☐
25644	$4.25	☐	☐	☐	☐

#J84 10¢ POSTAGE DUE

Wet Printed 4 Plates

Plate	Price	UL	UR	LL	LR
20619	$8.00	☐	☐	☐	☐
20620	$8.00	☐	☐	☐	☐
22821	$8.00	☐	☐	☐	☐
22822	$8.00	☐	☐	☐	☐

Dry Printed 2 Plates

Plate	Price	UL	UR	LL	LR
25645	$8.50	☐	☐	☐	☐
25646	$8.50	☐	☐	☐	☐

#J85 30¢ POSTAGE DUE

Wet Printed 4 Plates

Plate	Price	UL	UR	LL	LR
20623	$40.00	☐	☐	☐	☐
20624	$40.00	☐	☐	☐	☐

POSTAGE DUE ISSUES

1931-32 ISSUE Continued

#J85 30¢ POSTAGE DUE Cont.

		UL	UR	LL	LR
22829	$40.00	☐	☐	☐	☐
22830	$40.00	☐	☐	☐	☐

#J86 50¢ POSTAGE DUE

Wet Printed **4 Plates**

		UL	UR	LL	LR
20621	$52.50	☐	☐	☐	☐
20622	$52.50	☐	☐	☐	☐
22831	$52.50	☐	☐	☐	☐
22832	$52.50	☐	☐	☐	☐

ROTARY PRESS PERF. 10½ x 11

#J87 $1 POSTAGE DUE

Wet Printed **2 Plates**

		UL	UR	LL	LR
25243	$300.00	☐	☐	☐	☐
25244	$300.00	☐	☐	☐	☐

1959 ISSUE

Unwmkd. Perf. 11 x 10½
ROTARY PRESS

The plates for this issue print the design and the denominations are added in black by a method similar to that used in precancelling.

All of the plates could exist on any denomination but only those plates that have been reported on the value are shown.

(See Appendix A for gum and paper varieties)

#J88 ½¢ POSTAGE DUE

6 Plates		UL	UR	LL	LR
26289	$150.00	☐	☐	☐	☐
26290	$150.00	☐	☐	☐	☐
26291	$350.00	†	☐	†	†
26292	$350.00	☐	☐	†	†
26660	$150.00	☐	☐	☐	☐
26661	$150.00	☐	☐	☐	☐

#J89 1¢ POSTAGE DUE 20 Plates

		UL	UR	LL	LR
26289	$.40	☐	☐	☐	☐
26290	$.40	☐	☐	☐	☐
26291	$.40	☐	☐	☐	☐
26292	$.40	☐	☐	☐	☐
26660	$.40	☐	☐	☐	☐
26661	$.40	☐	☐	☐	☐
26833	$.40	☐	☐	☐	☐
26834	$.40	☐	☐	☐	☐
27072	$.40	☐	☐	☐	☐
27694	$.40	☐	☐	☐	☐

1959 ISSUE Continued

#J89 1¢ POSTAGE DUE Cont.

		UL	UR	LL	LR
27850	$.40	☐	☐	☐	☐
27851	$.40	☐	☐	☐	☐
29228	$.40	☐	☐	☐	☐
29229	$.40	☐	☐	☐	☐
34283	$.40	☐	☐	☐	☐
35283	$.40	☐	☐	☐	☐
35306	$.40	☐	☐	☐	☐
35307	$.40	☐	☐	☐	☐
37876	$.40	☐	☐	☐	☐
37877	$.40	☐	☐	☐	☐

#J90 2¢ POSTAGE DUE 21 Plates

		UL	UR	LL	LR
26289	$.50	☐	☐	☐	☐
26290	$.50	☐	☐	☐	☐
26291	$.50	☐	☐	☐	☐
26292	$.50	☐	☐	☐	☐
26660	$.50	☐	☐	☐	☐
26661	$.50	☐	☐	☐	☐
26833	$.50	☐	☐	☐	☐
26834	$.50	☐	☐	☐	☐
27072	$.50	☐	☐	☐	☐
27694	$.50	☐	☐	☐	☐
27850	$.50	☐	☐	☐	☐
27851	$.50	☐	☐	☐	☐
29228	$.50	☐	☐	☐	☐
29229	$.50	☐	☐	☐	☐
34283	$.50	☐	☐	☐	☐
35282	$.50	☐	☐	☐	☐
35283	$.50	☐	☐	☐	☐
35306	$.50	☐	☐	☐	☐
35307	$.50	☐	☐	☐	☐
37876	$.50	☐	☐	☐	☐
37877	$.50	☐	☐	☐	☐

#J91 3¢ POSTAGE DUE 19 Plates

		UL	UR	LL	LR
26289	$.60	☐	☐	☐	☐
26290	$.60	☐	☐	☐	☐
26660	$.60	☐	☐	☐	☐
26661	$.60	☐	☐	☐	☐
26833	$.60	☐	☐	☐	☐
26834	$.60	☐	☐	☐	☐
27072	$.60	☐	☐	☐	☐
27694	$.60	☐	☐	☐	☐
27850	$.60	☐	☐	☐	☐
27851	$.60	☐	☐	☐	☐
29228	$.60	☐	☐	☐	☐
29229	$.60	☐	☐	☐	☐
34283	$.60	☐	☐	☐	☐
35282	$.60	☐	☐	☐	☐
35283	$.60	☐	☐	☐	☐
35306	$.60	☐	☐	☐	☐
35307	$.60	☐	☐	☐	☐
37876	$.60	☐	☐	☐	☐
37877	$.60	☐	☐	☐	☐

1959 POSTAGE DUE ISSUES

#J92 4¢ POSTAGE DUE 18 Plates

		UL	UR	LL	LR
26289	$.75	☐	☐	☐	☐
26290	$.75	☐	☐	☐	☐
26291	$.75	☐	☐	☐	☐
26292	$.75	☐	☐	☐	☐
26660	$.75	☐	☐	☐	☐
26661	$.75	☐	☐	☐	☐
26833	$.75	☐	☐	☐	☐
26834	$.75	☐	☐	☐	☐
27072	$.75	☐	☐	☐	☐
27694	$.75	☐	☐	☐	☐
27850	$.75	☐	☐	☐	☐
27851	$.75	☐	☐	☐	☐
29228	$.75	☐	☐	☐	☐
29229	$.75	☐	☐	☐	☐
34283	$.75	☐	☐	☐	☐
35283	$.75	☐	☐	☐	☐
35306	$.75	☐	☐	☐	☐
35307	$.75	☐	☐	☐	☐

#J93 5¢ POSTAGE DUE 21 Plates

		UL	UR	LL	LR
*26289	—	☐	☐	☐	☐
26290	$.60	☐	☐	☐	☐
26291	$.60	☐	☐	☐	☐
26292	$.60	☐	☐	☐	☐
26660	$.60	☐	☐	☐	☐
26661	$.60	☐	☐	☐	☐
26833	$.60	☐	☐	☐	☐
26834	$.60	☐	☐	☐	☐
27072	$.60	☐	☐	☐	☐
27694	$.60	☐	☐	☐	☐
27850	$.60	☐	☐	☐	☐
27851	$.60	☐	☐	☐	☐
29228	$.60	☐	☐	☐	☐
29229	$.60	☐	☐	☐	☐
34283	$.60	☐	☐	☐	☐
35282	$.60	☐	☐	☐	☐
35283	$.60	☐	☐	☐	☐
35306	$.60	☐	☐	☐	☐
35307	$.60	☐	☐	☐	☐
37876	$.60	☐	☐	☐	☐
37877	$.60	☐	☐	☐	☐

#J94 6¢ POSTAGE DUE 17 Plates

		UL	UR	LL	LR
26289	$1.25	☐	☐	☐	☐
26290	$1.25	☐	☐	☐	☐
26291	$1.25	☐	☐	☐	☐
26292	$1.25	☐	☐	☐	☐
26660	$1.25	☐	☐	☐	☐
26661	$1.25	☐	☐	☐	☐
26833	$1.25	☐	☐	☐	☐
27072	$1.25	☐	☐	☐	☐
27694	$1.25	☐	☐	☐	☐
27850	$1.25	☐	☐	☐	☐
27851	$1.25	☐	☐	☐	☐
29228	$1.25	☐	☐	☐	☐
29229	$1.25	☐	☐	☐	☐
34283	$1.25	☐	☐	☐	☐

#J94 6¢ POSTAGE DUE Continued

		UL	UR	LL	LR
35283	$1.25	☐	☐	☐	☐
35306	$1.25	☐	☐	☐	☐
35307	$1.25	☐	☐	☐	☐

#J95 7¢ POSTAGE DUE 16 Plates

		UL	UR	LL	LR
26289	$1.50	☐	☐	☐	☐
26290	$1.50	☐	☐	☐	☐
26291	$1.50	☐	☐	☐	☐
26292	$1.50	☐	☐	☐	☐
26660	$1.50	☐	☐	☐	☐
26661	$1.50	☐	☐	☐	☐
26833	$30.00	☐	☐	†	☐
26834	$1.50	☐	☐	☐	☐
27072	$7.50	☐	☐	☐	☐
27694	$1.50	☐	☐	☐	☐
27850	$1.50	☐	☐	☐	☐
27851	$1.50	☐	☐	☐	☐
29228	$1.50	☐	☐	☐	☐
29229	$1.50	☐	☐	☐	☐
35306	$1.50	☐	☐	☐	☐
35307	$1.50	☐	☐	☐	☐

#J96 8¢ POSTAGE DUE 14 Plates

		UL	UR	LL	LR
26291	$1.50	☐	☐	☐	☐
26292	$1.50	☐	☐	☐	☐
26834	$7.50	☐	☐	☐	☐
27072	$1.50	☐	☐	☐	☐
27694	$1.50	☐	☐	☐	☐
27850	$1.50	☐	☐	☐	☐
27851	$1.50	☐	☐	☐	☐
29228	$1.50	☐	☐	☐	☐
29229	$1.50	☐	☐	☐	☐
34283	$1.50	☐	☐	☐	☐
35282	$8.00	☐	☐	☐	☐
35283	$1.50	☐	☐	☐	☐
35306	$1.50	☐	☐	☐	☐
35307	$1.50	☐	☐	☐	☐

#J97 10¢ POSTAGE DUE 21 Plates

		UL	UR	LL	LR
26289	$1.20	☐	☐	☐	☐
26290	$1.20	☐	☐	☐	☐
26291	$1.20	☐	☐	☐	☐
26292	$1.20	☐	☐	☐	☐
26660	$1.20	☐	☐	☐	☐
26661	$1.20	☐	☐	☐	☐
26833	$1.20	☐	☐	☐	☐
26834	$1.20	☐	☐	☐	☐
27072	$1.20	☐	☐	☐	☐
27694	$1.20	☐	☐	☐	☐
27850	$1.20	☐	☐	☐	☐
27851	$1.20	☐	☐	☐	☐
29228	$1.20	☐	☐	☐	☐
29229	$1.20	☐	☐	☐	☐
34283	$1.20	☐	☐	☐	☐
35282	$2.50	☐	☐	†	†
35283	$1.20	☐	☐	☐	☐
35306	$1.20	☐	☐	☐	☐
35307	$1.20	☐	☐	☐	☐
37876	$1.20	☐	☐	☐	☐
37877	$1.20	☐	☐	☐	☐

1959 POSTAGE DUE ISSUE

#J102 11¢ POSTAGE DUE 4 Plates

		UL	UR	LL	LR
34283	$4.50	☐	☐	☐	☐
35283	$4.50	☐	☐	☐	☐
35306	$1.50	☐	☐	☐	☐
35307	$1.50	☐	☐	☐	☐

#J103 13¢ POSTAGE DUE 4 Plates

		UL	UR	LL	LR
34283	$1.30	☐	☐	☐	☐
35283	$1.30	☐	☐	☐	☐
35306	$1.30	☐	☐	☐	☐
35307	$1.30	☐	☐	☐	☐

#J104 17¢ POSTAGE DUE 2 Plates

		UL	UR	LL	LR
35306	$17.50	☐	☐	☐	☐
35307	$17.50	☐	☐	☐	☐

#J98 30¢ POSTAGE DUE 19 Plates

		UL	UR	LL	LR
26289	$15.00	☐	☐	☐	☐
26290	$15.00	☐	†	☐	☐
26291	$3.50	☐	☐	☐	☐
26292	$3.50	☐	☐	☐	☐
26660	$3.50	☐	☐	☐	☐
26661	$3.50	☐	☐	☐	☐
26833	$15.00	☐	☐	☐	†
27072	$3.50	☐	☐	☐	☐
27694	$3.50	☐	☐	☐	☐
27850	$3.50	☐	☐	☐	☐
27851	$3.50	☐	☐	☐	☐
29228	$3.50	☐	☐	☐	☐
29229	$3.50	☐	☐	☐	☐
34283	$3.50	☐	☐	☐	☐
35283	$3.50	☐	☐	☐	☐
35306	$3.50	☐	☐	☐	☐
35307	$3.50	☐	☐	☐	☐
37876	$3.50	☐	☐	☐	☐
37877	$3.50	☐	☐	☐	☐

#J99 50¢ POSTAGE DUE 20 Plates

		UL	UR	LL	LR
26289	$5.00	☐	☐	☐	☐
26290	$5.00	☐	☐	☐	☐
*26291	—	☐	†	†	†
26660	$5.00	☐	☐	☐	☐
26661	$5.00	☐	☐	☐	☐
26833	$20.00	☐	☐	☐	☐
*26834	—	†	☐	†	†
27072	$5.00	☐	☐	☐	☐
27694	$5.00	☐	☐	☐	☐
27850	$5.00	☐	☐	☐	☐
27851	$5.00	☐	☐	☐	☐
29228	$5.00	☐	☐	☐	☐
29229	$5.00	☐	☐	☐	☐
34283	$5.00	☐	☐	☐	☐
35282	$5.00	☐	☐	☐	☐
35283	$5.00	☐	☐	☐	☐
35306	$5.00	☐	☐	☐	☐
35307	$5.00	☐	☐	☐	☐
37876	$5.00	☐	☐	☐	☐
37877	$5.00	☐	☐	☐	☐

1959 POSTAGE DUE ISSUE

#J100 $1 POSTAGE DUE 19 Plates

		UL	UR	LL	LR
26290	$7.50	☐	☐	☐	☐
26291	$7.50	☐	☐	☐	☐
26292	$7.50	☐	☐	☐	☐
26660	$7.50	☐	☐	☐	☐
26661	$7.50	☐	☐	☐	☐
26834	$7.50	☐	☐	☐	☐
27072	$7.50	☐	☐	☐	☐
27694	$7.50	☐	☐	☐	☐
27850	$7.50	☐	☐	☐	☐
27851	$7.50	☐	☐	☐	☐
29228	$7.50	☐	☐	☐	☐
29229	$7.50	☐	☐	☐	☐
34283	$7.50	☐	☐	☐	☐
35282	$7.50	☐	☐	☐	☐
35283	$7.50	☐	☐	☐	☐
35306	$7.50	☐	☐	☐	☐
35307	$7.50	☐	☐	☐	☐
37876	$7.50	☐	☐	☐	☐
37877	$7.50	☐	☐	☐	☐

#J101 $5 POSTAGE DUE 17 Plates

		UL	UR	LL	LR
26291	$35.00	☐	☐	☐	☐
26292	$35.00	☐	☐	☐	☐
26660	$35.00	☐	☐	☐	☐
26661	$35.00	☐	☐	☐	☐
27072	$35.00	☐	☐	☐	☐
27694	$35.00	☐	☐	☐	☐
27850	$35.00	☐	☐	☐	☐
27851	$35.00	☐	☐	☐	☐
29228	$35.00	☐	☐	☐	☐
29229	$35.00	☐	☐	☐	☐
34283	$35.00	☐	☐	☐	☐
35282	$35.00	☐	☐	☐	☐
35283	$35.00	☐	☐	☐	☐
35306	$35.00	☐	☐	☐	☐
35307	$35.00	☐	☐	☐	☐
37876	$35.00	☐	☐	☐	☐
37877	$35.00	☐	☐	☐	☐

BUREAU ISSUES ASSOCIATION 1930 · INCORPORATED 1938 · P.P.N.A. 1926 · KNOW YOUR COUNTRY'S STAMPS

OFFICIAL MAIL

Double Line Wmk. Perf. 12

#O121 2¢ BLACK

Imprint X

		T	L	R	B
5500	$225	☐	☐	☐	☐
5501	$225	☐	☐	☐	☐
5502	$225	☐	☐	☐	☐
5503	$225	☐	☐	☐	☐

#O122 50¢ DARK GREEN

Imprint X

5614	$2,000	☐	☐	☐	☐

#O123 $1 ULTRAMARINE

Imprint X

5615	$1750	☐	☐	☐	☐

Single Line Watermark Perf. 12

#O124 1¢ DARK VIOLET

Imprint X

5646	$125	☐	☐	☐	☐

#O125 2¢ BLACK

Imprint X

5500	$575	☐	☐	☐	☐
5501	$575	☐	☐	☐	☐
5502	$575	☐	☐	☐	☐
5503	$575	☐	☐	☐	☐

#O126 10¢ CARMINE

Imprint X

5613	$250	☐	☐	☐	☐

1983 ISSUE

Perf. 11 x 10½

The make-up of the printing plates of this issue is the forerunner of what is now called "quadrant printing". The result is that the entire plate is no longer either the same denomination or the same design in each of the four quarters that are normally issued as postoffice panes. One set of plates was made with a 1¢ in UL; a 1¢ in UR; a 17¢ in LL and a 4¢ in LR. The second set of plates was made with a $1 in UL; a 13¢ in UR; a $5 in LL and a non-denominated "D" in LR.

#O127 1¢ OFFICIAL MAIL 5 Plates

		UL	UR	LL	LR
2	$.15	☐	☐	‡	‡
3	$.15	☐	☐	‡	‡
4	$.15	☐	☐	‡	‡
5	$.15	☐	☐	‡	‡
6	$.15	☐	☐	‡	‡

1983 ISSUE Continued

#O128 4¢ OFFICIAL MAIL 5 Plates

		UL	UR	LL	LR
2	$.40	‡	‡	‡	☐
3	$.40	‡	‡	‡	☐
4	$.40	‡	‡	‡	☐
5	$.40	‡	‡	‡	☐
6	$.40	‡	‡	‡	☐

#O129 13¢ OFFICIAL MAIL 4 Plates

1	$1.30	‡	☐	‡	‡
2	$1.30	‡	☐	‡	‡
3	$1.30	‡	☐	‡	‡
4	$1.30	‡	☐	‡	‡

#O130 17¢ OFFICIAL MAIL 5 Plates

2	$1.70	‡	‡	☐	‡
3	$1.70	‡	‡	☐	‡
4	$1.70	‡	‡	☐	‡
5	$1.70	‡	‡	☐	‡
6	$1.70	‡	‡	☐	‡

#O132 $1 OFFICIAL MAIL 4 Plates

1	$10.00	☐	‡	‡	‡
2	$10.00	☐	‡	‡	‡
3	$10.00	☐	‡	‡	‡
4	$10.00	☐	‡	‡	‡

#O133 $5 OFFICIAL MAIL 4 Plates

1	$50.00	‡	‡	☐	‡
2	$50.00	‡	‡	☐	‡
3	$50.00	‡	‡	☐	‡
4	$50.00	‡	‡	☐	‡

#O138 "D" OFFICIAL MAIL 4 Plates

1	$1.40	‡	‡	‡	☐
2	$1.40	‡	‡	‡	☐
3	$1.40	‡	‡	‡	☐
4	$1.40	‡	‡	‡	☐

#O135 20¢ OFFICIAL MAIL COIL

1 Plate **STRIP OF 3**

1	$20.00	☐

#O139 "D" OFFICIAL MAIL COIL

1 Plate **STRIP OF 3**

1	$35.00	☐

ADDITIONAL ISSUES

....	☐	☐	☐	☐
....	☐	☐	☐	☐
....	☐	☐	☐	☐
....	☐	☐	☐	☐
....	☐	☐	☐	☐
....	☐	☐	☐	☐
....	☐	☐	☐	☐
....	☐	☐	☐	☐
....	☐	☐	☐	☐

NEWSPAPER & PERIODICAL STAMPS

The first issue printed by the Bureau of Engraving and Printing used plates that were supplied by the American Bank Note Company. Plate numbers in the regular postage stamp series were assigned to these plates but were never entered on the plates. Since the plate numbers appear only on the proof sheets with the assigned number written in pencil in the bottom margin, Scott Catalog numbers PR90-PR101 will not be listed.

The regulations in effect at the time the unwatermarked issue made its appearance stated that neither mint nor used stamps were to be given or sold to collectors. Since some clerks and postmasters chose to ignore these regulations, some examples of PR102-PR113 exist. Please consult Appendix HH for further information.

The early issues of the watermarked series exist without guide lines. The regulations pertaining to the sale and distribution of these stamps were still in effect. Please consult Appendix HH for further information.

In 1899 the government sold complete sets of PR114-PR125 to the public. It is from this act that the majority of the plate strips and blocks were obtained by collectors. Side plate blocks on the 1¢ thru 50¢ are either upper left or lower right with half imprint and split arrow. On the $2 thru $100, the side plates are with full imprint and exist as upper left, lower left, upper right and lower right positions. The top and bottom plate blocks of the 1¢ thru $100 will have plate number, full imprint, full arrow and vertical guideline.

Watermarked Double Line USPS with vertical guide line

#PR114 1¢ FREEDOM 2 Plates

		T	L	R	B
	Imprint III				
90	—	☐	☐	☐	☐
	Imprint VI				
262	—	☐	☐	☐	☐

#PR115 2¢ FREEDOM 2 Plates

		T	L	R	B
	Imprint III				
100	—	☐	☐	☐	☐
	Imprint VI				
*265	—	☐	☐	☐	☐

#PR116 5¢ FREEDOM 2 Plates

		T	L	R	B
	Imprint III				
93	—	☐	☐	☐	☐
	Imprint VI				
266	—	☐	☐	☐	☐

#PR117 10¢ FREEDOM 2 Plates

		T	L	R	B
	Imprint III				
105	—	☐	☐	☐	☐
	Imprint VI				
*269	—	☐	☐	☐	☐

#PR118 25¢ JUSTICE 1 Plate

		T	L	R	B
	Imprint III				
123	—	☐	☐	☐	☐

#PR119 50¢ JUSTICE 2 Plates

		T	L	R	B
	Imprint III				
109	—	☐	☐	☐	☐
	Imprint VI				
259	—	☐	☐	☐	☐

#PR120 $2 VICTORY 1 Plate

		T	L	R	B
	Imprint III				
136	—	☐	☐	☐	☐

#PR121 $5 CLIO 1 Plate

		T	L	R	B
	Imprint III				
137	—	☐	☐	☐	☐

#PR122 $10 VESTA 1 Plate

		T	L	R	B
	Imprint III				
138	—	☐	☐	☐	☐

#PR123 $20 PEACE 1 Plate

		T	L	R	B
	Imprint III				
139	—	☐	☐	☐	☐

#PR124 $50 COMMERCE 1 Plate

		T	L	R	B
	Imprint III				
135	—	☐	☐	☐	☐

#PR125 $100 INDIAN 1 Plate

		T	L	R	B
	Imprint III				
140	—	☐	☐	☐	☐

POSTAL SAVINGS STAMPS

FLAT PLATE PRINTING
Double Line Wmk. Perf. 12

#PS1 10¢ ORANGE

		T	L	R	B
Imprint X					
5504	$450	☐	☐	☐	☐
5505	$450	☐	☐	☐	☐
5506	$450	☐	☐	☐	☐
5507	$450	☐	☐	☐	☐

FLAT PLATE PRINTING
Single Line Wmk. Perf. 12

#PS4 10¢ DEEP BLUE

Imprint X					
5504	$175	☐	☐	☐	☐
5505	$175	☐	☐	☐	☐
5506	$175	☐	☐	☐	☐
5507	$175	☐	☐	☐	☐
Imprint XII					
5698	—	†	†	†	†
5700	—	†	†	†	†
5703	—	†	†	†	†
5704	—	†	†	†	†

FLAT PLATE PRINTINGS
Unwatermarked Perf. 11

UNASSIGNED IMPRINT NUMBER

#PS6 10¢ DEEP BLUE

		TL	TR	L	R	B
Imprint XV						
21485	$125	☐	☐	☐	☐	☐
21486	$125	☐	☐	☐	☐	☐

#PS7 10¢ DEEP ULTRAMARINE

22540	$225	☐	☐	☐	☐	☐
22541	$225	☐	☐	☐	☐	☐

#PS8 25¢ DARK CARMINE ROSE

22542	$350	☐	☐	☐	☐	☐
22543	$350	☐	☐	☐	☐	☐

#PS9 50¢ DARK BLUE GREEN

		TL	TR	L	R	B
22544	$850	☐	☐	☐	☐	☐

#PS10 $1 GRAY BLACK

22545	$1,850	☐	☐	☐	☐	☐

ROTARY PRESS PRINTINGS
Unwatermarked Perf. 11 x 10½

#PS11 10¢ ROSE RED

		UL	UR	LL	LR
22714	$9.00	☐	☐	☐	☐
22715	$9.00	☐	☐	☐	☐
22722	$9.00	☐	☐	☐	☐
22723	$9.00	☐	☐	☐	☐
148245	$9.00	☐	☐	☐	☐
148246	$9.00	☐	☐	☐	☐

#PS12 25¢ BLUE GREEN

22716	$22.50	☐	☐	☐	☐
22717	$22.50	☐	☐	☐	☐
22724	$22.50	☐	☐	☐	☐
22725	$22.50	☐	☐	☐	☐
148247	$22.50	☐	☐	☐	☐
148248	$22.50	☐	☐	☐	☐

#PS13 50¢ ULTRAMARINE

22718	$50.00	☐	☐	☐	☐
22719	$50.00	☐	☐	☐	☐
22726	$50.00	☐	☐	☐	☐
22727	$50.00	☐	☐	☐	☐

#PS14 $1 GRAY BLACK

22720	$100.00	☐	☐	☐	☐
22728	$100.00	☐	☐	☐	☐

FLAT PLATE PRINTING
Unwatermarked Perf. 11

#PS15 $5 SEPIA

		TL	TR	L	R	B
22730	$550	☐	☐	‡	‡	☐
22731	$550	☐	☐	‡	‡	☐
22732	$550	☐	☐	‡	‡	☐
22733	$550	☐	☐	‡	‡	☐
22734	$550	☐	☐	‡	‡	☐
22735	$550	☐	☐	‡	‡	☐
22736	$550	☐	☐	‡	‡	☐
22737	$550	☐	☐	‡	‡	☐
22740	$550	☐	☐	‡	‡	☐

1912-13 PARCEL POST ISSUE

Single Line Wmk. Perf. 12
FLAT PRESS

PLATE BLOCK SIZE SHOWN ( )

#Q1 1¢ POST OFFICE CLERK

Imprint IX **20 Plates**

Basic Price **T** (6) $95.00
Basic Price **L, R, B** (6) $90.00

6199 6200 6201 6202 6203
6204 6205 6206 6207 6208
6209 6210 6330 6331 6332
6333 6334 6335 6336 6337

Imprint XIV - ONE **17 Plates**

Basic Price **T, B** (4) $40.00
Basic Price **L, R** (6) $95.00

6199 6200 6204 6206 6330
6331 6332 6333 6334 6335
6336 6337 6377 *6378 *6388
*6393 *6399

#Q2 2¢ CITY CARRIER

Imprint IX **16 Plates**

Basic Price **T** (6) $115.00
Basic Price **L, R, B** (6) $110.00

6177 6178 6179 6180 6181
6182 6183 6184 6195 6196
6197 6198 6338 6339 6340
6341

Imprint XIV - TWO **13 Plates**

Basic Price **T, B** (4) $40.00
Basic Price **L, R** (6) $115.00

6195 6338 6339 6340 6341
6367 6370 6371 6374 6379
6384 *6390 6395

#Q3 3¢ RAILWAY POSTAL CLERK

Imprint XIV - THREE **4 Plates**

Basic Price **T, B** (4) $65.00
Basic Price **L, R** (8) $250.00

6254 6255 6256 6257

#Q4 4¢ RURAL CARRIER

Imprint IX **8 Plates**

Basic Price **T** (6) $750
Basic Price **L, R, B** (6) $700

6169 6170 6171 6172 6345
6346 6347 6350

Imprint XIV - FOUR **9 Plates**

Basic Price **T, B** (4) $325
Basic Price **L, R** (6) $900

6345 6346 6347 6350 6359
6360 6361 *6365 *6392

#Q5 5¢ MAIL TRAIN

Imprint IX **13 Plates**

Basic Price **T** (6) $775
Basic Price **L, R, B** (6) $725

6211 6212 6213 6214 6215
6216 6217 6218 6219 6220
6221 6222 6245

Imprint XIV - FIVE **12 Plates**

Basic Price **T, B** (4) $300
Basic Price **L, R** (6) $900

6217 6220 6221 6222 6245
6405 6407 6411 6417 6420
*6433 *6441

#Q6 10¢ STEAMSHIP

Imprint IX **8 Plates**

Basic Price **T** (6) $1,000
Basic Price **L, R, B** (6) $950

6161 6162 6163 6164 6165
6167 6168 6266

Imprint XIV - TEN **8 Plates**

Basic Price **T, B** (4) $350
Basic Price **L, R** (6) $1,250

6161 6162 6163 6164 6165
6167 6168 6266

#Q7 15¢ AUTOMOBILE

Imprint IX **4 Plates**

Basic Price **T** (6) $2,000
Basic Price **L, R, B** (6) $1,900

6258 6259 6260 6261

Imprint XIV - FIFTEEN **4 Plates**

Basic Price **T, B** (4) $550
Basic Price **L, R** (8) $2,250

6258 6259 6260 6261

#Q8 20¢ AEROPLANE

Imprint IX **4 Plates**

Basic Price **T** (6) $4,750
Basic Price **L, R** (6) $4,500

6191 6192 6193 6194

Imprint XIV - TWENTY **4 Plates**

Basic Price **T, B** (4) $1,250
Basic Price **L, R** (8) $5,250

6191 6192 6193 6194

1912-13 PARCEL POST ISSUE

#Q9 25¢ MANUFACTURING

Imprint IX **6 Plates**

Basic Price **T** (6) $2,250
Basic Price **L, R, B** (6) $2,000

6173 6174 6175 6176 *6186
*6189

Imprint XIV - TWENTY-FIVE **6 Plates**

Basic Price **T, B** (6) $2,500
Basic Price **L, R** (8) $2,750

6173 6174 6175 6176 *6186
*6189

#Q10 50¢ DAIRYING

Imprint XIV - FIFTY **4 Plates**

Basic Price **T, B** (4) $2,000
Basic Price **L, R** (6) $12,000

6423 6424 6427 6428

#Q11 75¢ HARVESTING

Imprint IX **4 Plates**

Basic Price **T** (6) —
Basic Price **L, R, B** (6) —

6287 6288 6296 6299

Imprint XIV - SEVENTY-FIVE **4 Plates**

Basic Price **T, B** (6) —
Basic Price **L, R** (8) —

6287 6288 6296 6299

#Q12 $1 FRUIT GROWING

Imprint IX **1 Plate**

Basic Price **T** (6) —
Basic Price **L, R, B** (6) —

6262

Imprint XIV - ONE DOLLAR **4 Plates**

Basic Price **T, B** (6) —
Basic Price **L, R** (8) —

6262 6263 6264 6265

PARCEL POST POSTAGE DUE ISSUE 1912 ISSUE

FLAT PRESS Block of 6
Single Line Wmk. Perf. 12

#JQ1 1¢ PARCEL POST DUE

Basic Price **T** $600
Basic Price **L, R, B** $575

Imprint IX

6225 6226 6227 6228

#JQ2 2¢ PARCEL POST DUE

Basic Price **T** —
Basic Price L, R, B —

Imprint IX

6241 6242 6243 6244

#JQ3 5¢ PARCEL POST DUE

Basic Price **T** $700
Basic Price **L, R, B** $650

Imprint IX

6229 6230 6231 6232 *6239
*6240

#JQ4 10¢ PARCEL POST DUE

Basic Price **T** —
Basic Price **L, R, B** —

Imprint IX

6250 6251 6252 6253

#JQ5 25¢ PARCEL POST DUE

Basic Price **T** —
Basic Price **L, R, B** —

Imprint IX

6246 6247 6248 6249

1925-29 SPECIAL HANDLING ISSUE

FLAT PRESS Perf. 11
Block of 6

#QE1 10¢ SPECIAL HANDLING

Wet Printed **4 Plates**

		TL	TR	L	R	B
19553	$30.00	☐	☐	☐	☐	☐
19554	$30.00	☐	☐	☐	☐	☐
19555	$30.00	☐	☐	☐	☐	☐
19556	$30.00	☐	☐	☐	☐	☐

Dry Printed **2 Plates**

		TL	TR	L	R	B
19553	$32.50	☐	☐	☐	☐	☐
19554	$32.50	☐	☐	☐	☐	☐

1925-29 SPECIAL HANDLING ISSUE

#QE2 15¢ SPECIAL HANDLING

Wet Printed — 4 Plates

Plate	Price	TL	TR	L	R	B
19557	$40.00	☐	☐	☐	☐	☐
19558	$40.00	☐	☐	☐	☐	☐
19559	$40.00	☐	☐	☐	☐	☐
19560	$40.00	☐	☐	☐	☐	☐

Dry Printed — 4 Plates

Plate	Price	TL	TR	L	R	B
19557	$42.50	☐	☐	☐	☐	☐
19558	$42.50	☐	☐	☐	☐	☐
19559	$42.50	☐	☐	☐	☐	☐
19560	$42.50	☐	☐	☐	☐	☐

#QE3 20¢ SPECIAL HANDLING

Wet Printed — 4 Plates

Plate	Price	TL	TR	L	R	B
19541	$45.00	☐	☐	☐	☐	☐
19542	$45.00	☐	☐	☐	☐	☐
19543	$45.00	☐	☐	☐	☐	☐
19544	$45.00	☐	☐	☐	☐	☐

Dry Printed — 4 Plates

Plate	Price	TL	TR	L	R	B
19541	$50.00	☐	☐	☐	☐	☐
19542	$50.00	☐	☐	☐	☐	☐
19543	$50.00	☐	☐	☐	☐	☐
19544	$50.00	☐	☐	☐	☐	☐

#QE4 25¢ SPECIAL HANDLING

Wet Printed — 8 Plates

Plate	Price	TL	TR	L	R	B
17095	$300.00	☐	☐	☐	☐	☐
17096	$300.00	☐	☐	☐	☐	☐
17097	$300.00	☐	☐	☐	☐	☐
17098	$300.00	☐	☐	☐	☐	☐
17099	$300.00	☐	☐	☐	☐	☐
17101	—	☐	☐	☐	☐	☐
17102	—	☐	☐	☐	☐	☐
17103	$300.00	☐	☐	☐	☐	☐

PROVISIONAL REVENUES

#R153 SMALL I.R.
1¢ FRANKLIN (#279)

		T	L	R	B
440	—	□	†	†	‡
494	—	†	†	†	‡
495	—	□	□	□	‡
534	—	□	□	□	‡
535	—	□	□	□	‡
536	—	□	□	□	‡
538	—	†	‡	†	‡
539	—	□	‡	†	‡
540	—	□	‡	†	‡
541	—	□	‡	†	‡
542	—	□	□	□	‡
543	—	□	□	□	‡
544	—	□	□	□	‡
545	—	□	□	□	‡
546	—	□	□	□	‡
547	—	□	□	□	‡
548	—	□	□	□	‡
549	—	□	□	□	‡

#R154 LARGE I.R.
1¢ FRANKLIN (#279)

		T	L	R	B
439	—	□	□	□	□
440	—	□	□	□	□
493	—	□	□	□	□
494	—	□	□	□	□
495	—	□	□	□	□
496	—	□	□	□	□
526	—	□	□	□	□
527	—	□	□	□	□
528	—	□	□	□	□
534	—	□	□	□	□
535	—	□	□	□	□
536	—	□	□	□	□
537	—	□	□	□	□
538	—	□	□	□	□
539	—	□	□	□	□
540	—	□	□	□	□
541	—	□	□	□	□
542	—	□	□	□	□
543	—	□	□	□	□
544	—	□	□	□	□
545	—	□	□	□	□
546	—	□	□	□	□
547	—	□	□	□	□
548	—	□	□	□	□
549	—	□	□	□	□

#R155 LARGE I.R.
2¢ WASHINGTON (#267)

		T	L	R	B
475	—	□	□	□	□
480	—	□	□	□	□
481	—	□	□	□	□
482	—	□	□	□	□
483	—	□	□	□	□
484	—	□	□	□	□
485	—	□	□	□	□
486	—	□	□	□	□

#R155 LARGE I.R.
2¢ WASHINGTON (#267) Cont.

		T	L	R	B
487	—	□	□	□	□
501	—	□	□	□	□
502	—	□	□	□	□
503	—	□	□	□	□

#R155 LARGE I.R.
2¢ WASHINGTON (#279B)

		T	L	R	B
505	—	□	□	□	□
506	—	□	□	□	□
507	—	□	□	□	□
508	—	□	□	□	□
509	—	□	□	□	□
510	—	□	□	□	□
511	—	□	□	□	□
512	—	□	□	□	□
513	—	□	□	□	□
514	—	□	□	□	□
515	—	□	□	□	□
516	—	□	□	□	□
517	—	□	□	□	□
522	—	□	□	□	□
523	—	□	□	□	□
524	—	□	□	□	□
*525	—	†	†	□	‡
550	—	□	□	□	□
551	—	□	□	□	□
552	—	□	□	□	□
553	—	□	□	□	□
556	—	□	□	□	□
557	—	□	□	□	□
558	—	□	□	□	□
559	—	□	□	□	□
560	—	□	□	□	□
561	—	□	□	□	□
562	—	□	□	□	□
563	—	□	□	□	□

#R159 O/P READING DOWN
$5 NEWSPAPER (#PR121)

		T	L	R	B
137	—	□	□	□	□

#R160 O/P READING UP
$5 NEWSPAPER (#PR121)

		T	L	R	B
137	—	□	□	□	□

The overprints on all stamps in the following listing are INVERTED.

#R154a LARGE I.R.
1¢ FRANKLIN (#279)

		T	L	R	B
495	—	‡	□	‡	□
534	—	‡	□	‡	□
535	—	‡	□	‡	□
536	—	‡	□	‡	□
542	—	□	□	□	□
543	—	‡	□	‡	□
544	—	‡	□	‡	□
545	—	‡	□	‡	□

PROVISIONAL REVENUES

The overprints on all stamps in the following listing are INVERTED.

#R155a LARGE I.R.
2¢ WASHINGTON (#267)

		T	L	R	B
475	—	□	□	□	□
480	—	‡	□	‡	□
481	—	‡	□	‡	□
482	—	‡	□	‡	□
483	—	‡	□	‡	□
501	—	‡	□	‡	□
502	—	‡	□	‡	□
503	—	‡	□	‡	□

#R155a LARGE I.R.
2¢ WASHINGTON (#279B)

505	—	‡	□	‡	□

PROVISIONAL REVENUES
#R155a LARGE I.R. Cont.

508	—	‡	†	‡	□
509	—	‡	□	‡	□
510	—	□	□	□	□
511	—	□	□	□	□
512	—	□	□	□	□
513	—	□	□	□	□
515	—	‡	□	‡	□
516	—	‡	□	‡	□
517	—	‡	□	‡	□
522	—	‡	□	‡	□
523	—	□	□	□	□
524	—	□	□	□	□
551	—	□	□	□	□
552	—	‡	□	‡	□
553	—	‡	□	‡	□
556	—	‡	□	‡	□
557	—	‡	□	‡	□
558	—	‡	□	‡	□
559	—	‡	□	‡	□

HUNTING PERMIT STAMPS

Although plates of RW 1 thru RW 25 and RW 31 are printed on flat plate presses, we will designate the positions in the same manner as is customary for the rotary press products. The prices are for plate blocks of six with the SIDE margin intact.

BLOCKS OF SIX WITHOUT SIDE MARGIN ARE VALUED AT 80% OF PRICE SHOWN

The placement of the letter F is not necessarily in the UR plate block. The exceptions are RW 3, RW 5 & RW 11. Starting with RW 13 the use of the letter F was discontinued.

UL (upper left)

UR (upper right)

LL (lower left)

LL (lower right)

1934 ISSUE

#RW 1 $1 MALLARDS

4 Plates		UL	UR	LL	LR
129199	$5,750	☐	☐	☐	☐
129200	$5,750	☐	☐	☐	☐
129201	$5,750	☐	☐	☐	☐
129202	$5,750	☐	☐	☐	☐

1935 ISSUE

#RW 2 $1 CANVASBACKS

4 Plates		UL	UR	LL	LR
131980	$7,000	☐	☐	☐	☐
131981	$7,000	☐	☐	☐	☐
131982	$7,000	☐	☐	☐	☐
131983	$7,000	☐	☐	☐	☐

1936 ISSUE

#RW 3 $1 CANADA GEESE

2 Plates		UL	UR	LL	LR
134317	$3,000	☐	☐	☐	☐
134318	$3,000	☐	☐	☐	☐

The "F" appears on the upper left pane of these plates.

1937 ISSUE

#RW 4 $1 SCAUP DUCKS

1 Plate		UL	UR	LL	LR
136267	$1,700	☐	☐	☐	☐

1938 ISSUE

#RW 5 $1 PINTAILS

1 Plate		UL	UR	LL	LR
138602	$1,700	☐	☐	☐	☐

The "F" appears on the upper left pane of these plates.

1939 ISSUE

#RW 6 $1 GREEN-WINGED TEALS

1 Plate		UL	UR	LL	LR
141428	$1,100	☐	☐	☐	☐

1940 ISSUE

#RW 7 $1 BLACK MALLARDS

2 Plates		UL	UR	LL	LR
143743	$1,000	☐	☐	☐	☐
143776	$1,000	☐	☐	☐	☐

HUNTING PERMIT STAMPS

1941 ISSUE

#RW 8 $1 RUDDY DUCKS

2 Plates		UL	UR	LL	LR
146271	$900	☐	☐	☐	☐
146282	$900	☐	☐	☐	☐

1942 ISSUE

#RW 9 $1 BALDPATES

2 Plates		UL	UR	LL	LR
149599	$900	☐	☐	☐	☐
149600	$900	☐	☐	☐	☐

1943 ISSUE

#RW 10 $1 WOOD DUCKS

2 Plates		UL	UR	LL	LR
152826	$400	☐	☐	☐	☐
152827	$400	☐	☐	☐	☐

1944 ISSUE

#RW 11 $1 WHITE-FRONTED GEESE

2 Plates		UL	UR	LL	LR
155590	$350	☐	☐	☐	☐
155603	$350	☐	☐	☐	☐

The letter F is separated from the plate number and appears in the selvedge of the stamp to the left of the plate number in the UR position.

1945 ISSUE

#RW 12 $1 SHOVELLER DUCKS

2 Plates		UL	UR	LL	LR
157248	$225	☐	☐	☐	☐
157249	$225	☐	☐	☐	☐

1946 ISSUE

#RW 13 $1 REDHEAD DUCKS

4 Plates		UL	UR	LL	LR
158448	$200	☐	☐	☐	☐
158449	$200	☐	☐	☐	☐
158456	$200	☐	☐	☐	☐
158457	$200	☐	☐	☐	☐

Inscription printed on back by Offset. The plate number of this offset plate appears in only one place. This is in the sheet margin of stamp #24 in the upper right pane. The Offset plate number is 47510.

1947 ISSUE

#RW 14 $1 SNOW GEESE

4 Plates		UL	UR	LL	LR
159461	$200	☐	☐	☐	☐
159462	$200	☐	☐	☐	☐
159463	$200	☐	☐	☐	☐
159464	$200	☐	☐	☐	☐

The back plate number is 47510.

1948 ISSUE

#RW 15 $1 BUFFLEHEADS

4 Plates		UL	UR	LL	LR
160099	$250	☐	☐	☐	☐
160100	$250	☐	☐	☐	☐
160101	$250	☐	☐	☐	☐
160102	$250	☐	☐	☐	☐

The back plate number is 47510.

1949 ISSUE

#RW 16 $1 GOLDENEYE DUCKS

4 Plates		UL	UR	LL	LR
160790	$250	☐	☐	☐	☐
160791	$250	☐	☐	☐	☐
160792	$250	☐	☐	☐	☐
160793	$250	☐	☐	☐	☐

The back plate number is 47510.

1950 ISSUE

#RW 17 $2 TRUMPETER SWANS

4 Plates		UL	UR	LL	LR
161533	$350	☐	☐	☐	☐
161534	$350	☐	☐	☐	☐
161535	$350	☐	☐	☐	☐
161536	$350	☐	☐	☐	☐

The back plate number is 47510.

1951 ISSUE

#RW 18 $2 GADWALL DUCKS

4 Plates		UL	UR	LL	LR
162125	$350	☐	☐	☐	☐
162126	$350	☐	☐	☐	☐
162127	$350	☐	☐	☐	☐
162128	$350	☐	☐	☐	☐

Starting with this issue the Offset plate number of the inscription on the back has been trimmed off and does NOT appear on subsequent issues.

1952 ISSUE

#RW 19 $2 HARLEQUIN DUCKS

4 Plates		UL	UR	LL	LR
162602	$350	☐	☐	☐	☐
162603	$350	☐	☐	☐	☐
162604	$350	☐	☐	☐	☐
162605	$350	☐	☐	☐	☐

HUNTING PERMIT STAMPS

FLAT PRESS **Plate Blocks of 6**
PERF. 11

1953 ISSUE

#RW 20 $2 BLUE-WINGED TEALS

4 Plates		UL	UR	LL	LR
163622	$350	☐	☐	☐	☐
163623	$350	☐	☐	☐	☐
163624	$350	☐	☐	☐	☐
163625	$350	☐	☐	☐	☐

1954 ISSUE

#RW 21 $2 RING-NECKED DUCKS

4 Plates		UL	UR	LL	LR
164744	$350	☐	☐	☐	☐
164745	$350	☐	☐	☐	☐
164746	$350	☐	☐	☐	☐
164747	$350	☐	☐	☐	☐

1955 ISSUE

#RW 22 $2 BLUE GEESE

4 Plates		UL	UR	LL	LR
165282	$350	☐	☐	☐	☐
165283	$350	☐	☐	☐	☐
165284	$350	☐	☐	☐	☐
165285	$350	☐	☐	☐	☐

1956 ISSUE

#RW 23 $2 MERGANSERS

4 Plates		UL	UR	LL	LR
165826	$350	☐	☐	☐	☐
165827	$350	☐	☐	☐	☐
165829	$350	☐	☐	☐	☐
165860	$350	☐	☐	☐	☐

1957 ISSUE

#RW 24 $2 EIDERS

4 Plates		UL	UR	LL	LR
166256	$350	☐	☐	☐	☐
166257	$350	☐	☐	☐	☐
166258	$350	☐	☐	☐	☐
166259	$350	☐	☐	☐	☐

1958 ISSUE

#RW 25 $2 CANADA GEESE

4 Plates		UL	UR	LL	LR
166753	$350	☐	☐	☐	☐
166754	$350	☐	☐	☐	☐
166755	$350	☐	☐	☐	☐
166756	$350	☐	☐	☐	☐

ROTARY PRESS **Plate Blocks of 4**
PERF. 11

1959 ISSUE

#RW 26 $3 LABRADOR RETRIEVER

2 Plates		UL	UR	LL	LR
167109	$300	☐	☐	☐	☐
167120	$300	☐	☐	☐	☐

1960 ISSUE

#RW 27 $3 REDHEAD DUCKS

2 Plates		UL	UR	LL	LR
167498	$300	☐	☐	☐	☐
167503	$300	☐	☐	☐	☐

1961 ISSUE

#RW 28 $3 MALLARDS

2 Plates		UL	UR	LL	LR
167768	$300	☐	☐	☐	☐
167772	$300	☐	☐	☐	☐

1962 ISSUE

#RW 29 $3 PINTAILS

1 Plate		UL	UR	LL	LR
168073	$350	☐	☐	☐	☐

1963 ISSUE

#RW 30 $3 BRANTS

2 Plates		UL	UR	LL	LR
168269	$350	☐	☐	☐	☐
168273	$350	☐	☐	☐	☐

1964 ISSUE

FLAT PRESS **Plate Blocks of 6**

#RW 31 $3 NENE GEESE

2 Plates		UL	UR	LL	LR
168629	$2,250	☐	☐	☐	☐
168630	$2,250	☐	☐	☐	☐

1965 ISSUE

ROTARY PRESS **Plate Blocks of 4**

#RW 32 $3 CANVASBACKS

2 Plates		UL	UR	LL	LR
168790	$300	☐	☐	☐	☐
168791	$300	☐	☐	☐	☐

HUNTING PERMIT STAMPS

ROTARY PRESS **Plate Blocks of 4**

1966 ISSUE

#RW 33 $3 WHISTLING SWANS

2 Plates		UL	UR	LL	LR
169058	$300	☐	☐	☐	☐
169063	$300	☐	☐	☐	☐

1967 ISSUE

#RW 34 $3 OLD SQUAW DUCKS

2 Plates		UL	UR	LL	LR
169457	$300	☐	☐	☐	☐
169487	$300	☐	☐	☐	☐

1968 ISSUE

#RW 35 $3 HOODED MERGANSERS

2 Plates		UL	UR	LL	LR
170436	$175	☐	☐	☐	☐
170443	$175	☐	☐	☐	☐

1969 ISSUE

#RW 36 $3 WHITE-WINGED SCOTERS

2 Plates		UL	UR	LL	LR
170765	$175	☐	☐	☐	☐
170767	$175	☐	☐	☐	☐

1970 ISSUE

#RW 37 $3 ROSS GEESE

2 Plates		UL	UR	LL	LR
171165	$150	☐	☐	☐	☐
171169	$150	☐	☐	☐	☐

1971 ISSUE

#RW 38 $3 CINNAMON TEALS

2 Plates		UL	UR	LL	LR
171586	$125	☐	☐	☐	☐
171587	$125	☐	☐	☐	☐

1972 ISSUE

#RW 39 $5 EMPEROR GEESE

2 Plates		UL	UR	LL	LR
171862	$100	☐	☐	☐	☐
171864	$100	☐	☐	☐	☐

1973 ISSUE

#RW 40 $5 STELLER'S EIDERS

2 Plates		UL	UR	LL	LR
172101	$85	☐	☐	☐	☐
172102	$85	☐	☐	☐	☐

ROTARY PRESS **Plate Blocks of 4**

1974 ISSUE

#RW 41 $5 WOOD DUCKS

2 Plates		UL	UR	LL	LR
172500	$50.00	☐	☐	☐	☐
172505	$50.00	☐	☐	☐	☐

1975 ISSUE

#RW 42 $5 CANVASBACK DECOY

2 Plates		UL	UR	LL	LR
172775	$50.00	☐	☐	☐	☐
172777	$50.00	☐	☐	☐	☐

1976 ISSUE

#RW 43 $5 CANADA GEESE

2 Plates		UL	UR	LL	LR
173029	$45.00	☐	☐	☐	☐
173030	$45.00	☐	☐	☐	☐

1977 ISSUE

#RW 44 $5 ROSS GEESE

2 Plates		UL	UR	LL	LR
173205	$45.00	☐	☐	☐	☐
173206	$45.00	☐	☐	☐	☐

1978 ISSUE

#RW 45 $5 HOODED MERGANSER

2 Plates		UL	UR	LL	LR
173331	$45.00	☐	☐	☐	☐
173333	$45.00	☐	☐	☐	☐

1979 ISSUE

#RW 46 $7.50 GREEN-WINGED TEAL

2 Plates		UL	UR	LL	LR
173422	$60.00	☐	☐	☐	☐
173423	$60.00	☐	☐	☐	☐

1980 ISSUE

#RW 47 $7.50 MALLARDS

2 Plates		UL	UR	LL	LR
173492	$60.00	☐	☐	☐	☐
173493	$60.00	☐	☐	☐	☐

1981 ISSUE

#RW 48 $7.50 RUDDY DUCKS

2 Plates		UL	UR	LL	LR
173572	$60.00	☐	☐	☐	☐
173573	$60.00	☐	☐	☐	☐

HUNTING PERMIT STAMPS

1982 ISSUE

#RW 49 $7.50 CANVAS BACKS

2 Plates

		UL	UR	LL	LR
173669	$60.00	☐	☐	☐	☐
173672	$60.00	☐	☐	☐	☐

1983 ISSUE

#RW 50 $7.50 PINTAILS

2 Plates

		UL	UR	LL	LR
173765	$60.00	☐	☐	☐	☐
173767	$60.00	☐	☐	☐	☐

1984 ISSUE

#RW 51 $7.50 WIGEONS

2 Plates

		UL	UR	LL	LR
173871	$47.50	☐	☐	☐	☐
173872	$47.50	☐	☐	☐	☐

1985 ISSUE

#RW 52 $7.50 CINNAMON TEAL

2 Plates

		UL	UR	LL	LR
174343	$47.50	☐	☐	☐	☐
174350	$47.50	☐	☐	☐	☐

1986 ISSUE

#RW 53 $7.50 FULVOUS WHISTLING

2 Plates

		UL	UR	LL	LR
176844	$47.50	☐	☐	☐	☐
176845	$47.50	☐	☐	☐	☐

1987 ISSUE

#RW 54 $10.00 RED HEAD

1 Plate

		UL	UR	LL	LR
178171	$57.50	☐	☐	☐	☐

1988 ISSUE

#RW 55 $10.00 SNOW GOOSE

1 Plate

		UL	UR	LL	LR
180059	$57.50	☐	☐	☐	☐

1989 ISSUE

#RW 56 $12.50 LESSER SCAUPS

1 Plate

		UL	UR	LL	LR
182531	$67.50	☐	☐	☐	☐

ADDITIONAL ISSUES

APPENDIX A

Prior to the issuance of the Great American Series of regular issues, the current stamps were printed on different papers and were gummed with changed formulations. Four general catagories are as follows:

A. Shiny gum. White paper.
B. Shiny gum. Tinted paper.
C. Dull gum. Tinted paper.
D. Dull gum. White paper.

The following is a list of the plate numbers that exist with more than one of the above types.

#1393 6¢ EISENHOWER

A. Shiny gum. White paper.

	UL	UR	LL	LR
31947	☐	☐	☐	☐
31948	☐	☐	☐	☐
32007	☐	☐	☐	☐
32008	☐	☐	☐	☐

D. Dull gum. White paper.

	UL	UR	LL	LR
31947	☐	☐	☐	☐
31948	☐	☐	☐	☐
32007	☐	☐	☐	☐
32008	☐	☐	☐	☐

#1289 20¢ MARSHALL

A. Shiny gum. White paper.

	UL	UR	LL	LR
38938	☐	☐	☐	☐
38939	☐	☐	☐	☐

D. Dull gum. White paper

	UL	UR	LL	LR
38938	☐	☐	☐	☐
38939	☐	☐	☐	☐

#1290 25¢ DOUGLASS

A. Shiny gum. White paper.

	UL	UR	LL	LR
37604	☐	☐	☐	☐
37605	☐	☐	☐	☐

D. Dull gum. White paper.

	UL	UR	LL	LR
37604	☐	☐	☐	☐
37605	☐	☐	☐	☐

#1292 40¢ PAINE

A. Shiny gum. White paper

	UL	UR	LL	LR
29537	☐	☐	☐	☐
34074	☐	☐	☐	☐
37044	☐	☐	☐	☐
37045	☐	☐	☐	☐

D. Dull gum. White paper.

	UL	UR	LL	LR
29537	☐	☐	☐	☐
34074	☐	☐	☐	☐
37044	☐	☐	☐	☐
37045	☐	☐	☐	☐

#1581 1¢ AMERICANA

B. Shiny gum. Tinted paper.

	UL	UR	LL	LR
38252	☐	☐	☐	☐
38256	☐	☐	☐	☐
38257	☐	☐	☐	☐
38258	☐	☐	☐	☐

#1581 1¢ AMERICANA Continued

C. Dull gum. Tinted paper.

	UL	UR	LL	LR
38252	☐	☐	☐	☐
38256	☐	☐	☐	☐
38257	☐	☐	☐	☐
38258	☐	☐	☐	☐

D. Dull gum. White paper.

	UL	UR	LL	LR
38257	☐	☐	☐	☐
38258	☐	☐	☐	☐

#1582 2¢ AMERICANA

B. Shiny gum. Tinted paper.

	UL	UR	LL	LR
38281	☐	☐	☐	☐
38287	☐	☐	☐	☐
38601	☐	☐	☐	☐
38602	☐	☐	☐	☐
38603	☐	☐	☐	☐
38604	☐	☐	☐	☐
38606	☐	☐	☐	☐

C. Dull gum. Tinted paper.

	UL	UR	LL	LR
38281	☐	☐	☐	☐
38287	☐	☐	☐	☐
38601	☐	☐	☐	☐
38602	☐	☐	☐	☐
38603	☐	☐	☐	☐
38604	☐	☐	☐	☐
38606	☐	☐	☐	☐

D. Dull gum. White paper.

	UL	UR	LL	LR
38281	☐	☐	☐	☐
38287	☐	☐	☐	☐
38601	☐	☐	☐	☐
38602	☐	☐	☐	☐
38603	☐	☐	☐	☐
38604	☐	☐	☐	☐
38606	☐	☐	☐	☐

#1584 3¢ AMERICANA

B. Shiny gum. Tinted paper

	UL	UR	LL	LR
38277	☐	☐	☐	☐
38278	☐	☐	☐	☐

C. Dull gum. Tinted paper.

	UL	UR	LL	LR
38277	☐	☐	☐	☐
38278	☐	☐	☐	☐

#1591 9¢ AMERICANA

B. Shiny gum. Tinted paper.

	UL	UR	LL	LR
38348	☐	☐	☐	☐
38349	☐	☐	☐	☐

APPENDIX A Continued

#1591 9¢ AMERICANA Continued

C. Dull gum. Tinted paper.

	UL	UR	LL	LR
38348	☐	☐	☐	☐
38349	☐	☐	☐	☐

#1592 10¢ AMERICANA

B. Shiny gum. Tinted paper.

	UL	UR	LL	LR
37248	☐	☐	☐	☐
37250	☐	☐	☐	☐
37251	☐	☐	☐	☐
37641	☐	☐	☐	☐

C. Dull gum. Tinted paper.

	UL	UR	LL	LR
37248	☐	☐	☐	☐
37250	☐	☐	☐	☐
37251	☐	☐	☐	☐
37641	☐	☐	☐	☐

#1604 28¢ AMERICANA

B. Shiny gum. Tinted paper.

	UL	UR	LL	LR
38772	☐	☐	☐	☐
38778	☐	☐	☐	☐

C. Dull gum. Tinted paper.

	UL	UR	LL	LR
38772	☐	☐	☐	☐
38778	☐	☐	☐	☐

#1605 29¢ AMERICANA

B. Shiny gum. Tinted paper.

	UL	UR	LL	LR
38485	☐	☐	☐	☐
38486	☐	☐	☐	☐

C. Dull gum. Tinted paper.

	UL	UR	LL	LR
38485	☐	☐	☐	☐
38486	☐	☐	☐	☐

#J90 2¢ POSTAGE DUE

A. Shiny gum. White paper

	UL	UR	LL	LR
34283	☐	☐	☐	☐

B. Shiny gum. Tinted paper.

	UL	UR	LL	LR
34283	☐	☐	☐	☐

#J91 3¢ POSTAGE DUE

A. Shiny gum. White paper.

	UL	UR	LL	LR
34283	☐	☐	☐	☐

B. Shiny gum. Tinted paper.

	UL	UR	LL	LR
34283	☐	☐	☐	☐

#J93 5¢ POSTAGE DUE

A. Shiny gum. White paper.

	UL	UR	LL	LR
34283	☐	☐	☐	☐
37876	☐	☐	☐	☐
37877	☐	☐	☐	☐

B. Shiny gum. Tinted paper.

	UL	UR	LL	LR
34283	☐	☐	☐	☐

APPENDIX A Continued

#J93 5¢ POSTAGE DUE Cont.

C. Dull gum. Tinted paper.

	UL	UR	LL	LR
37876	☐	☐	☐	☐
37877	☐	☐	☐	☐

#J96 8¢ POSTAGE DUE

A. Shiny gum. White paper.

	UL	UR	LL	LR
34283	☐	☐	☐	☐

B. Shiny gum. Tinted paper.

	UL	UR	LL	LR
34283	☐	☐	☐	☐

#J97 10¢ POSTAGE DUE

A. Shiny gum. White paper.

	UL	UR	LL	LR
34283	☐	☐	☐	☐
37876	☐	☐	☐	☐
37877	☐	☐	☐	☐

B. Shiny gum. Tinted paper.

	UL	UR	LL	LR
34283	☐	☐	☐	☐
37876	☐	☐	☐	☐
37877	☐	☐	☐	☐

C. Dull gum. Tinted paper.

	UL	UR	LL	LR
37876	☐	☐	☐	☐
37877	☐	☐	☐	☐

#J98 30¢ POSTAGE DUE

A. Shiny gum. White paper.

	UL	UR	LL	LR
37876	☐	☐	☐	☐
37877	☐	☐	☐	☐

C. Dull gum. Tinted paper.

	UL	UR	LL	LR
37876	☐	☐	☐	☐
37877	☐	☐	☐	☐

#J99 50¢ POSTAGE DUE

A. Shiny gum. White paper.

	UL	UR	LL	LR
34283	☐	☐	☐	☐

B. Shiny gum. Tinted paper.

	UL	UR	LL	LR
34283	☐	☐	☐	☐

#J100 $1 POSTAGE DUE

A. Shiny gum. White paper

	UL	UR	LL	LR
34283	☐	☐	☐	☐
37876	☐	☐	☐	☐
37877	☐	☐	☐	☐

B. Shiny gum. Tinted paper.

	UL	UR	LL	LR
34283	☐	☐	☐	☐
37876	☐	☐	☐	☐
37877	☐	☐	☐	☐

#J101 $5 POSTAGE DUE

A. Shiny gum. White paper.

	UL	UR	LL	LR
34283	☐	☐	☐	☐

B. Shiny gum. Tinted paper.

	UL	UR	LL	LR
34283	☐	☐	☐	☐

APPENDIX B

During the period when the private vending machine operators were purchasing imperforate sheets of stamps from the Post Office Department for use in their perforating and coiling machines, the use of the "Star plates" gave birth to two collectible varieties of panes of stamps. The configuration of the star plate created a problem for the vending machine operators. The star plate was created in an attempt to solve the problem of uneven shrinkage of wetted stamp paper. The 400 subject star plate consisted of twenty horizontal rows of stamps each of twenty vertical rows. The vertical spacing was constant but the horizontal spacing consisted of six outside rows spaced at 3mm; eight internal rows spaced at 2mm and six outside rows spaced at 3mm. Since the non-uniform spacing caused problems in the perforating and coiling operation, the vending machine operators persuaded the Post Office Department to sell them imperforate sheets consisting of the 8 rows that were spaced 2mm apart as a pane of 160 stamps. Since this left a remainder on hand of two panes of 120 stamps each, the decision was made to perforate these remainders 12 x 12 and to sell panes of sixty subjects at the post office instead of the normal 100 subjects. This action created the panes of sixty of Scott #374.

The collectible positions of Scott #374 are:

a) UL pane consisting of sixty subjects with a full imprint and plate number in the left margin and imprint only over the two top right stamps.

b) UR pane consisting of sixty subjects with a full imprint and plate number in the right hand margin and a full imprint and plate number in the top margin with a straight edge at left side of imprint.

c) LL pane consisting of sixty subjects with a full imprint and plate number in the left margin and imprint only under the two bottom right stamps.

d) LR pane consisting of sixty subjects with a full imprint and plate number in the right margin and a full imprint and plate number in the bottom margin with a straight edge at left side of imprint.

e) A plate block of six subjects with full imprint and plate number in top margin with a *full* margin straight edge at left side. This is a UR plate block.

f) A full plate block of six subjects with full imprint and plate number in bottom margin with a *full* margin straight edge at left side. This is a LR plate block.

There are no UL top or LL bottom plate blocks. The majority of reported panes are LR. The side position plate blocks cannot be distinguished from the plate blocks from the one hundred subject sheets.

Before the vending machine operators had purchased all of the stock of the 160 subject imperforates, another change in plate configuration was made which were the "A" plates that had a constant horizontal spacing of 2 3/4 mm. Since this spacing was satisfactory, the operators ceased purchasing the imperforate 160 subject panes. As a direct result, the Post Office Department sold the remainders of the 160 subject panes at the Philatelic Agency in Washington, DC. This action created the panes of 160 subjects of Scott #383.

The collectible position of Scott #383 is a pane of 160 stamps with a plate number *ONLY* over the top left stamp and a plate number ONLY under the bottom left stamp.

The plate numbers that have been reported for the above variations are:

5603	5604	5605	5607	5620
5622	5639	5640	5643	5644
5647	5651	5672	5673	

APPENDIX C

The Bureau of Engraving and Printing currently prints United States postage stamps on high speed sheet-fed and web-fed rotary presses. Multi-colored stamps are printed in a variety of ways such as line intaglio, combination line intaglio and offset, combination line intaglio and gravure, and gravure. In earlier days any of the combination type of printing required the use of more than one type of press for the production of the stamps.

The initial line-intaglio rotary presses in use at the BEP were the Stickney presses. These were designed by a Bureau employee and were in use from 1914 until 1962.

The next line intaglio rotary press was developed by the Huck Company. The first stamp printed was the International Red Cross commemorative (Scott #1002). The cross was added by a letterpress attachment.

Refinements were made to this design and new presses were supplied by Cottrell. The first stamp printed on these presses was the 3¢ Statue of Liberty of 1954 (Scott #1035). The first commemorative stamp printed was the Wheatland issue of 1956 (Scott #1081.) The Huck prototype and the Cottrells printed the bulk of the regular issues, including sheets and coils plus most of the single color commemoratives. The last Cottrell press was retired on Nov. 20, 1985.

New presses were being developed that were capable of printing in more than one color from a single intaglio plate. The sheet fed Giori press printed up to three colors from a single plate. It was first used to print the 1957 4¢ Flag Stamp (Scott #1094). Today, there are eight fourth generation descendants of this press designated I-8's used mostly for printing currency, but one is on call for stamp work. The I-8 is the only sheet-fed press in use currently for stamp production. The other presses are all web-fed.

A short-lived Huck nine color press designed to Bureau specifications was intended to be the most advanced stamp press in the world. It printed stamps from small plates attached to three separate printing cylinders with a capability of printing nine colors (three from each cylinder). The first stamp printed by this press was the 1968 Christmas issue (Scott #1363). The press produced an extremely high rate of spoilage. Since the press could only be used economically for very long press runs, the only stamps printed on it were the 1968 Christmas, the 1969 Christmas (Scott #1384), and the sheet and coil versions of the 6¢ (Scott #1338D and Scott #1338A), 8¢ (Scott #1338F and Scott #1338G), 10¢ (Scott #1509 and 1519) and 13¢ (Scott #1622 and 1625) Flag stamps of the regular issues. The press was junked in 1978.

The Andreotti gravure press was acquired in 1969 to print aerogrammes. It solved the problem of producing multi-colored stamps. Starting with the Missouri Statehood (Scott #1426) stamp of 1970, it has printed the major share of all commemorative stamps to date. This press uses one plate per color and has the capability of printing seven colors (normally six colors and the tagging compound).

The combination gravure/intaglio press designated as the A press was obtained in 1973. The first stamp produced was the 13¢ Christmas (Scott #1703). The early production from this press used only the gravure section by itself or the intaglio section by itself. The first combined use of the gravure and intaglio sections was the Touro Synagogue issue of 1982 (Scott #2017). The press can print five gravure colors (one from each gravure plate) plus three intaglio colors (from one intaglio plate). The press with an Andreotti gravure section was manufactured by Giori.

The three color intaglio press designated as the B press was obtained in 1973 to print multi-color coil and booklet stamps. The initial three color production was the $1.20 booklet pane (Scott #1892-93). This press produces coil stamps 18 rows across the web. The press has picked up the single color coil production that was formerly printed on the Cottrells.

The three color intaglio press designated as the C press was obtained in 1982. The press is faster than the B press when used for coil or booklet production. The press produces coil stamps 20 rows across the web. In addition the press has a "Cottrell" format and is capable of printing single or multi-color sheet stamps in either regular issue or commemorative issue format. The first production was the 20¢ Flag booklet (Scott #1896a). The press was manufactured by Goebel.

The combination offset/intaglio press designated as the D press was obtained in 1984. The press has the capability of printing six offset colors (one from each offset plate) plus three intaglio colors from one intaglio plate. The first stamp produced was the Smokey Bear commemorative of 1984 (Scott #2096). Since no acceptance run had been made prior to the production of the stamp, the rate of spoilage was extremely high. Since then the press has performed as expected. The press was manufactured by Goebel.

As of December 1985, there are five web-fed presses; the Andreotti gravure, the Giori A & B and the Goebel C & D, used for the production of our postage stamps. In an emergency one of the currency presses can be used for stamp production.

A change in production techniques using the A press has resulted in the capability of printing sheet stamps in the old familiar Cottrell press format of a plate number in each of the four corners instead of the product with the roving plate numbers.

APPENDIX D
ROTARY PRESS COIL PLATE NUMBERS

The stamps produced by the Stickney rotary presses of the 1911 Series of postage stamps for use as coil stamps have now been listed in the front section of this catalog. As an aid in determining the possible plate number to be deciphered from the partial plate number on the stamp, we will list all of the known plate numbers that were sent to press to produce the rotary press coils. The Scott Catalog numbers of 448, 449, 450, 452, 453, 454, 455, 456, 457, 458, 459, 486, 487, 488, 489, 490, 491, 492, 493, 494, 495, 496 and 497 were produced from these plates. Due to the procedure used to manufacture these coil stamps in rolls of 500, large quantities of printed paper that was perforated 10 in one direction were left over. Rather than destroy this surplus of printed paper, a decision was made to perforate at right angles to the existing perforations and produce sheets of 170 subjects which could be sold at the postoffices. A complete description may be found in The United States Specialist. This product is known as the coil waste stamps and is listed under Scott Catalog numbers 538, 539, 540, 541, 545 and 546. All of the coil waste issues are on unwatermarked paper so not all of the early plate numbers were used. Almost all of the known rotary press coil plate numbers from the 170 subject plates are from the coil waste issues. The extremely few known plate numbers on the coils produced from the 150 and 170 subject plates are partial numbers existing on off-centered stamps. To furnish the reader with a means for checking the partial plate numbers, we will list all of the plates used for printing. We will list the different marginal inscriptions that exist and then will break down the listing by the face value and the arrangement. We will not list the plates that were known not to be used and those that were not completed.

The changes in the listing are the result of the recent examination of all proof sheets by Dr. Wallace Cleland.

The following is a description of the marginal markings of the various arrangements that were used on the finished plates:

ARRANGEMENT #1 used on 150 subject plates has one plate number located to the left of stamps **#71.**

ARRANGEMENT #2 used on 170 subject plates has one plate number located above stamp **#9.**

ARRANGEMENT #3 used on 170 subject plates has a plate number located above stamp **#9** plus the symbol **S20** above stamp **#10.**

ARRANGEMENT #4 used on 170 subject plates has a plate number located above stamp **#9** plus the symbol **S40** above stamp **#10.**

ARRANGEMENT #5 used on 170 subject plates has a plate number located above stamp **#9** plus the symbol **S30** above stamp **#10.**

ARRANGEMENT #6 used on 150 subject plates has the symbol **S30** located to the left of stamp **#61** and the plate number to the left of stamp **#71.**

ARRANGEMENT #7 used on 150 subject plates has the symbol **S30** located to the left of stamp **#61,** the plate number to the left of stamp **#71** and a star to the left of stamp **#141.**

ARRANGEMENT #7a used on 150 subject plates has the symbol **S30** located to the left of stamp **#51,** the plate number to the left of stamp **#61** and a star to the left of stamp **#141.**

ARRANGEMENT #8 used on 170 subject plates has a star located above stamp **#1** and the plate number above stamp **#9.**

ARRANGEMENT #9 used on 150 subject plates has the plate number located to the left of stamp **#71** and a star to the left of stamp **#141.**

ARRANGEMENT #10 used on 170 subject plates has a star located above stamp **#1,** the plate number above stamp **#9** and the symbol **S30** above stamp **#10.**

ARRANGEMENT #11 used on 170 subject plates has both a star and a plate number located above stamp **#1.**

ARRANGEMENT #12 used on 150 subject plates has both a star and a plate number located to the left of stamp **#141.**

The 170 subject plates print sideways coils and the 150 subject plates print endwise coils.

1¢ Rotary Press Coil Plates

ARRANGEMENT #2 — **7 Plates**

170 Subject

7170	7171	7182	7183	7506
7507	7508			

ARRANGEMENT #5 — **15 Plates**

170 Subject

7552	7553	7558	7559	7565
7566	7567	7619	7626	7627
7690	7691	7744	7745	7763

ARRANGEMENT #8 — **12 Plates**

170 Subject

13445	13446	13447	13448	13491
13492	13575	13576	13611	13612
13615	13616			

ARRANGEMENT #10 — **74 Plates**

170 Subject

7766	7767	7957	7958	7963
7964	7978	7979	8081	8082
8336	8337	8339	8340	9099
9111	9112	9113	9114	9141

APPENDIX D Continued

1¢ Rotary Press Coil Plates

ARRANGEMENT #10 Continued

9142	9151	9152	9450	9451
9452	9453	9463	9464	9467
9468	10087	10088	10089	10090
10103	10104	10184	10185	10202
10203	10345	10346	10347	10348
10349	10350	10361	10640	10641
10642	10643	10686	10687	10688
10689	10690	10691	10692	10693
10694	10695	11740	11741	11742
11743	11764	11765	11766	11767
13312	13313	13314	13315	

ARRANGEMENT #11 — 28 Plates

170 Subject

13810	13811	13812	13813	13820
13821	13826	13827	13828	13829
13856	13857	13872	13873	13896
13897	13906	13907	13910	13911
13930	13931	13942	13943	13968
13969	13976	14104		

ARRANGEMENT #1 — 2 Plates

150 Subject

7433	7434

ARRANGEMENT #7 — 9 Plates

150 Subject

7563	7564	8079	8080	10081
10408	10409	10410	10411	

ARRANGEMENT #7a — 1 Plate

150 Subject

10082

ARRANGEMENT #12 — 2 Plates

150 Subject

13928	13929

2¢ Rotary Press Coil Plates

ARRANGEMENT #2 — 14 Plates

Type I ***170 Subject***

6856	6857	7174	7175	7230
7231	7270	7271	7408	7409
7417	7418	7422	7423	

ARRANGEMENT #2 — 12 Plates

Type II ***170 Subject***

7425	7426	7427	7428	7429
7430	7437	7438	7443	7444
7445	7446			

ARRANGEMENT #3 — 4 Plates

Type II ***170 Subject***

7457	7458	7462	7463

2¢ Rotary Press Coil Plates

ARRANGEMENT #4 — 12 Plates

Type II ***170 Subject***

7467	7468	7469	7470	7482
7483	7489	7490	7496	7497
7502	7503			

ARRANGEMENT #5 — 49 Plates

Type III ***170 Subject***

7510	7511	7512	7513	7521
7522	7523	7524	7617	7621
7624	7625	7630	7631	7636
7637	7661	7662	7672	7673
7677	7678	7679	7680	7686
7687	7688	7689	7738	7739
7746	7747	7751	7752	7782
7803	7804	7813	7814	7826
7827	7829	7830	7835	7836
7909	7910	7915	7916	

ARRANGEMENT #8 — 63 Plates

Type III ***170 Subject***

13397	13398	13399	13400	13401
13402	13413	13414	13417	13418
13425	13426	13427	13428	13505
13506	13507	13508	13509	13510
13511	13512	13514	13583	13584
13585	13586	13595	13596	13597
13598	13599	13600	13601	13602
13603	13604	13605	13606	13607
13608	13637	13638	13641	13642
13647	13648	13651	13652	13657
13658	13677	13678	13692	13693
13694	13695	13718	13719	13720
13721	13740	13764		

ARRANGEMENT #10 — 220 Plates

Type III ***170 Subject***

7852	7853	7939	7940	7953
7961	7962	7965	7967	7976
8049	8050	8051	8052	8056
8057	8061	8062	8071	8072
8073	8074	8075	8076	8169
8170	8171	8172	8326	8327
8328	8329	8928	8939	8940
9103	9104	9105	9106	9153
9154	9233	9234	9235	9236
9237	9457	9458	9465	9466
9469	9470	10097	10098	10115
10116	10175	10176	10177	10178
10183	10295	10296	10297	10306
10307	10308	10315	10316	10317
10318	10384	10386	10387	10388
10389	10444	10445	10446	10447
10448	10449	10450	10451	10452
10453	10466	10467	10468	10469
10470	10471N	10478	10479	10480

N The S30 is inverted with respect to the plate number.

APPENDIX D Continued

2¢ Rotary Press Coil Plates

ARRANGEMENT #10 Type III Cont.

10485	10486	10487	10488	10489
10491	10492	10648	10649	10650
10651	10652	10670	10671	10680
10681	10723	10724	10725	10726
10727	10728	10729	10730	10731
10732	10733	10738	10739	10740
10741	10750	11718	11719	11724
11725	11726	11727	11730	11731
11732	11733	11734	11735	11736
11737	11769	11770	11771	11772
11797	11798	11799	11800	11808
11809	11810	11811	12464	12465
12466	12469	12470	12471	12472
12473	12474	12475	12476	12483
12484	12485	12486	12513	12514
12515	12516	12517	12518	12519
12520	12529	12530	12531	12532
12601	12602	12603	12604	12918
12919	12920	12921	12922	12927
12928	12929	12970	12971	12972
12973	13002	13004	13005	13239
13240	13253	13254	13286	13287
13288	13289	13290	13291	13292
13293	13294	13295	13386	13387
13388	13536	13537	13538	13539

ARRANGEMENT #11 60 Plates

Type III *170 Subject*

13741	13742	13743	13765	13766
13767	13776	13777	13778	13779
13786	13787	13788	13789	13800
13801	13802	13803	13804	13805
13807	13809	13814	13815	13830
13831	13840	13841	13842	13843
13874	13875	13894	13895	13938
13939	13958	13959	13960	13961
13970	13971	13984	13985	14030
14031	14032	14033	14038	14039
14040	14041	14050	14051	14052
14053	14054	14055	14056	14057

ARRANGEMENT #1 2 Plates

Type I *150 Subject*

6279 6280

ARRANGEMENT #1 2 Plates

Type II *150 Subject*

7431 7432

ARRANGEMENT #6 4 Plates

Type III *150 Subject*

7561 7562 7628 7629

ARRANGEMENT #7 4 Plates

Type III *150 Subject*

8077 8078 10767 10768

2¢ Rotary Press Coil Plates

ARRANGEMENT #9 4 Plates

Type III *150 Subject*

13629 13630 13631 13632

3¢ Rotary Press Coil Plates

ARRANGEMENT #2 2 Plates

Type I *170 Subject*

7441 7442

ARRANGEMENT #8 34 Plates

Type I *170 Subject*

8107	8108	8109	8110	8124
8125	8151	8152	8153	8154
8155	8201	8202	8203	8216
8217	8218	8219	8226	8227
8228	8229	8233	8234	8237
8238	8239	8240	8244	8245
8247	8248	8250	8251	

ARRANGEMENT #8 46 Plates

Type II *170 Subject*

8269	8275	8276	8281	8282
8402	8408	8409	8428	8429
8442	8454	8455	8458	8459
8463	8464	8467	8468	8469
8470	8471	8472	8474	8475
8482	8483	8923	8924	8949
8950	8951	9107	9108	9109
9110	9133	9134	9135	9136
9143	9144	9145	9146	9181
9182				

ARRANGEMENT #9 4 Plates

Type I *150 Subject*

7634 7635 8111 8112

4¢ Rotary Press Coil Stamps

ARRANGEMENT #2 2 Plates

170 Subject

7440 7452

ARRANGEMENT #8 2 Plates

7675 7676

5¢ Rotary Press Coil Stamps

ARRANGEMENT #2 2 Plates

170 Subject

7435 7436

ARRANGEMENT #8 2 Plates

170 Subject

13633 13634

10¢ Rotary Press Coil Stamps

ARRANGEMENT #8 2 Plates

170 Subject

13625 13626

APPENDIX E

The plate numbers produced by the existing rotary presses vary in location and size depending upon the type of stamp being produced and the printing press used.

COTTRELL PRESS

The now obsolete intaglio presses produced sheet stamps with the five digit or single digit number in one corner (UL, UR, LL, LR) of a post office pane. A normal pad of panes consisted of one position with fifty sheets each of two alternating plate numbers.

The production of coil stamps was from two separate line engraved plates each 18 stamps wide by 24 stamps long. The plate number represented by a single or double digit, e.g. on the Transportation Coil Series, appears on a post office roll of coil stamps at the bottom of the stamp to the left of the join line. The companion plate number appears in the identical location 24 stamps further in the roll. These two numbers alternate throughout the 100, 500 or 3,000 subject coil rolls. Bureau precancels are produced by printing from mats located on a letterpress attachment and do not have a separate and distinct plate number.

Prior to the use of the single or double digit number representing the five digit plate number, the actual five digit number was entered on the plate below the first and last stamp of the eighteenth row of stamps and was intended to be cut off in the slitting operation. Mis slit join line pairs from this row may show partial five digit numbers. The join line pairs with partial numbers will show alternating numbers from each of the companion plates.

I-8 INTAGLIO PRESS

Sheet stamps produced by this press have post office panes with plate numbers in one corner (UL, UR, LL, LR). A normal pad consists of four different plate numbers repeated in groups of four throughout the pad. This applies to both single digit and five digit plate numbers.

ANDREOTTI GRAVURE PRESS

Current sheet stamps produced by this press have post office panes with a single digit representing each color used on one stamp in one corner (UL, UR, LL, LR). Only one set of plate numbers is found in a normal post office pad.

Current coil stamps produced by this press have one digit representing each color used located on one stamp. These numbers are repeated on another stamp 24 stamps further in the roll. There is no join line where the number appears.

Current Bureau precancels are produced on this press by using a separate gravure cylinder which may be indicated by an additional black plate number as on the 18¢ George Washington & Washington Monument coil stamp (Scott #2149a) or by changing the black line cylinder as was done with the 21.1¢ Letters coil (Scott #2150a). Although both the unprecanceled and the precanceled coil plate number stamps show apparently identical numbers (111111), the last digit (black) was printed by different cylinders as shown by the respective six digit numbers assigned in the miscellaneous numbers series.

When the five digit numbers appeared on the stamps printed on this press, there was one five digit number in the selvage of adjacent stamps. Each of these were printed in the color of the specific cylinder. The earlier plate blocks contained three, four, five or six of these five digit numbers.

This press was also used to print a coil version of the "D" stamps (Scott #2112). The plate number repeats every 38 stamps in these coils instead of the current 24.

NOTE: Some gravure cylinders are interchangeable for use on either the Andreotti gravure press or the gravure section of the "A" press.

A PRESS
(INTAGLIO/GRAVURE OR COMBINATION)

The initial production of stamps from this press had a distinctive characteristic, namely that the plate numbers roved instead of being in one finite location. The numbers were located in either the top and bottom margin or else the left and right margin. It is possible to collect 23 different positions of plate numbers in strips. The initial production from this press used only the gravure section. This was followed by a period of where either the intaglio or the gravure section was used and finally both sections were used at the same time. When using the five digit plate numbers, each of the numbers was entered three times on the printing cylinder with either three spaces or two spaces (each of stamp dimension) to fill out the 23 subject spaces. All five digit numbers were entered on gravure section cylinders only. When the changeover was made to the single digit or double digit, the result was that three distinct types of plate blocks were produced. One was a plate block consisting of only gravure digits over one stamp;

APPENDIX E Continued

A PRESS (Continued)

the second was only one intaglio digit over one stamp and the third was a group of gravure digits over one stamp and a single intaglio digit over the adjacent stamp. On the sheet stamps all of these numbers appear in the margin and not on the stamps themselves.

The current production from this press can utilize a change in cylinder or sleeve layout which results in the capability of printing sheet stamps with the numbers located in the four corners of the large sheet. The post office panes will have only the one number in one corner. This is not a permanent change so that should the need arise some of the regular issue sheet stamps can be produced by the old roving method so that a variety is not made deliberately.

B PRESS

When printing coil stamps this press utilizes sleeves that are 18 rows wide by 52 rows around. There is no join line in the coil stamps produced by this press. The same digit is used for the plate number on all eighteen stamps in the row. Therefore the same plate number is found 52 stamps apart in each of the rolls of coil stamps purchased at the post office.

When printing booklet panes, the sleeve layout is such that the identical number will appear in the tab over the booklet pane stamps. The plate number is located over the left stamp for the current production. All panes in one booklet will have the same plate number.

C PRESS

When printing coil stamps this press utilizes sleeves that are 20 rows wide by 48 rows around. There is no join line in the coil stamps produced by this press. The same digit is used for the plate number on all twenty stamps in the row. Therefore the same plate number is found 48 stamps apart in each of the rolls of coils purchased at the post office.

When printing booklet panes, the sleeve layout is such that the identical number will appear in the tab over the booklet pane stamps. The plate number is located over the left stamp for current production. All panes in one booklet will have the same plate number.

When printing sheet stamps on this press the format is such that all post office panes will have one number in one corner (UL, UR, LL, LR) in a normal pad.

D PRESS

When used to print sheet stamps, the offset plate numbers will appear in the selvage above one stamp and the intaglio number will appear in the selvage of the adjacent stamp. A normal post office pad will have a single combination of offset and intaglio numbers in one corner (UL, UR, LL, LR).

The announced use of this press to print multi-color stamp booklets stated that the offset plate numbers will be trimmed and that only the intaglio numbers will be available for collectors.

APPENDIX F

Reference is made to the original article on page 291 of the July 1983 UNITED STATES SPECIALIST. Many additions have been made and one style (6) has been deleted. However, there is a question that needs to be resolved.

When the Transportation coil series was initiated the Bureau of Engraving and Printing was producing precancels on the Cottrell presses. At that time the change had been made to eliminate the city and state and use only one pair of parallel lines (see our Style 2). This permitted the use of the stamps in any city instead of the original restricted use and accompanying initial printing costs of using specific locality designations.

With the advent of the newer presses, it was possible to print in more than one color on the intaglio section of the rotary press. Now, on some of the designs it is possible to add a service indicator on the stamp in another color using a single sleeve as the printing base. When the design is such that there is no room for the added wording, use is made of a "flexographic" plate to add the text in a manner comparable to precancelling. We have assigned separate style numbers to the flexographic plates and the intaglio sleeves that bear identical inscriptions.

Should we consider the "service indicator" to be the same as a precancel?

This immediately raises a very serious question. Refer to either your personal collection or the Scott Specialized Catalog and examine #1613 (3.1 Guitar), #1813 (3.5 Violin), #1614 (7.7 Saxhorn), #1615 (7.9 Drum) and #1615C (8.4 Piano). All of these stamps were issued for a specifically named service to be provided by the USPS. All were precancelled with either the two line city and state type or the newer two line only type (our style 2). The stamps without the precancel were furnished by the USPS for sale to collectors, who did not want precancels in their collections. In addition, the early Transportation coils #1900 (5.2 Sleigh), #1901 (5.9 Bicycle), #1903 (9.3 Mail Wagon) #1904 (10.9 Hansom Cab) and #1905 (11 Caboose) all show monocolored service indicators. Once again these were issued to appease stamp collectors who did not want to collect precancels. They were primarily printed with the Style 2 overprint for use by the quantitiy mailers.

Finally the USPS decided that it was too burdensome to keep giving in to collector's demands for non-overprinted stamps and have issued only the stamps clearly indicating the service that is applicable. At the same time the USPS also relaxed their regulation that only a valid precancel permit holder could use the stamps. Up to that ruling, it was ILLEGAL to have precancelled stamps with gum. Only a permit holder was permitted to purchase precancelled stamps and he was NOT permitted to sell them to collectors BY LAW.

Classify the stamps as you wish. We have shown the styles of wording that exist, so you can make a decision.

APPENDIX G

ROTARY PRESS BOOKLET PANES

Over the years many devices and/or methods have been used to attempt a determination of the percentage of the partial plate number that may appear on either rotary press printed coil stamps or rotary press printed booklet panes. Virtually all have required a "guesstimate" involving 10% of the number.

Finally, the gauge shown in the adjacent column evolved. The following is taken directly from the included instructions.

DIRECT READING PARTIAL PLATE NUMBER GAUGE

This plate number gauge usable on plate numbers 17700 and up. (Bureau Specialist Vol VII P145 Oct. 1936, H.M. Southgate)

Each black bar in the outside rows is 50% of the plate number. The inner rows are labled as to the % of the plate number. Thus at the 100% position it is possible to measure 100%, 150% (100 + 50) or 200% (100 + 50 + 50). Also, for example, at the 30% position 30%, 80%, and 130% may be measured. A word of caution, we have enlarged many plate numbers up to 30X and have found small variations in the heights of the digits within any number. Check one or more digits within each plate number for an average height.

The following pages list all of the rotary press booklet page plate numbers that were printed and issued from Scott *#583* thru the last use of the 5 digit plate numbers that appeared alongside of the stamps in the UL, LL, UR, and LR positions. The intent in the manufacturing process was that all of the plate numbers would be removed in the trimming operation. This was the case until the new plate numbering system started which shows the suffix number in the margin similar to the old flat plate press printing.

The percentages of plate numbers listed were measured using this gauge.

If you have any booklet panes showing a larger percentage of plate number, please report them to the editor.

P.O. Box 1047
Belleville, IL 62223-1047

PERCENTAGES

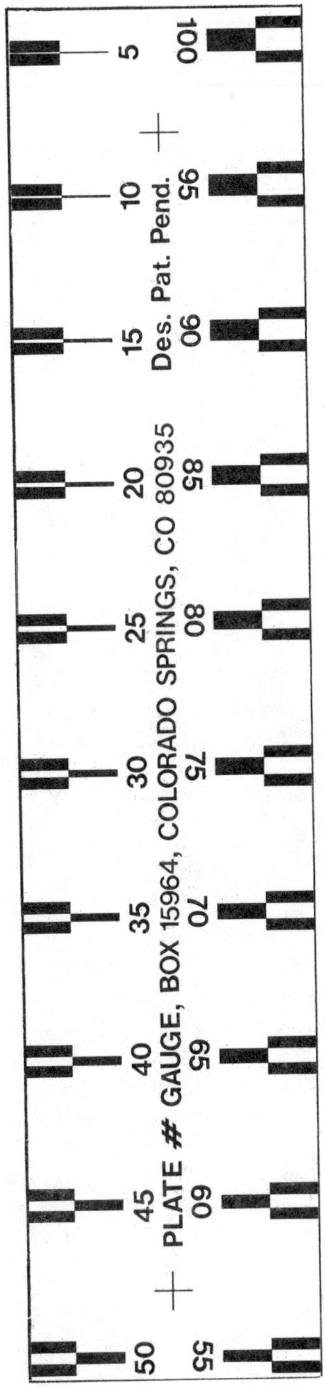

APPENDIX G

ROTARY PRESS BOOKLET PANES PERCENTAGES Cont.

#583a 2¢

	UL	LL	UR	LR
17450		60		
17451		65		
18550		45		
18551		35		
18662	22.5			
18663	25	30		
18695				
18696	30			
18697	40	50		
18698	40	55		
18705	40	70		
18706	30	30		
18707				
18708	40			
18710	40			

#632a 1¢

	UL	LL	UR	LR
18915	80	60		
18916	65	75		
18917	40	70		
18918	50	50		
19529	30	30		
19530	40	40		
19531	65	65		
19532	70	60		
19561	80	85	10	30
19562	80	55	15	20
19563	80	80	T	20
19564	80	70		20
19921	50	50		
19922	30	45		

#634d 2¢

	UL	LL	UR	LR
18662	30	45		
18663		35		
18695	NOT USED			
18696	NOT USED			
18697	85	70		
18698	75	75		
18705	35	35		
18706	20	40		
18707		15		
18708	70	20		
18709	25			
18710	70	25		
18711				
18712	25	10		
18716		35		
18717		15		
18718	65	55		
18719	35			
18720	80	100		
18721	40	30		
18842	30	75		
18843	40	60		
18844	90	40		
18845	85			

#634d 2¢ Contined

	UL	LL	UR	LR
19183	25*			
19184		35		
19193	35	55		
19194	40	60		
19199	55	65		
19200	60	50		
19274	65	55		
19275	70	55		
19276	60			
19277	60			
19278	60	50		
19279	90			
19314	35	65		
19315	60	55		
19316	60	75		
19317	30			
19357	80	70		
19358	65	55		
19359				
19360				
19361	45	20		
19362	30	15		
19404	30			
19405	60	40		
19406	75	35		
19407		40		
19408	45	40		
19409	60	55		
19760	80	20		
19761	45	55		
19762	40	45		
19763	60			
19834	100	100		
19835	90	90		
19844	70	100		
19845	67.5	95		
19846	70	100		
19847	65	100		
19848	100	100		
19849	100	100		
19850	100	100		
19851	100	100		
19962	55	100		
19963	65	100		10
19972	40			
19973	100	100	T	10
19990	100	90		
19991	100	95		
20041	40	95		10
20042	45	50		20
20096	100	100		5
20097	100	100		5
20100	65	60		10
20101	70	60	45	15
20106	40	100	20	20
20107	55	65		

* - PLATE SINGLE

APPENDIX G

ROTARY PRESS BOOKLET PANES PERCENTAGES Cont.

#720b 3¢

	UL	LL	UR	LR
20900	100	50		10
20901	90	30		
20902	60	60		
20903	50	45	70	
20904	80	100	37.5	T
20905	60	45	20	10
21010	100	80		T
21011	100	60		30
21012	60	75		30
21013	45	70		10
21489	45	95	27.5	27.5
21490	30	90	27.5	27.5
21515	50	60		T
21516	40	60		5
21519	20	80	10	5
21520	75	50		

#804b 1¢

	UL	LL	UR	LR
22007	25	15	10	10
22008	10	15	20	3
22009	100	100	45	40
22010	100	100	35	35
22234	95	100	20	35
22235	95	100	20	10
22389	95	50	15	T
22390	70	60	20	10
22402	100	100	10	10
22403	100	100	10	10
22930	100	80	25	30
22931	100	75	25	20
22977	100	95	35	15
22978	100	90	40	15

#806b 2¢

	UL	LL	UR	LR
22011	100	80	20	20
22012	100	100	85	25
22392	90	70	15	5
22404	95	80		
22405	65	90		
22461	80	60	20	10
24298	30	35	50	
24299	35	75	50	

#807a 3¢

	UL	LL	UR	LR
21995	100	100	60	40
21996	100	100	55	35
21997	100	100	50	25
21998	100	100	55	35
22170	100	100	45	40
22171	100	100	30	50
22434	100	100	35	25
22435	100	100	40	15
22436	100	100	30	25
22437	100	100	35	25

#807a 3¢ Continued

	UL	LL	UR	LR
22886	100	100	10	25
22887	100	100	20	10
22932	100	100	20	15
22933	100	100	25	10
22973	100	100	20	5
22974	100	100	20	10
22975	100	100	15	20
22976	100	100	20	15
23158	100	100		
23159	100	100		
23160	100	70	25	15
23161	70	50	15	15
23283	100	100	T	10
23284	100	100	T	10
23291	80	100	T	10
23292	70	70		10
23412	95	90	25	15
23413	90	80		T
23422	100	80	5	20
23423	100	90	15	25
23573	80	90	T	
23574	85	100	30	T
23594	80	80	20	30
23595	80	100	15	25
23758	90	85		25
23759	100	85		10
23770	70	100	15	25
23771	85	70	25	10
23847	70			
23848	70			
24089	80	100	20	25
24090	85	90	20	25
24255	100	95	10	20
24256	100	100	5	20
24257	100	100		10
24258	70	95		30
24412	100	95	20	T
24413	100	90	10	
24418	90	100	5	20
24419	75	90		
24420	95	100	20	15
24421	95	100	20	10
24422	60	30		
24423	100	100	25	5
24424	70	80	25	30
24425	80	80	25	25
24426	70	60	20	
24427	60	80	25	
24428	70	20		
24429	60	T		
24443	60	95		
24739				
24740				

Continued

APPENDIX G
ROTARY PRESS BOOKLET PANES PERCENTAGES Cont.

#1035a 3¢ WET PRINTED

	UL	LL	UR	LR
24975	90	100		
24976	85	90		
24980	100	70	20	20
24981	100	75	20	20
25002	100	95		T
25003	100	65	5	5
25006	100	65		
25007	100	90		5
25013	97.5	100		10
25014	100	100		10
25334	57.5	50		
25335	65	50		
25353	30	30	T	
25354	45	30	T	

#1035a 3¢ DRY PRINTED

	UL	LL
25355	55	45
25356		
25357	65	60
25358	60	80
25363	70	
25364	75	
25372	50	100
25373	100	20
25417	25	25
25418		10
25567	60	70
25568	45	42.5
25569	50	50
25570	60	72.5
25743	80	95
25744	85	90
25757	60	60
25758	65	70
25774	80	95
25775	75	90
25789	57.5	100
25790	57.5	100

#1036a 4¢ DRY PRINTED

	UL	LL	UR	LR
26013	75	65		
26014	65	50		
26032	75	90		
26033	70	100		
26038	100	45		
26039	85	50		
26111	60	100		
26112	100	65		
26154	75	70		
26155	70	75		
26191	80	85		
26192	80	75		
26287	100	90		
26288	90	95		
26468	90	100		

#1036a 4¢ DRY PRINTED Cont.

	UL	LL	UR	LR
26469	95	95		
26515	70	60		
26516	65	100		
26518	80	70		
26519	80	100		
26520	60	40		
26521	60	50		
26593	100	100		
26594	100	100		
26652	90	95		
26653	85	80		
26689	35	15		
26690	57.5	60		
26699	70	100		
26700	75	100		
26817	85	90		
26818	85	45		
26819	100	80		
26822	40	80		
26823	45	80		
26829	45	55		
26830	62.5	70		
26955	100	100		
26956	100	90		
27188	95	100		
27189	95	100		
27215	70	65		
27216	75	70		

#1213a 5¢ UNTAGGED "Your Mailman"

		UL	LL
27347	100	99	
27348		100	100
28349		50	70
27350		55	85
27351		85	90
27352		80	85
27357		90	100
27358		95	75
27412		35	62.5
27413		30	55
27435		60	75
27436		62.5	80
27438		100	95
27439		95	95

#1213a 5¢ UNTAGGED "Use Zone Nos."

	UL	LL
27498	100	55
27499	70	60
27503	42.5	40
27504	35	65
27505	60	40
27506	57.5	20
27523	T	17.5

APPENDIX G
ROTARY PRESS BOOKLET PANES PERCENTAGES Cont.

#1213a 5¢ UNTAGGED Cont.
"Use Zone Nos."

	UL	LL	UR	LR
27524	20	5		
27525	100	70		
27526	90	70		
27546	65	100		
27547	95	100		
27563	65	100		
27564	60	100		
27565	90	100		
27566	85	85		
27650	70	70		
27651	65	70		

#1213a 5¢ UNTAGGED
"Always Use"

	UL	LL	UR	LR
27669	100	80		
27670	55	85		
27671	90	100		
27672	90	95		
27675	72.5	55		
27676	50	100		
27678	72.5	100		
27679	80	100		
27723	50	80		
27724	55	85		
27734	50	100		
27735	50	100		
27736	62.5	50		
27737	50	50		
27738	100	55		
27739	100	55		
27827	70	80		
27828	70	55		
27829	75	55		
27830	70	55		
27833	80	55		
27834	75	55		
28013	45	40		
28014	50	40		
28039	85	100		
28040	60	40		
28080	20	80		
28081	30	60		
28084	100	100		
28085	100	100		
28090	55	60		
28091	55	60		
28214	97.5	100		
28215	100	100		
28216	95	65		
28217	90	57.5		
28338	50	60		
28339	100	100		
28345	100	100		
28346	50	60		
28440	60	85		

#1213a 5¢ UNTAGGED Cont.
"Always Use"

	UL	LL	UR	LR
28441	55	85		
28471	75	75		
28472	75	65		

#1213c 5¢ TAGGED
"Use Zone Nos.

	UL	LL	UR	LR
27563		60		
27564		50		

#1213c 5¢ TAGGED
"Always Use"

	UL	LL	UR	LR
27671		50		
27678	40	15		
27679	40	25		
27734	40	25		
27735	35	35		
27827	50	40		
27829	50	40		
28081		50		
28091	55	65		
28214	60	95		
28215	60	80		
28216		50		
28217		40		
28339	75	80		
28345	75	85		
28440	70	80		
28441	60	100		
28471	45	50		
28472	45	40		
28491	70	65		
28492	75	100		
28513	80	75		
28514	75	80		
28518	40	35		
28538	90	100		
28539	90	100		
28567	60	100		
28568	80	75		
28569	90	50		
28570	95	50	15	
28619	55	65		
28849	50	70		
28850	60	70		
28854	100	80		
28904	95	100		
28905	100	100		
29053	55	85		
29054	55	80		
29058	65	85		
29130	80	55		
29131	90	55	10	
29213	30	5		
29214	40			
29283				
29284				
29336	32.5	60		
29337	40	65		

APPENDIX G
ROTARY PRESS BOOKLET PANES PERCENTAGES Cont.

#1278a 1¢

	UL	UR	LL	LR
30656	85			
31775	100	100		

#1278b 1¢

	UL	UR	LL	LR
32904	90	100		
32905	80	85		
32906	65	100		
32907	70	100		

#1280a 2¢

	UL	UR	LL	LR
29558	85	90	12.5	
29559	85	85		
29561				
29562	10			

#1280c 2¢

	UL	UR	LL	LR
32966	100	100		
32967	100	100		
32996	55	100		
32997	100	47.5		
33985	50	100		
34102	50	100		
36882	30			
36883	25			
36884	22.5			
36885				

#1284b 6¢

	UL	UR	LL	LR
30137	75		20	10
30199	90			
30200	65			
30281	100	40		
30282		70		
30603		85		
30604		95		
30670			25	15
30835		100		

#1284c 6¢

	UL	UR	LL	LR
29556	50	75		
29557	50	75		
29565	70	80		
29566	90	100		
31244				

#1288c 15¢

No reported numbers

#1393a 6¢

	UL	UR	LL	LR
31932		100		
32011	100	100		

#1393b 6¢ (Pane of 5 + label)

	UL	UR	LL	LR
31955-Z	15	30		
31956-ME	15	25	10	

#1395a 8¢ (Pane of 8)

	UL	LL	UR	LR
32716	100			
32717		25		
32728		95		
32758		90		
32759		50		
32760	100		15	

#1395b 8¢ (Pane of 6)

	UL	LL	UR	LR
32908	100	90		
32909	100	100		
32910	99	100		
32900	100			

#1395d 8¢ (Pane of 7 + label)

	UL	LL	UR	LR
33767	100			
33768		100		

#1510b 10¢ (Pane of 5 + label)

	UL	LL	UR	LR
34729		100		
34730				
34731	30	100		
34732	15			
34957				
34958		40		

#1510c 10¢ (Pane of 8)

No reported numbers

#1510d 10¢ (Pane of 6)

	UL	LL	UR	LR
35211	100	20		
35212				

#1595a 13¢ (Panes of 6)

	UL	LL	UR	LR
36516				
36517				
36722	25	100		
36723	30	100		
36770		20		
36771		10		

#1595b 13¢ (Panes of 7)

	UL	LL	UR	LR
36725			15	

#1595c 13¢ (Panes of 8)

	UL	LL	UR	LR
36651				10
37031				30
37032			45	30
37033				12.5

#1595d 13¢ (Panes of 5)

	UL	LL	UR	LR
37253				
37254	25			
37255	37.5	27.5		
37256	37.5	35		

APPENDIX G
ROTARY PRESS BOOKLET PANES PERCENTAGES Cont.

#1595d 13¢ (Panes of 5) Cont.

	UL	LL	UR	LR
37258				
37321				
37327	30	25		
37328		40		
37377				
37572				
37573				

#1598a 15¢ (Panes of 8)
NO reported numbers

#C10a 10¢

	UL	LL	UR	LR
19414	10			
19425	15	65	30	
19426	25	20	40	5
19427	10	65	3	

#C25a 6¢

	UL	LL	UR	LR
22979	100	100		
22980	100	100		
22981	65	95	10	
22982	100	100	20	
23028	50	40		
23029	50	100		
23048	35	50		
23072	35	50		
23258				
23259				

#C39a 6¢ WET PRINTED

	UL	LL	UR	LR
24141	75	100	20	5
24142	70	100	20	30
24163	97.5	100	100	
24264	85	100	25	15
24564	60	30	T	15
24565	45	(50)*	T	10
24908		100		
24909		100		

#C39a 6¢ DRY PRINTED

	UL	LL	UR	LR
25359		10		
25360	50	30		
25376	50	40		
25377	(35)*	(25)*		

*PLATE SINGLE

#C51a 7¢ BLUE

	UL	LL	UR	LR
26042	80	65		
26043	90	65		
26175	75	55		
26176	75	80		
26458	45	30		
26459	50	27.5		

#C60a 7¢ RED

	UL	LL	UR	LR
26458	60	65		
26459	60	100		
26475	70	65		
26476	70	65		

#C64b 8¢ UNTAGGED "Your Mailman"

	UL	LL	UR	LR
27371	100	100		
27372	100	90		
27375	80	90		
27376	80	85		

#C64b 8¢ UNTAGGED "Use Zone Nos."

	UL	LL	UR	LR
27515	70	100		
2756	65	100		

#C64b 8¢ UNTAGGED "Always use"

	UL	LL	UR	LR
27646	90	100		
27673	100	60		
27674	65	75		
27677	100	90		
27697				
27698				

#C64c 8¢ TAGGED "Always Use"

	UL	LL	UR	LR
27646	37.5	57.5		
27673	25	40		
27674	25	100		
27677	40	50		
27697	10	75		
27698	15	75		
28030	70	85		
28031	40	20		
28032	70	80		
28050	35	40		
28115	95	95		
28116	90	90		
28317	55	70		
28403	65	65		
28404	77.5	85		
28405	80	80		
28469	75	60		
28470	75	60		
28480	85	100		
28481	85	100		
28496	90	90		
28497	85	90		
28575	35	55		
28576		60		

APPENDIX G
ROTARY PRESS BOOKLET PANES PERCENTAGES Cont.

#C72b 10¢ (Pane of 8)

Will list only reported numbers.

#C72c 11¢ (Pane of 5)

	UL	UR	LL	LR
29563	50	50		
29564	45	45		
29567		45		
29568	25			

#C78a 11¢ (Pane of 4)

	UL	UR	LL	LR
32964	100	100	10	10
32965	100	100		15

#C78a 11¢ (Pane of 4) Cont.

	UL	UR	LL	LR
32994	80	75		
32995	80	75		
33485	75	100		
33486	75	100		

#C79a 13¢ (Pane of 5)

	UL	UR	LL	LR
34795	100	100		
34796	100	85		
34843		100		
34844		20		
35338				
35339				

APPENDIX AA

EARLY IMPERFORATE PLATE NUMBERS

Although the following items were not issued in the normal manner by the Post Office Department, they have been given catalog status. For the record we list the plate numbers that have been reported for each of the stamps involved.

#252a 2¢ WASHINGTON

Imperforate Vertically
152

#253a 3¢ JACKSON

Imperforate
47

#254a 4¢ LINCOLN

Imperforate
50

#255b 5¢ GRANT

Imperforate
53

#255c 5¢ GRANT

Imperforate Horizontally
130

#256a 6¢ GARFIELD

Imperforate Horizontally
28

#258a 10¢ WEBSTER

Imperforate
63

#264b 1¢ FRANKLIN

Imperforate Vertically
24

#264c 1¢ FRANKLIN

Imperforate
314 334 336

#267a 2¢ WASHINGTON

Imperforate
319 340

#268a 3¢ JACKSON

Imperforate
103 107

#269a 4¢ LINCOLN

Imperforate
94 106

#270b 5¢ GRANT

Imperforate
251 351

#271b 6¢ GARFIELD

Imperforate
373

#272b 8¢ SHERMAN

Imperforate
249

#273a 10¢ WEBSTER

Imperforate
305

#274a 15¢ CLAY

Imperforate
52

#275b 50¢ JEFFERSON

Imperforate
75

#276b $1 PERRY

Imperforate
76

#277b $2 MADISON

Imperforate
84

#278a $5 MARSHALL

Imperforate
85

#E5a 10¢ SPECIAL DELIVERY

Imperforate
257

#J31 a 1¢ POSTAGE DUE

Imperforate
57

Other stamps in these issues have also been reported imperforate. However, there is no report of the plate numbers for any of the stamps.

APPENDIX BB—CANAL ZONE

Some of the basic stamps of the United States were overprinted for use in the Canal Zone. We have listed these using the Scott Canal Zone Catalog numbers. We have also shown the basic Scott United States Catalog number in parenthesis following the description. Other issues of Canal Zone were printed by the Bureau of Engraving and Printing but these were assigned from the miscellaneous series of numbers and we do not list them.

#4 1¢ FRANKLIN (#300) 11 Plates

2061 2062 2063 2064 2087
2088 2092 2141 2142 2143
2144

#5 2¢ SHIELD (#319) 21 Plates

2076 2133 2134 2135 2136
2169 2171 2172 2192 2201
2202 2203 2204 2205 2206
2208 2209 2210 2212 2214
2217

#6 5¢ LINCOLN (#304) 4 Plates

1885 1886 1887 1888

#7 8¢ MARTHA WASHINGTON (#306) 4 Plates

1497 1498 1499 1500

#8 10¢ WEBSTER (#307) 4 Plates

1590 1591 1592 1593

#70 ½¢ HALE (#551) 8 Plates

17017 17018 17020 17029 17078
17079 17080 17081

#71 1¢ FRANKLIN (#552) 12 Plates

15334 15358 15359 15374 15375
15384 15385 15437 15456 16556
16560 16561

#72 1½¢ HARDING (#553) 4 Plates

16829 16838 16848 16863

#73 2¢ WASHINGTON (#554) 14 Plates

15378 15402 15405 15496 15629
15630 15631 15632 16721 16722
16723 16724 17110 17115

#74 5¢ ROOSEVELT (#557) 4 Plates

15148 15204 15205 15206

#75 10¢ MONROE (#562) 4 Plates

15510 15511 15512 15513

#76 12¢ CLEVELAND (#564) 8 Plates

14404 14405 14406 14407 15350
15351 15352 15692

#77 14¢ INDIAN (#565) 4 Plates

14512 14513 14514 14515

#78 15¢ STATUE OF LIBERTY (#566) 4 Plates

14910 14911 14912 14913

#79 30¢ BISON (#569) 4 Plates

14436 14437 14438 14439

#80 50¢ AMPHITHEATRE (#570) 4 Plates

14042 14043 14044 14045

#81 $1 LINCOLN MEMORIAL (#571) 1 Plate

14268

#84 2¢ WASHINGTON (#554) 5 Plates

17430 17814 17842 17890 17892

#85 3¢ LINCOLN (#555) 4 Plates

16400 16401 16402 16474

#86 5¢ ROOSEVELT (#557) 12 Plates

15571 15952 16331 16332 16333
16363 16365 16366 16391 16392
16393 16394

#87 10¢ MONROE (#562) 4 Plates

16376 16377 16378 16379

#88 12¢ CLEVELAND (#564) 4 Plates

15350 15351 15352 15693

#89 14¢ INDIAN (#565) 4 Plates

14526 15795 15796 15797

#90 15¢ STATUE OF LIBERTY (#566) 12 Plates

14910 14911 14912 14913 17430
17431 17432 17433 18928 18929
18930 19139

#91 17¢ WILSON (#623) 8 Plates

18021 18022 18023 18024 18025
18026 18027 18028

#92 20¢ GOLDEN GATE (#567) 20 Plates

16646 16648 †17227 17228 17229
17230 17426 17427 17428 17429
17530 17531 19134 19468 19648
19872 20033 †20034 †20037 20038

APPENDIX BB Continued

#93 30¢ BISON (#569) 8 Plates

14436 14437 14438 14439 17446
17447 17448 17449

#94 50¢ AMPHITHEATRE (#570) 4 Plates

14042 14043 14044 14045

#95 $1 LINCOLN MEMORIAL (#571) 1 Plate

14268

#96 2¢ SESQUICENTENNIAL (#627) 4 Plates

18570 18577 18582 18583

#97 2¢ WASHINGTON (#583) 8 Plates

18632 18633 18809 18827 †18933
*18934

#98 3¢ LINCOLN (#584) 2 Plates

18445 18446

#99 10¢ MONROE (#591) 2 Plates

18532 18538

#100 1¢ FRANKLIN (#632) 2 Plates

18730 18731

#101 2¢ WASHINGTON (#634) 6 Plates

18809 18827 18933 18934 18985
18986

#102 3¢ LINCOLN (#635) 4 Plates

18126 18803 18831 18833

#103 5¢ ROOSEVELT (#637) 2 Plates

18851 18855

#104 10¢ MONROE (#642) 4 Plates

19234 19235 19256 19257

#115 3¢ WASHINGTON (#720) 9 Plates

20932 20933 20934 20950 20954
20959 20960 21000 21001

#116 14¢ INDIAN (#695) 2 Plates

20549 20550

#118 ½¢ FRANKLIN (#803) 10 Plates

21885 21887 21888 21889 21899
21900 22470 22471 22898 22899

#119 1½¢ MARTHA WASHINGTON (#805) 21 Plates

21877 21878 21879 21881 21882
21883 21884 21934 21937 22077
22078 22079 22080 22173 22174
22464 22466 22645 22646 22876
22877

BOOKLET PANES

#71e 1¢ FRANKLIN (#552a) 6 Plates

14269 14270 14271 14272 15961
15964

#73a 2¢ WASHINGTON (#554c) 4 Plate

15790 15792 16602 16603

#101a 2¢ WASHINGTON (#634d) 1 Plate

18721

POSTAGE DUES

#J1 1¢ POSTAGE DUE (#J45) 4 Plates

5510 5522 5534 5541

#J2 2¢ POSTAGE DUE (#J46) 4 Plates

6703 6704 6705 6706

#J3 10¢ POSTAGE DUE (#J49) 4 Plates

5525 5532 5540 6555

#J12 1¢ POSTAGE DUE (#J61) 2 Plates

13844 13845

#J13 2¢ POSTAGE DUE (#J62) 4 Plates

14026 14027 14028 14029

#J14 10¢ POSTAGE DUE (#J65) 4 Plates

5532 5540 6555 6556

#J15 1¢ FRANKLIN (#552) 4 plates

overprinted Postage Due
15334 15358 15359 15437

#J16 2¢ WASHINGTON (#554) 4 Plates

overprinted Postage Due
15629 15630 15631 15632

#J17 10¢ MONROE (#562) 4 Plates

overprinted Postage Due
15510 15511 15512 15513

#J18 1¢ POSTAGE DUE (#J61) 5 Plates

8214 13844 13845 13846 13847

#J19 2¢ POSTAGE DUE (#J62) 8 Plates

14026 14027 14028 14029 14596
14597 14598 14599

#J20 10¢ POSTAGE DUE (#J65) 3 Plates

6555 6556 18725

APPENDIX CC—CUBA

The overprinted stamps of Cuba are listed in the Scott Cuba Catalog number order with the basic United States stamp shown on the next line with number in parenthesis.

#221 CUBA 1¢ de PESO 23 Plates on 1¢ FRANKLIN (#279)

564 565 566 567 572
573 574 575 766 767
768 769 770 771 772
773 794 795 797 810
811 812 813

#222 CUBA 2¢ de PESO 2 Plates on 2¢ WASHINGTON (#267)

475 503

#222 CUBA 2¢ de PESO 34 Plates on 2¢ WASHINGTON (#279B)

556 559 560 561 562
563 568 569 570 571
593 594 595 596 745
746 747 748 753 754
755 756 758 759 760
761 762 763 764 765
774 775 776 777

#223 CUBA 2½¢ de PESO 3 Plates on 2¢ WASHINGTON (#267)

469 475 503

#223 CUBA 2½¢ de PESO 28 Plates on 2¢ WASHINGTON (#279B)

516 552 556 559 560
561 562 563 568 569
570 571 593 594 595
596 745 746 747 748
753 754 755 756 758
759 760 761

#224 CUBA 3¢ de PESO 4 Plates on 3¢ JACKSON (#268)

447 448 449 450

#225 CUBA 5¢ de PESO 94 Plates on 5¢ GRANT(#281)

389 390 391 392 407
408 409 410

#226 CUBA 10¢ de PESO 4 Plates on 10¢ WEBSTER (#282C)

302 303 305 306

#227 1¢ STATUE COLUMBUS 4 Plates

879 884 889 890

#228 2¢ ROYAL PALMS 4 Plates

871 872 873 874

#228b 2¢ BOOKLET PANE 1 Plate

†1323

#229 3¢ ALLEGORY "CUBA" 4 Plates

891 892 893 894

#230 5¢ OCEAN LINER 4 Plates

899 901 902 903

#231 10¢ CANE FIELD 1 Plate

900

#232 1¢ UN CENTAVO 4 Plates surcharged on #229

891 892 893 894

#E1 CUBA 10¢ de PESO 1 Plate on 10¢ SPECIAL DELIVERY (#E5)

492

#E2 10¢ IMMEDIATA 1 Plate

908

#E3 10¢ INMEDIATA 1 Plate

1432

#J1 CUBA 1¢ de PESO 2 Plates on 1¢ POSTAGE DUE (#J38)

246 267

#J2 CUBA 2¢ de PESO 2 Plates on 2¢ POSTAGE DUE (#J39)

247 268

#J3 CUBA 5¢ de PESO 2 Plates on 5¢ POSTAGE DUE (#J41)

71 255

#J4 CUBA 10¢ de PESO 2 Plates on 10¢ POSTAGE DUE (#J42)

72 256

SPECIAL PRINTINGS

The following is a list of the plate numbers that were used for the special printing made for the exhibit in Paris.

#221 CUBA 1¢ de PESO 1 Plate

†975

#222 CUBA 2¢ de PESO 1 Plate

†886

#223 CUBA 2½¢ de PESO 1 Plate

†885

#225 CUBA 5¢ de PESO 1 Plate

†950

#226A CUBA 10¢ de PESO 1 Plate

935

APPENDIX DD—GUAM

The overprinted stamps of Guam are listed in the Scott Guam Catalog number order with the basic United States stamp listed on the next line with number in parenthesis.

#1 "GUAM" overprint 12 Plates
on 1¢ FRANKLIN (#279)

794 795 796 797 810
811 812 813 830 831
832 833

#2 "GUAM" overprint 63 Plates
on 2¢ WASHINGTON (#279B)

758 759 760 761 762
763 764 765 777 778
779 780 781 782 783
784 785 786 787 788
789 798 799 800 801
802 803 804 805 814
815 816 817 838 840
841 842 843 845 850
851 852 853 858 859
860 861 866 867 869

*870 875 876 877 878
895 896 897 898 904
905 906 907

#3 "GUAM" overprint 4 Plates
on 3¢ JACKSON (#268)

447 448 449 450

#4 "GUAM" overprint 4 Plates
on 4¢ LINCOLN (#280a)

790 791 792 793

#5 "GUAM" overprint 8 Plates
on 5¢ GRANT (#281)

389 390 391 392 834
835 836 837

#6 "GUAM" overprint 4 Plates
on 6¢ GARFIELD (#282)

922 923 924 925

#7 "GUAM" overprint 4 Plates
on 8¢ SHERMAN (#272)

928 929 930 931

#8 "GUAM" overprint 4 Plates
on 10¢ WEBSTER (#282C)

518 519 520 521

#10 "GUAM" overprint 1 Plate
on 15¢ CLAY (#284)

264

#11 "GUAM" overprint 1 Plate
on 50¢ JEFFERSON (#275)

75

#12 "GUAM" overprint 1 Plate
on $1 PERRY (#276)

76

#E1 "GUAM" overprint 4 Plates
on 10¢ SPECIAL DELIVERY (#E5)

880 881 882 883

SPECIAL PRINTINGS

The following is a list of the plate numbers used for the special printing prepared for the exhibit at Paris.

#1 1¢ FRANKLIN (#279)

975

#2 2¢ WASHINGTON (#279B)

888

#3 3¢ JACKSON (#268)

447

#5 5¢ GRANT #281)

949

#8 10¢ WEBSTER (#282C)

932

#9 10¢ WEBSTER (#283)

932

#10 15¢ CLAY (#284)

264

#13 $1 PERRY (#276A)

76

#E1 10¢ SPECIAL DELIVERY (#E5)

881

APPENDIX EE—PHILIPPINES

Since there is some question concerning which positions were overprinted for the Philippines on all issues, we shall list only the plate numbers. The Scott Catalog number of the basic U.S. stamp is shown in parenthesis.

#212 PHILIPPINES on 50¢ JEFFERSON (#260) — **1 Plate**

75

#213 PHILIPPINES on 1¢ FRANKLIN (#279) — **83 Plates**

770	771	772	773	794
795	796	797	810	811
812	813	†818	819	820
821	822	823	824	825
†969	979	984	985	986
987	992	993	†994	995
1000	1001	1002	1003	†1004
†1005	1006	1007	1050	1051
1052	1053	1062	1063	1064
1065	1130	1131	1132	1133
1146	1147	1148	1149	1157
1158	1159	1160	1205	1207
1396	1397	1398	1399	1400
1401	†1402	1403	†1407	1408
1409	1410	1411	1420	1421
1422	1423	1424	1427	1453
1454	1455	†1456		

#214 PHILIPPINES on 2¢ WASHINGTON (#279B) — **119 Plates**

556	758	759	760	761
762	763	764	765	774
775	776	777	778	779
780	781	782	783	784
785	786	787	788	789
798	799	800	801	802
803	804	805	807	808
809	814	815	816	817
838	839	840	841	850
851	852	853	854	855
856	857	858	859	860
861	866	867	869	870
875	876	877	878	885
886	887	888	895	896
897	898	904	905	906
907	915	917	918	919
†1025	1026	1027	1032	1034
1039	1054	1056	1067	1068
1069	1070	1071	†1080	1081
†1082	1359	†1373	1381	1382
1383	1384	1385	1386	1387
1412	†1413	1414	1415	†1416
1417	1418	1419	1434	1435
1436	1438	1439	1440	

#215 PHILIPPINES on 3¢ JACKSON (#268) — **4 Plates**

447 448 449 450

#216 PHILIPPINES on 5¢ GRANT (#281) — **20 Plates**

389	390	391	392	407
408	409	410	980	981
982	983	1199	1200	1201
1202	†1217	1218	†1219	1220

#217 PHILIPPINES on 10¢ WEBSTER (#282C) — **8 Plates**

302	303	305	306	518
519	520	521		

#217A PHILIPPINES on 10¢ WEBSTER (#283) — **4 Plates**

1336 1337 1338 1339

#218 PHILIPPINES on 15¢ CLAY (#284) — **1 Plate**

264

#219 PHILIPPINES on 50¢ JEFFERSON (#275) — **1 Plate**

75

#220 PHILIPPINES on 4¢ LINCOLN (#280) — **5 Plates**

790 1100 1101 1102 1103

#221 PHILIPPINES on 6¢ GARFIELD (#282) — **4 Plates**

922 923 924 925

#222 PHILIPPINES on 8¢ SHERMAN (#272) — **4 Plates**

928 929 930 931

#223 PHILIPPINES on $1 PERRY (#276) — **1 Plate**

76

#223A PHILIPPINES on $1 PERRY (#276A) — **1 Plate**

76

#224 PHILIPPINES on $2 MADISON (#277) — **1 Plate**

84

#225 PHILIPPINES on $5 MARSHALL (#278) — **94 Plate**

85

APPENDIX EE Continued

#226 PHILIPPINES on 1¢ FRANKLIN (#300) — 92 Plates

1651	1653	†1654	1655	†1656
†1657	1658	1680	1682	†1683
†1721	†1722	†1723	1734	1735
†1737	†1738	1739	†1740	1793
1794	1801	†1804	1946	†2061
2062	†2063	†2064	†2141	†2142
†2143	†2144	2173	2174	2175
2176	2193	2194	†2196	2257
2258	2259	†2260	2310	2391
†2392	2393	2394	2407	2408
2409	2410	2415	2416	2417
2418	2451	2452	2453	2454
2468	2469	2470	2471	2484
2485	2486	2487	†2492	2493
2494	2495	2500	2501	2502
2503	2745	2761	2762	2763
2764	†2792	†2798	2799	2820
2821	†2822	2823	2907	2911
2915	2919			

#227 PHILIPPINES on 2¢ WASHINGTON (FLAG) (#301) — 27 Plates

1644	1645	1646	1668	1669
1670	1671	1672	1674	1675
1676	1677	1678	1679	1696
1697	1698	1699	1704	1705
1706	1707	1708	1709	1710
1711	1716			

#228 PHILIPPINES on 3¢ JACKSON (#302) — 8 Plates

1586	1587	1588	1589	2516
2517	2518	2519		

#229 PHILIPPINES on 4¢ GRANT (#303) — 4 Plates

1797 178 1799 1800

#230 PHILIPPINES on 5¢ LINCOLN (#304) — 12 Plates

1537	1538	1540	1663	1885
1886	1887	†1888	2225	2226
2227	2297			

#231 PHILIPPINES on 6¢ GARFIELD (#305) — 4 Plates

1598 1599 1600 1601

#232 PHILIPPINES on 8¢ MARTHA WASHINGTON (#306) — 4 Plates

1497 1498 1499 1500

#233 PHILIPPINES on 10¢ WEBSTER (#307) — 4 Plates

1590 1591 1592 1593

#234 PHILIPPINES on 13¢ HARRISON (#308) — 4 Plates

1473 1474 1475 1476

#235 PHILIPPINES on 15¢ CLAY (#309) — 2 Plates

1607 2330

#236 PHILIPPINES on 50¢ JEFFERSON (#310) — 1 Plate

1602

#237 PHILIPPINES on $1 FARRAGUT (#311) — 1 Plate

1629

#238 PHILIPPINES on $2 MADISON (#312) — 1 Plate

1630

#239 PHILIPPINES on $5 MARSHALL (#313) — 1 Plate

1620

#240 PHILIPPINES on 2¢ WASHINGTON (#319) — 23 Plates

2211	†2212	2214	2217	2439
2441	2459	2460	2461	2462
2712	2794	2795	2796	2810
2831	2835	2839	2840	2863
2864	2865	2866		

#E 1 PHILIPPINES on 10¢ SPECIAL DELIVERY (#E 5) — 4 Plates

880 881 882 883

#J 1 PHILIPPINES on 1¢ POSTAGE DUE (#J38) — 2 Plates

246 267

#J 2 PHILIPPINES on 2¢ POSTAGE DUE (#J39) — 3 Plates

247 268 1099

#J 3 PHILIPPINES on 5¢ POSTAGE DUE (#J41) — 2 Plates

71 255

#J 4 PHILIPPINES on 10¢ POSTAGE DUE (#J42) — 2 Plates

72 †256

#J 5 PHILIPPINES on 50¢ POSTAGE DUE (#J44) — 1 Plate

74

APPENDIX EE Continued

#J 6 PHILIPPINES on 3¢ POSTAGE DUE (#J40) **1 Plate**

254 1631

#J 7 PHILIPPINES on 30¢ POSTAGE DUE (#J43) **1 Plate**

73

SPECIAL PRINTINGS

Special printings were made in 1904 for exhibiting in the St. Louis World's Fair and again in 1907. Not more than one plate block or plate strip exists for either special overprinting and most have been accounted for. This act resulted in the only known use of plate 288 for the $5 Marshall (U.S. #278). Scott #E2A was also created by the overprinting of 1907. The stamp was never issued for use in the Philippines. For the record, we will list the Philippines Scott Catalog number and the plate number used to make the special overprints.

SCOTT #	PLATE NUMBER
218	264
221	924
223	76
224	84
225	288
226	3393
227	1553
228	2808
230	1887 & 3158
231	1600
232	2803
233	2289
234	1473 & 1474
235	3209
236	1602
237	1629
238	1630
239	1620
240	1913 & 3372
E1	881
E2A	1774
J1	1632
J2	1244
J3	1642
J4	1633
J5	74
J6	254 & 1631
J7	73

UR-top position based on examination of proof sheet by W. Cleland.

APPENDIX FF—PUERTO RICO

The overprinted stamps of Puerto Rico are listed in the Scott Puerto Rico Catalog order with the basic United States stamp listed on the next line.

#210 1¢ "PORTO RICO" 12 Plates on 1¢ FRANKLIN (#279)

564	565	566	567	574
575	768	769	770	771
772	773			

#211 2¢ "PORTO RICO" 36 Plates on 2¢ WASHINGTON (#279B)

556	561	562	563	593
594	595	596	745	746
747	748	753	754	755
756	758	759	760	761
762	763	764	765	774
775	776	777	778	779
780	781	782	783	784
785				

#212 5¢ "PORTO RICO" 6 Plates on 5¢ GRANT (#281)

389	390	391	392	408
†410				

#213 8¢ "PORTO RICO" 2 Plates on 8¢ SHERMAN (#272)

249 555

#214 10¢ "PORTO RICO" 8 Plates on 10¢ WEBSTER (#282C)

302	303	305	306	518
519	520	521		

#215 1¢ "PUERTO RICO" 23 Plates on 1¢ FRANKLIN (#279)

846	847	848	849	862
863	864	865	937	938
939	940	941	942	944
946	†947	†952	†953	954
955	958	†959		

#216 2¢ "PUERTO RICO" 36 Plates on 2¢ WASHINGTON (#279B)

838	839	840	841	850
851	852	853	854	855
856	857	858	859	860
861	866	867	869	870
875	876	877	878	885
886	887	888	895	896
897	898	904	905	906
907				

#J1 1¢ "PORTO RICO" 2 Plates on 1¢ POSTAGE DUE (#J38)

246 267

#J2 2¢ "PORTO RICO" 2 Plates on 2¢ POSTAGE DUE (#J39)

247 268

#J3 10¢ "PORTO RICO" 1 Plate on 10¢ POSTAGE DUE (#J42)

72

SPECIAL PRINTINGS

A special overprinting was made of certain values for exhibiting at the Paris Exposition. All of the special printings have the overprint "Puerto Rico" and as such some of the values overprinted have no Scott Catalog number. Only one plate number was used for all of the values.

#215 1¢ "PUERTO RICO" on 1¢ FRANKLIN (#279)

975

#216 2¢ "PUERTO RICO" on 2¢ WASHINGTON (#279B)

878

 # 5¢ "PUERTO RICO" on 5¢ GRANT (#281)

948

 # 8¢ "PUERTO RICO" on 8¢ SHERMAN (#272)

929

 # 10¢ "PUERTO RICO" on 10¢ WEBSTER (#282C)

†932

 # 10¢ "PUERTO RICO" on 10¢ WEBSTER (#283)

†932

#J 1¢ "PUERTO RICO" on 1¢ POSTAGE DUE (#J38)

267

#J 2¢ "PUERTO RICO" on 2¢ POSTAGE DUE (#J39)

268

#J 10¢ "PUERTO RICO" on 1¢ POSTAGE DUE (#J42)

256

APPENDIX GG — SHANGHAI

The Shanghai China overprints have been the subject of a study by Mr. Meyer Tuchinsky for many years. Since his study enables us to differentiate the plate positions of numbers K1 thru K15, we shall list those stamps in all eight possible plate block positions with the letter X and the unreported with the letter O. Should you own an unreported position, it would be appreciated if a photo or photocopy of your block be submitted to the editor.

The upper left position of the flat plate sheet includes a top and a left side plate block.

The upper right position of the flat plate sheet includes a top and a right side plate block.

The lower left position of the flat plate sheet includes a bottom and a left side plate block.

The lower right position of the flat plate sheet includes a bottom and a right side plate block.

#K1 2¢ on 1¢ — 16 Plates

	UL		UR		LL		LR	
	T	L	T	R	B	L	B	R
8168	O	O	X	O	X	X	X	X
8431	X	O	O	O	X	O	X	X
9478	O	O	X	O	X	X	X	X
9479	X	X	X	X	X	X	X	X
13219	O	O	O	O	X	X	X	X
13220	X	X	X	O	X	X	O	O
13221	X	O	X	O	O	X	O	O
13222	X	O	X	O	X	O	X	X
13257	O	O	X	X	O	O	O	O
13301	O	O	X	X	O	O	O	O
13307	X	O	X	X	O	O	O	O
13318	O	O	X	X	O	O	O	O
13341	O	O	O	O	O	X	O	X
13342	X	O	O	O	O	X	O	O
13343	X	O	X	O	O	O	O	X
13344	O	X	O	O	O	O	O	X

#K2 4¢ on 2¢ — 16 Plates

	UL		UR		LL		LR	
	T	L	T	R	B	L	B	R
9190	X	X	X	X	O	O	O	O
9198	O	X	O	X	O	O	O	O
9199	X	X	X	X	X	O	O	O
9200	X	O	X	X	O	O	X	X
13438	O	X	X	X	O	X	O	X
13440	X	X	O	O	O	X	O	X
13534	O	O	X	X	X	O	O	X
13535	O	O	X	X	O	O	O	O
13540	X	O	X	X	O	X	O	O
13541	O	O	X	X	X	O	O	O
13567	O	X	X	O	O	X	O	X
13588	O	O	X	O	O	X	O	X
*13738	O	O	O	O	O	O	O	O
*13739	O	O	O	O	O	O	O	O
*13746	X	O	O	O	O	O	O	O
13747	O	O	O	O	O	X	O	X

*Plate single left side on 738, 739, 746

#K3 6¢ on 3¢ — 8 Plates

	UL		UR		LL		LR	
	T	L	T	R	B	L	B	R
8386	O	O	O	O	X	O	X	X
8456	X	O	O	O	O	O	O	O
8462	O	X	X	X	O	O	O	X
8473	O	X	O	X	O	X	O	O
8476	X	X	X	X	X	X	O	X
8868	X	X	O	X	X	X	O	O
8869	O	O	X	X	X	X	O	X
8906	O	X	X	X	X	X	X	O

#K4 8¢ on 4¢ — 8 Plates

	UL		UR		LL		LR	
	T	L	T	R	B	L	B	R
8494	X	O	X	X	O	O	O	X
8495	O	O	O	X	X	O	O	X
8496	X	X	X	X	O	X	X	X
8497	O	O	X	X	X	X	X	X
12549	X	X	X	X	O	X	O	O
12550	X	O	X	X	X	X	X	X
12551	X	X	O	X	X	O	X	X
12552	X	X	X	X	X	O	X	O

#K5 10¢ on 5¢ — 8 Plates

	UL		UR		LL		LR	
	T	L	T	R	B	L	B	R
9115	O	X	O	O	X	X	X	O
9116	X	X	O	O	X	X	O	O
9117	O	X	O	O	X	X	O	X
9118	O	X	O	X	X	X	X	O
13272	O	X	O	O	X	O	X	X
13273	X	O	O	O	X	X	O	O
13274	X	X	O	O	X	X	O	O
13275	X	O	X	X	X	O	O	O

#K6 12¢ on 6¢ — 8 Plates

	UL		UR		LL		LR	
	T	L	T	R	B	L	B	R
7822	X	X	O	O	X	X	X	X
7828	X	X	X	O	O	O	X	X
7834	X	X	O	O	X	X	O	X
7837	X	X	X	O	X	X	X	X
13372	X	X	O	X	X	O	O	O
13373	X	O	X	X	O	X	X	O
13374	O	O	X	X	X	O	O	O
13375	X	X	X	X	O	O	X	O

#K7 14¢ on 7¢ — 8 Plates

	UL		UR		LL		LR	
	T	L	T	R	B	L	B	R
8490	X	O	X	X	X	O	O	O
8898	X	X	X	X	X	X	X	X
8899	O	O	X	X	X	O	X	O
8943	X	O	X	X	O	O	X	O
12561	X	O	X	X	O	X	O	O
12562	O	X	X	O	X	X	X	X
12563	X	O	X	X	X	X	X	X
12564	O	X	X	O	X	O	O	X

#K8 16¢ on 8¢ — 8 Plates

	UL		UR		LL		LR	
	T	L	T	R	B	L	B	R
7734	O	O	O	X	X	O	X	X
7740	O	X	O	X	O	X	X	X
7742	O	O	O	X	X	X	X	X
7748	O	X	O	X	X	X	X	X
10785	O	O	X	X	X	O	O	X
10786	O	O	X	O	O	O	O	O
10787	O	O	O	X	X	O	X	X
10788	X	X	X	X	X	O	O	O

APPENDIX GG Continued

#K9 18¢ on 9¢ — 8 Plates

Plate	UL T	UL L	UR T	UR R	LL B	LL L	LR B	LR R
6918	X	X	X	O	O	X	O	O
6922	X	X	X	X	O	X	O	X
6925	X	X	X	O	O	O	O	O
6930	X	X	X	O	O	X	O	O
11773	X	O	X	X	X	X	X	X
11774	O	O	X	X	O	O	X	O
11775	O	O	X	X	O	O	X	X
11776	O	O	X	X	X	O	X	X

#K10 20¢ on 10¢ — 8 Plates

Plate	UL T	UL L	UR T	UR R	LL B	LL L	LR B	LR R
8435	O	X	X	O	O	O	O	X
8436	X	X	X	O	X	O	X	X
8437	X	O	O	O	X	X	X	X
8438	X	X	X	X	O	O	X	X
13403	X	X	X	O	X	X	X	X
13404	X	X	X	O	X	O	X	X
13405	X	O	X	X	O	O	X	X
13406	O	X	O	O	O	O	O	X

#K11 24¢ on 12¢ — 8 Plates

Plate	UL T	UL L	UR T	UR R	LL B	LL L	LR B	LR R
6931	O	X	X	X	O	O	X	X
6934	X	X	X	O	X	X	X	X
7036	X	X	X	O	X	O	X	X
7037	X	X	X	X	O	O	X	X
10621	X	O	X	O	O	O	O	O
10622	O	X	O	X	O	O	O	X
10623	O	X	O	O	O	O	O	O
10624	O	O	X	O	O	O	X	O

#K12 30¢ on 15¢ — 8 Plates

Plate	UL T	UL L	UR T	UR R	LL B	LL L	LR B	LR R
7926	O	O	X	O	O	X	X	X
7927	X	O	X	X	O	X	X	X
7928	O	X	O	X	O	X	X	X
7929	O	O	O	O	O	O	X	X
12589	X	X	O	O	O	O	X	O
12590	O	X	X	X	X	X	X	O
12591	X	O	X	X	X	X	X	X
12592	O	O	O	X	O	O	O	O

#K13 40¢ on 20¢ — 8 Plates

Plate	UL T	UL L	UR T	UR R	LL B	LL L	LR B	LR R
6933	X	X	O	X	X	X	X	X
6935	X	O	O	X	O	O	O	X
6938	X	O	X	X	O	O	X	X
7033	X	O	X	X	X	O	O	X
12593	O	O	X	O	X	O	X	O
12594	X	X	X	X	X	X	O	X
12595	X	O	O	O	O	O	X	X
12596	O	O	X	X	O	O	X	X

#K14 60¢ on 30¢ — 5 Plates

Plate	UL T	UL L	UR T	UR R	LL B	LL L	LR B	LR R
6899	X	O	O	O	O	O	O	O
6921	X	O	O	O	X	X	X	X
6924	X	O	X	X	X	X	X	O
6927	X	X	X	X	X	X	X	O
6928	O	X	X	X	X	X	X	X

#K15 $1 on 50¢ — 4 Plates

Plate	UL T	UL L	UR T	UR R	LL B	LL L	LR B	LR R
7040	O	O	X	X	O	O	O	X
7042	X	X	X	O	X	X	X	O
7049	X	X	X	O	O	O	O	X
7057	X	X	X	X	X	X	O	O

On K16, K17 & K18 it is impossible to differentiate between panes.

#K16 $2 on $1 — 1 Plate

Plate	T	L	R	B
5782	X	‡	‡	X

#K17 2¢ on 1¢ — 10 Plates

Plate	T	L	R	B
10584	X	X	†	†
10592	X	X	†	†
10595	X	X	†	†
10599	X	X	†	†
*10600	X	X	†	†
11729	X	X	†	†
11787	X	X	†	†
11790	X	X	†	†
11791	X	O	†	†
11792	X	X	†	†

#K18 4¢ on 2¢ — 2 Plates

Plate	T	L	R	B
*13077	X	†	X	†
13129	X	†	X	†

IDENTIFYING POSITIONS ON SHANGHAI OVERPRINTS.

For each pane of 100 stamps, 4 blocks of 25 overprints (5 x 5) were made, clamped into a frame, and used to overprint 100 stamps at a time. Where 2 of the blocks met, there is usually more than the standard space. Thus on a plate block of 6, 4 stamps will show identical positions of the overprint, and 2 will show slightly different positions. For top and bottom plate blocks, the right 2 stamps differ on LL-L and LR-R, and the bottom 2 on UL-L and UR-R. Blocks of 4 can be identified on the basis of whether the spacings are the same, or different, but plate singles can not be assigned a unique position. The 'F' marking helps identify the UR-T position on plates 9478,9 (K1), 9198 (K2), 8495, 12550 (K4), 9116 (K5), 11729, 11787 (K17), and in both positions on 11776 (K9). Plates below 8000 and 8899 (K7), 10786 (K8), all K18 have no F. On 9199 (K2) the F is on the LR-R position.

APPENDIX HH

NEWSPAPER & PERIODICAL STAMPS

WITHOUT VERTICAL OR HORIZONTAL GUIDELINES

The following is a listing of potential plate positions on both the unwatermarked and the early watermarked series of stamps. Contrary to the information in the Scott Catalog, neither Series has vertical nor horizontal guidelines. We will list reported positions as ☐ and unreported as †. All strips or plate blocks will be Imprint III and there is only one plate number for each value. We show only top and bottom positions on the watermarked series, since side plates could not be distinguished from the later issues with guidelines, except on the 1¢-50¢ values if the panes were cut in such a manner that the absence of a horizontal guide line could be established.

Unwatermarked

Stamp	Plate	T	L	R	B
#PR 102 1¢ FREEDOM	90	☐	†	†	☐
#PR 103 2¢ FREEDOM	100	†	†	†	☐
#PR 104 5¢ FREEDOM	93	☐	†	†	☐
#PR 105 10¢ FREEDOM	105	☐	†	†	☐
#PR 106 25¢ FREEDOM	123	☐	†	†	†
#PR 107 50¢ JUSTICE	109	†	†	†	☐
#PR 108 $2 VICTORY	136	†	†	†	†
#PR 109 $5 CLIO	137	†	†	†	†
#PR 110 $10 VESTA	138	†	†	†	†
#PR 111 $20 PEACE	139	†	†	†	†
#PR 112 $50 COMMERCE	135	†	†	†	☐
#PR 113 $100 INDIAN	140	†	†	†	†

Watermarked Double Line USPS

Stamp	Plate	T	B
#PR 114 1¢ FREEDOM	90	☐	☐
#PR 115 2¢ FREEDOM	100	☐	†
#PR 116 5¢ FREEDOM	93	☐	☐
#PR 117 10¢ FREEDOM	105	†	☐
#PR 118 25¢ JUSTICE	123	☐	☐
#PR 119 50¢ JUSTICE	109	☐	†
#PR 120 $2 VICTORY	136	†	†
#PR 121 $5 CLIO	137	†	†
#PR 122 $10 VESTA	138	†	†
#PR 123 $20 PEACE	139	†	†
#PR 124 $50 COMMERCE	135	†	†
#PR 125 $100 INDIAN	140	†	†

We request that you report any unreported positions to the editor for inclusion in the next edition of the catalog.

APPENDIX JJ
ALLIED MILITARY GOVERNMENT

The initial plates prepared by the Bureau of Engraving and Printing for use by the Allied Military Government occupation forces consisted of ornamental frames with the wording "ALLIED MILITARY POSTAGE" in white roman letters plus a center ornament with white gothic numerals.

The plate numbers assigned for the various denominations were as follows:

PLATE NO.	DENOMINATION	COLOR
44460	30	Grey
44462	60	Yellow
44463	2	Red
44464	1	Green
44465	5	Blue
44466	10	Brown
44467	50	Purple
44687	15	Orange
44688	25	Olive

The intent was to prepare an additional plate for overprinting showing the country name above the denomination and the monetary unit below the denomination for each country requiring stamps for AMG usage.

The following overprinting plates were prepared and used; printed in black.

PLATE NO.	COUNTRY	MONETARY UNIT
44620	Italy	Centesimi
44621	Italy	Lira
44622	Italy	Lire

ALLIED MILITARY ITALIAN POSTAGE STAMPS

By combining the basic plate printing and the proper overprinting plate the following stamps were prepared for use in Italy.

PLATE NOS.	FACE VALUE
44687 + 44620	15 centesimi
44688 + 44620	25 centesimi
44460 + 44620	30 centesimi
44467 + 44620	50 centesimi
44462 + 44620	60 centesimi
44464 + 44621	1 Lira
44463 + 44622	2 Lire
44465 + 44622	5 Lire
44466 + 44622	10 Lire

SUPPLEMENTAL FRENCH POSTAGE STAMPS SERIES 1944

These issues had the country name as part of the basic design and also the face value.

PLATE NO.	FACE VALUE	BASIC COLOR
45440	5 centimes	Maroon
45472	10 centimes	Grey
45442	25 centimes	Brown
45437	50 centimes	Olive
45443	1 Franc	Green
45444	1.50 Francs (!)	Red
45445	2.50 Francs	Purple
45568	4 Francs	Blue
45446	5 Francs	Black
45475	10 Francs	Orange

APPENDIX JJ Continued

COMMITTEE FRENCH POSTAGE STAMPS SERIES 1944

These issues utilized one basic frame plate for all denominations showing country name. The frame plate was number 45891. This plate was printed in various colors and the denomination was then applied by an overprinting plate.

BASIC PLATE NO.	COLOR	OVERPRINTING PLATE NO.	DENOMINATION (Black)
45891	Orange	45965	30 centimes
45891	Grey	45966	40 centimes
45891	Olive	45967	50 centimes
45891	Purple	45968	60 centimes
45891	Yellow Green	45923	80 centimes
45891	Brown	45931	1.20 franc
45891	Light Red	45924	1.50 franc
45891	Yellow	45962	2 francs
45891	Rose Carmine	45925	2.40 francs
45891	Maroon	45963	3 francs

ALLIED MILITARY GERMAN POSTAGE STAMPS SERIES 1944

These issues were printed from separate plates for each value of an identical design.

PLATE NO.	COLOR	FACE VALUE
45865	Purple	3 pfennig
45866	Grey	4 pfennig
45867	Green	5 pfennig
45868	Yellow	6 pfennig
45869	Orange	8 pfennig
45870	Brown	10 pfennig
45871	Purple	12 pfennig
45882	Purple	12 pfennig
45883	Purple	12 pfennig
45872	Red	15 pfennig
45873	Blue	25 pfennig

ALLIED MILITARY POSTAGE STAMPS FOR AUSTRIA SERIES 1945

PLATE NO.	COLOR	DENOMINATION
46506	Orange	3 groschen
46508	Light Brown	4 groschen
46509, 46517	Green	5 groschen
46510	Maroon	6 groschen
46511	Claret	8 groschen
46494	Grey	10 groschen
46495	Brown	12 groschen
46496	Red	15 groschen
46499	Bistre	20 groschen
46497	Blue	25 groschen
46500	Magenta	30 groschen
46501	Slate Blue	40 groschen
46505	Olive Green	60 groschen
46512	Purple	1 schilling
46513	Yellow	2 schilling
46514	Indigo	5 schilling

SUPPLEMENTAL ALLIED POSTAGE STAMPS FOR AUSTRIA SERIES 1945

PLATE NO.	COLOR	DENOMINATION
46916	Blue	1 groschen